BERNSTEIN'S
REVERSE
DICTIONARY

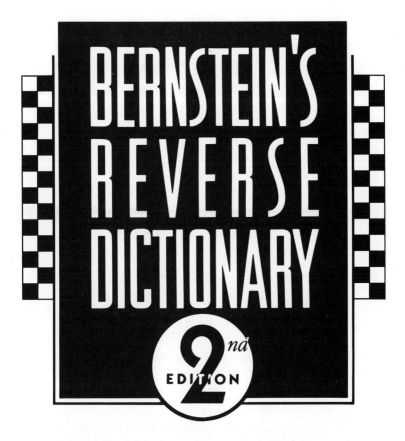

BERNSTEIN'S REVERSE DICTIONARY

2nd EDITION

THEODORE M. BERNSTEIN

revised and expanded by

DAVID GRAMBS

Times
BOOKS

The first edition was published by Quadrangle/the New York Times Book Company
in 1975.

Library of Congress Cataloging-in-Publication Data

Bernstein, Theodore Menline, 1904–
   Bernstein's reverse dictionary.
   Includes index.
   1. English language—Synonyms and antonyms.
2. English language—Dictionaries. I. Grambs,
David. II. Title. III. Title: Reverse dictionary.
PE1591.B45 1988 423'.1 87-40596
ISBN 0-8129-1593-3

Manufactured in the United States of America

9 8 7 6 5 4 3 2

BOOK DESIGN BY BETH MCNALLY

. . . and this one is for Ethel

Introduction to the Original Edition

A conventional dictionary lists words alphabetically and gives you their meanings. This unconventional dictionary lists an array of meanings alphabetically and gives you the words. That is why it is called a Reverse Dictionary.

The words it discovers for you are those you have momentarily forgotten or those you never knew or those of whose meanings you were not quite certain. If I tell you how the concept originated, it may make the idea more quickly understandable.

One evening a couple of us, in the course of conversation, got onto the subject of Chinese cuisine. My friend said he was especially fond of won ton soup. That led me to remark that the words "won ton" made perhaps even more sense if they were read backward. Whereupon my friend cried out, "Yes, just like that famous sentence, 'Madam, I'm Adam.' What *do* you call that kind of sentence?" I replied, "I know the word you want, but I'm damned if I can think of it at this moment. But anyway, 'won ton' is not what that word refers to, because then 'won ton' would have to read exactly the same backward as forward. And it doesn't."

On and off, between drinks, the two of us struggled for the rest of the evening to recall that word, elusive and yet familiar to both of us.

The next morning I telephoned him in triumph. "You know what we needed?" I said. "A reverse dictionary."

"A what?" said he.

"A reverse dictionary. When we couldn't think of that word last night we would have gone to the reverse dictionary and looked under the *b*'s for 'backward,' and it would have said something like 'backward—a sentence that reads backward the same as forward: PALINDROME.' Or we could have looked under the *r*'s for 'reverse' and it would have said, 'reverse—a sentence that reads the same in reverse as forward: PALINDROME.' Or if neither of those definitions had occurred to us, we could have tried under the *r*'s for 'right to left—a sentence that reads from right to left just as it does from left to right: PALINDROME.' Get it?"

He got it, all right, and that is how this project began.

It has entailed labor, to be sure, but it was lovable labor. I found it lovable and so did Jane Wagner, who toiled mightily and perceptively as my collaborator. Our labor involved two principal tasks. One was selecting the words to be included in this lexicon; the other was framing the definitions in ways that would make the words readily findable.

In selecting the entries, we had to hit a happy medium between commonplace, everyday words that everyone except a thirteen-month-old knows (and would never have to grope for) and words that are so remote from general use that only a specialist in a particular field would have occasion to employ them. Thus you won't find *and* or *the* or *boy* or *box* in this dictionary, nor will you find many words like *bradykinin* or *intratelluric* or *thysanuran.* But you will find *brouhaha* and *cholesterol* and *alliteration* and *danseur.*

Framing the definitions was somewhat more difficult. Let me first set forth two items of terminology that we used and that will be used in this introduction. The word to be defined—that is, the word the user of this dictionary is groping for—we call the *target word.* The first word or words of each definition—that is, the word or phrase that is a synonym for the target word, or at least bears a sense relation to it—we call the *clue word.* It is the clue words that are alphabetized in this vocabulary and it is the clue words that lead into definitions of the target words.

Naturally in most instances these clue words cannot be the first words that ordinarily appear in dictionary definitions, since dictionary definitions often begin with such things as "of or pertaining to" or "the act of" or "any of various substances." Phrases like those would not be helpful here; the first word of each entry must be meaningful. In addition, it must be a word that most likely would occur to the groper for a target word. Let's say the groper was groping for "Adonis"; most probably he would turn to the *h*'s and look for "handsome" or he would turn to the *m*'s and look for "man." Either way he would be rewarded: Under the *h*'s he would find "handsome man: ADONIS" and under the *m*'s he would find "man of great beauty: ADONIS." And he would be at grope's end.

Although we have tried to adhere to dictionary definitions—particularly, although not exclusively, to the concise ones in Funk and Wagnalls Standard College Dictionary—we have sometimes had to modify them so as to begin with meaningful clue words. Moreover, although our definitions give the sense of the target word accurately, their wording on a few occasions does not conform to the part of speech of the target word. For instance, one entry for the noun "agnosticism" is not a noun but rather a phrase: "God's existence questioned." Using that definition provides a helpful clue word—"God's"—and no damage is done to the word's meaning. This book is not, after all, a conventional dictionary.

Still, for a person momentarily lacking any kind of conventional dictionary whatever, this lexicon could help fill the gap. The target words appear alphabetically at the back of the book as an index, accompanied by page numbers that tell where their definitions or synonyms may be found. In other words, this reverse dictionary if used *in reverse* could be a conventional dictionary, though a very abridged one. That puts it one up on a normal dictionary, which can be used in only one direction. Of course, the definitions in this one are not so detailed nor so comprehensive as those in a conventional dictionary, and they are not intended to be. Yet they do give more than a hint of what each target word means.

This reverse dictionary is not a thesaurus either, yet within the limitation of the number of words it contains it can serve a similar purpose. The normal thesaurus throws masses of synonyms and closely or distantly related words at you, often leaving you to find your own way out of the jungle it has created. This lexicon gives you, by means of the clue words, synonyms or closely related expressions ranging from one to five or six for each target word. For the target word ACAUDAL, all that anyone needs for a synonym or a definition is "tailless." For the target word AMBIENCE, however, more is required, and in this vocabulary you will find five entries, as follows:

—atmosphere of a place or situation
—environmental distinctiveness
—feel of a place or situation
—milieu
—surroundings

Thus when using this dictionary for its principal purpose, if you could not recall the word AMBIENCE you could look under any one of those five entries and there the target word would be awaiting you. On the other hand, if you were looking for another way of saying "ambience," you could look in the index and be referred to all of those five entries. In doing that you would be using this work as a thesaurus.

Parenthetically, listing those five entries referring to AMBIENCE brings to mind one of the fascinating difficulties we encountered in devising this dictionary. We found we had to be seers—mind readers for thousands of people. We constantly kept asking ourselves the question, "If Jane Doe Smith couldn't recall Word A, what kindred word or expression to look under would pop into her mind?" We tried to think of as many relevant look-up words as we could and thus the clue words kept multiplying.

That process gave the book a lagniappe that hadn't occurred to us at first: the more entries the wider the opportunity for service to word fiends—vocabulary builders, crossword-puzzle workers and double-crostic solvers. After all, the pattern of this book is not unlike that of a crossword puzzle dictionary, though neither could replace the other. But if the crossword puzzle demanded a six-letter word for a "handsome man," you would find "Adonis" waiting for you in these pages.

If you wanted to get still more fun out of this basically serious book, you could use it to generate new word games in your living room. For instance, after the first round of cocktails, the host, leafing through these pages, could ask Guest A, "What's a word for an ancient adding machine?" If the guest came up with "abacus," the host could reward him with a second cocktail. Then the host could turn to Guest B and say, "Give me any one of a half a dozen definitions of 'abecedarian,'" and if Guest B scratched his head in vain, the host could say, "What you need is another cocktail," and give it to him. And so it could go.

Fundamentally, however, this book is designed with a serious purpose. It is intended to help all users of English, and particularly serious writers, to find words that temporarily are eluding them or words that they did not know even existed. It has as a chief purpose keeping them from settling for a second-best word by making easily available the precise word they require and should have. And needless to say, precision in language is a continuing imperative.

* * *

Now for three minor details that should be called to the attention of users of this dictionary:

1. The various kinds of phobias are not entered separately. They appear in a listing under the clue word "phobias."
2. Likewise, the various kinds of manias are not entered separately. They appear in a listing under the clue word "manias." This listing, as well as that of phobias, is derived in the main from Funk and Wagnalls Standard College Dictionary.
3. Terms for groups, males, females and the young of animals, birds, fish and other creatures are not entered separately, but appear in a chart headed "Creature Terms" under the letter C.

T.M.B.

New York, New York, September 1975

Editor's Postscript

In addition to the more than 2,500 new terms defined for this edition, two more special or omnibus listings—along the lines of those for phobias, manias, and "Creature Terms"—have been added:

1. A listing of terms for various fields of medicine appears as a box, "Medical Fields," under the letter M.

2. Nicknames for all fifty states of our country are listed in a box, "U.S. State Nicknames," under the letter S.

D.L.G.

New York, New York, March 1988

BERNSTEIN'S
REVERSE
DICTIONARY

abandon an undertaking: **SCUTTLE**

abandoned, deserted, wretched, cheerless: **FORLORN**

abandonment of one's faith, party or principles: **APOSTASY**

abandon, yield, give up: **RELINQUISH**

abate, calm, quiet: **SUBSIDE**

abbreviation or sign representing a word, such as the dollar sign: **LOGOGRAM**

abdominal pain resulting from muscular spasms: **COLIC**

abhorrence, disgust or dislike in the extreme: **LOATHING**

abide, continue unchanged: **SUBSIST**

ability, skill: **PROWESS**

ability to do something adroitly: **KNACK**

abnormal: **ANOMALOUS**

abnormal, diverging from the natural order: **PRETERNATURAL**

abnormal, monstrous: **TERATOID**

abominable, revolting, detestable: **EXECRABLE**

abominable snowman: **YETI**

abortion-inducing substance, procedure, etc.: **ABORTIFACIENT**

abortion opponent: **RIGHT-TO-LIFER**

about, approximately: **CIRCA**

about-face, complete reversal: **VOLTE-FACE**

about to happen without delay: **IMMINENT**

about to occur: **IMPENDING**

above all else in importance: **PARAMOUNT**

above comparison, preeminently: **PAR EXCELLENCE**

abridge, make concise: **CONDENSE**

abridgement that is brief but comprehensive: **COMPENDIUM**

abroad-living citizen: **EXPATRIATE**

abrogate, repeal, revoke: **RESCIND**

abrupt, brief, hasty: **CURSORY**

abruptly cause: **PRECIPITATE**

abrupt, sharp emphasis: **STACCATO**

absence of government: **ANARCHY**

absence of life: **ABIOSIS**

absent-minded: **DISTRAIT**

absent, not present: **IN ABSENTIA**

absolute and unquestioning, unreserved: **IMPLICIT**

absolute, complete, thoroughgoing: **UNMITIGATED**

absolute, full, complete: **PLENARY**

absolute government by an individual: **AUTOCRACY**

absolute, not to be questioned, final: **PEREMPTORY**

absolute power, supreme command: **IMPERIUM**

absolute rule: **AUTARCHY**

absolute, without any qualifications: **CATEGORICAL**

absorbed in completely: **RAPT**

absorb, occupy completely, monopolize: **ENGROSS**

absorption in one's thoughts: **BROWN STUDY**

abstainer from alcoholic drinks: **TEETOTALER**

abstaining from sexual intercourse: **CELIBATE**

abstract, concise summary: **PRÉCIS**

abstracted quality or essence of anything: **DISTILLATION**

abstractly or intellectually apprehended: **NOETIC**

abstract or speculative philosophy: **METAPHYSICS**

abstruse, hidden: RECONDITE

abstruse, secret, unknown except by a few: ESOTERIC

absurd appearance given to something or someone: STULTIFIED

absurdity ultimately of an argument or proposition demonstrated: REDUCTIO AD ABSURDUM

absurd, ridiculous: LUDICROUS

absurd, senseless: IRRATIONAL

abundant, lavish, generous: PROFUSE

abundant, numerous: GALORE

abundant, plentiful: RIFE

abuse by words, verbal attack: INVECTIVE

abuse, handle roughly, manhandle: MAUL

abuse or satirize in humorous prose or verse: LAMPOON

abuse, vilify: REVILE

abusive and defamatory words: OBLOQUY

abusive and loud: THERSITICAL

abusive, coarse in language: SCURRILOUS

abusive denunciation, harangue: DIATRIBE

abusive, disgracing: OPPROBRIOUS

abusive language: VITUPERATION

accented forcibly in music: SFORZANDO

accent mark consisting of two dots over a letter (ü): DIERESIS, UMLAUT

accent mark, hooklike, placed under a "c" (ç): CEDILLA

accent mark, in Arabic, like an apostrophe: HAMZA

accent mark in the form of an inverted "v" (^): CIRCUMFLEX

accent mark like a thick acute accent and used for syllable stress or letter differentiation (′): PRIME

accent mark like a wavy line (~): TILDE

accent mark that points upward to the left (`): GRAVE ACCENT

accent mark that points upward to the right (´): ACUTE ACCENT

accent, way of speaking a language: INTONATION

accept as true: POSTULATE

accepted, popular, everyday speech: VULGATE

accepted practice: PRAXIS

accessory: ACCOUTREMENT, ACCOUTERMENT

accessory: APPURTENANCE

accidental, fortunate by chance rather than design: FORTUITOUS

accidental homicide: CHANCE-MEDLEY

accidentally occurring or acquired: ADVENTITIOUS

accidental occurrence: HAPPENSTANCE

accidental, random: HAPHAZARD

accident in a car that is minor: FENDER BENDER

accompanying as a factor or circumstance: CONCOMITANT

accomplice at a carnival, con game, auction, etc., who poses as an onlooker or customer: SHILL

accomplice in crime: PARTICEPS CRIMINIS

accomplish, bring about: EFFECT

accomplished fact or irrevocable thing done: FAIT ACCOMPLI

accomplishment, creation or performance that is ingenious or impressive: TOUR DE FORCE

accomplishment or realization of things worked for: FRUITION

accord, harmonious relationship: RAPPORT

accordion-like small instrument: CONCERTINA

accumulation that is confusing; jumble, slew: WELTER

accurate, certain: UNERRING

accurate, exact, precise: NICE

accurately verbatim reproduction of a spelling or quotation followed by this word in parentheses: SIC

accurate reproduction: FIDELITY

accusation of a formal or serious nature: J'ACCUSE

accusation of wrongdoing made against a public official: IMPEACHMENT

accusation or denunciation that is virulent: INVECTIVE

accusation or the charging of a wrongdoing or fault: IMPUTATION

accusatory searching out and persecuting of certain people: WITCH-HUNT

accuse, charge with a crime: INDICT

accuse falsely: CALUMNIATE

accuse in return: RECRIMINATE

accuse of wrongdoing or imply guilt: INCRIMINATE

accustomed or used to, habituated: WONT

accustom or harden someone to something: CONDITION
accustom to something difficult: INURE
acme, highest point: PINNACLE
acorn-shaped: BALANOID
acquainted or familiar with a subject: CONVERSANT
acquit, free from accusation or blame: EXONERATE
acquit, justify: VINDICATE
acrid: PUNGENT
acrobat's or gymnast's canvas jumping sheet stretched on a frame: TRAMPOLINE
across: ATHWART
acrostic form in which the final letters of successive lines form a word: TELESTICH
acrostic form in which the middle letters of successive lines form a word: MESOSTICH
act as a judge: ADJUDICATE
act as an official: OFFICIATE
acting hastily: BRASH
actions that are devious or mischievous: SHENANIGANS
activator, leader, inspirer: SPARK PLUG
active, lively: VIVACIOUS
actor or actress: THESPIAN
actor or actress who feeds comedian lines: STRAIGHT MAN
actual or realized existence as opposed to mere potentiality: ENTELECHY
actual, real, important: SUBSTANTIVE
acute, keen, sharp, biting: INCISIVE
acutely or keenly experienced, as a particular pleasure: EXQUISITE
adage: APHORISM
add at the end: SUBJOIN
added clause appended to a legislative bill: RIDER
added syllable or syllables at the end of a word: SUFFIX
adding machine of ancients: ABACUS
additional and not inherent, acquired, extrinsic, supplementary: ADSCITITIOUS
additional feature or aspect: ADJUNCT
addition, increase, something added or gained: INCREMENT
addition, insertion or interruption in a discourse, process or series: INTERPOLATION
addition to a will: CODICIL

add or inject certain elements: INCORPORATE
addressing a person or thing absent or in a rhetorical way: APOSTROPHE
address to graduating class: BACCALAUREATE
adept at many things: VERSATILE
adhesive, sticky: VISCID
adjective linked to a noun to which it normally would not apply: TRANSFERRED EPITHET, HYPALLAGE
adjective used as a noun: ADNOUN
adjunct: APPURTENANCE
adjusted or resigned to a situation: RECONCILED
adjustment: ORIENTATION
adjustment to meet the demands of the environment: REALITY PRINCIPLE
adjustment to society's cultural norms: ACCULTURATION, ENCULTURATION
adjust, temper, soften or regulate: MODULATE
ad lib: EXTEMPORANEOUS
administration or manner of governing: GOVERNANCE
admirable, consummate: EXQUISITE
admittance: ACCESS
admonish or advise strongly, urge by earnest appeal: EXHORT
adolescent who is awkward: HOBBLEDEHOY
adorn magnificently, extol, celebrate: EMBLAZON
adroit, skillful: DEXTEROUS
adulterous spouse's named partner in a divorce suit: CORESPONDENT
adultery, in law: CRIMINAL CONVERSATION
adult-learning methods: ANDRAGOGY
advance announcer of the coming of someone or something: HARBINGER
advanced beyond what is usual for one's age: PRECOCIOUS
advantage-intended action, move or temporary sacrifice: GAMBIT
advantage or weapon held in reserve, secret winner: ACE IN THE HOLE
advantageous position: CATBIRD SEAT
advantage spot for observation: COIGN OF VANTAGE
advantage-taker who is sneaky: CHEAP-SHOT ARTIST
adverb that is misplaced so it could

modify either of two words:
SQUINTING MODIFIER

adverse, unfortunate: **UNTOWARD**

advertisement explaining or informing
in a formal way, as by a
corporation or union:
ADVERTORIAL

advertisement made to look like an
editorial: **ADVERTORIAL**

advertisement or notice distributed by
hand: **HANDBILL**

advertising billboard (British):
HOARDING

advertising offer of a low-priced item to
lure customers into purchasing a
higher-priced item:
BAIT-AND-SWITCH

advertising or promotion that is
sensational: **BALLYHOO**

advertising space measurement: **AGATE
LINE**

advise of a fault: **ADMONISH**

advise or recommend strongly, urge by
earnest appeal: **EXHORT**

adviser or critic who is frank and
severe: **DUTCH UNCLE**

advisers consulted, usually unofficially,
for their expertise: **BRAIN TRUST**

advisers, usually secret and unofficial:
CAMARILLA

advocacy or support, as of a cause:
ESPOUSAL

advocate or originator of a cause:
PROPONENT

aerial cablecar: **TELPHER**

aesthetic qualities associated with
ancient Greece and Rome:
CLASSICISM

affectation of style or peculiarity of
manner: **MANNERISM**

affected display of modesty: **PRUDERY**

affected in writing, behavior, etc.:
PRECIOUS

affectedly or cutely quaint (British):
TWEE

affectedly or effeminately prim, elegant
or dainty: **MINCING**

affecter of attitudes to impress others:
POSEUR

affecting superiority, ostentatious:
PRETENTIOUS

affection that is foolish or excessive:
DOTAGE

affirmative meaning expressed by
negating its opposite: **LITOTES**

affront, insult: **INDIGNITY**

African lute-like musical instrument:
OUD

African or African-modeled long and
colorfully patterned buttonless shirt
worn chiefly by men: **DASHIKI**

African village or native community:
KRAAL

after death: **POSTHUMOUS**

afterdinner: **POSTPRANDIAL**

aftereffect, reverberation:
REPERCUSSION

aftermath: **WAKE**

aftermath that is surprising and
unfortunate or harmful:
AFTERCLAP

after-the-event perception, retrospect:
HINDSIGHT

after the fact: **EX POST FACTO**

again, from the beginning, anew: **DE
NOVO**

against change or progress,
conservative: **REACTIONARY**

aged, infirm, doting: **SENILE**

age-estimate a fossil by carbon
measurement: **CARBON-DATE**

age, length of life: **LONGEVITY**

agency that sells articles, columns,
cartoons, etc., to a number of
periodicals: **SYNDICATE**

agent, deputy, substitute: **VICAR**

agent in financing: **FACTOR**

agent or adviser who is powerful but
unofficial: **ÉMINENCE GRISE**

agent planted in an organization to
incite trouble or dissension: **AGENT
PROVOCATEUR**

agent that remains unchanged while
changing other components:
CATALYST

agent who handles orders to buy and
sell securities: **BROKER**

agent who is an intermediary or
go-between in espionage: **CUT-OUT**

age of a girl before which intercourse is
statutory rape: **AGE OF CONSENT**

aggravated or distraught state: **SWIVET**

aggravate, worsen, make worse or more
severe: **EXACERBATE**

aggressive, obnoxious: **BUMPTIOUS**

aggressive, lively: **FEISTY**

aging and the aged as a scientific study:
GERONTOLOGY

aging, growing old: **SENESCENT**

agitated state: **SWIVET**

agitated, worried, tense, bewildered: **DISTRAUGHT**

agitating violently: **TURBULENT**

agitator, fiery upstart, stirrer-upper: **FIREBRAND**

agonizing, painful: **EXCRUCIATING**

agreeable in manner or style, apt, well-chosen: **FELICITOUS**

agreeableness: **COMPLAISANCE**

agreeable to persuasion or change: **AMENABLE**

agree exactly: **COINCIDE**

agree, go along with: **ACCEDE**

agreeing, conforming: **CONGRUENT**

agree, jell: **JIBE**

agreement: **CONCURRENCE**

agreement, compact, pledge: **COVENANT**

agreement guaranteed solely by the pledged word of the parties involved: **GENTLEMAN'S AGREEMENT**

agreement, harmony: **CONSONANCE**

agreement made provisionally or for practicality pending final accord: **MODUS VIVENDI**

agreement of all concerned: **UNANIMITY**

agreement or covenant, especially between church and state: **CONCORDAT**

agreement or opinion that is general: **CONSENSUS**

agreement that is mutual: **ENTENTE**

agreement, treaty, contract: **PACT**

agricultural: **AGRARIAN**

aiding, supporting, auxiliary: **ANCILLARY**

aid, succor: **SUBVENTION**

aimed straight at a target and close enough so the projectile does not fall appreciably: **POINT-BLANK**

aim, goal, purpose: **INTENT**

aimless, casual, disconnected, random: **DESULTORY**

aimless wandering: **MEANDERING**

air-attack a target with machine-gun fire from low-flying planes: **STRAFE**

air column swirling around a vertical axis: **WHIRLWIND**

aircraft carrier: **FLATTOP**

aircraft enclosure, especially one housing an engine: **NACELLE**

aircraft on a single military mission: **SORTIE**

aircraft workshop or shelter: **HANGAR**

air-cushion vehicle: **HOVERCRAFT**

air hole: **SPIRACLE**

air over a hot surface, such as a blacktop road, shimmering because of refraction of light rays: **LAURENCE EFFECT**

airplane for sophisticated surveillance: **AWACS (AIRBORNE WARNING AND CONTROL SYSTEM)**

airplane landing that is perfect: **THREE-POINT LANDING**

airplane's prospective passenger who fails to claim reservation: **NO-SHOW**

airport luggage conveyor belt: **BAGGAGE CAROUSEL**

airstream behind a propeller, moving vehicle, etc.: **SLIPSTREAM**

airtight: **HERMETIC**

airy, light, spiritual: **ETHEREAL**

alarm, bell signal: **TOCSIN**

alarm, call to arms: **ALARUM**

alarm, upset, disturb: **PERTURB**

alchemist's sought-after stone or substance to transmute other metals into gold: **PHILOSOPHER'S STONE**

alcohol: **AQUA VITAE**

alcoholically abstain or undergo treatment to stop drinking: **DRY OUT**

alcoholically inclined: **BIBULOUS**

alcoholic appetizer: **APERITIF**

alcoholic derelict: **WINO**

alcoholic hallucinatory delirium: **DELIRIUM TREMENS**

alcoholic liquor: to add in small quantity to a beverage: **LACE**

alcoholic strong liquor: **SCHNAPPS**

alcoholism, craving for alcohol: **DIPSOMANIA**

ale or beer and ginger ale mixed: **SHANDYGAFF**

alert, watchful: **VIGILANT**

alert, wide-awake; **ON THE QUI VIVE**

alienated, estranged: **DISAFFECTED**

alien or from beyond earth, nonhuman: **EXTRATERRESTRIAL**

alignment (in a straight line) of three celestial bodies, as during an eclipse: **SYZYGY**

aligned with or as a margin, not indented: **FLUSH**

alikeness of a trait, characteristic or viewpoint: **COMMON DENOMINATOR**

all at one time: **HOLUS-BOLUS**

alleviate, extenuate: **PALLIATE**

alley lined with dwellings that were formerly stables: **MEWS**

alliance: **COALITION**

alliance of two or more business concerns for a venture: **CONSORTIUM**

all-important thing: **BE-ALL AND END-ALL**

all kinds of things accepted, as by the mind: **OMNIVOROUS**

all life held as sacred: **AHIMSA**

all out, using all resources, furiously: **TOOTH AND NAIL**

all out, with energy and determination: **HAMMER AND TONGS**

allowable, permissible: **TOLERABLE**

allowable, permissible, worthy: **ADMISSIBLE**

allowance, salary, pension: **STIPEND**

allowing for or taking into consideration attendant differences: **MUTATIS MUTANDIS**

allowing unusual freedom, lenient: **PERMISSIVE**

all performers take part, in music: **TUTTI**

all right, fine, satisfactory: **HUNKY-DORY**

all the more forcefully or logically, even more: **A FORTIORI**

almighty: **OMNIPOTENT**

almond-flavored liqueur: **AMARETTO**

almost, nearly: **WELL-NIGH**

alms-giving, charitable: **ELEEMOSYNARY**

alone: **ISOLATED**

alphabetic characters of one language used to represent the letters of another: **TRANSLITERATION**

alphabet in small letters used in printing: **LOWER CASE**

alphabet, pertaining to the: **ABECEDARIAN**

also known as, otherwise called, alias: **A.K.A.**

altar boy: **ACOLYTE**

altar boy who carries the censer: **THURIFER**

alter a female animal by removal of the ovaries: **SPAY**

alteration, destruction, or mutilation, especially of a legal document: **SPOLIATION**

alternate, change places: **INTERCHANGE**

alter or deter the plans of someone by persuasion: **DISSUADE**

altitude-measuring instrument: **ALTIMETER**

altogether, entirely: **IN TOTO**

always prepared: **SEMPER PARATUS**

amaze, astound: **FLABBERGAST**

amazement, fear or panic that is sudden and paralyzing: **CONSTERNATION**

amazing, hard to believe: **INCREDIBLE**

amazing, wonderful: **PRODIGIOUS**

ambiguity that is usually unintentional and because of grammatical looseness: **AMPHIBOLOGY**

ambiguous, insincere: **LEFT-HANDED**

ambiguous or oracular: **DELPHIC**

ambiguous talk: **DOUBLE TALK**

ambiguous, uncertain in origin or character, double-meaninged, dubious: **EQUIVOCAL**

ambitious newcomer to success or wealth, upstart, parvenu: **ARRIVISTE**

ambush: **WAYLAY**

ambush: **AMBUSCADE**

amends, restoration to proper condition: **REPARATION**

American and British in mixture, as one's speech: **MID-ATLANTIC**

American Indian male who is married: **SANNUP**

American 19th-century doctrine of justified expansionism: **MANIFEST DESTINY**

ammunition belt worn over the shoulder: **BANDOLIER**

ammunition wagon: **CAISSON**

amnesia state or period: **FUGUE**

among other things: **INTER ALIA**

amount: **QUANTUM**

amount added to determine the selling price: **MARKUP**

amount by which a stock or bond may sell above its dollar value: **PREMIUM**

amount of stock an individual has sold even though he didn't own it and hasn't yet paid for it: **SHORT POSITION**

amount that must be paid by customer even though he uses his broker's credit for purchase: **MARGIN**

amputee's sensation of pain where the lost limb would be: **PHANTOM LIMB PAIN**

amulet, charm: TALISMAN
amuse, distract, entertain: DIVERT
amuse, entertain: REGALE
amusement: DIVERTISSEMENT
amusement park having a central
theme: THEME PARK
amusement, pastime: DIVERSION
amuse or occupy oneself, frisk about,
frolic: DISPORT
anachronism in the form of a wrongly
early date: PROCHRONISM
anachronism in the form of a wrongly
late date: METACHRONISM
anagram or word puzzle: LOGOGRIPH
analysis of something that has
happened: POSTMORTEM
analysis or interpretation of a word,
passage or work: EXEGESIS
analyze, break up or separate into parts:
RESOLVE
ancestor dating furthest back,
forefather: PRIMOGENITOR
ancestor worship: MANISM
ancestral line: PEDIGREE
ancestry, pedigree: LINEAGE
anchor for small boats: KILLICK
anchoring place, available port:
ANCHORAGE
anchor with sharp flukes or hooked
spikes: GRAPNEL
ancient, outmoded, old-fashioned, out of
step with the times: ANTEDILUVIAN
ancient, venerable, gray- or
white-haired: HOARY
ancient wedge-stroke writing:
CUNEIFORM
ancient writing: PALEOGRAPHY
and others (et alii): ET AL.
"and" symbol (&): AMPERSAND
and the following: ET SEQ.
anew, again, from the beginning: DE
NOVO
angel of the highest rank: SERAPH
angered easily, irascible, hot-tempered:
CHOLERIC
anger, embitter: RANKLE
anger, enrage: INCENSE
anger or offense shown: BRIDLE
anger roused by injustice or baseness:
INDIGNATION
angle iron or metal bracket used to
strengthen a corner or angle of a
structure: GUSSET
Anglo-Saxon bard: SCOP
Anglo-Saxon council: WITENAGEMOT

angrily and frowningly stare: GLOWER
angrily or sullenly look, scowl: LOWER
angry argument: ALTERCATION
angry behavior: BELLICOSITY
angry dispute, quarrel: WRANGLE
angry, enraged: IRATE
angry or irritated state: SNIT
angry or resentful to a great degree: IN
HIGH DUDGEON
anguish, distress, pain, suffering:
TRAVAIL
animal and plant comparison as a
science: BIOSTATICS
animal and plant functions and
processes as a science:
PHYSIOLOGY
animal and plant structures as a study
apart from function: MORPHOLOGY
animal, a rodent, believed to drown
itself in mass numbers: LEMMING
animal behavior in nature as a study:
ETHOLOGY
animal bereft of its horns: POLLARD
animal doctor: VETERINARIAN
animal group terms—see "creature
terms"
animal living in the nest or dwelling of
another species: INQUILINE
animal or plant selected as
representative of a new species:
HOLOTYPE
animal or plant surviving from an
earlier period or type: RELICT
animal preservation after death by
stuffing and mounting skins:
TAXIDERMY
animal's den: LAIR
animals living in a given area: FAUNA
animals or insects that are harmful or
offensive pests: VERMIN
animal's or organism's biological
development as an individual:
ONTOGENY
animals' survival or perpetuation
because of being the most fit or the
most adaptable: NATURAL
SELECTION
animals that are warm-blooded and
whose offspring are fed with milk
from female mammary glands:
MAMMALS
animal used for heavy work: BEAST OF
BURDEN
animal worship: ZOOLATRY
animate or pervade: INFORM

ankle bones as a group: **TARSUS**

annihilation or destruction of an entire people or national group: **GENOCIDE**

annotate a text between the lines: **INTERLINE**

announce officially, put into effect: **PROMULGATE**

annoyance, hindrance, snag, complication: **FLY IN THE OINTMENT**

annoyance that is always a problem: **BUGBEAR**

annoyed, offended, irritated: **MIFFED**

annoying, irritating: **VEXATIOUS**

annoying, provoking, prodding person: **GADFLY**

annoy or harass with taunts or questions: **HECKLE**

annoy or taunt by reminding of a fault: **TWIT**

annoy, weary, vex: **IRK**

annually recurring, said of certain Mediterranean summer winds: **ETESIAN**

annul: **INVALIDATE**

annul, as a law or a right: **ABROGATE**

answer sharply: **RETORT**

antagonistic, alien, not desirable: **REPUGNANT**

antagonistic, hostile: **INIMICAL**

antagonist or opposing thing that threatens retribution or defeat: **NEMESIS**

anthology of scholarly writings for a special occasion: **FESTSCHRIFT**

anti-abortion adherent: **RIGHT-TO-LIFER**

anti-aircraft gun used in pairs or more on ships: **POM-POM**

antic, caper: **DIDO**

antic, caper: **GAMBADO**

anticipatory: **PREVENIENT**

antidotal, countering poison or infection: **ALEXIPHARMIC**

antidote for a poison: **MITHRIDATE**

anti-drowning technique for a swimmer: **DROWNPROOFING**

anti-government in any form: **ANARCHIC**

anti-guerrilla government activity: **COUNTERINSURGENCY**

anti-machinery worker: **LUDDITE**

antiquated: **ANTEDILUVIAN**

antique: **MUSEUM PIECE**

anti-smoking viewpoint: **MISOCAPNIA**

anxiety: **DISQUIETUDE**

anxiety about one's health, often over imagined symptoms: **HYPOCHONDRIA**

anxiety, agitation, nervous excitement: **DITHER**

anxiety, fear, dread, apprehension: **ANGST**

anxious or in a state of suspense: **ON TENTERHOOKS**

anything: **AUGHT**

apartment consisting of a single room with kitchenette and bathroom: **EFFICIENCY APARTMENT**

apartment house in which occupants own shares of stock in the building: **COOPERATIVE**

apartment house in which units are owned separately by individuals: **CONDOMINIUM**

apartment or lodging, furnished, consisting of one room: **BED-SITTER**

apartment or lodging place that is part-time, occasional or temporary; **PIED-À-TERRE**

apartment whose rooms are in a straight line: **RAILROAD APARTMENT, RAILROAD FLAT**

apathetic: **PHLEGMATIC**

apathetic, lackadaisical, indifferent: **LISTLESS**

apathetic, unconcerned: **INDIFFERENT**

apathy, sluggishness, dullness: **LETHARGY**

apathy, stupor: **TORPOR**

ape-like: **SIMIAN**

ape-like or man-like primate: **HOMINID**

ape-like two-legged creature said to exist in remote areas of western North America: **SASQUATCH, BIGFOOT**

apex, top: **VERTEX**

aphrodisiac called Spanish fly: **CANTHARIDES**

apologetic: **DEPRECATORY**

apologetic, meek, shy person: **MILQUETOAST**

apparatus that functions by itself: **AUTOMATON**

apparently but not really correct: **SPECIOUS**

apparent, seeming: **OSTENSIBLE**

apparent to sight or understanding, evident, obvious: **MANIFEST**

apparition, ghost: **SPECTER**

apparition of a person thought to be alive, seen just before or after death: **WRAITH**

apparitions or images in a series, as in a dream: **PHANTASMAGORIA**

appeal earnestly, direct, command: **ADJURE**

appealing to emotions: **AFFECTIVE**

appealing to the audience's greed or financial concerns: **AD CRUMENAM**

appealing to the audience's sentiment rather than to reason or fact: **AD POPULUM**

appealing to prejudice rather than to reason: **AD HOMINEM**

appearance: **SEMBLANCE**

appearance, aspect: **GUISE**

appearance-improving: **COSMETIC**

appearance, manner: **MIEN**

appearance or aspect that is false in order to deceive: **GUISE**

appearance or likeness of truth or reality: **VERISIMILITUDE**

appearance or look of a person or thing: **PHYSIOGNOMY**

appearance or manifestation of a deity, a showing forth: **EPIPHANY**

appearing in various passages in a book: **PASSIM**

appear or come into view as through a mist, often ominously: **LOOM**

appeasement gift or bribe: **SOP**

appease or satisfy by deceit, put off by lies or evasion: **FOB OFF**

appease, pacify: **PLACATE**

appease, win goodwill: **PROPITIATE**

append: **SUBJOIN**

appendix to a will: **CODICIL**

appetite so great as to be pathological: **BULIMIA**

appetizer in the form of an alcoholic drink: **APERITIF**

appetizer of toast and a spread: **CANAPÉ**

appetizers: **HORS D'OEUVRES**

appetizers of raw vegetables, often with a dip: **CRUDITÉS**

appetizing, tasty: **SAVORY**

appetizing treat, delicious morsel, delicacy: **BONNE BOUCHE**

applauders hired for the purpose: **CLAQUE**

applause: **PLAUDITS**

applause outburst: **OVATION**

applicable, pertinent: **RELEVANT**

appointment or secret meeting, as of lovers: **TRYST**

appointment to meet, meeting place: **RENDEZVOUS**

appoint or preempt: **CO-OPT**

apprehension, doubt, qualm: **MISGIVING**

apprehension, fear, anxiety, dread: **ANGST**

apprentice, beginner: **NOVICE, TYRO**

approachableness: **ACCESS**

approach game or prey in a stealthy manner: **STALK**

appropriate, applicable: **RELEVANT**

appropriate or pirate the ideas, writings, music, etc., of another: **PLAGIARIZE**

appropriate or seize beforehand: **PREEMPT**

approval: **APPROBATION**

approved status granted an academic institution: **ACCREDITATION**

approve, permit, ratify: **SANCTION**

approve, support, encourage: **COUNTENANCE**

approximately: **CIRCA**

approximation, nonexact estimate: **BALLPARK FIGURE**

apse: **CHEVET**

apt, well-chosen, agreeable in manner or style: **FELICITOUS**

aquarium sediment at the bottom of the tank: **MULM**

Arab commandos: **FEDAYEEN**

Arabic diacritical mark like an apostrophe: **HAMZA**

Arabic or decimal system of counting: **ALGORISM**

Arab's headband: **AKAL**

Arab's hooded cloak: **BURNOOSE**

Arab's kerchief worn over head and shoulders: **KAFFIYEH**

Arab's sleeveless garment: **ABA**

Arab's sleeveless robe: **ABA, ABBA, ABAYA**

arbitrary, overbearing: **HIGH-HANDED**

arbor or walk with a latticework roof: **PERGOLA**

arcade or passageway open on one side: **LOGGIA**

arch composed of rows of tapered block-like elements or voussoirs: **ROWLOCK ARCH**

archeological excavation: **DIG**

architectural decorative patterns, as in stone over a large Gothic window: **TRACERY**

architectural harmony or balance:
EURHYTHMY
architectural leaf-like ornament:
ACANTHUS
architectural movement of the 1920s
and 1930s stressing functional
design and synthesis of all arts
with technology: **BAUHAUS**
architectural projecting block: **DENTIL**
architectural roof-like fronting that is
triangular, classical gable:
PEDIMENT
architecture order of Greece
characterized by fluted columns
and simple capitals: **DORIC**
architecture order of Greece
characterized by ornate,
bell-shaped capitals: **CORINTHIAN**
architecture order of Greece
characterized by scrolls on the
capitals: **IONIC**
arch's wedge-shaped piece fitted with
others in a curve: **VOUSSOIR**
arch that curves in a reverse way before
coming to a point: **OGEE ARCH**
arch that is narrow and acutely pointed:
LANCET ARCH
arctic, frigid: **HYPERBOREAN**
ardent, extremely fervid: **PERFERVID**
ardent, passionate: **TORRID**
ardent, violent, impetuous: **VEHEMENT**
ardor, intensity of emotion: **FERVOR**
area of authority or competency:
BAILIWICK
area that is unclaimed, unoccupied or
indefinite: **NO-MAN'S-LAND**
arena for horse shows or circuses:
HIPPODROME
arguable, open to question: **DISPUTABLE**
argue earnestly or debate: **CONTEND**
argue earnestly with someone about the
inadvisability of some action:
EXPOSTULATE
argue, oppose: **CONTROVERT**
argue or dispute noisily: **WRANGLE**
arguer or contender about trifling
matters: **STICKLER**
arguer who takes the opposing side
perversely: **DEVIL'S ADVOCATE**
arguing by proving the irrelevant:
IGNORATIO ELENCHI
arguing on the basis of new evidence or
by stressing unduly a minor point:
SPECIAL PLEADING
argument: **POLEMIC**

argumentation, debate: **FORENSICS**
argumentative: **AGONISTIC, ERISTIC**
argumentative, contentious:
DISPUTATIOUS
argument fine point: **QUODLIBET**
argument in which one of the premises
or the conclusion is not stated but
implied: **ENTHYMEME**
aristocrat, member of the upper classes:
PATRICIAN
armband: **BRASSARD**
armor hinged piece for the lower face,
chin plate: **BEAVER**
arm or leg stiffness or cramp: **CHARLEY
HORSE**
armor-like medieval garment of chain
mail: **HAUBERK**
armor piece protecting the torso or the
breast only, breastplate: **CUIRASS**
armpit: **OXTER**
aromatic substances in a ball:
POMANDER
around, about, approximately: **CIRCA**
arouse anger or bitterness: **RANKLE**
arouse interest or curiosity: **INTRIGUE**
arouse, startle, thrill: **ELECTRIFY**
arousing comment, as a piece of
furniture or art: **CONVERSATION
PIECE**
arrangement according to time of
occurrence: **CHRONOLOGY**
arrangement of five things, of which
four make a square and one is in
the middle: **QUINCUNX**
arrangement of parts: **CONFIGURATION**
arrangement of parts that is harmonious
and elegant: **CONCINNITY**
arrangement or progression that is
orderly or gradual: **GRADATION**
arrangement, plan or style of
presentation of a book, TV show,
etc.: **FORMAT**
arrange or organize: **COLLOCATE**
arrest made by a citizen who sees a
crime: **CITIZEN'S ARREST**
arrive at or reach a port: **FETCH**
arrogance arising from overbearing
pride or passion: **HUBRIS**
arrogance or conceit characterizing
one's ways or attitudes:
OVERWEENING
arrogant: **SUPERCILIOUS**
arrogant, domineering: **IMPERIOUS**
arrogant, forward: **PRESUMPTUOUS**

arrogant in assertion of beliefs:
DOGMATIC
arrow's feathers: **FLETCHING**
art and literary movement that tries to
express the workings and images of
the subconscious mind:
SURREALISM
art as an end in itself: **AUTOTELISM**
art cult that rejected conventions:
DADA
artery in the neck, one of two: **CAROTID
ARTERY**
artery walls thickened and degenerated:
ARTERIOSCLEROSIS
artery walls thickened and degenerated
with fatty substances deposited:
ATHEROSCLEROSIS
art for art's sake: **ARS GRATIA ARTIS**
art for art's sake, ars gratia artis: **L'ART
POUR L'ART**
artful moves or strokes: **MANEUVERS**
artful strategy, cunningness, craftiness:
FINESSE
article or book presenting facts on a
subject: **TREATISE**
articulate clearly and distinctly:
ENUNCIATE
artificial, counterfeit: **POSTICHE**
artificial grass used in baseball
stadiums: **ASTROTURF**
artificially elegant style of speech or
writing: **EUPHUISM**
artificial manner: **AFFECTATION**
artificial, not natural, sham: **FACTITIOUS**
artificial part of body: **PROSTHESIS**
artillery or cannon, military combat
materiel: **ORDNANCE**
artistically or imaginatively unifying or
shaping: **ESEMPLASTIC**
artistically thought-of ordinary object:
OBJET TROUVÉ
artistic design in the form of five joined
leaves, petals or lobes: **CINQUEFOIL**
artistic design in the form of four joined
leaves, petals or lobes: **QUATREFOIL**
artistic design in the form of three
joined leaves, petals or lobes:
TREFOIL
artistic imitator or follower: **EPIGONE**
artistic premise, given idea behind a
literary work: **DONNÉE**
artistic small article: **OBJET D'ART**
artistic work combining drama, poetry,
music, etc.: **GESAMTKUNSTWERK**
artistic work critically praised but not

commercially successful: **SUCCÈS
D'ESTIME**
artistic worth or fineness, or a taste for
objects possessing this quality:
VERTU, VIRTU
art is to conceal art, or true art
conceals its methods: **ARS EST
CELARE ARTEM**
artist or writer who doesn't sell his
services exclusively to one
employer: **FREE LANCE**
artists' group, literary group: **CENACLE**
artist's work as a whole: **OEUVRE**
artless, candid, sincere: **GUILELESS**
artless, unaffected, simple, candid:
NAIVE
art movement characterized by free or
distorted expressionist forms and
bold colors: **FAUVISM**
art movement that departs from reality
to reproduce inner experience:
EXPRESSIONISM
art, music or literature schools that
seek to produce moods through
quick glimpses of subject:
IMPRESSIONISM
art of curvilinear designs: **ART
NOUVEAU**
art of everyday realism by U.S. group:
ASHCAN SCHOOL
art of good eating: **GASTRONOMY**
art of strong outlines and geometric
forms: **ART DECO**
art or literature of a cheap, popular or
sentimental quality: **KITSCH**
art work consisting of arrangement of
flat materials pasted on a surface:
COLLAGE
art work painted directly on a wall:
MURAL
arty (British): **TWEE**
ascribe, attribute: **IMPUTE**
ashamed, degraded, sneaky: **HANGDOG**
ashes of a cremated body: **CREMAINS**
ashes-of-the-dead repository:
CINERARIUM
ash gray: **CINEREOUS**
aside directed to a person or thing:
APOSTROPHE
as, in the role or capacity of, acting as:
QUA
as it should be: **COMME IL FAUT**
ask for humbly, pray earnestly for
something: **SUPPLICATE**
ask questions, examine: **INTERROGATE**

aspect, phase or side of a person or subject: FACET

aspersion: SLUR

assassination or murder, as by secret governmental order: EXECUTIVE ACTION

assassination or murder order that is implicit in but euphemized by this term: EXTREME PREJUDICE

assault troops who are highly trained: SHOCK TROOPS

assault with intent to rob: MUG

assembled from various items or sources: CUT-AND-PASTE

assembling of separate parts into a whole: SYNTHESIS

assembly place: AGORA

assent: ACQUIESCENCE

assertion of something made by the negation of its opposite: LITOTES

assign, allot, divide up and give out: ALLOCATE

assimilation of thoughts or facts that is gradual: OSMOSIS

assist: ABET

assistance or money furnished to advance a venture: GRUBSTAKE

assistant, attendant: ACOLYTE

assistant or servant, as of a magician or scholar: FAMULUS

associate closely with someone: FRATERNIZE

associated item or piece of equipment, accessory: ACCOUTREMENT, ACCOUTERMENT

associate on close terms, mingle with: HOBNOB

association, fellowship: SODALITY

association of individuals to negotiate some business: SYNDICATE

assume as a fact: POSIT

assumed name or identity: INCOGNITO

assume to be true: POSTULATE

assumption based on evidence at hand or facts already known: EXTRAPOLATION

assumption provisionally accepted as basis for reasoning or argument: HYPOTHESIS

assure, guarantee: VOUCH

astonishing, fascinating, spectacular: EYE-POPPING

astound, confound: FLABBERGAST

astringent: ACERB

astrologer's chart of position of planets and stars for fortunetelling: HOROSCOPE

astrologer's table of planet and star positions: EPHEMERIS

astronomer's table or almanac: EPHEMERIS

astronomical alignment of three celestial bodies, as during an eclipse: SYZYGY

astronomy muse: URANIA

at-hand materials utilized for tools, decoration, etc.: BRICOLAGE

athlete paid a bonus to become a professional: BONUS BABY

athlete's leap over a high horizontal bar with the aid of a long pole: POLE VAULT

athlete who flaunts his skills or is a showoff: HOT DOG

athletically vigorous: STHENIC

athletic club, gymnast association: TURNVEREIN

athletic competition combining cross-country skiing and rifle marksmanship: BIATHLON

athletic competition combining swimming, bicycling and distance running: TRIATHLON

athletic contest in which each contestant participates in five events: PENTATHLON

athletic contest of ten track-and-field events in all of which each contestant participates: DECATHLON

athletic meet, automobile steeplechase or horsemanship competition: GYMKHANA

athletic or sturdy in body structure: MESOMORPHIC

atmosphere beginning at a height of about seven miles: STRATOSPHERE

atmosphere of a place or situation: AMBIENCE

atmosphere or influence that is unwholesome or noxious: MIASMA

atmospheric and weather phenomena as a science: METEOROLOGY

atomic bomb: A-BOMB

atomic particle carrying a negative charge: ELECTRON

atomic particle carrying a positive charge: PROTON

atomic particle carrying no charge: NEUTRON

atom splitting: NUCLEAR FISSION
atone for, make amends for: EXPIATE
atonement shown for wrongdoing:
    PENANCE
atoning: PIACULAR
atrocious, beyond decency:
    OUTRAGEOUS
atrocious, odious, wicked, evil:
    HEINOUS
atrocious, wicked: FLAGITIOUS
attachment of one thing to another:
    APPURTENANCE
attachment or learning by offspring that
    usually occurs early and is
    long-lasting in effect: IMPRINTING
attachment psychologically to somebody
    because of his or her perceived
    resemblance to one's parent,
    guardian, etc., in early childhood:
    ANACLISIS
attachment to a thing or a person:
    FIXATION
attach the property of a person so it
    can be used to pay a debt:
    GARNISHEE
attack, dispute or challenge the truth or
    validity of: IMPUGN
attacked, besieged,
    controversy-embroiled: EMBATTLED
attack in print: COUP DE PLUME
attack in writing or speech that is
    intentful or malicious: HATCHET
    JOB
attack that is swift and sudden, usually
    in war: BLITZKRIEG
attack that is violent: ONSLAUGHT
attack with scathing criticism: FLAY
attempting: CONATION
attendants of a person of rank, escort:
    RETINUE
attendants, retainers or followers in a
    group: ENTOURAGE
attention grabbing, overshadowing
    another: UPSTAGING
attentive: ASSIDUOUS
attentive to every detail: CIRCUMSPECT
at the home of: CHEZ
at the same or an equal rate,
    progressing together, side by side:
    PARI PASSU
at this time: HEREAT
attitudes and character of a community
    or individual: ETHOS
attract, cause or make likely: INVITE

attractive in a flashy way:
    MERETRICIOUS
attractive photographically:
    PHOTOGENIC
attractive physically, sexually appealing:
    FOXY
attractive, pleasing: PREPOSSESSING
attractive, sweet, engaging: WINSOME
attribute, ascribe: IMPUTE
attribute to another without just reason:
    ARROGATE
auction or sale that is public: VENDUE
audacity, boldness, impudence:
    EFFRONTERY
audacity, brassiness: CHUTZPAH
aunt-like: AMITULAR
aura, halo: NIMBUS
auspices: AEGIS
auspicious, favorably disposed:
    PROPITIOUS
austere: ASTRINGENT
austere person: ASCETIC
Australian back country, bush:
    OUTBACK
Australian wild dog: DINGO
authentic item: REAL MCCOY
authenticity being lacking:
    APOCRYPHAL
authoritative because of rank or office:
    EX CATHEDRA
authoritative, urgently necessary,
    unavoidable: IMPERATIVE
authority, government, etc., that is
    repressive and ever watchful: BIG
    BROTHER
authority or power that is absolute or
    supreme: IMPERIUM
authority shared: COLLEGIALITY
authorization: FIAT
authorize, empower: WARRANT
author's assumed name: NOM DE
    PLUME
automatically conditioned, involving
    trained responses: PAVLOVIAN
automatic electronic regulating
    mechanism using little power to
    control considerable power:
    SERVOMECHANISM
automatic, lifeless: MECHANICAL
automatic response to a stimulus:
    TROPISM
automaton, mechanical man: ROBOT
automobile accident that is minor:
    FENDER BENDER
automobile adjusted or reequipped for

quick starts and high speed: HOT
 ROD
automobile bought that is defective:
 LEMON
automobile device that detects nearby
 police speed-measuring radar:
 FUZZBUSTER
automobile engine that works on rotary
 combustion: WANKEL ENGINE
automobile for drag racing or its driver:
 DRAGSTER
automobile of standard make modified
 for racing: STOCK CAR
automobile sports car long-distance
 race: RALLY, RALLYE
automobile steeplechase, athletic meet
 or horsemanship competition:
 GYMKHANA
automobile steeplechase-like competition
 for small cars on a narrow and
 twisting course: AUTOCROSS
automobile wheel-locking clamp used
 against parking scofflaws: DENVER
 BOOT
automobile whose rear and rear window
 lift up: HATCHBACK
automobile with a convertible's design
 but with a rigid top: HARDTOP
auxiliary: ADMINICLE
auxiliary, aiding, supporting:
 ANCILLARY
available: UP FOR GRABS
avarice, greed: CUPIDITY
avenging, punitive: VINDICATORY
average, moderately good:
 RESPECTABLE

average person: HOMME MOYEN
 SENSUEL
avert or prevent: OBVIATE
avoidable: EVITABLE
avoidance of extremes; middle or
 average that is ideal: GOLDEN
 MEAN
avoidance strategies or techniques, as to
 forestall strikes or riots: CRISIS
 MANAGEMENT
avoider of paying, shirker, sponger:
 DEADBEAT
avoid, escape: ELUDE
avoid, outwit: CIRCUMVENT
avoid, turn aside, ward off: PARRY
awaiting, until: PENDING
away from the center: CENTRIFUGAL
awesome, imposing: AUGUST
awesome, intimidating, challenging:
 FORMIDABLE
awesome, ominous: PORTENTOUS
awkward: UNGAINLY
awkward, boorish: UNCOUTH
awkward, clumsy: GAUCHE
awkward, complicated or problematic
 situation, predicament: PLIGHT
awkward fellow, clown, boor: LOUT
awkward, incompetent, clumsy: INEPT
awkward or inexperienced person on
 board a ship: LANDLUBBER
awkward rustic: BUMPKIN
awkward youth: HOBBLEDEHOY
axiomatic, terse, pithy: SENTENTIOUS
ax- or hatchet-shaped: DOLABRIFORM
azure blue gem: LAPIS LAZULI

baby born in the United States between 1946 and 1965: **BABY BOOMER**

baby delivery by abdominal surgery: **CESAREAN SECTION**

baby delivery, childbirth: **PARTURITION**

baby-like cupid or cherub, especially in a work of art: **AMORETTO**

baby's first cry when born: **VAGITUS**

baccarat variation: **CHEMIN DE FER**

backboned creatures: **VERTEBRATES**

backcountry, remote area, inland region: **HINTERLAND**

backer of a cause: **PROPONENT**

back of a horse, ox or deer, between shoulder blades: **WITHERS**

back-of-the-head bag-like net for a woman's hair: **SNOOD**

back of the neck: **NAPE**

back of the skull: **INION**

back out of an agreement, revoke: **RENEGE**

backward looking, turning or bending: **RETROVERSION**

backward movement: **RECOIL**

backward movement, reversion: **REGRESSION**

backward moving, tending to recede: **RECESSIVE**

backward or remote place, stagnant area: **BACKWATER**

backward reading of a word or sentence being the same as normal, left-to-right reading: **PALINDROME**

backward reasoning, from consequence to antecedent, considered a logical fallacy: **HYSTERON PROTERON**

backward tending, worsening, declining: **RETROGRADE**

backward writing that is readable in a mirror: **MIRROR-WRITING**

bacon or pork slice used for larding meat: **LARDON**

bacon slice: **RASHER**

bad breath: **HALITOSIS**

bad check: **KITE**

bad counsel, false information or advice: **BUM STEER**

bad effect making a medical treatment inadvisable: **CONTRAINDICATION**

bad, evil, repulsive: **VILE**

badge-like rosette or knot of ribbons as worn on a hat: **COCKADE**

bad handwriting or spelling: **CACOGRAPHY**

bad in a conspicuous fashion, glaring, flagrant: **EGREGIOUS**

bad job: **BOTCH**

bad luck: **AMBSACE**

badminton feathery cone hit back and forth over the net: **SHUTTLECOCK**

bad money drives out good: **GRESHAM'S LAW**

bad morally: **UNSAVORY**

bad or incorrigible person who is atypical or is undesirable to others: **ROTTEN APPLE**

bad or vile person, villain, scoundrel: **BLACKGUARD**

bad-tempered: **ATRABILIOUS**

bad-tempered: **CANTANKEROUS**

bad-tempered and moody, peevish, morose: **SPLENETIC**

bad-tempered outburst: **TANTRUM**

bad-tempered, peevish, snappish: **WASPISH**

bad-tempered person: **CROSSPATCH**

bad-tempered, spiteful: **SPLENETIC**

baggage checkroom (British): **LEFT-LUGGAGE OFFICE**

baggage handler at a station, porter: **REDCAP**

baggage, supplies and equipment carried by an army: **IMPEDIMENTA**

bag of perfumed powder: **SACHET**

bagpipe part with finger holes: **CHANTER**

bagpipe's shrill sound: **SKIRL**

bag used by sailors for carrying personal belongings: **DITTY BAG**

bag worn over one shoulder: **HAVERSACK**

bag worn strapped across the shoulders and used for carrying supplies: **KNAPSACK**

bait, allurement, enticement: **GUDGEON**

balance: **EQUILIBRIUM**

balance by presenting as an opposite or contrast: **COUNTERPOSE**

balance, counteract or compensate for something else: **OFFSET**

balanced, calm, ordered, harmonious, rational: **APOLLONIAN**

balance or counterbalance: **EQUIPONDERATE**

balancing point: **FULCRUM**

balcony, window or porch with an excellent view, in Spanish architecture: **MIRADOR**

baldness: **ALOPECIA**

baldness, especially on top of the head: **CALVITIES**

balk, move restlessly sidewise or backward: **JIB**

balky, fretful, jittery: **RESTIVE**

ballet bending of the knees with the back kept upright: **PLIÉ**

ballet dancer, female: **BALLERINA**

ballet dancer, male: **DANSEUR**

ballet dancer's whirling on the toes: **PIROUETTE**

ballet dancer who performs only in groups: **FIGURANT**

ballet dancer who ranks between the soloists and the corps de ballet: **CORYPHEE**

ballet leap from one foot to the other: **JETÉ**

ballet leap with dancer activating legs in air: **ENTRECHAT**

ballet position on tiptoe: **EN POINTE**

ballet's principal female dancer: **PRIMA BALLERINA**

ballet's principal male dancer: **PREMIER DANSEUR, DANSEUR NOBLE**

ball game in which players hit a ball against a wall by striking it with their hands: **HANDBALL**

ball of small size: **PELLET**

ball's horizontal twist or spin: **ENGLISH**

baloney, bull: **BUSHWA**

banal, trite, commonplace remark: **PLATITUDE**

ban, curse: **ANATHEMA**

bandaged, bound with a band: **FASCIATE**

bandage used to compress an artery to stop the flow of blood: **TOURNIQUET**

bandleader's or soldier's tall and stiff cylindrical headdress with a visor and plume: **SHAKO**

band of commercial or political interests: **CARTEL**

band or group: **COHORT**

banish, exile: **RELEGATE**

bankrupt: **BELLY-UP**

bankruptcy procedure outlined in U.S. law: **CHAPTER 11**

bankrupt, lacking sufficient funds: **INSOLVENT**

banned, forbidden: **TABOO**

banner fixed to a crosspiece rather than a pole: **GONFALON**

banquet with celebrities featuring humorous mock attacks on the guest of honor: **ROAST**

banter: **CHAFF**

banter, flippant talk or writing: **PERSIFLAGE**

banter, jesting: **RAILLERY**

baptismal water receptacle, usually of stone, in a church: **FONT**

baptism by immersion: **HOLOBAPTISM**

barbecuing, roasting or broiling appliance with a rotating spit: **ROTISSERIE**

barbed wire that has sharp edges: **RAZOR RIBBON**

barefooted, as certain religious orders: **DISCALCED**

barely begun: **INCHOATE**

barely get, get with difficulty: **EKE OUT**

barely sufficient despite much work: **HARDSCRABBLE**

bar for drinks that is equipped with a sink and running water: **WET BAR**

bargain or argue about terms: **HAGGLE**

bargain-priced, at a good bargain: **À BON MARCHÉ**

baring parts of the body for sexual stimulation of oneself: **EXHIBITIONISM**

bark, yelp: **YAWP**

barrel maker: **COOPER**

barrel stave: **LAG**

barren, bleak: **STARK**

barren, fruitless, sterile: **INFECUND**

barren, insipid, dry, lacking interest: **JEJUNE**

barren, not pregnant: said of cows: **FARROW**

barren, unfruitful: **STERILE**

barren, weak: **EFFETE**

barrier made up of strong stakes: **PALISADE**

barrier to keep out disease: **CORDON SANITAIRE**

bar serving food and drink: **BRASSERIE**

bar that is upright and forms the principal support: **STANCHION**

bar used to prevent a vehicle from slipping backward on an incline: **SPRAG**

baseball: a ball grounded or bounced right back to the pitcher: **COMEBACKER**

baseball barely deflected by the bat: **FOUL TIP**

baseball batter fourth in the lineup: **CLEANUP HITTER**

baseball batter in the American League who bats throughout the game for the pitcher but does not function as a fielder: **DESIGNATED HITTER, DH**

baseball batter's fly ball or bunt that results in an out but enables a base runner to advance: **SACRIFICE**

baseball batter's long hit: **CLOUT**

baseball batter's stance in which the front foot is planted closer to the plate than the rear foot: **CLOSED STANCE**

baseball batter's stance in which the front foot is planted farther from the plate than the rear foot: **OPEN STANCE**

baseball batter's weakly hit ball: **BLOOPER**

baseball catcher's error in failing to catch a pitch, thus allowing a man on base to advance: **PASSED BALL**

baseball decision by a player to try to put out a baserunner rather than the batter: **FIELDER'S CHOICE**

baseball diamond space within the four base lines: **INFIELD**

baseball errant pitch that the catcher cannot handle, thereby allowing a runner to advance: **WILD PITCH**

baseball field perimeter strip along the outfield fence: **WARNING TRACK**

baseball fly hit in fielding practice by a batsman who tosses the ball up and strikes it as it descends: **FUNGO**

baseball game division during which each team has a turn at bat: **INNING**

baseball game with many hits and usually many runs scored by both teams: **SLUGFEST**

baseball hand-held device to measure the speed of a pitch: **RADAR GUN**

baseball hard hit so that it travels in an approximately horizontal trajectory: **LINE DRIVE**

baseball hit ball that rolls or bounces along the ground: **GROUND BALL, GROUNDER**

baseball hit in the air that falls between the infield and the outfield for a base hit: **TEXAS LEAGUER**

baseball hit on which the batter reaches second base: **DOUBLE**

baseball hit on which the batter reaches third base: **TRIPLE**

baseball hit so that it takes a high bounce in front of home plate: **BALTIMORE CHOP**

baseball hit that allows the batter to touch all bases and score a run: **HOME RUN, HOMER**

baseball hit that bounces into the stands or is interfered with by a spectator, whereupon the batter is permitted two bases: **GROUND RULE DOUBLE**

baseball home run hit when there is a runner on every base: **GRAND SLAM**

baseball illegal pitched ball that is moistened before being thrown: **SPITBALL**

baseball infielder stationed between second and third bases: **SHORTSTOP**

baseball infielder who on a given play

intercepts a throw from the outfield: CUTOFF MAN

baseball left-handed pitcher: SOUTHPAW

baseball light hit of the ball without swinging the bat: BUNT

baseball outfield areas between the centerfielder and the left and right fielders: POWER ALLEYS

baseball out made when a runner, forced from his base by a teammate's hitting the ball, fails to reach the next base before the ball is caught there: FORCE-OUT

baseball pitch by a right-hander that curves right or by a left-hander that curves left: SCREWBALL

baseball pitcher's illegal motion: BALK

baseball pitcher who replaces another: RELIEVER

baseball pitch like a fastball but that suddenly drops as it approaches home plate: SPLIT-FINGERED FASTBALL

baseball pitch that is fast and curves only slightly: SLIDER

baseball pitch that curves sharply downward as it approaches home plate: SINKER

baseball pitch thrown deliberately close to the batter to move him away from the plate or to intimidate him: BRUSHBACK PITCH

baseball pitch thrown wide to the catcher by prearrangement in hope of throwing out a base runner expected to be attempting a steal: PITCHOUT

baseball pitch thrown with a fast motion but that is slow in movement: CHANGEUP, CHANGE OF PACE

baseball player able to bat both left-handed and right-handed: SWITCH HITTER

baseball player's stirrup-like oversock: STIRRUP SOCK

baseball player who is not a starting player or likes to hector the opponents during the game: BENCH JOCKEY

baseball player who is used as a substitute in different positions: UTILITY PLAYER

baseball play in which a base runner trapped between two bases is put out: RUNDOWN

baseball play in which a man on base starts running with the pitch and the batter's role is to strike at the ball to protect him: HIT-AND-RUN PLAY

baseball play in which a runner is caught off base by a sudden throw: PICKOFF

baseball play in which the batter tries to bunt the ball to allow a man on third to score: SQUEEZE PLAY

baseball play in which three players are put out: TRIPLE PLAY

baseball play in which two players are put out: DOUBLE PLAY

baseball quick throw to a base to catch the baserunner off the bag: PICKOFF PLAY

baseball relief pitcher relied upon to pitch not more than a few innings near or at the end of the game: SHORT RELIEVER, SHORT MAN, CLOSER

baseball relief pitcher relied upon to replace a starting pitcher early in the game if necessary and to continue for four, five or more innings: LONG RELIEVER, LONG MAN

baseball retirement of a batter with three strikes: STRIKEOUT

baseball rule, applicable when there are runners at first and second or first, second and third with fewer than two outs, that a catchable infield fly is an automatic out and may not be deliberately dropped or missed by the infielder in order to trap other runners off base: INFIELD FLY RULE

baseballs caught on the fly in practice: SHAGGING

baseball stadium's area where pitchers warm up: BULLPEN

baseball surprise bunt for a base hit made with the batter already in motion toward first base: DRAG BUNT

baseball tactic, with fewer than two outs, whereby a runner on third base races home to try to score the moment the ball leaves the pitcher's hand: SUICIDE SQUEEZE baseball tactic, with fewer than two outs, whereby a runner on third base races toward home to try to score the instant the batter bunts the ball: **SQUEEZE PLAY**

baseball term for obscure minor leagues: **BUSH LEAGUES**

baseball: to not swing at a pitched ball: **TAKE**

baseball: the pitcher and the catcher: **BATTERY**

base, degraded, vile: **SORDID**

base, dishonorable, degraded: **IGNOBLE**

baseless: **UNFOUNDED**

baseness, vileness, depravity: **TURPITUDE**

base-of-cliff debris or rubble: **SCREE**

base something on known facts or conditions: **PREDICATE**

basic: **ABECEDARIAN**

basically, essentially, fundamentally, at bottom: **AU FOND**

basic, inherent in, fundamental: **ORGANIC**

basic unity in ecology, including both organisms and environment: **ECOSYSTEM**

basis for a discussion or conclusion: **PREMISE**

basis, fundamental principle: **HYPOSTASIS**

basketball defense with two players zoned on either side of the free-throw lane and the remaining defender guarding a particular opponent man-to-man: **BOX AND ONE**

basketball dribbling violation, or the taking of too many steps or moving of the pivot foot by the ball handler: **TRAVELING, WALKING, STEPS**

basketball field goal made by throwing the ball in a sweeping downward motion through the hoop: **SLAM DUNK**

basketball free throw: **FOUL SHOT**

basketball intensive defense by guarding opposing players man-to-man from one end of the court to the other: **FULL-COURT PRESS**

basketball interference by an offensive player with the ball around the backboard or rim in any of various ways, negating any subsequent basket: **GOALTENDING**

basketball offensive play in which a player momentarily screens an opponent, then whirls to receive a pass from the ball handler: **PICK AND ROLL**

basketball offensive strategy whereby a team upon gaining possession of the ball moves it quickly toward its own basket in hopes of scoring quickly, often the style of a team having swift personnel: **FAST BREAK**

basketball one-handed shot made sideways over the head: **HOOK**

basketball shot made by a player in the air during a jump: **JUMP SHOT**

basketball shot made with one hand from close to the basket: **LAYUP**

basketball shot that touches neither the backboard, rim nor net, or a complete miss: **AIR BALL**

basketball team's loss of possession of the ball because of a steal or other mistake: **TURNOVER**

basketball: to move by bouncing it with the hand: **DRIBBLE**

basket-like handicraft work, furniture, etc.: **WICKERWORK**

basket of fruit done in sculpture: **CORBEIL**

basket of fruit, often shown carried on the head, that was a fertility symbol in Greek and Roman antiquity: **CALATHUS**

basket, usually large and covered: **HAMPER**

bath, cleansing: **ABLUTION**

bathing suit for women that is two-piece and brief: **BIKINI**

batter cake that is crisp and baked in a griddle: **WAFFLE**

battle-ax with two sharp edges: **TWIBIL**

battle flag or other symbol to inspire courage: **ORIFLAMME**

battle formation: **DEPLOYMENT**

battle that is great or decisive: **ARMAGEDDON**

bawl, shout, exclaim loudly: **VOCIFERATE**

bay, bend in a river or coastline: **BIGHT**

bay or stream leading into the land from a larger body of water: **INLET**

bay window: **ORIEL**

beach bathhouse that is often a tent: **CABANA**

beam-emitting device that amplifies and concentrates light waves: **LASER**

beam going from wall to wall: **CROSSBEAM**

beam resting horizontally upon the walls of a building and supporting the ends of joists: **SUMMER**

beams placed parallel and horizontally from wall to wall: **JOISTS**

bearable: **TOLERABLE**

beard on the chin: **GOATEE**

beard that is long and somewhat rectangular: **PATRICIAN**

beard that is short and pointed: **VANDYKE**

bear-like: **URSINE**

beast-like in form: **THERIOMORPHIC**

beat at which the hand of the conductor is raised: **UPBEAT**

beat, cudgel: **FUSTIGATE**

beating with a stick as punishment: **BASTINADO**

beat, overcome: **DRUB**

beat rapidly, flutter, quiver: **PALPITATE**

beat, thrash severely, punish: **TROUNCE**

beat with the fists: **PUMMEL**

beautiful in having shapely buttocks: **CALLIPYGIAN**

beauty: **PULCHRITUDE**

beauty as a subject of study: **ESTHETICS**

because of one's official position: **EX OFFICIO**

because of this: **HEREAT**

become known, leak out: **TRANSPIRE**

become or make better: **AMELIORATE**

becoming sour: **ACESCENT**

bed covering for warmth, comforter, quilt: **DUVET**

bed cover that is quilted: **COMFORTER**

bed, grade, layer: **STRATUM**

bed of straw that lies on the floor: **PALLET**

bedridden, the person is not: **AMBULATORY**

bedroom and small living room combined: **BED-SITTER**

bedroom censoriousness by a wife: **CURTAIN LECTURE**

bedsore: **DECUBITUS**

bedspread, quilt: **COUNTERPANE**

bed that swings up easily into a closet for storing during the day: **MURPHY BED**

bed-wetting: **ENURESIS**

beef cattle male: **STEER**

beef cut from the loin end ahead of the rump: **SIRLOIN**

beef marinated in vinegar before cooking: **SAUERBRATEN**

beef tenderloin, lean and thick, broiled: **FILET MIGNON**

beehive, especially one made of straw: **SKEP**

beehives: **APIARY**

beer or ale and ginger ale mixed: **SHANDYGAFF**

before birth, unborn, in the uterus: **IN UTERO**

before, earlier: **ANTERIOR**

beforehand opinion, to form a: **PRECONCEIVE**

before noon: **ANTE MERIDIEM**

before now, previously: **HERETOFORE**

before the Civil War, especially the pre-1861 South: **ANTEBELLUM**

before the Flood: **ANTEDILUVIAN**

beg: **CADGE**

beget, produce: **PROCREATE**

beggar, sponger: **SCHNORRER**

begging: **MENDICANT**

begin, commence: **INAUGURATE**

begin, commence, originate: **INITIATE**

beginner: **ABECEDARIAN**

beginner: **FLEDGLING**

beginner, apprentice: **NOVICE**

beginner, novice: **TYRO**

beginner, recent convert: **NEOPHYTE**

beginning affixed to a word: **PREFIX**

beginning and end: **ALPHA AND OMEGA**

beginning a series of lines or sentences with the same word or phrase: **ANAPHORA**

beginning, commencement: **CONCEPTION**

beginnings, earliest stages of development: **INCUNABULA**

beginning, start: **INCEPTION**

beginning to appear, coming into existence: **INCIPIENT**

beg something of: **SUPPLICATE**

beg urgently, entreat: **IMPLORE**

behave (oneself): **DEMEAN**

behavior-altering treatment whereby undesired responses or habits become associated with unpleasant stimuli: **AVERSIVE CONDITIONING, AVERSION THERAPY**

behavior, conduct: **DEPORTMENT**

behavior, deportment: DEMEANOR
behavior that is seemly and proper:
   DECOROUS
behead: DECAPITATE
behind: BUTTOCKS
behind: DERRIÈRE
behind, after, later: POSTERIOR
behold: VOILÀ
being nowhere: NULLIBICITY
being, objective existence of something
   in the mind, actual being: ENTITY
belch: ERUCT
belief, doctrine or principle maintained
   as true by a person or a group:
   TENET
belief in a god: THEISM
belief in more than one god:
   POLYTHEISM
belief in one god without denying the
   existence of others: HENOTHEISM
belief in something with too little
   evidence: CREDULITY
belief or opinion contrary to established
   doctrine: HERESY
belief or particular conviction that is
   necessary, indispensable tenet:
   ARTICLE OF FAITH
beliefs or opinions held to be true and
   necessary: DOGMA
believability: CREDIBILITY
believable, apparently true but open to
   question: PLAUSIBLE
believed but not substantiated assertion,
   as one often printed or repeated:
   FACTOID
believing according to a particular
   religion or philosophy: SECTARIAN
belittle: DISPARAGE
belittle: DEPRECIATE
belittle, detract: DEROGATE
belittle, put down: DISPARAGE
belittle, speak disparagingly:
   POOH-POOH
bell casting and ringing:
   CAMPANOLOGY
belligerent's right to use or destroy
   neutral's property: ANGARY
bell ringing variations: CHANGE
   RINGING
bell rung at morning, noon and night:
   ANGELUS
bell-shaped woman's hat: CLOCHE
bell signal, alarm: TOCSIN
bell sounded slowly and at regular
   intervals: TOLLING

bells ringing: TINTINNABULATION
bells rung by hammers operated from a
   keyboard: CARILLON
bell tolling, especially one announcing a
   death: KNELL
bell tower, especially one that is not
   part of a building: CAMPANILE
belly button: NAVEL
belly button: UMBILICUS
belly that is big and prominent:
   PAUNCH
belt: CEINTURE
belt buckle's tongue-like part: TANG
belt or cord put around the waist:
   CINCTURE
benches not under a roof at a sporting
   event: BLEACHERS
bench that is upholstered and without
   arms: BANQUETTE
bendable, flexible: PLIABLE
bend, contort, twist: WRITHE
bend, curve in and out: SINUATE
bend in a river or coastline, bay: BIGHT
bending, curved or bent part: FLECTION
bending easily, graceful, limber: LITHE
bending of light or heat ray as it moves
   from one medium to another:
   REFRACTION
bending or winding, unsteady,
   wavering: FLEXUOUS
bend, misrepresent, twist: DISTORT
bend that is sharp or elbow-like:
   DOGLEG
bend the knee, as in worship:
   GENUFLECT
beneath, below: NETHER
beneath one's dignity: INFRA DIG
beneficial: SALUTARY
beneficiary or recipient of a legacy:
   LEGATEE
benefit owed because of status:
   PERQUISITE
bent backward: RETROFLEX
bent like a hook: UNCINATE
berate, upbraid, scold severely:
   OBJURGATE
beseeching: SUPPLIANT
beset by a difficult situation: HARD-SET
beset or surround: BELEAGUER
besides, in addition: WITHAL
beside the (real) point: ACCIDENTAL
besieged, attacked, beleaguered,
   controversy-embroiled: EMBATTLED
bespangled with fine stars: STELLULAR
best in a given field: ARISTOCRACY

best moment, most critical time:
PSYCHOLOGICAL MOMENT
best, most choice or elite people:
CRÈME DE LA CRÈME
best, most distinguished: ELITE
best or most appealing aspect: BEAUTY
PART
bestow, make known, disclose: IMPART
best quality, highest priced: GILT-EDGED
bet in which one chooses first- and
second-place finishers without
having to indicate in which order:
QUINIELA
bet in which one chooses the first- and
second-place finishers: PERFECTA
bet in which one chooses the first- ,
second- and third-place finishers:
TRIFECTA
bet-on choice that has little chance of
winning: LONG SHOT
bet on races in which those backing
winners share in the total wagered:
PARIMUTUEL
bet on winners in two races: DAILY
DOUBLE
betrayal: SELLOUT
betterment: MELIORATION
betterment of the world: MELIORISM
bet the winnings of a previous race on a
later one: PARLAY
between: INTERVENING
between acts: ENTR'ACTE
between the devil and the deep blue sea:
DILEMMA
between the lines: INTERLINEAR
between us: ENTRE NOUS
bevel a surface: CHAMFER
beverage of chocolate syrup, milk and
soda water: EGG CREAM
bewilder, amaze, stun: STUPEFY
bewilder, dumbfound, perplex:
NONPLUS
bewildered: BEMUSED
bewildered, tense, worried, agitated,
crazed: DISTRAUGHT
bewildered, uncertain, puzzled:
PERPLEXED
beyond earth in origin, nonhuman,
alien: EXTRATERRESTRIAL
beyond the lawful powers of, forbidden:
ULTRA VIRES
beyond words: INEFFABLE
biased: TENDENTIOUS
biased, favoring one party, prejudiced:
PARTIAL

bias, prejudice: PRECONCEPTION
bias that is favorable, partiality:
PREDILECTION
bible of information, reference, etc.,
easily carried around: VADE
MECUM
biblical interpretation: HERMENEUTICS
bids entered simultaneously for the
same stock are resolved by a flip of
a coin: MATCHED AND LOST
big and sudden change or increase:
QUANTUM LEAP, QUANTUM JUMP
big belly: PAUNCH
Big Board: NEW YORK STOCK
EXCHANGE
biggest portion (originally the whole
thing): LION'S SHARE
bigotry: INTOLERANCE
big, thick-skinned animals with hooves:
PACHYDERMS
big toe: HALLUX
bigwig, chief, important official:
POOH-BAH
big-word user, one with an inflated
vocabulary: LEXIPHANES
billboard (British): HOARDING
bill for merchandise sent or services
rendered: INVOICE
billiard ball caused to recoil after
impact: DRAW
billiard shot in which the ball first
strikes the cushion: BRICOLE
billiard shot in which the cue ball
strikes two others in succession:
CAROM
billiard stroke in which the cue is held
perpendicularly: MASSÉ
billionth of a second: NANOSECOND
bind one's arms to render helpless:
PINION
biographer, especially a devoted one:
BOSWELL
biological and medical technological
advances: BIOENGINEERING
biological cell division process having
two phases: MEIOSIS
biological classification that is a
subdivision of a genus: SPECIES
biological individual's development:
ONTOGENY
biologically deteriorating as a strain or
type, especially in man: DYSGENIC
biologically occurring in different or
isolated regions: ALLOPATRIC

biologically occurring in the same region: **SYMPATRIC**

bird cage, usually large: **AVIARY**

bird group terms and terms for young—see "creature terms"

bird-like, flying, extinct reptile with a long beak: **PTERODACTYL**

bird of Arabian legend that is huge and strong: **ROC**

bird of legend that rises from its ashes: **PHOENIX**

bird's rump or part that holds the tail feathers: **UROPYGIUM**

bird study: **ORNITHOLOGY**

birth by abdominal surgery: **CESAREAN SECTION**

birth control governing the number and spacing of offspring: **PLANNED PARENTHOOD**

birthday or nativity calculation: **GENETHLIALOGY**

birth-giving, involving childbirth: **PUERPERAL**

birthmark: **NEVUS**

birth with the buttocks first: **BREECH DELIVERY**

biscuit baked on a griddle: **SCONE**

biscuit for army and navy use that is hard and cracker-like: **HARDTACK**

bisexual: **AC/DC**

bisexual: **DOUBLE-GAITED**

bishopric, bishops collectively: **EPISCOPATE**

bishop's geographical area of jurisdiction: **DIOCESE**

bishop's staff or pole, pastoral staff: **CROSIER**

bishop who acts as assistant or auxiliary to another bishop: **SUFFRAGAN**

biting: **ASTRINGENT**

biting, caustic: **PUNGENT**

biting in taste: **ACRID**

biting, sarcastic: **CAUSTIC**

biting, sharp, keen: **INCISIVE**

bit, scrap: **SNIPPET**

bitter: **ACERB**

bitter: **ACRIMONIOUS**

bitter in taste: **ACRID**

bitterness: **ASPERITY**

bitter, rancorous: **VIRULENT**

bizarre, fantastic: **GROTESQUE**

black: **JET**

black alloy used in cut-in decorations in metal: **NIELLO**

black Americans' game of mutual insult, usually about relatives: **DOZENS**

black and blue: **LIVID**

black and blue mark, bruise: **ECCHYMOSIS**

black and white: **ACHROMATIC**

black and white, light and shade: **CHIAROSCURO**

black anti-glare pigment applied under the eyes, as by athletes: **LAMPBLACK**

blacken, disparage, defame: **DENIGRATE**

blackjack-like weapon: **COSH**

black letter type: **OLD ENGLISH**

black magic, fortune-telling, sorcery: **NECROMANCY**

blackmail of sorts of a company by buying much of its stock and posing a threatened takeover: **GREENMAIL**

blackness, darkness: **NIGRESCENCE**

black person in America of African descent: **AFRO-AMERICAN**

blacksmith, horseshoer: **FARRIER**

blacksmith's workshop: **SMITHY**

bladder examination: **CYSTOSCOPY**

bladder inflammation: **CYSTITIS**

bladder or bowel lack of control: **INCONTINENCE**

blame: **CENSURE**

blame, charge with fault: **INCULPATE**

blame, criticize, find fault with: **REPREHEND**

blamed person to whom mistakes of others are attributed: **SCAPEGOAT**

blame is mine: **MEA CULPA**

blameless: **IRREPROACHABLE**

blameless, faultless: **UNIMPEACHABLE**

blame, rebuke, disapproval: **REPROOF**

blame, reprove, censure: **REPROACH**

blameworthy: **CULPABLE**

bland, dull, tasteless, flat: **INSIPID**

blank check: **CARTE BLANCHE**

blank, fixed, uncomprehending: **GLASSY**

blank, gap: **LACUNA**

blank leaf at the beginning or end of a book: **FLYLEAF**

blasphemous: **IMPIOUS**

blather, hesitate, equivocate: **WAFFLE**

bleach or dry in the sun: **INSOLATE**

bleak, barren: **STARK**

bleeding condition caused by absence of a clotting factor: **HEMOPHILIA**

bleeding in large quantity: **HEMORRHAGE**

bleeding-stopping stick usually of alum: **STYPTIC PENCIL**

blemish, stain: **MACULATION**

blend: **AMALGAM**

blend and reconcile, as various philosophies: **SYNCRETIZE**

blend, combine: **INTERLACE**

blending of two vowels generally pronounced separately: **SYNERESIS**

blending together of variant readings of a text: **CONFLATION**

blend or fuse together: **COALESCE**

blessed, blissful, sublimely contented or happy: **BEATIFIC**

blessing: **BENEDICTION**

blight: **CANKER**

blind alley: **CUL-DE-SAC**

blindly devoted: **IDOLATROUS**

blindness or impaired vision for blue and yellow: **TRITANOPIA**

blind persons, printing method for: **BRAILLE**

blind spot: **SCOTOMA**

blissful, blessed, sublimely contented or happy: **BEATIFIC**

bliss, release from care and pain: **NIRVANA**

blister: **BLEB**

blister-producing: **VESICANT**

blockhead: **JACKASS**

blockhead, stupid person: **DOLT**

block, hinder, stop, impede: **OBSTRUCT**

block, obstruct: **STYMIE**

block or stone on which a column or statue stands: **PLINTH**

block, shut or close off: **OCCLUDE**

block that projects (architecture): **DENTIL**

blood clot in the heart or blood vessel: **THROMBOSIS**

blood clotting: **COAGULATION**

blood infection: **SEPTICEMIA**

blood poisoning: **TOXEMIA**

blood-pressure, cuff-like measuring device: **SPHYGMOMANOMETER**

blood relationship: **CONSANGUINITY**

blood vessels and heart, pertaining to: **CARDIOVASCULAR**

bloody: **SANGUINARY**

bloody or slaughterous site, place of bloodshed: **ACELDAMA**

bloody slaughter: **CARNAGE**

blossom, bloom forth, flower: **EFFLORESCE**

blossoming: **FLORESCENCE**

blossoming late: **SEROTINOUS**

blotched, spotted, streaked: **MOTTLED**

blouse-like garment gathered at the waist: **TUNIC**

blouse-like garment that hangs loose over a waistband or belt: **BLOUSON**

blow in puffs: **WHIFFLE**

blow low or almost out, as a candle flame: **GUTTER**

blow to back of the neck in boxing: **RABBIT PUNCH**

blue appearance of skin due to lack of oxygen in blood: **CYANOSIS**

blue blindness: **TRITANOPIA**

blue or shocking in content: **RISQUÉ**

bluffing by talk and posturing: **SHUCKING AND JIVING**

blundering, clumsy: **MALADROIT**

blunt, direct: **POINT-BLANK**

blunt, dull, insensible: **OBTUSE**

blurred piece of print, blemish or spot: **MACKLE**

blurring or softening colors or lines in a painting or drawing: **SCUMBLE**

bluster, bragging talk: **GASCONADE**

boardinghouse, rooming house: **PENSION**

boards arranged for nailing together into barrels or boxes: **SHOOK**

boardwalk-like flooring or slats over a wet surface, as behind a counter or bar: **DUCKBOARDS**

boardwalk or carnival booth game of any sort: **HANKY-PANK**

board with handle underneath used to hold plaster or mortar: **HAWK**

board, with letter and other markings, used for spiritualistic telepathy: **OUIJA**

boaster: **GASCON**

boastful defiance: **BRAVADO**

boastfully vain: **VAINGLORIOUS**

boastfulness, bragging: **RODOMONTADE**

boastful or bullying speech: **FANFARONADE**

boastful soldier: **MILES GLORIOSUS**

boasting that is ostentatious: **JACTITATION**

boasting that is pretentious: **BRAGGADOCIO**

boat basin for pleasure craft: **MARINA**

boat, flat-bottomed with battened sails, used by Chinese: **JUNK**

boat for armed antisubmarine combat,

disguised as a merchant ship:
Q-SHIP, Q-BOAT

boat for fishing: **SMACK**

boat for pleasure propelled by pedaling:
PEDAL BOAT

boat framework that extends beyond
the gunwale: **OUTRIGGER**

boat, narrow and light, for racing:
SCULL

boat or ship interior wall or partition:
BULKHEAD

boat or ship term for upper edge of
craft's side: **GUNWALE, GUNNEL**

boat or supplies carrying at a place
where a waterway is not navigable,
or the place where this is
necessary: **PORTAGE**

boat race or series of boat races:
REGATTA

boat's crosswise seat for a rower:
THWART

boat-shaped: **SCAPHOID**

boat, small and flat-bottomed, used
along the rivers and coasts of
China and Japan: **SAMPAN**

boat song, gondolier's song:
BARCAROLE

boat's or ship's pole, or spar, projecting
from the bow: **BOWSPRIT**

boat's or ship's triangular sail to the
front of the mainsail: **SPINNAKER**

boat stairway between decks:
COMPANIONWAY

boat that drags a net across a fishing
bank: **TRAWLER**

boat that services another at sea:
TENDER

boat with a double hull and sails:
CATAMARAN

boat with three parallel hulls and with
sails: **TRIMARAN**

bodily build and constitution as related
to disease: **HABITUS**

bodily disorders being caused by mental
or emotional conditions:
PSYCHOSOMATIC

bodily or involving the body's attributes
or elements: **CORPORAL,
CORPOREAL**

bodily pleasures or place that provides
them: **FLESHPOT**

bodily processes that continuously build
up and break down protoplasm:
METABOLISM

bodily waste matter: **EGESTA**

body chemical that stimulates other
people: **PHEROMONE**

body-covering tight garment often used
for exercise: **BODY STOCKING**

body of men summoned to assist a
peace officer: **POSSE**

body, preoccupied by the: **CARNAL**

body-related, as distinguished from the
soul: **SOMATIC**

body's inherent timing or cyclical
mechanisms: **BIOLOGICAL CLOCK**

body stealer: **RESURRECTIONIST**

bog down, sink in mud: **MIRE**

bog, marsh: **MORASS**

bog, swamp, backwater: **SLOUGH**

boil down, condense: **DECOCT**

boil gently: **SIMMER**

boiling or agitated condition: **CALDRON**

boil partly or quickly: **PARBOIL**

boisterous, unruly: **OBSTREPEROUS**

bold, dauntless, fearless: **INTREPID**

bold deeds or adventures: **DERRING-DO**

bold, indecent, self-assertive: **IMMODEST**

boldness, audacity, impudence:
EFFRONTERY

boldness, daring, audacity: **HARDIHOOD**

bold, saucy, brazen, shameless:
IMPUDENT

bombastic: **TUMID**

bombastic, grandiloquent: **TURGID**

bombastic, high-flown: **INFLATED**

bombastic, ornate, florid, showy:
FLAMBOYANT

bombastic or pretentious language:
FUSTIAN

bombastic, pompous: **GRANDILOQUENT**

bombing intensely concentrated to
obliterate: **SATURATION BOMBING**

bomb or grenade consisting of a bottle
containing flammable liquid:
MOLOTOV COCKTAIL

bomb that explodes into jagged pieces:
FRAGMENTATION BOMB

bond, connection, link: **NEXUS**

bond issued by a company with a
reputation for showing a profit:
GILT-EDGED

bond issue that may be redeemed by
the issuer before maturity:
CALLABLE BOND

bond not having the owner's name
registered with the issuing
company and payable to any
holder of the bond: **BEARER BOND**

bond often lacking a specific pledge of assets: DEBENTURE

bond of unity or union: VINCULUM

bond on which principal and interest are guaranteed by a company other than the issuer of the bond: GUARANTEED BOND

bond, tie that connects: LIGAMENT

bond value as it appears on the security: FACE VALUE

bond with a low rating and high yield: JUNK BOND

bone and muscle branch of surgery: ORTHOPEDICS

bone at lower end of the spine: COCCYX

bone-forming process: OSSIFICATION

bones-of-the-dead receptacle or vault: OSSUARY

bones united by muscles: SYSSARCOSIS

bookbinding leather: SKIVER

bookbinding style characterized by gilded ornamentation: GROLIER

bookbinding with leather on the spine and corners and cloth or paper on the sides: HALF BINDING

book bound in paper rather than cloth or leather: PAPERBACK

book bound in stiff cover as distinguished from paperback: HARDCOVER BOOK

book carrying various versions of a text: VARIORUM

book containing rules of spelling, punctuation and typography, used by editors: STYLEBOOK

book cover lining, especially when it is ornamental: DOUBLURE

book destroyer, book burner: BIBLIOCLAST

book for recording one's favorite quotations, literary passages and thoughts: COMMONPLACE BOOK

book installment prior to publication: FASCICLE

bookish or literary woman, pedantic female: BLUESTOCKING

book jacket matter that touts the volume: BLURB

book lover and collector: BIBLIOPHILE

bookmaker's advantage in the betting odds he creates: VIGORISH

book of daily prayers and offices for canonical house: BREVIARY

book or Bible peddler: COLPORTEUR

book or list of lessons for church service: LECTIONARY

book or passage written without using a particular letter: LIPOGRAM

book, pamphlet or article on a single subject: MONOGRAPH

bookplate, from the library of: EX LIBRIS

books kept in print year after year by a publisher: BACKLIST

books of an author or on a given subject listed: BIBLIOGRAPHY

books of no value, worthless literature: BIBLIA ABIBLIA

books or other writings on unusual topics, often pornography: CURIOSA

books printed before 1500 A.D.: INCUNABULA

book that is useful and handy to carry, handbook: VADE MECUM

boom-like platform for a worker that is raised from a truck: CHERRY PICKER

boor, clown, awkward fellow: LOUT

boorish: UNCOUTH

boor, yokel, hick: MUCKER

boot covering the leg to the knee in front but cut lower in back: WELLINGTON BOOT

booth, newsstand or bandstand usually lightly constructed and open: KIOSK

boot of sealskin or reindeer skin worn by Eskimos: MUKLUK

booty, loot: PILLAGE

booty, money: PELF

booty, stolen goods: PLUNDER

border, contrasting edge: LIMBUS

bordered or edged with waviness or even projections: SCALLOPED

border on: ABUT

bored, dull or depressed state of mind: DOLDRUMS

boredom, discontent or weariness: ENNUI

bore or displease: PALL

boring passage: LONGUEUR

boring, tedious: WEARISOME

boring, wearisome: TEDIOUS

born out of wedlock: MISBEGOTTEN

born with: INHERENT

borrower's property or securities pledged to insure repayment of a loan: COLLATERAL

borrowing stock expected to decline in

order to sell it at a higher price:
SHORT SALE
botany: **PHYTOLOGY**
botany as a descriptive study:
PHYTOGRAPHY
botch a job: **BUNGLE**
bother, disturb: **INCOMMODE**
bother, fluster, fuss: **POTHER**
bother, inconvenience, trouble:
DISCOMMODE
both hands being used equally well:
AMBIDEXTROUS
both sexes being united in one person:
ANDROGYNOUS
bottle for vinegar or oil: **CRUET**
bottle of glass that is decorative and
used for wine: **DECANTER**
bottom, basis or foundation that is
solid: **BEDROCK**
bottom-living or -dwelling, as certain
fish: **DEMERSAL**
bounce, jolt, shake up and down:
JOUNCE
boundary between the shore and the
ocean: **STRAND LINE**
boundary, limit: **PARAMETER**
boundary line of a figure or area:
PERIMETER
boundary line separating language
groups, dialects, etc.: **ISOGLOSS**
boundary, restriction: **PALE**
bound or consecrated by a vow or
promise: **VOTARY**
bound with a band, bandaged:
FASCIATE
bountiful, lavish, generous: **MUNIFICENT**
bow decoration on a ship: **FIDDLEHEAD**
bow decoration on a ship in the form of
a carved figure: **FIGUREHEAD**
bowel or bladder lack of control:
INCONTINENCE
bowel stimulant, cathartic: **PURGATIVE**
bowling knockdown of all ten pins on
the first bowled ball: **STRIKE**
bowling knockdown of all ten pins with
two deliveries of the ball, or in one
frame: **SPARE**
bowling pins still standing apart or in
two clusters after the first bowled
ball: **SPLIT**
bow of a stringed instrument made to
rebound slightly: **SPICCATO**
boxer belonging to lightest weight class,
weighing 112 pounds or less:
FLYWEIGHT

boxer or wrestler weighing between 113
and 118 pounds: **BANTAMWEIGHT**
boxer or wrestler weighing between 127
and 135 pounds: **LIGHTWEIGHT**
boxer or wrestler weighing between 136
and 147 pounds: **WELTERWEIGHT**
boxer or wrestler weighing between 148
and 160 pounds: **MIDDLEWEIGHT**
boxer or wrestler weighing between 161
and 175 pounds: **LIGHT
HEAVYWEIGHT**
boxer or wrestler weighing over 175
pounds: **HEAVYWEIGHT**
boxer's deformed ear: **CAULIFLOWER
EAR**
boxer weighing up to 126 pounds or a
wrestler up to 134 pounds:
FEATHERWEIGHT
boxes fitting into larger boxes: **CHINESE
BOXES**
boxing: **PUGILISM**
boxing and matters pertaining to
boxing: **FISTIC**
boxing victory based on points when
there has been no knockout:
DECISION
boxing victory in a fight halted by the
referee: **TECHNICAL KNOCKOUT**
box or case in which moisture is
retained, for storing cigars or
tobacco: **HUMIDOR**
box with feinting movements and light
blows: **SPAR**
boy (Spanish): **MUCHACHO**
boy's voice change: **PONTICELLO**
boy used in sodomy: **CATAMITE**
bragged about, praised profusely:
VAUNTED
bragging, blustering: **RODOMONTADE**
bragging, boastful: **THRASONICAL**
bragging talk or bluster: **GASCONADE**
braid: **PLAIT**
braided hairstyle as favored by
Rastafarians: **DREADLOCKS**
braid of fabric that is narrow and flat
and woven in a herringbone effect:
SOUTACHE
brain examination that traces brain
waves: **ELECTROENCEPHALOGRAM
(EEG)**
brain inflammation: **ENCEPHALITIS**
brain-lacking: **ANENCEPHALOUS**
brains, intellect: **GRAY MATTER**
brain's opium-like peptide: **ENDORPHIN**

brainwashed assassin: **MANCHURIAN CANDIDATE**

brake in which friction pads press on disc that is part of wheel: **DISC BRAKE**

branched: **RAMOSE**

branch, offshoot: **RAMIFICATION**

branch or spread out, diverge: **DIVARICATE**

branch or twig that is tough and flexible: **WITHE**

brand-nameless, as a discounted medication: **GENERIC**

brand-new, unused or original condition: **MINT CONDITION**

brandy goblet narrow at the top: **SNIFTER**

brass-rubbings executor or expert: **CHALCOTRIPT**

bravery pretended: **BRAVADO**

brave, staunch: **YEOMANLY**

brave, steadfast: **UNFLINCHING**

brave, strong, determined: **STALWART**

brave, warlike, disciplined: **SPARTAN**

brave when drunk: **POT-VALIANT**

brawl: **AFFRAY**

brawl, fight, conflict, uproar: **FRAY**

brawl marked by roughness, free-for-all: **DONNYBROOK**

brazen audacity: **CHUTZPAH**

brazenly display or parade: **FLAUNT**

brazen, shameless, bold, saucy: **IMPUDENT**

bread made of cornmeal, eggs, milk and shortening, baked soft enough to be served with a spoon: **SPOON BREAD**

bread that is baked yellow and then sliced and toasted: **ZWIEBACK**

bread, usually braided, eaten by Jews on holidays and by others: **HALLAH, CHALLAH**

breakable, brittle, fragile: **FRANGIBLE**

break apart: **RUPTURE**

break, as in electric service: **OUTAGE**

break away, separate from: **DISSOCIATE**

breakdown of social order: **ANOMIE**

breakdown or collapse that is sudden and ruinous, spectacular failure: **DEBACLE**

breakdown or interruption in electric power: **OUTAGE**

breakfast, late, or luncheon: **DÉJEUNER**

break in a relationship, parting of the ways: **RIFT**

break in continuity: **INTERREGNUM**

break in continuity to present an episode occurring earlier: **FLASHBACK**

breaking of a law or a pledge: **INFRACTION**

breaking off in the middle of a sentence without completing the idea: **APOSIOPESIS**

breaking-off or -up love letter: **DEAR JOHN**

breaking or rushing in: **IRRUPTION**

breaking up, dividing into parts, disintegrating: **FISSIPAROUS**

break off from an association, separate from an association: **DISSOCIATE**

break off relations with: **DISAFFILIATE**

break or pause in a line of verse: **CAESURA**

break or split, especially in layer: **SPALL**

break out or erupt afresh: **RECRUDESCE**

break, tear apart forcibly: **REND**

break up a group into small dissenting factions: **BALKANIZE**

break up or separate into parts, analyze: **RESOLVE**

breastbone: **STERNUM**

breast or chest, pertaining to: **PECTORAL**

breast of a woman: **POITRINE**

breastplate: **CUIRASS**

breast-removal surgery: **MASTECTOMY**

breasts being prominent with marked cleavage, deep-bosomed: **BATHYCOLPIAN**

breast separation line in a woman: **CLEAVAGE**

breathe: **RESPIRE**

breathe noisily, as a dog following a scent: **SNUFFLE**

breathe or blow into or upon: **INSUFFLATE**

breathing difficulty caused by swelling in some parts of the body: **EMPHYSEMA**

breathing excessively and thus depleting carbon dioxide: **HYPERVENTILATION**

breathing that is labored: **DYSPNEA**

breathlessness: **APNEA**

breeches loose above the knees and tight below: **JODHPURS**

breeches of old that were loose and wide: **GALLIGASKINS**

breeding of special races or strains of animals and plants: STIRPICULTURE

breed, multiply by natural reproduction: PROPAGATE

breed rapidly, swarm, teem: PULLULATE

brewing process of fermentation as a branch of chemistry: ZYMURGY

bribable, corrupt: VENAL

bribe of a small nature or a tip: BAKSHEESH

bribe or procure one to commit perjury: SUBORN

bribe or something given as appeasement: SOP

brick that is sun-dried: ADOBE

bride's outfit: TROUSSEAU

bridge bid that exceeds the preceding bid by more than the minimum: JUMP BID

bridge hand with no card higher than nine: YARBOROUGH

bridge-like framework for holding the rails of a traveling crane: GANTRY

bridge victory consisting of the winning of all thirteen tricks in a round of play: GRAND SLAM

brief and meaningful, terse, concise: SUCCINCT

brief, concise, terse: LACONIC

brief general view of a work: SYNOPSIS

brief, hasty, abrupt: CURSORY

bright, brilliant: INCANDESCENT

brighten by rubbing: FURBISH

bright idea: BRAINSTORM

bright, intense, clear: VIVID

bright, rational, clear, easily understood: LUCID

bright spot seen in a fog: FOGDOG

brilliance of action or effect: ÉCLAT

brilliance, radiance, splendor: REFULGENCE

brilliant in a light and playful fashion: LAMBENT

brilliantly wise or intelligent: LUMINOUS

brilliant or dashing performance: BRAVURA

brilliant, ostentatious oratory: PYROTECHNICS

brilliant, speedy, dazzling: METEORIC

brim at the front of a cap to shade the eyes: VISOR

brine for pickling: SOUSE

bring about, accomplish: EFFECT

bring forth, originate: SPAWN

bring on oneself: INCUR

bring something about quickly: PRECIPITATE

bring together: RALLY

bring up or train: NURTURE

bring up partly digested food: REGURGITATE

brisk, cheerful: CHIPPER

brisk, dashing, self-confident, stylish, lively: JAUNTY

briskly, lively, quickly, in music: VIVACE

bristly: SETACEOUS

bristly, spiny: ECHINATE

bristly, spiny: HISPID

Britain, England: ALBION

British and American in mixture, as one's speech: MID-ATLANTIC

British late-morning snack: ELEVENSES

British military concentric circle emblem on aircraft: ROUNDEL

British military orderly: BATMAN

British Parliament member who is not a party leader: BACKBENCHER

British record of proceedings in Parliament: HANSARD

British upper-class or public school speech or dialect: RECEIVED STANDARD

British yeoman of the guard: BEEFEATER

broadcaster who coordinates reports: ANCHORMAN, ANCHORWOMAN

broadheaded: BRACHYCEPHALIC

broad in tastes or understanding: CATHOLIC

broad jump: LONG JUMP

broadside or leaflet distributed free: THROWAWAY

broken bit of earthenware: POTSHERD, POTSHARD

broken down: DILAPIDATED

broken down, decrepit: FLEA-BITTEN

broken-hearted: INCONSOLABLE

broken, incomplete: FRAGMENTARY

broken-off piece: CANTLE

broken piece of pottery: SHARD

broken up into incidents, disjointed: EPISODIC

brokerage house that is fraudulent: BUCKET SHOP

broker holding securities in his own name rather than in the name of his customer: STREET NAME

broker on the floor of the stock

exchange handling transactions for other brokers: **TWO-DOLLAR BROKER**

brokers' broker: **SPECIALIST**

bromide, trite expression: **CLICHÉ**

bronze or silver gilt: **VERMEIL**

brook or stream that is small, rivulet: **RUNNEL**

brook, small stream: **RIVULET**

brothel: **BORDELLO**

brothel: **LUPANAR**

brother sharing only one of one's parents: **HALF BROTHER**

brothers or sisters: **SIBLINGS**

browbeat, bully, cow: **INTIMIDATE**

browbeat, torment, rant, bully, bluster: **HECTOR**

brown or reddish brown pigment or pictures done in this pigment: **SEPIA**

brown paper used for bags and wrapping: **KRAFT**

bruise by blow or impact: **CONTUSE**

bruise or black-and-blue mark: **ECCHYMOSIS**

brutish, stupid, foolish, unmoved: **INSENSATE**

bubble, ripple, heave: **POPPLE**

bubbling over with enthusiasm or excitement: **EBULLIENT**

bucket's or pail's wire handle: **BAIL**

Buddhist concept of birth-death-rebirth cycle: **SAMSARA**

Buddhist or Hindu religious law: **DHARMA**

buffet meal consisting of Scandinavian hors d'oeuvres: **SMORGASBORD**

buffet or sideboard, usually without legs: **CREDENZA**

buffoon, clown: **MERRY-ANDREW**

bugle call in the military indicating good-night or marking a military burial: **TAPS**

building construction as an art or science: **TECTONICS**

building of corrugated metal that is long, semicylindrical and prefabricated: **QUONSET HUT**

building of many stories: **HIGH RISE**

building or skyscraper exterior's indention or part of face squared inward: **SETBACK**

built in an ingeniously if impractically complicated way: **RUBE GOLDBERG**

bulging: **PROTUBERANT**

bulky, lumbering: **PONDEROUS**

bulky, of great volume: **VOLUMINOUS**

bull, baloney: **BUSHWA**

bulletin board for actors in a theater: **CALLBOARD**

bullets, missiles, rockets, etc., science of: **BALLISTICS**

bullfight: **CORRIDA**

bullfighter's (matador's) red cloak used to lure the bull: **CAPA**

bullfighter who kills the bull: **MATADOR**

bullfight horseman who pricks the bull's neck with a lance: **PICADOR**

bullfight waver of red cloak to distract the bull: **CAPEADOR**

bullish, like a bull: **TAURINE**

bully, browbeat, torment: **HECTOR**

bully, cow, make uneasy: **INTIMIDATE**

bulwark, fortification: **RAMPART**

bump or lump, protuberance: **KNURL**

bump, strike against: **JAR**

bums' section of a city: **SKID ROW**

bungle, do wrongly, lose an opportunity: **MUFF**

bungler and born loser: **SCHLIMAZEL**

bungling, clumsy, or domineering: **HEAVY-HANDED**

bungling, inept person: **SCHLEMIEL**

bun or knot of hair at the back of the head worn by women: **CHIGNON**

buoyancy, elasticity: **RESILIENCE**

buoyant, optimistic, cheerful: **SANGUINE**

burden: **MILLSTONE**

burden, discouraging or oppressive thing: **INCUBUS**

burden of proof: **ONUS PROBANDI**

burden, responsibility: **ONUS**

burdens, drawbacks: **IMPEDIMENTA**

burdensome: **ONEROUS**

bureaucrat, functionary: **APPARATCHIK**

bureau of drawers, often with a mirror: **CHIFFONIER**

burglar's crowbar: **JIMMY**

burial mound: **TUMULUS**

burial vault: **SEPULCHER**

burlesque imitation of a serious literary or musical work: **PARODY**

burlesque or imitation that is grotesque: **TRAVESTY**

burlesque rigmarole: **AMPHIGORY**

burning at the stake: **AUTO-DA-FÉ**

burning, caustic: **VITRIOLIC**

burn quickly with great heat and light: **DEFLAGRATE**

burn the midnight oil in writing or studying: LUCUBRATE
burn tissue: CAUTERIZE
burn up, cremate: INCINERATE
bursting or breaking in: IRRUPTION
bury, inter: INHUME
business licensed branch, outlet or subsidiary, or the main company's license to have such branches: FRANCHISE
businessperson who assumes full control and risk of an enterprise: ENTREPRENEUR
business source or dealer between the producer and the retailer: MIDDLEMAN
business that may hire nonunion workers, who are required to become union members by a specified time: UNION SHOP
bustle about, rush pell-mell: HURRY-SCURRY
bustle, excitement, fluster: POTHER
busybody: QUIDNUNC
busybody, nosy person: NOSEY PARKER, NOSY PARKER
butterfly, moth: LEPIDOPTERAN
butterfly still in cocoon: CHRYSALIS, PUPA
buttocks: DERRIÈRE
buttocks: FUNDAMENT
buttocks: NATES

buttocks that are fat, especially in women: STEATOPYGIA
buttonhole flower: BOUTONNIERE
buttress that juts out some distance away from the wall: FLYING BUTTRESS
buyer beware: CAVEAT EMPTOR
buying and selling the same stock simultaneously in two different cities to realize a profit: ARBITRAGE
buying and selling volume of stocks that is relatively low: THIN MARKET
buying or selling sacred things: SIMONY
buying securities at stated intervals at a fixed amount: MONTHLY INVESTMENT PLAN
buy or sell order for securities good only for the day on which it is entered: DAY ORDER
buy up goods for reselling at a profit: FORESTALL
buy up with the aim of selling at a higher price: REGRATE
buzzard or hawk: BUTEO
buzz, hum, drone: BOMBINATE
by-product, new application, incidental result: SPIN-OFF
by the very fact: IPSO FACTO
by virtue of one's official position: EX OFFICIO

C

cabal: **CAMARILLA**
cabal, intriguing group: **JUNTA**
cabaret, nightclub: **BOÎTE**
cabinet of shelves to display objects:
    ÉTAGÈRE
cabinet whose center projects:
    BREAKFRONT
cablecar that is aerial: **TELPHER**
cable or rope for mooring or towing:
    HAWSER
cable, wire or rope used to steady or
    secure something: **GUY**
café or restaurant that provides
    entertainment: **CABARET**
cafeteria for a movie studio:
    COMMISSARY
cage, usually large, for birds: **AVIARY**
cajole: **BLANDISH**
cake made of butter and eggs, with fruit
    or nuts added: **TORTE**
cake made of sugar, eggs and flour,
    containing no shortening and
    beaten very light: **SPONGE CAKE**
cake, small and made of unsweetened
    batter: **CRUMPET**
calamity: **CATASTROPHE**
calculating device with counters moving
    up and down on rods: **ABACUS**
calculator of risks and premiums for
    insurance: **ACTUARY**
calendar used in most of the world:
    GREGORIAN CALENDAR
calfskin or lambskin that is untanned:
    KIP
California gold miner: **ARGONAUT**
California hot dry wind: **SANTA ANA**
called, named (archaic): **YCLEPT**
called or considered so by oneself:
    SELF-STYLED

call in question, dispute, challenge:
    OPPUGN
call or whistle that is derisive: **CATCALL**
callow, immature, but opinionated:
    SOPHOMORIC
call, summon, draw forth: **EVOKE**
call to account, discipline or chastise:
    CALL ON THE CARPET
call to arms, alarm: **ALARUM**
call together, as a meeting: **CONVOKE**
call to troops for service, review, etc.:
    MUSTER
call upon for aid, protection or witness:
    INVOKE
calm: **DISPASSIONATE**
calm down, quiet, abate: **SUBSIDE**
calmness, composure, even temper:
    EQUANIMITY
calm, ordered, harmonious, balanced,
    rational: **APOLLONIAN**
calm, peaceful, tranquil: **PLACID**
calm, quietly assured, poised:
    SELF-POSSESSED
calm, quiet, serene: **TRANQUIL**
calm, serene, idyllic: **HALCYON**
calm, serene, unmoved: **IMPASSIVE**
calm, unruffled: **IMPERTURBABLE**
calm, untroubled, tranquil: **SERENE**
calories with no food value or gained
    without nutrition: **EMPTY
    CALORIES**
Cambridge and Oxford and the British
    tradition and prestige they
    represent: **OXBRIDGE**
Cambridge (U.K.) resident:
    CANTABRIGIAN
camel with one hump: **DROMEDARY**
camera in which the framing of the
    viewed image is identical to what

will appear in the finished print:
SINGLE LENS REFLEX, SLR

camera lens that shows 180-degree field
of vision: FISH-EYE LENS

camouflaging or imitative, as an animal
or insect blending into its
background: APATETIC

camp, temporary, usually without
shelter: BIVOUAC

campus-related, involving life within a
college: PARIETAL

cancel a passenger's place on a flight:
BUMP

cancel, recall, rescind, annul: REVOKE

cancer-causing substance: CARCINOGEN

cancer of the blood: LEUKEMIA

cancerous dark mole-like tumor:
MELANOMA

cancerous growth: CARCINOMA

candelabrum with seven branches used
in the Jewish religion: MENORAH

candidate almost unknown who wins a
nomination or election: DARK
HORSE

candidate list: SLATE

candidate put forward as a cover for
another person: STALKING HORSE

candid, sincere, artless: GUILELESS

candied or sugared, iced, frozen: GLACÉ

candlemaker: CHANDLER

candlestick that is branched:
CANDELABRUM

candy composed of nuts and fruits:
NOUGAT

canine tooth: CUSPID

cannibals: ANTHROPOPHAGI

cannon or artillery, military combat
materiel: ORDNANCE

cannon with a relatively high angle of
fire: HOWITZER

canoe made from a tree trunk: PIROGUE

canoe that is covered except for an
opening for the paddler: KAYAK

can opener: CHURCH KEY

canopy or large tent, summerhouse:
PAVILION

canopy over a pulpit or bed: TESTER

canopy used in religious processions:
BALDACHIN

can or cup that is small: CANNIKIN

cantankerous: CROTCHETY

cant, lingo: JARGON

canvas sheet stretched on a frame and
used for acrobatics or gymnastics:
TRAMPOLINE

capable of working, as a plan; able to
live: VIABLE

cap and bells of a jester: FOOLSCAP

cap cover with long rear flap:
HAVELOCK

caper, antic: DIDO

caper, antic: GAMBADO

caper, prance about: TITTUP

capital for a new or risky enterprise:
VENTURE CAPITAL

capitalist tycoon of the late 19th
century who was powerful and
exploitive: ROBBER BARON

capital-letter abbreviations for
government agencies or the like,
initialisms and acronyms:
ALPHABET SOUP

capital letters in type: UPPER CASE

capital punishment or execution as a
science: KTENOLOGY

capital that is hardly adequate used in
starting a business: SHOESTRING

cap, knitted and hood-like, with a
back-of-neck covering: BALACLAVA

cap of felt with a tassel, worn by
Moslem men: TARBOOSH

cap of loose and heavy material for
men, with a flattened top that can
often be snapped against the short
brim in front: TOURING CAP

cap or top being difficult to remove:
CHILDPROOF

caprice, whim, fanciful humor: WHIMSY

capricious, willful: WAYWARD

cap that is flat and round: BERET

cap that is square and stiff and worn by
clergy: BIRETTA

caption or explanatory description on
an illustration, chart or map:
LEGEND

capture or seize: CORRAL

cap worn by sailors for warmth that is
knitted, close-fitting and navy-blue:
WATCH CAP

car collision spectator event:
DEMOLITION DERBY

card game called twenty-one:
VINGT-ET-UN

card game series terminated when one
side has won two games: RUBBER

card game situation in which a winner
has made more than double his
opponent: LURCH

card game that breaks a tie between
players: RUBBER

card of a suit that outranks other suits during the playing of a hand: **TRUMP**

cards left on the table after the deal: **TALON**

cards used in fortune-telling: **TAROT**

career or biographical description or chronology, résumé: **CURRICULUM VITAE**

carefree: **FOOTLOOSE**

carefree and indifferent, easygoing, irresponsible: **GALLIONIC**

carefree existence, drink and play: **BEER AND SKITTLES**

carefree, lighthearted, gay: **ROLLICKING**

carefreeness: **RHATHYMIA**

carefree, unconcerned, lighthearted: **INSOUCIANT**

carefree, uninvolved, easygoing: **DÉGAGÉ**

carefree, worry-free: **SANS SOUCI**

careful about what one says, prudent, tactful: **DISCREET**

careful and diligent: **PAINSTAKING**

careful, cautious, frugal: **CHARY**

carefully, cautiously: **GINGERLY**

carefully or deliberately receive, consider seriously: **TAKE UNDER ADVISEMENT**

careful, prudent, discreet: **CIRCUMSPECT**

careful, scrupulous about detail or observance of forms: **PUNCTILIOUS**

careful, wise: **JUDICIOUS**

carelessly done: **SLIPSHOD**

careless, negligent: **REMISS**

careless or untidy person: **SLOVEN**

careless, reckless: **DEVIL-MAY-CARE**

careless, reckless, weak: **FECKLESS**

cargo cast overboard from an imperiled ship: **JETSAM**

carnival or boardwalk booth game of any sort: **HANKY-PANK**

carnival performer of repellent acts, such as biting the head off a live chicken: **GEEK**

carpet of velvety texture: **WILTON**

carp, raise trivial objections: **CAVIL**

carriage for four horses driven by one person: **FOUR-IN-HAND, TALLYHO**

carriage, four-wheeled and light, with two seats facing forward (one behind the other) and a more or less flat-bottomed chassis: **SURREY**

carriage, four-wheeled, low and open, in which passengers sit sideways on a bench (or astride it) with their feet near the ground: **DROSHKY**

carriage, four-wheeled, that has a simple flat and springless platform: **BUCKBOARD**

carriage, four-wheeled, the back section of whose covered body can be folded down: **LANDAU**

carriage, light and either two-wheeled (England) or four-wheeled (United States), drawn by one horse: **BUGGY**

carriage, light and two-wheeled, that has a simple seat and is drawn by one horse: **GIG**

carriage, two-wheeled and drawn by one horse, that is covered and has an elevated driver's seat to the rear: **HANSOM**

carriage, two-wheeled and drawn by one horse, with a folding top and usually a rear platform for a groom: **CABRIOLET**

carriage with four wheels, facing seats, a folding top and a high seat in front for the driver: **BAROUCHE**

carriage, with four wheels, in the form of a closed box with a driver's seat in front: **BROUGHAM**

carriage with hood and with high seat for horse driver: **CABRIOLET**

carried away by foolish love: **INFATUATED**

carried booth-like and upright box for one person, borne on poles by litter bearers: **SEDAN CHAIR**

carried enclosed horizontal shuttered box for one person, borne on poles by litter bearers: **PALANQUIN**

carrier of microorganisms: **VECTOR**

carry a person face down by the arms and legs: **FROG MARCH**

carry away wrongfully: **ABDUCT**

carry, haul, lug, drag: **SCHLEP**

carry or move gently, float: **WAFT**

carry through or accomplish something: **TRANSACT**

carry through, put into effect: **IMPLEMENT**

cart carrying prisoners to the guillotine during the French Revolution: **TUMBREL**

cartoon-like drawing, characterization, version, etc.: **CARICATURE** cart with two wheels for a passenger, pulled by one person: **RICKSHA, RICKSHAW**

carved design beneath the surface: **INTAGLIO**

carved ivory, stone or shells: **SCRIMSHAW**

carve, engrave, cut into: **INCISE**

carving or engraving, especially on gems: **GLYPTICS**

case for small articles that is often ornamental: **ETUI**

case, light and rectangular, for carrying papers: **ATTACHÉ CASE**

case or example: **INSTANCE**

cash in a prize coupon, gift certificate, etc.: **REDEEM**

cash-lacking: **ILLIQUID**

cash payment made by customer when he uses his broker's credit for purchase of a security: **MARGIN**

casino card game played against the bank: **BACCARAT**

casino game that is a variation of baccarat: **CHEMIN DE FER**

casket platform: **BIER**

cask holding half a barrel: **KILDERKIN**

cassock: **SOUTANE**

casting or molding of footprints, tire marks, etc., for use in criminal investigation: **MOULAGE**

castle battlement notch or opening between merlons: **CRENEL**

castle battlement solid or tooth-like part between crenels: **MERLON**

castle-like in structure: **CASTELLATED**

castle opening in a projecting support of a battlement: **MACHICOLATION**

castle tower at a drawbridge or gate: **BARBICAN**

castle tower or keep: **DONJON**

castle turret projecting or overhanging: **BARTIZAN**

cast off, as dead skin: **SLOUGH**

cast off or discard a sweetheart: **JILT**

cast out an evil spirit by prayers or incantations: **EXORCISE**

cast-out matter or refuse, as from a volcano: **EJECTA**

castrated animal, especially a horse: **GELDING**

castrated man or youth: **EUNUCH**

castrated rooster: **CAPON**

castrate, geld, weaken, make effeminate: **EMASCULATE**

casual, aimless, disconnected, random: **DESULTORY**

casual, minor, secondary: **INCIDENTAL**

casual or indiscriminate, especially sexually: **PROMISCUOUS**

casual, spontaneous, impromptu: **OFF-THE-CUFF**

casualties evaluated and sorted to fix priorities for treatment: **TRIAGE**

catalog with scholarly notes of particular books, paintings, etc.: **CATALOGUE RAISONÉE**

catching: **INFECTIOUS**

catch, snag, complication: **HITCH**

catch up with or get ahead of, as a ship: **FOREREACH**

categorize, classify: **PIGEONHOLE**

cat family member: **FELINE**

cathedral grounds: **CLOSE**

cathedral or church gallery above the side aisle: **TRIFORIUM**

cathedral or church upper wall, above a lateral roof, that contains windows and admits light: **CLERESTORY**

cat, particularly an old female one: **GRIMALKIN**

cat's-eye: **CHATOYANT**

Catskill and White Mountain hotels that provide entertainment: **BORSCHT CIRCUIT, BORSCHT BELT**

Catskill Mountains resort entertainer and activities director: **TUMMLER**

cat that is an adult female: **CATTA, QUEEN**

cattle food: **PROVENDER**

cattle herder: **COWBOY, COWHAND, COWPUNCHER**

cattle movement seasonally to more suitable pastures: **TRANSHUMANCE**

caught in the act: **IN FLAGRANTE DELICTO**

caught in the very act, incriminatingly: **RED-HANDED**

cause-and-effect theory in philosophy, especially of human behavior: **DETERMINISM**

cause a result creditable or discreditable: **REDOUND**

cause, bring about: **INDUCE**

caused estrangement, by another, between husband and wife: **ALIENATION OF AFFECTIONS**

cause or make likely, attract: INVITE
causes and origins as subjects of study:
    ETIOLOGY
cause something abruptly or
    unexpectedly: PRECIPITATE
cause that produces a result: FACTOR
cause to effect, prior to: A PRIORI
caustic: ACRIMONIOUS
caustic, biting: PUNGENT
caustic, burning: VITRIOLIC
caustic, cutting, sarcastic: MORDANT
caustic, mercilessly severe, withering:
    SCATHING
cautious: WARY
cautious, careful, frugal: CHARY
cautious checking of every detail:
    CIRCUMSPECT
cautiously, carefully: GINGERLY
cautiously shrewd: CANNY
cautious, moderate, opposed to change:
    CONSERVATIVE
cave entrance exposed to daylight:
    TWILIGHT ZONE
cave explorer: SPELUNKER
cave formation, cone-shaped, that is
    built up on the floor: STALAGMITE
cave formation, long and tapering, that
    hangs from the roof: STALACTITE
cave-like underground chamber or
    passageway: CATACOMB
cave man: TROGLODYTE
cave or cavern: GROTTO
cave or fall in, sink, collapse, fail:
    FOUNDER
caves as a subject of study:
    SPELEOLOGY
cavities in the skull leading into the
    nasal cavities: SINUSES
cease-fire, armistice: TRUCE
ceiling decorated with a painted or
    carved design: PLAFOND
ceiling with recessed panels: LACUNAR
celebrate, make merry, delight (in):
    REVEL
celebration, festival: FIESTA
celebrity banquet featuring humorous
    mock attacks on the guest of
    honor: ROAST
celebrity, fame: RENOWN
celebrity genius whose scandalous ways
    and actions are news: MONSTRE
    SACRÉ
celestial, heavenly: SUPERNAL
celestial, sublime, superior, fiery:
    EMPYREAL

cellar or underground shelter used
    during cyclones or tornadoes:
    CYCLONE CELLAR
cells: study of their structure,
    organization and function:
    CYTOLOGY
cement or plaster used to surface walls:
    STUCCO
cemetery for paupers: POTTER'S FIELD
censor by deleting offensive passages:
    BOWDLERIZE
censor by removing obscene or
    otherwise objectionable material:
    EXPURGATE
censorious prude: MRS. GRUNDY
censorship that is puritanical:
    COMSTOCKERY
censure, blame, rebuke: REPROACH
censure or rebuke severely: REPRIMAND
censure, scold, reproach: UPBRAID
censure vehemently: INVEIGH
center being in common: CONCENTRIC
centerless: ACENTRIC
center of attention, activity or interest:
    FOCAL POINT
center of attraction: CYNOSURE
central or essential element, core:
    NUCLEUS
central point, hub, navel: OMPHALOS
century-and-a-half observance:
    SESQUICENTENNIAL
century, era, period: SIÈCLE
century's end, especially the end of the
    19th century; also decadence: FIN
    DE SIÈCLE
ceremonial procession: CORTEGE
ceremonial soft drumroll and fanfare:
    RUFFLE AND FLOURISH
ceremonial washing of hands:
    ABLUTION
ceremonies commemorating the
    founding of a city or university or
    the consecration of a church:
    ENCAENIA
ceremony that is pretentious or
    hypocritical: MUMMERY
certain: APODICTIC
certain: COCKSURE
certain, accurate: UNERRING
certainly, without doubt: SANS DOUTE
certain, unavoidable: INEVITABLE
certain, unquestionable: INDUBITABLE
certificate acknowledging debt:
    DEBENTURE

certificate entitling the holder to receive shares of stock, money, etc.: SCRIP

cesspool, sewer: CLOACA

chain hanging from a woman's belt to hold keys or purse: CHATELAINE

chain of colored paper, ribbon or flowers hung in loops: FESTOON

chain of things or events: CONCATENATION

chain or closely connected series: CATENA

chair of wood with spindle back and slanting legs: WINDSOR CHAIR

chair, usually of leather, that is armless: BARCELONA CHAIR

chair with a high back and high side pieces: WING CHAIR

challenge: THROW DOWN THE GAUNTLET

challenge, dispute or attack the truth or validity of: IMPUGN

challenge the honesty or validity of: IMPEACH

challenge to combat, in the form of a glove being thrown down, in the Middle Ages: GAGE

chamberpot in a low chair or cabinet: COMMODE

champagne bottle's metal bands over the cork: COIFFE, AGRAFE

champagne designation for moderately dry: SEC

chance occurrence: HAPPENSTANCE

changeable: AMBIVALENT

changeable, erratic: INCONSISTENT

changeable, inconstant: FICKLE

changeable in luster: CHATOYANT

changeable into different forms or shapes: PROTEAN

changeable, lively, clever: MERCURIAL

changeable person: CHAMELEON

changeable, transformable: MUTABLE

changeable, unstable: LABILE

change a person's personal convictions by coercion: BRAINWASH

change in the form, character or appearance: METAMORPHOSIS

change into a different shape: TRANSMOGRIFY

change in vowel for changed tense: ABLAUT

change of opinion that is complete: ABOUT-FACE

change one substance into another: TRANSUBSTANTIATE

change or movement that is constant: FLUX

change or vary often and in an irregular manner: FLUCTUATE

change places, alternate: INTERCHANGE

change plans of someone by persuasion against: DISSUADE

change sides, apostatize: TERGIVERSATE

changes in price that can be absorbed by the market in a particular security: LIQUIDITY

changes in series of plant or animal formations: SERE

changes or variations occurring irregularly, as of fortune: VICISSITUDES

change the appearance of: TRANSFIGURE

change the form or quality of: TRANSMUTE

changing or confusingly shifting situation: MUSICAL CHAIRS

changing rapidly and intricately: KALEIDOSCOPIC

channel for water, as under a road: CULVERT

chant: INTONE

chanted formula or magic words: INCANTATION

chanted, nonmetrical hymn: CANTICLE

chanting by monks unaccompanied and without harmonizing: GREGORIAN CHANT

chaos, disorder, confusion: CHINESE FIRE DRILL

chapel for private prayer: ORATORY

character and attitudes of a community or individual: ETHOS

character in a play or novel who comments: RAISONNEUR

characteristic or typifying factor or element: PARAMETER

characterization, often disparaging, of a person or thing: EPITHET

characterless: INVERTEBRATE

characterless, not distinctive: NONDESCRIPT

character, mark or stamp that is distinctive: IMPRESS

charcoal pencil or a sketch or drawing done in charcoal: FUSAIN

charge a public official with a crime or misdemeanor: IMPEACH

charge at cabarets, hotels or clubs for

entertainment or service: COVER CHARGE

charged, filled: FRAUGHT

charge with a crime, accuse: INDICT

charging of a wrongdoing or fault, accusation: IMPUTATION

charitable, alms-giving: ELEEMOSYNARY

charity case, a very poor person: PAUPER

charity to aid mankind: PHILANTHROPY

charlatan, vendor of quack medicines: MOUNTEBANK

charm: AMULET

charm: ENAMOR

charm, amulet: TALISMAN

charm as if by magic: BEWITCH

charm, divert: BEGUILE

charm, talisman: GRIGRI

chart or diagram of the stages of a process: FLOW CHART

chart showing a line or lines representing changes in growth, value, etc.: GRAPH

chasm or fissure, as in a glacier: CREVASSE

chastise or rebuke severely: CASTIGATE

chat, gossip: CONFABULATE

chat, informal conversation: CAUSERIE

chat, talk idly: SCHMOOZE

chatter, talk senselessly: PRATE

chauvinist: JINGO

cheap and showy: BRASSY

cheap and showy: TAWDRY

cheap and showy, designed merely to sell: CATCHPENNY

cheap and showy, gaudy, tawdry, phony: BRUMMAGEM

cheap, flashy dress or ornamentation: FRIPPERY

cheap-looking, shabby, seedy: TACKY

cheap or sensational talk: CLAPTRAP

cheap, poor quality: SCHLOCK

cheap red wine: VIN ORDINAIRE

cheap, shoddy, tacky: SLEAZY

cheap, trashy, measly: CHINTZY

cheat: BAMBOOZLE

cheat, dawdle, or pass time: DIDDLE

cheated or fooled easily: GULLIBLE

cheat, fool, deceive, frustrate, con: SNOOKER

cheating on taxes by concealing full profits: SKIMMING

cheat or deceive in a petty way: COZEN

cheat or defraud a person: MULCT

cheat or extort: GOUGE

cheat, outwit: EUCHRE

cheat, swindle: ROOK

cheat, swindler, corrupt official: HIGHBINDER

cheat, trick: HOODWINK

cheat, trick, deceive: FINAGLE

checkered, mosaic-like: TESSELLATED

checkered or plaid pattern of dark lines on a light ground: TATTERSALL

checking-out of validity, good faith, authentication or verifications, credentials: BONA FIDES

check or restrain, as an impulse: INHIBIT

check or stop the flow of: STANCH

check out, examine for validity or acceptability, authenticate: VET

check stub or stub of money order kept as record: COUNTERFOIL

cheerful: BLITHE

cheerful: BUOYANT

cheerful, brisk: CHIPPER

cheerful, buoyant, optimistic: SANGUINE

cheerful, gay: JOCUND

cheerful, lively, urbane: DEBONAIR

cheerful, optimistic: ROSEATE

cheerful willingness: ALACRITY

cheese-and-crumbs crust: AU GRATIN

cheese, Italian, that is hard and is sprinkled on spaghetti or soup: PARMESAN

cheese, melted and cooked, often with beer or ale added, and served on toast or crackers: WELSH RABBIT

cheese, to turn into or become like: CASEFY

chemist's shallow glass dish for cultures: PETRI DISH

chess draw resulting when a player can make no move without placing his or her king in check: STALEMATE

chess player's explanation that he or she is only adjusting a piece: J'ADOUBE

chess player who is a beginner or blunderer: PATZER

chess position in which no move by a player will be advantageous: ZUGZWANG

chest of drawers, high and often with a mirror: CHIFFONIER

chest of drawers, on short legs, about table height: LOWBOY

chest of drawers, usually in two sections, the lower on legs: HIGHBOY

chest or respiratory high vibrating sound or whistling: STRIDOR

chest pain recurrent because of lack of oxygen in heart muscles: ANGINA PECTORIS

chest rattling or whistling sound from bronchial obstruction: RHONCHUS

chewing food thoroughly as an aid to good health: FLETCHERISM

chew noisily, munch: CHAMP

chewy, as lightly cooked spaghetti: AL DENTE

chic, elegant, showy, arty: CHICHI

chicken a few months old: SPRING CHICKEN

chicken-and-leeks soup: COCK-A-LEEKIE

chicken pox: VARICELLA

chicken stewed in wine: COQ AU VIN

chicken stewed Italian style: CHICKEN CACCIATORE

chief, bigwig, important official: POOH-BAH

chief commodity of a place or region: STAPLE

chief, leader: COCK OF THE WALK

chief, leader: HONCHO

chief of a political party: SACHEM

child being related to parents: FILIAL

childbirth, delivery: PARTURITION

childbirth pangs: TRAVAIL

childbirth ritual among primitive people in which father of newly born goes through motions as if he had given birth: COUVADE

childbirth time: ACCOUCHEMENT

childish talk: PRATTLE

childish, trivial, silly: PUERILE

child left alone at home for part of the day: LATCHKEY CHILD

child murder: INFANTICIDE

child murder by a parent: FILICIDE

child prodigy: WUNDERKIND

children, aversion to or dislike of: MISOPEDIA

children's diseases and hygienic care as a study: PEDIATRICS

child's nurse or female caretaker, nursemaid: NANNY

child who because of neglect spends his or her time in the streets: GUTTERSNIPE

child with extraordinary aptitude or talent: PRODIGY

chilling: FRIGORIFIC

chimney channel or duct: FLUE

china or porcelain that is very thin and delicate: EGGSHELL CHINA

Chinese dumpling appetizers: DIM SUM

Chinese karate-like art of self-defense: KUNG-FU

Chinese-originated use of needles in medical practice: ACUPUNCTURE

Chinese ornate decoration or an object so decorated: CHINOISERIE

Chinese shrine or temple: JOSS HOUSE

Chinese system for transliterating Chinese into the Western (Latin) alphabet, in 1979 officially succeeding (e.g., "Beijing" instead of "Peking") the Wade-Giles system: PINYIN

chivalric, romantic or daring in intentions but impractical: QUIXOTIC

chivalry: KNIGHT-ERRANTRY

chocolate (or other flavor) chilled pudding-like dessert: MOUSSE

choice: OPTION

choice between what is offered and nothing: HOBSON'S CHOICE

choice, excellent, of exceptional quality: VINTAGE

choice that must be made between two equally undesirable alternatives: DILEMMA

choke to death: STRANGLE

choking: lifesaving countermeasure by squeezing the victim's upper abdomen from behind: HEIMLICH MANEUVER

choose, elect: OPT

choose with care: HANDPICK

choral songs and dance muse: TERPSICHORE

chord's notes played in quick succession: ARPEGGIO

Christian Creed, beginning "I believe in God," part of the Mass: CREDO

Christian embrace or handshake as a gesture of fellowship in a church: KISS OF PEACE

Christian Holy Communion, Christ's Body and Blood: EUCHARIST

Christian "Lord have mercy upon us"

prayer and part of the Mass: **KYRIE**

Christian penitential 40-day period from Ash Wednesday to Easter: **LENT**

Christian prayer beginning "Glory be to God on High," part of the Mass: **GLORIA**

Christian prayer beginning "Holy, holy, holy, Lord God of hosts," part of the Mass: **SANCTUS**

Christian prayer to Christ as Savior (Lamb of God) and a part of the Mass: **AGNUS DEI**

Christian who emphasizes spiritual zeal or ecstasy and the power of healing: **CHARISMATIC**

Christmas display of stable, scene of Jesus' birth: **CRÈCHE**

chronic worrier: **WORRYWART**

chronology as estimated by growth rings on trees: **DENDROCHRONOLOGY**

chuckle with glee: **CHORTLE**

church-and-state conflict: **KULTURKAMPF**

church architecture and decoration as a study: **ECCLESIOLOGY**

church area behind the altar: **RETROCHOIR**

church area or community under jurisdiction of a bishop: **DIOCESE**

church baptismal basin, usually on a stone pedestal: **FONT**

church building with a nave and side aisles, clerestory, transept or crossing and apse: **BASILICA**

church caretaker: **SEXTON**

churchman of high rank: **PRELATE**

church or cathedral crossing near the choir: **TRANSEPT**

church or cathedral gallery above the side aisle: **TRIFORIUM**

church or cathedral upper wall, above a lateral roof, that contains windows and admits light: **CLERESTORY**

church plainsong chanted by monks: **GREGORIAN CHANT**

church rule by prelates: **PRELACY**

church's usually semicircular projection behind the altar, bay at the eastern end of the nave: **APSE**

church vestibule or portico: **NARTHEX**

church wall repository for sacraments: **AMBRY**

church whose side aisle roofing rises as

high or almost as high as the nave: **HALL CHURCH**

cigar that is cut square at both ends: **CHEROOT**

cigar that is long and slim: **PANATELA**

cigar that is long, slender and inexpensive: **STOGIE**

cigar that is strong and dark: **MADURO**

cigar that tapers at both ends: **PERFECTO**

circle boundary: **CIRCUMFERENCE**

circle-closing or -opening motion picture shot, using an iris lens: **IRIS SHOT**

circle of prehistoric monumental stone slabs, as at Stonehenge: **CROMLECH**

circle, persons having an interest or interests in common: **COTERIE**

circle's circumference in relation to its diameter: **PI**

circle with locked arms as formed by dancers in this Romanian and Israeli folk dance: **HORA**

circling back to the original problem results after its solution raises other problems: **VICIOUS CIRCLE**

circular graph divided into proportionate sections: **PIE CHART**

circular, revolving or whirling in motion: **GYRAL**

circulate, permeate: **DIFFUSE**

circumference, especially of the waist: **GIRTH**

circumlocution, wordiness: **PERIPHRASIS**

circus springboard, like a small seesaw, for launching a person at one end into the air: **TEETERBOARD**

cite for proof or example: **ADDUCE**

citizen, middle-class resident, town dweller: **BURGHER**

citizen of the world: **COSMOPOLITE**

citizenship bestowal, freeing from slavery: **ENFRANCHISEMENT**

city area where vice and corruption flourish: **TENDERLOIN**

civic or local promotionalism and optimism: **BOOSTERISM**

civic or town resident: **OPPIDAN**

civilian clothes, especially when worn by one who usually wears a uniform: **MUFTI**

civilians arming spontaneously in times of military emergency: **LEVY EN MASSE**

civilities: **AMENITIES**

civility: COMITY
civil liberties advocate: LIBERTARIAN
civil magistrate, officer representing a government: SYNDIC
claim on property in payment of or as security for a debt: LIEN
claim without right: ARROGATE
clairvoyance, telepathy: CRYPTESTHESIA
clam: QUAHOG
clam of the littleneck variety but larger: CHERRYSTONE
clam that is the young of the quahog: LITTLENECK
clannish set: CLIQUE
clarify, enlighten, illuminate, light up: IRRADIATE
clarify, explain: INTERPRET
clarinet's lowest register: CHALUMEAU
classical-music lover: LONGHAIR
classic, venerable, time-honored: VINTAGE
classification laws and principles, especially in biology and botany: TAXONOMY
classified biologically or botanically according to the binomial system of Swedish botanist Carl von Linne: LINNAEAN
classify, categorize: PIGEONHOLE
classify under or within, subordinate: SUBSUME
classiness or nobleness in being generous, understanding, etc.: NOBLESSE OBLIGE
class or group in society: CASTE
class, sort, kind: ILK
clattering or rattling noise: BRATTLE
clauses in a sentence with connectives and dependent syntax: HYPOTAXIS
clauses of a sentence without connectives between them: PARATAXIS
claw, hoof, nail: UNGUIS
clay-like: FICTILE
clay pottery: CERAMICS
clean, correct, flawless: IMMACULATE
cleanse or wipe off: DETERGE
cleansing: ABLUTION
clean slate: TABULA RASA
clear and resounding: CLARION
clear, bright, intense: VIVID
clear, comprehensible: INTELLIGIBLE
clear, definite, straightforward, outspoken: EXPLICIT

clear, easily understood, rational, bright, shining: LUCID
clearing area in a fog bank: FOGDOG, SEADOG
clearing in the woods: GLADE
clear, lucid, understandable: PERSPICUOUS
clear of accusation: VINDICATE
clear of blame or accusation, acquit: EXONERATE
clear, rounded or full in voice: OROTUND
clear the throat audibly: HAWK
clear, transparent, lucid, pure: LIMPID
clear, understandable: PELLUCID
clear, understandable in one way only: UNEQUIVOCAL
cleavage-prominent, deep-bosomed: BATHYCOLPIAN
clergyperson jointly officiating at a communion service: CONCELEBRANT
clergyperson officiating at a Mass or service: CELEBRANT
clergyperson's residence: RECTORY
clergyperson's salary paid out of church revenues: PREBEND
clerical cap that is square and stiff: BIRETTA
clerical cloak with a clasp at the neck: COPE
clerical full-length white vestment with sleeves: ALB
clerical knee-length garment that is loose and white and has wide sleeves: SURPLICE
clerical or professional worker: WHITE-COLLAR WORKER
clerical scarf-like garment: TIPPET
clerical sleeved garment worn over the alb: DALMATIC
clerical sleeveless garment hanging loosely from the shoulders: SCAPULAR
clerical sleeveless mantle worn by priest at a communion service: CHASUBLE
clever person, thinker: SOPHIST
clever remark: BON MOT
clever, skillful, inventive: INGENIOUS
cliché: BROMIDE
clichéd and no longer vivid metaphor: DEAD METAPHOR
clichéd idea: RECEIVED IDEA
clicking or clapper pieces used

percussively by Spanish dancers:
CASTANETS
cliff at the rim of a plateau: **SCARP**
cliff debris or rubble piled at the base:
SCREE
cliff on the side of a hill: **SCAR**
cliff projecting into the water:
HEADLAND
cliff's edge: **PRECIPICE**
cliff that extends a distance: **PALISADES**
climax: **APOGEE**
climax in sexual intercourse: **ORGASM**
climb, as a tree, by clasping with the
arms and legs: **SWARM**
clinging closely: **OSCULANT**
clinging mollusk: **LIMPET**
clinging, retentive: **TENACIOUS**
clique: **CAMARILLA**
clique or group: **FACTION**
clockwise: **DEASIL**
close association, confidential friendship:
INTIMACY
close call, near accident: **NEAR MISS**
closed or secret, as a session: **IN**
CAMERA
closed session, as of a legislature, to
consider confidential business:
EXECUTIVE SESSION
closed to others' opinions or beliefs:
INTOLERANT
closed to outside influence, incapable of
being passed through: **IMPERVIOUS**
closely contested with the advantage
going back and forth: **NIP AND**
TUCK
closemouthed, reserved: **TACITURN**
closeness: **PROPINQUITY**
close off, block or shut up: **OCCLUDE**
close one's eyes to something as if it
had not happened: **CONDONE**
close one's eyes to wrongdoing:
CONNIVE
close quarters or close contact, at or in:
HAND-TO-HAND
close together, jammed: **CHOCKABLOCK**
close, touching: **CONTIGUOUS**
clot formation causing dead tissue:
INFARCTION
cloth containing an intricate design that
usually includes loops ending in
curlicues: **PAISLEY**
clothed negligently or partly as a state:
DISHABILLE
clothe richly: **CAPARISON**

cloth for the head on a chair or sofa:
ANTIMACASSAR
clothing, accoutrements, furnishings:
HABILIMENTS
clothing-related: **SARTORIAL**
cloth laid on the lap of a bishop
officiating at a mass or ordination:
GREMIAL
cloth of yellowish brown: **KHAKI**
cloud formation at low altitude that is
stretched horizontally and almost
even along the bottom: **STRATUS**
cloud formation that is dense and
usually white, with a domed top
and horizontal base, seen in fair
weather: **CUMULUS**
cloud of rounded mass appearing before
a thunderstorm: **THUNDERHEAD**
clouds in a fine, whitish veil, giving a
hazy appearance: **CIRROSTRATUS**
clouds in a mass of fleecy globular
cloudlets: **CIRROCUMULUS**
clouds in large globular masses,
disposed in waves, groups or
bands: **STRATOCUMULUS**
clouds in white wispy tufts or bands
across the sky: **CIRRUS**
clouds, long and fibrous, supposed to
foretell a storm: **MARE'S TAIL**
cloud streamers or wisps of
precipitation: **VIRGA**
cloud study as a branch of meteorology:
NEPHOLOGY
cloudy, foggy, obscure, indefinite:
NUBILOUS
cloudy, murky: **TURBID**
cloudy, overcast: **LOWERY**
clown, buffoon: **MERRY-ANDREW**
clown face painted with exaggerated
features: **AUGUSTE**
club, cudgel, stick for beating:
TRUNCHEON
clubfoot: **TALIPES**
clump along pompously: **GALUMPH**
clump or tuft, as of grass or hair:
TUSSOCK
clumsily done: **BOTCHED**
clumsily handle, botch the job: **BUNGLE**
clumsiness in handling things:
BUTTERFINGERS
clumsy, awkward, heavy in appearance
or movement: **LUMBERING**
clumsy, awkward, incompetent: **INEPT**
clumsy, blundering: **MALADROIT**

clumsy, boorish, awkward: **GAUCHE**
clumsy, bungling, domineering:
HEAVY-HANDED
clumsy, labored: **PONDEROUS**
clumsy or stupid person: **CLODHOPPER**
clumsy person: **KLUTZ**
clumsy rustic: **BUMPKIN**
coal mining by stripping off soil rather
than sinking a shaft: **STRIP MINING**
coarse food: **ROUGHAGE**
coarse, loud, rough in sound: **RAUCOUS**
coarsely or vulgarly joking: **RIBALD**
coarse or abusive in language:
SCURRILOUS
coarse, unrefined, natural: **EARTHY**
coastal inlet, estuary: **FIRTH**
coastal land projection: **CAPE**
coastal narrow sea inlet between steep
cliffs: **FJORD**
coat a metal protectively: **ANODIZE**
coat lapel: **REVERS**
coat-of-arms-possessing or -worthy,
having a heraldic device:
ARMIGEROUS
coat of which the sleeves are in one
piece up to the collar: **RAGLAN**
coat or covering, as of a seed: **TEGMEN**
coats of arms, genealogies, etc.:
HERALDRY
coat with tails for formal wear by a
man: **CUTAWAY**
coax or flatter to persuade: **WHEEDLE**
coax with flattery: **CAJOLE**
cocked in angle, as the way a hat is
worn: **ARAKE**
cock less than a year old: **COCKEREL**
cocktail discount hour: **HAPPY HOUR**
coddle: **COCKER**
code deciphering: **CRYPTANALYSIS**
coded message in decoded form:
PLAINTEXT
coded writing: **CRYPTOGRAPHY**
code of words representing each letter
of the alphabet, such as *Alpha* for
A and *Zulu* for Z, used in radio
communication: **ALPHABET CODE**
codfish that is young: **SCROD**
coercion, compulsion: **DURESS**
coercive measures taken to force a
country to comply with demands:
SANCTIONS
coffee, black: **CAFÉ NOIR**
coffee or coffee-flavored: **MOCHA**

coffeepot basket holding the grounds:
BIGGIN
coffee, small cup of: **DEMITASSE**
coffee with milk: **CAFÉ AU LAIT**
coffin of stone: **SARCOPHAGUS**
coffin platform: **BIER**
coffin-supporting framework:
CATAFALQUE
coherence-lacking: **DISJOINTED**
coiled: **TORTILE**
coiled spirally: **HELICOID**
coin a word: **MINT, NEOLOGIZE**
coincidence: **CONJUNCTION**
coined money: **SPECIE**
coin or medal disc apart from lettering
or a stamped design: **FLAN**
coin or medal space for date, place of
coining, etc.: **EXERGUE**
coins, medals, etc., as a study:
NUMISMATICS
cold in the head: **CORYZA**
cold-like condition from inflamed
mucous membranes: **CATARRH**
cold sore: **HERPES LABIALIS**
collaborator with the enemy, traitorous
leader: **QUISLING**
collapse, fail, sink: **FOUNDER**
collapse inward violently: **IMPLODE**
collapsible or barely-holding-together
structure, plan, etc.: **HOUSE OF
CARDS**
collar or cord used to strangle:
GARROTE
colleague or fellow member: **CONFRERE**
collected excerpts from literary works:
ANALECTS
collect, gather or store: **GARNER**
collect, incorporate, make part of a
whole: **EMBODY**
collection during a religious ceremony:
OFFERTORY
collection, gathering, treasure: **TROVE**
collection of choice extracts for
instruction in a language:
CHRESTOMATHY
collection of poems, stories, etc.:
ANTHOLOGY
collection of things, mass, heap:
CONGERIES
collection of works and roles of a
performance or company:
REPERTORY
collection or cluster that is
heterogeneous: **CONGLOMERATE**

collective farm in the Soviet Union:
KOLKHOZ
collective farm or settlement in Israel:
KIBBUTZ
collector or connoisseur of works of art:
VIRTUOSO
college athlete not in varsity sports for
a year: **REDSHIRT**
college enrollment: **MATRICULATION**
colleges all of which were once
all-female and which are
considered prestigious Eastern
women's colleges (Barnard, Bryn
Mawr, Mount Holyoke, Radcliffe,
Smith, Vassar, and Wellesley):
SEVEN SISTERS
collegiate with regard to rules:
PARIETAL
collusion in a lawsuit to get a share of
the matter sued for: **CHAMPERTY**
color blending or changing by skillfully
smooth gradations: **SFUMATO**
color blindness: **ACHROMATOPSIA**
color blindness: **DALTONISM**
color change showing in different lights:
VERSICOLOR
colored differently in different parts:
PARTICOLORED
colored material of fluorescent hue:
DAY-GLO
colored variously, as wires or pipes, to
ease identification: **COLOR-CODED**
coloring matter: **PIGMENT**
colorless or not refracting light into
colors; neutral in hue; black and
white: **ACHROMATIC**
colorless, pale: **PALLID**
color or tint uniform throughout:
ISOCHROMATIC
color slightly: **TINGE**
colors of the rainbow in shifting hues
and patterns: **IRIDESCENCE**
color study: **CHROMATICS**
column in the form of a female figure:
CARYATID
columns that are regularly spaced:
COLONNADE
combative: **PUGNACIOUS**
comb for horses: **CURRYCOMB**
combination of circumstances or events:
CONJUNCTURE
combination of two or more substances:
AMALGAM
combine, blend and reconcile, as
various philosophies: **SYNCRETIZE**

combustible substance that will ignite
with a spark: **TINDER**
come between, especially as a barrier:
INTERPOSE
comedian who is the star: **TOP BANANA**
comedy that is broad or exaggerated:
FARCE
comedy that is loud, physical and
crude: **SLAPSTICK**
come forth into the open, emerge:
DEBOUCH
come into office or dignity: **ACCEDE**
come into view or appear as through a
mist, often ominously: **LOOM**
come out or be channeled into a larger
area, as into a river or valley:
DEBOUCH
comer into a country not his or her
own: **IMMIGRANT**
comforter, quilt: **DUVET**
comfort in grief: **SOLACE**
comic antics: **HARLEQUINADE**
comic muse: **THALIA**
coming from without, unrelated to the
matter at hand: **EXTRANEOUS**
coming in continually, as of people or
things: **INFLUX**
coming into existence, beginning to
appear: **INCIPIENT**
coming together, crowd: **CONCOURSE**
comma: erroneous use, instead of a
period or semicolon: **COMMA
FAULT, COMMA SPLICE**
comma-minimal punctuation style:
OPEN PUNCTUATION
commandeer a plane in transit: **HIJACK**
command level: **ECHELON**
command, order, forbid: **ENJOIN**
comma-rich punctuation style: **CLOSE
PUNCTUATION**
commence, begin: **INAUGURATE**
commencement headgear with a flat,
square top: **MORTARBOARD**
commence, originate, begin: **INITIATE**
commendation: **PLAUDIT**
commendatory: **LAUDATORY**
comment-arousing object:
CONVERSATION PIECE
commentary, explanatory note: **GLOSS**
comment critically on another's action,
choice, etc.: **SECOND-GUESS**
commenting character in a play or
novel: **RAISONNEUR**
comment that is not binding, a remark
made in passing: **OBITER DICTUM**

commerce, communication, exchange: **INTERCOURSE**

commissions and other costs of distribution included in the price paid by the purchaser of securities: **LOAD**

commit or carry out, as a crime or hoax: **PERPETRATE**

committed, involved, earnest: **ENGAGÉ**

committee consisting of all members of a legislative body: **COMMITTEE OF THE WHOLE**

committee determining the order of business: **STEERING COMMITTEE**

committee formed for a specific purpose: **AD HOC COMMITTEE**

common, everyday speech: **VULGATE**

common good, public or civic welfare: **COMMONWEAL**

common notion: **RECEIVED IDEA**

common people, masses: **HOI POLLOI**

common people, pertaining to: **DEMOTIC**

commonplace: **TOLERABLE**

commonplace, basic: **BREAD-AND-BUTTER**

commonplace, dull: **STODGY**

commonplace, ordinary, simple: **EXOTERIC**

commonplace, trite idea or expression: **CLICHÉ**

commonplace, trite statement: **PLATITUDE**

commonplace, uninspired, unimaginative: **PROSAIC**

common rather than literary language: **VERNACULAR**

common run, ordinary people: **RUCK**

common sense: **MOTHER WIT**

common stock earnings as affected by bond interest and preferred stock dividends: **LEVERAGE**

common to the masses: **VULGAR**

common, vulgar: **PLEBEIAN**

common, widely practiced: **PREVALENT**

commotion: **TURBULENCE**

commotion, fluster, bustle: **POTHER**

communication, exchange, commerce: **INTERCOURSE**

communication of minds by other than normal sensory means: **TELEPATHY**

communication system for immediate, direct exchange in an emergency: **HOT LINE**

communication system that is secret and usually person to person: **GRAPEVINE**

communication that is primitive, as in the jungle: **BUSH TELEGRAPH**

Communion received as bread dipped in wine: **INTINCTION**

Communism seen as spreading from one takeover to another: **DOMINO THEORY**

Communist emblem: **HAMMER AND SICKLE**

community laws against drinking, dancing, etc.: **BLUE LAWS**

community promotionalism and optimism: **BOOSTERISM**

compact, agreement, pledge: **COVENANT**

companionship: **SODALITY**

company's or corporation's breakup or selling off of holdings: **DIVESTITURE**

company that uses its capital to invest in other companies: **INVESTMENT TRUST**

compare critically, as writings or facts: **COLLATE**

comparison implied in a figure of speech: **METAPHOR**

compass holder or stand on a boat: **BINNACLE**

compatible, congenial: **SIMPATICO**

compelling, fascinating: **IRRESISTIBLE**

compel or force to go: **HALE**

compensate for or counteract something else: **OFFSET**

compensate, make up, offset: **COUNTERVAIL**

compensate, pay back: **REIMBURSE**

compensate, pay for: **REMUNERATE**

compensate, repay in kind: **REQUITE**

compensate, right a wrong: **REDRESS**

compensational unconscious behavior opposite to one's repressed desires: **REACTION FORMATION**

compensation for injury to the feelings: **SOLATIUM**

compensation for loss or damage, exemption from penalties or liabilities: **INDEMNITY**

compensation, pay, fee, or tip: **EMOLUMENT**

compete: **VIE**

competent legally to take care of one's own affairs: **SUI JURIS**

competition, rivalry: **CONTENTION**

competitive field day: **GYMKHANA**

competitor not among the top winners or finishers: **ALSO-RAN**

competitor on a team who is a fill-in or outsider: **RINGER**

complacent, self-satisfied: **SMUG**

complain: **CARP**

complain about being poor: **POOR-MOUTH**

complainer, irritable or whining person: **CRAB**

complain, fret: **REPINE**

complaining, whining: **QUERULOUS**

complaint, grievance: **PLAINT**

complaint receiver in government, consumer organizations, etc.: **OMBUDSMAN**

complain, whine: **KVETCH**

complement or mate to another: **COUNTERPART**

complete, absolute: **UNMITIGATED**

complete, absolute, full: **PLENARY**

complete confidence: **CERTITUDE**

complete, entire: **INTEGRAL**

completely organized and active: **FULL-FLEDGED**

completely, to the fullest, thoroughly: **À FOND**

completeness: **INTEGRITY**

complex, subtle, highly intellectual: **METAPHYSICAL**

compliant, manageable: **TRACTABLE**

complicate, confuse, entangle: **EMBRANGLE**

complicated, involved, puzzling: **INTRICATE**

complicated, involved, twisted or intricate: **CONVOLUTED**

complicate, disconcert, hamper: **EMBARRASS**

complicatedly constructed in an ingenious if impractical way: **RUBE GOLDBERG**

complicated or confused state of affairs: **IMBROGLIO**

complicated or problematic situation, predicament: **PLIGHT**

complicated or refined in design: **SOPHISTICATED**

complication, annoyance, hindrance, snag: **FLY IN THE OINTMENT**

complication, intertwining, entanglement: **INVOLUTION**

complication, snag, catch: **HITCH**

compliment that is dubious or insulting: **LEFT-HANDED COMPLIMENT**

comply, either in fact or only apparently: **TEMPORIZE**

comport (oneself): **DEMEAN**

compose, write out: **REDACT**

composure, coolness: **SANGFROID**

composure, even temper, calmness: **EQUANIMITY**

composure, serenity, self-assurance: **POISE**

comprehension or awareness independent of the senses: **ESP (EXTRASENSORY PERCEPTION)**

compromising too readily or out of weakness, adapting to the opposing party or view: **ACCOMMODATIONIST**

compulsive, excessive preoccupation with a thought or feeling: **OBSESSION**

compulsively neat, finicky and rigid: **ANAL-RETENTIVE**

compulsory service: **CONSCRIPTION**

computer basic unit of information: **BIT, BINARY DIGIT**

computer design and apparatus: **HARDWARE**

computer group of adjacent bits, commonly eight, processed as a unit: **BYTE**

computer information delivered in printed form: **PRINTOUT**

computer information fed into the apparatus: **INPUT**

computerized, robotic or mechanical autonomy, as in performing tasks, solving problems or playing games: **ARTIFICIAL INTELLIGENCE**

computer or equipment being linked up to a main computer system: **ON-LINE**

computer products not yet existing: **VAPORWARE**

computer programs: **SOFTWARE**

computers: designed to be easily understood and used: **USER-FRIENDLY**

computers and human nervous system under study: **CYBERNETICS**

computer screen symbol that moves or blinks: **CURSOR**

conceal, disguise, feign, make a false show of: **DISSEMBLE**

concealed: **ABSTRUSE**

concealed priority: **HIDDEN AGENDA**

concealed, secret or sheltered: **COVERT**

concealing language: AESOPIAN
LANGUAGE
concealment by a public official of an
offense, crime or wrongdoing by
another official: MISPRISION
concealment of one's real activities,
designs or misdeeds: COVER-UP
concealment of profits or theft of
money off the books: SKIMMING
conceal, pretend, dissemble:
DISSIMULATE
conceited, arrogant: BUMPTIOUS
conceited, boastful: VAINGLORIOUS
conceited or arrogant in one's ways or
attitudes: OVERWEENING
conceit, egotism: EGO
concentration of psychic energy upon a
person, idea, fantasy: CATHEXIS
concern, anxious attentiveness:
SOLICITUDE
concerned: SOLICITOUS
concerning, in the matter of: IN RE
conciliate opposing sides: MEDIATE
conciliate, win over: PROPITIATE
conciliatory present: DOUCEUR
concise: TERSE
concise summary or abstract: PRÉCIS
concise, terse, brief: LACONIC
concise, terse, meaningful: SUCCINCT
conclude or accept from evidence:
INFER
conclude or suppose from incomplete
evidence: CONJECTURE
conclusion in a sentence that follows
from the protasis, or condition:
APODOSIS
conclusive test: LITMUS TEST
concrete example or proof: OBJECT
LESSON
concretize, make real: REIFY
concubine, harem slave: ODALISQUE
concurrent: SIMULTANEOUS
condemn: CENSURE
condemn or denounce: DECRY
condemn, prohibit, outlaw: PROSCRIBE
condense: ABBREVIATE
condense: ABRIDGE
condense, boil down: DECOCT
condescend: DEIGN
condescend to, grant or permit:
VOUCHSAFE
conditional transaction authorized for
when, as and if a security is issued:
WHEN ISSUED

conditioned, involving trained
responses, automatic: PAVLOVIAN
condition existing at a particular time:
STATUS QUO
conditioning in which the pairing of
one stimulus, as a bell, with
another, as food, induces a
response to the first: CLASSICAL
CONDITIONING
conditioning of behavior by immediate
reward or punishment: OPERANT
CONDITIONING
condition set forth in a clause that leads
to apodosis, or conclusion:
PROTASIS
condition, stipulation: PROVISO
conduct, behavior: DEPORTMENT
cone-like mound in volcanic area:
CINDER CONE
cone- or funnel-shaped:
INFUNDIBULIFORM
cone or pyramid with top sliced off:
FULSTRUM
conference: POWWOW
conference of opposing sides, talk:
PARLEY
conference or conversation that is
formally arranged: COLLOQUY
conference or seminar of scholars:
COLLOQUIUM
confidence game, operation to defraud
or swindle: STING
confidence lack, timidity, shyness:
DIFFIDENCE
confidential friendship, close association:
INTIMACY
confidential or private conversation:
TÊTE-À-TÊTE
confined without means of
communication: INCOMMUNICADO
confine, imprison: INCARCERATE
confinement that is forced,
imprisonment: DURANCE
confine or detain, as during war:
INTERN
confine, surround, enclose within walls,
imprison: IMMURE
confining or checking item, as a rope:
TETHER
conflicting, mismated, discordant:
INCOMPATIBLE
con, fool, deceive, cheat, frustrate:
SNOOKER
conforming, done in accordance with:
PURSUANT

conforming or agreeing: CONGRUENT

conformity-forcing ruthlessly:
PROCRUSTEAN

confused: ADDLED, ADDLE-BRAINED,
ADDLEPATED

confused and hurried: HELTER-SKELTER

confused condition, mess: MARE'S NEST

confused, disjointed: INCOHERENT

confused, disorderly situation (from
military slang acronym "situation
normal, all fucked up"): SNAFU

confuse, defeat the plans of, frustrate:
DISCOMFIT

confuse, distract, upset, throw off:
DISCOMBOBULATE

confuse, divert: DISTRACT

confused mixture, medley: FARRAGO

confused or complicated state of affairs:
IMBROGLIO

confused or meaningless talk:
GALIMATIAS

confused, random: INDISCRIMINATE

confused, vague: HAZY

confuse, mix up: DISORIENT

confuse, muddle: EMBROIL

confuse, obscure: OBFUSCATE

confuse or mix up, as ideas or things:
CONFOUND

confuse, upset, frustrate: DISCONCERT

confusion, chaos, disorder: CHINESE
FIRE DRILL

confusion, hodgepodge:
KATZENJAMMER

confusion that is noisy: BEDLAM

congenial, compatible: SIMPATICO

congratulate: FELICITATE

congratulation on a witty retort or a
successful point made: TOUCHÉ

conjunctions omitted: ASYNDETON

con man's confederate who directs
potential victims to the place,
game, etc.: STEERER

connection, bond, link: NEXUS

connection or common boundary point:
INTERFACE

connect like links of a chain: CATENATE

connect with a crime or fault:
IMPLICATE

connive, conspire: COLLUDE

connoisseur: MAVEN, MAVIN

connoisseur, collector of works of art:
VIRTUOSO

consciously or deliberately done:
WITTINGLY

consciousness: SENTIENCE

conscious of oneself as being observed
by others, ill at ease:
SELF-CONSCIOUS

conscious perception: APPERCEPTION

consecrated or bound by a vow or
promise: VOTARY

consecrate, make holy: HALLOW

consent: ACCEDE

consent given passively: SUFFERANCE

consent quietly: ACQUIESCE

consequence: AFTERMATH

consequence: SEQUELA

consequence or result that is normal:
COROLLARY

conservative in beliefs, especially in
politics: TORY

conservative or entrenched element,
traditionalists: OLD GUARD

conservative or old-fashioned person:
FOGY, MOSSBACK

conservative or reactionary worker:
HARD HAT

conservative, reactionary: RIGHTIST

consider as real: HYPOSTATIZE

consider carefully, think about, reflect:
PONDER

considered or called so by oneself:
SELF-STYLED

consider seriously: TAKE UNDER
ADVISEMENT

consign, as to an obscure place or
inferior position: RELEGATE

consistency brought about, as in ideas:
RECONCILED

consolation in grief: SOLACE

consonant or combination of
consonants, such as "s," "sh," "f"
or "v," pronounced with breath
friction: SPIRANT

conspicuous public position: LIMELIGHT

conspicuous, striking, standing out:
SALIENT

conspiracy, plot, secret and
underhanded activity: INTRIGUE

conspire, connive: COLLUDE

conspire, scheme: MACHINATE

constant: INVARIABLE

constantly cause irritation, rankle:
FESTER

constantly changing or confusingly
shifting situation: MUSICAL CHAIRS

constant movement or change: FLUX

constipated: COSTIVE

constructed in an ingeniously if

impractically complicated way:
RUBE GOLDBERG
construction as a science: TECTONICS
construction material of plaster and
fiber that is temporary: STAFF
consumers susceptible to mass-media
persuasion: ADMASS
contact at a single point, as of a curved
line: TANGENT
contacting and sharing with others in a
profession: NETWORKING
contagious disease that breaks out
suddenly and affects many
individuals at the same time:
EPIDEMIC
container: RECEPTACLE
container of miscellaneous things:
CATCHALL
container's weight deducted to find
weight of contents: TARE
container usually of metal, as for tea or
spices: CANISTER
contain or include: COMPRISE
contemplation of the navel:
OMPHALOSKEPSIS
contemporary: COEVAL
contemptible, trivial, petty: PALTRY
contemptible, vile: DESPICABLE
contemptuous sound: BRONX CHEER
contender or arguer about trifling
matters: STICKLER
contentious, argumentative:
DISPUTATIOUS
contentious, railing, carping:
RABULISTIC
contentment or smugness:
COMPLACENCY
contestant not among the top winners
or finishers: ALSO-RAN
contest in which each player engages
every other player: ROUND ROBIN
contest won without much opposition:
WALKAWAY
continue unchanged, abide: SUBSIST
continuing, lasting a long time:
CHRONIC
continuing throughout the year, lasting
a long time: PERENNIAL
continuing, undecided: PENDING
continuing without interruption:
INCESSANT
continuity interrupted to present an
episode occurring earlier:
FLASHBACK
continuous, pitiless: RELENTLESS

continuum of four dimensions—three of
space plus time: SPACE-TIME
contraceptive medication for women:
PILL (THE PILL)
contraceptive or anti-infection sheath
for the penis: CONDOM
contraceptive pessary: DIAPHRAGM
contract between union official and
management that betrays the
interests of the union membership:
SWEETHEART CONTRACT
contract obligating a person to work for
another for a period: INDENTURE
contradict, deny, oppose: GAINSAY
contradiction between two individually
reasonable statements, laws, etc.,
thoughts inconsistent as a pair:
ANTINOMY
contradiction, inconsistency:
DISCREPANCY
contradictory-appearing statement that
is in some sense true: PARADOX
contradictory feelings: DISSONANCE
contradictory feelings, attitudes, etc.,
held at once by a person:
COGNITIVE DISSONANCE
contradictory terms combined in one
phrase: OXYMORON
contradictory thoughts or attitudes:
AMBIVALENCE
contradict, repudiate, deny: DISAFFIRM
contrary, nonconforming: PERVERSE
contrary to: ATHWART
contrast: ANTITHESIS
contrast by reverse parallelism in
phraseology: CHIASMUS
con trick or job, swindle: FIDDLE
contrition: PENITENCE
control and communication as they
apply to the operation of complex
machines and functions of human
organisms: CYBERNETICS
control artfully: MANIPULATE
controlled course of living: REGIMEN
controversy-embroiled, besieged,
attacked: EMBATTLED
conveniently introduced person or event
to untangle a story plot: DEUS EX
MACHINA
conventional person uninformed about
culture or aesthetics: PHILISTINE
conventional, proper: ORTHODOX
conversation about unimportant things:
SMALL TALK
conversational: COLLOQUIAL

conversational wit: **REPARTEE**

conversation or conference that is formally arranged: **COLLOQUY**

conversation or dialogue participant: **INTERLOCUTOR**

conversation that is informal, chat: **CAUSERIE**

convert by intensive indoctrination: **BRAINWASH**

convert ill-gained money to an unsuspicious form or area: **LAUNDER**

convert into a different shape: **TRANSMOGRIFY**

convert or try to convert a person to one's religion or cause: **PROSELYTIZE**

convert the energy of instinctual drives into socially acceptable manifestations: **SUBLIMATE**

convert, transform: **RESOLVE**

convincing: **COGENT**

convincing, influential: **POTENT**

convulsive: **SPASMODIC**

convulsive seizure, as in pregnancy or childbirth: **ECLAMPSIA**

cooked in a simple way or uncooked: **AU NATUREL**

cookery or the kitchen, pertaining to: **CULINARY**

cook gently: **CODDLE**

cooking, its style and quality: **CUISINE**

cooking pot that is airtight and prepares food quickly under pressure: **PRESSURE COOKER**

cool, casually indifferent: **NONCHALANT**

coolness, composure: **SANGFROID**

cooperate secretly: **COLLUDE**

cooperative, working together: **SYNERGETIC**

coop or pen for small animals: **HUTCH**

coordinator of a broadcasting team: **ANCHORMAN, ANCHORWOMAN**

copy, duplicate made by the originator: **REPLICA**

copy, imitation of a person or thing: **CLONE**

copy in form, as a legislative bill: **ENGROSS**

copying device, as for duplicating a map, made up of four rods in parallelogram shape: **PANTOGRAPH**

copying process employing electrostatic attraction: **XEROGRAPHY**

copy or reproduction that is exact: **FACSIMILE**

copyright or patent has run out: **PUBLIC DOMAIN**

cord: **LANYARD, LANIARD**

cordiality: **EMPRESSEMENT**

cord-like decoration used on clothes: **PIPING**

cord or belt worn around the waist: **CINCTURE**

cord or metal collar used to strangle: **GARROTE**

cord that is elastic, often with hooked ends, and used to secure large packages, luggage, etc.: **BUNGEE CORD, SHOCK CORD**

corduroy ridge: **WALE**

core, central or essential element: **NUCLEUS**

core group: **CADRE**

cork-holding wire on a champagne bottle: **COIFFE, AGRAFE**

cornmeal dough ball fried in deep fat: **HUSH PUPPY**

cornstalks: **STOVER**

corny political rhetoric: **BOMFOG (BROTHERHOOD OF MAN, FATHERHOOD OF GOD)**

coronary tissue death (necrosis) caused by obstruction: **INFARCTION**

corporation embracing companies in unrelated industries: **CONGLOMERATE**

corporation's total amount of securities issued: **CAPITALIZATION**

corporation that holds securities of another corporation that it normally controls: **HOLDING COMPANY**

corporeal, physical: **SOMATIC**

corpulent, very fat: **OBESE**

correctable, reformable: **CORRIGIBLE**

correct a manuscript, edit: **BLUE-PENCIL**

correctness of judgment, uprightness: **RECTITUDE**

correct or change a literary work, especially after scholarly study: **EMEND**

correct speech that is strained and actually erroneous: **HYPERCORRECTION**

corrupt: **ADULTERATE**

corrupt: **PERVERT**

corrupting, destructive or diseased thing, blight: **CANKER**

corrupt, invalidate, debase: VITIATE
corruption in officeholding:
MALVERSATION
corrupt, morally degraded:
SCROFULOUS
corrupt official, swindler, cheat:
HIGHBINDER
corrupt or dishonest profiting in politics
or business: GRAFT
corrupt, pervert: DEPRAVE
corrupt, rotten: PUTRID
corrupt, seduce, deprave: DEBAUCH
corrupt, sinful: PECCANT
corrupt, subject to bribery: VENAL
corrupt, undermine the morale of:
SUBVERT
cosmopolitan person, sophisticate:
COSMOPOLITE
costs of transaction included in the
price paid by a purchaser of
securities: LOAD
costs or continuous operating expenses
of a business: OVERHEAD
cottage cheese: SMEARCASE
cottage, duplex apartment: MAISONETTE
couch-like chair with an elongated seat
to support one's legs: CHAISE
LONGUE
couch or sofa that is upholstered and
without a back or arm rests: DIVAN
couch without arms or a back:
OTTOMAN
cough drop: TROCHE
cough up (phlegm): HAWK
couldn't-care-less in feeling: APATHETIC
counterbalance: EQUIPONDERATE
countercharge: RECRIMINATION
counterclockwise: WIDDERSHINS
counterfeit, artificial: POSTICHE
counterfeit, illegitimate: SPURIOUS
counterpart: OBVERSE
counting time in reverse: COUNTDOWN
countries that are underdeveloped and
belong to neither the communist
nor the capitalist bloc: THIRD
WORLD
country home in Russia: DACHA
country person who is awkward:
BUMPKIN
country that is dependent: CLIENT
STATE
country, to live in or adopt a rural way
of life: RUSTICATE
courage, initiative, shrewd common
sense: GUMPTION

courage inspired by alcohol: DUTCH
COURAGE
courageous: GAME
courageous, valiant: METTLESOME
courage, pluck, spirit: METTLE
course for advanced study: SEMINAR
court agreement prompting the
defendant to plead guilty to a
lesser charge: PLEA BARGAIN
court clerk who is chief:
PROTHONOTARY
court command that a thing be done:
MANDAMUS
court engaged in arbitrary or illegal
procedures: STAR CHAMBER
courteous, gallant, generous:
CHIVALROUS
courtesan: HETAERA
courtesy: COMITY
court fool's cap: FOOLSCAP
court has it under consideration: SUB
JUDICE
courtly or gallant man: CAVALIER
court-martial in the field for an offense
committed during operations:
DRUMHEAD COURT-MARTIAL
court official's cry to obtain silence:
OYEZ
court or central spacious recess:
ATRIUM
court order to appear and testify:
SUBPOENA
court-summoned person called in to
advise, "friend of the court":
AMICUS CURIAE
court that is unauthorized and
irregular: KANGAROO COURT
court writ ordering production of
documents or other evidence:
SUBPOENA DUCES TECUM
coverall worn by paratroops, mechanics,
etc., or a similar one-piece garment
worn as streetwear: JUMPSUIT
covered with matted woolly hair:
TOMENTOSE
covered with matted woolly masses:
FLOCCULENT
covering or outer coating, especially a
natural covering: INTEGUMENT
cover oneself for alternative possibilities
or outcomes: HEDGE ONE'S BETS
cover or suffuse with a liquid or color:
PERFUSE
cover up, gloss over: WHITEWASH
coward: POLTROON

cowardly: CRAVEN
cowardly, timid: CHICKEN-HEARTED, CHICKEN-LIVERED
cowardly, unfaithful: RECREANT
cowardly, weak: PUSILLANIMOUS
coward, sneak: DASTARD
cowboy's leather trousers: CHAPS
cow not pregnant: FARROW
cow that is young and hasn't yet produced a calf: HEIFER
coy, shy, modest, reserved: DEMURE
cozily, privately with one other person: À DEUX
coziness, friendliness, hospitality: GEMÜTLICHKEIT
crablike: CANCROID
crack, cleft, chink: CREVICE
cracked or fissured, chinky: RIMOSE
crackle, rattle: CREPITATE
cracklings: GREAVES
cracks in the surface of a painting: CRAQUELURE
crack, small space: INTERSTICE
cracks that intersect, as in glazed pottery: CRAZE
craft, cunning: SLEIGHT
craftiness, cunning: WILES
craftsman: ARTIFICER
crafty, fox-like, sly: VULPINE
crafty, insincere: DISINGENUOUS
cramped, uncomfortably small: INCOMMODIOUS
cramp, muscle pain: MYALGIA
cranky, stubborn: PERVERSE
crashing noisily, as waves: PLANGENT

crash or run into a person from the side and unseen: BLINDSIDE
craven, mean-spirited person: POLTROON
crave, yearn, desire: HANKER
craving: APPETENCE
crawl face downward, lie prostrate: GROVEL
crawl-into unfinished level in a house or building: CRAWL SPACE
crazed: DISTRAUGHT
craze for or irrational interest in one thing: MONOMANIA
craze, obsession: MANIA
crazy: CRACKBRAINED
crazy: DAFT
crazy: HAYWIRE
crazy: MESHUGA, MESHUGGA
crazy, absurd: COCKAMAMIE
cream of the crop: CRÈME DE LA CRÈME
creating ill will or dislike: INVIDIOUS
creation that turns on its creator or becomes uncontrollable: FRANKENSTEIN'S MONSTER
creation theory founded on belief in the Bible: CREATIONISM
creative efforts to devise new products and services: RESEARCH AND DEVELOPMENT, R & D
creative force or power: DEMIURGE
creative, original: PROMETHEAN
creative principle in living things, life force: ÉLAN VITAL
creative, productive, potential, germinal: SEMINAL

CREATURE TERMS

Creature	Group	Male	Female	Young
antelope	herd	buck	doe	kid
ass	herd, drove, pace	jack	jenny	colt, foal
badger	cete	boar	sow	
bear	sloth			cub
beaver				kitten
bee	swarm, hive	drone	queen	
boar	sounder			squeaker, calf
buffalo	herd	bull	cow	
camel	herd, flock	bull	cow	foal, calf, colt
cat	kindle (young), clowder, cluster	tom	she-cat, queen (fancy breed)	kitten
cattle	herd, drove	bull	cow	calf, heifer (female)

CREATURE TERMS *(Continued)*

Creature	Group	Male	Female	Young
chicken	brood, flock	rooster, cock	hen	chicken, pullet (female), cockerel (male)
cod			codling, sprag	
crane	herd			
crow	murder			
deer	herd	buck, stag	doe	fawn
dog	pack, kennel	hound	bitch	puppy, whelp
duck	team (in flight), paddling (in water)	drake	duck	duckling
eagle	convocation			eaglet
eel	swarm, congeries			elver
elephant	herd	bull	cow	calf
elk	gang	bull	cow	calf
ferret	business	dog	bitch	
finch	charm			
fish (general)	shoal, school, run			fry
frog	army			tadpole
fox	earth, skulk	vix	vixen	cub
giraffe	herd			
goat	flock, herd, tribe	billy	nanny	kid
goose	flock, skein (on the wing), gaggle (on water)	gander	goose	gosling
grouse	covey (family), pack (larger group)			
gull	colony			
hare	drove, trace	buck	doe	leveret
hawk	flight			eyas
heron	siege			
herring	army, glean, shoal			
hippopotamus				calf
horse	herd, stable	stallion	mare	colt, foal, filly
hummingbird	charm			
jay	band			
kangaroo	troop			joey
lark	exaltation			
leopard	leap	leopard	leopardess	cub
lion	pride, flock, troop	lion	lioness	cub
lobster			hen	chicken lobster
mackerel	shoal			spike, blinker, tinker
monkey	troop, tribe			

CREATURE TERMS *(Continued)*

Creature	Group	Male	Female	Young
moose		bull	cow	calf
mouse	nest			
mule	barren, rake			
nightingale	watch			
owl	parliament			owlet
otter		dog	bitch	
ox	herd, drove			
parrot	flock			
partridge	covey			squeaker
peafowl	muster	peacock	peahen	
pheasant	nye (young), brood			
pigeon	flight, flock			squab, squealer, squeaker
pig	herd	boar	sow	pig, farrow, shote, shoat
polecat		hob	jill	
porpoise	school			
quail	bevy			
raven	unkindness			
rhinoceros	crash			
seal	crash, herd, pod			cub
sheep	flock	ram	ewe	lamb
sparrow	host			
squirrel	dray			
starling	chattering			
stork	mustering			
swallow	flight			
swan	herd, wedge	cob	pen	cygnet
swine	sounder	boar	sow	
tiger		tiger	tigress	cub
toad	knot			
trout	hover			
turkey	flock	tom	hen	poult
turtle	bale			
whale	herd, school, gam, pod	bull	cow	calf
wolf	herd, rout, pack	dog wolf	bitch	whelp, cub
wren	herd			
zebra	herd	stallion	mare	foal, colt

credit amount that may legally be advanced by brokers to customers for purchase of securities: **REGULATION T**

credit for an achievement: **KUDOS**

credits in a film or TV show that move upward vertically on screen: **CRAWL**

credulous, unaffected, simple, candid, artless: **NAIVE**

creek, stream, channel: **KILL**

creep who charms and lives off women: **LOUNGE LIZARD**

cremate, burn up: **INCINERATE**

cremation repository: **CINERARIUM**

crescent or crescent-shaped item:
MENISCUS
cricket noises: STRIDULATION
cricket over, or period, in which no
runs are scored: MAIDEN OVER
cricket set of three upright sticks, or
stumps, with two small crosspieces,
or bails, at which the ball is
bowled: WICKET
cricket: to deflect a ball by a slight turn
of the bat: DRAW
crier, or caller to prayer, from a
minaret: MUEZZIN
crime, criminals and prisons as a study:
PENOLOGY
crime or concealment of an offense by a
public official: MISPRISION
crime, proof of a: CORPUS DELICTI
crime shocking for its wanton cruelty
or sadism: ATROCITY
crime study: CRIMINOLOGY
crime such as murder, rape, arson or
burglary: FELONY
crime syndicate chief: CAPO
crime syndicate chief's
second-in-command: CAPOREGIME
crime syndicate leader's close adviser:
CONSIGLIERE
crime syndicate member of low rank:
BUTTON, SOLDIER
criminal, evildoer: MALEFACTOR
cringe fondly, toady: FAWN
crinkled and light fabric usually with a
striped pattern: SEERSUCKER
cripple by shooting in the knee:
KNEECAP
crisis, critical situation: CONJUNCTURE
crisis or conflict between opposing
groups: CONFRONTATION
criterion or standard for testing the
qualities of something:
TOUCHSTONE
critical: CAPTIOUS
critical and biased article, book or
speech: HATCHET JOB
critical comment, harsh remark:
BRICKBAT
critical, demanding immediate action,
urgent: EXIGENT
critical in a detached or scientific way:
CLINICAL
critical in a harsh way, acid, unsparing:
ACIDULOUS
critical to an excessive degree, hard to
please: HYPERCRITICAL

critical year or period: CLIMACTERIC
criticism: ANIMADVERSION
criticism or difficulties from both sides:
GANTLET, GAUNTLET
criticism that is bitter or malicious:
DIATRIBE
criticism that is petty: QUIBBLE
criticism that is severe: STRICTURE
criticize as if by perforation: RIDDLE
criticize by hindsight: SECOND-GUESS
criticize, find fault with, rebuke, blame:
REPREHEND
criticize sharply: SCARIFY
criticizing angrily or caustically:
VITRIOLIC
critic or adviser who is frank and
severe: DUTCH UNCLE
critic who is strict but fair: ARISTARCH
cross bearer: CRUCIFER
crossbreed: INTERBREED
cross-country race along a course
containing obstacles:
STEEPLECHASE
cross-country runner: HARRIER
cross-country skiing run: LANGLAUF
crosser of the equator by ship:
SHELLBACK
cross-eyed condition: STRABISMUS
cross-fertilization: XENOGAMY
cross from one side to another:
TRANSVERSE
cross in form of an X, intersect:
DECUSSATE
cross-shaped: CRUCIATE
cross-shaped: CRUCIFORM
cross surmounted: CRUX ANSATA
cross surmounted by a loop, the ancient
Egyptian symbol of life: ANKH
cross threads in cloth: WEFT
cross whose arms narrow toward the
center and have V-shaped ends:
MALTESE CROSS
cross with a circle behind the
crossbeam: CELTIC CROSS
cross woman who is old-fashioned in
dress: FRUMP
crossword puzzle doer:
CRUCIVERBALIST
crouch or shrink in servility: CRINGE
crowbar used by burglars: JIMMY
crowd: RUCK
crowd, a coming together: CONCOURSE
crowd, a flocking together:
CONFLUENCE
crowded, densely populated: IMPACTED

crowded dwelling: WARREN
crowd or push roughly, shake up, elbow, shove: JOSTLE
crown, headband: DIADEM
crown-like, jeweled headdress worn by women: TIARA
crucially important, essential: PIVOTAL
crucial or ultimate test: ACID TEST
crucifixion of Jesus site: GOLGOTHA
crude: INDELICATE
crude and stupid person, boor: YAHOO
crude, backward and stupid person: NEANDERTHAL
crude, unpolished, uncultured: INCULT
crude, unrefined, rough: UNCOUTH
cruel exercise of power: TYRANNY
cruel, harsh or severe to an extreme degree: DRACONIAN
cruel or hideous being: OGRE
cruel or wantonly pitiless person: HELLKITE
cruel, stubborn: TRUCULENT
cruel, vicious, inhuman: FELL
crumb, food scrap: ORT
crumbly, pulverizable: FRIABLE
crusade, fanatic campaign: JIHAD
crusading: MESSIANIC
crushable, crumbly: FRIABLE
crush, subdue utterly, silence: SQUELCH
cry from the heart, passionate appeal or lament: CRI DE COEUR
crying out or shouting together: CONCLAMANT
cry loudly, scream, bawl: SQUALL
cry or whine with low, broken sounds: WHIMPER
cry, wail, whimper: PULE
cuddle: SNUGGLE
cuddle, snuggle for comfort: NESTLE
culminating or highest point: ZENITH
culminating point: SOLSTICE
cultivable, as land: ARABLE
cultivate deliberately the confidence or favor of others: INGRATIATE
cultural change in one society being effected by the culture of another: ACCULTURATION
cunning, craft: SLEIGHT
cunning, craft, deceit: GUILE
cunning, craftiness: WILE
cunning, ingenious, intricate: DAEDAL
cunningness, artful strategy, craftiness: FINESSE
cunning, treacherous, wily: INSIDIOUS

cup for drinking that is large, often with a cover: TANKARD
cup holder into which a handleless mug fits: ZARF
cupid or cherub, especially in a work of art: AMORETTO
cup or glass filled to the brim: BUMPER
cup or glass for measuring liquor: JIGGER
cup or goblet: CHALICE
cup-shaped: CALATHIFORM
cup that is the object of the quest in Arthurian legend: HOLY GRAIL
curative, healing: THERAPEUTIC
curb around a hatchway or skylight to keep out water: COAMING
cure-all, remedy for all ailments: PANACEA
cure-all, remedy, panacea: ELIXIR
cure oneself of alcoholism through special treatment: DRY OUT
cure or solution that is or would be miraculous: MAGIC BULLET
curious to an offensive degree: INQUISITORIAL
curling: competitor's broom used to sweep the ice before the sliding stone: BESOM
curling: to play the stone gently: DRAW
curly- or wavy-haired: CYMOTRICHOUS
curse against someone, slander, calumny: MALEDICTION
curse, call down a calamity: IMPRECATE
curse, denounce violently: EXECRATE
curse or ban: ANATHEMA
cursing: BLASPHEMY
curtain across a doorway: PORTIÈRE
curtain at the rear of a stage: BACKDROP
curvature of the spine: LORDOSIS
curved and tapered furniture leg: CABRIOLE
curved or arch-like long corrugated metal prefabricated building: QUONSET HUT
curved or bent part, bending: FLECTION
curved wall or screen usually containing pictures: CYCLORAMA
curve, especially inward: INCURVATE
curve in and out, bend: SINUATE
curve pattern that circles around a central point or in either direction around an axis: SPIRAL
curve shaped like a bell in statistics: BELL-SHAPED CURVE

curving inward: CONCAVE
curving outward: CONVEX
cushion for sitting or the feet: HASSOCK
custard dessert with caramel topping:
    FLAN
custard or a similar easily digested dish:
    FLUMMERY
custodian or superintendent in charge
    of a museum or similar institution:
    CURATOR
customary practice, habit: WONT
custom-made (British): BESPOKE
customs officer: DOUANIER
customs or folkways of a social group:
    MORES
cut across, divide: INTERSECT
cutely or affectedly quaint (British):
    TWEE
cut expenses: RETRENCH
cut into, carve, engrave: INCISE
cutlet, especially veal: SCHNITZEL
cut off by ecclesiastical authority:
    EXCOMMUNICATE
cutoff of operation or service by
    accident: OUTAGE
cut or mark the edge of a border with
    notches: INDENT

cut or notch carved out by a saw or ax:
    KERF
cut or part into two sections:
    DICHOTOMIZE
cut or split into long thin pieces:
    SLIVER
cut or trim branches, as from a tree:
    LOP
cutout decorating art in which snippets
    are lacquered: DÉCOUPAGE
cut out, excise: EXSCIND
cut, scratch: SCOTCH
cut the top or end from: TRUNCATE
cutting, intersecting: SECANT
cutting off: ABSCISSION
cutting, splitting: SCISSION
cutting teeth, teething: DENTITION
cut up or stir the surface, as of topsoil:
    SCARIFY
cyclone in the western Pacific:
    TYPHOON
cymbals mounted vertically as a pair on
    a rod and brought together by a
    drummer by means of a pedal:
    HIGH-HAT CYMBALS
cynical, sneering, scornful: SARDONIC

dabbler with a superficial interest in an art or science: **DILETTANTE**

dagger mark, double, in printing (‡): **DIESIS**

dagger or sword with wavy-edged blade: **KRIS**

daily expense allowance: **PER DIEM**

daily in cycle or recurrence: **DIURNAL**

daily in occurrence: **QUOTIDIAN**

daily prayers said by Catholic clergy: **BREVIARY**

daily walk for exercise: **CONSTITUTIONAL**

dainty, elegant, affectedly or effeminately prim: **MINCING**

dainty, oversensitive: **FASTIDIOUS**

damage as if by perforation: **RIDDLE**

damage or destruction done deliberately to obstruct, thwart, delay, etc.: **SABOTAGE**

damages awarded in excess of actual loss: **EXEMPLARY DAMAGES**

damage to a person's reputation done through a false or malicious written statement or graphic representation: **LIBEL**

damaging or destruction of property willfully: **VANDALISM**

damnation, hell: **PERDITION**

damning with faint praise: **DIASYRM**

dam placed in a stream to divert the water, as in irrigation: **WEIR**

damp, moist: **HUMID**

damp, moist, humid: **DANK**

dam side channel or apron to divert excess flow: **SPILLWAY**

dance and choral songs muse: **TERPSICHORE**

dance in which couples form sets in squares: **SQUARE DANCE**

dance in which the performer's shoes sharply accentuate the rhythm with the toes and heels: **TAP DANCE**

dance like a slow polka: **SCHOTTISCHE**

dance movement in which a couple swing round with hands joined: **POUSETTE**

dance notation: **CHOREOLOGY**

dance of Romanians and Israelis in which dancers lock arms in a circle: **HORA**

dance of Slavs in which a man performs the prisiadka, a step in which from a squatting position each leg is kicked out alternately: **KAZATSKY**

dancer: **TERPSICHOREAN**

dancing art: **CHOREOGRAPHY**

dancing mania, characteristic of a nervous disorder: **TARANTISM**

dandified man or one who dresses overfastidiously: **FOP**

dandruff: **FURFUR**

dandruff or similar scales shed by the skin: **SCURF**

dandy, fop, man who dresses flashily: **DUDE**

danger: **JEOPARDY**

danger on both sides: **BETWEEN SCYLLA AND CHARYBDIS**

danger or trap always possible or to be feared: **PITFALL**

dangerous, as a degree of speed: **BREAKNECK**

dangerous or potentially explosive situation or place: **TINDERBOX**

dangerous, perilous, risky: **PARLOUS**

dangerous to society: **PESTILENT**

danger-signaling or -warning, as by an animal: **SEMATIC**

danger that is looming or imminent:
SWORD OF DAMOCLES

daredevil, bravo, swaggering adventurer:
SWASHBUCKLER

daring, audacity, impudence, boldness:
HARDIHOOD

daring deeds or adventures:
DERRING-DO

dark: **APHOTIC**

dark and threatening, as the weather:
LOWERING

dark-complexioned, dusky: **SWARTHY**

darken, dim, make opaque: **OPACATE**

darkened or tinged with brown, as a
part of an insect's wing:
INFUSCATE

dark, gloomy: **CIMMERIAN**

dark, gloomy: **TENEBROUS**

dark, gloomy, infernal: **STYGIAN**

dark in appearance or pigmentation:
MELANOID

dark, obscure, misty: **MURKY**

dark shape or profile with light
background: **SILHOUETTE**

dash, enthusiasm, vivacity: **ÉLAN**

dashing, gay, smart: **RAKISH**

dashing, large, vigorous, swift:
SPANKING

dashing, self-confident, stylish, lively,
brisk: **JAUNTY**

dash, spirited style: **PANACHE**

dash, vigor: **VERVE**

date on which a loan or bond comes
due: **MATURITY**

daughter's sexual attachment to her
father: **ELECTRA COMPLEX**

dauntless, fearless, bold: **INTREPID**

dawdle, pass time, cheat: **DIDDLE**

dawdle, waste time: **DILLYDALLY**

dawdle, waste time: **PIDDLE**

dawn: **COCKCROW**

day blindness: **HEMERALOPIA**

day-by-day account of events:
CHRONOLOGY

daydreamer, one with his or her head
in the clouds: **LUFTMENSCH**

daydreaming, musing: **REVERIE**

daydreaming tendency that removes one
from reality: **AUTISM**

day or month being added to the
calendar: **INTERCALARY**

days and nights are equal at these
times, March 21 and September 21:
VERNAL EQUINOX and **AUTUMNAL
EQUINOX**

daytime rather than nighttime:
DIURNAL

day when night and day are of equal
length, marking the start of spring
or autumn: **EQUINOX**

dazzling, brilliant, swift: **METEORIC**

dazzling, shining with brilliance, vividly
bright: **RESPLENDENT**

dead at birth: **STILLBORN**

deaden, paralyze with fear: **PETRIFY**

dead, extinct: **DEFUNCT**

deadlocked situation: **STALEMATE**

deadly-eyed or fatal to look at:
BASILISK

deadly, fatal: **LETHAL**

deadly, injurious, malicious:
PERNICIOUS

deadly to both sides of a group:
INTERNECINE

dead or rotten flesh: **CARRION**

dead person: **DECEDENT**

dead; say nothing but good about them:
DE MORTUIS NIL NISI BONUM

dead's oppressive influence on the
living: **DEAD HAND**

deaf-mute alphabet: **DACTYLOLOGY**

dealer, trader: **MONGER**

dealing with people or situations
delicately and without giving
offense: **TACT**

deal maker, operator, shrewd business
person: **WHEELER-DEALER**

death: **DEMISE**

death anniversary observed by Jews:
YAHRZEIT

death blow, mortal blow: **COUP DE
GRACE**

death house: **CHARNEL HOUSE**

death investigation: **INQUEST**

deathly looking: **CADAVEROUS**

death-near, at the point of death: **IN
EXTREMIS**

death omen: **KNELL**

death only apparent and not real:
ANABIOTIC

death or mortality reminder: **MEMENTO
MORI**

death, resurrection and immortality as a
subject of study: **ESCHATOLOGY**

death that is painless and peaceful:
EUTHANASIA

debase: **ADULTERATE**

debase, corrupt, invalidate: **VITIATE**

debase oneself out of fear or servility:
GROVEL

debatable, academic or so hypothetical as to be without significance: MOOT

debate, argumentation: FORENSICS

debate or argue earnestly: CONTEND

debate that is formal: DISPUTATION

debating fine point: QUODLIBET

debauched, immoral: DISSOLUTE

debt-acknowledging certificate: DEBENTURE

debt acknowledgment that is non-negotiable and usually exchangeable for goods or services: DUE BILL

debt acquittal or payment, recompense: QUITTANCE

debt or liability extinguished gradually, as by installment payments: AMORTIZED

debutante-type young woman: JUNIOR LEAGUER

decayed: CARIOUS

decayed, neglected, shabby: DILAPIDATED

decay or decline, as in art or morals: DECADENCE

decay, rot: PUTREFY

deceit, cunning, craft: GUILE

deceit, dishonest dealing: INDIRECTION

deceitful: MENDACIOUS

deceitfulness, trickery, double-dealing: DUPLICITY

deceitfulness, trickery, rascality: KNAVERY

deceitful, treacherous: DOUBLE-DEALING

deceive: BEGUILE

deceive, cheat, trick: FINAGLE

deceive, mislead: EQUIVOCATE

deceive or cheat in a petty way: COZEN

deceiver: IMPOSTOR

deception or pretended blow meant to distract: FEINT

deception, trickery: HOCUS-POCUS

deceptively appearing to be true or correct: SPECIOUS

deceptive, pretended, sham: FEIGNED

deceptive talk: SHUCKING AND JIVING

decided previously by judicial authority: RES JUDICATA

deciding statement: CLINCHER

deciding vote: CASTING VOTE

decimal system of counting: ALGORISM

decision maker in a dispute: ARBITER

decisive, final, absolute, positive: PEREMPTORY

declare relevant and operative, as a law: INVOKE

declare solemnly: ASSEVERATE

decline or decay, as in art or morals: DECADENCE

declining market: BEAR MARKET

declining, worsening, going backward: RETROGRADE

decoded message: PLAINTEXT

decoding: CRYPTANALYSIS

decomposing naturally, as bacterially, in the environment: BIODEGRADABLE

decorate an initial page or word of a manuscript with designs or bright colors: ILLUMINATE

decorate, dress up: TITIVATE

decorated with material embedded flush with the surface: INLAID

decorate lavishly, as with jewels: INCRUST, ENCRUST

decorate or dress up with showy ornaments: PRANK

decorate or enrich with engraved or inlaid work: ENCHASE

decorate, ornament: EMBELLISH

decorate or ornament the edge, adorn the border: PURFLE

decoration à la Chinoise: CHINOISERIE

decoration, patch or trimming glued or sewn on: APPLIQUÉ

decorative glitter on a fabric: DIAMANTÉ

decorative horizontal strip, as along the top of a wall: FRIEZE

decorative inlaid work: MARQUETRY

decorative plan of a room: DECOR

decrease, lessening, diminution: DECREMENT

decree: RESCRIPT

decree, command or prohibition: EDICT

decree, establish: ORDAIN

decree, law: STATUTE

decree that is official and arbitrary: UKASE

dedicate or sign a book for presentation: INSCRIBE

dedicatory words or lines at the end of a poem: ENVOY

deduce by logical methods: RATIOCINATE

deduce, conclude from evidence: INFER

deduction, conjecture: INFERENCE

deduction, discount: REBATE

deduction, inference: ILLATION

deductive reasoning formula:
SYLLOGISM
deep-freezing the dead or diseased in
hope of future revival or cure:
CRYONICS
deep in intellect or feeling: PROFOUND
deep involvement: IMMERSION
deeply established habits: SECOND
NATURE
deeply felt or suffered: DE PROFUNDIS
deep red or purplish red: CARMINE
deep-rooted, firmly established:
INGRAINED
deep-sea chamber: BATHYSPHERE
deep-sea-fishing boat's anchored chair:
FIGHTING CHAIR
deep-sea navigable research vessel with
a spherical cabin, submersible
exploratory craft: BATHYSCAPHE
deer meat: VENISON
deer's tail: FLAG
defamation that is spoken: SLANDER
defamatory and abusive words:
OBLOQUY
defame, dishonor: SMIRCH
defame, disparage, blacken: DENIGRATE
defame, disparage, despise: VILIPEND
defame, revile: VILIFY
defame, say malicious things: TRADUCE
defame, traduce: MALIGN
defeat another force but with great
losses: CADMEAN VICTORY,
PYRRHIC VICTORY
defeat by cleverness: OUTWIT
defeat by skillful maneuver:
CHECKMATE
defeated officeholder having time
remaining in office: LAME DUCK
defeatist or pacifist propaganda:
BOLOISM
defeat, nullify, prevail over: OVERRIDE
defeat suffered abruptly: REBUFF
defeat that is final or decisive:
WATERLOO
defeat the plans or purposes of,
frustrate, vanquish: DISCOMFIT
defeat utterly: DRUB
defect existing at birth: CONGENITAL
DEFECT
defendable, maintainable: TENABLE
defending-oneself system that is a form
of jujitsu: JUDO
defenseless or not defendable, as an
attitude: UNTENABLE
defense or justification: APOLOGIA

defensive tactic: PARRY
defer, put off, postpone: WAIVE
defiance of established doctrine: HERESY
defiant in an aggressive way:
TRUCULENT
deficiency: INSUFFICIENCY
defile, besmirch, soil: SULLY
defile, dirty: POLLUTE
defined word or term: DEFINIENDUM
definite, clear, straightforward,
outspoken: EXPLICIT
definition part of a dictionary entry:
DEFINIENDUM
definitive, judicial, established by
decree: DECRETORY
deflect, turn aside, distract, amuse,
entertain: DIVERT
deformation of the earth's crust,
forming mountains, continents:
DIASTROPHISM
defraud or cheat a person: MULCT
defy, scoff, mock, jeer: FLOUT
degrade: DEMEAN
degraded, base, dishonorable: IGNOBLE
degraded, morally debased:
SCROFULOUS
degraded, sneaky, skulking: HANGDOG
degree of personal excellence: CALIBER
degree or range of occurrence:
INCIDENCE
degree or strength of a feeling, quality
or action: INTENSITY
deification: APOTHEOSIS
deign to grant or permit: VOUCHSAFE
dejected: CHAPFALLEN
dejected: DISPIRITED
dejected: INCONSOLABLE
dejected, depressed: CRESTFALLEN
dejected, gloomy, saddened:
DISCONSOLATE
dejection, despair: SLOUGH OF
DESPOND
dejection of spirits, hopelessness:
DESPONDENCY
delayed effect in physics, electricity or
magnetism: HYSTERESIS
delayed reaction to a joke or unusual
situation: DOUBLE TAKE
delay, hinder, put obstacles in the way
of: IMPEDE
delay, hinder, slow: RETARD
delaying: DILATORY
delay or suspension authorized in some
specific activity: MORATORIUM

delay, postponement, interval of relief or rest: **RESPITE**

delay that is temporary: **ABEYANCE**

delete obscene or otherwise objectionable material: **EXPURGATE**

deletion, erasure: **EXPUNCTION**

deliberate decision: **VOLITION**

deliberately or consciously done: **WITTINGLY**

delicate, flimsy substance: **GOSSAMER**

delicious morsel, appetizing treat, delicacy: **BONNE BOUCHE**

delicious, richly sweet: **LUSCIOUS**

delightful, entrancing: **RAVISHING**

delight, give unusual pleasure, entertain: **REGALE**

delight (in), celebrate, make merry: **REVEL**

deliver up or surrender an accused individual to another state or country: **EXTRADITE**

delusion, insane notion: **DELIRAMENT**

delusion, misleading phenomenon: **WILL-O'-THE-WISP**

delusion shared by two people: **FOLIE À DEUX**

delusions of persecution or grandeur: **PARANOIA**

demagnetize: **DEGAUSS**

demand for a customer to put money or securities with his broker: **MARGIN CALL**

demanding constant hard work: **EXACTING**

demanding insistently: **IMPORTUNATE**

demand rigorously, require as a matter of justice: **EXACT**

demand, summons: **REQUISITION**

demolish, level to the ground: **RAZE**

demon-like carved figure on a building: **GARGOYLE**

demon-possessed: **DEMONIAC**

demonstrable: **APODICTIC**

demonstrate convincingly, show clearly: **EVINCE**

demon that takes possession of a living person: **DYBBUK**

denial, as of a charge, by a government or official body: **DEMENTI**

denominational: **SECTARIAN**

denounce, condemn: **DECRY**

denounce violently, curse: **EXECRATE**

dense, incomprehensible: **IMPENETRABLE**

dentistry branch that is devoted to gums and bones supporting the teeth: **PERIODONTICS**

dentistry branch that strives to prevent and correct tooth irregularities: **ORTHODONTICS**

denunciation: **REPROBATION**

denunciation or accusation that is violent: **INVECTIVE**

denunciation or threat, especially from a divine source: **COMMINATION**

denunciation that is loud and violent: **FULMINATION**

denunciatory speech: **TIRADE**

denying believability of excuses in case things go wrong: **DENIABILITY**

deny oneself something: **ABSTAIN**

deny, oppose, contradict: **GAINSAY**

deny or renounce one's own rights, desires, etc.: **ABNEGATION**

deny, repudiate: **DISAFFIRM**

depart suddenly: **ABSCOND**

departure in mass numbers, general flight, group emigration: **EXODUS**

departure that is furtive or without a farewell: **FRENCH LEAVE**

dependable, firm: **STAUNCH**

dependent clauses used in syntax: **HYPOTAXIS**

dependent country: **CLIENT STATE**

dependent on luck: **ALEATORY**

deportment, manner in which one bears oneself: **DEMEANOR**

deposit eggs or roe: **SPAWN**

deprave, corrupt, seduce: **DEBAUCH**

depravity, baseness, vileness: **TURPITUDE**

depreciatory or derogatory: **PEJORATIVE**

depressed, bored, or dull state of mind: **DOLDRUMS**

depressed, dejected: **CRESTFALLEN**

depressed, downhearted: **DISPIRITED**

depressed, gloomy, dusky: **SOMBER**

depressed mood: **FUNK**

depressing person, pessimist, killjoy: **CRAPEHANGER, CREPEHANGER**

depressing, unhappy: **DOWNBEAT**

deprive as a punishment: **AMERCE**

deprive of rights or possessions: **DIVEST**

deprive of rights or privileges, as of a citizen's right to vote: **DISFRANCHISE, DISENFRANCHISE**

deprive of, strip, rob: **DESPOIL**

deputy, agent, substitute: **VICAR**

deranged or twisted mentality: **ABERRATION**

derelict's section of a city: SKID ROW

deride, sneer, laugh coarsely, jeer:
FLEER

derisive or mocking speech or manner:
JEER

derisive sound: BRONX CHEER

derivations and development of words
as a study: ETYMOLOGY

derogatory or depreciatory: PEJORATIVE

descendant, offspring: SCION

descended from the same parent,
language, etc.: COGNATE

descent of an individual traced from a
certain ancestor: GENEALOGY

describe, portray, paint, draw: LIMN

description of a person, as of a criminal
for identification: SIGNALMENT

desecrate, pollute: PROFANE

desert, change sides: TERGIVERSATE

deserted, wretched, abandoned,
cheerless: FORLORN

deserter, traitor: RENEGADE

desertion of faith or principles:
APOSTASY

desert monument of a mythical
creature: SPHINX

deserved or suitable, as a punishment:
CONDIGN

design cut on a gem: GLYPTOGRAPH

design in nature, as studied in
cosmology: TELEOLOGY

design in relief, as in metal: REPOUSSÉ

design of five things of which four
make a square and one is in the
middle: QUINCUNX

design of interlaced foliage or flowers,
geometric tendrils, etc.:
ARABESQUE

design or shape that doesn't adhere to
any rigid pattern: FREE-FORM

desire: APPETENCE

desire, crave, yearn: HANKER

desired, wanted or aimed-for thing:
DESIDERATUM

desire, feel the need for or the lack of:
DESIDERATE

desire or lust for something belonging
to another: COVET

desolate or saddened through loss:
BEREAVED

despair, dejection: SLOUGH OF
DESPOND

despise, defame, disparage: VILIPEND

despise, scorn: CONTEMN

despotic subordinate governor: SATRAP

despotism: ABSOLUTISM

dessert of custard topped with caramel:
FLAN

dessert that is pudding-like: MOUSSE

destroy completely, wipe out:
OBLITERATE

destroyer of images or of venerated
objects or ideas: ICONOCLAST

destroy or kill a large proportion of:
DECIMATE

destroy or weaken the affection of:
DISAFFECT

destroy utterly, pull up by the roots,
uproot, erase: ERADICATE

destroy wholly, root out: EXTIRPATE

destruction, mutilation or alteration,
especially of a legal document:
SPOLIATION

destruction of great scope, especially by
fire: HOLOCAUST

destruction or extermination of an
entire people or national group:
GENOCIDE

destruction, ruin: HAVOC

destructive, diseased or corrupting
thing, blight: CANKER

destructive force that is slow and
relentless: JUGGERNAUT

detached, isolated: INSULAR

detachedly observant or analytical:
CLINICAL

detached, unbiased: OBJECTIVE

detail, declare, state: EXPOUND

detailed examination or discussion:
CANVASS

detain or confine, as during war:
INTERN

detective: HAWKSHAW

detective novel stressing realistic police
investigation: POLICE PROCEDURAL

detective or private detective: GUMSHOE

deteriorated, rickety: RAMSHACKLE

deteriorating biologically, as a strain or
type, especially of man: DYSGENIC

determined, brave, strong: STALWART

determinedly, energetically, all out:
HAMMER AND TONGS

determined, resolved, unflinching:
RESOLUTE

deter or alter the plans of someone by
persuasion against: DISSUADE

detest: ABHOR

detestable, revolting, abominable:
EXECRABLE

detestation: ABHORRENCE

detraction: DISPARAGEMENT
detract, take away from: DEROGATE
developed or advanced more rapidly
    than is usual: PRECOCIOUS
develop or work out gradually: EVOLVE
develop, sit on and hatch eggs:
    INCUBATE
develop to the utmost, make the most
    of: OPTIMIZE
deviating from the normal rule:
    ANOMALOUS
deviating from what is generally
    accepted: PERVERSE
deviation: ABERRATION
deviation from the main current: EDDY
deviation from the normal: PERVERSION
devil, in Moslem countries: SHAITAN
devilish: CLOVEN-HOOFED
devious: AMBAGIOUS
devious: TORTUOUS
devise, make up: CONCOCT
devise, think out carefully: EXCOGITATE
devitalize, sap the strength of, weaken:
    ENERVATE
devoted: ASSIDUOUS
devoted admirer or follower: VOTARY
devoted blindly: IDOLATROUS
devotee: AFICIONADO
devotee of a particular pursuit,
    enthusiast: VOTARY
dew formation: DEWFALL
dexterity or skill in manipulation:
    SLEIGHT
dexterous: ADROIT
diabetics' needed protein hormone:
    INSULIN
diagonal: CATERCORNERED
diagonal or oblique line: BIAS
diagram or chart of the stages of a
    process: FLOW CHART
diagrams, charts, drawings, etc., used as
    explanatory matter: GRAPHICS
diagram showing a sequence of
    operations for a program or
    process: FLOW CHART
diagram, synopsis or summary, as of a
    process: SCHEMA
dialect closest to the standard major
    language of a country: ACROLECT
dialect dictionary: IDIOTICON
dialect, especially one that is crude:
    PATOIS
dialect least like the standard major
    language of a country: BASILECT
dialect midway between an acrolect and

basilect in likeness to the standard
    major language of a country:
    MESOLECT
dialect of a region that has become the
    language of a larger area: KOINE
dialect or jargon mixed with English:
    PIDGIN ENGLISH
dialogue: INTERLOCUTION
dialogue or conversation participant:
    INTERLOCUTOR
diameter-measuring instrument:
    CALIPERS
diametrically opposed: ANTIPODAL
diamond or rhombus, as used in decor
    or heraldry: LOZENGE
diarrhea and nausea afflicting a tourist
    in a foreign country: TURISTA,
    TOURISTA
diarrhea or stomach upset:
    COLLYWOBBLES
dictatorial, imperious: PEREMPTORY
dictionary compiling: LEXICOGRAPHY
dictionary, especially a polyglot
    dictionary: CALEPIN
dictionary of proper names:
    ONOMASTICON
die: BUY THE FARM
died without having made a will:
    INTESTATE
dieting establishment: FAT FARM
difference: DISSIMILITUDE
difference, as of opinion: DIVERGENCE
difference of opinion, discord, quarrel:
    DISSENSION
difference or remainder paid to equalize
    a business transaction: OWELTY
differences in outlook between
    individuals: PERSONAL EQUATION
different: DIVERSE
different directions, move in: DIVERGE
different, dissimilar, distinct: DISPARATE
differing: DISSIDENT
differing in names that show a
    relationship: HETERONYMOUS
differing, not all alike: HETEROGENEOUS
differ in opinion: DIVERGE
difficult and interminable: SISYPHEAN
difficulties or criticism from both sides:
    GAUNTLET, GANTLET
difficult or puzzling problem: STICKLER
difficult or tricky situation (British):
    STICKY WICKET
difficult position: QUAGMIRE
difficult situation: MORASS

difficult, stubborn, unruly: **INTRACTABLE**

difficult to accomplish: **HERCULEAN**

difficult to deal with: **SCABROUS**

difficult to understand: **ABSTRUSE**

diffuse or scatter, as if by sowing: **DISSEMINATE**

diffusion of a fluid through a membrane: **OSMOSIS**

digestion that is good: **EUPEPSIA**

digest, summary: **CONSPECTUS**

digital watch display-reading mechanism: **LED (LIGHT-EMITTING DIODE)**

dignified and well-bred: **DISTINGUÉ**

dig out the facts: **PLUMB**

digression: **APOSTROPHE**

digressive, rambling: **EXCURSIVE**

digress, wander or stray from the subject: **DIVAGATE**

digs, the study of: **ARCHEOLOGY**

dig up a corpse or some buried thing: **EXHUME**

diligent and careful: **PAINSTAKING**

diligent, constant, working steadily: **SEDULOUS**

diminish: **ABATE**

diminish, lessen: **DWINDLE**

diminution, lessening, decrease: **DECREMENT**

diminutive: **LILLIPUTIAN**

dimming of lights: **BROWNOUT**

dim, obscure, pertaining to twilight: **CREPUSCULAR**

dimple, small depression: **FOSSETTE**

dining hall in a college or monastery: **REFECTORY**

dinner menu with a complete meal at a set price: **TABLE D'HÔTE**

dinner menu with each item having a separate price: **À LA CARTE**

dinner precooked and frozen, often in an aluminum-foil-covered tray: **TV DINNER**

dinosaur-age flying reptile: **PTERODACTYL**

dinosaur, herbivorous, having a large rounded body, long neck and small head: **BRONTOSAUR**

dinosaur that was large and carnivorous and walked on two legs: **TYRANNOSAUR**

dinosaur with a small head and large tooth-like bony plates along its curved back and tail: **STEGOSAURUS**

dinosaur with hooves, three horns, a beak-like mouth and a bony fan-like crest around the neck: **TRICERATOPS**

diphtheria test: **SCHICK TEST**

dip into liquid for pickling: **SOUSE**

dip lightly or suddenly into water, as a bird does: **DAP**

diplomatic etiquette: **PROTOCOL**

diplomatic move, response or statement of position: **DÉMARCHE**

diplomatic, prudent, wise: **POLITIC**

direct, blunt: **POINT-BLANK**

directed firmly, unwavering, steadfast: **INTENT**

direct into set channels: **CANALIZE**

direction or sense of direction lost or mixed up: **DISORIENTATION**

direct opposite: **ANTITHESIS**

direct, plain: **FLAT-FOOTED**

direct relationship, freedom from intervention: **IMMEDIACY**

dirge, funeral hymn: **EPICEDIUM**

dirge, funeral song: **THRENODY**

dirty, defile: **POLLUTE**

dirty, foul, appearing neglected: **SQUALID**

dirty language: **COPROLALIA**

dirty, squalid: **SORDID**

dirty, stain or soil another's name or reputation, sully: **BESMIRCH**

disable: **INCAPACITATE**

disadvantage: **DRAWBACK**

disadvantage imposed on contestants of superior ability in a contest or race: **HANDICAP**

disagree: **DISSENT**

disagreeable, offensive: **UNSAVORY**

disagreeable, ugly, unpleasant in appearance: **ILL-FAVORED**

disagreeing, quarreling: **AT LOGGERHEADS**

disagreement: **DISSIDENCE**

disagreement, quarrel, estrangement: **FALLING-OUT**

disappear by degrees, vanish gradually: **EVANESCE**

disappearing by normal biological action, decomposing: **BIODEGRADABLE**

disappointment or distress over one's own acts, plight, etc.: **CHAGRIN**

disapproval: **ANIMADVERSION**

disapprove, plead against: DEPRECATE
disarrayed, partly dressed: DISHABILLE
disassemble a weapon for cleaning:
   FIELD STRIP
disaster that brings violent change:
   CATACLYSM
disavow a former belief: RECANT
disbelief or denial of any purpose in
   existence or in customary
   institutions: NIHILISM
disbelieving, doubting: INCREDULOUS
discard or cast off a favored sweetheart:
   JILT
discard something that hampers:
   JETTISON
discerning, perceptive, keen:
   PERSPICACIOUS
discernment, wisdom: SAGACITY
discharged debt, recompense:
   QUITTANCE
discharge of repressed emotions:
   CATHARSIS
discharge suddenly and quickly,
   exclaim: EJACULATE
disciplinarian of extreme militaristic
   severity: MARTINET
disciplinary action that is swift:
   CRACKDOWN
discipline or chastise, call to account:
   CALL ON THE CARPET
disclose, bring to light, reveal: EXHUME
disclose, make known, bestow: IMPART
disclose, reveal, give vent to: UNBOSOM
disclose, reveal, tell: DIVULGE
disclosure in a trial or hearing that a
   defendant is compelled to make:
   DISCOVERY
discolored or stained, as pages of an old
   book: FOXED
disconcerted by some occurrence:
   ABASHED
disconcert, embarrass:
   DISCOUNTENANCE
disconcert, impede, complicate:
   EMBARRASS
disconnect: UNCOUPLE
disconnected, aimless, casual, random:
   DESULTORY
disconnected, lacking in coherence:
   DISJOINTED
disconnected, separate: DISCRETE
discontent or illness, a chronic feeling
   of either: DYSPHORIA
discordant: ABSONANT

discordant, conflicting, mismated:
   INCOMPATIBLE
discordant or harsh sound: JANGLE
discordant sound: CACOPHONY
discord, harsh disagreement:
   DISSONANCE
discord, quarrel, difference of opinion:
   DISSENSION
discourage: DISHEARTEN
discourteous or rude manner:
   INCIVILITY
discover with the eye, discern, observe:
   DESCRY
discovery and investigation as a way of
   learning: HEURISTICS
discreet fee or token of appreciation:
   HONORARIUM
discreet, prudent, careful: CIRCUMSPECT
discriminate against or keep out specific
   people: BLACKLIST
discriminate, distinguish: SECERN
discriminating taster or enjoyer of food
   and drink: GOURMET
discrimination against black people
   historically in the United States:
   JIM CROW
discrimination against older people:
   AGEISM
discrimination perceived as existing in
   effect against the group originally
   cited for discriminatory practices:
   REVERSE DISCRIMINATION
discussing or discussed in a way that is
   informal and rambling:
   CRACKER-BARREL
discussion, conversational get-together:
   PALAVER
discussion or series of remarks:
   DESCANT
disdainful, arrogant: SUPERCILIOUS
disease breaking out suddenly and
   affecting many individuals at the
   same time: EPIDEMIC
disease causing tics, twitches and
   uncontrollable vocal outbursts:
   TOURETTE'S SYNDROME
disease correction by manipulation of
   parts of the body: OSTEOPATHY
diseased, destructive or corrupting
   thing, blight: CANKER
disease moving from one part of the
   body to another: METASTASIS
disease of the intestine usually caused

by eating undercooked pork:
TRICHINOSIS
disease of the nervous system causing
jerkiness and uncontrollable
movements, chorea: **SAINT VITUS'S
DANCE**
disease-preventing treatment:
PROPHYLAXIS
disease-producing: **MORBIFIC**
diseases and their nature as a branch of
medicine: **PATHOLOGY**
diseases classified and described:
NOSOGRAPHY
disease treatment effected by producing
incompatible conditions:
ALLOPATHY
disembowel or remove vital part of:
EVISCERATE
disentangle, free from entanglement:
EXTRICATE
disgrace attached to a person or group:
STIGMA
disgraceful: **INGLORIOUS**
disgraceful, shocking, notorious:
FLAGRANT
disgrace, infamy: **OBLOQUY**
disgracing, abusive: **OPPROBRIOUS**
disguise, feign, conceal, make a false
show of: **DISSEMBLE**
disguise, shelter: **COVERTURE**
disguise to avoid recognition:
INCOGNITO
disguise to blend with the environment:
CAMOUFLAGE
disgusting, offensive, hateful, repugnant:
ODIOUS
disgusting, offensive, stinking, noxious:
NOISOME
disgust or dislike in the extreme,
abhorrence: **LOATHING**
dishes other than the main course, side
dishes, dessert: **ENTREMETS**
disheveled, untidy: **UNKEMPT**
dish-like concave large antenna used for
extensive television signal
reception: **DISH ANTENNA**
dish made light by adding beaten egg
whites: **SOUFFLÉ**
dish of chopped meat, eggs, onions,
anchovies: **SALMAGUNDI**
dish of veal or chicken stuffed or
layered with ham and cheese
before sautéing: **CORDON BLEU**

dishonest or corrupt profiting in politics
or business: **GRAFT**
dishonesty, deceitfulness, trickery:
KNAVERY
dishonesty, lack of integrity: **IMPROBITY**
dishonorable: **IGNOMINIOUS**
dishonorable, degraded, base: **IGNOBLE**
dishonor, defame: **SMIRCH**
dish served at the end of a meal or as
an appetizer: **SAVORY**
dish that is deep and covered, for
serving soup: **TUREEN**
disintegrating, dividing into parts,
breaking up: **FISSIPAROUS**
disinterested, free from bias, fair:
IMPARTIAL
disjoin, dislocate: **LUXATE**
disjointed, broken up into separate
incidents: **EPISODIC**
disjointed, confused: **INCOHERENT**
dislike of children: **MISOPEDIA**
dislike of debate, argument or
reasoning: **MISOLOGY**
dislike or disgust in the extreme,
abhorrence: **LOATHING**
dislocate, throw out of joint: **LUXATE**
dismayed: **AGHAST**
dismissal, leavetaking: **CONGÉ**
dismiss in disgrace: **CASHIER**
disobedient: **INSUBORDINATE**
disobedient, insolently so:
CONTUMACIOUS
disobedient, stubborn, rebellious:
RECALCITRANT
disorder and inertness as an irreversible
tendency of a system: **ENTROPY**
disorder, confusion: **HUGGER-MUGGER**
disorder, destruction or carnage, scene
of: **SHAMBLES**
disordered, jumbled, topsy-turvy:
HIGGLEDY-PIGGLEDY
disorderly and wildly in haste:
PELL-MELL
disorderly, boisterous, rude:
RAMBUNCTIOUS
disorderly, loud: **RAUCOUS**
disorder, purposelessness, anxiety,
lawlessness, malaise: **ANOMIE**
disorder resulting from lack of a leader
or a plan: **ANARCHY**
disorganized, giddy, frivolous, screwy:
SCATTERBRAINED
disorientation in a foreign or alien
environment: **CULTURE SHOCK**

disown, reject, refuse to accept:
REPUDIATE
disparage, defame, blacken: DENIGRATE
disparage, treat with contempt:
VILIPEND
disparaging term used to describe
something neutral or inoffensive:
DYSPHEMISM
dispassionately critical: CLINICAL
dispel, waste, squander: DISSIPATE
displaced, uprooted, away from one's
native place: DERACINATED
display or parade brazenly or gaudily:
FLAUNT
display ostentatiously: FLOURISH
displease, bore: PALL
dispose of a matter quickly: DISPATCH
dispose of by fraud or trickery: FOB
OFF
dispose of, make unnecessary: OBVIATE
dispose of swiftly: MAKE SHORT SHRIFT
OF
dispose quickly of a matter: DISPATCH
disposition, tendency, leaning:
PROCLIVITY
dispossession that is unlawful:
DISSEIZIN
disproportionate, inadequate:
INCOMMENSURATE
disprove, demonstrate an error: REFUTE
dispute: ALTERCATION
dispute, challenge, attack the truth or
validity of: IMPUGN
dispute, challenge, call in question:
OPPUGN
disregard, forgetfulness: OBLIVION
disregard for the rules or for fact to
achieve artistic effect: POETIC
LICENSE
disregard, neglect: SLIGHT
disreputable, ill-tempered, perverse
woman, hussy: JADE
disreputable, tawdry, vulgar: RAFFISH
disrespectful, insulting: INSOLENT
disrespect toward one to whom
deference is due: LESE MAJESTY,
LÈSE MAJESTÉ
dissension, disagreement, lack of
harmony: DISCORD
dissenter: RECUSANT
dissimilar, distinct, different: DISPARATE
dissimilar, unrelated, unlike:
HETEROGENEOUS
dissolute, lustful: WANTON
dissolve out, filter, percolate: LEACH

distance around: CIRCUMFERENCE
distance light travels in a vacuum in
one year: LIGHT-YEAR
distance measured by determination of
angles: TELEMETRY
distance of an eighth of a mile:
FURLONG
distance of 3,280.8 feet: KILOMETER
distance-traveled recording instrument:
ODOMETER
distant and unknown region: ULTIMA
THULE
distended, swollen: TURGID
distinct, different, dissimilar: DISPARATE
distinctive mark: CACHET
distinct, separate, disconnected from
others: DISCRETE
distinguish, discriminate: SECERN
distinguished: PRESTIGIOUS
distinguished, dignified, well-bred:
DISTINGUÉ
distinguished, renowned: ILLUSTRIOUS
distinguishing characteristic, facial
contour or feature: LINEAMENT
distorted vision or view: ASTIGMATISM
distortion of shape: ANAMORPHISM
distort, misapply: PERVERT
distract, amuse, entertain: DIVERT
distraction from the real issue: RED
HERRING
distract, turn aside, deflect: DIVERT
distress, cause of: BANE
distress or disturb the mind or feelings
painfully: HARROW
distress, pain, suffering, anguish:
TRAVAIL
distribute or divide in proportion:
PRORATE
district of a city in which a minority
lives: GHETTO
distrustfully, suspiciously: ASKANCE
distrust or hatred of mankind:
MISANTHROPY
disturb, alarm, upset: PERTURB
disturbance, civil disorder: DISTEMPER
disturbance of the peace: AFFRAY
disturb, bother: INCOMMODE
disturb, ruffle: DISTEMPER
disturb the mind or feelings painfully,
distress: HARROW
disturb the smoothness of: RUFFLE
disturb, trouble, inconvenience:
DISCOMMODE
ditch-like depression in a desert region:
WADI

ditch or moat artificially created: FOSSE

dive down suddenly, as a whale when harpooned: SOUND

dive in which one does a back flip and plunges into the water headfirst and facing the board: HALF GAINER

divergency, inconsistency: DISCREPANCY

diverge, spread apart or branch out at a wide angle: DIVARICATE

diverse in sources used: ECLECTIC

diverse, varied to a great degree: MULTIFARIOUS

diversify or vary by adding something different: INTERLARD

diversion: RED HERRING

diver's rapture of the deep caused by excess nitrogen: NITROGEN NARCOSIS

diver's sickness, sometimes fatal, caused by bloodstream nitrogen bubbles: DECOMPRESSION SICKNESS, THE BENDS, CAISSON DISEASE

divert, confuse: DISTRACT

diverted by thought, preoccupied: BEMUSED

dive that is perilous or suicidal: BRODIE

divide, branch into two parts, separate: BIFURCATE

divide by cutting or passing across: INTERSECT

divided in half: DIMIDIATE

divide into opposing groups or views: POLARIZE

divide into two sections: DICHOTOMIZE

dividend, either regular or scheduled, that has been omitted: PASSED DIVIDEND

dividend on stock, paid in securities instead of cash: STOCK DIVIDEND

divide or distribute in proportion: PRORATE

divide or shape a voting area to advance the interests of one political party: GERRYMANDER

divide or spread out into divisions: RAMIFY

divide, separate, part: DISSEVER

divide up and give out, assign, allot: ALLOCATE

dividing evenly into another number, as 3 into 9: ALIQUOT

dividing into parts, breaking up, disintegrating: FISSIPAROUS

dividing not evenly into another number, as 4 into 9: ALIQUANT

divination by means of figures formed when particles of earth are thrown down at random: GEOMANCY

divination by use of a divining rod: RHABDOMANCY

divinatory, mystical or magical: OCCULT

divine or supernatural intervention in human affairs: THEURGY

division: SCISSION

division of a church or other organization into factions: SCHISM

dizziness: VERTIGO

dizzy, whirling, spinning: VERTIGINOUS

do away with, as a law or a right: ABROGATE

dock on a river or waterway, landing place: EMBARCADERO

dock post for mooring a ship: BOLLARD

doctor-prompted as an illness: IATROGENIC

doctor's auxiliary or assistant: PARAMEDIC

doctor serving apprenticeship in a hospital: INTERN

doctor's hammer used on the knee: PERCUSSOR

doctor who is a fraud or charlatan: QUACK

doctor who treats animals: VETERINARIAN

doctrine, belief or principle maintained as true by a person or a group: TENET

doctrine holding that reality has existence independent of the mind: OBJECTIVISM

doctrines held to be true and necessary: DOGMA

doctrine that all life is sacred: AHIMSA

document accrediting an envoy to a foreign power: LETTER OF CREDENCE

document wholly in the handwriting of the person whose signature it bears: HOLOGRAPH

dodge, avoid: SIDESTEP

dodge or device to avoid, conceal, etc.: SUBTERFUGE

dog family member: CANINE

dog lover: PHILOCYNIC

dogmatic, arrogant, haughty, pompous: PONTIFICAL

dogmatic or unproved assertion: IPSE
DIXIT
dog of the Australian outback: DINGO
dogs and their history as a subject:
CYNOLOGY
dog's short and vestigial claw or digit:
DEWCLAW
doings that are devious or mischievous:
SHENANIGANS
dollar per share of stock: POINT
doll collecting: PLANGONOLOGY
doll made of wood representing spirit
ancestors of Pueblo Indians:
KACHINA
doll of painted wood, Russian and
somewhat bowling-pin-shaped, that
is one of a "nest" of such dolls
that fit one within the other:
MATRUSHKA
domain: DEMESNE
domain of authority: BAILIWICK
domelike Buddhist shrine: STUPA
dome-like structure of polygonal
sections: GEODESIC DOME
dome, roof that is rounded: CUPOLA
dominant, prevalent: REGNANT
dominate thoughts, engross:
PREOCCUPY
domination of one state over another or
leadership: HEGEMONY
domineering, arrogant: IMPERIOUS
domineering, overwhelming:
OVERBEARING
done-beyond-recall action, accomplished
fact: FAIT ACCOMPLI
done or said thing for effect or as a
formality: GESTURE
done with great effort: LABORED
doomed, in great trouble, in a hopeless
situation: UP THE CREEK
doomed person or thing: GONER
doomed-to-failure situation: FORLORN
HOPE
do or commit something, as a crime or
hoax: PERPETRATE
door divided horizontally so that either
half can be opened separately:
DUTCH DOOR
door, entrance: PORTAL
doorkeeper of a building: CONCIERGE
door or window part, above the opening
and supporting structure above it:
LINTEL
doorway curtain that replaces a door:
PORTIÈRE

doorway or window drapery that covers
only the top half of the opening:
LAMBREQUIN
doorway side post: JAMB
do penance, be humbled: GO TO
CANOSSA
dormant: LATENT
dots of many colors used as a method
of painting: POINTILLISM
dots or hyphens in a horizontal row
serving to guide the eye across a
page: LEADER
dots or shadings used in
photoengraving: BENDAY
dots over the second of two adjacent
vowels to indicate it is pronounced
separately (ö): DIERESIS
dots used to indicate the omission of
words: POINTS OF ELLIPSIS
dotted pattern woven into fabric:
SHARKSKIN
dotted, spotted, marked with minute
spots: PUNCTULATE
double, become doubled: GEMINATE
double chin: BUCCULA
double-dagger symbol used in printing
(‡): DIESIS
double dealing, trickery: DUPLICITY
double image, blot: MACKLE
double in meaning: AMBIGUOUS
double in meaning, ambiguous,
uncertain in origin or character,
dubious: EQUIVOCAL
double in pulse beat with each
heartbeat: DICROTIC
double meaning attributable to
grammatical looseness:
AMPHIBOLOGY
double meaning, equivocation, pun:
EQUIVOQUE
double seat or small sofa: LOVE SEAT
double-spouted cruet or bottle: GEMEL
double tablet, picture or carving, often
depicting a religious subject:
DIPTYCH
double, twofold: DUPLE
double, two or paired: BINARY
double vision: DIPLOPIA
doubling of a syllable or sound in a
word: REDUPLICATION
doubling the stakes in gambling to
recover previous losses:
MARTINGALE
doubter: SKEPTIC
doubtful: DUBIOUS

doubtfulness: INCERTITUDE
doubtful state: DUBIETY
doubting, disbelieving: INCREDULOUS
doubting, resisting, ignoring attitude:
    NEGATIVISM
doubt, qualm, apprehension: MISGIVING
doughnut in elongated, twisted shape:
    CRULLER
dowdy, sometimes ill-tempered woman:
    FRUMP
down in spirits, dejected: DISPIRITED
down-in-the-dumps feeling,
    down-in-the-mouth state:
    DOLDRUMS
down in the mouth: CHAPFALLEN
down to earth, practical rather than
    speculative: PRAGMATIC
downward trend in stock market prices:
    DOWNSIDE
down with: À BAS
downy, covered with soft fine hair:
    LANUGINOUS
dowry, woman's marriage portion: DOT
drab, frumpish, not smartly dressed:
    DOWDY
draft: CONSCRIPTION
drag, haul, lug: SCHLEP
drag in the mud, lag, follow slowly:
    DRABBLE
dragon breathing fire: FIREDRAKE
dramatic or sudden change or increase:
    QUANTUM LEAP, QUANTUM JUMP
dramatic repartee in classical and
    Elizabethan theater:
    STICHOMYTHIA
drapery or board across the top of a
    window: VALANCE
draw a line around: CIRCUMSCRIBE
draw back, as claws: RETRACT
drawback, burden: IMPEDIMENTA
draw forth, call or summon: EVOKE
draw forth, evoke, bring to light: ELICIT
drawing a conclusion based on
    reasoning from the general to the
    particular: DEDUCTION
drawing or model with the exterior left
    off to show the interior: CUTAWAY
drawing together, reconciliation:
    RAPPROCHEMENT
drawn-out, as speech or writing:
    LONG-WINDED
drawn parallel-line shading to show
    elevation or steepness: HACHURE
draw or a tie, as in a game: STANDOFF
draw or scribble aimlessly: DOODLE

draw, paint, engrave with dots instead
    of lines: STIPPLE
draw so as to create the illusion of
    depth and distance while keeping
    the proper proportions:
    FORESHORTEN
dread, abnormal and persistent, of a
    particular thing: PHOBIA (also see
    listing under that word)
dreaded or hated object or person: BÊTE
    NOIRE
dreaded thing: BUGBEAR
dread, fear, anxiety, apprehension:
    ANGST
dreamer, visionary: FANTAST
dream interpreter: ONEIROCRITIC
dream-like apparitions or images in a
    series: PHANTASMAGORIA
dream-like, visionary: HYPNAGOGIC
dreamy repose caused by smoking
    narcotics: KEF
dregs of wine or liquor: LEES
dregs or lees, grain refuse from
    breweries and distilleries: DRAFF
drench or stain, especially with blood:
    IMBRUE
dress fussily: PRIMP
dress hanging straight from the
    shoulders: CHEMISE
dress in clothes of the opposite sex:
    CROSS-DRESS
dressing gown of a woman, negligee:
    PEIGNOIR
dressing in garments of the opposite
    sex, a compulsion to do so:
    TRANSVESTISM
dressing room for a woman: BOUDOIR
dressmaker: COUTURIER
dress showily, primp: PREEN
dress that is long, simple and shapeless:
    MOTHER HUBBARD
dress that is negligent or partial:
    DISHABILLE
dress up, decorate: TITIVATE
dress up, make showy: ENGAUD
dressy person: CLOTHESHORSE
dribbling of saliva: SLAVER
dried meat used as rations: PEMMICAN
drink: IMBIBE
drinkable: POTABLE
drink and play, carefree existence: BEER
    AND SKITTLES
drink, given to: BIBULOUS
drink greedily or to excess: GUZZLE
drink heartily: QUAFF

drinking at a festive time, carousal, revelry: WASSAIL

drinking bowl or its contents: JORUM

drinking cup or goblet: MAZER

drinking glass like a goblet but narrowed at the top: SNIFTER

drinking glass of large size for beer: SCHOONER

drinking sparingly: ABSTEMIOUS

drink liquor: TIPPLE

drink of chocolate syrup, milk and soda water: EGG CREAM

drink of mild nature to wash down hard liquor: CHASER

drink or eat greedily, gorge: INGURGITATE

drinks-at-a-reduced-price time at a bar: HAPPY HOUR

drink that is drugged: MICKEY FINN

drive a sharp stake through: IMPALE

drive away, dispel: DISSIPATE

drive away or remove, as by scattering: DISPEL

drive back, ward off: REPEL

drivel, talk incoherently: MAUNDER

driven by idealistic or religious zeal: MESSIANIC

drive off, dispel, scatter: DISPERSE

drive on roads other than toll roads and highways, motor via back roads: SHUNPIKE

drive or force to action, urge on: IMPEL

drive out of hiding: FERRET OUT

driving force: IMPETUS

driving too closely behind another vehicle: TAILGATING

droop gradually, pine, weaken: LANGUISH

droop, hang down loosely: LOP

droop, hang loosely: LOLL

drooping: NUTANT

droop, weaken: FLAG

drop heavily and clumsily, flop: FLUMP

drop of liquid, in pharmacy: GUTTA

drop or plunge straight down: PLUMMET

dropping a sound at the end of a word: APOCOPE

dropping of sounds or letters from the middle of a word: SYNCOPE

dropping the initial letter or sound in a word: APHERESIS

dropping to earth of particles after a nuclear explosion: FALLOUT

drowning as a form of execution: NOYADE

drowsy: SOMNOLENT

drudge, one who hires himself out to do routine or tedious work: HACK

drug being neither harmful nor healing: ADIAPHOROUS

druggist: APOTHECARY

drugs as a science: PHARMACOLOGY

drugs, to use them occasionally: JOYPOP

drug that overcomes effects of sedatives: ANALEPTIC

drug users' and sellers' illicit meeting place: SHOOTING GALLERY

drug withdrawal: COLD TURKEY

drum: TAMBOUR

drumbeat repetitions, drum sounds: RATAPLAN

drumbeat with two sticks striking almost simultaneously: FLAM

drumhead with jingles in its rim, held in the hand and shaken or rapped: TAMBOURINE

drum in the form of a hemisphere with a parchment top: KETTLEDRUM

drum-like: TYMPANIC

drumming continously: TATTOO

drumming with the fingers or feet: DEVIL'S TATTOO

drum or tap monotonously: THRUM

drum or trumpet signal for a parley: CHAMADE

drums, in a pair, used in Indian (Asian) music and played with the hands: TABLA

drum, small and double-headed, with a wire string across the bottom: SNARE DRUM

drunk: BESOTTED

drunk: INEBRIATED

drunkard: TOPER

drunkard: TOSSPOT

drunken, gluttonous: CRAPULENT

drunkenly brave but only then: POT-VALIANT

drunken revelry: BACCHANAL

drunk-making liquid: INTOXICANT

drunk straight or iceless and without anything added: NEAT

drying: SICCATIVE

dry in taste, as a champagne: BRUT

dry, lacking interest, naive, barren, insipid: JEJUNE

dry, low in moisture: XERIC

dry or roast by exposing to heat: **TORREFY**

dry up, make thirsty: **PARCH**

dry up or out: **EXSICCATE**

dualism in theology, belief in two coequal gods: **DITHEISM**

dualistic religiously or philosophically: **MANICHAEAN**

dubious use of ploys to gain an advantage: **GAMESMANSHIP**

duck feathers used for pillows and quilts: **EIDERDOWN**

ducking chair on a long pole once used for punishment: **DUCKING STOOL**

dueling sword with sharp point and no cutting edge: **ÉPÉE**

dull: **LACKLUSTER**

dull, blunt or make stupid: **HEBETATE**

dull, commonplace: **STODGY**

dull, depressed or bored state of mind: **DOLDRUMS**

dulled from overindulgence, worn-out, exhausted, sated: **JADED**

dull, heavy, lethargic: **LOGY**

dull, inactive, sluggish: **TORPID**

dull, insensible, not acute: **OBTUSE**

dull, lifeless, insipid, flat: **VAPID**

dull, light-resistant: **OPAQUE**

dull, mediocre, prosaic: **PEDESTRIAN**

dull, monotonous: **HUMDRUM**

dullness, apathy, sluggishness: **LETHARGY**

dullness, stagnation, weakness, fatigue, dreaminess, spiritlessness: **LANGUOR**

dullness, yawning: **OSCITANCY**

dull, ordinary, uninspired: **PROSAIC**

dull, tasteless, flat, bland, vapid: **INSIPID**

dull, trite: **BANAL**

dull, zestless: **PERFUNCTORY**

dumbfound, perplex, bewilder: **NONPLUS**

dunghill: **MIDDEN**

dupe, tool: **CAT'S-PAW**

duplicate of a work made by the originator, close copy: **REPLICA**

duplicate the foregoing or the above: **DITTO**

durable, binding: **INDISSOLUBLE**

durable, permanent: **PERDURABLE**

durable products such as automobiles, refrigerators and furniture: **HARD GOODS**

dusky, dark-complexioned: **SWARTHY**

dusky, gloomy, depressed: **SOMBER**

dusty, powdery: **PULVERULENT**

duty to be nobly generous, understanding, etc.: **NOBLESSE OBLIGE**

dwarf, midget: **HOMUNCULUS**

dwelling: **ABODE**

dwelling, house, home, abode: **DOMICILE**

dwelling that is wretched and small, shed: **HOVEL**

dwell or stay temporarily: **SOJOURN**

dying: **IN EXTREMIS**

dying work, as of a writer or composer: **SWAN SONG**

dynamically active person: **BALL OF FIRE**

eager for food in quantity: **VORACIOUS**
eagerly curious or excited: **AGOG**
eagle-eyed: **ARGUS-EYED**
earache: **OTALGIA**
ear deformed by blows: **CAULIFLOWER EAR**
ear diseases as a study: **OTOLOGY**
ear-inspecting instrument used by doctors: **OTOSCOPE**
earlier, before: **ANTERIOR**
earliest stages of development, beginnings: **INCUNABULA**
ear-like projections for holding something, as a pot or a kettle: **LUGS**
early edition of a newspaper: **BULLDOG EDITION**
early in the morning: **MATUTINAL**
early morning: **COCKCROW**
early or youthful works by a writer or artist: **JUVENILIA**
early spring, pertaining to: **PRIMAVERAL**
early-retirement incentive offered to an older employee: **GOLDEN HANDSHAKE**
earnest, committed, involved: **ENGAGÉ**
earnestly appeal: **ADJURE**
earnest, warm, glowing: **FERVENT**
earnings of common stock as affected by bond interest and preferred stock dividends: **LEVERAGE**
ear reception, pertaining to: **AURAL**
ear's largest, shell-like hollow: **CONCHA**
ears ringing: **TINNITUS**
earthenware piece in broken condition: **POTSHERD, POTSHARD**
earthenware that is glazed, usually blue and white: **DELFT**
earth inhabitant: **TELLURIAN**

earthly: **TERRESTRIAL**
earthquake: **TEMBLOR**
earthquake center at the earth's surface: **EPICENTER**
earthquake-measuring scale: **RICHTER SCALE**
earthquake phenomena as a science: **SEISMOLOGY**
earth's physical structure as a science: **GEOLOGY**
earth's shape and surface points, determination and study of: **GEODESY**
earth's structure and the forces that change it as a scientific study: **TECTONICS**
earth's surface above sea level treated as a science: **HYPSOGRAPHY**
earth study of materials, their structure and characteristics: **GEOGNOSY**
earthy and extravagant or bold in humor: **RABELAISIAN**
earwax: **CERUMEN**
easily: **HANDILY**
easily achieved, ready or quick in performance, skillful: **FACILE**
easily, effortlessly, without any question about it: **HANDS DOWN**
easily-taken-advantage-of person, sucker: **SOFT TOUCH**
easing, as of discord, between nations: **DETENTE**
easterly wind in Mediterranean regions: **LEVANTER**
Eastern Hemisphere: **ORIENT**
easy for the consumer to learn and use, as a personal computer: **USER-FRIENDLY**
easygoing, carefree, uninvolved: **DÉGAGÉ**
easy mark: **GULL**

easy-money position, situation, source, etc.: GRAVY TRAIN

easy to approach: AFFABLE

eater and drinker with discriminating taste: GOURMET

eater of much food: TRENCHERMAN

eater to excess: GOURMAND

eat, especially with someone: BREAK BREAD

eat greedily: ENGORGE

eating all kinds of food both animal and vegetable: OMNIVOROUS

eating as an art: GASTRONOMY

eating at the same table: COMMENSAL

eating disorder characterized by dieting to the point of emaciation: ANOREXIA NERVOSA

eating implements: CUTLERY

eating many foods: POLYPHAGIA

eating or wearing away of a substance: CORROSION

eating sparingly: ABSTEMIOUS

eating to excess: GLUTTONOUS

eating varied foods: PLEOPHAGOUS

eat, nibble, snack: NOSH

eat or drink greedily, gorge: INGURGITATE

eat ravenously: GUTTLE

eat voraciously or gluttonously: GOURMANDIZE

ebb, flowing back: REFLUX

ebbing, flowing back: REFLUENT

eccentric, irregular, nonconforming: ERRATIC

eccentric, queer: CRANKY

ecclesiastical council: SYNOD

ecclesiastical cutting off of one from fellowship of a church: EXCOMMUNICATION

ecclesiastical property being transferred to laymen: IMPROPRIATED

echoic as pertaining to words: ONOMATOPOEIC, ONOMATOPOETIC

echoing loudly: REBOANT

echo, response: REPLICATION

ecology: nonavailable water of the soil: ECHARD

ecology of plant and animal communities: SYNECOLOGY

ecology: plant adjustment to a new habitat: ECESIS

ecology's basic unit, including both organisms and environment: ECOSYSTEM

ecology: soil rather than climate as an affective factor: EDAPHIC

ecology: zone wherein two different species contend for dominance: ECOTONE

economical: SPARING

economically favoring governmental money and tax management to increase employment and control inflation: KEYNESIAN

economically favoring tax reduction and encouragement of the business sector: SUPPLY-SIDE

economical, worth the investment or expense: COST-EFFECTIVE

economic self-sufficiency: AUTARKY

economic union of Belgium, Netherlands and Luxembourg: BENELUX

economic union of Western Europe: COMMON MARKET, EUROPEAN ECONOMIC COMMUNITY

economize, save in expenditures, be frugal: SCRIMP

economy or thrift in managing: HUSBANDRY

economy spur of governmental expenditures financed by borrowing: DEFICIT FINANCING

ecstasy of a religious nature: THEOPATHY

edge-adorn, decorate a border: PURFLE

edge of fabric so woven as not to ravel: SELVAGE

edge of paper that resembles the ragged edge of handmade paper: DECKLE EDGE

edge, outer part: PERIPHERY

edge that slopes: BEVEL

edging decorated with a series of indentations: ENGRAILED

edging of small loops of ribbon or thread: PICOT

edging, selvage, strip, as of cloth: LIST

edible: ESCULENT

edit: REDACT

edit, correct a manuscript: BLUE-PENCIL

editing of a text by reference to varying manuscripts: RECENSION

editorial-we use or overuse: NOSISM

editor of manuscripts in newspaper or publishing house: COPY EDITOR

editor's insertion mark (∧): CARET

editor who contracts authors for a publishing house, often conceiving book ideas and dealing with agents: **ACQUISITIONS EDITOR**

edit prudishly: **BOWDLERIZE**

educated people or individuals collectively: **INTELLIGENTSIA**

eel fishing by putting bait into the eels' hiding places: **SNIGGLING**

eel-shaped: **ANGUILLIFORM**

eerie, strange, weird, unnatural: **UNCANNY**

eerie, weird: **ELDRITCH**

efface, destroy completely: **OBLITERATE**

effective: **POTENT**

effective as of or from a specified past time: **RETROACTIVE**

effective, moving, working: **OPERATIVE**

effect or symptom making a certain medical treatment inadvisable: **CONTRAINDICATION**

effect, result: **RAMIFICATION**

effect to cause: **A POSTERIORI**

effeminate: **EMASCULATED**

effeminately or affectedly prim, elegant or dainty: **MINCING**

effeminate, sexless: **EPICENE**

efficacy, potency: **VIRTUE**

efficient quickness: **DISPATCH**

eggs baked with crumbs in a buttered dish: **SHIRRED EGGS**

eggs cooked and served on toast spread with anchovy paste: **SCOTCH WOODCOCK**

eggs laid at one time: **CLUTCH**

egg white: **ALBUMEN**

egg-white glaze: **GLAIR**

egg yolk: **VITELLUS**

Egyptian monument of a mythical creature: **SPHINX**

Egyptian symbol of life: **CRUX ANSATA**

Egyptian symbol of life, a cross having as its top piece a loop: **ANKH**

eight-fold: **OCTUPLE**

eight-fold or based on the number 8: **OCTONARY**

eight tones above or below a given one: **OCTAVE**

eight-year period: **OCTENNIAL**

elaborate, speak or write more fully: **EXPATIATE**

elasticity, buoyancy: **RESILIENCE**

elated: **COCK-A-HOOP**

elate or excite to a degree of rapture, frenzy, etc.: **INTOXICATE**

elderly woman companion, governess, chaperon: **DUENNA**

elderly woman of dignified bearing and wealth: **DOWAGER**

eldest or senior member of a group: **DOYEN, DOYENNE**

elect, choose: **OPT**

electioneer on a political trip, campaign on the road: **STUMP**

election held between regular ones: **BY-ELECTION**

election that finally decides: **RUN-OFF**

electrical device for adjusting or varying current, as to brighten or dim light: **RHEOSTAT**

electrical plug third prong in addition to two standard blades: **GROUNDING PRONG**

electric strength, unit that measures: **AMPERE**

electromotive force measured in volts: **VOLTAGE**

electronic devices without moving parts or heated elements: **SOLID STATE**

electronic solid-state device that controls flow of current without use of a vacuum: **TRANSISTOR**

elemental, original, primitive: **PRIMORDIAL**

elementary: **ABECEDARIAN**

elementary: **RUDIMENTARY**

elementary in stage or form of instruction: **PROPAEDEUTIC**

element that causes a thing to be what it is: **FACTOR**

elephant keeper and driver, in India: **MAHOUT**

elephant-like extinct mammal with curved tusks, a shaggy coat and (unlike the mammoth) complex teeth: **MASTODON**

elephant male's period (in rut) of unpredictable violence and sexual frenzy: **MUSTH**

elephant rider's seat: **HOWDAH**

elevator for conveying food from floor to floor: **DUMBWAITER**

eleven-sided figure: **HENDECAGON**

elf: **OUPHE, OUPH**

elf, sprite: **PIXIE**

elite group, place or level: **PANTHEON**

elite group within an organization: **CADRE**

elk, large North American deer: **WAPITI**

emaciate, become thin: **MACERATE**

emaciated, haggard, hollow-eyed, gloomy, desolate: **GAUNT** emaciation: **MARASMUS**

emanate, exude: **EFFUSE**

emanation: **EFFLUX**

emanation, especially foul-smelling exhalation from decaying matter: **EFFLUVIUM**

emancipate, liberate, free: **MANUMIT**

emasculate: **CASTRATE**

embarrass, disconcert: **DISCOUNTENANCE**

embarrassed: **ABASHED**

embarrassed smiling: **DRY GRINS**

embarrassing occurrence: **CONTRETEMPS**

embarrassment or distress, as at one's own acts, plight, etc.: **CHAGRIN**

embed a material such as gold or ivory into a surface so as to form a decorative pattern: **INLAY**

embellish a speech or writing with quotations, etc.: **LARD**

embellish, as with ornamental lines or figures: **FLOURISH**

embellishment: **GARNITURE**

embezzle or misappropriate: **DEFALCATE**

embezzle, steal funds, especially public funds: **PECULATE**

embitter: **ENVENOM**

embitter, stir enduring ire: **RANKLE**

embodiment of an attribute or a quality in a person: **PERSONIFICATION**

embroidery at the ankle of a sock or stocking: **CLOCK**

embroidery that is rich: **ORPHREY**

emerge, come forth into the open: **DEBOUCH**

emergency medical squad member: **PARAMEDIC**

emergency or temporary, as applied to a ship's rigging: **JURY-RIGGED**

emergency program that has top priority: **CRASH PROGRAM**

emergency solution or remedy: **QUICK FIX**

emigration of scientists, technicians, etc., for better opportunity or pay: **BRAIN DRAIN**

emotional for effect, theatrical: **HISTRIONIC**

emotional in appeal: **AFFECTIVE**

emotional intensity, ardor: **FERVOR**

emotional or mental block: **INHIBITION**

emotional or sentimental, tearfully so: **MAUDLIN**

emotional shock, injury: **TRAUMA**

emotionless: **APATHETIC**

emotionless, unfeeling, dispassionate: **AFFECTLESS**

emotion, subjective aspect of: **AFFECT**

employees tend to rise to their level of incompetence: **PETER PRINCIPLE**

employer's barring employees from work until they accept his terms: **LOCKOUT**

employer who is excessively demanding: **SLAVE DRIVER**

employment of more workers than needed: **FEATHERBEDDING**

empower, authorize: **WARRANT**

emptiness: **VACUITY**

empty compliment or flattery: **FLUMMERY**

empty, flow out of, pour out from: **DISEMBOGUE**

empty tomb: **CENOTAPH**

enact, establish, decree: **ORDAIN**

enamel-and-metal work: **CLOISONNÉ**

enamel- or lacquer-ornamented metalware: **TOLE**

enchantress who changed men into swine: **CIRCE**

enclosed feeling of boredom or restlessness: **CABIN FEVER**

enclosed grounds or yard, as around a cathedral: **CLOSE**

enclosed yard, close: **GARTH**

enclose within walls, imprison, confine, surround: **IMMURE**

encourage: **ABET**

encourage: **HEARTEN**

encouraging, exhorting: **HORTATORY**

encroach, infringe: **IMPINGE**

end a parliamentary session: **PROROGUE**

end, cease: **SURCEASE**

ending of debate in parliamentary procedure: **CLOSURE, CLOTURE**

ending of one or more syllables affixed to a word: **SUFFIX**

ending section of a book or a play that adds commentary or explanation: **EPILOGUE**

ending that is unsurprising or disappointing, unexciting conclusion, letdown: **ANTICLIMAX**

endless: **INTERMINABLE**

endless and difficult: **SISYPHEAN**

end of the world: **CRACK OF DOOM**

end-of-the-world battle between good and evil: **ARMAGEDDON** end or withdraw by plan: **PHASE OUT**

endowment: **APPANAGE**

endowment, gift, estate or inheritance, as of a church: **PATRIMONY**

ends being tangent or touching: **ABUTTING**

end, termination: **EXPIRY**

end unexpectedly: **ABORT**

endurance test: **MARATHON**

endurance test, painful experience: **ORDEAL**

endurance, vigor, strength: **STAMINA**

enemy-aiding internal force or group: **FIFTH COLUMN**

energetic doer, fast worker: **BALL OF FIRE**

energetic, in music: **VIGOROSO**

energy and matter as a science: **PHYSICS**

energy, enthusiasm: **VERVE**

energy or force held as the basis for phenomena of the universe: **DYNAMISM**

enfeebled, worn out by age or use: **DECREPIT**

engine mounted on the rear of a small boat: **OUTBOARD MOTOR**

England, Britain: **ALBION**

English dessert consisting of sponge cake soaked in wine and topped with jam, custard and whipped cream: **TRIFLE**

English holiday, November 5, honoring the man who attempted to blow up the Houses of Parliament in 1605: **GUY FAWKES DAY**

English provincial university, apart from Oxford and Cambridge: **RED-BRICK UNIVERSITY**

English sporting cap with front and back visors and earflaps that can be tied together atop: **DEERSTALKER**

engrave, cut into, carve: **INCISE**

engraver of precious stones: **LAPIDARY**

engross, dominate thoughts: **PREOCCUPY**

engrossed intensely: **RAPT**

engross, involve deeply: **IMMERSE**

enigmatic, mysterious: **INSCRUTABLE**

enigmatic, prophetic: **ORACULAR**

enjoyment: **DELECTATION**

enjoyment of possessions: **FRUITION**

enlarge: **AGGRANDIZE**

enlarge a hole: **REAM**

enlarge excessively, increase unduly, puff up: **INFLATE**

enlargement: **AMPLIFICATION, AMPLIATION**

enlarging, growing, waxing: **INCRESCENT**

enlighten, benefit, uplift: **EDIFY**

enlighten, illuminate, light up, make clear: **IRRADIATE**

enmity, ill feeling, hostility: **BAD BLOOD**

enmity, malice: **RANCOR**

enormous, hideous: **MONSTROUS**

enormous, unwieldy, ponderous: **ELEPHANTINE**

enormous, vast: **PRODIGIOUS**

enrage, anger: **INCENSE**

enraged, angry: **IRATE**

enroll or register in a college or university as a candidate for a degree: **MATRICULATE**

entangle, complicate, confuse: **EMBRANGLE**

entangle, intertwine, involve: **IMPLICATE**

entanglement, complication, intertwining: **INVOLUTION**

enter office, assume dignity: **ACCEDE**

entertain, amuse, distract: **DIVERT**

entertain, delight, give unusual pleasure to: **REGALE**

enter without leave or invitation: **INTRUDE**

enthusiasm, dash, vivacity: **ÉLAN**

enthusiasm, energy: **VERVE**

enthusiasm, zest: **GUSTO**

enthusiast: **AFICIONADO**

enthusiastic, excited, bubbling: **EBULLIENT**

enthusiastic, fervent: **ZEALOUS**

entice by flattery or guile, draw, cajole: **INVEIGLE**

entirely: **TOUT À FAIT**

entirely, altogether: **IN TOTO**

entire range of anything: **GAMUT**

entrance, going in, place or means to enter: **INGRESS**

entrance hall, lobby: **FOYER**

entrance or gate: **PORTAL**

entrance or passageway, as into a mine: **ADIT**

entreating earnestly and humbly: **SUPPLIANT**

entreaty or appeal for assistance: **INVOCATION**

entreaty or prayer in behalf of others: **INTERCESSION**

entrée, sure means of admission or success, access: OPEN SESAME
entry: ACCESS
envelope markings used instead of stamps: INDICIA
environmental distinctiveness: AMBIENCE
environment in relation to organisms: ECOLOGY
environment, setting: MILIEU
epic poetry muse: CALLIOPE
epidemic among animals: EPIZOOTIC
episode that is minor: INCIDENT
epithet or title substituted for one's proper name: ANTONOMASIA
equal before the law or in ability or social position: PEER
equal in number of parts: ISOMEROUS
equal in size: COMMENSURATE
equal intervals of time, characterized by: ISOCHRONAL
equality in dimensions or measurements: ISOMETRIC
equality in rank, power, condition, etc.: PARITY
equality or mingling of racial and ethnic groups: INTEGRATION
equal or equivalent: TANTAMOUNT
equal political power in a government: ISOCRACY
equal socially and politically: EGALITARIAN
equal time given to opposing viewpoints as a policy in radio and television: FAIRNESS DOCTRINE
equestrian execution of trotting slowly in place: PIAFFE
equilibrium of an organism: HOMEOSTASIS
equipment, gear, personal effects: PARAPHERNALIA
equipment or skills needed, as in medicine: ARMAMENTARIUM
equivalent, equal: TANTAMOUNT
equivocate, be evasive: TERGIVERSATE
equivocate, hesitate, blather: WAFFLE
equivocate, lie: PREVARICATE
eradicate, dislocate, uproot: DERACINATE
era, period, century: SIÈCLE
erase, delete: EXPUNGE
erase, destroy utterly, pull up by the roots, uproot: ERADICATE
erase, rub out, cancel, obliterate: EFFACE

erection of the penis as a persistent pathological condition: PRIAPISM
ermine in its brown summer coat: STOAT
errata: CORRIGENDA
erratic, unexpected: WAYWARD
erring, wicked: PERVERSE
erroneous, misleading: FALLACIOUS
erroneous name: MISNOMER
erroneous placement of something in time: ANACHRONISM
erroneous situating of something, something out of place or inappropriate to a country: ANACHORISM
error in reading or speaking lines: FLUFF
error in speaking that is thought to disclose a person's true feelings or thinking: FREUDIAN SLIP
errorless, faultless, flawless: IMPECCABLE
errors in a book noted as needing correction: CORRIGENDA
errors in a list: ERRATA
escape, avoid: ELUDE
escape from the law by secret departure: ABSCOND
escapism or aloofness: IVORY TOWER
escort, attendants of a person of rank: RETINUE
Eskimo boot or one similar in style: MUKLUK
Eskimo-type heavy pullover jacket with a hood, parka: ANORAK
essence of a legal complaint or accusation: GRAVAMEN
essence of something: QUIDDITY
essence of something in concentrated form: QUINTESSENCE
essence or abstracted quality of anything: DISTILLATION
essential, inherent: INTRINSIC
essentially, basically, fundamentally, at bottom: AU FOND
essential matter, crux: BOTTOM LINE
essential qualities of anything: DISTILLATION
essential source of life, actions, energy: ANIMA
essential theme or part, gist: PITH
essential thing, indispensable ingredient: SINE QUA NON
essential, whole: INTEGRAL

established firmly by long continance:
INVETERATE
established firmly, deep-rooted:
INGRAINED
established rule or principle: CANON
esteem, high regard: REPUTE
estimate based on a guess:
GUESSTIMATE
estimate from evidence at hand, project
on the basis of facts already
known: EXTRAPOLATE
estranged, alienated: DISAFFECTED
estrangement, disagreement, quarrel:
FALLING-OUT
estuary, coastal inlet: FIRTH
eternity or period of time that is
incalculable: EON
ethical consequences of all one's acts
(Buddhism and Hinduism): KARMA
ethics, science of moral obligation:
DEONTOLOGY
ethnic or racial slur: ETHNOPHAULISM
etiquette in diplomacy: PROTOCOL
Eucharist as given just before death:
VIATICUM
eulogy or praise formally delivered:
ENCOMIUM
European Economic Community:
COMMON MARKET
European or white gentleman or official
in imperial India: SAHIB
European or white woman in imperial
India, lady: MEMSAHIB
European rooming house: PENSION
European time of peace and cultural
progress before World War I
(1871–1914): BELLE EPOQUE
evangelist preacher: REVIVALIST
evasion of main point by stressing a
trivial point: QUIBBLE
evasion of painful emotions or
unacceptable impulses by adjusting
behavior or mental attitude:
DEFENSE MECHANISM
evasive action to gain time:
TEMPORIZATION
evasive talk or explanation, beating
around the bush: SONG AND
DANCE
even beat, as in music or speech:
CADENCE
even horizontally, level, flattened:
COMPLANATE
evening prayers or services: VESPERS
evening star: HESPERUS

even more so, all the more forcefully or
logically: A FORTIORI
even on the same line or with a margin:
FLUSH
evergreen: INDECIDUOUS
everyday speech, popular or accepted
parlance: VULGATE
everything included: OVERALL
every two weeks: BIWEEKLY
everywhere in presence, omnipresent,
universal: UBIQUITOUS
everywhere present simultaneously:
OMNIPRESENT
evidence or proof of wrongdoing, crime,
etc.: SMOKING GUN
evidence that a defendant is compelled
to disclose in a trial or hearing:
DISCOVERY
evidence that if unrefuted establishes
the fact alleged: PRIMA FACIE CASE
evident, manifest, obvious: PATENT
evident, obvious, plainly apparent:
MANIFEST
evident, open, unconcealed: OVERT
evildoer, criminal: MALEFACTOR
evildoer, villain: MISCREANT
evildoing, treachery, murder: FOUL
PLAY
evil-eye-protection charm: AMULET
evilly treacherous person: SNAKE IN
THE GRASS
evil notoriety: INFAMY
evil omens be absent, heaven help us,
knock on wood: ABSIT OMEN
evil person: SHAITAN
evil, repulsive, flagrantly bad: VILE
evil, vile: NEFARIOUS
evil, wicked, odious, atrocious:
HEINOUS
evoke, draw forth, bring to light: ELICIT
evolution of any animal or plant group:
PHYLOGENY
evolution theory according to the Bible,
not Darwin: CREATIONISM
evolving at a slower rate: BRADYTELIC
evolving at a faster rate: TACHYTELIC
evolving at a standard rate: HOROTELIC
exact, accurate: PRECISE
exact copy or reproduction: FACSIMILE
exact, honest: SCRUPULOUS
exact in rendering the words of the
original: LITERAL
exact, precise, accurate: NICE
exact, scrupulous about detail or
observance of forms: PUNCTILIOUS

exaggerate a narrative with fictitious details: **EMBROIDER**

exaggerated drawing, characterization, version, etc.: **CARICATURE**

exaggerated praise or promotion: **PUFFERY**

exaggerated sense of buoyancy and vigor: **EUPHORIA**

exaggeration or overstatement intended for effect and not to be taken seriously: **HYPERBOLE**

exalting human to divine status: **APOTHEOSIS**

examination of prospective witnesses and jurors: **VOIR DIRE**

examination of something that has already happened: **POSTMORTEM**

examination of tissue removed from a living organism: **BIOPSY**

examination or discussion that is detailed: **CANVASS**

examine by feeling or touching: **PALPATE**

examine carefully: **SCRUTINIZE**

examine for validity or acceptability, authenticate, check out: **VET**

examine or analyze minutely, sift: **WINNOW**

examine or read thoroughly, scrutinize: **PERUSE**

examine or scrutinize carefully: **TRAVERSE**

example in practical terms or real life: **OBJECT LESSON**

example, model: **PARADIGM**

example of excellence: **PARAGON**

example or case: **INSTANCE**

excavation for archeological purposes: **DIG**

excavations as a historical study: **ARCHEOLOGY**

exceed a limit: **TRANSCEND**

exceed, excel: **OUTSTRIP**

exceed or surpass in cruelty or extravagance: **OUT-HEROD HEROD**

excel: **TRANSCEND**

excel, beat, surpass: **TRUMP**

excel, exceed: **OUTSTRIP**

excellence exemplified: **PARAGON**

excellent, fine: **COPACETIC**

excellent, of exceptional quality, choice: **VINTAGE**

excerpts or selections from literary works: **ANALECTS**

excess, abundance beyond need: **SUPERFLUITY**

excess in eating or drinking: **SURFEIT**

excessive: **INORDINATE**

excessive beyond usual limits: **EXORBITANT**

excessive, extreme: **INTEMPERATE**

excessive, insincere: **FULSOME**

excessively: **UNDULY**

excessiveness, extremeness, overenthusiasm: **OVERKILL**

excessive, unrestrained: **WANTON**

excess merchandise, money or value: **OVERAGE**

excess word or phrase: **PLEONASM**

exchange, as ideas: **INTERCHANGE**

exchange of something for something else: **QUID PRO QUO**

exchange or mutual granting, as by two countries, of concessions: **RECIPROCITY**

excited, confused, hasty: **HECTIC**

excited to a feverish pitch: **FRENETIC**

excite, enliven, stimulate: **QUICKEN**

excite, exhilarate, intoxicate: **INEBRIATE**

excitement that is great and intense: **WHITE HEAT**

excite or elate to a degree of rapture, frenzy, etc.: **INTOXICATE**

excite, rouse to action, stimulate: **GALVANIZE**

excite, stimulate, raise the spirits of: **ELATE**

excite, stimulate, sharpen: **WHET**

exciting or producing similar reactions in others: **INFECTIOUS**

exclaim, discharge suddenly and quickly: **EJACULATE**

exclaim loudly, shout, bawl: **VOCIFERATE**

exclamation, often profane: **EXPLETIVE**

exclamation point: **ECPHONEME**

exclamation that is usually one word: **INTERJECTION**

exclude from sacraments and solemn services, as in the Roman Catholic Church: **INTERDICT**

exclude, make impossible, shut out: **PRECLUDE**

exclude, shut out: **OSTRACIZE**

exclusive control of a product or service: **MONOPOLY**

exclusive set: **CLIQUE**

excrement: **DEJECTA**

excrement: **FECES**

excrement of humans as fertilizer:
NIGHT SOIL
excrete waste matter: **DEFECATE**
excusable or pardonable, as a fault:
VENIAL
excuse or exempt, as from a regulation:
DISPENSE
excuse or reason for being: **RAISON
D'ÊTRE**
excuse or try to excuse from blame:
EXTENUATE
excuse that clears from censure,
criticism or suspicion:
EXCULPATION
excuse that is not quite honest: **SALVO**
execute or attack with a cord or metal
collar that is tightened: **GARROTE**
execution or capital punishment as a
science: **KTENOLOGY**
executive recruiter: **HEADHUNTER**
executive's lavish contractual
assurances: **GOLDEN PARACHUTE**
exemption, as from a rule or law:
DISPENSATION
exemption from local law granted to
members of the diplomatic corps:
DIPLOMATIC IMMUNITY
exemption from obligation or penalty:
IMMUNITY
exemption from penalties or liabilities,
compensation for loss or damage:
INDEMNITY
exemption or freedom from
punishment, harm or unpleasant
consequences: **IMPUNITY**
exercise by lifting weights at different
speeds in a continuous motion, as
with certain machines: **ISOTONIC
EXERCISE**
exercise by using one muscle against an
object or another muscle without
motion: **ISOMETRIC EXERCISE**
exercise or conditioning to improve the
heart, lungs and circulation
through increased oxygen
consumption: **AEROBICS**
exercises to promote bodily grace and
health: **CALISTHENICS**
exhausted, helpless, lying flat:
PROSTRATE
exhibit in which modeled figures are set
in a naturalistic foreground, which
blends into a painted background:
DIORAMA

exhibition or parade that is spectacular:
PAGEANT
exhibit, show or present to advantage:
SHOWCASE
exhilarate, excite: **INEBRIATE**
exhorting, encouraging: **HORTATORY**
existing, surviving: **EXTANT**
exit, going out, place or means to leave:
EGRESS
expand a business by increasing the
variety of its products: **DIVERSIFY**
expand, grow, increase step by step:
ESCALATE
expanding with age: **ACCRESCENCE**
expand, stretch out, swell: **DISTEND**
expand, widen, swell: **DILATE**
expectorated matter: **SPUTUM**
expedient and wise: **POLITIC**
expedition, journey: **SAFARI**
expenditures being limited or regulated,
as by law: **SUMPTUARY**
expense account: **SWINDLE SHEET**
expense allowance for each day: **PER
DIEM**
expenses or continuous costs of
operating a business: **OVERHEAD**
experience alone as the source of
knowledge: **EMPIRICISM**
experience or moment spiritually or
existentially transcendent: **PEAK
EXPERIENCE**
experiment subject: **GUINEA PIG**
expert: **ADROIT**
expert: **MAVEN, MAVIN**
expert in matters of art and taste:
CONNOISSEUR
expertness, manual skill: **HANDINESS**
expert on recorded music: **DISCOPHILE**
expert on social elegance or aesthetic
taste: **ARBITER ELEGANTIAE,
ARBITER ELEGANTIARUM**
expert unofficial advisers or consultants:
BRAIN TRUST
explain actions or happenings on
rational grounds, which may not
be the real motives: **RATIONALIZE**
explain away: **GLOZE**
explain away: **RESOLVE**
explainer or interpreter, scholarly critic:
EXEGETE
explainer or promoter: **EXPONENT**
explain, make clear: **INTERPRET**
explain or interpret: **EXPLICATE**
explanation for something complex but

that is too simple or broad:
PANCHRESTON
explanation of a word, passage or work:
EXEGESIS
explanation that is detailed:
EXPLICATION
explanatory description or caption on a
chart, map or illustration: **LEGEND**
explanatory note, commentary: **GLOSS**
explicit, most accurate and complete:
DEFINITIVE
explode suddenly and with violence:
DETONATE
exploitive and powerful capitalist
tycoon of the late 19th century:
ROBBER BARON
exploration of enemy positions:
RECONNAISSANCE
explosive force of a thousand tons of
TNT: **KILOTON**
explosive's effect: **BRISANCE**
explosive sound, or a throwing off of
small particles, as by frying meat:
SPLUTTER
explosive that is trinitrotoluene: **TNT**
expose actual or alleged corruption:
MUCKRAKE
expose to the sun, as for bleaching:
INSOLATE
exposure to risk to achieve some end:
BRINKMANSHIP
express by gestures: **GESTICULATE**
expressing much in a single word or
phrase: **HOLOPHRASTIC**
expressing something by negating its
opposite: **LITOTES**
expressive style: **FAÇON DE PARLER**
expurgate: **BOWDLERIZE**
extemporize: **AD LIB**
extended to great subtlety: **FINE-DRAWN**
extend, spread out: **SPLAY**
extension: **AMPLIFICATION**
extent, scope, range: **PURVIEW**
extenuate, alleviate: **PALLIATE**
extermination or destruction of an
entire people or national group:
GENOCIDE
extinct, dead: **DEFUNCT**
extinct marine arthropod, found in
rocks, like a flattened oval with
two furrows: **TRILOBITE**
extinguish or satisfy thirst: **QUENCH**
extirpate, uproot, dislocate, eradicate:
DERACINATE
extort: **EXACT**

extortionist: **SHYLOCK**
extort or swindle to get goods or
money: **FLAY**
extract or passage, especially from the
Bible: **PERICOPE**
extra day in leap year: **BISSEXTILE DAY**
extraneous, superfluous:
SUPEREROGATORY
extra or complementary payment to
close a deal: **OWELTY**
extraordinary happening: **PHENOMENON**
extrasensory: **PARANORMAL**
extrasensory perception of distant
objects: **TELESTHESIA**
extra something given beyond
obligation: **LAGNIAPPE**
extravagance to impress: **CONSPICUOUS
CONSUMPTION**
extravagant, as in entertaining or in
style of living: **LUCULLAN**
extravagant in ornamentation:
BAROQUE
extravagantly, broadly and grossly
humorous: **RABELAISIAN**
extravagantly praise: **ADULATE**
extravagant, pompous: **HIGHFALUTIN**
extravagant, wasteful, lavish: **PRODIGAL**
extra vowel inserted into word:
ANAPTYXIS
extreme, excessive: **INTEMPERATE**
extremely, radically, to the utter limit:
À OUTRANCE
extremist or pretentious person:
HIGHFLIER
extrinsic: **ADVENTITIOUS**
exude, emanate: **EFFUSE**
exult over another's bad luck: **GLOAT**
eyeballs being protruding or bulging:
EXOPHTHALMIC
eyebrows being bushy and prominent:
BEETLE-BROWED
eye disease marked by pressure within
the eyeball: **GLAUCOMA**
eye disorder in which both eyes cannot
be focused simultaneously on the
same spot: **STRABISMUS**
eye examination to determine response
to light and shadow: **SKIASCOPY**
eye examiner: **OPTOMETRIST**
eye for an eye, a tooth for a tooth:
RETALIATION
eyeglass dealer: **OPTICIAN**
eyeglasses that grip the bridge of the
nose: **PINCE-NEZ**

eyeglasses with handle into which they may be folded: **LORGNETTE**

eyeglasses with three-part lenses: **TRIFOCALS**

eyeglasses with two-part lenses: **BIFOCALS**

eye-handicapped in having divergent strabismus, having the eye directed outward: **WALLEYED**

eye in which the iris is light-colored: **WALLEYE**

eyelet of metal or a flexible loop: **GROMMET**

eyelid or eye wrinkles surgery: **BLEPHAROPLASTY**

eye, make eyes at suggestively: **OGLE**

eye or sight, involving: **OCULAR**

eyes as a medical study: **OPHTHALMOLOGY**

eyes being dark and velvety: **SLOE-EYED**

eye's circular dark aperture, within the iris, that admits light: **PUPIL**

eye's colored circular diaphragm, perforated by the pupil: **IRIS**

eye sees an object double: **DIPLOPIA**

eye's membrane covering over the iris and pupil: **CORNEA**

eyes see what appear to be specks or threads: **MUSCAE VOLITANTES**

fable or tale with a moral: APOLOGUE
fabrication, fiction: FIGMENT
fabric edge so woven as not to ravel:
  SELVAGE
fabric gathered in parallel rows:
  SHIRRING
fabric having fibers that make the
  surface fuzzy: NAPPED
fabric piece, usually triangular, inserted
  in a garment for reinforcement or
  roomier fit: GUSSET
fabric sample: SWATCH
fabric surface of velvet, plush or
  corduroy: PILE
fabric that is light, crinkled and usually
  striped: SEERSUCKER
fabric with a soft pile: VELOUR
fabric woven with a dotted pattern:
  SHARKSKIN
fabulous or treasure-filled place: EL
  DORADO
facade, fakery or show to hide an
  unvarnished truth, false front:
  POTEMKIN VILLAGE
face-down, lying on the stomach:
  PRONE
face, facial expression: VISAGE
face that is pale and sallow: WHEYFACE
face to face: VIS-À-VIS
face-to-face meeting: CONFRONTATION
face upward, lying on the back: SUPINE
facial contour or feature, distinguishing
  characteristic: LINEAMENT
facial expression indicative of pain or
  annoyance: GRIMACE
facial features regarded as clues to
  character: PHYSIOGNOMY
facile, too glib: PAT
facilitate, quicken, speed up: EXPEDITE

facing each other directly to compete,
  man to man, dueling: MANO A
  MANO
facing toward one: OBVERSE
factual condition as distinguished from
  legal or official condition: DE
  FACTO
fail disastrously: COME A CROPPER
fail, sink, collapse: FOUNDER
fail to carry out a mission: ABORT
fail to keep a promise: RENEGE
failure in duty, willful omission or
  neglect: DERELICTION
failure or neglect to meet an obligation:
  DEFAULT
failure that is complete or humiliating:
  FIASCO
failure to do one's duty or what is
  required: NONFEASANCE
failure to realize one's intentions:
  MISCARRIAGE
faint, hidden, unclear: OBSCURE
faintness or a tendency to faint:
  LIPOTHYMIA
faint wish or desire, inclination,
  tendency: VELLEITY
fair, disinterested: IMPARTIAL
fair, impartial: UNBIASED
fair, impartial, reasonable: EQUITABLE
fairness, impartiality, justness: EQUITY
fairy, elf, goblin: SPRITE
faithful devotion to obligations:
  FIDELITY
faithful follower: MYRMIDON
faithful forever: SEMPER FIDELIS
faithfulness, obligation owed, loyalty:
  FEALTY
fake, false, sham, counterfeit, phony:
  BOGUS

falconry term for the short strap on each leg of a hawk, used for attaching a leash: JESS

fallacy of a proof that misses the point: IGNORATIO ELENCHI

fallacy that a book can be interpreted from biographical information about the author: BIOGRAPHICAL FALLACY

fallacy that a sequence of occurrences implies a causative connection (after this, therefore on account of this): POST HOC, ERGO PROPTER HOC

falling-behind or slow person, straggler: LAGGARD

falling objects always roll to the most inaccessible spot: BERNSTEIN'S FIRST LAW

falling off or shedding, as petals, leaves or fruit: DECIDUOUS

falling out of hair: PSILOSIS

falling short or the amount or degree of this: SHORTFALL

fall on or pass to, as a responsibility: DEVOLVE

fall or cave in, sink, collapse, fail: FOUNDER

fall straight down, plunge: PLUMMET

fall that is heavy: CROPPER

fall upon, strike against: IMPINGE

false appearance, pretense: GUISE

false charges: ASPERSIONS

false conception or deceptive appearance: ILLUSION

false, fraudulently invented: TRUMPED-UP

false front: FACADE

false front: POTEMKIN VILLAGE

falsehood: FABRICATION

falsehood, lying, prevarication, deception: MENDACITY

false information or advice, bad counsel: BUM STEER

false, invented, not real: FICTITIOUS

false lead: RED HERRING

falsely alarm others: CRY WOLF

falseness in word, treachery, perfidy: PUNIC FAITH

false, not genuine: SPURIOUS

false or malicious written statement or graphic representation that damages a person's reputation: LIBEL

false pathos: BATHOS

false sentimentality: MAWKISHNESS

false, sham, counterfeit, phony, fake: BOGUS

false step, mistake, error, especially in etiquette: FAUX PAS

false story circulated for political purposes: ROORBACK

false story, rumor: CANARD

falsetto and normal chest tones alternated in song: YODEL

false verdict, unfair or undeserved accusation or judgment: BUM RAP

falsify, misrepresent: BELIE

fame, celebrity: RENOWN

fame, publicity, fashionableness: RECLAME

familiar phrase or person that represents a type: BYWORD

family, branch of a family: STIRPS

family, clan or group symbolic object, revered emblem: TOTEM

family name: COGNOMEN

family name: PATRONYMIC

family or kindred, collectively: COUSINRY

family tree, descent of an individual from a certain ancestor: GENEALOGY

famous: RENOWNED

famous and fashionable luminaries, party-going elite: GLITTERATI

famous, distinguished: ILLUSTRIOUS

fan: AFICIONADO

fanatical enthusiast, one possessed by evil spirits: ENERGUMEN

fanatical, raging: RABID

fanatic, partisan who is rabid: ZEALOT

fanciful humor, caprice: WHIMSY

fanciful idea or notion that emerges suddenly: WHIM

fanciful thought or expression: CONCEIT

fancy trappings, finery: REGALIA

fancy, whim, peculiarity: CROTCHET

fanfare, as of trumpets: FLOURISH

fan who literally follows a rock star or other entertainer: GROUPIE

fan-oriented or amateurs' magazine, as for science fiction buffs: FANZINE

fan-shaped: FLABELLATE

fan-shaped structure: FLABELLUM

fantastic: CHIMERICAL

Far East two-wheeled passenger vehicle pulled by one person: RICKSHA, RICKSHAW

farewell: ADIEU

farewell: VALE
farewell-bidding, as a speech:
 VALEDICTORY
farewell drink: STIRRUP CUP
farm horse: DOBBIN
farming: HUSBANDRY
farming-related, rural: GEORGIC
farm on which vegetables are grown for
 market: TRUCK FARM
farm operated cooperatively:
 COLLECTIVE
farseeing: PRESCIENT
farsightedness as an abnormal condition
 of the eye: HYPERMETROPIA
farsightedness that accompanies aging:
 PRESBYOPIA
farthest possible point: ULTIMA THULE
fascinate, beguile: INTRIGUE
fascinating, enchanting: IRRESISTIBLE
fascinating, spectacular, astonishing:
 EYE-POPPING
fascist party member: BLACKSHIRT
fashionable: DE RIGUEUR
fashionable adoption of a radical or
 minority cause by the rich:
 RADICAL CHIC
fashionable and famous luminaries,
 party-going elite: GLITTERATI
fashionable dresser: FASHION PLATE
fashionable, in style: À LA MODE
fashionable, wealthy people: JET SET
fashionable world, high society: BEAU
 MONDE
fashion-conscious person:
 CLOTHESHORSE
fasten firmly: RIVET
fastening in the form of a hook and
 loop: AGRAFE
fasten, tie together: COLLIGATE
faster than the speed of sound:
 SUPERSONIC
fastidious, overly exacting: FINICKY
fasting or other ascetic practices to keep
 from sinning: MORTIFICATION
fast-talk to bluff or deceive, glib
 posturing: SHUCKING AND JIVING
fast time in music: ALLEGRO
fast worker, energetic doer: BALL OF
 FIRE
fat: ADIPOSE
fatal, deadly: LETHAL
fatal or ruinous act: KISS OF DEATH
fat and red-faced: BLOWZY
fat and short person: SQUAB
fate: KISMET

fat, fleshy: CORPULENT
fatherly: PATERNAL
father of a newly born child in
 primitive tribes going through
 motions as if he had given birth, as
 by taking to bed: COUVADE
father's side of the family, in kinship:
 AGNATE
fatigue, spiritlessness, dreaminess,
 dullness, stagnation: LANGUOR
fat-like substance: LIPOID
fatness: EMBONPOINT
fat of beef or mutton used in making
 soap and candles: TALLOW
fat of hogs in melted form: LARD
fats that limit cholesterol level are:
 POLYUNSATURATED
fatten: BATTEN
fatty buttocks, especially in women:
 STEATOPYGIA
fatty pocked or lumpy flesh, as on the
 upper thigh: CELLULITE
fatty substance linked to atherosclerosis:
 CHOLESTEROL
fat, very stout: OBESE
faucet or valve used to drain off water
 or air: PETCOCK
faultfinder: MOMUS
faultfinding: CAPTIOUS
faultfinding: CENSORIOUS
faultfinding, berating: VITUPERATION
faultfinding, complaining, whining:
 QUERULOUS
fault in character that is minor: FOIBLE
faultless, blameless: UNIMPEACHABLE
faultless, flawless, errorless:
 IMPECCABLE
fault, trivial sin: PECCADILLO
faulty or illogical reasoning:
 PARALOGISM
favorable, mild, gentle: BENIGN
favorable, opportune, promising:
 AUSPICIOUS
favorably disposed, auspicious, gracious:
 PROPITIOUS
favoring one party, prejudiced, biased:
 PARTIAL
favoritism shown to relatives in jobs:
 NEPOTISM
fawn, cower: CRINGE
fawning, servile, overly obedient:
 OBSEQUIOUS
fawning, servile person: TOADY
fawn upon: ADULATE
fear, abnormal and persistent, of a

particular thing: PHOBIA (also see listing under that word)

fear, amazement or panic that is sudden and paralyzing: CONSTERNATION

fear, anxiety, dread, apprehension: ANGST

feared thing: BUGBEAR

fearful anxiety: TREPIDATION

fearful feeling that something is about to happen: PRESENTIMENT

fearful or nervously timid person: SCAREDY-CAT

fearful, timid: TIMOROUS

fearful, timid, trembling: TREMULOUS

fear-inspiring, formidable: REDOUBTABLE

fearless, bold, dauntless: INTREPID

fear of losing sexual power: APHANISIS

fearsome, awesome: FORMIDABLE

feast, picnic or pleasure trip: JUNKET

feather beginning to emerge through the skin: PINFEATHER

feathers, from a sea duck, used for pillows and quilts: EIDERDOWN

feather shaft: RACHIS

feathers on the neck of a rooster or pigeon or hairs on the neck of a dog: HACKLES

feces, waste matter from bowels: EXCREMENT

federal funds appropriated to help an official with his constituents: PORK BARREL

federally regulated amount of credit that a bank may extend to a customer for the purchase of stock: REGULATION U

feebleminded: ANILE

feebleminded person: AMENT

feeding on other animals, exploiting others: PREDATORY

feeding on vegetables, plant-eating: HERBIVOROUS

feeding through a stomach tube: GAVAGE

feed or fodder for cattle: STOVER

feed or supply to excess: SURFEIT

feed, support, rear, train: NURTURE

feel about with the hands, grope, sprawl, flounder: GRABBLE

feeling for language: SPRACHGEFÜHL

feeling or feelings shared: COMPATHY

feelings or desires related to childhood repression newly directed toward

the psychiatrist or another person: TRANSFERENCE

feelings or emotions shared with another: EMPATHY

feel of a place or situation: AMBIENCE

feel or examine by touching: PALPATE

fee paid to obtain the services of an attorney or a consultant: RETAINER

feet or toes being characteristically turned in: PIGEON-TOED

feign, conceal, disguise, make a false show of: DISSEMBLE

fellow member, colleague: CONFRERE

fellowship: CAMARADERIE

fellowship, association: SODALITY

female and male sexual organs in one individual: HERMAPHRODITE

female demon: SUCCUBUS

female external genitals: PUDENDUM

female figure forming a column or pillar: CARYATID

female genitalia or the vulva represented as the female principle in Hinduism: YONI

female genitals subjected to oral stimulation: CUNNILINGUS

female line of kinship, involving the: ENATE

female line or maternal branch of family: DISTAFF SIDE

female nightclub singer: CHANTEUSE

female office worker with varied responsibilities: GIRL FRIDAY, GAL FRIDAY

female opera singer of note, prima donna: DIVA

female professional singer: CANTATRICE

female sex hormone: ESTROGEN

female singer in the principal role: PRIMA DONNA

female spirit, in Irish folklore, whose wail portends somebody's death: BANSHEE

feminine in conduct or role: FEMME

femininity, womanhood: MULIEBRITY

fence of rails crossed at ends so that the fence zigzags: WORM FENCE

fence or wall placed in a ditch so as not to interfere with the view: HA-HA

fermentation, as in brewing: ZYMOLYSIS

ferocious, stubborn, defiant: TRUCULENT

fertile: PROLIFIC

fertile, fruitful: FERACIOUS

fertile, fruitful, prolific: FECUND

fertilizer composed of bird or bat droppings: GUANO

fertilize, saturate, permeate: IMPREGNATE

fervid to an extreme, ardent: PERFERVID

fester, form pus: SUPPURATE

festival, celebration: FIESTA

fetus death by killing: FETICIDE

fetus's connection, a vascular organ, to the uterus: PLACENTA

fetus that is malformed, monstrosity: TERATISM

feud, usually a blood feud, involving families: VENDETTA

fever: PYREXIA

feverish: FEBRILE

feverishly excited: FRENETIC

feverless: AFEBRILE

fewer-words-than-the-original book or article: ABRIDGMENT

few in varieties, inferior in growth or numbers, underdeveloped: DEPAUPERATE

fewness, small quantity: PAUCITY

few words being characteristic: LACONIC

fickle: INCONSTANT

fickle: SKITTISH

fickle, frivolous, shallow: FLIGHTY

fickleness, lightness, gaiety that is inappropriate, frivolity: LEVITY

fickle person, variable thing: WEATHERCOCK

fickle, unstable, fleeting, transient: VOLATILE

fiction, fabrication: FIGMENT

fictitious: MYTHICAL

fictitious name, pen name: PSEUDONYM

fiddle-shaped: PANDURATE

fidgety, unruly, restless: RESTIVE

field near a stable where horses are exercised: PADDOCK

fiendish: DEMONIAC

fierce, harsh: FELL

fierce, malicious, unruly: VICIOUS

fierce, wild, unsociable: FAROUCHE

fiery upstart, agitator, stirrer-upper: FIREBRAND

fifth of a gallon, especially of liquor: FIFTH

fight among people that is confused and noisy: MELEE

fight, brawl or dispute that is noisy: FRACAS

fight, conflict, uproar, brawl: FRAY

fighter in an independent raiding band: GUERRILLA

fighting in public: AFFRAY

fighting or contending with spirit, unfaltering, courageous, plucky: GAME

fighting over words, verbal contention: LOGOMACHY

fighting with an imaginary or make-believe foe: SCIAMACHY

fig-shaped: CARICOUS, SYCOSIFORM

figure of a demon or grotesque creature on a building: GARGOYLE

figure of any shape with straight-line sides: POLYGON

figure of speech endowing inanimate things with human qualities: PERSONIFICATION

figure of speech, figurative turn of language: TROPE

figure of speech implying a comparison: METAPHOR

figure of speech in which an assertion is made by the negation of its opposite: LITOTES

figure of speech in which an attribute or an associated term is substituted for the name of the thing itself: METONYMY

figure of speech in which a word relating to or modifying two others accords grammatically with only one of them: ZEUGMA

figure of speech in which contradictory ideas are combined: OXYMORON

figure of speech in which the normal order of things or events is reversed: HYSTERON PROTERON

figure of speech in which two words are joined by "and" instead of the more literal, correct wording: HENDIADYS

figure of speech or construction in which a word relating to or modifying two or more words acquires different meanings: SYLLEPSIS

figure of speech that describes an event as happening before it could have happened: PROLEPSIS

figure of speech that makes a comparison by use of "as" or "like": SIMILE

figure or letter above and to the side of a character: SUPERSCRIPT figure or letter below and to the side of a character: SUBSCRIPT

file of particular information, accumulated records or data: DOSSIER

filled, laden: FRAUGHT

filler for holes or cracks: BEAUMONTAGE

fill-in in a job: LOCUM TENENS

fill-in team member brought in from outside: RINGER

fill or impregnate thoroughly, permeate: SATURATE

film director or maker regarded as having a notable personal style: AUTEUR

film documentary close to reality: CINEMA VERITÉ

film of part of a television series used for trial purposes: PILOT FILM

film of tiny size for reproducing texts, pictures, etc.: MICROFILM, MICROFICHE

filter, dissolve out, percolate: LEACH

filth or indecency in art or literature: COPPROLOGY

filthy or foul sediment: FECULENCE

filthy or very corrupt situation or problem: AUGEAN STABLES

final and deciding election: RUN-OFF

final contestant of a team, as in a relay race: ANCHORMAN

finalism, final causes as studied in cosmology: TELEOLOGY

final lines of a poem, usually a dedication: ENVOY

final unraveling or solution in a plot: DENOUEMENT

financial: FISCAL

fine change or gradation in meaning: NUANCE

fine, delicate or lace-like surface ornamentation or design: FILIGREE

fine, excellent: COPACETIC

finely or carefully made: WROUGHT

fine point of behavior or etiquette: PUNCTILIO

fine point, subtlety: NICETY

finery, fancy trappings: REGALIA

finger: DIGIT

finger beside the little finger: RING FINGER

fingerboard bar, movable, to change the pitch of a guitar: CAPO

fingerless: ADACTYLOUS

fingerprint: DACTYLOGRAM

fingerprint ridge: WHORL

finger snap or quick tap with the nail of a finger that has been snapped: FILLIP

fingertip infection that is painful: WHITLOW

finicky, fussy: NIGGLING

finish used to coat fabrics, paper or other surfaces: SIZE

firearm of old used with the butt held against the chest: PETRONEL

fire-breathing monster, part goat, lion and serpent: CHIMERA

firecracker that burns with a spitting sound before exploding: SQUIB

fire engine's hydraulic ladder mounted on a turntable: TOWER LADDER

firefighter who parachutes into or near a forest fire: SMOKE JUMPER

fireflies' fire: LUCIFERIN

fire-like: IGNEOUS

fireplace, furnace floor: HEARTH

fireplace support for wood: ANDIRON

fireproof: INCOMBUSTIBLE

fire that is great and destructive: CONFLAGRATION

fireworks: PYROTECHNICS

firework that rotates: GIRANDOLE

firm, dependable: STAUNCH

firm, durable: INDISSOLUBLE

firm foundation of anything, bedrock: HARDPAN

firm, hard, obdurate: FLINTY

firm in chewing, as lightly cooked spaghetti: AL DENTE

firmly committed, ardent, thoroughgoing: DYED-IN-THE-WOOL

firmly established by long continuance: INVETERATE

firmly faithful, unwavering: STEADFAST

firm, solid, forthright: FOURSQUARE

firm, unshakable: IMPREGNABLE

first among equals: PRIMUS or PRIMA INTER PARES

first in rank: PREMIER

first mention or suggestion, to make: BROACH

first, original, principal: PRIMAL

first principle, fundamental: RUDIMENT

fish as a branch of zoology: ICHTHYOLOGY

fish basket used by anglers: CREEL

fish cured by splitting and drying in the air, without salting: STOCKFISH

fish eggs, especially in masses: SPAWN
fish group terms—see "creature terms"
fishing boat's anchored chair for use in
reeling in large fish: FIGHTING
CHAIR
fishing by dragging a hook and line
near the surface: TROLLING
fishing pronged spear: LEISTER
fish net, large, that hangs vertically
from surface floats: SEINE
fish or hunt illegally: POACH
fish resembling a sardine: SPRAT
fish stew of several kinds of fish:
BOUILLABAISSE
fish with suction discs that clings to
sharks: REMORA
fissured or cracked, chinky: RIMOSE
fissure or chasm, as in a glacier:
CREVASSE
fitness, agreement: CONGRUITY
fit of bad temper: TANTRUM
fitting, as to proportion:
COMMENSURATE
fit together nicely or fit together with,
mesh: DOVETAIL
fit together, unify, bring together into a
whole: INTEGRATE
five-element design of four squared
things and one in the middle:
QUINCUNX
five-fold: QUINTUPLE
five-fold or based on the number 5:
QUINARY
five-line stanza: CINQUAIN
five-year period: LUSTRUM
fixed amount, as of work to be done in
a specified time: STINT
fixed, blank, uncomprehending: GLASSY
fixed idea: IDÉE FIXE
fixed in one place: STABILE
fixed price for a whole meal: PRIX FIXE
fixed, unchangeable: INFLEXIBLE
fix in place: IMMOBILIZE
fix the eyes or attention of: RIVET
fix upon a sharp stake: IMPALE
flabby, intellectually or morally:
INVERTEBRATE
flabby, not firm or vigorous, weak,
limp: FLACCID
flag fixed to a crosspiece rather than a
pole: GONFALON
flagrant, glaring, conspicuously bad:
EGREGIOUS
flag's upper inner corner or the box
part of its design: CANTON

flaming, flaring: IGNESCENT
flaming, said of food served flaming
with ignited brandy or other
liquor: FLAMBÉ
flaring, flaming: IGNESCENT
flash like lightning: FULGURATE
flashy, cheap dress or ornamentation:
FRIPPERY
flask-shaped: LAGENIFORM
flat and broad blade-like instrument for
spreading, as plaster or cake icing:
SPATULA
flat and open country: CHAMPAIGN
flat, bland, dull, tasteless: INSIPID
flat, broad piece: SLAB
flat, dull, lifeless, insipid: VAPID
flattened, made horizontal or level:
COMPLANATE
flatterer who is servile, parasite:
SYCOPHANT
flatter or coax to persuade: WHEEDLE
flatter, wheedle: BLANDISH
flatter worshipfully: ADULATE
flattery, empty compliment: FLUMMERY
flattery or blather contrived as a means
of persuasion: SNOW JOB
flatulence remedy: CARMINATIVE
flavor-enhancing chemical:
MONOSODIUM GLUTAMATE
flavor or odor imbued in a substance:
TINCTURE
flavor, taste: SAPOR
flawless, errorless, faultless:
IMPECCABLE
flawless, warranting no criticism:
UNEXCEPTIONABLE
fleeting, quickly passing: FUGACIOUS
fleeting, transient, fickle, unstable:
VOLATILE
fleeting, transitory: EVANESCENT
fleet of large merchant ships: ARGOSY
flesh-eating mammals: CARNIVORES
fleshly: CARNAL
flesh of the mid-body that is uneven
and unattractive: CELLULITE
fleshy, fat: CORPULENT
fleshy part below the lower jaw: JOWL
flexible, bendable: PLIABLE
flexible, easily bending or shifting:
SUPPLE
flexible, pliable: MALLEABLE
flickering, radiating softly: LAMBENT
flicker low, as a candle flame: GUTTER
flight overnight or late at night:
RED-EYE

flighty, giddy, foolish: **HAREBRAINED**
flighty, haughty: **HOITY-TOITY**
flimsily built: **JERRYBUILT**
flimsy, delicate substance: **GOSSAMER**
flimsy, delicate, thin: **TENUOUS**
flippant, light manner of talk or
    writing: **PERSIFLAGE**
flippantly humorous, jesting: **FACETIOUS**
flirtatious glance, ogling look: **OEILLADE**
flirtatious woman who stays a virgin:
    DEMI-VIERGE
flirt or act in a trifling manner: **COQUET**
float, carry or move gently: **WAFT**
floating cylinder or boat to support a
    temporary bridge: **PONTOON**
floating goods after a shipwreck,
    flotsam: **WAVESON**
floating objects on a body of water:
    FLOTSAM
floating or living near the water's
    surface, as certain aquatic
    organisms: **EMERSAL**
floating, swimming: **NATANT**
floating wreckage: **FLOTSAM**
flocking together, a crowd:
    CONFLUENCE
floodlight used in making motion
    pictures: **KLIEG LIGHT**
flood of the tide in an estuary: **EAGRE**
flood or overwhelm with abundance or
    excess: **INUNDATE**
flood, pertaining to, especially the flood
    at the time of Noah: **DILUVIAL**
floors of inlaid woodwork: **PARQUETRY**
floral essence for perfume: **ATTAR**
florid, overelaborate, profusely or finely
    baroque: **ROCOCO**
florid, showy, bombastic, ornate:
    FLAMBOYANT
florid, showy, excessively ornamented:
    ORNATE
flounder, splash: **SLOSH**
flourish at the end of a signature:
    PARAPH
flourishing, happy, prosperous: **PALMY**
flower and ornamental-plant culture:
    FLORICULTURE
flower, bloom forth, blossom:
    EFFLORESCE
flower bunch, small bouquet, posy:
    NOSEGAY
flowering, flourishing: **INFLORESCENCE**
flowerless: **ANANTHOUS**
flowers, in a bunch: **BOUQUET**

flowers or foliage planted in an abstract
    design: **CARPET BEDDING**
flower that is small: **FLORET**
flowery, excessively ornate: **FLORID**
flowery, metaphorical: **FIGURATIVE**
flowery speech or writing: **EUPHUISM**
flowing and sweet-sounding:
    MELLIFLUOUS
flowing back, ebb: **REFLUX**
flowing back, ebbing: **REFLUENT**
flowing, discharge: **FLUX**
flowing in: **INFLUENT**
flowing out: **EFFLUENCE**
flowing together: **CONFLUENCE**
flow into a larger area, as into a river
    or valley: **DEBOUCH**
flow of water beneath and opposite to
    the surface current: **UNDERTOW**
flow out of, pour out from, empty:
    DISEMBOGUE
fluctuate, swing back and forth:
    OSCILLATE
fluffy-particle-like, woolly in loose bits,
    like soft flakes: **FLOCCULENT**
fluid, in mythology, that flows in the
    veins of the gods: **ICHOR**
fluidless: **ANEROID**
flushed, ruddy: **FLORID**
fluster, excitement, bustle: **POTHER**
fluted or crimped ornamentation, as
    along the edge of fabric: **GOFFER**
flute played while held outward from
    the mouth and having a plug, or
    fipple, near the mouthpiece:
    RECORDER
flutter, beat rapidly: **PALPITATE**
flying, able to fly: **VOLANT**
flying horse: **PEGASUS**
flying or gliding one-person apparatus
    like a kite: **HANG GLIDER**
flying saucers as a field of inquiry:
    UFOLOGY
foam, scum, froth: **SPUME**
fodder, food suitable for horses and
    cattle: **FORAGE**
fodder or feed for cattle: **STOVER**
fog containing ice particles: **POGONIP**
foggy, misty, indefinite: **NUBILOUS**
fog, mist: **BRUME**
foil, frustrate, obstruct: **THWART**
folded backward: **REPLICATE**
folded fan-like: **PLICATED**
fold of cloth doubled back and pressed
    flat: **PLEAT**

foliage that has fallen in a forest: DUFF
folklore as a study: STORIOLOGY
folk singers' meeting for a public performance: HOOTENANNY
folkways or customs of a social group: MORES
follies or vices attacked by ridicule or wit: SATIRE
follow closely upon something: SUPERVENE
follower or favorite who behaves servilely: MINION
followers or companions in a group: COHORT
followers, retainers or attendants in a group: ENTOURAGE
follower with material or selfish motives, opportunistic parasite: HANGER-ON
following, as an effect or conclusion: CONSEQUENTIAL
following in time: SUBSEQUENT
fond overly of or submissive to one's wife: UXORIOUS
fond of others' company: GREGARIOUS
fond overly of or submissive to one's husband: MARITORIOUS
food: ALIMENT
food: NUTRIMENT
food, cheap and popular among Southern blacks: SOUL FOOD
food, especially a choice type or morsel: VIAND
food expert: EPICURE
food for body or mind: ALIMENT
food, means of support, livelihood: SUSTENANCE
food mixture of oatmeal, nuts, raisins, etc.: GRANOLA
food-poisoning bacteria: PTOMAINE
food poisoning often fatal: BOTULISM
food prepared by highly skilled chefs: HAUTE CUISINE
food reheated: RECHAUFFÉ
food scrap, crumb: ORT
food suitable for horses or cattle, fodder: FORAGE
food that is coarse: ROUGHAGE
fool around or hesitate, dawdle, be irresolute, vacillate: SHILLY-SHALLY
fool around, waste time, be idle: FUTZ
fool around, waste time, dawdle: LALLYGAG, LOLLYGAG

fool, deceive, cheat, frustrate, con: SNOOKER
fooled or cheated easily: GULLIBLE
foolhardiness, heedlessness: TEMERITY
foolish appearance given to something or someone: STULTIFIED
foolish, flighty, giddy: HAREBRAINED
foolish, idiotic, stupid: FATUOUS
foolish love, unreasoning passion: INFATUATION
foolishly wasteful and involved procedure: RIGMAROLE
foolish or excessive affection: DOTAGE
foolish or senseless talk: DRIVEL
foolish, stupid, brutish, unmoved: INSENSATE
foolish, talkative person: BLATHERSKITE
fool, stupid person: BONEHEAD
foot and toenail treatment: PEDICURE
football action after the ball has been snapped by the center: SCRIMMAGE
football area between the goal line and the end line where a touchdown may be scored: END ZONE
football catch, indicated to officials by an arm signal by the waiting receiver, upon which the receiver may not advance or be tackled: FAIR CATCH
football change in the planned play or formation called out at the line of scrimmage: AUDIBLE
football defense in which extra backs or extra linebackers are used to thwart a long pass: PREVENT DEFENSE
football defense using five backs, or one extra back instead of a linebacker: NICKEL DEFENSE
football defense using six backs, or two extra backs instead of linebackers: DIME DEFENSE
football defensive player stationed just behind the linemen: LINEBACKER
football field corner at the goal line: COFFIN CORNER
football illegality consisting of blocking from behind an opponent who is not carrying the ball: CLIPPING
football kicked after being dropped from the hands but before touching the ground: PUNT
football kick in which the ball is

dropped, then kicked as it bounces up from ground: **DROP KICK**

football kickoff method tried by the losing team to recover the ball immediately, usually through a low and oblique kick easily fumbled by the opponent: **ONSIDE KICK**

football lineman between the guard and the end: **TACKLE**

football line parallel to the goal line along which teams take positions at the start of play: **LINE OF SCRIMMAGE**

football maneuver in which one back hands the ball to another: **HANDOFF**

football offensive formation with the quarterback behind the center and the fullback behind him flanked by the halfbacks: **T FORMATION**

football offensive play in which two backs from opposite sides run toward the quarterback with one receiving a handoff and the other feigning it: **CROSS BUCK**

football official supervising at the sidelines: **LINESMAN**

football pass having little probability of being completed, as a long and high one coming down near a cluster of players in the end zone: **HAIL MARY PASS**

football pass play initiated to look like a running play, as with a faked handoff: **PLAY-ACTION PASS**

football pass that moves parallel to the passer's goal line rather than forward: **LATERAL PASS**

football place kick that starts play at the beginning of each half or following a touchdown: **KICKOFF**

football player, one of a pair who with the quarterback and fullback make up the backfield: **HALFBACK**

football players behind the linemen: **BACKFIELD**

football players providing protection for the ball carrier: **INTERFERENCE**

football player stationed behind the quarterback: **FULLBACK**

football player who calls the signals: **QUARTERBACK**

football play involving both a lateral pass or handoff and a forward pass in either order: **FLEA-FLICKER**

football play in which a player grounds the ball behind his own goal line after it has been moved there by an opponent: **TOUCHBACK**

football play in which the ball is thrown toward the passer's goal: **FORWARD PASS**

football play that goes awry: **BROKEN PLAY**

football play whereby the quarterback retreats as though to pass but hands off to a back who exploits the opening left by the onrushing defenders: **DRAW PLAY**

football score of six points made by touching the ball down or catching it behind the opponent's goal line: **TOUCHDOWN**

football scoring of one or two extra points after a touchdown: **CONVERSION**

football sideline officials who move the box showing the down and the ten-yard measuring chain: **BOX-AND-CHAIN CREW**

football tactic of a concerted rush by several defenders at the quarterback: **BLITZ**

football term for a player's touching the ball to the ground or catching it behind his own goal line at the cost of two points: **SAFETY**

football term for being ahead of the ball before it is snapped by the center: **OFFSIDE**

football term for charging the opposing quarterback by rushing through the line: **BLITZ**

football term for putting the ball in play: **SNAP**

footprint or other trace of a wild animal: **SPOOR**

foot race 26.2 (42.2 kilometers) long: **MARATHON**

footrest or stool-like seat that is padded: **HASSOCK**

foot section above the arch, on the upper side, between the ankle and the toes: **INSTEP**

footstool, usually upholstered: **HASSOCK**

foot that is flat and turned out: **SPLAYFOOT**

foot medical treatment: **PODIATRY**

forbearance, patient endurance or suffering: **LONGANIMITY**

forbid a person to have or do
something: **INTERDICT**
forbidden: **VERBOTEN**
forbidden, banned: **TABOO**
forbidden, beyond the lawful powers of:
ULTRA VIRES
forbidden but clandestinely printed
literature in the U.S.S.R.:
SAMIZDAT
forbidding by law reporters or others
from disclosing details of a case to
the public: **GAG ORDER**
forced feeding: **GAVAGE**
forced labor, particularly for repairing
roads: **CORVÉE**
force of destruction that is slow and
irresistible: **JUGGERNAUT**
force oneself or one's opinion on
someone else: **OBTRUDE**
force oneself upon others: **INTRUDE**
force or compel to go: **HALE**
force or drive to action, urge on: **IMPEL**
force or pack down by repeated
pressure: **TAMP**
force or spirit from within that guides:
NUMEN
force others aboard a ship through use
of violence or intoxicants:
SHANGHAI
forces at work in any field: **DYNAMICS**
force that balances another force:
COUNTERPOISE
force that is overpowering or coercive:
FORCE MAJEURE
force that sets a body in motion:
IMPETUS
force unjustly: **EXACT**
force, use of: **DURESS**
forcible separation, as surgically or by a
flood: **AVULSION**
foreboding: **PREMONITION**
foreboding: **PRESENTIMENT**
forefather, earliest ancestor:
PRIMOGENITOR
forefather, source: **PROGENITOR**
forefinger: **INDEX FINGER**
forefront, as of technological research
or progress: **CUTTING EDGE**
forehead just above the nose and
between the eyebrows: **GLABELLA**
forehead mark worn by Hindus: **TILAK**
foreign dweller but a native of another
country: **EXPATRIATE**
foreign geographical name, place name
in a different language: **EXONYM**

foreignness or uncertainty as a feeling
in a very different place: **CULTURE
SHOCK**
foreign workers or influence thought to
be excessive, foreign infiltration:
ÜBERFREMDUNG
foreknowledge: **PRESCIENCE**
foreknowledge by God theorized as well
as salvation and damnation being
preordained: **PREDESTINATION**
forerunner, preliminary comer or
manifestation: **PRECURSOR**
foreshadow: **ADUMBRATE**
foreshadow, warn: **PORTEND**
foresight, prudent economy:
PROVIDENCE
foreskin: **PREPUCE**
forest fire spreading at treetops: **CROWN
FIRE**
forests of a certain region and their
characteristics: **SILVA**
foretell: **VATICINATE**
foreteller of events: **SOOTHSAYER**
foretell, indicate beforehand:
PROGNOSTICATE
foretelling by omens: **AUGURY**
foretelling the future, prophecy:
DIVINATION
forethought: **CALCULATION**
forever: **AD INFINITUM**
for example, by way of example: **E.G.
(EXEMPLI GRATIA)**
forgetfulness, disregard: **OBLIVION**
forgetfulness, forgetting, obliviousness:
OBLIVESCENCE
forgetfulness, oblivion: **LETHE**
forgetting temporarily a word,
tip-of-the-tongueness:
LETHOLOGICA
forgivable, as sins: **REMISSIBLE**
forgiveness: **ABSOLUTION**
forgo, relinquish, give up: **WAIVE**
forked, branching: **FURCATE**
forked twig or branch popularly
thought to be effective in finding
underground water: **DIVINING ROD**
fork with three broad tines, one sharp:
RUNCIBLE SPOON
formal in an artificial way, pompous:
STILTED
form a point of view beforehand:
PRECONCEIVE
formation in ranks or steps, as with
troops, fleets or airplanes:
ECHELON

formed, fashioned: WROUGHT
formed into a rounded mass:
    GLOMERATE
former: QUONDAM
former, onetime, previous: ERSTWHILE
formidable, fear-inspiring:
    REDOUBTABLE
form-lacking or indefinite: AMORPHOUS
formless: INCHOATE
form only: PRO FORMA
form, shape, outline: FIGURATION
forsaking one's faith, party or
    principles: APOSTASY
forte, one's occupation for which he or
    she is particularly suited: MÉTIER
for the time being, temporary,
    provisional: PRO TEMPORE
forthright, firm, solid: FOURSQUARE
fortification, bulwark: RAMPART
fortification, stronghold, remote and
    secure place: FASTNESS
fortified place: BASTION
fortnightly: BIWEEKLY
fortune-teller, sorceress: SIBYL
fortune-telling card deck: TAROT
fortune-telling from the lines of the
    palm: PALMISTRY
fortune-telling, sorcery, black magic:
    NECROMANCY
for want of something better: FAUTE DE
    MIEUX
forward, overconfident, arrogant:
    PRESUMPTUOUS
forward-thrusting or -moving:
    POSIGRADE
fossil study or examination of
    prehistoric forms of life:
    PALEONTOLOGY
foul or filthy sediment: FECULENCE
foul-smelling: MEPHITIC
foul-up, malfunction, snag: GLITCH
foundation of stones thrown together:
    RIPRAP
foundation or basic facilities of a
    community: INFRASTRUCTURE
four-dimensional continuum—three of
    space plus time: SPACE-TIME
four-fold: QUADRUPLE
four-fold or based on the number 4:
    QUATERNARY
four, group of four: TETRAD
four-year period: QUADRENNIUM
fox hunter's usually scarlet coat: PINK
    COAT, PINKS
fox-like, sly, crafty: VULPINE

fracas, rough-and-tumble clash:
    SCRIMMAGE
fragilely delicate or collapsible
    structure, plan, etc.: HOUSE OF
    CARDS
fragment, as of pottery: SHARD
fragments or particles separated from
    rock masses by erosion or glaciers:
    DETRITUS
fragments or selections from literary
    works: ANALECTS
fragrant, suggestive of something:
    REDOLENT
frame of mind: DISPOSITION
frame of mind: POSTURE
frame of wood used for sawing wood:
    SAWHORSE
framework like a bridge for holding the
    rails of a traveling crane: GANTRY
framework, structure: FABRIC
France's nuclear strike force: FORCE DE
    FRAPPE
frank and private: HEART-TO-HEART
frank, innocent, simple, naive,
    straightforward: INGENUOUS
fraudulently invented, false:
    TRUMPED-UP
fraudulent or illegitimate doctor,
    charlatan: QUACK
fraudulent or tricky action: JOCKEYING
freakish, strange: OUTLANDISH
freckle: LENTIGO
free advance to the next round, as by a
    highly ranked competitor: BYE
free and easy, offhand: CAVALIER
freedom from restrictions: LATITUDE
freedom or exemption from
    punishment, harm or unpleasant
    consequences: IMPUNITY
free, emancipate, liberate: MANUMIT
free-for-all, brawl marked by roughness:
    DONNYBROOK
free from blame, prove innocent:
    EXCULPATE
free from bondage or restraint:
    EMANCIPATE
free from fever: AFEBRILE
free from slavery, admit to citizenship:
    ENFRANCHISE
free of charge: GRATIS
free ticket, pass: ANNIE OAKLEY
free-ticket possessor or user: DEADHEAD
free, unpaid-for thing or privilege:
    FREEBIE

free will denied or minimized in regard to human behavior: DETERMINISM

freezing the dead or diseased in hope of future revival or cure: CRYONICS

freight train's rear car: CABOOSE

French city district: ARRONDISSEMENT

French cooking stressing light sauces, vegetables and less richness or fat: NOUVELLE CUISINE

French for "good-bye," "till next time": AU REVOIR

French for "good day": BON JOUR

French for "good evening": BON SOIR

French for "thank you": MERCI

French iris-like symbol: FLEUR-DE-LIS

French king's oldest son: DAUPHIN

French kiss: CATAGLOTTISM

French quotation marks (« »): GUILLEMETS

French strong liqueur containing wormwood (now illegal): ABSINTHE

French working girl, especially one with free and easy manners: GRISETTE

frenzied, raging: MADDING

frequently occurring: PREVALENT

frequent visitor to a place: HABITUÉ

fresh, springlike, youthful: VERNAL

fret, complain: REPINE

fretful, jittery, balky: RESTIVE

fried rapidly with little fat: SAUTÉD

friendliness, hospitality, coziness: GEMÜTLICHKEIT

friendliness that is warm and effusive: EMPRESSEMENT

friendly: AFFABLE

friendly: AMICABLE

friendly and solicitous toward guests: HOSPITABLE

friendship and mutual help among influential female comrades: OLD GIRL NETWORK

friendship and mutual help among influential male comrades: OLD BOY NETWORK

friendship or loyalty weakened or destroyed: DISAFFECTION

friend who is exceedingly close to one: ALTER EGO

friend who is no friend, cunning betrayer: SNAKE IN THE GRASS

frightened easily: SKITTISH

frightened, panicky mood: FUNK

frighten with threats: INTIMIDATE

frightful: HORRENDOUS

frigid, arctic: HYPERBOREAN

fringed, as a plant: LACINIATE

frisk about, frolic: DISPORT

frisk about or prance: CAVORT

frivolity, fickleness, lightness, gaiety that is inappropriate: LEVITY

frivolous, impulsive, irresponsible: FLIGHTY

frivolous, restless, superficial: YEASTY

frolic or amuse oneself, frisk about: DISPORT

frolic, skip or leap about: GAMBOL

frolic with hilarity: SKYLARK

from another source, not from the document or evidence at hand: ALIUNDE

from nothing: EX NIHILO

from the beginning, again, anew: DE NOVO

from the depths of sorrow or anguish: DE PROFUNDIS

frontal, in front of: ANTERIOR

front end of a boat: BOW

front or phony corporation: DUMMY CORPORATION

front or primary side of something, such as a coin: OBVERSE

froth, foam, scum: SPUME

frozen, icy: GELID

frozen layered dessert of ice cream, syrup and fruit in a slender glass: PARFAIT

frugal, careful, cautious: CHARY

fruit-bearing: FRUITION

fruit-eating: FRUGIVOROUS

fruitful: PROCREANT

fruitful, fertile: FERACIOUS

fruitful, fertile, prolific: FECUND

fruitful, inventive, productive: PREGNANT

fruitless, unsuccessful: INEFFECTUAL

fruit's (citrus) white covering beneath the rind: ALBEDO

fruits stewed in syrup: COMPOTE

frustrate, confuse, defeat the plans of: DISCOMFIT

frustrate, obstruct, foil: THWART

frying pan of iron and with a long handle: SPIDER

fulfillment: FRUITION

full, absolute, complete: PLENARY

full and rounded, as a voice: OROTUND

full attendance, as in a legislative body: PLENUM

fuller statement, addition for fuller explanation: EPEXEGESIS

full length: IN EXTENSO
full moon after the harvest moon:
    HUNTER'S MOON
fullness of a container lacking by this
    amount: ULLAGE
full of meaning: PREGNANT
full, overflowing: TEEMING
full power being conferred:
    PLENIPOTENTIARY
full, sated, amply supplied: REPLETE
full-sounding, loud: SONOROUS
fully and energetically, with
    determination, all out: HAMMER
    AND TONGS
fumble, bungle, misplay: FOOZLE
fumbler who drops things:
    BUTTERFINGERS
functionary, bureaucrat: APPARATCHIK
fundamental, basic, inherent: ORGANIC
fundamental principle, basis:
    HYPOSTASIS
fund invested so that its gradual
    accumulations will pay a debt:
    SINKING FUND
funds for a new or risky enterprise:
    VENTURE CAPITAL
funeral hymn, dirge: EPICEDIUM
funeral hymn, lament: DIRGE
funeral loving, pleasure in attending
    obsequies: TAPHOPHILIA
funeral pile: PYRE
funeral rites: OBSEQUIES
funeral song, dirge: THRENODY
funnel- or cone-shaped:
    INFUNDIBULIFORM
funny to a great degree, hilarious:
    UPROARIOUS
fun, quip, playfulness: JEST
fun that is noisy and rough:
    HORSEPLAY
fur hat that is cylindrical, worn by

hussars, marching band leaders,
    etc.: BUSBY
Furies: EUMENIDES
furious, enraged: LIVID
furiously angry, maddened: HORN-MAD
furnace floor, fireplace: HEARTH
furnace or oven for baking or drying
    bricks, pottery, cement: KILN
furnished one-room apartment:
    BED-SITTER
furnishings, clothing, accoutrements:
    HABILIMENTS
furnishings, equipment, interior decor:
    APPOINTMENTS
furnish, supply: PURVEY
furniture leg that is curved and tapered:
    CABRIOLE
fur, or other covering of a mammal:
    PELAGE
furtive: CLANDESTINE
furtively move about: SKULK
furtive, sneaky, sly: WEASELLY
fuse or blend together: COALESCE
fuss, commotion in a relatively simple
    situation: TSIMMES
fuss over something trivial: FOOFARAW
fussy, old-fashioned person:
    FUDDY-DUDDY
fussy, overprecise, finicky: NIGGLING
fussy person: FUSSBUDGET
fussy, precise, overly fastidious,
    exacting: FINICKY
futile endeavor: WILD-GOOSE CHASE
futilely sought thing that is a delusion:
    WILL-O'-THE-WISP
futile, unsuccessful: UNAVAILING
future event referred to as if it had
    already happened: PROLEPSIS
future generations: POSTERITY
fuzzy or hairy, in botany: COMATE

gad about, walk about idly or aimlessly: **TRAIPSE**

gadget or device, the name of which is forgotten: **DINGUS**

gaiety: **JOLLITY**

gaiety or merriment that is exuberant and noisy: **HILARITY**

gaiety that is inappropriate, frivolity, fickleness, lightness: **LEVITY**

gains equaling losses in a system, game, etc.: **ZERO-SUM**

gallant, courteous, generous: **CHIVALROUS**

gallant or courtly man: **CAVALIER**

gallery or portico at the side of a building and usually roofed: **VERANDA**

gallery or portico that is arcaded and built into the side of a building: **LOGGIA**

gallows: **GIBBET**

gambling or luck being a cause or reason: **ALEATORY**

gambling system in which one doubles the stakes to recover previous losses: **MARTINGALE**

game in which one team fails to score: **SHUTOUT**

game of ball, popular in Latin America, played with a curved basket fastened to the arm: **JAI ALAI**

game with shells or cups that is a con game, calling for the bettor to guess under which covering a pea or similar object lies: **THIMBLERIG**

gang once empowered to seize and force men into naval or military service: **PRESS-GANG**

gangrenous: **SPHACELATE**

gap, blank: **LACUNA**

gape, stare stupidly: **GAWK**

gap in a mountain through which a torrent passes: **FLUME**

gaping or expanse of open mouth: **RICTUS**

gap, opening, break or interruption of continuity: **HIATUS**

garbage or refuse, large container for: **DUMPSTER**

garden cultivation: **HORTICULTURE**

garden for quiet pleasure: **PLEASANCE**

garden's protective ground covering, as of compost, sawdust or moss: **MULCH**

garden party or picnic on a grand scale: **FÊTE CHAMPÊTRE, FÊTE GALANTE**

garlic-like or onion-like in taste or smell: **ALLIACEOUS**

garment like a skirt worn by both sexes in the Malay Archipelago: **SARONG**

garment of one piece often worn over regular clothes: **COVERALL**

garment, one-piece and tight-fitting, worn by dancers and acrobats: **LEOTARD**

garments that dry quickly after washing and need no ironing are: **DRIP-DRY**

garments that need no ironing after washing are: **WASH-AND-WEAR**

garment that blouses over a waistband or belt: **BLOUSON**

garment with no sleeves worn by Arabs: **ABA**

garment worn by an official or a clergyman: **VESTMENT**

gash, cut: **INCISION**

gas in the intestine: **FLATUS**

gasoline that vaporizes at a relatively low temperature: **HIGH-TEST** gate controlling the flow of water into a canal lock: HEAD GATE

gate controlling water flow: PENSTOCK

gate raised or lowered at a fortress entrance: PORTCULLIS

gate that revolves to admit passengers after deposit of fare: TURNSTILE

gateway or porch, covered, at the entrance of a building: PORTE-COCHÈRE

gathered into a mass: AGGLOMERATE

gathering, collection, treasure: TROVE

gathering of people, animals or things: CLUTCH

gather or store, accumulate: GARNER

gather sheets of manuscript into a unified whole: COLLATE

gauge or pattern used to copy something accurately, as in woodworking: TEMPLATE

gaunt, pale, ghastly: CADAVEROUS

gaunt, wild or worn looking, as from fatigue, hunger or anxiety: HAGGARD

gay, carefree, lighthearted: ROLLICKING

gay, cheerful: JOCUND

gay, puckish, strange: FEY

gay, smart, dashing: RAKISH

gear, equipment, personal effects: PARAPHERNALIA

geld, weaken, castrate, make effeminate: EMASCULATE

gem cutting, engraving or polishing, pertaining to: LAPIDARY

gems as a study: GEMOLOGY

gem that is cut in oblong shape: BAGUETTE

gem unit of weight (200 milligrams): CARAT

genealogies, armorial bearings, etc.: HERALDRY

general and undetailed, sweeping: BROAD-BRUSH

general good, public or civic welfare: COMMONWEAL

general handyman, all-purpose worker, jack-of-all-trades: FACTOTUM

general idea, vague concept: NOTION

generalization to particular instances: A PRIORI

generally epidemic, widespread, universal: PANDEMIC

general pardon: AMNESTY

general store: EMPORIUM

general to the particular, as in reasoning: DEDUCTION

general, undirected, unfocused, uncommitted: FREE-FLOATING

generous: BOUNTEOUS

generous, bountiful, lavish: MUNIFICENT

generous, high-minded, great of soul: MAGNANIMOUS

generous in giving or spending: LAVISH

genitalia wig, once popular during smallpox epidemics: MERKIN

Gentile: GOY

Gentile man or boy: SHEGETZ

Gentile woman or girl: SHIKSA

gentle, mild, favorable: BENIGN

gentle reproof: ADMONITION

genuine thing: REAL McCOY

genus-and-species classifying is: LINNAEAN

geographic measured angular distance from a so-called zero meridian, shown as vertical parallels on a map or globe: LONGITUDE

geographic measured angular distance from the equator and shown as horizontal parallels on a map or globe: LATITUDE

geological groundwater source, as for springs and wells: AQUIFER

geometry that deals with three-dimensional figures: SOLID GEOMETRY

German black-letter type: FRAKTUR

German double-S letter resembling a capital B (β): ES-ZET, ESZETT

German for "so long": AUF WIEDERSEHEN

German for "thank you": DANKE SCHÖN

German leather shorts worn especially in Bavaria: LEDERHOSEN

German military iron cross symbol: CROSS-PATTÉE

German prisoner-of-war camp: STALAG

German Rhine wine: LIEBFRAUMILCH

German song: LIED

germfree, sterilized: AXENIC

germ killer: GERMICIDE

gestures as a communicational science: PASIMOLOGY

gestures without words: PANTOMIME

get by begging: CADGE

get-rich-quick scheme involving an initial investment, recruitment of other participants and presumed returns that multiply with doubling and redoubling membership: **PYRAMID SCHEME**

get rid of, shed: **SLOUGH**

get something from a person by violence or threats: **EXTORT**

getting even with someone: **REPRISAL**

getting somebody to do something by pretending one doesn't want this or doesn't care: **REVERSE PSYCHOLOGY**

ghost: **REVENANT**

ghost, apparition: **SPECTER**

ghost believed to cause sounds: **POLTERGEIST**

ghostly double of someone: **DOPPELGANGER**

ghostly, weird: **EERIE**

gibberish: **GALIMATIAS**

gibberish, speech that is confused or meaningless: **JARGON**

gibberish, unintelligible speech, jargon: **BARAGOUIN**

gibe, witty remark: **QUIP**

giddy, flighty: **HOITY-TOITY**

giddy, flighty, foolish: **HAREBRAINED**

gift given as an apology or for conciliation: **DOUCEUR**

gift given at start of new year or new venture: **HANDSEL**

gift of money, tip: **GRATUITY**

gift reclaiming: **INDIAN GIVING**

gifts bestowed liberally: **LARGESS**

gift that is small and comes from one who can barely afford it: **WIDOW'S MITE**

gift to a beggar: **HANDOUT**

gigantic: **BROBDINGNAGIAN**

gigantic, strong, having enormous power: **HERCULEAN**

gigantic unidentified water beast: **LEVIATHAN**

gilt of bronze or silver: **VERMEIL**

gin or vodka mixed with bouillon as a cocktail: **BULLSHOT**

gin or vodka mixed with dry vermouth as a cocktail: **MARTINI**

gin or vodka mixed with water and sweetened lime juice as a cocktail: **GIMLET**

giraffe: **CAMELOPARD**

girdle or belt: **CEINTURE**

girls in a group: **BEVY**

girl (Spanish): **MUCHACHA**

gist, essential theme or part: **PITH**

give and take: **BANDY**

give back: **RETROCEDE**

give cause for just complaint: **AGGRIEVE**

give grudgingly: **STINT**

given idea behind a literary work, artistic premise: **DONNÉE**

given without requirement of payment or return: **GRATUITOUS**

give off or send forth, as light or heat: **EMIT**

give out, distribute: **DISPENSE**

giver of benefits or favors: **BENEFACTOR**

give to another in a will: **BEQUEATH**

give up: **ABDICATE**

give up, abandon, yield: **RELINQUISH**

give up or turn over something to someone: **CONSIGN**

give up, relinquish, forgo: **WAIVE**

give up rights, powers, etc.: **ABNEGATE**

give up something: **CEDE**

give up something as a penalty: **FORFEIT**

give up, usually conditionally: **CAPITULATE**

give vent to, reveal, disclose: **UNBOSOM**

giving of something back or in retaliation: **TIT FOR TAT**

giving or spending generously: **LAVISH**

giving something equivalent in return, repayment in kind, retaliation: **TIT FOR TAT**

giving up or resigning an office: **DEMISSION**

glacial snow or snow on high mountains that becomes ice: **NÉVÉ**

glaciers as a scientific study: **GLACIOLOGY**

gladiator who fought with a short sword and a long shield: **SAMNITE**

gladiator who fought with a small and often curved sword: **THRACE**

gladiator who fought with a standard sword and shield: **MIRMILLON**

gladiator who fought with a trident and a net: **RETIARIUS**

gladly, willingly: **FAIN**

glance at, read quickly: **SCAN**

glance over or read hastily: **SKIM**

glandular secretion that is internal: **ENDOCRINE**

glass, broken or refuse, that is gathered for remelting: **CULLET**

glasses with three lenses: TRIFOCALS
glasses with two lenses: BIFOCALS
glass-like, transparent: HYALINE
glass of large size for drinking beer:
    SCHOONER
glass or cup filled to the brim: BUMPER
glass or cup for measuring liquor:
    JIGGER
glass or plastic small sealed container
    for liquid in medicine: AMPULE
glass showcase, as for art objects:
    VITRINE
glass that is colored and used in
    mosaics: SMALTO
glassware with embedded ornaments of
    colored glass: MURRHINE GLASS
glassy: VITREOUS
glaze made of raw egg white: GLAIR
gleefully chuckle: CHORTLE
glib and swift talk: PATTER
glib, talkative, speaking fluently:
    VOLUBLE
glide or skim over water: SKITTER
glide or slide, as a snake: SLITHER
gliding, sinuous motion: UNDULATION
glitter: SPANGLE
glitter, flash, sparkle: SCINTILLATE
glittering brilliants, glass spangles, etc.,
    on a garment: DIAMANTÉ
glittering, tinsely, showy: CLINQUANT
gloating over another's troubles:
    SCHADENFREUDE
globe of the world's attached metal
    semicircle, with calibrations and
    anchored to pins at the poles:
    MERIDIAN
globular: CONGLOBATE
gloomy, dark: CIMMERIAN
gloomy, dark: TENEBROUS
gloomy, dejected: DISCONSOLATE
gloomy, depressed, murky: SOMBER
gloomy, desolate, haggard: GAUNT
gloomy, grave, morose: SATURNINE
gloomy, ill-humored, sullen: MOROSE
gloomy, infernal, dark: STYGIAN
gloomy, melancholy: SEPULCHRAL
gloomy, peevish: DYSPEPTIC
gloomy, saddened, dejected:
    DISCONSOLATE
gloomy, stern, morose, ill-tempered:
    DOUR
Gloria Patri, Gloria in excelsis Deo:
    DOXOLOGY
glorification: APOTHEOSIS
glorify, idealize: TRANSFIGURE

glory of the world thus passes away:
    SIC TRANSIT GLORIA MUNDI
gloss over, cover up: WHITEWASH
gloss-producing machine, used on paper
    or fabric: CALENDER
glove-containing protective or sterilized
    container used in laboratories:
    GLOVE BOX
glove part joining back and front parts
    of adjacent fingers: FOURCHETTE
glove thrown down as a medieval
    challenge to combat: GAGE
glowing: LUMINOUS
glowing by living organisms:
    BIOLUMINESCENCE
glowing or luminous with heat:
    INCANDESCENT
glue: MUCILAGE
glum, resentfully morose: SULLEN
glut, offer more than enough: SATIATE
gluttonous, drunken: CRAPULENT
gnome who lives underground, in
    German folklore: KOBOLD
go about, roam in search of diversion:
    GALLIVANT
goad, incite, foment, provoke, spur on
    to some drastic action: INSTIGATE
go along with, agree: ACCEDE
goat-like, lustful: HIRCINE
goat or sheep newly born: YEANLING
gobbledygook: BAFFLEGAB
go-between: INTERMEDIARY
go-between: INTERNUNCIO
goblet, large drinking cup: MAZER
God as the uncaused creator of all
    things: FIRST CAUSE
God conceived as having human
    characteristics: THEANTHROPISM
God evidenced in every feature of the
    universe: PANTHEISM
God's existence denied: ATHEISM
God's existence questioned:
    AGNOSTICISM
God viewed as human in nature:
    ANTHROPOPHUISM
going before, preceding: PREVENIENT
going in, entrance, place or means to
    enter: INGRESS
going or traveling from place to place:
    ITINERANT
going out, exit, place or means to leave:
    EGRESS
go in peace: VADE IN PACE
gold-colored alloys used in cheap
    jewelry and ornaments: ORMOLU

Golden Fleece searchers with Jason:
ARGONAUTS

golden mean, especially as a
government policy: **JUSTE-MILIEU**

gold-rich paradise: **EL DORADO**

golf ball being on the green on a line
perpendicular to the line of
approach: **HOLE-HIGH**

golf course obstacle or trap: **HAZARD**

golfer's shouted warning that the ball is
about to be hit: **FORE**

golf: one stroke over par on a hole:
BOGEY

golf: one stroke under par on a hole:
BIRDIE

golf play in which the ball goes into the
hole on the drive from the tee:
HOLE IN ONE

golf shot, short and lofted, made in
approaching the green: **CHIP SHOT**

golf situation in which an opponent's
ball lies on the green in a direct
line between a player's ball and the
hole: **STYMIE**

golf stroke on the green to move the
ball into or near the hole: **PUTT**

golf: three strokes under par: **DOUBLE
EAGLE**

golf: two strokes over par: **DOUBLE
BOGEY**

golf: two strokes under par on a hole:
EAGLE

gondolier's song, boat song:
BARCAROLE

good breeding, sophistication:
SAVOIR-VIVRE

good-bye (French): **ADIEU**

good-bye (German): **AUF WIEDERSEHEN**

good-bye (Spanish): **HASTA LA VISTA,
HASTA LUEGO, HASTA MAÑANA**

good deed (Hebrew): **MITZVAH**

good, dignified and mature person:
MENSCH

good faith, authentication or
verifications, credentials: **BONA
FIDES**

good life (the), the sweet life: **DOLCE
VITA**

good living: **CAKES AND ALE**

good luck: **MAZEL TOV**

good-luck piece: **AMULET**

good nature: **BONHOMIE**

good-natured, polite remark:
PLEASANTRY

goodness, moral excellence: **VIRTUE**

good-or-bad personal judgment about
something: **VALUE JUDGMENT**

good or benevolent spirit: **EUDEMON**

good or proper to a fulsome degree:
GOODY-GOODY

goods accumulated as a reserve:
STOCKPILE

goods paid for by dealer only after
they've been sold: **ON
CONSIGNMENT**

goods sold in a miscellany collection to
a retailer: **JOB LOT**

goods that may not be imported or
exported: **CONTRABAND**

good things of life: **AMENITIES**

good-versus-evil-oriented: **MANICHAEAN**

goof, social blunder: **FAUX PAS**

goose flesh: **HORRIPILATION**

gory drama or theater: **GRAND
GUIGNOL**

gospel-spreading through preaching and
revival meetings: **EVANGELISM**

gossip, chat: **CONFABULATE**

gossipmonger, teller of secrets and
rumors: **TALEBEARER**

Gothic or historical romance novel:
BODICE RIPPER

gourd musical percussion instrument
played by scraping with a stick:
GUIRO

gourmet, sensualist: **EPICURE**

gout: **PODAGRA**

government administration by routine
procedures or by stolid or inflexible
officials: **BUREAUCRACY**

governmental or diplomatic denial:
DEMENTI

governmental organization of a state or
society: **POLITY**

government, authorities, etc., that are
repressive and ever watchful: **BIG
BROTHER**

government by a few: **OLIGARCHY**

government by holy men: **HAGIARCHY,
HAGIOCRACY**

government by men only: **PATRIARCHY**

government by priests or members of
the clergy: **HIEROCRACY**

government by the military:
STRATOCRACY

government by the old: **GERONTOCRACY**

government by the rich: **PLUTOCRACY**

government by women or a woman:
GYNARCHY

government council, local or national, in the Soviet Union: SOVIET

government expenditures financed by borrowing in order to increase productivity and consumption: DEFICIT FINANCING

government in which people as a whole control production and distribution of goods: COLLECTIVISM

government-must-go theory: ANARCHISM

government or authority shared jointly by two men: DUUMVIRATE

government seizure, usually sudden and often accompanied by violence: COUP D'ÉTAT

government's seizure or punishment of foreigners to counter a similar measure by their government: ANDROLEPSY

government's unlimited authority: ABSOLUTISM

government with absolute power: AUTARCHY

go without sleep, keep vigil: WATCH

gown, loose and flowing, gathered from the neckline: MUUMUU

graceful in bending, bending easily, limber: LITHE

graceful in structure or movement: EURYTHMIC

graceful, slender young woman: SYLPH

graceful, smooth, expressive: FLUENT

gracious: BENIGNANT

gracious gesture: BEAU GESTE

gradation or subtle change in meaning: NUANCE

grade, layer, bed: STRATUM

gradually slow down, recover or stretch after exercise: COOL DOWN

gradually, slowly but surely: INCHMEAL

gradual reduction and extinction of debt or liability, as by installment payments: AMORTIZATION

graduation address: BACCALAUREATE

graduation speech of farewell: VALEDICTORY

grain that has been or is to be ground, meal: GRIST

grammatical change of construction within a sentence: ANACOLUTHON

grammatically analyze a sentence by giving the form, function and syntactical relationship of its words: PARSE

grammatical or syntactical violation: SOLECISM

grammatical system consisting of a set of rules for producing sentences: GENERATIVE GRAMMAR

grammatical term for possessive case: GENITIVE

grammatical theory that holds that all sentences are kernel sentences or transformations of them in accordance with transformational rules: TRANSFORMATIONAL GRAMMAR

grandiloquent: TURGID

grandiloquent political oratory: BOMFOG (BROTHERHOOD OF MAN, FATHERHOOD OF GOD)

grand, imposing: GRANDIOSE

grand-jury report on an offense, based on its own knowledge and with no indictment: PRESENTMENT

grandparental: AVAL

grand, stately, impressive: IMPOSING

grant with condescension: VOUCHSAFE

grape cultivation for wine: VINICULTURE

grape growing: VITICULTURE

grape refuse after pressing, from which brandy is distilled: MARC

graphic symbol representing an object or idea: IDEOGRAPH

graph in the form of a circle divided into proportionate sections: PIE CHART

graph's statistics or frequency curve shaped like a bell: BELL-SHAPED CURVE

graph using rectangular columns: BAR GRAPH, BAR CHART

grasping, greedy: RAPACIOUS

grasping, holding: PREHENSION

grass-covered land, turf: SWARD

grass-eating: GRAMINIVOROUS

grass in second growth after regular cutting, usually tall and rank: FOG

grassland or open country of South Africa: VELDT

gratify, yield to one's own or another's desires: INDULGE

grating, shrill: STRIDENT

gratuity, something extra given: LAGNIAPPE

grave, gloomy, morose: SATURNINE

grave robber, revolting monster: GHOUL

grave robber, stealer of bodies: **RESURRECTIONIST**

graveyard of the West, gunfighters' cemetery: **BOOT HILL**

graveyard shift in newspaper work: **LOBSTER SHIFT**

gravy in natural form included: **AU JUS**

grayish, often with a mottled appearance: **GRISEOUS**

grayish painting or decoration with a sculptural look: **GRISAILLE**

gray or graying, gray-haired: **GRIZZLED**

gray- or white-haired, ancient, venerable: **HOARY**

grease, oil: **LUBRICATE**

greasy, slippery-feeling: **UNCTUOUS**

great of soul, generous, high-minded: **MAGNANIMOUS**

great style: **BRAVURA**

great work, masterpiece: **MAGNUM OPUS**

greed, avarice: **CUPIDITY**

greedy and opportunistic woman in her relations with men: **GOLD DIGGER**

greedy, envious: **COVETOUS**

greedy, grasping: **RAPACIOUS**

greedy, insatiable, immoderate: **VORACIOUS**

greedy, rapacious person: **HARPY**

greedy, wanting ever more: **INSATIABLE**

Greek architecture characterized by elaborateness: **CORINTHIAN**

Greek architecture characterized by ornamental scrolls on capitals: **IONIC**

Greek architecture characterized by simplicity and plain capitals on columns: **DORIC**

Greek folk dance, traditionally but not exclusively danced by men: **SYRTAKI**

Greek long-necked stringed instrument: **BOUZOUKI**

Greek monster with the head and trunk of a man, the body and legs of a horse: **CENTAUR**

Greek red or white wine flavored with resin: **RETSINA**

green all year long, not deciduous: **EVERGREEN**

green coating on bronze or copper: **PATINA**

green crops for animal fodder: **SOILAGE**

green, grassy: **VERDANT**

greenish: **VIRESCENT**

greenish dull color common in military uniforms: **OLIVE DRAB**

greenish-yellow: **LUTEOUS**

green pigment in plant cells involved in photosynthesis: **CHLOROPHYLL**

greeting: **SALUTATION**

greeting in chiefly Islamic countries consisting of a low bow with the right palm at the forehead: **SALAAM**

greet overenthusiastically or somewhat insincerely: **GLAD-HAND**

grief or sorrow, to cause: **AGGRIEVE**

grief or weeping that is false: **CROCODILE TEARS**

grievance: **GRAVAMEN**

grievance, complaint: **PLAINT**

grieve or sympathize with someone: **CONDOLE**

grim, severe, strict: **STARK**

grinding of teeth, especially during sleep: **BRUXISM**

grind or scrape harshly, cut, pierce: **GRIDE**

grin, laugh: **RISUS**

gritty like sand: **SABULOUS**

groggy: **PUNCH-DRUNK**

grooved, striped: **STRIATED**

grooved with long, rounded channels: **FLUTED**

grotesque carved figure on a building: **GARGOYLE**

ground, as of a region or territory: **TERRAIN**

ground plan of a building or other structure: **ICHNOGRAPHY**

ground that is solid and unbroken: **HARDPAN**

group arranged by rank: **HIERARCHY**

group behavioral tendencies that reflect the personality of one individual: **SYNTALITY**

group, clique: **FACTION**

group of girls: **BEVY**

group of persons sharing same interest or interests: **COTERIE**

group of two or more business concerns for a venture: **CONSORTIUM**

group spirit: **ESPRIT DE CORPS**

group that is select and supreme, place or level for the elite: **PANTHEON**

group with common interests living together: **COMMUNE**

grove of small trees: **COPSE, COPPICE**

grow, increase, expand step by step:
ESCALATE
growing along the ground, lying down:
DECUMBENT
growing old, aging: **SENESCENT**
growing or blooming indefinitely, not
seasonal: **PERENNIAL**
growing or coming together:
CONCRETION
growing plants in solutions rather than
in soil: **HYDROPONICS**
growing, waxing, enlarging:
INCRESCENT
growing white: **ALBESCENT**
growing with age: **ACCRESCENCE**
growth arrested: **ATROPHY**
growth-favoring, as a particular climate:
GROWTHY
growth on a field, as of corn: **STAND**
growth rings on trees as a means of
determining approximate dates of
past events: **DENDROCHRONOLOGY**
growth that is abnormal:
HYPERTROPHY
growth that is gradual: **ACCRESCENCE**
gruesome, horrible, ghastly: **MACABRE**
gruesomeness theatrically: **GRAND**
GUIGNOL
gruff or irritable person, usually elderly:
CURMUDGEON
grumble, complain: **GROUSE**
G-string: **CACHE-SEXE**
guarantee: **WARRANTY**
guarantee, assure: **VOUCH**
guarantee, promise: **STIPULATE**
guard against, hinder or prevent in
advance: **FORESTALL**
guardian, trustee: **FIDUCIARY**
guarding and watching carefully: **WARY**
guard line, as of men or ships enclosing
an area: **CORDON**
guard, watchman, keeper: **WARDER**
guess: **CONJECTURE**
guess correctly, surmise: **DIVINE**
guessing game based on pantomimed
actions: **CHARADES**
guesswork-involving, random:
STOCHASTIC
guidebook, especially for travelers:
BAEDEKER
guidebook, manual: **HANDBOOK**
guideline, factor or element that is
signally informative: **PARAMETER**
guide or interpreter for travelers in the
Near East: **DRAGOMAN**

guide who explains to tourists:
CICERONE
guiding or animating spirit from within:
NUMEN
guiding principle or example:
LODESTAR
guillotine hole for victim's head:
LUNETTE
guilt feeling: **COMPUNCTION**
guilt feeling, self-reproach: **REMORSE**
guilt felt by a survivor when others
perish: **SURVIVOR GUILT**
guilt or wrongdoing implied:
INCRIMINATION
guitar string clamp to change the key:
CAPO
Gulf State inhabitant, Spanish
American or West Indian of
European descent: **CREOLE**
gulley or ravine in a desert region:
WADI
gullibility: **CREDULITY**
gully that is deep and dry: **ARROYO**
gum inflammation: **GINGIVITIS**
gunfighters' cemetery, graveyard of the
West: **BOOT HILL**
gunfire that sweeps across the length of
a trench or a troop of men:
ENFILADE
gun that is mounted and used in pairs
or more on ships as an antiaircraft
weapon: **POM-POM**
gush forth, squirt: **SPURT**
gushing, overdemonstrative: **EFFUSIVE**
gush or spurt of liquid from a narrow
orifice: **JET**
gut reaction, deeply felt: **VISCERAL**
gutter or channel of a street: **KENNEL**
gymnastics (men's) cross-like position
held between the rings: **IRON**
CROSS
gymnastics to promote grace and
health: **CALISTHENICS**
gymnastic wheeling vertically, forward
or backward, from feet to hands
and back to feet: **WALKOVER**
gymnasts' association, athletic club:
TURNVEREIN
gymnast's or acrobat's canvas jumping
sheet stretched on a frame:
TRAMPOLINE
gypsy: **TZIGANE**

habitat protected for an animal or
    species: **ECONICHE**
habit, customary practice: **WONT**
habit-ridding treatment whereby
    undesired responses become
    associated with unpleasant stimuli:
    AVERSIVE CONDITIONING,
    AVERSION THERAPY
habits deeply established: **SECOND**
    NATURE
habitual or hardened in a particular
    character or opinion: **INVETERATE**
habitual or usual way of reacting:
    DISPOSITION
habituated, accustomed, used to: **WONT**
habitué, inhabitant: **DENIZEN**
hack, mangle, cut unskillfully: **HAGGLE**
hack writers: **GRUB STREET**
Hades: **ACHERON**
hag: **CRONE**
haggard, hollow-eyed, gloomy, desolate,
    emaciated: **GAUNT**
hag, hateful old woman: **HARRIDAN**
hag who is ugly and malicious:
    BELDAM
hair being smooth or straight:
    LISSOTRICHOUS, LEIOTRICHOUS
hair being woolly or crisp:
    ULOTRICHOUS
hair covering that is matted and woolly:
    TOMENTOSE
hair covering that is soft like velvet:
    VELUTINOUS
hairdo in which the hair is bound by a
    ribbon in back and hangs loosely
    below it: **PONYTAIL**
hairdresser (female): **COIFFEUSE**
hairdresser (male): **COIFFEUR**
hair dressing that glosses and is
    scented: **BRILLIANTINE**

hair growing to a point on the
    forehead: **WIDOW'S PEAK**
hair in a braided style as favored by
    Rastafarians: **DREADLOCKS**
hair loss: **PSILOSIS**
hair net for women that is bag-like and
    for the back of the head: **SNOOD**
hair of a woman: **TRESSES**
hair remover: **DEPILATORY**
hairs in the nostrils: **VIBRISSA**
hair sticking up: **COWLICK**
hair that is matted or tangled as if by
    elves: **ELFLOCKS**
hair that is styled, on a man, like a
    brush: **EN BROSSE**
hair that is woolly or crispy is:
    ULOTRICHOUS
hairy: **HIRSUTE**
hairy or fuzzy, in botany: **COMATE**
hairy two-legged creature said to exist
    in remote areas of western North
    America: **SASQUATCH, BIGFOOT**
half-baked, small-time: **TINHORN**
half-breed, someone or something of
    mixed origin: **HYBRID**
half-man, half-horse monster of Greek
    mythology: **CENTAUR**
half-moon shape: **LUNETTE**
half, portion, share: **MOIETY**
half turn made by horse with rider:
    CARACOLE
hallucination-causing or
    mind-intensifying: **PSYCHEDELIC**
hallucinations from drunkenness:
    DELIRIUM TREMENS
halo: **AUREOLE**
halo: **GLORIOLE**
halo, aura: **NIMBUS**
halved: **DIMIDIATE**

hammered or stamped, as the figure or design on a coin: INCUSE
hammer-shaped: MALLEIFORM
ham that is smoked or cured: GAMMON
ham that is spicy and thin: PROSCIUTTO
handbag that is small, used by women: RETICULE
handbook: VADE MECUM
handbook, manual: ENCHIRIDION
handcuff, fetter, shackle: MANACLE
hand down, transmit, grant in a will: BEQUEATH
handle, especially of a knife, sickle, sword: HAFT
handle or move skillfully: MANIPULATE
hand measure, with the thumb and little finger extended: SPAN
hand-operated portable musical organ: HURDY-GURDY, BARREL ORGAN
hand over or give up something to someone: CONSIGN
handrail supported by balusters: BALUSTRADE
handsome man: ADONIS
hands on hips, having: AKIMBO
hand's V-shaped space between the thumb and the forefinger: PURLICUE
handwriting analysis: GRAPHOLOGY
handwriting art: CHIROGRAPHY
handwriting or spelling that is bad: CACOGRAPHY
handwriting or type that resembles it: SCRIPT
handwriting that is illegible: GRIFFONAGE
handwritten by the signer: HOLOGRAPH
handwritten signature's flourish: PARAPH
hang around, waste time, loiter: DAWDLE
hang down, droop loosely: LOP
hanger-on: CAMP FOLLOWER
hanging in a loose position: PENSILE
hanging in a swinging position: PENDULOUS
hanging on in spite of difficulties: TENACIOUS
hang loosely, droop: LOLL
haphazard: RANDOM
happening at the same rate: SYNCHRONOUS
happening, event: INCIDENT
happen or come into being as a final outcome: EVENTUATE

happen, take place: SUPERVENE
happiness or well-being as found in a life of moderation: EUDEMONIA
happiness, relaxation, well-being: EUPHORIA
happy and healthy: EUPEPTIC
happy condition: SEVENTH HEAVEN
happy-go-lucky behavior: RHATHYMIA
happy, optimistic: UPBEAT
happy, prosperous, flourishing: PALMY
hara-kiri: SEPPUKU
harangue, abusive denunciation: DIATRIBE
harangue that is lengthy: SCREED
harass or annoy with taunts or questions: HECKLE
harass with persistency: IMPORTUNE
harass, worry: CHIVY, CHIVVY
hard, cruel, obdurate: FLINTY
harden, become rigid: OSSIFY
harden, deaden, paralyze with fear: PETRIFY
hardened, unfeeling: INDURATE
hardening of the arteries: ARTERIOSCLEROSIS
hardening of the arteries with fatty substances deposited: ATHEROSCLEROSIS
harden or accustom someone to something: INURE
hardhearted, stubborn, pitiless: OBDURATE
hard legendary mineral: ADAMANT
hardness: CALLOSITY
hard or impossible to explain, as of something causing wonder: UNCANNY
hard problem or test for a beginner, stumbling block: PONS ASINORUM
hard-shelled: TESTACEOUS
hard, stony: PETROUS
hard to believe, amazing: INCREDIBLE
hard-to-express quality: JE NE SAIS QUOI
hard to grasp: ELUSIVE
hard to handle because of size, strength or difficulty: FORMIDABLE
hard to please: FASTIDIOUS
hard to please, excessively critical: HYPERCRITICAL
hard to understand: ABSTRUSE
hard-worked-for with meager returns: HARDSCRABBLE
harem: SERAGLIO
harem slave, concubine: ODALISQUE

harmful, injurious: NOCUOUS
harmful, mischievous: MALEFICENT
harmful, noxious: VIRULENT
harmful, unwholesome: NOXIOUS
harmful with intent, spiteful:
  MALICIOUS
harmless: INNOCUOUS
harmless or concocted person or thing:
  STRAW MAN
harmless substance given to comfort a
  patient or as a test control:
  PLACEBO
harmonious, calm, ordered, balanced,
  rational: APOLLONIAN
harmonious or pleasing in sound,
  smooth: EUPHONIOUS
harmonious relationship, accord:
  RAPPORT
harmonizing of old popular songs:
  BARBERSHOP
harmony, agreement: CONSONANCE
harmony and elegance in arrangement
  of parts: CONCINNITY
harmony, in sympathy: EN RAPPORT
harmony restored: RECONCILED
harm the reputation of: DISCREDIT
harpsichord, small piano: SPINET
harsh: ACERB
harsh, caustic, withering: SCATHING
harsh, cruel or severe to an extreme
  degree: DRACONIAN
harsh cry or sound like a donkey's:
  BRAY
harsh, discordant sound: JANGLE
harsh, fierce: FELL
harsh, merciless: INCLEMENT
harshness: ASPERITY
harsh or high in sound: STRIDENT
harsh, pitiless: RELENTLESS
harsh sound: CACOPHONY
harsh, stern: ASTRINGENT
hasten, hurry: HIE
hastening the tempo, in music:
  STRINGENDO
haste, turmoil, excitement: HECTIC
hasty, brief, abrupt: CURSORY
hasty or impulsive in actions or speech:
  HALF-COCKED
hasty, rash, impulsive: IMPETUOUS
hatchet- or ax-shaped: DOLABRIFORM
hate, deep enmity: RANCOR
hated or dreaded object or person: BÊTE
  NOIRE
hateful, repugnant, loathsome,
  disgusting, offensive: ODIOUS

hat for a woman that is stylishly
  wide-brimmed and plumed or
  flower-decked: GAINSBOROUGH,
  PICTURE HAT
hat for men of soft felt with a low and
  creased crown: FEDORA
hat for men of soft felt with an
  indented crown: TRILBY
hat for men with a high, creased crown
  and stiff brim with a curled edge:
  HOMBURG
hat for men with a low and flat crown
  and brim usually turned up or
  down: PORKPIE
hat for tropical climates that is hard
  and brimmed: PITH HELMET
hat of soft felt with a wide brim, for
  men: BORSALINO
hat, often of silk, that is high and stiff:
  TILE
hatred: ANIMUS
hatred of men: MISANDRY
hat rosette or knot of ribbons: COCKADE
hat that is round and close-fitting:
  TOQUE
hat with a broad brim turned up at the
  sides: SHOVEL HAT
hat with its brim turned up to form
  three sides: TRICORN
hat worn by a soldier or bandleader
  that is tall and stiff, cylindrical in
  shape, with visor and plume:
  SHAKO
haughty, arrogant: CAVALIER
haughty, arrogant, pompous, dogmatic:
  PONTIFICAL
haughty, cultivated person: BRAHMIN
haughty person who sets great store by
  social status, wealth, etc.: SNOB
haul, drag, lug: SCHLEP
haunt, place to which one often returns:
  PURLIEU
have a warning or negative effect, be
  adverse or dissuasive to: MILITATE
  AGAINST
have-it-made state or situation,
  prosperity: EASY STREET
Hawaiian feast with entertainment:
  LUAU
Hawaiian salutation: ALOHA
Hawaii newcomer or stranger:
  MALIHINI
hawk or buzzard: BUTEO
hay fever: POLLENOSIS

hay or grain raked into a long ridge or pile: WINDROW

haystack with the top fashioned to protect the interior from rain: RICK

hazy, misty, vague, unclear: NEBULOUS

headache on one side, as in migraine: HEMICRANIA

headband: BANDEAU

headband, crown: DIADEM

head being broad: BRACHYCEPHALIC

head cold: CORYZA

headdress, crown-like and jeweled, worn by women: TIARA

headdress of Moslems consisting of wound cloth: TURBAN

head enlargement caused by an excess of fluid in the cranium: HYDROCEPHALUS

head-in-the-clouds person, impractical daydreamer: LUFTMENSCH

headland, high land extending into the sea: PROMONTORY

headless: ACEPHALOUS

head of a human being joined to animal body: ANDROCEPHALOUS

head of the line: VAN

head to foot: CAP-A-PIE

healing: SANATIVE

healing, curative: THERAPEUTIC

health-conscious person unduly anxious about illness: VALETUDINARIAN

healthful: SALUBRIOUS

healthful and spiritual, natural: HOLISTIC

health resort: SANITARIUM

health, spirits: FETTLE

health that is sound and vigorous, robust: HALE

healthy and happy: EUPEPTIC

heap, mass or collection of things: CONGERIES

heard at a frequency range beyond that of human hearing: ULTRASONIC

heard information that is not positively known to be true: HEARSAY

hearing diminution that accompanies aging: PRESBYCUSIS

hearing distance: EARSHOT

heart and blood vessels, pertaining to: CARDIOVASCULAR

heart area tissue death (necrosis) caused by obstruction: INFARCTION

heart attack: CORONARY THROMBOSIS

heart attack factor, according to experimental evidence: CHOLESTEROL

heartbeat being abnormal, with double pulse beat: DICROTIC

heartbeat instability correcting by emergency procedures: DEFIBRILLATION

heartbeat regulating device that is implanted: PACEMAKER

heartbeats that are weak and irregular: FIBRILLATION

heartburn: PYROSIS

heart examination that traces changes in electric potential: ELECTROCARDIOGRAM (EKG)

heartfelt cry, passionate appeal or lament: CRI DE COEUR

heart rhythm disturbance: EXTRASYSTOLE

heart-shaped: CORDIFORM

heart's regular contraction: SYSTOLE

heart's regular dilatation: DIASTOLE

heat and cold sensitivity: THERMESTHESIA

heat and then cool to soften and strengthen, as glass or steel: ANNEAL

heat being oppressive or overpowering: SWELTERING

heat-causing or -producing: PYROGENIC

heated room with dry air rather than steam: SAUNA

heat energy being employed after nuclear fusion: THERMONUCLEAR

heat measurement: CALORIMETRY

heat or light ray bent in passage from one medium to another: REFRACTION

heat- or warmth-producing, like a mustard plaster: CALEFACIENT

heat-producing: CALORIFIC

heat-producing medical treatment: DIATHERMY

heave, convulse or strain to vomit: RETCH

heaven help us: ABSIT OMEN

heavenly, celestial: SUPERNAL

heavens, sky: FIRMAMENT

heavy, clumsy, awkward in appearance or movement: LUMBERING

heavy shoe: BROGAN

hedge or wall set low in a ditch so as not to obstruct the view: HA-HA

heedless, inattentive: UNAWARE

heedlessness, foolhardiness: TEMERITY
heel-stamping Spanish dance, flamenco-like: ZAPATEADO
height, instrument for measuring: ALTIMETER
height of power, thriving period, exuberance: HEYDAY
held notes, prolonged tempo, in music: SOSTENUTO
held or sustained, in music: TENUTO
helicopter landing place: HELIPORT
hell: INFERNO
hell: NETHER WORLD
helmet-like woolen cap with a back-of-neck covering: BALACLAVA
helmet that bears a spike, as worn by Prussians: PICKELHAUBE
helmet, often of pith, worn as protection against the sun: TOPEE
help: ABET
help, form of assistance: ADMINICLE
helpful person, rescuer: GOOD SAMARITAN
helping to make possible: CONDUCIVE
helpless, ineffective: IMPOTENT
helplessly distraught person: BASKET CASE
helplessly vulnerable person: SITTING DUCK
hence: ERGO
hen that has been spayed: POULARD
heraldically worthy or possessing a coat of arms: ARMIGEROUS
heraldic blue banner with three fleurs-de-lis of gold: ORIFLAMME
heraldic vertical band through the middle of the shield: PALE
heraldic white or silver: ARGENT
herald or announcement of the coming of something or someone: HARBINGER
heraldry depiction of an animal lying down: COUCHANT
heraldry depiction of an animal reared on its hind legs: RAMPANT
heraldry depiction of an animal sitting with the forelimbs upright: SEJANT
heraldry depiction of an animal walking with a forepaw raised: PASSANT
heraldry depiction of a square table set diagonally, displaying arms of a deceased person: HATCHMENT
heraldry depiction of two coats of arms placed side by side on an escutcheon: IMPALE
heraldry design including many small figures, as stars: SEMÉ
heraldry device placed above the shield in a coat of arms: CREST
heraldry division of the quarter, usually on the dexter side: CANTON
heraldry: left: SINISTER
heraldry: vertical bands of alternating colors: PALY
here and there in a book: PASSIM
heredity biochemical basis: GENETIC CODE
heredity study to improve quality of humans: EUGENICS
hermaphroditic: ANDROGYNOUS
hermit: ANCHORITE
hermit: EREMITE
hero as a rogue in fiction, involving the: PICARESQUE
heroic deeds or adventures: DERRING-DO
hero, knight, chivalrous rescuer: PALADIN
"he," "she" or "one" used instead of "I": ILLEISM
hesitancy or uneasiness regarding a question of ethics, morality or conscience: SCRUPLE
hesitate, equivocate, blather: WAFFLE
hesitate foolishly, dawdle, be irresolute, vacillate: SHILLY-SHALLY
hesitate in speaking: HEM AND HAW
hesitate, take exception, object: DEMUR
hesitating: IRRESOLUTE
hick, boor, yokel: MUCKER
hidden: ABSTRUSE
hidden goods or articles: CACHE
hidden or unknown difficulty: JOKER
hidden, profound: RECONDITE
hidden, secret: ARCANE
hidden tendency: UNDERCURRENT
hidden, unclear, faint: OBSCURE
hide, obscure: CAMOUFLAGE
hideous, enormous: MONSTROUS
hideous or cruel being: OGRE
hiding of one's real activities, designs or misdeeds: COVER-UP
hiding or safety place for an animal: CREEPHOLE
hiding place for goods or articles: CACHE
hieroglyphics key: ROSETTA STONE

high and level land formation: PLATEAU
high and mighty: HAUGHTY
high-and-mighty position: CATBIRD SEAT
high-born or high in rank: AUGUST
higher price on a stock transaction than the preceding transaction price: UP TICK, PLUS-TICK
highest bid to buy and lowest offer to sell a given stock at a given time: QUOTATION
highest grade, usually said of diamonds and pearls: FIRST WATER
highest honors awarded at graduation: SUMMA CUM LAUDE
highest in kind, quality, or degree: SUPERLATIVE
highest in rank: PARAMOUNT
highest or culminating point: ZENITH
highest point: APOGEE
highest point: PINNACLE
highest point of anything, zenith: MERIDIAN
highest point, topmost stone: CAPSTONE
highest priced or of the best quality: GILT-EDGED
high fashion: HAUTE COUTURE
high, harsh, as a sound: STRIDENT
high-minded, great of soul, generous: MAGNANIMOUS
high or culminating point: SOLSTICE
high platform for a worker that is raised from a truck: CHERRY PICKER
high-pressure peddling by phone of stocks of dubious value: BOILER ROOM
high priest, prelate: HIERARCH
high regard, esteem: REPUTE
high society: HAUT MONDE
high society, the fashionable world: BEAU MONDE
high spirits, elated: COCK-A-HOOP
high-strung, overexcited or easily excitable, worked up: HYPER
high-up dwelling on a hill or mountain, as a house or stronghold: AERIE
high voice above natural register: FALSETTO
highway around a city or urban area: BELTWAY
highway interchange with overpass and curved ramps: CLOVERLEAF
high-wire acrobat: AERIALIST
high-wire walker: FUNAMBULIST

hillock or knoll: HUMMOCK
hillside hollow serving as a shelter: ABRI
hillside vineyard: COTE
hill, small round mound: KNOLL
hill that is rocky or its craggy peak: TOR
hilly, having mounds: TUMULOSE
hinder, block or guard against in advance: FORESTALL
hinder, impede, crowd with useless additions: ENCUMBER
hinder, interfere with the movements of, impede: HAMPER
hinder, obstruct: CRIMP
hinder, put obstacles in the way of, retard: IMPEDE
hinder, slow, delay: RETARD
hindrance, impediment: TRAMMEL
Hindu ascetic philosophy that involves deep meditation: YOGA
Hindu loincloth: DHOTI
Hindu mythology triad of Brahma, Vishnu and Siva: TRIMURTI
Hindu or Buddhist religious law: DHARMA
Hindu system of exercises practiced in the self-freeing Yoga discipline: YOGA
Hindu women's garment consisting of a long piece of fabric artfully wound about the body: SARI
hint at, signify: IMPLY
hint, imply: INTIMATE
hint, notion, slight suggestion, vague idea: INKLING
hint, sly intimation: INSINUATION
hint, suggestion, insinuation, usually derogatory: INNUENDO
hip raised in a pose: HIPSHOT POSE
hired applauders: CLAQUE
Hispanic grocery store: BODEGA
hissing, making "s" sounds: SIBILANT
historical subjects represented in ornamental design: STORIATION
history muse: CLIO
history study based on excavations: ARCHAEOLOGY
hit and rebound: CAROM
hit or graze along the side: SIDESWIPE
hit or run into a person from the side and unseen: BLINDSIDE
hit repeatedly: PELT
hit repeatedly with the fists: PUMMEL
hives, nettle rash: URTICARIA

hoarding riches: **AVARICE**
hoarse, husky-voiced: **ROUPY**
hoax: **SPOOF**
hockey enclosure to seat players
     removed because of a penalty:
     PENALTY BOX
hockey feint or faked movement by the
     puck handler: **DEKE**
hockey foul of touching the opponent's
     body with the stick held in both
     hands: **CROSS-CHECK**
hockey movement of the puck with
     light taps of the stick: **DRIBBLE**
hockey pass in which the puck is
     suddenly or deceptively left for or
     tapped back to a trailing teammate:
     DROP PASS
hockey penalizing call for illegal entry
     into opponent's zone ahead of the
     puck: **OFFSIDE**
hockey player substitution without a
     stopping of play: **CHANGING ON
     THE FLY**
hockey rectangular area in front of the
     goal cage: **CREASE, GOAL CREASE**
hockey starting of a play by dropping
     the puck between the sticks of two
     opposing players: **FACE-OFF**
hockey team's preventing of a score by
     the opponent while it is short a
     player or players because of a
     penalty: **PENALTY KILLING**
hockey: uncharacteristically physical or
     rough in style of play: **CHIPPY**
hocus-pocus, sleight of hand, trickery:
     LEGERDEMAIN
hodgepodge, confusion:
     KATZENJAMMER
hodgepodge, hash: **GALLIMAUFRY**
hodgepodge, medley: **MÉLANGE**
hoggish, piggish, swinish: **PORCINE**
hold back from something: **ABSTAIN**
hold forth, discuss: **DESCANT**
hold forth with cant, talk in a windy
     way, speechify: **BLOVIATE**
holding, as of land or a term of office:
     TENURE
holding of an office: **INCUMBENCY**
holding temporarily of money, property,
     etc., by a third party: **ESCROW**
holding together: **COHERENT**
hold someone by binding the arms:
     PINION
hole drilled through the ocean floor:
     MOHOLE

hole in a paved road: **POTHOLE**
hole or pit at the bottom of a shaft or
     hole to collect water: **SUMP**
holiday spent in activity similar to one's
     regular work: **BUSMAN'S HOLIDAY**
holiness or righteousness pretended:
     SANCTIMONIOUS
hollowed-out recess or space, cavern:
     GROTTO
hollow in a wall, as for a bust or statue:
     NICHE
Holy Communion: **EUCHARIST**
Holy Communion plate for consecrated
     bread: **PATEN**
Holy Communion received as bread
     dipped in wine: **INTINCTION**
Holy Communion wafer receptacle: **PYX**
holy men as the hierarchy of a
     government: **HAGIARCHY,
     HAGIOCRACY**
holy objects or relics repository, as a
     box or a shrine: **RELIQUARY**
holy of holies, most sacred place:
     SANCTUM SANCTORUM
holy oil: **CHRISM**
holy-water basin: **STOUP**
holy-water sprinkler held in the hand:
     ASPERGILLUM
homage, respect, reverence: **OBEISANCE**
home: **ABODE**
home, house or dwelling: **DOMICILE**
homeless person forced by a war to live
     in a foreign country: **DISPLACED
     PERSON**
homeless, roaming: **NOMADIC**
homeless rover, vagabond: **VAGRANT**
homeless wanderer: **WAIF**
homeless, wandering youngster: **GAMIN**
homeless woman of the streets with her
     possessions: **BAG LADY**
home stayer, one remaining in the same
     place: **SEDENS**
homosexual female: **LESBIAN**
homosexuality, especially among males:
     URANISM
homosexual male: **URANIST, URNING**
honest and straightforward dealing:
     PLAIN-DEALING
honest, conscientious: **SCRUPULOUS**
honest, morally proper: **UPRIGHT**
honesty: **VERACITY**
honesty, probity: **INTEGRITY**
honorable, respectable, in good usage:
     REPUTABLE

honoree for excellence in his or her achievements: LAUREATE

honors awarded according to property owned, as a form of government: TIMOCRACY

honors awarded at graduation: CUM LAUDE

honor with festivities: FETE

hood and mask worn at masquerades: DOMINO

hooded: COWLED

hooded cloak: BURNOOSE

hoof, nail, claw: UNGUIS

hook at the end of the pole for landing large fish: GAFF

hooked, curved: AQUILINE

hooked or claw-like anchor: GRAPNEL

hook-like: UNCIFORM

hoot, wail, howl: ULULATE

hopeless, incapable of being reformed: INCORRIGIBLE

hopelessness, dejection of spirits: DESPONDENCY

hopeless plight: CHANCERY

hope that is desperate or futile: FORLORN HOPE

horizon arc measurement in navigation and astronomy: AZIMUTH

hormone associated with male or masculine drives: TESTOSTERONE

horn-bereft animal: POLLARD

hornlike, horny: CORNEOUS

horn overflowing with fruit, vegetables, grain: CORNUCOPIA

horn that is low-pitched, especially one used on ships to signal alarms: KLAXON

horrible fancy: CHIMERA

horrified: AGHAST

horror in a lurid dramatic or sensational form: GRAND GUIGNOL

hors d'oeuvres in the form of raw vegetables: CRUDITÉS

horseback riding: EQUITATION

horse, bred near Trieste, that is white or gray, finely shaped, spirited and noted as a dressage performer: LIPPIZANER

horse breed notable for its trotters and pacers: STANDARDBRED

horse comb: CURRYCOMB

horse command word meaning to turn left: HAW

horse command word meaning to turn right: GEE

horse-drawn two-wheeled vehicle for one person: SULKY

horse, in breeding, that is a female parent: DAM

horse less than a year old: FOAL

horse-like: EQUINE

horse-like mythical animal with one horn: UNICORN

horsemanship competition, athletic meet or automobile steeplechase: GYMKHANA

horsemanship execution of trotting slowly in place: PIAFFE

horsemen symbolizing pestilence, war, famine and death: FOUR HORSEMEN OF THE APOCALYPSE

horse of heavy build with feathered or brush-like pasterns and fetlocks: CLYDESDALE

horse of light tan color with ivory-colored mane and tail: PALOMINO

horse of medium size used for ordinary driving or riding: HACKNEY

horse race in which any entry is subject to purchase at a previously set price: CLAIMING RACE

horse race in which the competitors are selected far in advance: FUTURITY

horse race with only one starter: WALKOVER

horse-racing informant or consultant: TOUT

horse-racing information sheet: DOPE SHEET

horse-racing term for the designated weight carried by a horse in a handicap race: IMPOST

horseshoer, blacksmith: FARRIER

horseshoe-shaped: HIPPOCREPIFORM

horse's lifting of a forefoot and the opposite hind foot without moving forward or backward: PIAFFER

horses or horsemanship, relating to: EQUESTRIAN

horses or oxen in a matched pair: SPAN

horse that has been castrated: GELDING

horse that is a female foal: FILLY

horse that is a male parent or in breeding: SIRE

horse that is a mature female: MARE

horse that is a mature male: STALLION

horse that is gentle and plodding, farm horse: DOBBIN

horse that is male and four years of age or under, male foal: COLT

horse that is male and uncastrated: STALLION

horse that is spirited, as for riding or use in combat: STEED

horse that is worn out or useless: RIP

horse that races well on a muddy track: MUDDER

horse-trained gait whereby the horse moves partly sidewise: VOLT

horse training for performance of precise movements: DRESSAGE

horse used for heavy work: PERCHERON

horse whose coloring is permeated with gray or white: ROAN

hospital cot or stretcher with wheels: GURNEY

hospital department in which outpatients are treated: POLYCLINIC

hospitality, friendliness, coziness: GEMÜTLICHKEIT

hospitality, pertaining to: XENIAL

hospital or program for the terminally ill: HOSPICE

hospital or ship for the treatment of contagious diseases: LAZARETTO

hospital teenage nursing aide: CANDY STRIPER

hostile, antagonistic: INIMICAL

hostile behavior: BELLICOSITY

hostile feeling: ANIMUS

hostile, inharmonious, incongruous: DISSONANT

hostility, enmity, ill feeling: BAD BLOOD

hot days of July and August: DOG DAYS

hotel designed to accommodate motorists: MOTEL

hotel system in which the price includes room, service and meals: AMERICAN PLAN

hotel system of charging for room and service without meals: EUROPEAN PLAN

hotheaded person: HOTSPUR

hot, scorched: TORRID

hourly: HORAL

household: MÉNAGE

household gods: LARES AND PENATES

house used by spies as a secret refuge or meeting place: SAFE HOUSE

housewife who is extremely efficient and tidy: BALEBOSTE

house with a steep triangular shape or roof reaching to the ground: A-FRAME

house with a view: BELVEDERE

house with each floor half a story above or below the adjacent one: SPLIT-LEVEL

housing for low-income people scattered rather than concentrated in a middle-class area: SCATTERSITE HOUSING

howl, hoot, wail: ULULATE

H-shaped: ZYGAL

hubbub, turmoil: HURLY-BURLY

huge: TITANIC

huge: BROBDINGNAGIAN

huge and powerful creature or thing, monstrosity: BEHEMOTH

huge or powerful thing or creature: LEVIATHAN

human attributes ascribed to inanimate things: PATHETIC FALLACY

human nature, form, etc., ascribed to the inanimate in figurative speech: PERSONIFICATION

human behavior as a study: PRAXEOLOGY

human being requiring artificial parts, respiration system, etc., to function in an alien environment: CYBORG

human character, mores, etc., as a study: ETHOLOGY

human embodiment: INCARNATION

human emotions or passions attributed to gods or objects: ANTHROPOPATHY

human excrement as fertilizer: NIGHT SOIL

human form or characteristics ascribed to something not human: ANTHROPOMORPHISM

human improvement through control of environment: EUTHENICS

human improvement through control of factors that affect heredity: EUGENICS

human knowledge as a subject of study, cognition: EPISTEMOLOGY

human-looking robot: ANDROID

humanly made object or art: ARTIFACT

human nature attributed to God: ANTHROPOPHUISM

human settlements as a study: EKISTICS

human-shaped: ANDROID

human Upper Paleolithic precursor:
CRO-MAGNON
humbly and earnestly entreating:
SUPPLIANT
hum, buzz, drone: **BOMBINATE**
humid, damp, moist: **DANK**
humiliate: **ABASE**
humor directed against danger, death,
   etc.: **GALLOWS HUMOR**
humorous: **WAGGISH**
humorously extravagant, caricatural and
   ribald: **RABELAISIAN**
humorous, witty or ribald writings:
   FACETIAE
humpback, curvature of the spine:
   KYPHOSIS
hundred-fold: **CENTUPLE**
hunger that is abnormal and continual:
   BULIMIA
hungry, greedy: **ESURIENT**
hungry in a wild or greedy way:
   RAVENOUS
hunted creature: **QUARRY**
hunt or fish illegally: **POACH**
hurl from a height: **PRECIPITATE**
hurried and confused: **HELTER-SKELTER**
hurry: **POSTHASTE**
hurry, hasten: **HIE**
hurry off, run: **SCAMPER**
hurtful: **DELETERIOUS**
hurtful or touching to the feelings,
   affecting: **POIGNANT**
hurtle through air: **CATAPULT**
husbandly to an excessive degree, fond
   of or submissive to one's wife:
   UXORIOUS

husband of an unfaithful wife:
   CUCKOLD
husband of a reigning female sovereign:
   PRINCE CONSORT
husband or wife: **CONSORT**
husband who murders his wife:
   UXORICIDE
hush-hush or involving intrigue,
   plotting, spying, etc.:
   CLOAK-AND-DAGGER
husk, shell, pod: **SHUCK**
husky-voiced, hoarse: **ROUPY**
hussy: **JADE**
hybrid offspring of a stallion and a
   female ass: **HINNY**
hymn for the dead: **REQUIEM**
hymn or verse in praise of God:
   DOXOLOGY
hype: **PUFFERY**
hypocrisy: **PHARISAISM**
hypocrisy: **SANCTIMONY**
hypocrite: **TARTUFFE**
hypocrite: **WHITED SEPULCHER**
hypocrite who is fawning and scheming:
   URIAH HEEP
hypocritical behavior: **DISSEMBLANCE**
hypocritical, insincere: **PECKSNIFFIAN**
hypocritically pious expression: **CANT**
hypocritical, pretentious or ostentatious
   ceremony: **MUMMERY**
hypothetical, academic, debatable:
   MOOT
hysterical outburst, rage: **CONNIPTION**

I adjust my chess piece only (and do not move it): **J'ADOUBE**

I am at fault: **MEA CULPA**

I came, I saw, I conquered: **VENI, VIDI, VICI**

ice cream frozen layered dessert with syrup and fruit in a slender glass: **PARFAIT**

iced or chilled beverage as a dessert: **FRAPPÉ**

ice game, in which heavy stones are slid toward a goal: **CURLING**

ice-surface-smoothing tractor-like vehicle: **ZAMBONI**

icy, frozen: **GELID**

idea conference: **BRAINSTORMING**

idea forming, entertaining or relating: **IDEATION**

idealize, glorify: **TRANSFIGURE**

identification card: **ID CARD**

identification with another usually well-known person as an unconscious disorder: **APPERSONATION**

identifying journalistic sources: **ATTRIBUTION**

identifying oneself with other persons or objects: **INTROJECTION**

idiocy: **AMENTIA**

idiom, language, speaking style: **PARLANCE**

idiot: **AMENT**

idiotic, inane, stupid: **FATUOUS**

idle chatter: **PALAVER**

idle, dormant: **FALLOW**

idle, lazy: **OTIOSE**

idler, do-nothing: **FAINÉANT**

idle tramp who is subject to arrest: **VAGRANT**

idle, unoccupied: **VACUOUS**

idly talk, chatter: **PRATE**

idyllic, serene, calm: **HALCYON**

if anything can go wrong, it will: **MURPHY'S LAW**

if you please, please: **S'IL VOUS PLAÎT**

ignorance: **NESCIENCE**

ignorance or alibi backup planned as self-protective excuse: **DENIABILITY**

ignorance pretended to expose errors of opponent's argument: **SOCRATIC IRONY**

ignorant: **BENIGHTED**

ignore the indicated correction and let the original stand (a direction used in proofreading): **STET**

ignoring the complexity of problems, oversimplifying: **SIMPLISTIC**

I have found it: **EUREKA**

ill-assorted, incongruous: **DISSOCIABLE**

ill-disposed, wishing evil toward others: **MALEVOLENT**

illegal bargain made in a lawsuit to get a share of the matter sued for: **CHAMPERTY**

illegal commerce in goods that may not be exported or imported: **CONTRABAND**

illegal influencing of a judge or jury: **EMBRACERY**

illegal-money trafficker, payoff messenger: **BAGMAN**

illegal resident without authorized papers: **ILLEGAL ALIEN**

illegible handwriting: **GRIFFONAGE**

illegitimate, counterfeit: **SPURIOUS**

ill-humored, cross, gloomy: **SULKY**

ill-humored, sullen, gloomy: **MOROSE**

illiterate, uneducated: **UNLETTERED**

ill-natured or rude person: **CHURL**

illness, disorder: **DISTEMPER**

illness or discontent, a chronic feeling of either: DYSPHORIA
illness or disorder of the mind or body: DISTEMPER
illness that is slight: INDISPOSITION
illogical or faulty reasoning: PARALOGISM
ill-starred: STAR-CROSSED
ill-tempered or peevish: BILIOUS
ill temper, spitefulness, peevishness: SPLEEN
illusion of reality, in art or decoration: TROMPE L'OEIL
illusion that a new experience has happened before: DÉJÀ VU
illusory or unreal, as an imagined banquet: BARMECIDAL
illustrate a book already in print with illustrations removed from another book: GRANGERIZE
illustrative: EXEMPLARY
ill will, spitefulness: RANCOR
image: EIDOLON
image in the mind, specter: PHANTASM
image, likeness or picture, usually an object of veneration: ICON
image, likeness or representation, usually crudely done, of a disliked person: EFFIGY
images in works of art studied to determine the thematic significance of the subject: ICONOGRAPHY
imaginable, possible, secular: EARTHLY
imaginary, assumed, supposed: HYPOTHETICAL
imaginary, flimsy: INSUBSTANTIAL
imaginary grotesque monster: CHIMERA
imaginary or visionary semblance: SIMULACRUM
imaginary romantic and picturesque kingdom: RURITANIA
imaginary sought thing, delusion, misleading phenomenon: WILL-O'-THE-WISP
imaginary, unrealistic: VISIONARY
imaginative resources: INGENUITY
imagined or recalled with photographic vividness: EIDETIC
imagined or unreal, as a banquet that is an illusion: BARMECIDAL
imagined symptoms as part of anxiety about one's health: HYPOCHONDRIA
imitate in attempt to equal or surpass: EMULATE

imitate, look or act like someone or something: SIMULATE
imitating a sound, as an expressive word: ECHOIC
imitation, especially in literature and art: MIMESIS
imitation marble: SCAGLIOLA
imitation of a literary or musical work, meant humorously: PARODY
imitation of a person or thing, copy: CLONE
imitation or burlesque that is farcical: TRAVESTY
imitation or reproduction of the original: ECTYPE
immature: CALLOW
immature, callow but opinionated: SOPHOMORIC
immature, inexperienced: UNFLEDGED
immediate: INSTANTANEOUS
immediately: TOUT DE SUITE
immediately following this: HEREUPON
immigrant without proper papers, unlawful resident: ILLEGAL ALIEN
immoral, debauched: DISSOLUTE
immoral man, roué: RAKE
immortality: ATHANASIA
immovable: ADAMANT
immune, resistant: INSUSCEPTIBLE
immune to injury, unconquerable: INVULNERABLE
immunity to disease as a study: IMMUNOLOGY
immunize by an injection: INOCULATE
impair secretly, weaken by degrees: UNDERMINE
impair, spoil: VITIATE
impart gradually: INSTILL
impartial, fair: UNBIASED
impartial, fair, reasonable: EQUITABLE
impartiality, justness, fairness: EQUITY
impartial, objective: DISPASSIONATE
impartial, unbiased: DISINTERESTED
impassioned: FERVID
impassive, unaffected by pain or pleasure: STOICAL
impassive, unfeeling: STOLID
impede, block, hinder, stop: OBSTRUCT
impede, disconcert, complicate: EMBARRASS
impede, hinder, obstruct, crowd with useless additions: ENCUMBER
impede, restrain, interfere with the movements of: HAMPER
impediment, hindrance: TRAMMEL

impending, threatening: IMMINENT
imperialistic or expansionist doctrine of
    the 19th-century United States:
    MANIFEST DESTINY
imperious, dictatorial: PEREMPTORY
impetuous: BRASH
impetuous, ardent, violent: VEHEMENT
impetus of a body in motion:
    MOMENTUM
impish, mischievously merry: PUCKISH
implanted device to regulate heartbeat
    electronically: PACEMAKER
implant ideas or opinions: INSEMINATE
implanting synthetic replacement
    material in the human body:
    ALLOPLASTY
implicate: INVOLVE
implication of a word, an expression or
    a text: CONNOTATION
implied, not directly stated: TACIT
implied or understood matter in
    addition to what is expressed:
    SUBAUDITUR
imply, hint: INTIMATE
imply or give the appearance of fact,
    often falsely: PURPORT
important: CONSEQUENTIAL
important, conclusive or inescapable
    consideration, essential matter,
    crux: BOTTOM LINE
important, essential: PIVOTAL
important, highly regarded:
    PRESTIGIOUS
important official, chief, bigwig:
    POOH-BAH
important or outstanding feature:
    HIGHLIGHT
important person: HIGH MUCK-A-MUCK
important person in a group: KINGPIN
impose, introduce or insert
    unwelcomely: FOIST
imposing, awesome: AUGUST
imposing, pretentiously grand:
    GRANDIOSE
impossible to extricate oneself from,
    impossible to disentangle or undo:
    INEXTRICABLE
impressive, grand, stately: IMPOSING
impress on the mind, instill: INCULCATE
imprison: INCARCERATE
imprison, confine, surround, enclose
    within walls: IMMURE
imprisonment, forced confinement:
    DURANCE

improbable person or event introduced
    to untangle a story plot: DEUS EX
    MACHINA
impromptu, spontaneous, casual:
    OFF-THE-CUFF
improper: UNSEEMLY
improper, unseemly: UNTOWARD
improve: AMELIORATE
improvements to property: CAPITAL
    EXPENDITURE
improvise: AD LIB
improvised: EXTEMPORANEOUS
improvised measure to fill a need
    temporarily: STOPGAP
improvised musical passage: CADENZA
improvised, temporary, substitute:
    MAKESHIFT
imprudent: IMPOLITIC
imprudent, unwise: INDISCREET
impudence: CHUTZPAH
impudence, boldness, audacity:
    EFFRONTERY
impudently or ostentatiously display:
    FLAUNT
impudent young woman: BAGGAGE
impulse that is creative: AFFLATUS
impulsive, hasty, rash: IMPETUOUS
impulsive or hasty in action or speech:
    HALF-COCKED
impulsive, without forethought:
    SPONTANEOUS
impure, to make: ADULTERATE
inability to decide or act, loss of
    willpower: ABULIA
inability to experience pleasure or
    happiness: ANHEDONIA
inability to swallow: APHAGIA
inability to understand or use objects:
    APRAXIA
inactive for a period, especially winter:
    HIBERNATING
inactive, indolent, listless: SUPINE
inactive, settled, seated a great part of
    the time: SEDENTARY
inactive, sluggish, dull: TORPID
inactive, still, placid: QUIESCENT
in addition, besides: WITHAL
inadequate, disproportionate:
    INCOMMENSURATE
inadequate, not quite enough: SCANT
inadvertent or random action,
    accidental homicide:
    CHANCE-MEDLEY
in a hopeless situation, in great trouble,
    doomed: UP THE CREEK

in a living organism, not in a laboratory or artificial environment: IN VIVO

in an artificial environment or test tube, not within the living body or organism: IN VITRO

inane or idle thing: VACUITY

inanimate objects possess souls, as a belief: ANIMISM

in an undertone, softly or privately spoken, whispered: SOTTO VOCE

inappropriate, at odds with, unsuitable: INCONGRUOUS

inappropriate, out of place: MALAPROPOS

inattentive, heedless: UNAWARE

inaudible to humans: INFRASONIC

inborn: INHERENT

inborn: INNATE

incantation, magical unintelligible words: MUMBO JUMBO

incantation used to conjure an evil spirit: INVOCATION

incapable of being passed through: IMPERVIOUS

incapable of being transferred or removed: INALIENABLE

incarnation of a quality or idea: AVATAR

incautious, thriftless, rash: IMPROVIDENT

incense ingredient: TACAMAHAC

incentive, motivating force: IMPETUS

incentive, stimulus: FILLIP

inch by inch: INCHMEAL

incidental result, by-product, new application: SPIN-OFF

incident or controversy attracting wide attention: CAUSE CÉLÈBRE

incised carving: INTAGLIO

incite, foment, provoke, spur on or goad, especially to some drastic action: INSTIGATE

incite, instigate, stir up: FOMENT

inclination, slope of countryside: VERSANT

inclination, tendency: BENT

inclination, tendency, bent: PROPENSITY

incline downward, be of greater weight: PREPONDERATE

incline that links different levels: RAMP

include, embrace: COMPRISE

include or take in as a part of the whole: INCORPORATE

include within or beneath, subordinate: SUBSUME

incoherent, rapid talk: GIBBERISH

incoherent talk: GABBLE

income in dollars of individuals adjusted to take account of inflation: REAL INCOME

incompetence tends to be the level achieved by the promotion of employees: PETER PRINCIPLE

incompetent, clumsy, awkward: INEPT

incomplete, broken: FRAGMENTARY

incomprehensible, dense: IMPENETRABLE

incongruity, lack of harmony: DISSONANCE

incongruous, ill-assorted: DISSOCIABLE

incongruously nonsensical statement, droll self-contradiction: IRISH BULL

inconsistency, contradiction: DISCREPANCY

inconsistent, opposed, undesirable: REPUGNANT

inconstant, changeable: FICKLE

inconvenience, bother, trouble: DISCOMMODE

incorporate, collect, make part of a whole: EMBODY

incorrect though popular idea of the origin of a word: FOLK ETYMOLOGY

increase, addition, something added or gained: INCREMENT

increase, grow, expand step by step: ESCALATE

increase power, rank or wealth: AGGRANDIZE

increase unduly, puff up, enlarge excessively: INFLATE

increasing, enlarging, growing: INCRESCENT

increasing the number of shares of a company by dividing the outstanding shares: SPLIT

incriminate: INCULPATE

incriminatingly, in the very act: RED-HANDED, IN FLAGRANTE DELICTO

incurable, unremediable: IRREMEDIABLE

indecency or pornography in art or literature: COPROLOGY

indecent: UNSEEMLY

indecent, bold, self-assertive: IMMODEST

indecent, risqué: SCABROUS

indecisive: VACILLATING

indefinable something: JE NE SAIS QUOI

indefinite, misty, foggy: NUBILOUS
indefinite, vague: INTANGIBLE
indention of all lines of a paragraph
except the first, as in the format of
this entry: HANGING INDENTION
independent: AUTONOMOUS
independent and dangerous adventurer,
individual deemed loose and
beyond the control of a group:
ROGUE ELEPHANT
independent and supreme in authority:
SOVEREIGN
independent in resources: SUBSTANTIVE
independent, needing no help:
SELF-SUFFICIENT
independent of an original or main
body or group: SPLINTER
independent of outside control:
AUTONOMOUS
independent person, particularly in
politics: MUGWUMP
indescribable, ineffable: INENARRABLE
index to the individual words in a
particular book: CONCORDANCE
Indian (Asian) drums, played as a pair
with the hands: TABLA
Indian (Native American) conical tent:
TEPEE
Indian (Native American) feast in
which the host bestows lavish gifts
or destroys possessions with the
guests expected to follow suit:
POTLATCH
Indian (Native American) group
dwelling or dwellings often of
adobe, terraced and having ladders
for access: PUEBLO
Indian (Native American) rounded hut
of skins, mats or bark supported by
poles: WIGWAM
indicate, point out, signify: DENOTE
indicator or forerunner of something:
BELLWETHER
indifference, dullness, stagnation,
weakness, fatigue, spiritlessness:
LANGUOR
indifferent: APATHETIC
indifferent, apathetic: PHLEGMATIC
indifferent, apathetic, lackadaisical:
LISTLESS
indifferent in a casual way, cool:
NONCHALANT
indifferently careless, easygoing or
irresponsible: GALLIONIC
indifferent to pleasure or pain: STOICAL

indifferent, uncaring: POCOCURANTE
indigenous: ABORIGINAL
indigenous, native: ENCHORIAL
indignity: AFFRONT
indirect mention: ALLUSION
indirect, not obvious: SUBTLE
indirect, roundabout: CIRCUITOUS
indirect, slanted: OBLIQUE
indirect wording used to say something:
PERIPHRASIS
indiscretions of youth: WILD OATS
indiscriminate, especially sexually:
PROMISCUOUS
indispensable, essential, whole:
INTEGRAL
indispensable, required: REQUISITE
indispensable thing, that without which
there is nothing: SINE QUA NON
indisputable: APODICTIC
indisputable, uncontestable:
IRREFRAGABLE
indisputable, unquestionable:
INCONTESTABLE
individual deemed loose and beyond the
control of a group, independent
and dangerous adventurer: ROGUE
ELEPHANT
individual's language or dialect:
IDIOLECT
individuals or items chosen in the
expectation they will be
representative of a whole group:
RANDOM SAMPLE
indoctrination that is coercive:
BRAINWASHING
indolent and irresponsible individual:
LOTUS-EATER
indolent, listless, inactive: SUPINE
indoor swimming pool: NATATORIUM
induced by a physician or his
treatment: IATROGENIC
induce or bribe one to commit perjury:
SUBORN
indulgence that is excessive:
DISSIPATION
industrial worker: BLUE COLLAR
WORKER
indwelling, existing within: IMMANENT
inebriate: INTOXICATE
ineffable, indescribable: INENARRABLE
ineffective, lazy, useless: FAINÉANT
ineffectual person: WEAK SISTER
ineffectual, useless: OTIOSE
inequality, unlikeness: DISPARITY

inertness and disorder as an irreversible tendency of a system: ENTROPY

inevitability: FATALISM

inevitable, unavoidable: INELUCTABLE

inexperienced: CALLOW

inexperienced: VERDANT

inexperienced: WET BEHIND THE EARS

inexperienced or new person, newcomer, novice: GREENHORN

infallible authority, wise person: ORACLE

infamy, disgrace: OBLOQUY

infantile concept of a parent or loved one persisting in the adult: IMAGO

infantry, soldiers vulnerable to artillery: CANNON FODDER

inference, deduction: ILLATION

inference resulting from concealment or misrepresentation of facts: SUBREPTION

infer from incomplete evidence: CONJECTURE

inferior as a substitute: ERSATZ

inferior in any way: SUBORDINATE

inferior in quality: SHODDY

inferior in rank, subordinate: SUBALTERN

inferior, paltry, pitiable: SORRY

inferior to an appalling degree: EXECRABLE

infernal: AVERNAL

infernal, dark, gloomy: STYGIAN

infinitive in which an adverb intervenes between the "to" and the verb: SPLIT INFINITIVE

inflamed, sore: IRRITATED

inflated or a bombastic, as a style of speech: TURGID

inflated, overloaded: PLETHORIC

inflated, pompous: TUMID

inflated, pretentious: OVERBLOWN

inflation designed by government to bring back a former price structure: REFLATION

inflection of words: ACCIDENCE

inflexible, rigid: HARD-SHELL

inflict or enforce in an arbitrary fashion: IMPOSE

influence another with talk or insinuations: EARWIG

influential or powerful person in determining political candidates, power broker: KINGMAKER

inform: APPRISE

informal noisy gathering: CLAMBAKE

informal word or phrase: COLLOQUIALISM

information exchanging, useful professional intercommunication: NETWORKING

information gathered on a person or subject: DOSSIER

information that is false and deliberately disseminated by a government, intelligence agency, etc.: DISINFORMATION

informed, acquainted with the facts: AU FAIT

informed on current things: AU COURANT

informer for the police: STOOL PIGEON

in front of, frontal: ANTERIOR

ingenious, cunning, skillful: DAEDAL

ingenious, refined: SUBTLE

in great trouble, in a hopeless situation, doomed: UP THE CREEK

inhabitant, habitué: DENIZEN

inharmonious, incongruous, hostile: DISSONANT

inharmonious state or quality: DISSONANCE

inherent: INNATE

inherent, essential: INTRINSIC

inherited racial memory: COLLECTIVE UNCONSCIOUS

inhuman, cruel, vicious: FELL

initial, beginning: INCEPTIVE

initialisms and acronyms: ALPHABET SOUP

initial letter or sound dropped in the development of a word: APHERESIS

initial letter or sound the same in a series of words: ALLITERATION

initial letters of a series of words combined to form a word: ACRONYM

initial letters of lines forming a word: ACROSTIC

initiate someone by subjecting him to pranks and humiliating horseplay: HAZE

injection under the skin: HYPODERMIC

inject or add certain elements: INCORPORATE

injured feeling, resentment: UMBRAGE

injured or victimized by one's plans to injure another: HOIST BY ONE'S OWN PETARD

injurious: DELETERIOUS

injurious, deadly, malicious:
PERNICIOUS
injurious, harmful: **NOCUOUS**
injurious, unwholesome: **NOXIOUS**
injury, damage: **LESION**
injury, harmful action, ill service:
DISSERVICE
injury or emotional shock that is severe:
TRAUMA
ink blot test used to analyze
personality: **RORSCHACH TEST**
inland region, remote area,
backcountry: **HINTERLAND**
inlet of the sea between steep cliffs:
FJORD
inlet of the sea or mouth of a river
where tide and current meet:
ESTUARY
inmost parts, as in a house of worship:
PENETRALIA
in name alone, not in fact: **NOMINAL**
innards, internal organs such as the
stomach, heart, lungs: **VISCERA**
inner force that animates or guides:
NUMEN
inn, hostelry: **CARAVANSARY**
innkeeper: **BONIFACE**
innocence, peace and simplicity being
portrayed as associated with rural
life: **PASTORAL**
innocence-proving: **EXCULPATORY**
innocent or simple in style in a
deliberate and often somewhat false
way: **FAUX NAÏF**
innocent young woman: **INGENUE**
innumerable, vast indefinite number:
MYRIAD
in on a secret: **PRIVY TO**
in opposition to: **ATHWART**
in or by itself, as such, by nature: **PER
SE**
in passing: **EN PASSANT**
in place, in proper position: **IN SITU**
in place of: **IN LIEU OF**
in place of a parent: **IN LOCO PARENTIS**
in private, secretly: **IN PETTO**
in proper position, in place: **IN SITU**
insane: **DAFT**
insane notion, delusion: **DELIRAMENT**
insanity: **ALIENATION**
insatiable, immoderate, greedy:
VORACIOUS
inscribe or adorn with names or
symbols: **BLAZON**

inscription on a tomb or monument:
EPIGRAPH
inscriptions or their deciphering or
interpreting: **EPIGRAPHY**
inscriptions, scribblings or drawings on
walls: **GRAFFITI**
insect chirping sound, as made by
crickets and grasshoppers:
STRIDULATION
insect encased or cocoon stage:
CHRYSALIS, PUPA
insect noises: **FRITINIENCY**
insect study: **ENTOMOLOGY**
insensible, blunt, dull: **OBTUSE**
insert an organ within the body:
IMPLANT
insert an unacknowledged addition into
a text: **INTERPOLATE**
insert, as an additional day in the
calendar: **INTERCALATE**
inserting one's own ideas into a text
being explained: **EISEGESIS**
insertion, as in a wooden joint, to hide
a bad fitting or to replace a broken
piece: **DUTCHMAN**
insertion of a sound or letter into a
word: **EPENTHESIS**
insertion of a word between the parts of
a compound word: **TMESIS**
insertion of one thing into another:
INTROMISSION
insertion sign in typewritten or printed
matter (∧): **CARET**
insert-one's-hand protective or sterilized
container, as used in laboratories,
with interior gloves attached to
holes for the hands: **GLOVE BOX**
insert, throw in between other things,
introduce abruptly: **INTERJECT**
inside exclusive group: **CLIQUE**
inside of a curved surface: **CONCAVITY**
insider, one in the know: **COGNOSCENTE**
inside talk of a special group: **CANT**
insightful impression, immediate
perception, intuition: **APERÇU**
insignia that is V-shaped: **CHEVRON**
insignificant amount: **IOTA**
insignificant or trifling in size or
amount: **NEGLIGIBLE**
insignificant, trifling, tiny: **MINUTE**
insignificant, unimportant, trifling:
PETTY
insincere, ambiguous: **LEFT-HANDED**
insincere, crafty: **DISINGENUOUS**
insincere, excessive: **FULSOME**

insincere, hypocritical: **PECKSNIFFIAN**

insincere religious or moralistic talk: **CANT**

insincere support, avowal, etc.: **LIP SERVICE**

insincere sympathy: **BATHOS**

insinuation, hint, suggestion, usually derogatory: **INNUENDO**

insipid, dry, lacking interest, naive, barren: **JEJUNE**

insipid, flat, dull, lifeless: **VAPID**

insolence, rudeness: **IMPERTINENCE**

insolent: **BRASSY**

insolent, rebellious: **CONTUMACIOUS**

insolent treatment: **AFFRONT**

inspection of one or a few typical things out of many, to insure quality: **SPOT CHECK**

inspirer, activater, leader, as of a group: **SPARK PLUG**

inspire with ideas: **IMBUE**

install, as an official: **INAUGURATE**

installment ceremony: **INVESTITURE**

install or place in office formally: **INVEST**

instantly: **IN A TRICE**

instigate an evil act: **SUBORN**

instigate, incite, stir up: **FOMENT**

instill, impress on the mind: **INCULCATE**

institute legal proceedings: **PROSECUTE**

instruct in doctrines, principles or systems of belief: **INDOCTRINATE**

instructional, boringly pedagogical: **DIDACTIC**

instrument recording distance traveled: **ODOMETER**

instrument similar to the xylophone: **MARIMBA**

instrument that is long and tubular with a curving stem: **BASSOON**

instrument to measure diameter or thickness: **CALIPERS**

insubstantial, nonmaterial, spiritual: **INCORPOREAL**

insult, affront: **INDIGNITY**

insult game about relatives traditional among some black Americans: **DOZENS**

insulting: **ABUSIVE**

insulting, disrespectful: **INSOLENT**

insulting rudeness in speech: **CONTUMELY**

insult openly: **AFFRONT**

insult that is wittily veiled: **CHARIENTISM**

insurance risk and premium calculator: **ACTUARY**

insurrection: **INSURGENCE**

intact: **INVIOLATE**

intangible: **IMPALPABLE**

integrity, honesty: **PROBITY**

integrity lack, dishonesty: **IMPROBITY**

intellect, brains: **GRAY MATTER**

intellectually or abstractly apprehended: **NOETIC**

intellectual perception of something unknowable through the senses: **NOUMENON**

intellectual quickness, keenness: **ACUMEN**

intellectuals' center for interdisciplinary problem solving and research: **THINK TANK**

intemperance: **DISSIPATION**

intensify: **AGGRANDIZE**

intensify, elevate: **HEIGHTEN**

interbreeding of races: **MISCEGENATION**

inter, bury: **INHUME**

interchangeable or worthy as a replacement, as with a debt: **FUNGIBLE**

interesting and agreeable: **SAPID**

interest not compounded but computed on the original principal alone: **SIMPLE INTEREST**

interferer in a plan, project, etc.: **MARPLOT**

interferer, meddler: **BUTTINSKY**

intermediary, intercessor: **GO-BETWEEN**

intermediate point between two extremes, sometimes an average: **MEAN**

interminable and difficult: **SISYPHEAN**

internal aider of the foreign enemy: **FIFTH COLUMNIST**

internal-examining machine: **FLUOROSCOPE**

internal falling or slipping of an organ: **PROLAPSE**

internal organs, innards, such as stomach, heart, lungs: **VISCERA**

internal rhyme, in which a word within a line of verse rhymes with the final word of the line: **LEONINE RHYME**

International Criminal Police Organization: **INTERPOL**

interpolation of one's own ideas into a text being explained: **EISEGESIS**

interpretation, especially of the Bible:
HERMENEUTICS

interpretation of a word, passage or
work: EXEGESIS

interpretation of words in a spiritual
and mystical sense: ANAGOGE

interpretation or performance of a text,
role, etc.: RENDITION

interpretation that is facetious rather
than literal: PICKWICKIAN SENSE

interpreter, annotator or commentator
in scholarship: SCHOLIAST

interpreter or explainer, scholarly critic:
EXEGETE

interpreter or guide for travelers in the
Near East: DRAGOMAN

interpret, explain: EXPLICATE

interrupted, broken: DISCONTINUOUS

interruption, as of electric service:
OUTAGE

interruption, break in continuity:
INTERREGNUM

interruption, insertion or addition in a
discourse, process or series:
INTERPOLATION

intersect, cross so as to form an X:
DECUSSATE

intersecting, cutting: SECANT

intertwining, entanglement,
complication: INVOLUTION

interval between events or activities,
recess: INTERMISSION

intervene in behalf of another or to
mediate: INTERCEDE

interweave: PLEACH

intestinal: ENTERIC

intestinal disease usually caused by
eating undercooked pork:
TRICHINOSIS

intestinal inflammation: COLITIS

intestinal waves of contraction that
push the contents outward:
PERISTALSIS

in the matter of, concerning: IN RE

in the morning, early: MATUTINAL

in the place cited: LOC. CIT. (LOCO
CITATO)

intimate friend: ALTER EGO

intimately: CHEEK BY JOWL

intimately, privately with one other
person: À DEUX

intimidating, awesome, challenging:
FORMIDABLE

intricate: INVOLVED

intricate, skillful, cunning, ingenious:
DAEDAL

intriguers, cabal: JUNTA

intriguing secret group: CABAL

introduce abruptly, throw in between
other things: INTERJECT

introduce additions, comments, or
interruptions into a discourse or
process: INTERPOLATE

introduce, bring in something new:
INNOVATE

introduced (conveniently or improbably)
person or event to untangle a story
plot: DEUS EX MACHINA

introduce, impose, insert fraudulently:
FOIST

introduce some new element into:
INJECT

introduce subtly and gradually:
INSINUATE

introducing one's own ideas into a text
being explained: EISEGESIS

introduction, as to a field of study:
ISAGOGE

introduction, preface: PREAMBLE

introduction to a book or thesis:
PREFACE

introductory, as to an art or science:
PROPAEDEUTIC

introductory remark, foreword:
PROLEGOMENON

introductory statement, preface: PROEM

intrude gradually, make inroads,
trespass, advance beyond the
proper limit: ENCROACH

intrude, meddle in the affairs of others:
INTERLOPE

intrude oneself or one's opinion on
someone else: OBTRUDE

intuition, insightful impression,
immediate perception: APERÇU

intuitive, emotional: VISCERAL

intuitive knowledge, direct awareness:
IMMEDIACY

invalid: VALETUDINARIAN

invalidate, debase, corrupt: VITIATE

invasion, raid: INCURSION

invasion that is sudden: IRRUPTION

invent a word: MINT, NEOLOGIZE

invent details to compensate for loss of
memory: CONFABULATE

invented, false, not real: FICTITIOUS

inventive, clever, skillful: INGENIOUS

inventive, fruitful, productive:
PREGNANT

invent or make up as a story or a lie:
    FABRICATE
invent, produce, perform without
    previous thought or preparation:
    IMPROVISE
inversion in order of words:
    ANASTROPHE
inversion of the structure of the second
    of two parallel clauses: CHIASMUS
inverted "V" placed under a line to
    indicate insertion: CARET
inverted word order: HYPERBATON
investigate or search for information:
    DELVE
investigation and discovery as a way of
    learning: HEURISTICS
investigation, officially done, of the
    beliefs and activities of individuals:
    INQUISITION
investment swindle: PONZI, PONZI
    GAME, PONZI SCHEME
invigorate, cheer up, pep up, stimulate:
    EXHILARATE
inviolable, as an oath: STYGIAN
inviting attack, vulnerable: PREGNABLE
involved, committed, earnest: ENGAGÉ
involved, complicated, puzzling:
    INTRICATE
involved, complicated, twisted or
    intricate: CONVOLUTED
involved or foolishly wasteful
    procedure: RIGMAROLE
involve, entangle, intertwine: IMPLICATE
involve in trouble: EMBROIL
involve necessarily or naturally: IMPLY
invulnerable, unfeeling: IMPASSIBLE
inward carrying or conducting, as
    neural pathways conveying
    impulses to the brain: AFFERENT
inward violent collapse: IMPLOSION
in wine there is truth: IN VINO VERITAS
iota: TITTLE
Iranian language: FARSI
iridescence: OPALESCENCE
iridescence, especially on pottery:
    REFLET
iridescent: VERSICOLOR
iridescent, pearl-like: NACREOUS
iridescent, resembling a peacock's tail:
    PAVONINE
Irish pronunciation: BROGUE
iron for pressing clothes that is pointed
    at both ends: SADIRON
irony: ANTIPHRASIS
irregular: ANOMALOUS

irregular, eccentric, nonconforming:
    ERRATIC
irregularity: ABNORMALITY
irregular, occasional: SPORADIC
irrelevant: INAPPOSITE
irrelevant ("nothing to the matter"):
    NIHIL AD REM
irrelevant remark: NON SEQUITUR
irreligious, unbelieving: HEATHEN
irresistibly attractive: BEWITCHING
irresponsible, reckless, wild:
    HARUM-SCARUM
irreverent: IMPIOUS
irreverent remarks about God or sacred
    things: BLASPHEMY
irritability or excitability in any part of
    the body to an abnormal degree:
    ERETHISM
irritableness, peevishness: PETULANCE
irritable or gruff person, usually elderly:
    CURMUDGEON
irritable person: CROSSPATCH
irritable, quick-tempered: IRASCIBLE
irritable, touchy: TETCHY
irritable, unruly, cranky, rebellious:
    FRACTIOUS
irritated, annoyed, offended: MIFFED
irritated or angry state: SNIT
irritate, embitter: RANKLE
irritate or upset: RUFFLE
irritating, annoying: VEXATIOUS
irritating thing: BUGBEAR
is it not so? (German): NICHT WAHR?
Islamic fasting period: RAMADAN
Islamic prophet or messiah expected
    before the end of the world:
    MAHDI
Islamic respected scholar: AYATOLLAH
Islamic spiritual ruler: IMAM
island of coral that is ring shaped
    (almost closed): ATOLL
island or reef, especially one of coral,
    that is low and beside a coast: KEY
islands, chain of: ARCHIPELAGO
Isle of Man native: MANXMAN
isn't it so? (French): N'EST-CE PAS?
isolate: INSULATE
isolate a thought: PRESCIND
isolated, detached: INSULAR
isolated or private room: SANCTUM
isolated, separated: SPORADIC
Israeli and Romanian folk dance in
    which dancers lock arms in a
    circle: HORA

Israeli collective farm or settlement:
  KIBBUTZ
Israeli Constituent Assembly: **KNESSET**
Israeli native: **SABRA**
Italian appetizers: **ANTIPASTO**
Italian bowling played outdoors on a
  narrow dirt court: **BOCCIE**
Italian dessert containing layers of
  different ice creams: **SPUMONI**
Italian for "enough" or "stop": **BASTA**
Italian for "goodbye": **ARRIVEDERCI**
Italian frothy dessert made of eggs,
  sugar and wine: **ZABAGLIONE**
Italian greeting used at meeting or
  parting: **CIAO**

Italian ice cream low in butterfat:
  GELATO, GELATI
Italian pastry confections shaped like
  tubes: **CANNOLI**
Italian small eating place: **TRATTORIA**
itemized list of securities held by a
  person or an institution:
  PORTFOLIO
items too small or too numerous to be
  separately specified: **SUNDRIES**
ivory, bone or shells ornamented by
  cutting or carving: **SCRIMSHAW**

jabbering: **BLITHERING**

jacket that binds the arms to the body to restrain a violent person: **STRAITJACKET**

jacket that is short and sleeveless for a woman: **HUG-ME-TIGHT**

jack-of-all-trades: **FACTOTUM**

jai alai building or stadium: **FRONTON**

jai alai court: **CANCHA**

jammed, close together: **CHOCKABLOCK**

Japanese-American born in the United States: **NISEI**

Japanese-American born in the United States but educated in Japan: **KIBEI**

Japanese-American, third generation, born in the United States: **SANSEI**

Japanese art of paperfolding: **ORIGAMI**

Japanese broad sash with a bow in the back: **OBI**

Japanese classical drama: **NO, NOH**

Japanese dish of raw fish sliced thin: **SASHIMI**

Japanese dish of shaped pieces of raw fish atop cold rice: **SUSHI**

Japanese dish of thinly sliced meat and vegetables usually cooked rapidly at the table: **SUKIYAKI**

Japanese fencing with bamboo weapons and body-protective equipment: **KENDO**

Japanese feudal-military code of honor: **BUSHIDO**

Japanese floor mat: **TATAMI**

Japanese for "thank you": **ARIGATO**

Japanese gardening art of dwarfed shaped trees: **BONSAI**

Japanese gateway shaped somewhat like the pi symbol (Π): **TORII**

Japanese immigrant to the United States: **ISSEI**

Japanese Kabuki actor who plays female roles: **ONNAGATA**

Japanese marinated chicken: **YAKITORI**

Japanese play on popular or comic themes: **KABUKI**

Japanese ritual suicide by disembowelment: **HARA-KIRI, SEPPUKU**

Japanese stone collecting and arranging: **SUISEKI**

Japanese stringed musical instrument: **KOTO**

Japanese suicidal air attack: **KAMIKAZE**

Japanese syllabic writing: **KANA**

Japanese thin mattress used as a floor bed: **FUTON**

Japanese translucent paper screen used as a partition or door: **SHOJI**

Japanese upright wrestling engaged in by large and obese men: **SUMO**

Japanese verse form: **HAIKU**

Japanese wide and bowl-like cooking pan: **WOK**

Japanese wrestling system that uses size and strength of an opponent against him: **JUJITSU**

Japan's influential conglomerates in business, finance and industry: **ZAIBATSU**

jargon: **ARGOT**

jargon, gibberish, unintelligible speech: **BARAGOUIN**

jargon or vocabulary of a profession or class: **LINGO**

jargon that is mystifying, gibberish, gobbledygook: **BAFFLEGAB**

jar of antiquity that is narrow at the top and base and has two handles: **AMPHORA**

jar or pot that is broad-mouthed and of earthenware: OLLA
jaundice: ICTERUS
jaunty, gay, dashing: RAKISH
jaw, pertaining to: GNATHIC
jazz improvised singing in nonsense syllables: SCAT
jazz that is loud and improvised: BARRELHOUSE
jeer, defy, scoff, mock: FLOUT
jeer, deride, sneer, laugh coarsely: FLEER
jeer or reproach sarcastically: TAUNT
jeer, taunt: GIBE
jell, agree: JIBE
jelly-making substance: PECTIN
jerkiness and uncontrollable movements as a nervous disorder, chorea: SAINT VITUS'S DANCE
jerky, unsteady movement: JIGGLE
jester's cap: FOOLSCAP
jesting, flippantly humorous: FACETIOUS
jesting, playful: JOCOSE
jesting, teasing talk: RAILLERY
Jesus' sayings not found in Bible: AGRAPHA
jewelers' or watchmakers' magnifying glass: LOUPE
jewelers' weights system: TROY
jewelry: BIJOUTERIE
jewels set so closely as to hide metal are: PAVÉ
Jewish boy's coming-of-age ceremony at 13: BAR MITZVAH
Jewish civil and religious law and commentaries thereon: TALMUD
Jewish culture, customs or literature: JUDAICA
Jewish daughter supposedly having materialistic values or spoiled: JAP (JEWISH AMERICAN PRINCESS)
Jewish day of atonement: YOM KIPPUR
Jewish doorpost faith symbol, a holy scripture on parchment in a small case or tube: MEZUZAH
Jewish eight-day commemoration of the Temple of Jerusalem's rededication: HANUKKAH
Jewish folklore robot like a human being: GOLEM
Jewish food in which dietary standards are observed is: KOSHER
Jewish girl's coming-of-age ceremony: BAS (or BAT or BATH) MITZVAH
Jewish greeting: SHALOM

Jewish holiday commemorating deliverance by Esther from Haman's massacre: PURIM
Jewish holiday commemorating the revelation of the Ten Commandments: SHABUOTH, SHAVUOTH
Jewish law and literature, the Pentateuch: TORAH
Jewish leather cases containing scriptural passages that are placed on the forehead and left arm during morning prayers: PHYLACTERIES
Jewish marriage broker: SCHATCHEN
Jewish mourning prayer: KADDISH
Jewish New Year: ROSH HASHANA
Jewish observance of mourning period: SIT SHIVA
Jewish Passover feast commemorating the exodus from Egypt: SEDER
Jewish school or college: YESHIVA
Jewish seven-day period of mourning: SHIVA
Jewish seven- or nine-branched candelabrum: MENORAH
Jewish thanksgiving festival: SUKKOTH, FEAST OF TABERNACLES
Jewish traditional toy spun like a top: DREIDEL
Jewish village of Eastern Europe: SHTETL
Jews' dispersion: DIASPORA
Jews of German or Eastern European descent: ASHKENAZIM
Jews of Spanish or Portuguese descent: SEPHARDIM
jittery, balky, fretful: RESTIVE
jobholder who does little: CHAIRWARMER
job that is monumentally dirty: AUGEAN STABLES
jockey's (short) whip: BAT
joined together: CONJUNCTIVE
jointed: ARTICULATED
joint formed in carpentry: MITER
joint government or authority shared by two men: DUUMVIRATE
joke, mischief: WAGGERY
joke, mock: JAPE
joke or witticism that is brief and self-contained: ONE-LINER
joker: WAG
joker in a card deck: MISTIGRIS
joker, wag: FARCEUR

joke that is a one-liner with an adverbial pun: **TOM SWIFTIE**

jolt, bounce, shake up and down: **JOUNCE**

jolting of the neck or base of the brain, as in an automobile crash: **WHIPLASH**

jot: **TITTLE**

journalism advocating a cause or purveying a viewpoint or opinion: **ADVOCACY JOURNALISM**

journalism that is irresponsibly sensational or exploitive: **YELLOW JOURNALISM**

journalism that is routine and hackneyed in style: **MORKRUMBO**

journalistically spontaneous, unconventional and often outrageous in approach or style: **GONZO**

journalists' corps or profession, the press: **FOURTH ESTATE**

journey, expedition: **SAFARI**

journey, laborious trip: **TREK**

journey made for safety or as an escape: **HEGIRA**

journey, usually short and for pleasure: **JAUNT**

joyful, triumphant: **JUBILANT**

joyful, vigorous, vital, spirited: **EXUBERANT**

joy of living: **JOIE DE VIVRE**

joy to the utmost, ecstasy: **RAPTURE**

J-shaped: **UNCIFORM**

jubilant, triumphant, joyful: **EXULTANT**

judge: **ADJUDICATE**

judge: **ARBITER**

judge's private room in court: **CAMERA**

judgment being lacking: **INJUDICIOUS**

judgment, personally, as to something's being either good or bad: **VALUE JUDGMENT**

judicial, definitive, established by decree: **DECRETORY**

judicial order requiring one to take, or refrain from, certain action: **INJUNCTION**

jug or mug in the form of an old man wearing a three-cornered hat: **TOBY**

jug or pitcher with a wide mouth: **EWER**

jug that is narrow-necked and often enclosed in wickerwork: **DEMIJOHN**

juice of grapes or other fruit that is unfermented: **MUST**

juicy: **SUCCULENT**

July and August hot sultry days: **DOG DAYS**

jumbled heap: **AGGLOMERATE**

jumbled, topsy-turvy, disordered: **HIGGLEDY-PIGGLEDY**

jumble, slew, accumulation that is confusing: **WELTER**

jumping-off place: **SPRINGBOARD**

jumpy, shy: **SKITTISH**

jungle or wilds primitive communication: **BUSH TELEGRAPH**

junk dealer, seller of trash: **SCHLOCKMEISTER**

junk, trash, rubbish: **DRECK**

junky, showy and worthless: **GIMCRACK**

jurors summoned to fill vacancies: **TALES**

jury of twelve selected after each party strikes a given number of names from a panel: **STRUCK JURY**

justice, prudence, temperance and fortitude: **CARDINAL VIRTUES**

justice that is ideal, with the good rewarded and the evil punished: **POETIC JUSTICE**

justify, acquit, restore: **VINDICATE**

justify, provide sufficient grounds for: **WARRANT**

just right, appropriate: **PAT**

juvenile, trivial, silly: **PUERILE**

juxtaposition of words, one to explain the other: **APPOSITION**

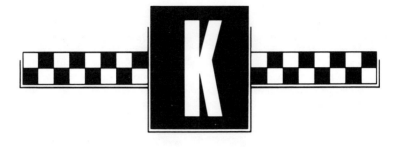

Kabuki actor playing female roles:
ONNAGATA
karate hand-held sticks joined by a
chain or rope: NUNCHAKU,
NUNCHAKUS, NUN-CHUCKS,
KARATE STICKS
karate-like but more aggressive
(Korean) martial art stressing
punches, chokes and leaping kicks:
TAE KWON DO
karate-like Chinese art of self-defense:
KUNG-FU
karate-like martial art emphasizing
balance and slow, stylized
movements: T'AI CHI CH'UAN
karate-like martial art emphasizing
gripping of the opponent's arms:
AIKIDO
keen, acute as in pleasure or pain:
EXQUISITE
keen, cutting, acute, sharp: INCISIVE
keen, discerning, perceptive:
PERSPICACIOUS
keen, discriminating: SUBTLE
keen, incisive: TRENCHANT
keenly desirous, as for food: SHARP-SET
keenness of mind: ACUMEN
keep back, suppress: STIFLE
keeper, guard, watchman: WARDER
keeper or withholder of something he
or she doesn't need: DOG IN THE
MANGER
keep out or discriminate against certain
people: BLACKLIST
keep vigil, go without sleep: WATCH
kept man: GIGOLO
kerchief worn by Arabs over the head
and shoulders: KAFFIYEH
kerchief worn on head: BABUSHKA
kettledrums: TIMPANI

keyhole-shaped: CLITHRIDIATE
key that is all-purpose, passkey, master
key: PASSE-PARTOUT
key to admission or success, entrée,
access: OPEN SESAME
key to hieroglyphics: ROSETTA STONE
kidnap: ABDUCT
kidney bean and other edible beans:
HARICOT
kidney disease: NEPHRITIS
kidney removal by surgery:
NEPHRECTOMY
kidney stone: NEPHROLITH
kill by choking: STRANGLE
killer who pathologically murders
repeatedly and often
indiscriminately: SERIAL KILLER
killing action: QUIETUS
killing a person upon secret official
order or contract: EXECUTIVE
ACTION
killing of a human being by another:
HOMICIDE
killing of a king: REGICIDE
killing of a legislative bill by a chief
executive: VETO
killing of one's brother or one's
countryman: FRATRICIDE
killing of one's sister: SORORICIDE
killjoy, pessimist, depressing person:
CRAPEHANGER, CREPEHANGER
kill or destroy a large portion of:
DECIMATE
kilt: FILLEBEG, FILEBEG
kind in disposition: BENIGN
kindly disposed, auspicious: PROPITIOUS
kind or type, as in art or literature:
GENRE
kind, sort, class: ILK

King Arthur's legendary court site: **CAMELOT**

kingdom, imaginary, of proverbial romance and picturesqueness: **RURITANIA**

king-killing: **REGICIDE**

king's deputy who rules a country, colony, etc.: **VICEROY**

kinship, nearness: **PROPINQUITY**

kissing: **OSCULATION**

kiss of betrayal or treachery: **JUDAS KISS**

kiss-off love letter: **DEAR JOHN**

kitchen utensil with small holes through which potatoes and other foods are pressed: **RICER**

kite-like glider with a pilot harness for gliding off a cliff: **HANG GLIDER**

knack: **INSTINCT**

knapsack: **RUCKSACK**

knee and back-of-thigh tendon: **HAMSTRING**

kneecap: **PATELLA**

knee (hammered) reflex, knee jerk: **PATELLAR TENDON REFLEX**

knee inflammation: **HOUSEMAID'S KNEE**

kneel on one knee, as in worship: **GENUFLECT**

knickerbockers extra long and sporty: **PLUS-FOURS**

knickknacks: **BRIC-A-BRAC**

knife-sharpening stone: **WHETSTONE**

knife that is sword-like: **SNICKERSNEE**

knife with a folded-in blade that springs open when a button is pressed: **SWITCH-BLADE KNIFE**

knife with a handle at each end: **DRAWKNIFE**

knife with the blade at a right angle to the handle: **FROE**

knight's usually sleeveless garment worn over the armor: **TABARD**

knitted fabric that is machine-made: **TRICOT**

knitted to follow the contour of the leg or body: **FULL-FASHIONED**

knitting stitch that gives a ribbed appearance: **PURL**

knobby: **TOROSE**

knob, knot, or swelling: **NODE**

knock about, cuff: **BUFFET**

knock-kneed condition: **VALGUS**

knock on wood: **ABSIT OMEN**

knoll or hillock: **HUMMOCK**

knot or bun of hair worn by women at the back of the head: **CHIGNON**

knot that forms a loop having no free ends: **HARNESS HITCH**

knowing all things, all-knowing: **OMNISCIENT**

knowing, perception: **COGNITION**

knowing something before it occurs: **PRESCIENCE**

knowledge: **KEN**

knowledgeable or familiar with a subject: **CONVERSANT**

knowledge derived from sense perception: **PERCEPT**

knowledge of something without conscious attention or reasoning: **INTUITION**

knowledge of the right thing to say or do: **SAVOIR-FAIRE**

knowledge or cognition as a subject of study: **EPISTEMOLOGY**

knowledge, skill: **EXPERTISE**

knowledge that is superficial: **SCIOLISM**

known or able to be known, characterized by awareness: **PRESENTATIVE**

"l" pronounced like "r" or "w," or "r"
  pronounced like "l": **LALLATION**
label someone as infamous: **BRAND**
labored, clumsy: **PONDEROUS**
laborer on river vessels or on the
  waterfront: **ROUSTABOUT**
laborer, unskilled worker (British):
  NAVVY
labor, toil: **TRAVAIL**
labyrinth monster with a human body
  and a bull's head: **MINOTAUR**
lace in which patterns are held together
  by connecting threads rather than
  by a net ground: **GUIPURE**
lace-like ornamental work or design:
  FILIGREE
lackadaisical: **LANGUID**
lackadaisical, indifferent, apathetic:
  LISTLESS
lacking animation, weak, listless:
  LANGUID
lacking any easing: **UNMITIGATED**
lacking common measure or a standard
  of comparison:
  INCOMMENSURABLE
lacking fulfillment, unsuccessful:
  MANQUÉ
lacking particular character, not
  distinctive: **NONDESCRIPT**
lacking understanding: **PURBLIND**
lack in meeting a goal or the amount or
  degree of this deficiency:
  SHORTFALL
lack of control of urinating or
  defecating: **INCONTINENCE**
lack of energy: **ANERGY**
lack of power or ability, impotence:
  IMPUISSANCE
lack of understanding between two
  generations: **GENERATION GAP**

lack, scarcity, famine: **DEARTH**
ladder hung over the side of a ship:
  ACCOMMODATION LADDER
ladies' man, seducer of women:
  LOTHARIO
lady's maid: **ABIGAIL**
lag, follow slowly, drag in the mud:
  DRABBLE
lake-like or involving a lake or lakes:
  LACUSTRINE
lake or pond that is shallow and near a
  larger body of water or that is
  enclosed by an atoll: **LAGOON**
lake surface waving movement: **SEICHE**
lamb chunks broiled on a skewer:
  SHASHLIK
lamb or other meat chunks skewered
  and broiled with tomatoes, onions,
  peppers: **SHISH KEBAB**
lambskin or calfskin that is untanned:
  KIP
lamentation or mourning in verse or
  song: **ELEGY**
lament by wailing for the deceased:
  KEEN
lament, woeful tale, complaint:
  JEREMIAD
lampshade framework or spokes:
  SPIDER
lampshade's metal loop above the
  lightbulb: **HARP**
lamp with light directed upward by a
  bowl reflector: **TORCHIER**
land-and-water vehicle or creature:
  AMPHIBIAN
land between hills, especially along a
  river: **INTERVALE**
land cultivation based on scientific
  principles: **AGRONOMY**

land extending in a narrow point from the shore into the water: **SPIT**

land extending into the sea, the high point of it: **PROMONTORY**

landing of a plane using only electronic signals: **INSTRUMENT LANDING**

landing of a spacecraft on water: **SPLASHDOWN**

landing place, dock on a river or waterway: **EMBARCADERO**

landlord who lets slum dwellings run down: **SLUMLORD**

land or soil being capable of being cultivated: **ARABLE**

land or territory projection, narrow extension: **PANHANDLE**

land projecting into water: **PENINSULA**

land strip plowed or cleared to prevent the spread of fire: **FIREBREAK**

land tenure or distribution, involving: **AGRARIAN**

land that is unclaimed, unoccupied or indefinite: **NO-MAN'S-LAND**

land, usually a narrow strip, extending into a body of water and connecting two larger land masses: **ISTHMUS**

language aptitude or instinct, feeling for idiom and usage: **SPRACHGEFÜHL**

language as a science or a study: **LINGUISTICS**

language expert, word authority: **LOGOGOGUE**

language, idiom, speaking style: **PARLANCE**

language, informal and substandard, that consists of coined words, new meanings of existing words and often colorful metaphors: **SLANG**

language invented for international use: **ESPERANTO**

language lacking sincere meaning or intention: **RHETORIC**

language making no sense: **JABBERWOCKY**

language mixture: **POLYGLOT**

language native to an area, common rather than literary language: **VERNACULAR**

language, official, that is deliberately ambiguous and deceptive (Orwell coinage): **NEWSPEAK**

language or grammatical forms that are customary: **USAGE**

language-origin theory that mankind's first utterances were imitative of sounds in nature, such as those of animals, water or thunder: **BOWWOW THEORY**

language-origin theory that mankind's first utterances were interjections that gradually acquired meanings: **POOH-POOH THEORY**

language-origin theory that mankind's first utterances were spontaneous vocal reactions: **DINGDONG THEORY**

language-related, linguistic: **LINGUAL**

language's smallest meaningful unit: **MORPHEME**

language study that assumes a formal system of signs and examines their nature and arrangement: **STRUCTURAL LINGUISTICS**

language that conceals: **AESOPIAN LANGUAGE**

language that is an amalgam of two different languages and evolves as a simplified form of one of them: **PIDGIN**

language that is pretentious gibberish: **GOBBLEDYGOOK**

language that was a pidgin but has become the native form of speech in a community: **CREOLE**

language theory that stresses tagmemes, the smallest meaningful grammatical forms: **TAGMEMICS**

language, usually hybrid, that is used as a common speech by people having different tongues: **LINGUA FRANCA**

lapel of a coat: **REVERS**

large and powerful creature or thing, monstrosity: **BEHEMOTH**

large, as capital letters: **MAJUSCULE**

large groups involved make something: **MACROSCOPIC**

large system regarded as a unity: **MACROCOSM**

lasso, lariat: **RIATA**

last and often inferior remnant: **RUMP**

lasting a short time, transitory, fleeting: **EPHEMERAL**

lasting condition, sometimes specifically for life: **PERPETUITY**

lasting or continuing a long time: **CHRONIC**

lasting through the year: **PERENNIAL**

last part or remnant, usually of no further use: **FAG END**

last resort or recourse, expedient alternative: **PIS ALLER**

last stage of any journey or project: **HOMESTRETCH**

late-blossoming: **SEROTINOUS**

latecomer or newcomer: **JOHNNY-COME-LATELY**

later, soon, shortly: **ANON**

latest fashion, trend or word: **DERNIER CRI**

latest stage, as of technological research or progress: **CUTTING EDGE**

Latin American of mixed ancestry: **LADINO, MESTIZO**

Latin American term for a foreigner, especially an American or Englishman: **GRINGO**

latitude, additional space for freedom of action: **LEEWAY**

laughable or having the power to laugh: **RISIBLE**

laugh at with contempt: **DERIDE**

laugh immoderately or noisily: **CACHINNATE**

laughing: **RIANT**

laughing gas: **NITROUS OXIDE**

laugh or laughter outburst: **YUK**

laughter in a loud and boisterous burst: **GUFFAW**

laughter that is uproarious and irrepressible: **HOMERIC LAUGHTER**

launch at high speed: **CATAPULT**

lavish, bountiful: **MUNIFICENT**

lavish, copious, generous: **PROFUSE**

lavish, overflowing: **EXUBERANT**

lavish, wasteful, extravagant: **PRODIGAL**

law and its administration, as a science: **JURISPRUDENCE**

law based on usage rather than legislation: **UNWRITTEN LAW**

lawbreaker whose violations are habitual: **SCOFFLAW**

law case in which an accident's mere occurrence indicates defendant's negligence: **RES IPSA LOQUITUR**

law derived from custom, usage or court opinions: **COMMON LAW**

law, especially of a municipal body: **ORDINANCE**

law-establishing, legislative: **NOMOTHETIC**

lawful: **LICIT**

lawful act performed in an unlawful way: **MISFEASANCE**

law jargon: **GRIMGRIBBER**

lawless confusion: **ANARCHY**

lawmaker, particularly a wise one: **SOLON**

law of locality not applied to foreign diplomats: **DIPLOMATIC IMMUNITY**

laws that are puritanically strict and prohibitive: **BLUE LAWS**

laws to protect investors against securities frauds: **BLUE SKY LAWS**

lawsuit: **LITIGATION**

lawsuit on behalf of a group: **CLASS ACTION**

law that limits the time during which a particular legal action may be brought: **STATUTE OF LIMITATIONS**

law violation less serious than a felony: **MISDEMEANOR**

lawyer expelled from the profession is: **DISBARRED**

lawyer, not highly competent, who deals with small cases: **PETTIFOGGER**

lawyer who is unethical or deceitful: **SHYSTER**

lawyer who opportunistically seeks out accident victims for business: **AMBULANCE CHASER**

laxative: **APERIENT**

layer, bed, grade: **STRATUM**

laziness in self-assertion: **LACHES**

lazy: **SHIFTLESS**

lazy: **SLOTHFUL**

lazy, idle: **INDOLENT**

lazy person: **SLUGGARD**

lazy person, idler: **FAINÉANT**

lazy person, loafer: **LAYABOUT**

lazy, useless, futile: **OTIOSE**

lead astray: **DELUDE**

leader: **BELLWETHER**

leader, chief: **COCK OF THE WALK**

leader, chief: **HONCHO**

leader, inspirer or activator, as of a group: **SPARK PLUG**

leaderless: **ACEPHALOUS**

leader of singing in church: **PRECENTOR**

leader, one who sets an example: **FUGLEMAN**

leadership or domination of one state over another: **HEGEMONY**

leadership person lacking real power: **FIGUREHEAD**

leadership quality that captures imagination and inspires loyalty: CHARISMA

leaders of new movements, especially in the arts: AVANT-GARDE

leader who appeals to prejudices and passions: DEMAGOGUE

leading character in a drama or a cause: PROTAGONIST

leading to: CONDUCIVE

lead poisoning: PLUMBISM, SATURNISM

lead taker, setter of a pace for others: PACESETTER

leaf-like architectural ornament: ACANTHUS

leafy: FOLIATE

leak out, become known: TRANSPIRE

lean in body structure: ECTOMORPHIC

leaning, bent, liking, tendency: INCLINATION

leaning, lying down, reclining: RECUMBENT

leaning, usually toward something objectionable: PROCLIVITY

leaning, weighing or resting upon something: INCUMBENT

lean, thin: SPARE

leap year's extra day, Feb. 29: BISSEXTILE DAY

learned person: PUNDIT

learned person in many fields, polyhistor: POLYMATH

learned person in many fields, polymath: POLYHISTOR

learned person, scholar: SAVANT

learned response: CONDITIONED REFLEX

learned, scholarly: ERUDITE

learner: ABECEDARIAN

learning, a branch of: DISCIPLINE

learning or attachment by offspring that usually occurs early and is long-lasting in effect: IMPRINTING

learning or teaching through discovery and investigation: HEURISTICS

learn the facts, fathom: PLUMB

least amount possible: AMBSACE

leather-like: CORIACEOUS

leather produced by some process not using tanning liquor: TAW

leather shorts worn with suspenders in Bavaria: LEDERHOSEN

leather used for bookbinding: SKIVER

leave one country to settle in another: EMIGRATE

leavetaking or dismissal: CONGÉ

leaving in mass numbers, general flight, group emigration: EXODUS

leaving one's faith, party or principles: APOSTASY

leaving quickly or sneakily: FRENCH LEAVE

lecherous, lewd, obscene: SALACIOUS

lecherous man: SATYR

lecherous or malicious look: LEER

lecture or political dinner circuit: RUBBER CHICKEN CIRCUIT

lecturer, tutor, teacher without faculty rank: DOCENT

lecture, sermonize: PRELECT

lecture that is brief and sets forth details: BRIEFING

lecture with diagrams made on blackboard: CHALK TALK

left- and right-handed: AMBIDEXTROUS

left-handed: SINISTRAL

left-handedness: MANCINISM

left-hand page of a book: VERSO

leftover: REMNANT

leftover or miscellaneous item, remnant: ODDMENT

leftover part, remainder: RESIDUE

left side as opposed to the right side or dexter, especially in heraldry: SINISTER

left side of a vessel or plane as one faces forward: PORT

legal arrangement by which diplomatic corps members are exempt from local law: DIPLOMATIC IMMUNITY

legal authority to act for another: POWER OF ATTORNEY

legalistic gobbledygook: GRIMGRIBBER

legal, legitimate, respectable: ON-THE-UP-AND-UP

legally based, or authorized, by law: DE JURE

legally settled matter: CHOSE JUGÉE

legal questions to which medical knowledge is applied: MEDICAL JURISPRUDENCE

legal-rights advisory read to apprehended suspects (based on *Miranda* v. *Arizona*, 1966): MIRANDA WARNING

legal right to use and profit from the property of another: USUFRUCT

leg instep and above-ankle cloth or leather covering above the shoe: GAITER, SPAT legislative bill's added clause or section: **RIDER**

legislative body's calling to account of an administrative official: **INTERPELLATION**

legislative, law-establishing: **NOMOTHETIC**

legislatively having two houses or chambers: **BICAMERAL**

legislative receptacle, figuratively, for bills to be taken up at a future time: **HOPPER**

legitimize in appearance illegal moneys: **LAUNDER**

leg or arm stiffness or cramp: **CHARLEY HORSE**

legs far apart: **ASTRIDE**

legs kicked out alternately from a squatting position in this Slavic folk dance by a male: **KAZATSKY**

leg-warming footless stockings for dance classes, exercise, etc.: **LEG WARMERS**

leisurely gait: **AMBLE**

lender of his or her name: **PRÊT-NOM**

lender who charges illegal rates of interest: **LOAN SHARK**

lengthened toward the poles: **PROLATE**

length measurement of old, from elbow to the tip of the middle finger, or approximately 20 inches: **CUBIT**

lenient: **INDULGENT**

lenient, tolerating unusual freedom: **PERMISSIVE**

lens used in a camera or projector that adjusts rapidly for close-up or distance shots while holding focus: **ZOOM LENS**

lesbian and acting as a feminine partner: **FEMME**

lesbian and acting as a masculine partner: **BUTCH**

lesbianism: **SAPPHISM**

lesbianism: **TRIBADISM**

lessen: **ABATE**

lessen: **ABRIDGE**

lessen, diminish: **DWINDLE**

lessening, decrease, diminution: **DECREMENT**

lessening of productivity in proportion to increase in expenditure: **DIMINISHING RETURNS**

lessening of speed: **RETARDATION**

lessen in quality or value, make worse: **IMPAIR**

lessen the guilt or odiousness of an offense: **EXTENUATE**

less severe, more moderate, milder: **MITIGATED**

less than one would expect: **NOMINAL**

let go, give up: **RELINQUISH**

lethargy: **HEBETUDE**

let it stand (a direction used in proofreading): **STET**

letter delivered from the same post office at which it was posted: **DROP LETTER**

lettered in forms like rounded capitals, as in ancient Greek and Latin manuscripts: **UNCIAL**

letter jilting a person: **DEAR JOHN**

letter or figure above and to the side of a character: **SUPERSCRIPT**

letter or figure below and to the side of a character: **SUBSCRIPT**

letter- or letters-related, involving correspondence: **EPISTOLARY**

letter or sound inserted into a word: **EPENTHESIS**

letter that each member of a group signs: **ROUND ROBIN**

letter that is long and formal: **EPISTLE**

letter with flourishes that is ornamental: **SWASH LETTER**

letting business act without regulation: **LAISSEZ-FAIRE**

level land with few or no trees: **SAVANNA**

level, made horizontal, flattened: **COMPLANATE**

level of command: **ECHELON**

level to the ground, demolish: **RAZE**

lewd, grossly ribald: **ITHYPHALLIC**

lewd, lascivious: **LUBRICIOUS**

lewd, lustful: **LECHEROUS**

lewd, obscene, lecherous: **SALACIOUS**

lewd or dissipated person: **DEBAUCHEE**

lewd or wanton: **CYPRIAN**

lewd, sexually abandoned: **LICENTIOUS**

lewd, sexually aroused: **RANDY**

liability or debt gradually extinguished, as by installment payments, is: **AMORTIZED**

liability to conviction and punishment: **JEOPARDY**

liable, possible: **CONTINGENT**

liable to err, to be misled or to be deceived: **FALLIBLE**

liable to injury, attack or criticism: **VULNERABLE**

liar: **ANANIAS**
liberal or radical political figure: **LEFTIST**
liberal or unorthodox in attitudes or beliefs: **LATITUDINARIAN**
liberate, free, emancipate: **MANUMIT**
lie: **PREVARICATE**
lie detector: **POLYGRAPH**
lie, equivocate: **PALTER**
lie, falsehood: **FABRICATION**
lie or lean in a relaxed manner: **LOLL**
lie that is trivial and told to be polite or spare someone's feelings: **WHITE LIE**
life and matter viewed as inseparable: **HYLOZOISM**
life force, creative principle in living things: **ÉLAN VITAL**
life generation from living organisms only: **BIOGENESIS**
life insurance policy in which the payment is double the face value in case of accidental death: **DOUBLE INDEMNITY**
life is like that: **C'EST LA VIE**
lifeless, automatic: **MECHANICAL**
lifeless state: **ABIOSIS**
life-like three-dimensional image produced by a laser process: **HOLOGRAM**
life-manifesting: **VITAL**
lifesaving anti-choking squeeze of the upper abdomen: **HEIMLICH MANEUVER**
lifesaving technique involving mouth-to-mouth resuscitation: **CPR (CARDIOPULMONARY RESUSCITATION)**
life-size drawing or illustration: **MACROGRAPH**
life's work of an artist: **OEUVRE**
lift to test weight or gauge: **HEFT**
lift up your hearts (part of the Mass): **SURSUM CORDA**
light according to wavelengths: **SPECTRUM**
light-admitting but not transparent: **TRANSLUCENT**
light, airy, spiritual: **ETHEREAL**
light and frothy dish fixed in that condition by adding beaten egg whites: **SOUFFLÉ**
light and shade, black and white: **CHIAROSCURO**
light beam that passes over a surface for television or other production: **SCAN**
lightbulb thread-like conductor that glows: **FILAMENT**
light emanating from certain organisms: **BIOLUMINESCENCE**
light emitted by a substance after exposure to some form of energy: **PHOSPHORESCENCE**
lighthearted: **BUOYANT**
lighthearted, carefree, unconcerned: **INSOUCIANT**
lighthearted, gay, carefree: **ROLLICKING**
lightheartedness: **RHATHYMIA**
lighthouse: **PHAROS**
light meal: **COLLATION**
lightness, gaiety that is inappropriate, frivolity, fickleness: **LEVITY**
lightning without thunder, in fitful play usually near the horizon on hot evenings: **HEAT LIGHTNING**
light or heat ray bent in its passage from one medium to another: **REFRACTION**
light-producing or light-conveying: **LUMINIFEROUS**
light reflected by a celestial body, cloud, snow, etc.: **ALBEDO**
light-resistant, dull: **OPAQUE**
light thrown by a candle on one square foot of surface one foot away: **FOOT-CANDLE**
light up, make clear, enlighten, illuminate: **IRRADIATE**
light-wave or sound-wave change that seems to accompany a change in distance between source and observer: **DOPPLER EFFECT**
light wind: **CAT'S-PAW**
like it or not: **WILLY-NILLY**
likeness, image, representation, usually crudely done, of a disliked person: **EFFIGY**
likeness in sound: **ASSONANCE**
likeness to what is real or true, truthful representation: **VERISIMILITUDE**
likening one thing to something else in a figure of speech using "like" or "as": **SIMILE**
liking for something: **PENCHANT**
liking, tendency, trend, leaning or bent: **INCLINATION**
limber, bending easily and gracefully: **LITHE**
limit, boundary: **PARAMETER**

limited, as by human or natural conditions: FINITE

limited, narrow, provincial: PAROCHIAL

limit freedom: TRAMMEL

limiting of damage, loss, adverse publicity, etc.: DAMAGE CONTROL

limitless: AD INFINITUM

limitless, vast: INFINITE

limit or range, as of power or action: TETHER

limits: AMBIT

limp, flabby, not firm or vigorous, weak: FLACCID

linear markings: STRIATION

line, as of men or ships, enclosing an area: CORDON

lined: LINEATE

linen for a household: NAPERY

line over a vowel indicating a long sound: MACRON

lines-in-parallel marking on a product to indicate classification and price electronically: BAR CODE, UNIVERSAL PRODUCT CODE (UPC)

lines that make up a page, an article, an ad, etc.: LINAGE

line that slants, used in printing or writing: VIRGULE

linger, walk aimlessly: LOITER

lingo, cant: JARGON

linguistical study of the structure of words: MORPHOLOGY

linguistic boundary line: ISOGLOSS

linguistic law accounting for certain exceptions to Grimm's law: VERNER'S LAW

linguistic law accounting for consonant changes in languages from Proto-Indo-European to Germanic: GRIMM'S LAW

link, connection, bond: NEXUS

linked things or events: CONCATENATION

lion-like: LEONINE

lip deformity consisting of a cleft, usually on the upper lip: HARELIP

lip-like: LABIATE

lip movement without sound: MUSSITATION

lip-piercing ornament: LABRET

liqueurs served in layers: POUSSE-CAFÉ

liquid measure of 63 or more gallons: HOGSHEAD

liquid medicine: POTION

liquid poured ceremonially, as in honor of a deity: LIBATION

liquid-surface-with-solid attraction or repulsion: CAPILLARY ACTION

liquor mixed with water, soda or ginger ale and served in a tall glass: HIGHBALL

liquor quantity, a fifth of a gallon: FIFTH

listen: HARK

listener whose patience, response or opinion is useful: SOUNDING BOARD

listen in at a college class: AUDIT

listening distance: EARSHOT

listless: LACKADAISICAL

listless discontent or weariness, boredom: ENNUI

listless, inactive, indolent: SUPINE

listless, lacking animation, weak: LANGUID

list of acknowledgments in film or TV show: CREDITS

list of acknowledgments in film or TV show that moves upward vertically on screen: CRAWL

list of articles on hand with description and quantity of each: INVENTORY

list of candidates: SLATE

list of goods being shipped: WAYBILL

list of merchandise sent or services rendered as well as price to purchaser: INVOICE

list of names: ROSTER

list of securities held by a person or an institution: PORTFOLIO

list of supplications, with a fixed response after each: LITANY

list, with definitions, of technical, obscure or foreign words of a work or field: GLOSSARY

literal translation of a word or construction from one language to another: LOAN TRANSLATION

literary attack: COUP DE PLUME

literary club: ATHENEUM

literary composition in a mixture of languages: MACARONIC

literary effort that is labored and pedantic: LUCUBRATION

literary group, artists' group: CENACLE

literary imitator or follower: EPIGONE

literary or artistic premise: DONNEE

literary or bookish woman, pedantic female: BLUESTOCKING

literary passage used as a classic or illustrative model: LOCUS CLASSICUS

literary professional, man or woman of letters: LITTERATEUR

literary rendering of the thoughts and feelings of a character: INTERIOR MONOLOGUE

literary study or scholarship: PHILOLOGY

literary thought, cogent or provocative observation: PENSÉE

literary work that is short, depicting something subtly: VIGNETTE

literature: BELLES-LETTRES

literature or art of a cheap, popular or sentimental quality: KITSCH

lithe, pliant, supple, agile: LISSOME

little by little: INCHMEAL

little or a bit, rather, somewhat: TAD

little universe: MICROCOSM

live in distressing conditions: LANGUISH

live in the country or adopt a country way of life: RUSTICATE

livelihood, food, means of support: SUSTENANCE

liveliness: ALACRITY

liveliness: BRIO

lively, active, spirited: VIVACIOUS

lively, aggressive: FEISTY

lively behavior: TITTUP

lively, brisk, dashing, self-confident: JAUNTY

lively, changeable, volatile: MERCURIAL

lively, cheerful, urbane: DEBONAIR

lively, energetic: VIBRANT

lively or playful movement in music: SCHERZO

lively person: GRIG

lively, quickly, briskly, in music: VIVACE

lively, racy: PIQUANT

lively, saucy: PERT

lively spirits, vivacity, gaiety, sparkle: EFFERVESCENCE

live now, seize the day: CARPE DIEM

live or reside in, occupy as a home: INHABIT

live passively, monotonously or dully: VEGETATE

liver degenerative disease: CIRRHOSIS

liver inflammation: HEPATITIS

live together: COHABIT

live well at another's expense: BATTEN

living, biologically, in different or isolated regions: ALLOPATRIC

living, biologically, in the same region: SYMPATRIC

living together of dissimilar organisms, usually in a mutually advantageous partnership: SYMBIOSIS

load that a missile can lift and carry to a target: THROW-WEIGHT

loafer, lazy person: LAYABOUT

loafer or idler who lives off others: DRONE

loafer, spendthrift: WASTREL

loan or prepayment of money from public funds: IMPREST

loan that may be terminated at any time: CALL LOAN

loathing: ABHORRENCE

loathsome, hateful, repugnant, disgusting: ODIOUS

lobby, entrance hall: FOYER

lobster liver, considered a delicacy: TOMALLEY

local or civic promotionalism and optimism: BOOSTERISM

locking hinged metal plate with a slot used with a padlock or pin: HASP

lock in the form of a springless bolt shifted by turning a key: DEAD BOLT

lockjaw: TRISMUS

locomotive's jutting triangular frame to clear tracks (steam locomotive): COWCATCHER

lodging for soldiers in a private home: BILLET

lodging place that is part-time, occasional or temporary: PIED-À-TERRE

lofty, extravagant, overly ambitious, pretentious: HIGH-FLOWN

lofty, impressive or noble, as in quality or style: SONOROUS

logical argument in examining ideas or opinions: DIALECTIC

logical pedanticism: ERGOISM

logical rather than intuitive: DIANOETIC

logical reasoning from the general to the particular: DEDUCTION

logic formula in which two premises are laid down and a conclusion is drawn from them: SYLLOGISM

logic, reasoning from the particular to the general: INDUCTION logic that is faulty or specious: **CHOPLOGIC**

logic with regard to truth and error: **ALETHIOLOGY**

loincloth or waistcloth of printed calico worn by Samoan natives: **LAVALAVA, PAREU**

loincloth worn by Hindus: **DHOTI**

loiter, waste time: **DAWDLE**

Londoner of the East End: **COCKNEY**

London press: **FLEET STREET**

loner, outsider, person apart from others: **ODD MAN OUT**

long and boring passage: **LONGUEUR**

long and polysyllabic, as a word or words: **SESQUIPEDALIAN**

long and wordy, tedious: **PROLIX**

long-drawn-out explanation or narrative: **MEGILLAH**

long-drawn-out story or anecdote that is humorously pointless: **SHAGGY DOG STORY**

longheaded: **DOLICHOCEPHALIC**

longing for something distant in time or place: **NOSTALGIA**

long jump, as formerly known: **BROAD JUMP**

long life: **LONGEVITY**

long live: **VIVE, VIVA**

long or lengthy in shape: **ELONGATE**

long-sleeved robe, sashed, worn in Mediterranean countries: **CAFTAN**

long-term study or experiment: **LONGITUDINAL STUDY**

long time: **MONTH OF SUNDAYS**

long-winded: **DIFFUSE**

long-windedness: **CIRCUMLOCUTION**

longwindedness: **AEOLISM**

look at closely, scrutinize: **SCAN**

look, countenance, face: **VISAGE**

look like or act like someone or something: **SIMULATE**

look or appearance lacking reality: **SEMBLANCE**

look that implies malice, lechery or slyness: **LEER**

loop that is flexible, eyelet: **GROMMET**

loose in morals: **WANTON**

loosening-up remark, gesture, etc.: **ICEBREAKER**

loosen or limber up after exercise: **COOL DOWN**

loose, not rigid: **LAX**

loose, weak: **SLACK**

lopsided, unsymmetrical: **SKEWED**

Lord's Prayer, the Our Father: **PATERNOSTER**

Lord's Supper: **EUCHARIST**

lose heart, withdraw in fear: **QUAIL**

loser, hapless bungler: **SCHLIMAZEL**

losing contender, one expected to lose: **UNDERDOG**

loss from sale of assets: **CAPITAL LOSS**

loss of an unaccented vowel at the beginning of a word: **APHESIS**

loss of consciousness that is brief: **SYNCOPE**

loss of income anticipated from eventual reduction in the supply of natural resources: **DEPLETION**

loss of memory: **AMNESIA**

loss of muscular coordination: **ATAXIA**

loss of power of speech: **APHASIA**

loss of scientists, technicians, etc., to a country offering them more: **BRAIN DRAIN**

loss of sight without organic defect: **AMAUROSIS**

loss of willpower, inability to decide or act: **ABULIA**

loss or impairment of sense of taste: **AGEUSIA**

lottery, often based on a horse race, in which all the wagers may be won by one or a few bettors: **SWEEPSTAKES**

loud and abusive: **THERSITICAL**

loud and noisy: **UPROARIOUS**

loud, full-sounding: **SONOROUS**

loudness measure: **DECIBEL**

loud, rough in sound: **RAUCOUS**

loud to an extreme: **STENTORIAN**

loud-voiced person: **STENTOR**

Louisiana descendant of the Acadian French: **CAJUN**

louse infestation: **PEDICULOSIS**

love affair that is secret or illicit: **INTRIGUE**

love insincerely (applied to a man): **PHILANDER**

love letter: **BILLET-DOUX**

love of other people: **ALTRUISM**

love of women: **PHILOGYNY**

love potion: **PHILTER**

lover, illicit sexual companion: **PARAMOUR**

lover or gallant of a married woman: **CICISBEO**

lovers, secret meeting of: **ASSIGNATION**

love unbridled: **AMOUR FOU**

loving, inviting or seductive glances: **GOO-GOO EYES**

loving or fellowship feast: **AGAPE, LOVE FEAST**

low blood sugar: **HYPOGLYCEMIA**

lowdown, rumor, gossip: **SCUTTLEBUTT**

lower: **NETHER**

lower-class and considered shiftless: **LUMPEN**

lower in dignity or reputation: **DEMEAN**

lowering of esteem: **DISPARAGEMENT**

lower middle class: **PETITE BOURGEOISIE**

lower oneself to do something: **CONDESCEND**

lower price on a stock transaction than on the preceding transaction: **DOWN TICK, MINUS-TICK**

lower someone in prestige or estimation: **ABASE**

lowest point: **NADIR**

lowest point in an orbit: **PERIGEE**

low in condition or state, hopelessly downcast, desperate: **ABJECT**

low neckline in a dress: **DÉCOLLETAGE**

low-priced stocks, selling at less than $1 a share: **PENNY STOCKS**

loyal: **STAUNCH**

loyal adherent: **MYRMIDON**

loyalty, obligation owed, faithfulness: **FEALTY**

loyalty or friendship weakened or destroyed: **DISAFFECTION**

lozenge that is medicated, as for a sore throat: **TROCHE**

lucid, clear, understandable: **PERSPICUOUS**

lucid, pure, clear, transparent: **LIMPID**

lucky and unexpected gain or acquisition: **WINDFALL**

lucky discoveries made accidentally: **SERENDIPITY**

lucky stroke, good luck: **FLUKE**

ludicrous or ridiculous situation: **FARCE**

lukewarm: **TEPID**

lumbering, bulky: **PONDEROUS**

luminous, glowing with heat: **INCANDESCENT**

lump, bump, protuberance: **KNURL**

lunatic, maniacal: **DEMONIAC**

lunching at work or school on food brought from home: **BROWN BAGGING**

lurch or twist from side to side: **CAREEN**

lust for or desire something belonging to someone else: **COVET**

lustful: **LASCIVIOUS**

lustful: **LIBIDINOUS**

lustful, amorous: **RANDY**

lustful, dissolute: **WANTON**

lustful, lewd: **LECHEROUS**

lust, sexual desire: **CONCUPISCENCE**

luxurious, sensual: **VOLUPTUOUS**

luxury-loving person: **VOLUPTUARY**

lying: **MENDACIOUS**

lying abnormally: **MYTHOMANIA**

lying down, growing along the ground: **DECUMBENT**

lying down, reclining, leaning: **RECUMBENT**

lying face down: **PRONE**

lying flat, helpless, exhausted: **PROSTRATE**

lying-in, confinement for childbirth: **ACCOUCHEMENT**

lying on the back, face upward: **SUPINE**

lying, prevarication, falsehood, deception: **MENDACITY**

lying under oath: **PERJURY**

lyric poetry muse: **ERATO**

machine for giving gloss to paper or
fabric: **CALENDER**

machinery or technology opposer in the
workplace: **LUDDITE**

"madam-I'm-Adam" type of reversible
sentence: **PALINDROME**

madam (in imperial India): **MEMSAHIB**

mad, crazy: **DAFT**

maddened, furiously angry: **HORN-MAD**

made of different pieces or elements,
pieced together: **PATCHWORK**

made to order (British): **BESPOKE**

Mafia chief: **CAPO**

Mafia chief's second-in-command:
CAPOREGIME

Mafia code of silence: **OMERTÀ**

Mafia leader's close adviser:
CONSIGLIERE

Mafia member of low rank: **BUTTON,
SOLDIER**

magazine oriented to fans or amateurs,
as to science fiction buffs: **FANZINE**

magic: **CONJURATION**

magic: **THEURGY**

magical, mystical or divinatory arts:
OCCULT

magical, occult, relating to alchemy:
HERMETIC

magical, unintelligible words,
incantation: **MUMBO JUMBO**

magician: **THAUMATURGE**

magician, sorcerer: **CONJURER**

magic tricks: **PRESTIDIGITATION**

magic tricks: **SLEIGHT OF HAND**

magic word: **ABRACADABRA**

magic words or formula: **INCANTATION**

magnifying glass used by jewelers or
watchmakers: **LOUPE**

maiden name of a married woman
preceded by this word: **NÉE**

maid role in a play or the actress
playing it: **SOUBRETTE**

maid to a lady, lady's maid: **ABIGAIL**

mail piece undeliverable because of an
illegible or inadequate address:
NIXIE

mail sent without charge, as by
congressmen: **FRANKED MAIL**

maim by shooting in the knee:
KNEECAP

main clause of a sentence at the
beginning: **LOOSE SENTENCE**

main clause of the sentence completed
at the end: **PERIODIC SENTENCE**

main course of a meal: **ENTRÉE**

main dish or chief item in a collection:
PIÈCE DE RÉSISTANCE

main idea or substance of an argument,
discussion, question: **GIST**

main or central attraction: **FOCAL
POINT**

main or principal vein of ore: **MOTHER
LODE**

maintainable, defendable: **TENABLE**

majestic: **AUGUST**

make a face: **GRIMACE**

make amends for, atone for: **EXPIATE**

make eyes at suggestively, stare at:
OGLE

make known, disclose, bestow: **IMPART**

make merry, delight (in), celebrate:
REVEL

make noteworthy, call attention to:
SIGNALIZE

make or become better: **AMELIORATE**

make outwardly real: **EXTERNALIZE**

make over, renovate: **REVAMP**

make poor or fruitless: **IMPOVERISH**

makeshift materials utilized for tools,
decoration, etc.: **BRICOLAGE**

make specific: CONCRETIZE
make stupid or obtuse: HEBETATE
make to seem sweeter, more pleasant or appealing, etc.: SUGARCOAT
make up, be the parts or elements of, represent: CONSTITUTE
make up, compensate: COUNTERVAIL
make up, devise: CONCOCT
makeup of a book, newspaper, etc.: FORMAT
make up or invent, as a story or lie: FABRICATE
make worse or more severe, aggravate, worsen: EXACERBATE
making sense: COHERENT
male adoption of female clothing and mannerisms: EONISM
male and female sexual organs in one individual make him/her a: HERMAPHRODITE
male ballet dancer: DANSEUR
male ballet dancer who is the principal performer: PREMIER DANSEUR
male counterpart of a ballerina: DANSEUR NOBLE
male dominance or favoritism: ANDROCENTRISM
male figure used as a supporting pillar: TELAMON
male figure with pointed ears, horns and goat's legs, in Greek mythology: SATYR
male flirt: PHILANDERER
male genitalia or the phallus represented as the male principle in Hinduism: LINGAM
male genitals subjected to oral stimulation: FELLATIO
male government: PATRIARCHY
male head of household, father: PATERFAMILIAS
male homosexual: URANIST, URNING
male line of kinship, involving the: AGNATE
male of beef cattle: STEER
male sex hormone: ANDROGEN
male sex hormone, a type of androgen: TESTOSTERONE
male singer in the principal role: PRIM'ORO
male sterilization by surgery: VASECTOMY
malevolent: ILL-DISPOSED
malformation: ABNORMALITY
malfunction, foul-up, snag: GLITCH

malice, hate: RANCOR
malice, spite: VENOM
malicious, cutting: SNIDE
malicious, fierce, unruly: VICIOUS
malicious or lecherous look: LEER
malicious or mean behavior: DOGGERY
malicious, unprovoked, unjust: WANTON
malicious, wicked: PERNICIOUS
malicious, wishing evil toward others: MALEVOLENT
malignant, as a disease: VIRULENT
malnutrition: CACHEXIA
mammals bringing forth living young are: VIVIPAROUS
man about town: BOULEVARDIER
manageable, compliant: TRACTABLE
management, superintendance: INTENDANCE
manager of another's affairs: PROCURATOR
manager, sponsor or organizer of performers for entertainment: IMPRESARIO
manage shrewdly: MANIPULATE
manage to live: SUBSIST
man as center: ANTHROPOCENTRIC
maneuver by craftiness: FINAGLE
maneuver, especially in diplomacy: DÉMARCHE
maneuver for an advantage: JOCKEY
maneuvering, methods or management to gain an end: TACTICS
maneuvering with ploys to gain an advantage: GAMESMANSHIP
maneuver or stratagem to outwit someone: PLOY
maneuver, trick, device for obtaining advantage: STRATAGEM
mangle, cut unskillfully, hack: HAGGLE
mangle, tear raggedly: LACERATE
manhandle, abuse, handle roughly: MAUL
man hatred: MISANDRY
mania: CACOËTHES
maniacal, lunatic: DEMONIAC
manias (In the following list read the words obsession with ahead of each entry.)
alcoholic liquor: DIPSOMANIA
animals: ZOOMANIA
ballet: BALLETOMANIA
bees: APIMANIA
birds: ORNITHOMANIA
books: BIBLIOMANIA
cats: AILUROMANIA

children: PEDOMANIA
crowds: OCHLOMANIA
dancing: CHOREOMANIA
dogs: CYNOMANIA
eating: SITOMANIA
fire: PYROMANIA
fish: ICHTHYOMANIA
flowers: ANTHOMANIA
gaiety: CHEROMANIA
grandiose things: MEGALOMANIA
horses: HIPPOMANIA
ideas: IDEOMANIA
insects: ENTOMOMANIA
money: CHREMATOMANIA
nakedness: GYMNOMANIA
one subject or thing: MONOMANIA
pleasure: HEDONOMANIA
reptiles: OPHIDIOMANIA
roaming: DROMOMANIA
solitude: AUTOMANIA
speech: LALOMANIA
stealing: KLEPTOMANIA
stillness: EREMIOMANIA
wandering: DROMOMANIA
wealth: PLUTOMANIA
women: GYNEMANIA
manic-depressive condition that is mild:
　CYCLOTHYMIA
manifestation or appearance of a deity,
　showing forth: EPIPHANY
manifest, demonstrate convincingly,
　show clearly: EVINCE
manifest, evident, obvious: PATENT
man in relation to environment:
　ANTHROPONOMY
manipulation of parts of the body to
　correct diseases: OSTEOPATHY
manipulator of another person:
　SVENGALI
mankind hater: MISANTHROPE
man-like: ANDROID
man-like: HOMINOID
man-like or ape-like primate: HOMINID
manly vigor: VIRILITY
man (male) hater: MISANDRIST
manner: MIEN
manner in which one bears oneself,
　deportment: DEMEANOR
mannerism, personal peculiarity: QUIRK
mannerism, quirk, habit peculiar to an
　individual: IDIOSYNCRASY
manner of operating: MODUS OPERANDI
manner of speaking, way of talking,
　natural wording: FAÇON DE
　PARLER

manner of speech: LOCUTION
man of great beauty: ADONIS
man-of-prehistory specimen remains
　that proved to be a hoax:
　PILTDOWN MAN
man or boy who is not Jewish:
　SHEGETZ
man's nature regarded as consisting of
　decisive actions rather than inner
　dispositions: EXISTENTIALISM
man supported by a woman to whom
　he is not married: GIGOLO
man to man, in direct competition,
　dueling: MANO A MANO
man to whom a woman is engaged:
　FIANCÉ
manual, guidebook: HANDBOOK
manual, handbook: ENCHIRIDION
manual laborer (British): NAVVY
manual skill, expertness: HANDINESS
manual training system: SLOYD
manual worker: BLUE-COLLAR WORKER
manure heap: MIDDEN
manuscript copier: AMANUENSIS
manuscript of a play, film or television
　show: SCRIPT
manuscript sheets being gathered into a
　unified whole: COLLATED
manuscripts sent unsolicited to a
　publisher: SLUSH PILE
man who dresses flashily: DUDE
man-woman relationship without sexual
　activity is: PLATONIC
many and varied in form: MANIFOLD
many-headed serpent of classical
　mythology: HYDRA
many-sided: VERSATILE
maple sap tree spike that is hollow and
　drips into a pail: SPILE
mapmaking: CARTOGRAPHY
map of the earth with parallel longitude
　lines intersected by parallel latitude
　lines: MERCATOR PROJECTION
map or chart circle-and-star symbol:
　COMPASS ROSE
map or survey used for taxation basis:
　CADASTER
mapping of regions or districts:
　CHOROGRAPHY
mapping or charting of area in detail:
　TOPOGRAPHY
marble used for shooting: TAW
marching exercises or discipline:
　DISMOUNTED DRILL

marching in precise movements and formations: CLOSE-ORDER DRILL

marching manner that is close together: LOCKSTEP

marginal note of explanation: SCHOLIUM

marginal, not essential: PERIPHERAL

marijuana: CANNABIS

marijuana: GANJA

marine animal and plant organisms that drift or float: PLANKTON

marital: CONJUGAL

marital: CONNUBIAL

mark as questionable or doubtful (with an obelus, or dagger symbol): OBELIZE

mark between parts of a compound word: HYPHEN

marked with lines, striped: LINEATE

marker or memorial of heaped-up stones: CAIRN

marketable: VENDIBLE

market influence by several producers: OLIGOPOLY

market on the decline: BEAR MARKET

market on the rise: BULL MARKET

market, outdoor, for dealing in secondhand goods: FLEA MARKET

marketplace: AGORA

mark, in Arabic, like an apostrophe: HAMZA

marking of a spotted animal or plant: MACULATION

markings on an envelope used in place of stamps: INDICIA

mark like a hook under the letter "c" (ç): CEDILLA

mark, mark as infamous: BRAND

mark of authenticity: CACHET

mark of identification: EARMARK

mark of infamy or disgrace: STIGMA

mark or proof of genuineness or high quality: HALLMARK

mark or spot on a domino, die or playing card: PIP

mark out boundaries or limits, separate: DEMARCATE

mark out extent or limits: CIRCUMSCRIBE

mark, stamp or character that is distinctive: IMPRESS

mark used over or under certain foreign letters: DIACRITICAL MARK

marriageable because of physical maturity: NUBILE

marriage after the death or divorce of first spouse: DIGAMY

marriage a man is forced into because of prior sexual relations with the woman: SHOTGUN WEDDING

marriage between royal or noble unequals in which titles and estates are not passed on to the inferior partner is: MORGANATIC

marriage broker, Jewish: SCHATCHEN

marriage estrangement or breakup caused by another: ALIENATION OF AFFECTIONS

marriage for the second time: DEUTEROGAMY

marriage for the second time: DIGAMY

marriage in trial form: COMPANIONATE MARRIAGE

marriage late in life: OPSIGAMY

marriage outside the group or tribe: EXOGAMY

marriage within the group or tribe, inbreeding: ENDOGAMY

marriage with one of lower position: MÉSALLIANCE

married male American Indian: SANNUP

married man who was a long-time bachelor: BENEDICT

married woman: FEME COVERT

married woman's acknowledged lover or gallant: CICISBEO

married woman's legal status: COVERTURE

marrying while already married: BIGAMY

Mars as a study: AREOLOGY

marsh, bog: MORASS

marshy body of water: BAYOU

marshy ground, bog: QUAGMIRE

marshy low ground: SWALE

martial art (chiefly Japanese) of blows used in self-defense: KARATE

martial art emphasizing balance and slow, stylized movements: T'AI CHI CH'UAN

martial art emphasizing gripping of the opponent's arms: AIKIDO

martial arts sticks joined by a chain or rope: NUNCHAKU, NUNCHAKUS, NUN-CHUCKS, KARATE STICKS

martial art that is Korean and more aggressive than karate, stressing punches, chokes and leaping kicks: TAE KWON DO

martini served with pickled onion:
GIBSON
marvelous, wonderful: **PRODIGIOUS**
marvelous, wonderful to tell: **MIRABILE
DICTU**
Mary holding the body of Jesus
represented in art: **PIETÀ**
masculine in conduct or role: **BUTCH**
masculine, strong, sturdy: **VIRILE**
masculine woman: **AMAZON**
masculinity: **VIRILITY**
masculinity, aggressive virility:
MACHISMO
mask for the eyes, worn at
masquerades: **DOMINO**
masochism or sadism: **ALGOLAGNIA**
massacre, especially directed against
Jews: **POGROM**
massacre, slaughter: **CARNAGE**
massage system concentrating on the
feet and hands to benefit other
parts of the body: **REFLEXOLOGY**
massage that uses acupressure on
specific points of the body:
SHIATSU
masses: **DEMOS**
masses, common people: **HOI POLLOI**
masses, pertaining to: **DEMOTIC**
mass, heap or collection of things:
CONGERIES
mass-market advertising or the public
so influenced: **ADMASS**
mass of things indiscriminately thrown
together: **AGGLOMERATE**
master: **SAHIB**
master of technique: **VIRTUOSO**
masterpiece: **CHEF D'OEUVRE**
masterpiece, great work: **MAGNUM
OPUS**
masterstroke, sudden telling blow,
brilliant stratagem: **COUP**
mast-located high-up lookout platform
on a ship: **CROW'S NEST**
mast or boom on a sailboat: **SPAR**
masturbation: **AUTOEROTICISM**
masturbation or interruption of coitus:
ONANISM
masturbatory rubbing against another:
FROTTAGE
matador's red cloak used to lure the
bull: **CAPA**
matchbook striking surface: **FRICTION
STRIP**
matchless: **INIMITABLE**
matchless, unequaled: **NONPAREIL**

mate or complement to another:
COUNTERPART
materialize, concretize: **REIFY**
material, real, having definite shape:
TANGIBLE
maternal or female line of a family:
DISTAFF SIDE
maternal-side family name:
MATRONYMIC
mathematically incapable of being
expressed in rational numbers:
SURD
mathematical progression in which the
difference between numerical terms
remains constant: **ARITHMETIC
PROGRESSION**
mathematical sequence in which the
ratio between each two numbers is
the same: **GEOMETRIC
PROGRESSION**
mathematical term indicating parts into
which the whole is to be divided:
DENOMINATOR
mat or small napkin for table
decoration or under something:
DOILY
matter and energy as a science:
PHYSICS
mattress of straw: **PALLIASSE**
mature: **FULL-FLEDGED**
maxim: **APOTHEGM**
maxim: **AXIOM**
maxim, rule, moral guide: **PRECEPT**
maxim, wise saying: **GNOME**
maze, intricate structure: **LABYRINTH**
meal: **REPAST**
meal at which guests serve themselves:
BUFFET
meal-related, particularly dinner:
PRANDIAL
meals and room included in the hotel
rate: **AMERICAN PLAN**
meal served in a restaurant complete at
a fixed price: **TABLE D'HÔTE**
meal that is light: **REFECTION**
meal that is light and informal:
COLLATION
mean: **PETTY**
meaningless language or utterance:
JABBERWOCKY
meaningless or merely sociable as talk:
PHATIC
meaningless performance: **CHARADE**
meaningless speech: **BALDERDASH**
meaningless talk: **ABRACADABRA**

meaningless, worthless: NUGATORY

meaning, purport, general course: TENOR

meaning-related as applying to words or language forms: SEMANTIC

meanings of language forms as a subject of study: SEMANTICS

meaning that is exact as stated: LITERAL

meaning that is suggested, significance: PURPORT

mean keeper or withholder of something he or she doesn't need: DOG IN THE MANGER

meanly stingy or petty: MINGY

mean or malicious behavior: DOGGERY

mean or stingy practice: CHEESEPARING

means of support, livelihood, food: SUSTENANCE

meantime, time between periods or events: INTERIM

measure (about 9 inches), as made by the hand with the thumb and little finger extended: SPAN

measurement from side to side: BREADTH

measurement of advertising space: AGATE LINE

measurement of distance by determination of angles: TELEMETRY

measure of length for yarn: SPINDLE

measure that is practical rather than scientifically accurate: RULE OF THUMB

measure the depth of water: PLUMB

meat-and-vegetable stew and its broth: POT-AU-FEU

meat broiled on a skewer: BROCHETTE

meat chunks marinated: KEBAB

meat pie topped with mashed potatoes: SHEPHERD'S PIE

meat portion that is small: COLLOP

mechanical man, automaton: ROBOT

mechanical way of doing something or doing it solely by memory: ROTE

medal or coin disc apart from lettering or a stamped design: FLAN

meddle, intrude in the affairs of others: INTERLOPE

meddler in a plan, project, etc.: MARPLOT

meddler, interferer: BUTTINSKY

meddler in the affairs of others: KIBITZER

mediating factor between opposite things: TERTIUM QUID

medical and biological technological advances: BIOENGINEERING

medical-appearing substance given to comfort a patient or as a test control: PLACEBO

medical auxiliary or assistant: PARAMEDIC

medical effect making a treatment or procedure inadvisable: CONTRAINDICATION

medical graduate serving in and living at a hospital for clinical training: INTERN

medical insertion of a tube into the larynx: INTUBATION

medical-instruments sterilizing heater: AUTOCLAVE

medical instrument to widen a body opening for inspection or treatment: SPECULUM

medical knowledge applied to questions of law: FORENSIC MEDICINE

medical oath setting forth a code of ethics: HIPPOCRATIC OATH

medical profession symbol, wand or staff of Mercury: CADUCEUS

medical radiographic instrument for three-dimensional images: CAT SCAN (COMPUTERIZED AXIAL TOMOGRAPHY SCAN)

medical technique employing needles inserted into body: ACUPUNCTURE

medical term for the branch of medicine dealing with functions and diseases of women: GYNECOLOGY

medicinal liquid injected into the colon as a purgative: ENEMA

medicine obtainable without prescription: OFFICINAL

medicine of one's own invention, quack medicine, cure-all: NOSTRUM

medicines described and listed in a book: PHARMACOPOEIA

medicine that causes vomiting: EMETIC

medicine that eases irritation: ABIRRITANT

medicine that increases the flow of urine: DIURETIC

medieval chemistry: ALCHEMY

mediocre: INDIFFERENT

mediocre, prosaic, dull: PEDESTRIAN

meditate, ponder: RUMINATE

MEDICAL FIELDS

aging: **GERONTOLOGY, GERIATRICS**
allergies: **ALLERGOLOGY**
anesthesia: **ANESTHESIOLOGY**
bacteria: **BACTERIOLOGY**
birth: **OBSTETRICS, TOCOLOGY**
blood: **HEMATOLOGY**
body functions: **PHYSIOLOGY**
body movement: **KINESIOLOGY**
bones: **OSTEOLOGY**
bones (manipulation): **OSTEOPATHY***
bones, muscles, ligaments:
    ORTHOPEDICS
cells: **CYTOLOGY**
children: **PEDIATRICS**
digestive system:
    GASTROENTEROLOGY
disease, autopsies: **PATHOLOGY**
disease causes and factors: **ETIOLOGY**
disease classification: **NOSOLOGY**
disease description: **NOSOGRAPHY**
disease identification: **DIAGNOSTICS**
ears: **OTOLOGY**
ears, nose, and throat:
    OTORHINOLARYNGOLOGY
    (OTOLARYNGOLOGY)
epidemic diseases: **EPIDEMIOLOGY**
eyes: **OPHTHALMOLOGY**
eye testing, vision correction:
    OPTOMETRY*
feet: **PODIATRY,* CHIROPODY***
female health: **GYNECOLOGY**
glands: **ADENOLOGY**
gums: **PERIODONTICS**
hearing: **AUDIOLOGY***
heart: **CARDIOLOGY**
hernias: **HERNIOLOGY**
hormones and glands:
    ENDOCRINOLOGY
immune system: **IMMUNOLOGY**
internal organs: **INTERNAL MEDICINE**
intestines: **ENTROLOGY**
joints: **ARTHROLOGY**
kidneys: **NEPHROLOGY**
ligaments and tendons:
    DESMOPATHOLOGY
liver: **HEPATOLOGY**
lungs and respiration:
    PULMONOLOGY

lymphatic system: **LYMPHOLOGY**
malformations and monstrosities:
    TERATOLOGY
medicinal dosage: **POSOLOGY**
mental disease: **PSYCHOPATHOLOGY**
mouth: **STOMATOLOGY, ORALOGY**
muscles: **MYOLOGY**
nervous system: **NEUROLOGY,**
    NEUROPATHOLOGY
newborn children: **NEONATOLOGY**
nose: **RHINOLOGY**
parasites: **PARASITOLOGY**
physical medicine and therapy:
    PHYSIATRICS
plastic surgery: **PLASTIC SURGERY**
poisons: **TOXICOLOGY**
rectum: **PROCTOLOGY**
rheumatic diseases:
    RHEUMATOLOGY
secretions: **ECCRINOLOGY**
serums: **SEROLOGY**
sexually transmitted diseases:
    VENEREOLOGY
skin: **DERMATOLOGY**
skull: **CRANIOLOGY**
spine (adjustment):
    CHIROPRACTIC*
stomach: **GASTROLOGY**
surgery for major injuries:
    TRAUMATOLOGY
symptoms: **SYMPTOMATOLOGY**
teeth: **DENTISTRY**
teeth alignment and correction:
    ORTHODONTICS
tissue: **HISTOLOGY**
tumors: **ONCOLOGY**
ulcers: **HELCOLOGY**
urinary and genitourinary tracts:
    UROLOGY
veins: **PHLEBOLOGY**
vessels (blood and lymph):
    ANGIOLOGY
viruses: **VIROLOGY**
vomiting agents or causes:
    EMETOLOGY
X rays, radiation therapy:
    RADIOLOGY

*Practitioners are not M.D.s or D.D.S.s.

meditative or religious commune:
ASHRAM
medium or moderate, in music: **MEZZO**
medium, person speaking for a spirit:
CHANNEL
medley: **SALMAGUNDI**
medley, confused mixture: **FARRAGO**
medley, mixture: **POTPOURRI**
meek, apologetic or shy person:
MILQUETOAST
meeting at the same point,
simultaneous: **CONCURRENT**
meeting or secret appointment, as of
lovers: **TRYST**
meeting place, meeting or appointment
to meet: **RENDEZVOUS**
meeting to achieve communication with
the dead: **SÉANCE**
meeting to confer on a particular
subject: **SYMPOSIUM**
melancholy: **ATRABILIOUS**
melancholy, gloomy: **SEPULCHRAL**
melancholy, pessimism, romantic
world-weariness: **WELTSCHMERZ**
melodic, songlike: **ARIOSE**
melodious, musical: **CANOROUS**
melodious, soothing, sweetly pleasant:
DULCET
melody added to another melody:
COUNTERPOINT
melting: **LIQUESCENT**
membership on a stock exchange: **SEAT**
members or body of an organization
apart from the leaders: **RANK AND
FILE**
members or items chosen out of a
group in the expectation they will
be representative of the whole
group: **RANDOM SAMPLE**
memorable or prominent object in the
landscape: **LANDMARK**
memorable or vivid in a photographic
way: **EIDETIC**
memorandum to remind one of
something in the future: **TICKLER**
memory: **RETENTION**
memory abnormally keen:
HYPERMNESIA
memory aid: **MNEMONIC**
memory alone as a way of doing
something, mechanical action:
ROTE
memory blocks, speech errors or faulty
actions: **PARAPRAXIS**

memory helper, reminder,
memorandum: **AIDE-MÉMOIRE**
memory involving clear visualization of
objects previously seen: **EIDETIC
IMAGERY**
memory loss: **AMNESIA**
memory loss concerning muscular
movements: **APRAXIA**
memory with precise visual images:
PHOTOGRAPHIC MEMORY
menacing, threatening: **MINACIOUS,
MINATORY**
men's furnishings: **HABERDASHERY**
menstruation cessation: **MENOPAUSE**
menstruation's beginning in a female's
life: **MENARCHE**
mental age, as tested, divided by
chronological age and multiplied
by 100: **INTELLIGENCE QUOTIENT
(IQ)**
mental confusion: **AMENTIA**
mental derangement: **ALIENATION**
mental disorder marked by separation
of thought from emotions:
SCHIZOPHRENIA
mental disorders treated by study of the
unconscious: **PSYCHOANALYSIS**
mental lapse: **ABERRATION**
mentally defective person brilliant in
one skill or field: **IDIOT SAVANT**
mentally deficient person: **AMENT**
mentally imagined, vividly or
photographically: **EIDETIC**
mentally retarded person: **IMBECILE**
mentally sound, sane: **COMPOS MENTIS**
mentally unsound: **NON COMPOS
MENTIS**
mental or emotional block: **INHIBITION**
mental or emotional rather than
physical: **PSYCHOGENIC**
mental position, frame of mind:
POSTURE
mental powers impaired: **DEMENTIA**
mental quickness, keenness: **ACUMEN**
mental telepathy: **CRYPTESTHESIA**
mental torpor, pathological: **ACEDIA**
mention of something by saying it will
not be mentioned: **APOPHASIS**
mention or suggest for the first time:
BROACH
menu with each item having a separate
price: **À LA CARTE**
mercenary, subject to bribery: **VENAL**
merciless: **RUTHLESS**
merciless, unrelenting: **IMPLACABLE**

mercy killing: EUTHANASIA

merge gradually one into another: INTERGRADE

merging into one of two vowels generally pronounced separately: SYNERESIS

merited or deserved, as a punishment: CONDIGN

merriment, spirited gaiety: MIRTH

merry-go-round: WHIRLIGIG

mess, confused condition: MARE'S NEST

messenger, especially one on urgent or diplomatic business: COURIER

messiah or prophet in Islam: MAHDI

messily difficult, troublesome or risky situation: HORNET'S NEST

metal-and-enamel work: CLOISONNÉ

metal condition as regards hardness and elasticity: TEMPER

metal disk, spangle: PAILLETTE

metals and alloys as a science: METALLURGY

metalware with enameled or lacquered design: TOLE

metaphorical, flowery: FIGURATIVE

metaphor that is stale and lifeless: DEAD METAPHOR

meteors as a study: AEROLITHOLOGY

meter being mixed within a poem: LOGAOEDIC

metrical or poetic unit of time equivalent to that of a short syllable or sound: MORA

metric basic unit of weight ($\frac{1}{16}$ pound): GRAM

Mexican-American settlement or district in the Southwest: COLONIA

Mexican blanket-like cloak worn by men: SERAPE

Mexican dish of hot-seasoned meat and corn wrapped in corn husks: TAMALES

Mexican farm laborer who enters the United States illegally: WETBACK

Mexican flat, round cake: TORTILLA

Mexican strong liquor: TEQUILA

microfilm sheet for filing: MICROFICHE

microscopic animal: ANIMALCULE

microscopic cell-less or one-celled animal, usually water-dwelling and often a parasite: PROTOZOAN

microscopic one-celled organism (protozoan): AMOEBA

microscopic ovoid organism with cilia: PARAMECIUM

microscopic, small to the point of being incalculable: INFINITESIMAL

middle-class: BOURGEOIS

middle-class resident, citizen, town dweller: BURGHER

Middle Eastern cylindrical men's hat, usually with a tassel: FEZ

middle finger: MEDIUS

middle ground, especially as a government policy: JUSTE-MILIEU

middle letters inserted into a word: INFIX

middleman handling transactions between a company issuing new securities and the public: INVESTMENT BANKER

middle number in a series of statistics: MEDIAN

middle or average that is ideal, avoidance of extremes: GOLDEN MEAN

middle way: VIA MEDIA

midget, dwarf: HOMUNCULUS

midway in the action rather than at the start: IN MEDIAS RES

mighty, powerful: PUISSANT

milder, less severe, more moderate: MITIGATED

mild, gentle, favorable: BENIGN

mildly given reproof: ADMONITION

mild or bland word substituted for one that might give offense or pain: EUPHEMISM

milieu: AMBIENCE

military aircraft on a single mission: SORTIE

military campsite after a day's march: ETAPE

military class in command of the government: STRATOCRACY

military court: COURT-MARTIAL

military detachment designated to do a particular job: DETAIL

military dull shade of green: OLIVE DRAB

military equipment and supplies: MATERIEL

military equipment of the heavy variety: HARDWARE

military expedition: ANABASIS

military headgear with a visor and a flat top: KEPI

military hierarchy arrangement: CHAIN OF COMMAND

military inspection without warning:
SHOWDOWN INSPECTION
military intervention used as a threat in
diplomacy: **GUNBOAT DIPLOMACY**
military materiel, cannon: **ORDNANCE**
military or naval academy freshman:
PLEBE
military persecution: **DRAGONNADE**
military position taken on the enemy
side of a river, defile, etc.:
BRIDGEHEAD
military post in the western United
States: **PRESIDIO**
military science that deals with
procurement, maintenance,
movement and disposition of
supplies and personnel: **LOGISTICS**
military-strategy game played in
miniature: **KRIEGSPIEL**
milk fermented by a bacterium:
YOGURT
milk from mare or camel, fermented:
KUMISS
milk included: **AU LAIT**
milk-like: **LACTESCENT**
milk's thin part that separates from
solids, as in making cheese: **WHEY**
milky: **LACTEAL**
milky liquid: **EMULSION**
million tons of TNT as the
measurement of an explosive:
MEGATON
mimic, play the part of: **IMPERSONATE**
mind controlling matter:
PSYCHOKINESIS
mind-originating rather than physical:
PSYCHOGENIC
mine entrance passage: **ADIT**
mineral-springs treatment of disease:
BALNEOLOGY
mingle in a friendly fashion with people
of an enemy or conquered country:
FRATERNIZE
mingle with, associate on close terms:
HOBNOB
minister's or clergyperson's residence:
MANSE
minister's or clergyperson's residence:
PARSONAGE
minister's or priest's residence:
RECTORY
minority incursion into a neighborhood
used to frighten homeowners into
selling: **BLOCKBUSTING**

minor leagues of no note: **BUSH
LEAGUES**
minor player, member, participant, etc.:
SPEAR CARRIER
minor, secondary, casual: **INCIDENTAL**
miracles as a study: **THAUMATOLOGY**
miraculous cure or solution: **MAGIC
BULLET**
miraculous sought-after stone or other
substance to transmute other
metals into gold: **PHILOSOPHER'S
STONE**
mirage, especially as observed in the
Strait of Messina: **FATA MORGANA**
mirror between two windows: **PIER
GLASS**
mirror for signaling by flashes of light:
HELIOGRAPH
mirror, hung on horizontal pivots, that
is full-length and tiltable in a floor
frame: **CHEVAL GLASS, PSYCHE**
misapply, distort: **PERVERT**
misappropriate, embezzle: **DEFALCATE**
miscarry: **ABORT**
miscarry (said of animals): **SLINK**
miscellaneous collection, variety of
things: **OMNIUM-GATHERUM**
miscellany: **POTPOURRI**
miscellany, hodgepodge: **OLIO**
mischief, joke: **WAGGERY**
mischief-maker: **HELLION**
mischief, pranks, roguish sportiveness,
frolicking: **ESPIEGLERIE**
mischievous, harmful: **MALEFICENT**
mischievously merry, impish: **PUCKISH**
misconduct of an official: **MISPRISION**
miser: **SKINFLINT**
miserable person: **WRETCH**
miserliness: **PARSIMONY**
miserly: **AVARICIOUS**
miserly and hard man: **SCROOGE**
misery, suffering: **TRIBULATION**
misfortune: **AMBSACE**
misgiving, fear: **QUALM**
mishaps in actions, speech or memory:
PARAPRAXIS
misinformation or deception that is
deliberate by a government,
intelligence agency, etc.:
DISINFORMATION
mislead: **BAMBOOZLE**
mislead: **DELUDE**
mislead, deceive: **EQUIVOCATE**
misleading talk: **HUMBUG**

mismated, conflicting, discordant:
INCOMPATIBLE
misrepresent: BELIE
misrepresent, twist, bend: DISTORT
missile's forward separable section
designed to stand intense heat:
NOSE CONE
missile's nose containing the explosive:
WARHEAD
missile with two or more warheads
aimed at separate targets: **MIRV**
(MULTIPLE INDEPENDENTLY
TARGETABLE REENTRY)
misstroke, misplay: FOOZLE
mistake, blunder, faux pas (British):
BLOOMER
mistake, error, false step: FAUX PAS
mistakes in a book noted as needing
correction: CORRIGENDA
mist, fog: BRUME
mistress of any fashionable household:
CHATELAINE
misty, unclear, dark: MURKY
misunderstanding between two
generations: GENERATION GAP
misuse of words: CATACHRESIS
miswriting of words or phrases,
generally caused by cerebral injury:
PARAGRAPHIA
mixed fruits or vegetables as a dessert
or salad: MACÉDOINE
mixed metaphor: CATACHRESIS
mixed-meter poem: LOGAOEDIC
mixed of origin, half-breed: HYBRID
mixed-up: ADDLED, ADDLE-BRAINED,
ADDLEPATED
mixture, hodgepodge: OLIO, OLLA
PODRIDA
mixture, in an artistic composition, of
features from various sources:
PASTICHE
mixture in a society of ethnic, racial,
religious or cultural groups:
PLURALISM
mixture, medley: POTPOURRI
mixture of a confused mass of elements:
MEDLEY
mixture of languages in one literary
composition: MACARONIC
mix up, confuse: DISORIENT
mix up ingredients for a drink or a
dish: CONCOCT
mobile-home area: TRAILER PARK
mob rule: OCHLOCRACY

mock, jeer, defy, scoff: FLOUT
mock, joke: JAPE
model of an apparatus or structure:
MOCKUP
model of the human body used to show
off clothes: MANNEQUIN
model or drawing with the exterior left
off to show the interior: CUTAWAY
model or exemplary literary passage:
LOCUS CLASSICUS
model, pattern, typical example:
EXEMPLAR
model, perfect standard: PROTOTYPE
moderate, cautious, opposed to change:
CONSERVATIVE
moderately good, average:
RESPECTABLE
moderate, restrained: TEMPERATE
moderate tempo in music: ANDANTE
moderation produced by addition of
another element: TEMPER
modernization, bringing up to date:
AGGIORNAMENTO
modest, shy, coy, reserved: DEMURE
modesty: PUDENCY
modesty and self-control, prudence,
restraint, temperance: SOPHROSYNE
Mohammedan fasting period:
RAMADAN
Mohammedan respected scholar:
AYATOLLAH
Mohammedan spiritual ruler: IMAM
moist, damp: HUMID
moist, damp, humid: DANK
moisten and rub the body with oil:
EMBROCATE
moisture-absorbing: DELIQUESCENT
moisture formation: DEWFALL
moisture measurement in the air:
HYGROMETRY
moldable: PLASTIC
moldable or shapable as a material,
clay-like: FICTILE
molding around the walls and close to
the ceiling: CORNICE
molding or casting of footprints, tire
marks, etc., for use in criminal
investigation: MOULAGE
mold in which something is cast or
shaped: MATRIX
mole that becomes lethally cancerous:
MELANOMA
molten rock within the earth: MAGMA

molting or shedding of skin:
EXUVIATION

moment or experience spiritually or existentially transcendent: **PEAK EXPERIENCE**

monetary matters, concerning: **PECUNIARY**

money: **DO-RE-MI**

money acquisition as a science: **CHREMATISTICS**

money bet or invested by supposedly knowing people: **SMART MONEY**

money, booty: **PELF**

money carried by a woman on a date to let her get home alone if need be: **MAD MONEY**

money-changing, foreign exchange: **AGIOTAGE**

money for a new or risky enterprise: **VENTURE CAPITAL**

money given to one who helped a person or company obtain a job or contract: **KICKBACK**

money in circulation lessened and resulting in a decline in prices: **DEFLATION**

money kept secretly aside for corrupt purposes: **SLUSH FUND**

moneylender who extorts: **SHYLOCK**

money-making: **LUCRATIVE**

money-making position, situation, source, etc., requiring little effort: **GRAVY TRAIN**

money-making recruiting scheme promising ever multiplying profits, as through stocks or a chain letter: **PYRAMID SCHEME**

money or assistance furnished to advance a venture: **GRUBSTAKE**

money or payment associated with murder: **BLOOD MONEY**

money paid to a person to prevent his disclosing something: **HUSH MONEY**

money pooled for any specific purpose: **KITTY**

money pursuer: **CHREMATIST**

money-related, concerning money circulation: **MONETARY**

money that is ill-gotten, to "clean" or channel to respectability: **LAUNDER**

money to start a venture or attract investors: **SEED MONEY**

money used for corrupt political purposes: **SLUSH FUND**

mongolism: **DOWN'S SYNDROME**

monkey or ape: **SIMIAN**

monk's haircut, with the crown of the head shaved: **TONSURE**

monologue: **SOLILOQUY**

monopolistic association: **CARTEL**

monopolistic power by several buyers: **OLIGOPSONY**

monopoly of a single buyer: **MONOPSONY**

monotonous or repetitive, narrow, belabored: **ONE-NOTE**

monster of classical mythology with many heads: **HYDRA**

monstrosity, in biology: **TERATISM**

monstrous: **BROBDINGNAGIAN**

monstrous act, wickedness: **ENORMITY**

monthly: **MENSAL**

monument to a dead person, which contains no body: **CENOTAPH**

moody to extremes or psychologically alternating between elation and depression: **MANIC-DEPRESSIVE**

moo like a cow: **LOW**

moon as a study: **SELENOLOGY**

moon, pertaining to the: **SELENIAN**

moon's dark side facing earth: **NEW MOON**

moon showing a thick sickle shape: **GIBBOUS MOON**

moon showing a thin sickle shape: **CRESCENT MOON**

moon's surface as a subject of scientific study: **SELENOGRAPHY**

mooring rope or cable: **HAWSER**

moral corruption: **DRY ROT**

moral decline or decay: **DECADENCE**

moral guide, maxim, rule: **PRECEPT**

moralizing, pedantic: **DIDACTIC**

moralizing, trite: **SENTENTIOUS**

morally bad: **UNSAVORY**

morally debased, degraded: **SCROFULOUS**

morally degraded: **DEGENERATE**

morally neutral: **ADIAPHOROUS**

morally unrestrained, unchaste: **LIBERTINE**

morbid humor: **GALLOWS HUMOR**

more than one wife or husband at once: **POLYGAMY**

more than usual in number: **SUPERNUMERARY**

morning call by a bugle or drum signaling the time to rise: **REVEILLE** morning snack (British): ELEVENSES

morose, gloomy, grave: SATURNINE

mortal blow or death blow: COUP DE GRACE

mortar that is thin and used to fill crevices between bricks or tiles: GROUT

mosaic-like in pattern, checkered: TESSELLATED

mosaic piece, as of stone or glass: TESSERA

mosaic woodwork style, popular in Renaissance Italy: INTARSIA

Moses' books in the Bible: TORAH, PENTATEUCH

Moslem fasting period: RAMADAN

Moslem law as observed by the orthodox: SUNNA

Moslem prince or commander, especially in Arabia: EMIR

Moslem scholars: ULEMA

Moslem's sacred book: KORAN

Moslems who slew during Crusades: ASSASSINS

Moslem term for the devil: SHAITAN

Moslem title of respect for one who has memorized the Koran: HAFIZ

most advanced stage, as of technological research or progress: CUTTING EDGE

moth, butterfly: LEPIDOPTERAN

mother being the head of the family: MATRIARCHY

mother considered legally as a child bearer: VENTER

mother-of-pearl shellfish: ABALONE

mother's side of the family, in kinship: ENATE

mother who is full of advice and overprotective: JEWISH MOTHER

motionless: STOCK-STILL

motionless, not moving: IMMOBILE

motionless with horror or awe: TRANSFIXED

motion picture abrupt-movement effect achieved usually by cutting film from the middle of a continuous shot: JUMP CUT

motion picture art and production: CINEMATOGRAPHY

motion picture back-and-forth sequencing between two different but parallel scenes or actions: CROSS-CUTTING

motion picture computerized process of coloring black-and-white films: COLORIZATION

motion picture continuous-movement shot by a camera on tracks, a dolly or a vehicle: TRACKING SHOT, TRAVELING SHOT, DOLLY SHOT

motion picture effect in which the scene in view is seemingly gradually edged off the screen by the next scene: WIPE

motion picture fast and blurred pan shot: FLASH PAN

motion picture gradual superimposition shot: DISSOLVE

motion picture initial shot indicating place, situation or mood: ESTABLISHING SHOT

motion picture or recording term for an uninterrupted run of a camera or recording apparatus: TAKE

motion picture recording of sound following filming, as for a clearer sound track or to dub in voices: POSTSYNCHRONIZATION

motion picture shot combining live action with a prephotographed or fake background: MATTE SHOT

motion picture shot in which the camera keeps pace with the person or object in motion: RUNNING SHOT

motion picture shot that opens from or closes to a central circle, made with an iris lens: IRIS SHOT

motion picture special effect in which the camera is briefly stopped and a change is made, as to make somebody or something suddenly appear, disappear or move in the viewed scene: STOP-MOTION, STOP-ACTION

motion picture still image effect, with motion stopped: FREEZE FRAME

motion picture studio projection of a still or moving image from behind a translucent screen to provide background for the live-action actors: BACK PROJECTION

motion picture transition from one scene to a different one by gradual fading of the former: LAP DISSOLVE, DISSOLVE

motion study without reference to

particular forces or bodies:
KINEMATICS
motivating force, incentive: IMPETUS
motivation or reward offered for an
    action: INDUCEMENT
motor mounted on the rear of a small
    boat: OUTBOARD MOTOR
mottled, especially in white and black:
    PIEBALD
motto or quotation prefixed to a book:
    EPIGRAPH
mound, small round hill: KNOLL
mound that is manmade, often of great
    size and very old: TUMULUS
mound-possessing, hilly: TUMULOSE
mountain base, foot of a mountain:
    PIEDMONT
mountain climber's spike: PITON
mountaineering descent of a cliff using
    a rope: RAPPEL
mountaineer's rope-fastening ring:
    CARABINER, KARABINER
mountaineer's spiked shoe plate for use
    on ice: CRAMPON
mountain lake: TARN
mountain mass of separate peaks:
    MASSIF
mountain nymph: OREAD
mountain on the sea floor: SEAMOUNT
mountain or hill in the midst of glacial
    ice: NUNATAK
mountain range or chain: SIERRA
mountain ridge, saddle or pass between
    two peaks: COL
mountains as a study: OROGRAPHY
mountainside area that is bowl-like or a
    wide semicircular depression:
    CIRQUE
mountainside gorge or gully: COULOIR
mountaintop's reddish glow before
    sunrise or after sunset:
    ALPENGLOW
mountain with steep sides and a usually
    level top: BUTTE
mournful, sad in a ludicrous manner:
    LUGUBRIOUS
mournful, sad, painful: DOLOROUS
mournful, sorrowful: PLAINTIVE
mournful, wretched: WOEBEGONE
mourning or lamentation in verse or
    song: ELEGY
mouth and its diseases as a branch of
    medicine: STOMATOLOGY
mouth gaping, expanse of open mouth:
    RICTUS

mouth, jaws or gullet of an animal:
    MAW
mouth, opening: ORIFICE
move across: TRAVERSE
move ahead slowly but steadily: FORGE
move a light boat by means of a long
    pole: PUNT
move backward, withdraw: RECEDE
move designed to gain an advantage:
    GAMBIT
move dreamily or idly: MAUNDER
move, especially in diplomacy:
    DÉMARCHE
move heavily and clumsily: FLUMP
movement of inanimate objects without
    apparent external cause:
    TELEKINESIS
movement or change that is constant:
    FLUX
movement or shift to the eye of an
    object due to a different point of
    observation: PARALLAX
movement or structure that is graceful
    or proportioned is: EURYTHMIC
movements or strokes that are artful:
    MANEUVERS
move or roll tumultuously: WELTER
move rapidly, scour, search: SKIRR
move sideways: SIDLE
move swiftly and with force: HURTLE
move the camera so as to photograph
    an entire scene, in movies or
    television: PAN
move unsteadily or irregularly at sea:
    YAW
move with exaggerated tosses of the
    body: FLOUNCE
move with rumbling noise, move
    clumsily: LUMBER
movie: FLICK
movie change in the sound track from
    the original language to another:
    DUBBING
movie device to translate dialogue from
    one language to another by
    superimposing lines low on the
    screen: SUBTITLE
moviemaking: CINEMATOGRAPHY
moviemaking hand-held blackboard
    with hinged top that is "clapped"
    to begin a take: CLAPPER
movie showing in advance of regular
    showings: SNEAK PREVIEW
movies of post-World War II America
    notable for their grim urban

realism and usually in black and white: **FILM NOIR**

movie studio cafeteria or lunchroom: **COMMISSARY**

movie theater that is run-down or dirty: **FLEAPIT**

moving imperceptibly but harmfully: **INSIDIOUS**

moving in an emotional way, touching: **POIGNANT**

moving out in a different direction: **DIVERGENT**

moving rapidly: **SPANKING**

moving sideways: **LATERIGRADE**

moving-water-dwelling; living in rivers, seas, etc.: **LOTIC**

much, very much, in music: **MOLTO**

muddled, confused: **TURBID**

muddle, obscure: **OBFUSCATE**

muddle or confuse: **EMBROIL**

mud or silt deposited by flowing water: **SULLAGE**

mug or jug in form of an old man wearing a three-cornered hat: **TOBY**

multilingual: **POLYGLOT**

multiply by natural reproduction, breed: **PROPAGATE**

mummies as a study: **MOMIOLOGY**

mumps: **PAROTITIS**

munch or chew noisily: **CHAMP**

municipal government by elected commission: **COMMISSION PLAN**

mural painting using pigments mixed with water glass: **STEREOCHROMY**

murder, evildoing, treachery: **FOUL PLAY**

murder of husband by wife or wife by husband: **MARITICIDE**

murder or assassination, as by secret governmental order: **EXECUTIVE ACTION**

murder or assassination order that is implicit in but euphemized by this term: **EXTREME PREJUDICE**

murderous: **HOMICIDAL**

murmuring softly, rustling, whispering: **SUSURRANT**

murmuring sound, as of the wind: **SOUGH**

muscle along the front of the thigh: **QUADRICEPS**

muscle-and-bone branch of surgery: **ORTHOPEDICS**

muscle pain or cramp: **MYALGIA**

muscles as a scientific study: **MYOLOGY**

muscle sense: **KINESTHESIA**

muscle spasm that pulls the head to one side: **TORTICOLLIS**

muscle-strength measuring device: **ERGOMETER**

muscle that is triangular and covers the shoulder joint: **DELTOID**

muscle that surrounds an opening or tube in the body and can open or close it: **SPHINCTER**

muscular coordination loss: **ATAXIA**

muscular development that is light: **ASTHENIA**

muscular rigidity and irresponsiveness to stimuli: **CATALEPSY**

muscular rigidity, stupor, occasional mental agitation: **CATATONIA**

muscular spasm: **CLONUS**

muscular strength: **BRAWN**

muse of astronomy: **URANIA**

muse of comedy: **THALIA**

muse of dance and choral songs: **TERPSICHORE**

muse of epic poetry: **CALLIOPE**

muse of history: **CLIO**

muse of lyric poetry: **ERATO**

muse of music: **EUTERPE**

muse of religious music or sacred poetry: **POLYHYMNIA**

muse of tragedy: **MELPOMENE**

museum or library overseer: **CURATOR**

musical bass instrument, large, of brass and having three to five valves: **TUBA**

musical brass valved instrument shorter than a trumpet and less brilliant in tone: **CORNET**

musical brass valved instrument with a coiled-tube body and a wide bell pointing down and backward when played: **FRENCH HORN**

musical brass wind instrument with long, doubled-up tube: **TROMBONE**

musical composition, especially for piano, that is free in form and lively in tempo: **CAPRICCIO**

musical composition for a story that is sung but not acted: **CANTATA**

musical composition for several male voices having no accompaniment: **GLEE**

musical composition for solo instruments and orchestra: **CONCERTO** musical composition in which a theme is repeated contrapuntally: FUGUE

musical composition on a religious subject for voices and orchestra: ORATORIO

musical composition suggestive of improvisation: RHAPSODY

musical composition that is playful or whimsical: HUMORESQUE

musical direction meaning more: PIÙ

musical direction to perform tenderly: AFFETTUOSO

musical double-reed woodwind instrument: OBOE, HAUTBOY

musical, dramatic or ballet offering given between acts of play or opera: INTERMEZZO

musical flourish: CADENZA

musical instrument in the flute category: PICCOLO

musical instrument like a piano in which strings are plucked: HARPSICHORD

musical instrument that has wooden bars of graduated length that are struck with wooden hammers: XYLOPHONE

musical instrument with double reed and low pitch: ENGLISH HORN

musical instrument with metal bars that produce bell-like tones when struck: GLOCKENSPIEL

musical instrument with metal strings that is played with two small hammers: DULCIMER

musical, melodious: CANOROUS

musical mouth instrument somewhat oval in shape, with finger holes and a mouthpiece not at the end: OCARINA, SWEET POTATO

musical notation for some stringed instruments that indicates rhythm and fingering: TABULATURE

musical notes that are short and detached: STACCATO

musical note that ornaments or embellishes a more important note: GRACE NOTE

musical once considered essential to a proper performance but now often optional: OBBLIGATO

musical passage ending a composition: CODA

musical passage or movement that is stately: MAESTOSO

musical pendulum device for keeping the beat: METRONOME

musical percussion instrument in the form of a serrated gourd that the player scrapes with a stick: GUIRO

musical piece consisting of parts of different songs: MEDLEY

musical play in a light vein: OPERETTA

musical sliding effect: GLISSANDO

musical solo composition or an exercise designed to perfect some technique: ÉTUDE

musical stringed table-played instrument: ZITHER

musical string instrument, like a zither, played by touching buttons: AUTOHARP

musical style of the West Indies: CALYPSO

musical term for gradual slackening of tempo: RITARDANDO

musical term for medium, moderate: MEZZO

musical term for quick: PRESTO

musical term for repeating from the beginning: DA CAPO

musical term for slightly, somewhat: POCO

musical term for slowing down gradually: RALLENTANDO

musical term for very fast: PRESTISSIMO

musical term for very soft: PIANISSIMO

musical trembling effect caused by rapid, tiny variations in pitch: VIBRATO

musical use of vocal syllables: SOLMIZATION

musical use vocally of the syllables do, re, mi, etc.: SOLFEGGIO

musical valved brass instrument mellower than the cornet and having a wider bore and larger bell: FLÜGELHORN

music at performer's pleasure: A CAPRICCIO

music by a small group, as a string quartet: CHAMBER MUSIC

music direction calling for slowness: LENTO

music direction to perform very loudly: FORTISSIMO

musician of eminence or a master in any art: MAESTRO

musician's book of lead sheets for standard songs: FAKE BOOK

musician's shift in style to increase audience appeal: CROSSOVER

music intended to be depictive in evoking or reflecting a place, event, mood of nature, etc.: PROGRAM MUSIC

music lacking tonality because of disregard of key: ATONALITY

music muse: EUTERPE

music played between stanzas of a hymn or acts of a play: INTERLUDE

music style that is smooth and flowing: LEGATO

music swelling in loudness: CRESCENDO

music teacher or critic strict about rules: BECKMESSER

music tempo that is moderate: ANDANTE

music tempo that is slow: LARGO

music with fast time: ALLEGRO

music with two or more voices, parts or melodies that blend harmonically: POLYPHONY

musing, daydreaming: REVERIE

Muslim respected scholar: AYATOLLAH

Muslim spiritual ruler: IMAM

muslin of a thin weave: TARLATAN

mustard plaster: POULTICE

mustard plaster: SINAPISM

musty, moldy, old-fashioned: FUSTY

mutilate a book by cutting out the illustrations: GRANGERIZE

mutilation, destruction or alteration, especially of a legal document: SPOLIATION

mutual: RECIPROCAL, BILATERAL

mysterious: ARCANE

mysterious: CABALISTIC

mysterious, defying understanding: INSCRUTABLE

mystery novel stressing realistic police investigation: POLICE PROCEDURAL

mystery story: WHODUNIT

mystical: ANAGOGIC

mystical or secret system: CABALA

mystical poem or song: RUNE

mystical status attributed to a person, institution, activity, etc.: MYSTIQUE

mystifying, secret, hidden, puzzling: CRYPTIC

mythical creature part lion and part eagle: GRYPHON, GRIFFIN

mythological fluid in the veins of the gods: ICHOR

mythological monster with a human body and a bull's head: MINOTAUR

mythology's Greek Furies: EUMENIDES

myths explained on the premise that they are based on actual events: EUHEMERISM

nag at: **BADGER**

nagging, petty: **NIGGLING**

nag, pest, whiner: **NUDGE, NOODGE**

nail biting: **ONCHYOPHAGY**

nail, claw, hoof: **UNGUIS**

nail that is slender and small with a small head: **BRAD**

naive, insipid, dry, lacking interest, barren: **JEJUNE**

naive or artless in style in a deliberate and often somewhat false way: **FAUX NAÏF**

naive, straightforward, frank, innocent, simple: **INGENUOUS**

naked: **AU NATUREL**

name: **APPELLATION**

named, called (archaic): **YCLEPT**

name derived from a place, place name: **TOPONYM**

name, in antonomasia, devised to be characterizing or descriptive, such as "Miss Neat": **APTRONYM**

nameless, anonymous: **INNOMINATE**

namely: **VIZ**

namely, that is to say: **TO WIT**

namely, to wit: **SCILICET**

name of a place in a different language, foreign geographical name: **EXONYM**

name of a plant or creature in common rather than scientific language: **VERNACULAR**

name of the broker rather than the customer used in securities holdings: **STREET NAME**

name of one person taken by another: **ALLONYM**

name of the person from which the name of a state or institution is derived: **EPONYM**

name of the writer at the head of an article: **BYLINE**

name or title only, nominal: **TITULAR**

name plate, signature, trademark, etc., on a single type plate: **LOGOTYPE**

name replaced by a title or epithet: **ANTONOMASIA**

names as a study: **ONOMASTICS**

name spelled backward as a pseudonym: **ANANYM**

names, terminology: **NOMENCLATURE**

names that are several for one thing: **POECILONYMY**

naming a parent after his or her child: **TEKNONYMY**

naming a thing by substituting one of its attributes or a term it suggests: **METONYMY**

naming journalistic sources: **ATTRIBUTION**

nape: **SCRUFF**

nape, back of the neck: **NUCHA**

narcotic made from Indian hemp: **HASHISH**

narrow, close or small margin or space: **HAIRBREADTH**

narrow elevated walking space: **CATWALK**

narrow focus or outlook, narrow-mindedness: **TUNNEL VISION**

narrow, limited, provincial: **PAROCHIAL**

narrow-minded: **PETTY**

narrow-mindedness, narrow focus or outlook: **TUNNEL VISION**

narrow-minded, obstinate: **HIDEBOUND**

narrow or limited in outlook, provincial: **INSULAR**

narrow, unsophisticated: **PROVINCIAL**

nasal tone: **SNUFFLE**

nation's total production of goods and services: GROSS NATIONAL PRODUCT (GNP)

native, indigenous: AUTOCHTHONOUS

native, indigenous: ENCHORIAL

native language of a place: VERNACULAR

native of one country living in another: EXPATRIATE

native person, animal or thing: INDIGENE

native to a given area, peculiar to a given country or people: ENDEMIC

native to a place: ABORIGINAL

native to a region: INDIGENOUS

natural accompaniment, attribute or endowment: APPANAGE

natural attraction: AFFINITY

natural, coarse, unrefined: EARTHY

natural, existing from birth: INBORN

natural, healthful and spiritual: HOLISTIC

naturally rough or showing a lack of polish: AGRESTIC

natural resources diminishing in supply and therefore reducing income from them: DEPLETION

natural response to stimulus: INSTINCT

natural virtues: CARDINAL VIRTUES

naughtiness: HANKY-PANKY

nauseated: QUEASY

nauseated or shocked easily, prudish: SQUEAMISH

nautical whistle that is slender and silver: BOATSWAIN'S WHISTLE

Navaho log-and-mud dwelling: HOGAN

navel: UMBILICUS

navel contemplation: OMPHALOSKEPSIS

navigating by deduction, record checking and guesswork: DEAD RECKONING

navigation by means of the heavens: CELESTIAL NAVIGATION

Nazi storm trooper: BROWNSHIRT

Nazi symbol (卐): SWASTIKA, HAKENKREUZ

near accident, close call: NEAR MISS

nearly, almost: WELL-NIGH

near, neighboring, adjoining: VICINAL

nearness: CONTIGUITY

nearness: PROXIMITY

nearness, kinship: PROPINQUITY

nearsighted, obtuse: MYOPIC

neat, finicky and rigid in a compulsive way: ANAL-RETENTIVE

necessarily: PERFORCE

necessary changes having been made: MUTATIS MUTANDIS

necessary means: WHEREWITHAL

neck ailment caused by muscle contraction: TORTICOLLIS, WRYNECK

neck artery, one of two: CAROTID ARTERY

neck-chain ornament, pendant: LAVALIERE

neck cloth on the back of a soldier's hat, protecting against the sun: HAVELOCK

necklace worn high around the throat: CHOKER

neckline cut low in a dress: DÉCOLLETAGE

neck or base of the brain jolted, as in an automobile crash: WHIPLASH

neck's back part: SCRUFF

neck thyroid swelling that is grotesque: GOITER

necktie knot that is a simple slip knot: FOUR-IN-HAND

necktie knot wider than a four-in-hand: WINDSOR

necktie, scarf: CRAVAT

necktie, Western-style, consisting of a cord or thong and an ornamental clasp: BOLO TIE

needful or right to be: BEHOOVE

needle-pricking of body tissues to diagnose or remedy ills: ACUPUNCTURE

needles, scissors, etc., small case for: ETUI

negative of a statement's opposite used to express an affirmative: LITOTES

neglect, disregard: SLIGHT

neglected, abandoned, unused condition: DESUETUDE

neglected, decayed, in disrepair: DILAPIDATED

neglect or failure to meet an obligation: DEFAULT

neglect or willful omission, failure in duty: DERELICTION

neglect, overlook, disregard: PRETERMIT

negligee: PEIGNOIR

negligee jacket or underwear concealer: CAMISOLE

negligence, carelessness or laxity in self-assertion: LACHES

negligence in duty or responsibility:
NONFEASANCE

negligent, careless: **REMISS**

negotiations between organized workers
and their employers: **COLLECTIVE
BARGAINING**

neighboring, near: **VICINAL**

neither good nor bad, middling, so-so:
COMME ÇI, COMME ÇA

nerve inflammation: **NEURITIS**

nervous excitement, anxiety, agitation:
DITHER

nervously excited, overstrained:
OVERWROUGHT

nervously or restlessly move: **FIDGET**

nervous system and its disorders as a
study: **NEUROLOGY**

nest of a predatory bird in high place:
AERIE

net-like: **RETICULAR**

network: **RETICULATION**

network, complicated interconnection of
parts: **PLEXUS**

network or system to catch a criminal:
DRAGNET

neurotic condition caused by feelings of
inferiority: **INFERIORITY COMPLEX**

nevertheless: **NOTWITHSTANDING**

new birth, revival: **RENASCENCE**

newcomer, novice: **GREENHORN**

newcomer to an organization, cult,
fraternity: **INITIATE**

new convert, beginner, novice:
NEOPHYTE

New England or New Englandish:
NOVANGLIAN

new enterprise, money to begin: **SEED
MONEY**

new life, restoration, reconstitution:
REGENERATION

newly born sheep or goat: **YEANLING**

newly conceived, just developing:
NASCENT

newly introduced element: **INNOVATION**

newly married man who was a
long-time bachelor: **BENEDICT**

newly rich or influential, upstart:
PARVENU

new-movement leaders, especially in the
arts: **AVANT-GARDE**

news copy, ready-to-print for
syndication and usually standard
or unremarkable: **BOILERPLATE**

news correspondent who works

part-time for a paper elsewhere:
STRINGER

newspaper brief follow-up item:
SHIRTTAIL

newspaper or magazine listing of
editors, staff and owners:
MASTHEAD

newspaper page opposite the editorial
page: **OP-ED PAGE**

newspaper's early edition: **BULLDOG
EDITION**

newspaper section in European papers
and usually at the bottom of the
page, where fiction is printed:
FEUILLETON

newspaper with sheets half the standard
size and usually emphasizing
pictures: **TABLOID**

newspaper work shift beginning during
the late-night hours: **LOBSTER
SHIFT**

news reporting that is irresponsibly
sensational or exploitive: **YELLOW
JOURNALISM**

newsstand, bandstand or booth, usually
lightly constructed and open:
KIOSK

news writing that is routine and
hackneyed in style: **MORKRUMBO**

new word or expression: **NEOLOGISM**

New York Stock Exchange: **BIG BOARD**

next: **PROXIMATE**

next to nothing: **AMBSACE**

next to the last: **PENULTIMATE**

niches for cinerary urns or as vaults for
the dead: **COLUMBARIUM**

nickname: **SOBRIQUET**

nickname, epithet or character name
use instead of a full name, such as
"Eric the Red," "a Silas Marner":
ANTONOMASIA

night and day of equal length, marking
the start of spring or autumn:
EQUINOX

night blindness: **NYCTALOPIA**

nightcap, sleeping cap: **BIGGIN**

nightclub, cabaret: **BOÎTE**

nightclub with recorded music for
dancing: **DISCOTHEQUE**

nightmare: **INCUBUS**

night or moon blindness: **NYCTALOPIA**

night-sky luminous streaks in the
Northern Hemisphere, northern
lights: **AURORA BOREALIS**

night vigil over a body before burial:
WAKE
nine-day prayer recitation: **NOVENA**
nine-fold: **NONUPLE**
nine-fold or based on the number 9:
NOVENARY
nine-inch measurement: **SPAN**
90-to-100-year-old person:
NONAGENARIAN
nip, pinch, tickle, twitch: **VELLICATE**
nipple coverings worn by strippers,
showgirls, etc.: **PASTIES**
nipple's dark circular background:
AREOLA
nobility's obligations: **NOBLESSE OBLIGE**
noble, lofty or impressive, as in quality
or style: **SONOROUS**
no-contest plea in criminal case without
admission of guilt: **NOLO**
CONTENDERE
nodding of the head: **NUTATION**
no ifs, ands or buts: **CATEGORICAL**
noise measure: **DECIBEL**
noise that is clattering: **BRATTLE**
noise that is shrill, creaking or grating:
STRIDOR
noisily crashing, as waves: **PLANGENT**
noisy: **CLAMOROUS**
noisy: **VOCIFEROUS**
noisy and loud: **UPROARIOUS**
noisy celebration around newlyweds:
CHARIVARI, SHIVAREE
noisy commotion of a crowd: **TUMULT**
noisy confusion: **BEDLAM**
noisy confusion, din of voices: **BABEL**
noisy disturbance: **FRACAS**
noisy gaiety, boisterous merriment:
HILARITY
noisy ghost: **POLTERGEIST**
nominal, in name only: **TITULAR**
nonconforming, contrary: **PERVERSE**
nonconformist: **MAVERICK**
nonconformist: **RECUSANT**
nonconformity: **DISSENT**
nonessential attribute: **ACCIDENTAL**
noninterference, especially by
government in business:
LAISSEZ-FAIRE
nonmaterial, spiritual, insubstantial:
INCORPOREAL
nonsense: **ABRACADABRA**
nonsense: **AMPHIGORY**
nonsense: **BALDERDASH**

nonsense, meaningless chatter:
SKIMBLE-SCAMBLE
nonsense, rubbish: **TRUMPERY**
nonsensical and drolly self-contradictory
statement: **IRISH BULL**
nontraditional medically or
scientifically: **HOLISTIC**
nonviolent civil disobedience or
resistance: **SATYAGRAHA**
nonviolent opposition: **PASSIVE**
RESISTANCE
noodles, broad and flat, served with
butter or a sauce: **FETTUCCINE**
normal consequence: **COROLLARY**
North African city's crowded section:
CASBAH
northern lights, or night-sky luminous
streaks in the Northern
Hemisphere: **AURORA BOREALIS**
North Star: **POLARIS**
nose and its diseases as a branch of
medicine: **RHINOLOGY**
nosebleed: **EPISTAXIS**
nose, humorous name for a large nose:
PROBOSCIS
nose inflamed or red from drunkenness:
COPPERNOSE
nose plastic surgery, nose job:
RHINOPLASTY
nose ridge above the lip and separating
the nostrils: **COLUMELLA**
nose-thumb somebody: **COCK A SNOOT,**
COCK A SNOOK
nostalgia for the common or earthy life,
"nostalgia for the mud":
NOSTALGIE DE LA BOUE
nostrils-separating ridge of flesh:
COLUMELLA
nosy person, busybody: **NOSEY**
PARKER, NOSY PARKER
not audible to human beings:
ULTRASONIC
not characterized by fraud or trickery:
ABOVEBOARD
notched at the edge: **SERRATED**
notched or indented, as a battlement on
a fortress: **CRENELATED**
notched pattern on edge of fabric:
PINKED
notches along an edge or border, space
from a margin: **INDENTION**
notch or cut carved out by a saw or ax:
KERF
not concrete: **ABSTRACT**

notes in music lengthened or shortened arbitrarily: **RUBATO**

notes in music that are short and detached: **STACCATO**

notes of a chord played in quick succession: **ARPEGGIO**

note well: **N.B. (NOTA BENE)**

not hearable by humans: **INFRASONIC**

nothing (Spanish): **NADA**

nothing to all intents and purposes, piddling thing or amount, peanuts: **BUPKES**

notify: **APPRISE**

not inherent: **ADVENTITIOUS**

notion or fancy that emerges suddenly: **WHIM**

not letting up: **CONTINUOUS**

not mixable: **IMMISCIBLE**

not moving, motionless: **IMMOBILE**

notoriety that is evil: **INFAMY**

notoriously bad: **ARRANT**

notoriously bad, odious, vile in reputation: **INFAMOUS**

"not to mention . . .": **APOPHASIS**

nouns linked by a conjunction to express the same thought as a noun with a modifier: **HENDIADYS**

nourishment: **ALIMENT**

nourish, rear, train: **NURTURE**

novel about a young person's development or maturing: **BILDUNGSROMAN**

novel of great length or several volumes that chronicles the life of a family or a society: **ROMAN-FLEUVE**

novel that includes actual persons under fictitious names: **ROMAN À CLEF**

novel that is brief and often contains a moral: **NOVELLA**

novice: **ABECEDARIAN**

novice, beginner: **NEOPHYTE**

novice, beginner: **TYRO**

noxious, harmful: **VIRULENT**

noxious, unwholesome atmosphere, influence, effect, etc.: **MIASMA**

nuclear bomb: **A-BOMB**

nuclear bomb lethal to people but causing less physical damage: **NEUTRON BOMB**

nuclear explosion's precise detonation point: **GROUND ZERO**

nucleus or core of a group: **CADRE**

nudge or touch with a slight jar, shake lightly, stimulate: **JOG**

null and void: **DIRIMENT**

null and void: **INVALID**

numb: **TORPID**

number divided into another: **DIVISOR**

number in arithmetic from which the subtrahend is to be subtracted: **MINUEND**

number indicating relative position or sequence adjectivally, such as 1st, 2nd or 3rd: **ORDINAL NUMBER**

numberless: **MYRIAD**

number midway between the highest and the lowest numbers in a series: **MEDIAN**

number of members necessary for an assembly to transact business: **QUORUM**

number or figure 1 followed by 100 zeros, or 10^{100}: **GOOGOL**

number or figure 1 followed by zeros for a total of $10^{10^{100}}$: **GOOGOLPLEX**

number representing the ratio of the speed of a body to that of the immediate speed of sound: **MACH NUMBER**

number sequence in which the difference between numerical terms remains constant: **ARITHMETIC PROGRESSION**

number sequence in which the ratio between each two numbers is the same: **GEOMETRIC PROGRESSION**

numbers expert or accountant who is a short-sighted bureaucrat: **BEAN COUNTER**

number symbols from 0 to 9: **DIGITS**

number that is divisible by two or more numbers: **COMMON MULTIPLE**

number the pages of a book: **FOLIATE, PAGINATE**

number to be divided: **DIVIDEND**

number to be multiplied: **MULTIPLICAND**

number to be subtracted from another: **SUBTRAHEND**

number used in counting, rather than adjectivally, such as 1, 2 or 3: **CARDINAL NUMBER**

number-using computer: **DIGITAL COMPUTER**

numerous, great numbers: **MULTITUDINOUS**

nun's headdress covering head, cheeks and neck: **WIMPLE**

nuptial poem or song: **EPITHALAMIUM**

nursemaid, child's nurse or female caretaker: NANNY

nurse's teenage helper: CANDY STRIPER

nurse who rears a child without suckling it: DRY NURSE

nut coated with sugar: DRAGÉE

nutrition and diet as a science: SITOLOGY

nutrition-related: TROPHIC

nutrition that is defective or perverted: DYSTROPHY

nutritious snack: GORP

nymph dwelling in or presiding over woods and trees: DRYAD

nymph fabled to live and die in the tree that she inhabited: HAMADRYAD

oath plus a written statement:
AFFIDAVIT
oath taker: **JURANT**
obedient: **DUTEOUS**
obedient to an excessive degree, servile:
OBSEQUIOUS
objectionable, offensive: **OBNOXIOUS**
objection that is trivial: **QUIDDITY**
objective, impartial, unbiased:
DISPASSIONATE
objective, unbiased: **DISINTERESTED**
objectivity: **DISINTEREST**
object made by man: **ARTIFACT**
object of attention: **CYNOSURE**
object regarded as having magical
powers: **FETISH**
object serving as a boundary mark or
guide to travelers: **LANDMARK**
object to, hesitate, take exception to:
DEMUR
obligation or penalty established by
authority: **IMPOSITION**
obligation owed, faithfulness, loyalty:
FEALTY
obligation to be nobly generous,
understanding, etc.: **NOBLESSE
OBLIGE**
obligatory: **INCUMBENT**
obligatory: **IRREMISSIBLE**
obligatory, required: **MANDATORY**
obligingness: **COMPLAISANCE**
oblique direction taken: **SKEW**
oblique or diagonal line: **BIAS**
oblivion, forgetfulness: **LETHE**
oblivion-producing potion: **NEPENTHE**
oblong-shaped cut gem: **BAGUETTE**
obscene: **SCATOLOGICAL**
obscene, lecherous, lewd: **SALACIOUS**
obscene talk: **COPROLALIA**
obscene talk or conduct: **BAWDRY**

obscene, vulgar: **FESCENNINE**
obscure: **AMBIGUOUS**
obscure: **INCOMPREHENSIBLE**
obscure, dim, pertaining to twilight:
CREPUSCULAR
obscure, muddle: **OBFUSCATE**
obscure or ambiguous saying, riddle,
puzzle: **ENIGMA**
obscure, overshadow, surpass: **ECLIPSE**
obscure poem or song: **RUNE**
obscure, unclear, misty, dark: **MURKY**
obsequious, servile: **SUBSERVIENT**
observation and analysis of one's own
thoughts and feelings:
INTROSPECTION
observation area built on the roof of a
house: **WIDOW'S WALK**
observation, experiment, actuality, etc.,
being the basis: **A POSTERIORI**
observation spot or point: **COIGN OF
VANTAGE**
observe, discern, discover with the eye:
DESCRY
obsession: **IDÉE FIXE**
obsession, craze: **MANIA** (*For a listing of
such conditions see* "manias.")
obsolete object: **MUSEUM PIECE**
obsolete, outdated, discarded:
SUPERANNUATED
obstacle: **IMPEDIMENT**
obstinacy: **PERTINACITY**
obstinately resistant: **DIEHARD**
obstinate, narrow-minded: **HIDEBOUND**
obstinate, shrewd, practical:
HARDHEADED
obstinate, sinful: **UNREGENERATE**
obstinate, unmanageable: **REFRACTORY**
obstruct, block: **STYMIE**
obstruct, frustrate, foil: **THWART**
obstruct, hinder: **CRIMP**

obstructing: OBSTRUENT
obstruction of action through
    time-killing tactics: FILIBUSTER
obtain by entreaty: IMPETRATE
obtrude, force oneself or one's will on
    another without right: IMPOSE
obtrusive, forward, pushy: OFFICIOUS
obtuse, nearsighted: MYOPIC
obvious, manifest, evident: PATENT
occasional: SPORADIC
occult doctrine, art or matter: CABALA
occult sciences: HERMETICS
occupation, avocation, interest: PURSUIT
occupation, career: VOCATION
occupation for which one is suited and
    well equipped: MÉTIER
occupy, amuse oneself: DISPORT
occupy completely, monopolize, absorb:
    ENGROSS
occurring or existing at the same time:
    SIMULTANEOUS
occurring together: CONCOMITANT
ocean grave of the drowned: DAVY
    JONES'S LOCKER
oceanic: PELAGIC
oceanic: THALASSIC
ocean wave, destructive, caused by an
    underwater earthquake: TSUNAMI
odd, freakish: WHIMSICAL
odd item, remnant, scrap: ODDMENT
odd-jobs worker or itinerant:
    ROUSTABOUT
odd, unconventional: OUTRÉ
odd, wild idea: VAGARY
odious, bad or vile in reputation:
    INFAMOUS
odor from decaying matter: EFFLUVIUM
odors as a scientific study: OSMICS
off-color, suggestive: RISQUÉ
offended, annoyed, irritated: MIFFED
offense against sovereign authority,
    treason: LESE MAJESTY, LÈSE
    MAJESTÉ
offense given or taken: UMBRAGE
offense not so serious as a felony, in
    law: MISDEMEANOR
offensive because of excessiveness or
    insincerity: FULSOME
offensive, disagreeable: UNSAVORY
offensive, disgusting, stinking, noxious:
    NOISOME
offensive, objectionable: OBNOXIOUS
offer: PROFFER
offer, as money: TENDER
offhand: CASUAL

offhand, free and easy: CAVALIER
offhand, spur-of-the-moment:
    IMPROMPTU
officeholder who does little:
    CHAIRWARMER
office or position that pays but involves
    few or no duties: SINECURE
officer's servant in the British army:
    BATMAN
offices filled through political power:
    PATRONAGE
official approval, as of a literary work:
    IMPRIMATUR
official arbitrary decree: UKASE
official defeated in an election but filling
    out an unexpired term: LAME
    DUCK
official denial: DEMENTI
official or politician who is inept:
    THROTTLEBOTTOM
officials, leaders, etc., arranged by rank:
    HIERARCHY
official who is foolish or stupid:
    DOGBERRY
official who is pompous or pretentious:
    PANJANDRUM
official who is tyrannical: SATRAP
offset: COUNTERBALANCE
offset, make up for, compensate:
    COUNTERVAIL
offshoot, branch: RAMIFICATION
offspring: PROGENY
offspring, descendant: SCION
offspring of a stallion and a female ass:
    HINNY
offspring of parents of different racial
    stock: HALF-BREED
offstage waiting room for performers:
    GREEN ROOM
ogling look, flirtatious glance: OEILLADE
oil consecrated for use in church:
    CHRISM
oil or grease something: LUBRICATE
oil prospector: WILDCATTER
oil well from which oil spouts: GUSHER
oily: OLEAGINOUS
oily, greasy: PINGUID
oily in flattery, ingratiating, phony and
    sweet: SMARMY
oily-tongued, fulsomely suave:
    UNCTUOUS
okay, fine, all right, satisfactory:
    HUNKY-DORY
old age as a branch of medicine:
    GERIATRICS

old age, senility: DOTAGE
old-age weakness: CADUCITY
old and forgotten object: MUSEUM
    PIECE
Old English bard: SCOP
old-fashioned: ANTEDILUVIAN
old-fashioned: DÉMODÉ
old-fashioned: PASSÉ
old-fashioned, fussy person:
    FUDDY-DUDDY
old-fashioned, musty, moldy: FUSTY
old-fashioned or conservative person:
    FOGY
old-fashioned, out of date, old hat:
    VIEUX JEU
old-fashioned, out of step with the
    times, ancient, outmoded:
    ANTEDILUVIAN
old, infirm, doting: SENILE
old maid: SPINSTER
old men forming a governing body:
    GERONTOCRACY
old or extremely long-lived person:
    METHUSELAH
old or former government or social
    system, order no longer existing:
    ANCIEN RÉGIME
old-process photograph on a metal
    plate: DAGUERREOTYPE
old salt, veteran sailor: SHELLBACK
Old Testament interpretation that is
    largely mystical: ANAGOGE
old-woman-like: ANILE
omelet containing a sauce of tomato,
    onion and green pepper: SPANISH
    OMELET
omelet prepared with ham, onion and
    green pepper: WESTERN OMELET
omen of death: KNELL
omen, portent: AUGURY
omen, warning, portent: PRESAGE
ominous, awesome: PORTENTOUS
omission of a letter or sound in
    pronunciation: ELISION
omission of conjunctions: ASYNDETON
omission of understood word or words:
    ELLIPSIS
omit a vowel or syllable in
    pronunciation: ELIDE
omitting, passing over: PRETERITION
omnipresent: UBIQUITOUS
one behind the other, as on a bicycle
    built for two: TANDEM
one-colored: MONOCHROME
one dollar per share of stock: POINT

one-eyed giant, or Cyclops, blinded by
    Ulysses: POLYPHEMUS
one following another: SERIATIM
"one," "he" or "she" used instead of
    "I": ILLEISM
one hundred years: CENTENARY,
    CENTENNIAL
one husband at a time: MONANDROUS
one leg on each side of something:
    ASTRIDE
one-man rule with absolute power:
    AUTOCRACY
one of a kind, unique: SUI GENERIS
one-sided: UNILATERAL
one-sided in heaviness or disproportion:
    LOPSIDED
one-sided, partisan: EX PARTE
onetime, former, previous: ERSTWHILE
onion-like or garlic-like in taste or
    smell: ALLIACEOUS
onomatopoeia: ECHOISM
on the agenda for consideration: ON
    THE TAPIS
on the alert, wide-awake: ON THE QUI
    VIVE
on the contrary: AU CONTRAIRE
on the up-and-up: ABOVEBOARD
ooze or trickle forth: EXUDE
open: ABOVEBOARD
open-handed in giving: MUNIFICENT
opening, break or interruption of
    continuity, gap: HIATUS
opening cut in an interior wall of a
    church to allow those in a side
    aisle to see the main altar:
    HAGIOSCOPE
opening flared or slanted outward for a
    window or door: EMBRASURE
opening for dropping missiles on
    attackers, one of several sheltered
    apertures in a projecting support of
    a battlement: MACHICOLATION
opening, mouth: ORIFICE
opening move in chess: GAMBIT
opening oration at a commencement:
    SALUTATORY
opening or slit in the upper part of a
    dress or skirt: PLACKET
opening performance: PREMIERE
open level path or grass area that is
    often scenic, promenade:
    ESPLANADE
open or in open air, outdoors:
    ALFRESCO
open out, develop: EVOLVE

open paved area adjoining a home:
PATIO

open to injury, attack or criticism:
VULNERABLE

open to question, arguable: **DISPUTABLE**

open to the sky, unroofed: **HYPETHRAL**

open, unconcealed, evident: **OVERT**

opera hat, flattenable when not being
used: **GIBUS**

opera in which music is subordinated to
words: **SINGSPIEL**

opera singer of note: **DIVA**

opera's verbal text: **LIBRETTO**

operatic singing technique that is light
but precise: **BEL CANTO**

operator, deal-maker, shrewd business
person: **WHEELER-DEALER**

operetta form in Spain: **ZARZUELA**

opinion adopted beforehand:
PRECONCEPTION

opinionated but immature:
SOPHOMORIC

opinionated political or philosophical
theorist: **IDEOLOGUE**

opinion or agreement that is general:
CONSENSUS

opinion or belief contrary to established
doctrine: **HERESY**

opinion that is conventional: **RECEIVED
IDEA**

opium addiction: **MECONISM**

opium preparation or tincture:
LAUDANUM

opponent, pursuer, or antagonist who is
unusually troublesome or
tenacious: **NEMESIS**

opponent who takes the wrong side
perversely: **DEVIL'S ADVOCATE**

opportune, favorable, promising:
AUSPICIOUS

opportune time to accomplish
something: **WINDOW**

oppose, argue: **CONTROVERT**

oppose, contradict, deny: **GAINSAY**

opposed, inconsistent, undesirable:
REPUGNANT

opposed to change or progress,
conservative: **REACTIONARY**

opposed to usual beliefs: **HETERODOX**

oppose or balance with an opposite or
alternative: **COUNTERPOSE**

oppose or protest by pleading:
REMONSTRATE

oppose, thwart: **TRAVERSE**

opposing or antagonistic in nature,

purpose or relationship:
ADVERSARIAL

opposite: **POLAR**

opposite meaning to words said
sarcastically or humorously or with
opposite result to what is
seemingly said: **IRONY**

opposite or reversed in order or effect:
INVERSE

opposite-sided: **ANTIPODAL**

opposite terms combined in one phrase:
OXYMORON

opposite word: **ANTONYM**

opposition expressed: **ADVERSATIVE**

opposition that is nonviolent: **PASSIVE
RESISTANCE**

opposition to shared knowledge,
deliberate abstruseness or
mystification: **OBSCURANTISM**

oppressed, tormented: **HAGRIDDEN**

oppressive thing, burden: **INCUBUS**

optical device in which pictures on both
sides of a card or disk appear to
blend when the card is twirled:
THAUMATROPE

optimistic about rising prices, as in the
stock market: **BULLISH**

optimistic, buoyant, cheerful: **SANGUINE**

optimistic, happy: **UPBEAT**

optimistic to a foolish degree,
credulously innocent:
PANGLOSSIAN

optimist to such a degree that he or she
is foolish, blindly or naively
positive: **POLLYANNA**

oracular, ambiguous: **DELPHIC**

oral defamatory statement: **SLANDER**

oral, not written (referring especially to
wills): **NUNCUPATIVE**

oral sex that is simultaneous by two
partners: **SOIXANTE-NEUF,
SIXTY-NINE**

oral, spoken: **VIVA VOCE**

oral teaching: **CATECHESIS**

oration opening a commencement:
SALUTATORY

oratory that is bombastic and artificial:
DECLAMATION

orbital point of a celestial body or
satellite that is farthest from the
earth: **APOGEE**

orbital point of a celestial body or
satellite that is nearest to the earth:
PERIGEE

orbital point of a celestial body or

satellite that is nearest to the sun: **PERIHELION**

orbiting man-made body: **SATELLITE**

orchestra keyboard player: **CEMBALIST**

orchestra seats in a theater: **PARQUET**

order, command, forbid: **ENJOIN**

order, decree, enact: **ORDAIN**

order of military rank or authority: **CHAIN OF COMMAND**

order requiring certain action: **MANDAMUS**

order requiring one to take, or refrain from, a certain action: **INJUNCTION**

order, send back: **REMAND**

order that is positive and authoritative: **FIAT**

order to buy or sell at the most advantageous price: **MARKET ORDER**

order to buy or sell securities that is good only for the day on which it was entered: **DAY ORDER**

ordinary, commonplace: **MUNDANE**

ordinary, hackneyed: **BANAL**

ordinary people, common run: **RUCK**

ordinary, simple, commonplace: **EXOTERIC**

ordinary, standard, usual, commonplace: **GARDEN VARIETY**

ordinary, uninspired, commonplace: **PROSAIC**

organic equilibrium: **HOMEOSTASIS**

organic whole has a reality other and greater than the sum of its parts: **HOLISM**

organisms derived asexually from a common ancestor: **CLONES**

organisms in relation to their environment: **ECOLOGY**

organization's members apart from its leaders: **RANK AND FILE**

organizer, manager or sponsor of performers for entertainment: **IMPRESARIO**

organ-like instrument with steam whistles: **CALLIOPE**

organ out-of-placeness internally: **PROLAPSE**

organ that uses reeds and resembles a harmonium: **MELODEON**

orgasmically incapable, not sexually responsive: **ANORGASTIC**

orgiastic, wild, frenzied, pagan, passionate: **DIONYSIAN**

orgy: **BACCHANAL**

Oriental art (chiefly Japanese) of blows used in self-defense: **KARATE**

origin: **PROVENANCE**

original condition, unused, brand new: **MINT CONDITION**

original, creative: **PROMETHEAN**

original, first, principal: **PRIMAL**

original pattern: **ARCHETYPE**

original, primitive, elemental: **PRIMORDIAL**

originate, begin, commence: **INITIATE**

originate, bring forth: **SPAWN**

ornamental designs representing historical subjects: **STORIATION**

ornamental elaborate foliage or flower design: **ARABESQUE**

ornamental italic capital letter: **SWASH LETTER**

ornamental openwork usually composed of interlaced parts: **FRETWORK**

ornamental relief work in metal: **TOREUTICS**

ornamental stand with shelves: **ÉTAGÈRE**

ornamental vertical grooves, as in architectural columns: **FLUTING**

ornamentation done with tools, as on leather: **TOOLING**

ornamentation or style that is extravagant: **BAROQUE**

ornamentation with wavy lines or patterns, or with inlaying or etching, as on iron or steel: **DAMASCENE**

ornament, decorate: **EMBELLISH**

ornamented excessively: **ORNATE**

ornamented tastelessly, showy and cheap: **TAWDRY**

ornament or mark used in typography: **DINGBAT**

ornament or trinket either gaudy or trifling: **FALLAL**

ornament resembling a twisted cable or cord: **TORSADE**

ornament that hangs: **PENDANT**

ornament the edge with a series of indentations: **ENGRAIL**

ornament topping a spire, gable, etc.: **FINIAL**

ornament with raised figures worked on a surface as decoration: **EMBOSS**

ornament worn on a neck chain, pendant: **LAVALIERE**

ornate, excessively flowery: **FLORID**
ornate, florid, showy, bombastic:
 FLAMBOYANT
ornateness to excess: **FROUFROU**
ornate writing: **PURPLE PROSE**
ostentatious, affecting superiority:
 PRETENTIOUS
ostracize: **BLACKBALL**
ostracize, banish from society: **SEND TO
 COVENTRY**
other person to whom one is talking:
 INTERLOCUTOR
other times, other customs: **AUTRES
 TEMPS, AUTRES MOEURS**
O the times! O the customs!:
 O TEMPORA! O MORES!
Our Father prayer, Lord's Prayer:
 PATERNOSTER
out and out: **ARRANT**
outbreak of violence: **RAMPAGE**
outburst of passion or emotion: **ACCESS**
outburst that is sudden and turbulent:
 PAROXYSM
outcast, one socially rejected: **PARIAH**
outcome in a plot: **DENOUEMENT**
outcome that is possible: **EVENTUALITY**
outcry, clamor, shouting: **HUE AND CRY**
outdated, obsolete, discarded:
 SUPERANNUATED
outdo in cruelty or extravagance:
 OUT-HEROD HEROD
outdoor banquet or entertainment: **FÊTE
 CHAMPÊTRE, FÊTE GALANTE**
outdoor celebration, especially a dinner
 or bazaar: **FETE**
outdoors, in open air: **ALFRESCO**
outer coating or covering, especially a
 natural covering: **INTEGUMENT**
outermost limit: **JUMPING-OFF PLACE**
outflow: **EFFLUENT**
outgoing person: **EXTROVERT**
outgrowth that is unnatural, such as a
 wart: **EXCRESCENCE**
outlaw, condemn, prohibit: **PROSCRIBE**
outline: **PROSPECTUS**
outline, form, shape: **FIGURATION**
outline of a film plot or television play:
 TREATMENT
outline of the main points of a course
 of study: **SYLLABUS**
outline or structure of something:
 CONFORMATION
outline sketchily: **ADUMBRATE**
outline, trace out, describe: **DELINEATE**

outlying area: **PURLIEU**
outmoded, old-fashioned, ancient, out of
 step with the times: **ANTEDILUVIAN**
out of action: **HORS DE COMBAT**
out of business: **DEFUNCT**
out of control: **RAMPANT**
out-of-date, not current: **OBSOLETE**
out-of-date, old-fashioned, old hat:
 VIEUX JEU
out-of-date or no longer useful thing:
 MUSEUM PIECE
out of nothing: **EX NIHILO**
out of place, inappropriate:
 MALAPROPOS
out of proportion, not in accordance:
 INCOMMENSURABLE
out-of-the-blue element introduced to
 untangle a story plot: **DEUS EX
 MACHINA**
out of work, laid off (British):
 REDUNDANT
outpatient department of a hospital:
 POLICLINIC
outpouring, as of words: **SPATE**
outrageous, notorious, shocking,
 disgraceful: **FLAGRANT**
outside, not central: **PERIPHERAL**
outsider, person apart from others,
 loner: **ODD MAN OUT**
outside the jurisdiction of a state or
 country: **EXTRATERRITORIAL**
outside the nature of something:
 EXTRINSIC
outspoken, definite, clear,
 straightforward: **EXPLICIT**
outstanding: **PREEMINENT**
outstanding, important feature:
 HIGHLIGHT
outward carrying or conducting, as
 neural pathways conveying
 impulses from a nerve center:
 EFFERENT
outwardly real, or made outwardly real:
 EXTERNALIZED
outwit, avoid: **CIRCUMVENT**
outwit, cheat: **EUCHRE**
ovary removal from a female animal:
 SPAYING
oven or furnace for baking or drying
 bricks, pottery, cement: **KILN**
overabundance: **PLETHORA**
overbearing, arbitrary: **HIGH-HANDED**
overcoat that is heavy: **GREATCOAT**
overcome, beat: **DRUB**

overdemonstrative: EFFUSIVE
overdevelopment, excessive growth:
   HYPERTROPHY
overdo, as an argument: BELABOR
overelaborate, florid, profusely or finely
   baroque: ROCOCO
overexcited or easily excitable, worked
   up, high-strung: HYPER
overflowing: INUNDANT
overflowing, full: TEEMING
overflowing, lavish: EXUBERANT
overflow or rise of a stream occurring
   suddenly: FRESHET
overland bearing of a boat or supplies
   where a waterway is not navigable,
   or the place for this: PORTAGE
overlapping condition: IMBRICATION
overlapping edges, as of tiles or
   shingles: IMBRICATE
overloaded, inflated: PLETHORIC
overlook, disregard: PRETERMIT
overlook something as if it had not
   happened: CONDONE
overly polite: CEREMONIOUS
overnice, squeamish: FASTIDIOUS
overprecise, finicky: NIGGLING
overreacher, attempter of something
   beyond his or her abilities:
   ULTRACREPIDARIAN
overrefined in behavior, writing, etc.:
   PRECIOUS
overrun, occur in large numbers so as
   to be annoying or dangerous:
   INFEST
overseeing to supervise or monitor:
   OVERSIGHT

overshadowing: ADUMBRAL
overshadow, obscure, surpass: ECLIPSE
oversight: INADVERTENCE
oversimplifying: SIMPLISTIC
oversleeping, profound sleepiness:
   HYPERSOMNIA
overspread, as with color: SUFFUSE
overstatement or exaggeration intended
   for the effect and not to be taken
   seriously: HYPERBOLE
overstrained, nervously excited:
   OVERWROUGHT
overthrow of a government, usually
   sudden and often accompanied by
   violence: COUP D'ÉTAT
overthrow, reversal or disruption,
   disorder, confusion, upset:
   BOULEVERSEMENT
overthrow, undermine: SUBVERT
overweight condition: EMBONPOINT
overwhelming, domineering:
   OVERBEARING
overwhelm, swallow up: ENGULF
owned by a proprietor, protected as by
   patent or copyright: PROPRIETARY
owner or tycoon of the late 19th
   century who was powerful and
   exploitive: ROBBER BARON
ownership of securities: LONG
Oxford and Cambridge and the British
   tradition and prestige they
   represent: OXBRIDGE
Oxford or Cambridge English:
   RECEIVED STANDARD
Oxford resident: OXONIAN
oxygen in liquid form: LOX

pacesetter, leader: FUGLEMAN
pacifist or defeatist propaganda:
    BOLOISM
pacify, appease, quiet down: MOLLIFY
pacifying measures to avoid or temper
    popular discontent: BREAD AND
    CIRCUSES
pacify, soothe: SALVE
packaging of clear plastic affixed to
    cardboard: BLISTER PACK
pack animal, beast of burden: SUMPTER
packed or wedged firmly, thickly
    populated: IMPACTED
packing material composed of thin
    wood shavings: EXCELSIOR
pack or force down by repeated
    pressure: TAMP
pagan, wild, frenzied, orgiastic,
    passionate: DIONYSIAN
page at the start of a book:
    FRONTISPIECE
page in a book or magazine that is
    larger than page size and can be
    unfolded: GATEFOLD
page number in a book: FOLIO
page on the left-hand side of a book:
    VERSO
page on the right-hand side of a book:
    RECTO
pages of a magazine or newspaper that
    face each other and include related
    material: DOUBLE TRUCK, SPREAD
paid for in cash without delivery: CASH
    AND CARRY
pail's or bucket's wire handle: BAIL
pain-combating: ANALGESIC
pain-free state: ANALGESIA
painful, agonizing: EXCRUCIATING
painful experience, endurance test:
    ORDEAL

painful inflammation near the shoulder:
    BURSITIS
painful, sad, mournful: DOLOROUS
painful sensation of a lost limb felt by
    amputees: PHANTOM LIMB PAIN
pain inflicted on others as a source of
    pleasure for the inflicter: SADISM
pain-relieving: ANODYNE
painstaking, overly precise about details:
    METICULOUS
pains that are violent: THROES
pain, suffering, anguish, distress:
    TRAVAIL
paint atomizer for delicate work or
    photographic retouching:
    AIRBRUSH
paint, engrave or draw with dots
    instead of lines: STIPPLE
painter's (housepainter's) paste for
    filling surface cracks: SPACKLE
painting by splattering, dripping,
    smearing, etc., for a spontaneous or
    random effect: ACTION PAINTING
painting in open air to render natural
    atmosphere and light: PLEINAIRISM
painting in water colors on wet plaster:
    FRESCO
painting in which pigment is applied
    thickly to a surface: IMPASTO
painting-like, finely artistic or
    descriptive: PAINTERLY
painting medium like oils but made of
    resin-based dilutable paint:
    ACRYLICS
painting medium made from a mixture
    of water and other substances such
    as egg yolks or glue: TEMPERA
painting method of using varicolored
    dots: POINTILLISM
painting, using shades of gray only,

often in imitation of bas-relief:
GRISAILLE
painting with opaque watercolors:
GOUACHE
paired, double, two: BINARY
paired, separated into pairs:
DICHOTOMIZED
pair of matched horses or oxen: SPAN
pair of objects considered as a single
unit: DUAD
pale and thin: PEAKED
pale, colorless: PALLID
pale, ghastly, gaunt: CADAVEROUS
pale or sallow face: WHEYFACE
pale, pallid, wan: PEAKED
palmistry: CHIROMANCY
palm off: FOB OFF
palm of the hand, sole of the foot:
VOLAR
palm of the hand's rounded part below
the thumb: THENAR
paltry, pitiable, inferior: SORRY
paltry, trivial: PICAYUNE
pamper: CODDLE
pampered, overindulged: SPOON-FED
pamper, pet: COSSET
panacea: CATHOLICON
pancakes that are thin and have a
filling: CRÊPES
pancakes that are thin and rolled in hot
orange sauce: CRÊPES SUZETTE
paneled lower part of an inner wall:
WAINSCOT
panel of prospective jurors: VENIRE
panic, amazement or fear that is sudden
and paralyzing: CONSTERNATION
pantomime, especially in which
Harlequin and a clown play
leading parts: HARLEQUINADE
pantomime in shadows thrown on a
screen or wall: GALANTY SHOW
pants for leisure that end just below the
knee: CLAM DIGGERS
pants for men that are wide and
gathered just below the knees:
KNICKERBOCKERS, KNICKERS
pants of old that were loose and wide:
GALLIGASKINS
panty-like garment that is tiny and
revealing: CACHE-SEXE
papal envoy who carries insignia to new
cardinals: ABLEGATE
papal letter addressed to the bishops of
the world: ENCYCLICAL

papal letter replying to an ecclesiastical
question: DECRETAL
paper at the front and back of a book,
one half of which is pasted to the
binding: END PAPER
paper being of high grade with a
smooth surface: WIRE-WOVE
paper chewed into a wet wad for
throwing: SPITBALL
paper cover slipped around a book:
DUST JACKET
paper fastener made of thin wire:
STAPLE
paper hole reinforcing ring for loose-leaf
sheets: REINFORCEMENT
paper in a unit of 480 to 516 sheets:
REAM
paper-like pulp that can be molded:
PAPIER-MÂCHÉ
paper mark of translucent lines or
designs: WATERMARK
paper money in small amounts: SCRIP
paper piece or scrap: SCRIP
paper size, 23 by 31 inches: IMPERIAL
paper that does not carry the marks of
the wire gauze on which it was
laid: WOVE PAPER
paper that measures 13 by 16 inches:
FOOLSCAP
paper used by lawyers and usually
measuring about 8½ by 13 inches:
LEGAL CAP
paper watermarked with fine parallel
lines: LAID PAPER
parade: CAVALCADE
parade of slaves, prisoners or animals
fastened together: COFFLE
parade or display brazenly or gaudily:
FLAUNT
parade or exhibition that is spectacular:
PAGEANT
paradise: ELYSIAN FIELDS
paradise for riches or opportunity: EL
DORADO
paragon, unequaled: NONPAREIL
paragraph symbol (¶): PILCROW
parallel lines slanting on each side of a
spine: HERRINGBONE
parallelogram with oblique angles and
its opposite sides equal: RHOMBOID
paralysis of both arms and both legs or
from the neck down:
QUADRIPLEGIA

paralysis of one side of the body: HEMIPLEGIA

paralysis of the lower part of the body: PARAPLEGIA

paralyze with fear, harden, deaden: PETRIFY

parasite and opportunist around another or others: HANGER-ON

parched, arid: TORRID

parchment or tablet on which earlier writing has been erased to make room for a new inscription: PALIMPSEST

pardonable, as sins: REMISSIBLE

pardonable or excusable, as a fault: VENIAL

pardon by a government given in general: AMNESTY

parentage, line of descent: FILIATION

parentally replacing, acting in lieu of a mother or father: IN LOCO PARENTIS

parent killing: PARRICIDE

parents of an adopted child: ADOPTIVE PARENTS

Paris shopgirl or seamstress: MIDINETTE

parka: ANORAK

parking meter support emplaced in the sidewalk: PIPE STANDARD

parley to gain time: TEMPORIZE

parroting, rote repetition in speech: PSITTACISM

part, divide, separate: DISSEVER

partiality or bias held in advance: PREDILECTION

particle hypothesized by physicists: QUARK

particle, speck: MOTE

particular in application, not general: AD HOC

particular instances to generalization: A POSTERIORI

particularize: INDIVIDUATE

particular to the general, as in reasoning: INDUCTION

parting of the ways, break in a relationship: RIFT

partisan, doctrinal: SECTARIAN

partisan who is rabid, fanatic: ZEALOT

partnership of dissimilar organisms: SYMBIOSIS

partnership or company distinguished from a corporation: FIRM

part of a debt or of a serial story: INSTALLMENT

part-of-speech shifting, as when a noun is used as a verb: FUNCTIONAL SHIFT

part that is the best or the most appealing: BEAUTY PART

part-time amusement: DIVERSION

part-time, occasional or temporary lodging place: PIED-À-TERRE

part used to stand for the whole: SYNECDOCHE

party given in the evening: SOIREE

passage of ornate writing: PURPLE PROSE

passage or extract, especially from the Bible: PERICOPE

passageway, as between a house and garage: BREEZEWAY

passageway or arcade open on one side: LOGGIA

passageway or entrance, as into a mine: ADIT

passageway that is narrow, especially at an English cathedral: SLYPE

pass assuring the bearer protection on a journey, as in time of war: SAFE-CONDUCT

pass away, slip by (said of time): ELAPSE

pass imperceptibly from one shade or degree to another: GRADATE

passing lightly from one subject to another, wandering from the point: DISCURSIVE

passing out of use, becoming obsolete: OBSOLESCENT

passionate, ardent: TORRID

passion or love that is foolish or unreasoning: INFATUATION

passive consent: ACQUIESCENCE

passive consent: SUFFERANCE

passive resistance: SATYAGRAHA

passkey, master key: PASSE-PARTOUT

Passover book containing story of the Exodus: HAGGADAH

passport endorsement granting entry into or passage through a country: VISA

pass through or survive, as a crisis: WEATHER

pass through tissue: TRANSPIRE

pass to the next round by a competitor: BYE

password, rallying cry: WATCHWORD
password, test word: SHIBBOLETH
pasta in the form of dumplings:
GNOCCHI
pastoral and simple, rustic, peaceful:
ARCADIAN
pastoral, rustic: BUCOLIC
pastry shell, fried, in which food may
be served: TIMBALE
pastry shell to be filled with meat or
fish: VOL-AU-VENT
pastry store: PATISSERIE
patch, decoration or trimming glued or
sewn on: APPLIQUÉ
path: ACCESS
path of an object moving through
space: TRAJECTORY
patient endurance or suffering,
forbearance: LONGANIMITY
patient treated at a hospital but not
staying there: OUTPATIENT
patient waiting as a strategy: WAITING
GAME
patriotism that is overzealous:
CHAUVINISM
patriot of an aggressive and boastful
nature: JINGO
patrol wagon: BLACK MARIA
patronizing: CONDESCENDING
patron of the arts: MAECENAS
pattern, model, example: PARADIGM
pattern, model, typical example:
EXEMPLAR
pattern or gauge used to copy
something accurately, as in
woodworking: TEMPLATE
pause or interruption of continuity, gap,
opening: HIATUS
pause temporarily, stop at intervals:
INTERMIT
pawn, pledge: IMPIGNORATE
pay back, compensate: REIMBURSE
pay, fee or a tip, compensation:
EMOLUMENT
pay for, compensate: REMUNERATE
paying back money originally invested:
SELF-LIQUIDATING
payment by each of his own meal
ticket, party fee, etc.: DUTCH
TREAT
payment extorted to prevent disclosure:
BLACKMAIL
payment for exclusive stories,
interviews, etc.: CHECKBOOK
JOURNALISM

payment for release of a seized person
or stolen property: RANSOM
payment, from earnings of a
corporation, to be made to
shareholders: DIVIDEND
payment immediately on delivery: SPOT
CASH
payment in addition to salary, such as
pension, insurance, etc.: FRINGE
BENEFIT
payment offered for something
ordinarily not remunerated:
HONORARIUM
payment or favor beyond regular salary
or profit: PERQUISITE
payoff messenger, illegal-money
trafficker: BAGMAN
pay out: DISBURSE
pay that is more than normal given to a
dismissed employee: SEVERANCE
PAY
pay to a clergyman from church
revenues: PREBEND
peaceable, showing goodwill: AMICABLE
peace be with you: PAX VOBISCUM
peaceful civil disobedience:
SATYAGRAHA
peaceful in purpose: IRENIC
peaceful, placid: PACIFIC
peaceful, tranquil, calm: PLACID
peace of mind: ATARAXIA
peace pipe: CALUMET
peace terms imposed by a dominant
country, or a state of peace that is
precarious: PAX ROMANA
peanuts, piddling thing or amount,
nothing to all intents and purposes:
BUPKES
pearl-like, iridescent: NACREOUS
pear-shaped: PYRIFORM
peculiarity in behavior or speech,
affectation of style: MANNERISM
peculiarity, whim, fancy: CROTCHET
peculiar to a given country or people,
native to a given area: ENDEMIC
pedantic: DIDACTIC
pedantic, dogmatic teacher: PEDAGOGUE
pedantic literary effort: LUCUBRATION
pedantic love of logic: ERGOISM
pedantic, moralizing: DIDACTIC
pedantic music teacher or critic:
BECKMESSER
pedantic or affected erudite word:
INKHORN WORD

pedantic, smug or overexacting person: **PRIG**

peddler of Bibles and other books: **COLPORTEUR**

peddler of food, liquor, etc. to an army: **SUTLER**

peddle, sell goods in the street: **HAWK**

pedestal on which a statue or column stands: **PLINTH**

pedestal part between the base and the cornice: **DADO**

pedestrian who disregards traffic rules: **JAYWALKER**

pedigree record of thoroughbred stock: **STUD BOOK**

peeping Tom: **VOYEUR**

peep show, street show: **RAREE SHOW**

peevish: **PETTISH**

peevish, bad-tempered, snappish: **WASPISH**

peevish, gloomy: **DYSPEPTIC**

peevish, ill-tempered: **BILIOUS**

peevishness, ill temper, spitefulness: **SPLEEN**

peevishness, irritableness: **PETULANCE**

pelt, shower, spatter: **PEPPER**

penalty in which something is given up or taken away: **FORFEIT**

penalty or obligation established by authority: **IMPOSITION**

pencil lead: **GRAPHITE**

pencil-like stick, often of alum, used to stop bleeding: **STYPTIC PENCIL**

pendant, neck-chain ornament: **LAVALIERE**

pendulum's length of swing: **RATING**

penetrate, spread through completely: **PERMEATE**

peninsula: **CHERSONESE**

penis erection as a persistent pathological condition: **PRIAPISM**

penis in rigid, enlarged condition: **ERECTION**

penis-like: **PHALLIC**

penis-like representation: **PHALLUS**

penis-representing or -symbolizing in a prominent way, as in certain primitive art: **ITHYPHALLIC**

penmanship as an art: **CHIROGRAPHY**

penmanship that is beautiful: **CALLIGRAPHY**

pen name: **NOM DE PLUME**

penniless, poor: **IMPECUNIOUS**

pension, allowance, salary: **STIPEND**

pension drawing while holding another job: **DOUBLE-DIPPING**

pension recipient, retired person: **PENSIONER**

Pentateuch, Jewish law and literature: **TORAH**

people collectively, especially those outside a specific profession or occupation: **LAITY**

people forced by circumstances to listen: **CAPTIVE AUDIENCE**

people's protector or champion: **TRIBUNE**

pep up, cheer up, stimulate, invigorate: **EXHILARATE**

perceived below the threshold of consciousness: **SUBLIMINAL**

perceive, recognize as different: **DISCERN**

percentage of total that must be paid by customer when the broker's credit is used to buy a security: **MARGIN**

perception after the event: **HINDSIGHT**

perception independent of senses: **EXTRASENSORY PERCEPTION (ESP)**

perception of distant objects by other than normal sensory means: **TELESTHESIA**

perception of one's own consciousness: **APPERCEPTION**

perception or knowing of a fact: **COGNIZANCE**

perception that has no external stimulus: **HALLUCINATION**

perceptive, keen, discerning: **PERSPICACIOUS**

perfect example: **ARCHETYPE**

perfection: **NE PLUS ULTRA**

perform a ceremony: **SOLEMNIZE**

performance added in response to audience demand: **ENCORE**

performance or interpretation of a text, role, etc.: **RENDITION**

performance that is dazzling or a triumph: **STAR TURN**

performer having a very small part, as in a play: **WALK-ON**

performer's special talent or piece of business: **SHTICK**

performing services for a fixed payment: **STIPENDIARY**

performing to win applause or approval: **GRANDSTAND PLAY**

perform, invent or produce without

previous thought or preparation:
IMPROVISE
perform the functions of an office:
OFFICIATE
perfumed powder in a bag: **SACHET**
perfume floral essence or ingredient:
ATTAR
perfume or oil from the East Indies:
PATCHOULI
peril that is imminent: **SWORD OF**
DAMOCLES
period, century, era: **SIÈCLE**
periodical of a company for its
employees: **HOUSE ORGAN**
period of happiness, comfort or wealth:
MILLENNIUM
period of temporary amity or
agreement: **HONEYMOON**
period of time that is incalculable,
eternity: **EON**
periods used to indicate the omission of
words: **POINTS OF ELLIPSIS**
period that divides some longer or
periodic process: **INTERLUDE**
period when work is not being done,
equipment is broken, etc.:
DOWNTIME
perjure oneself: **FORSWEAR**
permanence of position: **TENURE**
permanent: **INDELIBLE**
permanent, durable: **PERDURABLE**
permeable through pores: **POROUS**
permeate, circulate: **DIFFUSE**
permeate, fertilize: **IMPREGNATE**
permeate, fill or impregnate thoroughly:
SATURATE
permeation gradually of thoughts or
facts: **OSMOSIS**
permissible, allowable, worthy:
ADMISSIBLE
permission given or implied by failure
to prohibit: **SUFFERANCE**
permit, ratify, approve: **SANCTION**
permit with condescension: **VOUCHSAFE**
perplex, dumbfound, bewilder:
NONPLUS
perplexing situation: **QUANDARY**
persecution complex: **PARANOIA**
persecution imposed by the military:
DRAGONNADE
persecutor, torturer: **TORQUEMADA**
persecutory campaign to blame or
punish certain people: **WITCH-HUNT**
persevering: **ASSIDUOUS**
persevering, stubborn: **INDOMITABLE**

persistent: **ASSIDUOUS**
persistently demand: **IMPORTUNE**
persistent striving: **PERSEVERANCE**
persistent, stubborn: **PERTINACIOUS**
persistent, tough, stubborn: **TENACIOUS**
persister in error: **MUMPSIMUS**
persnickety person: **FUSSBUDGET**
person acting as if mechanically:
AUTOMATON
personal-attack propaganda, political
slander, reputation-damaging
campaign: **CHARACTER**
ASSASSINATION
personal excellence: **CALIBER**
personal feelings of one's mind being
the source of judgment, as opposed
to objective criteria: **SUBJECTIVE**
personality characterized
psychologically as aggressive,
impatient and competitive and
hence making the individual
possibly more prone to heart
disease: **TYPE-A PERSONALITY**
personality characterized
psychologically as relaxed, patient
and tolerant and hence making the
individual possibly less prone to
heart disease: **TYPE-B**
PERSONALITY
personality test involving interpretation
of standard ink blots: **RORSCHACH**
TEST
personal need as motivation:
BREAD-AND-BUTTER
personal property: **CHATTEL**
personal property, one's own possession:
PECULIUM
person, animal or plant that lives off
another: **PARASITE**
person apart from others, outsider,
loner: **ODD MAN OUT**
person from whom a family descends:
STIRPS
person from whom a nation, city or
epoch is said to derive its name:
EPONYM
personification: **PROSOPOPEIA**
personified: **INCARNATE**
person moved out of a destroyed or
threatened area: **EVACUEE**
personnel reduction through retirement,
etc.: **ATTRITION**
personnel specialist who recruits
executives: **HEADHUNTER**
person of the same age: **AGEMATE**

person seeking wealth: CHREMATIST

person thought of as a perfect example: PERSONIFICATION

person to whom secrets are confided: CONFIDANT

person who buys and sells for another, on commission: BROKER

person who drops things: BUTTERFINGERS

person who enjoys good living: BON VIVANT

person who goes beyond his or her abilities: ULTRACREPIDARIAN

person who identifies with the opposite sex and undergoes surgery and hormone treatments to that end: TRANSSEXUAL

person who is a cultured or aristocratic snob: BRAHMIN

person who is admirable but not polished: DIAMOND IN THE ROUGH

person who is decent, reliable and mature: MENSCH

person who remains in the same locale: SEDENS

person whose success is short-lived: FLASH IN THE PAN

person who utters prophecies of disaster: CASSANDRA

person with specialized knowledge, expert: COGNOSCENTE

person with two or more distinct personalities, a psychiatric disorder: MULTIPLE PERSONALITY

perspective point in a linear drawing where parallel lines converge: VANISHING POINT

perspiration that is copious: DIAPHORESIS

perspiration that smells bad: BROMIDROSIS

perspiration that smells bad, bromidrosis: KAKIDROSIS

persuadable, tractable: PLIANT

persuade one to act or speak: INDUCE

persuade or try to persuade by flattery: WHEEDLE

persuasive, insincere flattery or blather: SNOW JOB

persuasively forceful: COGENT

persuasive pressure or intimidation, especially by a president: JAWBONING

pertinent, appropriate: RELEVANT

pertinent, related to what is being discussed, relevant: GERMANE

Peruvian corded device for counting: QUIPU

pervade, animate: INFORM

pervade, saturate, wet thoroughly: IMBUE

pessimism, melancholy, romantic world-weariness: WELTSCHMERZ

pessimist, depressing person, killjoy: CRAPEHANGER, CREPEHANGER

pessimistic about stock prices: BEARISH

pester, press a debtor for payment: DUN

pest, nag, whiner: NUDGE, NOODGE

pests: VERMIN

pet idea or notion: MAROTTE

petitioner: POSTULANT

pet name or endearing diminutive: HYPOCORISM

pet phrase: BYWORD

petty, cheap, sleazy: CHINTZY

petty, contemptible, trivial: PALTRY

petty, nagging: NIGGLING

petty, trivial: INSIGNIFICANT

petty, trivial, mean: PICAYUNE

petulant, self-important: HOITY-TOITY

phallus-representing or -symbolizing in a prominent way, as in certain primitive art: ITHYPHALLIC

phantom: EIDOLON

pharmacist: APOTHECARY

phase, side or aspect of a person or subject: FACET

philosophical or political enthusiast with a definite viewpoint or bias: IDEOLOGUE

philosophical rule that theories or concepts should be simple: OCCAM'S RAZOR

phobias (In the following listing read the words irrational fear of ahead of each entry.)

air or drafts: AEROPHOBIA

aloneness: AUTOPHOBIA

animals: ZOOPHOBIA

bad men: SCELEROPHOBIA

being touched: HAPTEPHOBIA

blood: HEMOPHOBIA

blushing: ERYTHROPHOBIA

bridges: GEPHYROPHOBIA

burial alive: TAPHEPHOBIA

cats: AILUROPHOBIA

children: PEDOPHOBIA

cold: PSYCHROPHOBIA

confinement: CLAUSTROPHOBIA

contamination: MYSOPHOBIA
crowds: DEMOPHOBIA,
    OCHLOPHOBIA
dead bodies: NECROPHOBIA
death: THANATOPHOBIA,
    NECROPHOBIA
defecation: RHYPOPHOBIA
depths: BATHOPHOBIA
dirt: MYSOPHOBIA, RUPOPHOBIA
dogs: CYNOPHOBIA
dust: AMATHOPHOBIA
eating: PHAGOPHOBIA
England, the English: ANGLOPHOBIA
failure: KAKORRHAPHIOPHOBIA
fire: PYROPHOBIA
floods: ANTLOPHOBIA
foreigners, strangers: XENOPHOBIA
ghosts: PHASMOPHOBIA
heights: ACROPHOBIA
high objects: BATOPHOBIA
ideas: IDEOPHOBIA
infinity: APEIROPHOBIA
insects: ACAROPHOBIA,
    ENTOMOPHOBIA
knives: AICHMOPHOBIA
lice: PEDICULOPHOBIA
marriage: GAMOPHOBIA
men: ANDROPHOBIA
mice: MUSOPHOBIA
missiles: BALLISTOPHOBIA
movement: KINESOPHOBIA
night: NYCTOPHOBIA
noise: PHONOPHOBIA
novelty: NEOPHOBIA
number 13: TRISKAIDEKAPHOBIA
ocean: THALASSOPHOBIA
open spaces: AGORAPHOBIA
pain: ALGOPHOBIA
poison: TOXICOPHOBIA
precipices: CREMNOPHOBIA
red: ERYTHROPHOBIA
responsibility: HYPENGYOPHOBIA
ridicule: CATAGELOPHOBIA
robbers: HARPAXOPHOBIA
sexual intercourse: COITOPHOBIA
sharp objects: AICHMOPHOBIA
sinning: PECCATIPHOBIA
sleep: HYPNOPHOBIA
snakes: OPHIDIOPHOBIA
snow: CHIONOPHOBIA
solitude: AUTOPHOBIA
speaking: LALOPHOBIA
spiders: ARACHNEOPHOBIA
stillness: EREMIOPHOBIA
stars: ASTROPHOBIA

thunderstorms: ASTRAPHOBIA,
    BRONTOPHOBIA
touched, being: HAPHEPHOBIA
venereal disease: CYPRIDOPHOBIA
women: GYNOPHOBIA
phonograph-record catalog, as one of
    those by a particular artist:
    DISCOGRAPHY
phonograph-record collector or
    connoisseur: DISCOPHILE
phony and sweet, oily in flattery,
    ingratiating: SMARMY
phony corporation or front: DUMMY
    CORPORATION
phony, false, sham, counterfeit, fake:
    BOGUS
phony in speech, not frank:
    MEALYMOUTHED
photographer of celebrities: PAPARAZZO
photograph improvement through
    handwork to remove blemishes or
    add details: RETOUCHING
photograph on a silver or copper plate,
    an old process: DAGUERREOTYPE
photographs attractively: PHOTOGENIC
phrase, clause or word inserted in a
    sentence to add explanation or
    comment: PARENTHESIS
phraseology peculiar to a language or
    region and accepted though it may
    differ from the normal pattern:
    IDIOM
phraseology, verbal expression:
    LOCUTION
phrase or put into words: COUCH
phrase or watchword of a group:
    SHIBBOLETH
physical build and constitution as
    related to disease: HABITUS
physically strong: POTENT
physically suitable for marriage: NUBILE
physician's training period at a hospital:
    RESIDENCY
piano-like instrument: CLAVICHORD
pickle in a spicy and vinegary solution:
    MARINATE
pick, sort out, select: CULL
picnic or garden party on a grand scale:
    FÊTE CHAMPÊTRE, FÊTE GALANTE
picnic, pleasure trip, feast, banquet:
    JUNKET
picture, image, likeness, usually an
    object of veneration: ICON
picture-like scene represented by silent

and motionless persons: TABLEAU VIVANT

picture or symbol representing a word, sound or object: HIEROGLYPHIC

picture painted on transparent curtains: DIORAMA

picture printed from an engraving made with a hard needle: DRYPOINT

picture produced by superimposing different pictorial elements to make a single composition: MONTAGE

picturesque, pleasant: IDYLLIC

piddling thing or amount, nothing to all intents and purposes, peanuts: BUPKES

piece cut or broken off: CANTLE

pierced or perforated for design purposes, openwork: À JOUR, AJOURÉ

pierce through, impale: TRANSFIX

pier or wharf to protect a harbor or beach: JETTY

pie that is custard-like and made of cheese, bacon, etc., and served hot: QUICHE LORRAINE

pigeon, especially when an unfledged nestling: SQUAB

pigheaded, stubborn, unyielding: OBSTINATE

pig-like, swinish, hoggish: PORCINE

pigmentation deficiency: ALBINISM

pike with a battle-ax as a head: HALBERD

pile of stones as a marker, monument or grave: CAIRN

pile of wood, etc., for burning a dead body: PYRE

piles: HEMORRHOIDS

pilfer: FILCH

pillage during a search: RANSACK

pillage, plunder, prey upon: DEPREDATE

pillage, ruin, wreck: RAVAGE

pillar in the shape of a female figure: CARYATID

pillar in the shape of a male figure: TELAMON

pimp: PANDER

pimp (British): PONCE

pincers of small size: TWEEZERS

pincers, small tongs: FORCEPS

pinch, nip, tickle, twitch: VELLICATE

pineapple-shaped: PINEAL

pine cone's wood-like petal: SCALE

pine, weaken, droop gradually: LANGUISH

pin for locking inserted into a wheel's shaft or axle: LINCHPIN

pink-eyed and white-skinned person: ALBINO

pinkie: LITTLE FINGER

pin someone or something with or upon a sharp stake: IMPALE

pins, ribbons and other small miscellaneous articles for sale: NOTIONS

pin that is split with ends that can be bent to affix after passing through a hole: COTTER PIN

pinwheel-like firework: CATHERINE WHEEL

pipe exclusive of the stem, including the bowl and the shank: STUMMEL

pipe for smoking made of light white silicate material and often with a flared bowl: MEERSCHAUM

pipe that is vertical or tower for water: STANDPIPE

pipe with a tube passing through water to cool the smoke: HOOKAH

pirate: PICAROON

pirate black flag with a white skull and crossbones: JOLLY ROGER

pirate or appropriate the ideas, writings, music, etc., of another: PLAGIARIZE

pitcher or jug with a wide mouth: EWER

pitching-speed hand-held measuring device used at baseball games: RADAR GUN

pithy saying: APOTHEGM

pitiable, inferior, paltry: SORRY

pitiful, causing sorrow, sad: PATHETIC

pitiless, hardhearted, stubborn: OBDURATE

pitiless, harsh: RELENTLESS

pit of the stomach: SOLAR PLEXUS

pivot about: SLUE

pivotal, pivoting on its own axis: TROCHOID

place for storing goods: REPOSITORY

place in a female mammal where young are generated and developed: UTERUS, WOMB

place name, or name derived from a place: TOPONYM

place names, pertaining to: TOPONOMASTIC

place of rest or shelter: HOSPICE

place or install in office formally: INVEST

place or position forces according to a plan: DEPLOY

place's general atmosphere, feeling or spirit: GENIUS LOCI

place to stand on: POU STO

place to withdraw from reality or practicality: IVORY TOWER

place where a crime is committed or a trial is to be held: VENUE

place where criminals, addicts, etc., are helped to readjust to society: HALFWAY HOUSE

placing or situating of something erroneously: ANACHORISM

plaid or pattern of colored lines forming squares of solid background: TATTERSALL

plain: UNVARNISHED

plain, clear, obvious, evident: MANIFEST

plain devoid of forest, especially one of the extensive plains in Russia: STEPPE

plain, direct: FLAT-FOOTED

plain of Arctic regions, treeless and vast: TUNDRA

plain, rolling tract of open land: WOLD

plain, simple, rough: RUSTIC

plait: PLEACH

plane designed for short takeoffs and landings: STOL

plane designed for vertical takeoffs and landings: VTOL

planets and stars shown as models or images on a circular dome: PLANETARIUM

planing tool having a blade set between two handles: SPOKESHAVE

planned deliberately, premeditated: STUDIED

planning for the future, prudence: PROVIDENCE

plan of top priority to meet an emergency: CRASH PROGRAM

plan, proposal, undertaking: PROJECT

plant adapted to extreme changes of weather: TROPOPHYTE

plant and animal comparison as a science: BIOSTATICS

plant and animal periodicity as a study: PHENOLOGY

plant and animal structures, apart from function, as a study: MORPHOLOGY

plant-eating, feeding on vegetables: HERBIVOROUS

plant-growing method using nutrient mineral solutions rather than soil: HYDROPONICS

planting of flowers or foliage in an abstract design: CARPET BEDDING

plant or animal selected as representative of a new species: HOLOTYPE

plant or animal series of changes in formation: SERE

plant or animal surviving from an earlier period or type: RELICT

plants growing in a given region: FLORA

plaster of Paris and glue mixed as a base for painting or for making of bas-reliefs: GESSO

plaster or a similar wall coating: PARGET

plastic disk flipped and sailed in a game of catch: FRISBEE

plastic that is transparent or translucent: LUCITE

plateau that is small and steep-walled: MESA

platform for a coffin: BIER

platform, low and wheeled: DOLLY

platform or small porch with steps, at the entrance to a house or apartment building: STOOP

platform that an orchestra conductor or a speaker stands on: PODIUM

platform that is raised and on which guests of honor or speakers are seated: DAIS

platitude: BROMIDE

plausible but not true: SPECIOUS

player in sports who is not on the regular team: SCRUB

playful conversation: BANTER

playful, jesting: JOCOSE

playfully leap about: CAPER

playful mischief, pranks, roguish sportiveness, frolicking: ESPIÈGLERIE

playfulness, fun, quip: JEST

playful or lively movement in music: SCHERZO

playful teasing: BADINAGE

play rehearsal, usually the final one, performed exactly as the play will be on opening night: DRESS REHEARSAL

play side by side: COLLOCATE

play written for reading rather than performance: **CLOSET DRAMA**

plead against, disapprove: **DEPRECATE**

plead in protest or opposition: **REMONSTRATE**

plead poverty: **POOR-MOUTH**

pleasantness: **AMENITY**

pleasant-tasting, savory: **SAPID**

please, if you please: **S'IL VOUS PLAÎT**

please reply: **RÉPONDEZ S'IL VOUS PLAÎT (R.S.V.P.)**

pleasing: **PREPOSSESSING**

pleasing, attractive: **WINSOME**

pleasing in sound, harmonious, smooth: **EUPHONIOUS**

pleasing-the-people measures to avoid or temper discontent: **BREAD AND CIRCUSES**

pleasurable and unpleasurable states as a psychological study: **HEDONICS**

pleasurably excited: **TITILLATED**

pleasure as the only good and proper goal or moral behavior: **HEDONISM**

pleasure at one's own suffering or pain: **MASOCHISM**

pleasure in another's troubles: **SCHADENFREUDE**

pleasure-loving and luxury-loving person: **SYBARITE**

pleasure or self-indulgence as a way of life: **PRIMROSE PATH**

pleasure-seeking and pain-avoiding drive of the ego: **PLEASURE PRINCIPLE**

pleasure trip, banquet, picnic, feast: **JUNKET**

pleated or plaited, as a fan: **PLICATED**

pleats that resemble bellows folds of an accordion: **ACCORDION PLEATS**

pledged property set aside by a borrower to insure repayment of a loan: **COLLATERAL**

pledge of securities or property as collateral for a loan: **HYPOTHECATION**

pledge, pawn: **IMPIGNORATE**

pledge, security, challenge: **GAGE**

plentiful: **BOUNTEOUS**

plentiful, abundant: **RIFE**

pliable: **PLASTIC**

pliable, flexible: **MALLEABLE**

pliant, supple, agile, lithe: **LISSOME**

plod, as through mud: **SLOG**

plot, conspiracy, secret and underhanded activity: **INTRIGUE**

plotting group of evildoers: **CAMORRA**

plot to foil another, oppose in a secret way: **COUNTERMINE**

plucking an instrument's strings: **PIZZICATO**

plucking handpiece for playing a stringed instrument: **PLECTRUM**

plucking out, forcible extracting, uprooting: **EVULSION**

pluck, spirit, courage: **METTLE**

plucky: **GAME**

plug or seal edges or crevices: **CAULK**

plume on a helmet: **PANACHE**

plump in a pleasing way, well-rounded, buxom, as a woman: **ZOFTIG, ZAFTIG**

plump in body structure: **ENDOMORPHIC, PYKNIC**

plumpness: **EMBONPOINT**

plump, rounded out: **ROTUND**

plunder: **PILLAGE**

plunder during a search: **RANSACK**

plunder, invade for booty, raid: **MARAUD**

plunder or destroy a city: **RAPE**

plunder, pillage, prey upon: **DEPREDATE**

plunder, pillage, raid: **FORAY**

plunge straight down: **PLUMMET**

pocket for a watch: **FOB**

pod, husk, shell: **SHUCK**

poem being metrically complete: **ACATALECTIC**

poem in which one poet mourns the death of another: **MONODY**

poem of a short, pastoral nature: **ECLOGUE**

poem of eight lines and two rhymes with two of the lines repeated: **TRIOLET**

poem of ten or thirteen lines with two rhymes: **RONDEAU**

poem of three stanzas and an envoy, the last lines of which are the same: **BALLADE**

poem or arrangement of words in which certain letters of each line spell a word: **ACROSTIC**

poem or composition in which the end letters of successive lines form a word: **TELESTICH**

poem or composition in which the middle letters of successive lines form a word: **MESOSTICH**

poem or stanza of four lines: **QUATRAIN**

poem retracting something stated in an earlier one: PALINODE

poem, using only two rhymes, of five three-line stanzas followed by a quatrain (aba aba aba aba aba abaa): VILLANELLE

poem usually of fourteen lines in rhymed iambic pentameter: SONNET

poem with a "where are" theme of the fleetingness of life: UBI SUNT

poet: BARD

poetic forms as a study: PROSODY

poetic, involving poetry: PARNASSIAN

poetic irregular rhythm similar to that of normal speech and using initial stresses and an undetermined number of unstressed syllables: SPRUNG RHYTHM

poetic line of 12 syllables in iambic meter, usually with a caesura following the third foot: ALEXANDRINE

poetic metrical foot consisting of three syllables, the first accented, the others not: DACTYL

poetic metrical foot consisting of three syllables with the middle one accented: AMPHIBRACH

poetic metrical foot consisting of two equally accented syllables: SPONDEE

poetic metrical foot consisting of two syllables, the first accented and the second not: TROCHEE

poetic metrical foot consisting of two syllables, the first unaccented and the second accented: IAMB, IAMBUS

poetic metrical foot consisting of two unaccented syllables followed by one accented: ANAPEST

poetic or metrical unit of time equivalent to that of a short syllable or sound: MORA

poetic pair of rhymed lines in iambic pentameter: HEROIC COUPLET

poetic use of different meters in the same poem: POLYMETRY

poet in the Old English tongue: SCOP

poet regarded as scorned and downtrodden: POÈTE MAUDIT

poetry free of conventional meter and rhyme: FREE VERSE

poetry (lyric) muse: ERATO

poetry with the final lines usually in the form of a dedication: ENVOY

poet without much talent: POETASTER

pointed, sharp-edged: CULTRATE

pointed three-part flower symbol: FLEUR-DE-LIS

point in a linear drawing where parallel lines converge: VANISHING POINT

pointless, merely hypothetical: ACADEMIC

pointless, silly, empty-headed: INANE

point made by showing the contrary to be absurd: APAGOGE

point of contact, interaction or communication: INTERFACE

point of view from which facts or matters are seen or judged: PERSPECTIVE

point or rod on which something rotates: PIVOT

point out, signify, indicate: DENOTE

points on sole of shoe to prevent slipping: CALK

poison: ENVENOM

poison antidote: MITHRIDATE

poisonous: TOXIC

poison-proofing or achieving immunity to poison by ingesting gradually increased doses: MITHRIDATISM

poisons as a science: TOXICOLOGY

poker demanding of a disclosure of hands: CALL

poker game in which the first card is dealt face down, the four others face up: STUD POKER

poker hand having only four cards of a suit: FOUR FLUSH

poker hand made up of three of a kind and a pair: FULL HOUSE

poker hand of cards all of one suit: FLUSH

poker hand of cards in sequence: STRAIGHT

pole a boat forward: PUNT

police car, ambulance, etc., roof light whose beam rotates: ROTATING BEACON, CHERRY

police elite squad with paramilitary training: S.W.A.T. TEAM (SPECIAL WEAPONS AND TACTICS or SPECIAL WEAPONS ATTACK)

police officer on a naval vessel: MASTER-AT-ARMS

police patrol wagon: BLACK MARIA

police spy: MOUCHARD

police surveillance of a suspect or suspected place: STAKEOUT
polish, burnish: FURBISH
polished appearance: SPIT AND POLISH
polishing rock that is porous and lightweight rock: PUMICE
polite and good-natured remark: PLEASANTRY
polite behavior: AMENITIES
politeness stalemate between two mutually deferring people: ALPHONSE AND GASTON
polite, suave, refined: URBANE
political appearance that is brief: WHISTLE-STOP
political candidate unexpectedly nominated: DARK HORSE
political corruption: MALVERSATION
political determination by an area or culture to be absorbed by a kindred state and get rid of foreign control: IRREDENTISM
political device of altering the bounds of a voting area to promote the interests of one political party: GERRYMANDER
political dinner or lecture circuit: RUBBER CHICKEN CIRCUIT
political disorder: ANARCHY
politically amoral and unscrupulously cunning: MACHIAVELLIAN
political organization, machinery of government or power: APPARAT
political or governmental organization: POLITY
political or philosophical enthusiast with a definite viewpoint or bias: IDEOLOGUE
political pact between church and state: CONCORDAT
political party chief: SACHEM
political party meeting to select candidates and plan campaign: CAUCUS
political power to appoint to offices: PATRONAGE
political professional, party politician: POLITICO
political slander, personal-attack propaganda, reputation-damaging campaign: CHARACTER ASSASSINATION
political rhetoric that is corny and high-flown: **BOMFOG**

(BROTHERHOOD OF MAN, FATHERHOOD OF GOD)
political theory that one Communist takeover leads to another: DOMINO THEORY
politician from outside who is resented: CARPETBAGGER
politician or public officeholder who is inept: THROTTLEBOTTOM
politician's declared final refusal to be a candidate: SHERMAN
politicians' practice of trading votes and influence: LOGROLLING
politician's route in campaigning: HUSTINGS
politician who appeals to prejudices and passions: DEMAGOGUE
politicking in rural districts: BARNSTORMING
politics of power: REALPOLITIK
pollens and spores as a study: PALYNOLOGY
poll tax: CAPITATION
pollute, desecrate: PROFANE
polo time period: CHUKKER
polysyllabic, long (as a word): SESQUIPEDALIAN
pompous, artificially formal: STILTED
pompous, dogmatic, arrogant, haughty: PONTIFICAL
pompous, inflated: TUMID
pompous in speech: OROTUND
pompously conceited: VAINGLORIOUS
pompous official jargon: GOBBLEDYGOOK
pompous or bombastic language: FUSTIAN
pompous or bombastic style of speaking: GRANDILOQUENCE
pompous person: BASHAW
ponder, meditate upon: RUMINATE
poor judgment shown: INJUDICIOUS
poorly made, cheap, shoddy, tacky: SLEAZY
poorly made, underdone: SLACK-BAKED
poor, penniless: IMPECUNIOUS
poor person, charity case: PAUPER
poor, stingy: PENURIOUS
Pope's ambassador to a foreign government: NUNCIO
Pope's letter replying to an ecclesiastical question: DECRETAL
popular: DEMOTIC
popular, accepted, everyday speech: VULGATE

popular but incorrect idea of the origin of a word: FOLK ETYMOLOGY
populated densely, crowded: IMPACTED
population science: DEMOGRAPHY
populous large urban region of many cities: MEGALOPOLIS
porcelain or china that is very thin and delicate: EGGSHELL CHINA
porch: VERANDA
porch or platform, relatively small, with steps, at the entrance to a house or apartment building: STOOP
porch with room held up by columns: PORTICO
pores admit fluids, air or light: POROUS
pornographic movie in which a person is actually murdered: SNUFF FILM
pornography: SMUT
pornography as a study: COPROLOGY
porous and lightweight volcanic rock used in polishing: PUMICE
portent, omen: AUGURY
portent, omen, warning: PRESAGE
port for anchoring: ANCHORAGE
portion, serving: DOLLOP
portion, share, half: MOIETY
portray, trace out, outline: DELINEATE
port side of a ship: LARBOARD
Portuguese sad folk song: FADO
pose with one hip higher than the other: HIPSHOT POSE
posing or fake customer working with the pitchman or seller: SHILL
posing under a false name or character: IMPOSTURE
position or office that pays but involves few or no duties: SINECURE
position specially suited to a person: NICHE
positive declaration: ASSEVERATION
positive, final, decisive, absolute: PEREMPTORY
positive or arrogant in assertion of opinion: DOGMATIC
positive, with no qualifications: CATEGORICAL
possession that is more trouble than it's worth: WHITE ELEPHANT
possessive case in grammar: GENITIVE
possible but not in existence: POTENTIAL
possible, imaginable, secular: EARTHLY
possible, liable: CONTINGENT
possible outcome: EVENTUALITY
postage stamp sold at a higher price,

the markup going to a charity or public service: SEMIPOSTAL
post at end of handrail of a staircase: NEWEL
poster: PLACARD
poster or large sheet of paper with a printed message: BROADSIDE
postponement, delay, interval of relief or rest: RESPITE
postponement of punishment or pain: REPRIEVE
postpone or forgo a right: WAIVE
postpone, put off habitually: PROCRASTINATE
posts supporting a handrail: BALUSTER
posture: STANCE
potatoes prepared with finely sliced fried onions: LYONNAISE
potency, efficacy: VIRTUE
pot or jar that is broad-mouthed and of earthenware: OLLA
pottery, glazed, usually blue and white: DELFT
pottery-like or involving pottery: FICTILE
pottery of a very hard variety: STONEWARE
pot that is airtight and cooks food quickly under pressure: PRESSURE COOKER
pot that is small and made of earthenware: PIPKIN
pouch-like receptacle on the abdomen of a female marsupial for carrying the young: MARSUPIUM
pouch-shaped: BURSIFORM
pouch worn hanging in front of a kilt: SPORRAN
pour off a liquid without disturbing its sediment: DECANT
pour or spread out in all directions: DIFFUSE
pouting facial expression: MOUE
poverty: INDIGENCE
powdered, demolished: PULVERIZED
powdery, dusty: PULVERULENT
power equal to a thousand watts: KILOWATT
powerful manipulator: POWER BROKER
powerful, mighty: PUISSANT
powerful only seemingly and actually ineffective: PAPER TIGER
powerful or influential person in determining political candidates, power broker: KINGMAKER

powerful or wealthy man: NABOB

powerful to a prodigious degree, gigantic: HERCULEAN

power interruption or breakdown: OUTAGE

powerless: IMPUISSANT

powerless, incapable of producing the effect desired: INEFFECTUAL

powerless to act or accomplish anything: IMPOTENT

powerless, worthless: NUGATORY

power of thought or feeling: INTENSITY

power or high office used to exhort: BULLY PULPIT

power or might in arms, weaponry-rich status: ARMIPOTENCE

power that is absolute: DESPOTISM

practicable, workable: VIABLE

practical, not theoretical: PRAGMATIC

practical, obstinate, shrewd: HARDHEADED

practical or functional only, utilitarian, prosaic: BANAUSIC

practical rather than scientific as a measure: RULE OF THUMB

practical, suitable: FEASIBLE

practical, useful or valuable in a functional way: UTILITARIAN

practice rather than theory: PRAXIS

praise: LAUD

praised profusely, bragged about: VAUNTED

praise, especially when formal and delivered publicly: EULOGY

praise extravagantly: ADULATE

praise for an achievement: KUDOS

praise in the highest terms, exalt, laud: EXTOL

praise or eulogy formally delivered: ENCOMIUM

praise that is elaborate, laudation: PANEGYRIC

praise that is exaggerated, hype, ballyhoo: PUFFERY

prance, caper about: TITTUP

prance, frisk about: CAVORT

prank, spree, fling, reckless behavior: ESCAPADE

pray earnestly for something, ask for humbly: SUPPLICATE

prayer at the opening of a ceremony: INVOCATION

prayer caller or crier from a minaret: MUEZZIN

prayer consisting of a long list of supplications with a fixed response after each: LITANY

prayer or entreaty in behalf of others: INTERCESSION

prayer shawl worn by Orthodox and Conservative Jewish men: TALLITH

prayers made on nine days: NOVENA

prayers or services in the evening: VESPERS

prayer stand with a shelf for a book: PRIE-DIEU

prayer stool, usually folding and cushioned: FALDSTOOL

prayer that is brief: EJACULATION

prayer that is short and suitable to an occasion: COLLECT

pray for or call down a calamity or a curse: IMPRECATE

pray for us: ORA PRO NOBIS

precarious position: SWORD OF DAMOCLES

precarious state of peace or peace terms imposed by a dominant country: PAX ROMANA

preceding: PREVENIENT

pre-Christmas season: ADVENT

precipice that extends a distance: PALISADES

precise about details, overly painstaking: METICULOUS

precise, accurate, exact: NICE

precisely, meticulously, "to the fingernail": AD UNGUEM

precise, overly fastidious, fussy, exacting: FINICKY

preconceived judgment: PARTI PRIS

predecessor, forerunner, something in advance: PRECURSOR

predetermination: FATALISM

predetermined fate of the soul as a belief: PREDESTINATION

predicament: QUANDARY

predicament, complicated or problematic situation: PLIGHT

predicament entailing a choice between two undesirable alternatives: DILEMMA

prediction, forecast: PROGNOSIS

predictor of the future: SOOTHSAYER

predisposition to certain forms of disease: DIATHESIS

preempt or appoint: CO-OPT

preface, introductory remark: PROLEGOMENON

preface, introductory statement: PROEM

preference preconceived: **PREDILECTION**

preferred stock on which unpaid dividends do not accrue: **NONCUMULATIVE**

preferred stock that is entitled to dividends beyond those stated: **PARTICIPATING PREFERRED**

pregnancy: **GESTATION**

pregnant: **ENCEINTE**

pregnant: **GRAVID**

pregnant-for-the-first-time mother or the mother of just one: **PRIMIPARA**

prehistoric circle of monumental stone slabs, as at Stonehenge: **CROMLECH**

prehistoric human remains that proved to be a hoax: **PILTDOWN MAN**

prehistoric monument of one stone (capstone) atop two others (megaliths): **DOLMEN**

prehistoric monument of one upright stone, monolith: **MENHIR**

prejudice another with talk or insinuations: **EARWIG**

prejudice, bias: **PRECONCEPTION**

prejudiced, biased, favoring one party: **PARTIAL**

prejudicial or emotional in appeal: **AD HOMINEM**

prelate, high priest: **HIERARCH**

prelate with the highest rank in the country: **PRIMATE**

preliminary work for a project: **SPADEWORK**

prematurely born animal, especially a calf: **SLINK**

prematurely bring forth young: **ABORT**

prematurely developed: **PRECOCIOUS**

premeditated, deliberately designed: **STUDIED**

preoccupation with a thought or feeling that is compulsive and excessive: **OBSESSION**

preoccupied: **BEMUSED**

preparatory work for a project: **SPADEWORK**

preposition used to end a sentence: **ADDISONIAN TERMINATION**

prerequisite: **POSTULATE**

Presbyterian minister's residence: **MANSE**

present everywhere at once: **UBIQUITOUS**

present or tip, gratuity: **CUMSHAW**

present period or occasion: **NONCE**

present tense used to narrate a past event: **HISTORICAL PRESENT**

President's or other leader's unofficial advisers: **KITCHEN CABINET**

preside over, as a meeting: **MODERATE**

press a debtor for payment: **DUN**

pressed against, lying flat against, close to: **APPRESSED**

press food, drinks, etc., on a person: **PLY**

press, journalists' corps or profession: **FOURTH ESTATE**

pretend, dissemble, conceal: **DISSIMULATE**

pretended blow or deception meant to distract: **FEINT**

pretended, deceptive, sham: **FEIGNED**

pretended indifference to or dislike of what one doesn't or can't have: **SOUR GRAPES**

pretend, feign: **SIMULATE**

pretending to be important: **TINHORN**

pretending to be someone else in order to deceive: **IMPOSTURE**

pretending to be what one is not or to be better than one is, pretending to be virtuous or good: **HYPOCRISY**

pretend not to see wrongdoing: **CONNIVE**

pretense, false appearance: **GUISE**

pretentious behavior: **AFFECTATION**

pretentious boasting: **BRAGGADOCIO**

pretentious, inflated: **OVERBLOWN**

pretentious language: **CLAPTRAP**

pretentious, lofty, extravagant, overly ambitious: **HIGH-FLOWN**

pretentiously grand, imposing: **GRANDIOSE**

pretentiousness, windy promposity: **FLATULENCE**

pretentious official: **PANJANDRUM**

pretentious or extremist person: **HIGHFLIER**

pretentious, ostentatious or hypocritical ceremony: **MUMMERY**

pretentious, overdignified, self-important: **POMPOUS**

prevalent, dominant: **REGNANT**

prevent, avert: **OBVIATE**

prevent, guard against or hinder in advance: **FORESTALL**

preventing sleep: **AGRYPNOTIC**

preventive treatment against disease: **PROPHYLAXIS**

prevent, render impossible, exclude:
PRECLUDE
previously, before now: **HERETOFORE**
previous, onetime, former: **ERSTWHILE**
previous to consideration or
examination: **A PRIORI**
prey, game: **QUARRY**
prey upon, pillage, plunder: **DEPREDATE**
price at which a bond may be redeemed
before it reaches maturity:
REDEMPTION PRICE
price at which a person is ready to buy
a security: **BID**
price at which a person is ready to sell
a security: **OFFER**
price changes that can be absorbed by
the market in a particular security:
LIQUIDITY
price fall caused by decrease of money
in circulation: **DEFLATION**
price is fixed for a whole meal: **PRIX
FIXE**
price last reported at which security
was sold: **MARKET PRICE**
priceless: **INESTIMABLE**
priceless: **INVALUABLE**
price level reduced to increase
purchasing power but avoid
deflation: **DISINFLATION**
price of a stock transaction higher than
the preceding transaction: **UP TICK,
PLUS-TICK**
price range of buyer and seller of a
given stock at a given time:
QUOTATION
price rise and fall in value of money:
INFLATION
price that is the lowest at which
something will be sold at an
auction: **UPSET PRICE**
prickly: **SPINOUS**
prickly heat: **MILIARIA**
pride, especially in someone else's
accomplishments (Yiddish):
NACHUS
priestly: **SACERDOTAL**
priestly, sacerdotal: **HIERATIC**
priest or minister jointly officiating at a
communion service:
CONCELEBRANT
priest or minister officiating at a
communion service: **CELEBRANT**
priest's forgiveness of sin, in confession:
ABSOLUTION

priests or clergy in charge of
government: **HIEROCRACY**
priest's or minister's residence:
RECTORY
priest's sacrament and anointing for the
critically ill or injured: **EXTREME
UNCTION, LAST RITES**
prima donna, female operatic singer:
DIVA
primary in which people rather than
delegates select candidates: **DIRECT
PRIMARY**
primitive: **ABORIGINAL**
primitive, pure: **PRISTINE**
primitive state, reversion to: **ATAVISM**
primp, dress showily: **PREEN**
principal commodity, regularly in
demand: **STAPLE**
principal, original, first: **PRIMAL**
principle, belief or doctrine maintained
as true by a person or a group:
TENET
print a line, paragraph, etc., in from the
margin: **INDENT**
printed character containing two or
more letters joined together:
LIGATURE
printed sheets, loosely bound together:
CAHIER
printer's jumble, bollixed-up type: **PI**
printer's opening cut in a plate for the
insertion of type: **MORTISE**
printer's part of a letter that extends
downward: **DESCENDER**
printer's part of a letter that extends
upward: **ASCENDER**
printer's shallow tray for holding type
before it is put into a form:
GALLEY
printer's thinnest of metal spaces
separating letters or words: **HAIR
SPACE**
printing being even with the outside
margin: **FLUSH**
printing from a flat stone or metal plate
on which the material to be printed
is treated with grease that absorbs
ink: **LITHOGRAPHY**
printing from raised surfaces: **LETTER
PRESS**
printing impression that is blurred:
MACKLE
printing machines that cast type in
single characters: **MONOTYPE**

printing ornament or symbol: DINGBAT

printing or writing with flowing lines: CURSIVE

printing press that prints both sides of a sheet simultaneously: PERFECTING PRESS

printing press that uses webs, or rolls of paper, rather than separate sheets: WEB PRESS

printing press using curved plates and rolls of paper: ROTARY PRESS

printing process in which subjects are reproduced by photography on plates in relief: PHOTOENGRAVING

printing process in which the impression is transferred to a rubber roller and then to the paper: OFFSET

printing receptacle for broken or battered type: HELLBOX

printing sign (☞) to direct attention: INDEX FIST

printing type characteristic consisting of a fine line that finishes off a stroke: SERIF

printing type group containing all the characters in one size and style: FONT

printing type set in excess of the space available: OVERSET

printing type that is bold and somewhat fancy: OLD ENGLISH

printing type with thin light lines: LIGHTFACE

prints transferred from specially prepared paper to glass or wood: DECALCOMANIA

prisoner delivering-up or transfer to the jurisdiction of another state or country: EXTRADITION

prisoner of captors who are setting terms for his release: HOSTAGE

prissily good or proper in behavior: GOODY-GOODY

private and frank: HEART-TO-HEART

private, isolated room: SANCTUM

privately said, in an undertone: SOTTO VOCE

privately with one other person, intimately, cozily: À DEUX

private or confidential conversation: TÊTE-À-TÊTE

private or side entrance: POSTERN

private property, one's own possession: PECULIUM

privilege extended to stockholders ahead of others, to buy new issues, usually at lower than market price: RIGHTS

privilege or benefit owed or expected because of status: PERQUISITE

privilege or exemption, as in right to send mail without charge: FRANK

prize that is the biggest one possible to win: JACKPOT

problem of choosing between unpleasant alternatives: DILEMMA

problem-solving group or research center bringing together people from different disciplines: THINK TANK

problems pile up as the solution of one raises another and leads back to the original one: VICIOUS CIRCLE

problem that is complicated: GORDIAN KNOT

proclamation, decree, edict: UKASE

proclamation, public declaration: PRONUNCIAMENTO

prod, incite: GOAD

produce, beget: PROCREATE

produce, perform or invent without previous thought or preparation: IMPROVISE

producing many or much: PROLIFIC

producing or capable of producing a desired effect: EFFICACIOUS

production of goods and services by a nation: GROSS NATIONAL PRODUCT (GNP)

productive, creative, potential, germinal: SEMINAL

productive equipment owned by businesses: CAPITAL GOODS

productive, inventive, fruitful: PREGNANT

product striped marking to indicate classification and price electronically: BAR CODE, UNIVERSAL PRODUCT CODE (UPC)

profane, use sacrilegiously: DESECRATE

profaning, violation of anything sacred: SACRILEGE

professional or clerical worker: WHITE-COLLAR WORKER

profile or dark shape with a light background: SILHOUETTE

profitable: LUCRATIVE

profitable: REMUNERATIVE

profitable source: PAY DIRT

profit amount added by the seller to what he or she paid originally: MARKUP

profit anticipated but not yet realized on a security still held: PAPER PROFIT

profit from the sale of assets: CAPITAL GAIN

profound, hidden: RECONDITE

progression in which the difference between numerical terms remains constant: ARITHMETIC PROGRESSION

progression in which the ratio between each two numbers is the same: GEOMETRIC PROGRESSION

progression or arrangement that is orderly or gradual: GRADATION

progress resulting from planning: TELESIS

prohibit, debar, forbid a person to have or do something: INTERDICT

prohibited by convention or tradition: TABOO

prohibited, unlawful: ILLICIT

prohibiting by law reporters or others from disclosing details of a case to the public: GAG ORDER

prohibition: INJUNCTION

prohibit, outlaw, condemn: PROSCRIBE

projecting part of a battle line: SALIENT

projecting point of land at a coast: CAPE

projecting structure supported at only one end: CANTILEVER

project on the basis of facts already known, infer from evidence at hand: EXTRAPOLATE

proliferate, sprout: BURGEON

prolific, fruitful, fertile: FECUND

prolific or fond of children: PHILOPROGENITIVE

prologue: PROLUSION

prolonged or held, in music: SOSTENUTO

promenade, open level path or grass area that is often scenic: ESPLANADE

promenade, strut: CAKEWALK

prominent or memorable object in the landscape: LANDMARK

promiscuous woman, slut: SLATTERN

promiscuous woman, tramp: BIMBO

promise, guarantee: STIPULATE

promising, opportune, favorable: AUSPICIOUS

promotion awarded on the battlefield: BREVET

promotion or advertising that is sensational: BALLYHOO

promotion that is exaggerated, hype, ballyhoo: PUFFERY

promptness, speed: DISPATCH

pronounced without stress when in combination with a following word: PROCLITIC

pronounced without stress when in combination with a preceding word: ENCLITIC

pronounced with the back of the tongue touching or near the soft palate, as the "c" in "cool": VELAR

pronouncement: DICTUM

pronounce with a sound omitted: ELIDE

pronouncing "r" like "l" or "l" like "r" or "w": LALLATION

pronunciation mark over or under a letter: DIACRITICAL MARK

pronunciation standards: ORTHOEPY

proof of a crime: CORPUS DELICTI

proof of printed matter used for making corrections: GALLEY

proof of the genuineness of a document such as a will: PROBATE

proof or evidence of wrongdoing, crime, etc.: SMOKING GUN

proof or safe against attack: UNASSAILABLE

proof, the burden of: ONUS PROBANDI

propensity: APPETENCE

proper, advisable, suitable: EXPEDIENT

proper, conventional: ORTHODOX

properness, conformity with accepted usage: PROPRIETY

proper or customary act or procedure: FORMALITY

proper or fitting, appropriate, respectable: COMME IL FAUT

proper, seemly in behavior: DECOROUS

property improvement: CAPITAL EXPENDITURE

property ownership as the key to political power: TIMOCRACY

property reverting to government in absence of legal heirs: ESCHEAT

property seizure in a legal proceeding: ATTACHMENT

property transfer: CONVEYANCE

prophesying, foretelling the future:
    DIVINATION
prophetess of doom: CASSANDRA
prophetic, enigmatic: ORACULAR
prophetic, having divinatory power:
    MANTIC
prophetic, inspired: PYTHONIC
prophetic, oracular: VATIC
prophet-like in zeal of leadership:
    MESSIANIC
prophet or messiah in Islam: MAHDI
proportionate: COMMENSURATE
proposal in outline form for a written
    work or business project:
    PROSPECTUS
propose, suggest: PROPOUND
proposition that is demonstrably true,
    as in geometry: THEOREM
propriety or aptness of behavior:
    CONVENANCES
prosaic, dull, mediocre: PEDESTRIAN
prose style that is simple and
    straightforward: PLAIN STYLE
prose that is long and tiresome: SCREED
prosperity: EASY STREET
prosperous, especially as a mark of the
    times: FLUSH
prosperous, happy, flourishing: PALMY
prosperous or successful period:
    FLORESCENCE
prostitute: COCOTTE
prostitute: DOXY
prostitute: FILLE DE JOIE
prostitute: HARLOT
prostitute: HOOKER
prostitute: STRUMPET
prostitute: TROLLOP
prostitute: TRULL
prostitute catering to men of wealth or
    high rank: COURTESAN
prostitute's agent: PIMP
prostitutes as a group: DEMIMONDE
prostitute's customer: JOHN
prostitute who works in response to
    telephone calls: CALL GIRL
prostitution, as of talent or office, for
    gain: VENALITY
protect against loss or damage:
    INDEMNIFY
protected against malfunctioning:
    FAIL-SAFE
protected legally by patent or copyright,
    owned by a proprietor:
    PROPRIETARY

protection against disease:
    PROPHYLAXIS
protective influence: AEGIS
protective medieval garment of chain
    mail: HAUBERK
protector of the people: TRIBUNE
Protestant clergyperson's residence:
    MANSE
Protestant clergyperson's residence:
    PARSONAGE
protest or oppose by pleading:
    REMONSTRATE
protoplasm building and breaking down
    as continuous bodily processes:
    METABOLISM
prototype: ARCHETYPE
protozoan with a long and rounded
    body with cilia: PARAMECIUM
protruding: EXSERTILE
protruding-eyed, having bulging
    eyeballs: EXOPHTHALMIC
protrusion or slipping of one internal
    organ, as part of the intestines, into
    another: INTUSSCEPTION,
    INVAGINATION
protuberance, swelling: TUBEROSITY
prove false, contradict: BELIE
proverb: ADAGE
proverb: APHORISM
prove someone or something wrong:
    CONFUTE
provincial in regarding one's own ethnic
    or racial group as central:
    ETHNOCENTRIC
provincial, limited in outlook: INSULAR
provincial, limited, narrow: PAROCHIAL
provisions for a journey: VIATICUM
provoker of punishable acts: AGENT
    PROVOCATEUR
provoking anger or resentment by being
    unjustly discriminatory: INVIDIOUS
provoking, annoying person: GADFLY
prude: MRS. GRUNDY
prudence: CALCULATION
prudent, careful, discreet: CIRCUMSPECT
prudent, diplomatic, wise: POLITIC
prudent, tactful, careful about what one
    says: DISCREET
prudent, wary: CANNY
prudish editing: BOWDLERIZATION
prudish euphemism, refined but affected
    term: GENTEELISM
prudish, shocked or nauseated easily:
    SQUEAMISH

Prussian helmet with a spike:
PICKELHAUBE
prying or offensively curious:
INQUISITORIAL
pry or break open, as with a crowbar:
JIMMY
pseudonym in the form of one's name
spelled backward: ANANYM
psychiatric disorder marked by
separation of thought from
emotions: SCHIZOPHRENIA
psychiatric disorder marked by two or
more distinct personalities:
MULTIPLE PERSONALITY
psychic: PARANORMAL
psychic phenomenon or phenomena: PSI
psychoanalysis patient: ANALYSAND
psychoanalyst, psychiatrist: SHRINK
psychoanalytical arrested development:
FIXATION
psychological attachment to somebody
because of his or her perceived
resemblance to one's parent,
guardian, etc., in early childhood:
ANACLISIS
psychological conditioning in which the
pairing of one stimulus, as a bell,
with another, as food, induces a
response to the first: CLASSICAL
CONDITIONING
psychological conditioning of behavior
by immediate reward or
punishment: OPERANT
CONDITIONING
psychological dream-like period with
loss of memory: FUGUE
psychological persuading of another by
pretending the opposite of what
one actually desires: REVERSE
PSYCHOLOGY
psychological school holding that only
objective observation and
experiment constitute valid
evidence: BEHAVIORISM
psychological unconscious tendency to
do the opposite of one's repressed
desires: REACTION FORMATION
psychotherapeutically involving
comment by the therapist:
DIRECTIVE
puberty voice change in a boy:
PONTICELLO
pubic wig, once popular during
smallpox epidemics: MERKIN

public attention or notice: LIMELIGHT
public brawl: AFFRAY
public display: BLAZON
public finance as a science:
CAMERALISTICS
public forum place: AGORA
public good being the objective, as in
lawyering: PRO BONO PUBLICO
publicity, great popularity,
fashionableness: RÉCLAME
publicize officially, put into effect:
PROMULGATE
publicizer of real or alleged corruption:
MUCKRAKER
public offices offered as rewards of
partisan service: SPOILS SYSTEM
public sale or auction: VENDUE
publisher of books at the author's
expense: VANITY PRESS
publisher's mockup or layout: DUMMY
publisher's trademark: COLOPHON
publishing right to quote or reprint
without permission when done
fairly: FAIR USE
puckish, gay, strange: FEY
pudding baked under a roast to catch
the drippings: YORKSHIRE
PUDDING
pudding-like chilled dessert: MOUSSE
puff, blow in gusts: WHIFFLE
pugnacious in a disagreeable way:
TRUCULENT
pull or force away by violent twisting:
WREST
pulsatory: SPHYGMIC
pulsing, throbbing: VIBRANT
pulverize: COMMINUTE
pulverize: TRITURATE
pulverize: LEVIGATE
pun: PARONOMASIA
punch holes into: PERFORATE
punctuation style that is minimal and
uses few commas: OPEN
PUNCTUATION
punctuation style using commas freely:
CLOSE PUNCTUATION
pun, double meaning: PLAY ON WORDS
pungent: ACRID
punish, beat or thrash severely:
TROUNCE
punish by an arbitrary fine: AMERCE
punishment for evil: RETRIBUTION
punishment that corresponds to the
nature of the crime: TALION

punitive, avenging: VINDICATORY
punning: PARONOMASIA
pupil absent from school without
    permission: TRUANT
puppy: WHELP
purchase or considered object of
    undisclosed worth or value: PIG IN
    A POKE
purchasing power of individuals: REAL
    INCOME
pure essential part: QUINTESSENCE
pure, primitive: PRISTINE
purging or purifying of emotions:
    CATHARSIS
purify by a sacrifice or ceremony:
    LUSTRATE
purify by exposure to air: AERATE
purify by washing and straining or
    decanting: ELUTRIATE
purifying: DEPURATIVE
purifying, distilling or transforming
    thing or phenomenon: ALEMBIC
purify, refine: RAREFY
purplish red: MURREY
purpose, aim, goal: INTENT
purposeful: TELIC
purposeless, haphazard: RANDOM
purposelessness, anxiety, disorder,
    lawlessness, malaise: ANOMIE
pursue an undertaking: PROSECUTE
pursuit, search, adventure: QUEST
push down, thrust away from: DETRUDE
push or crowd roughly, shake up,
    elbow, shove: JOSTLE
push out, make protrude: EXSERT
pushy, nosy, obtrusive, forward:
    OFFICIOUS

put-down, acid remark: ZINGER
put down, belittle: DISPARAGE
put down by force, allay: QUELL
put down, suppress forcibly: QUASH
put in gradually by drops: INSTILL
put in or inject a comment or
    digression in a speech or argument:
    INTERPOSE
put in prison: INCARCERATE
put into words, phrase: COUCH
put off or postpone habitually:
    PROCRASTINATE
putting into effect, carrying through:
    IMPLEMENTATION
putting out of one's consciousness
    unacceptable memories, desires and
    impulses: REPRESSION
put together by combining bits and
    pieces: CUT-AND-PASTE
puzzled, confused, stupefied:
    BEFUDDLED
puzzled, uncertain, bewildered:
    PERPLEXED
puzzle in which the sound of a word or
    phrase is represented by letters,
    numerals, pictures: REBUS
puzzle out, interpret, understand:
    FATHOM
puzzling, complicated, involved:
    INTRICATE
puzzling, secret, hidden, occult,
    mystifying: CRYPTIC
pyramid or cone with the top sliced off:
    FULSTRUM
Pyrrhic victory: CADMEAN VICTORY

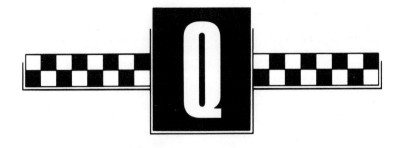

quack medicine, cure-all, medicine of one's own invention: **NOSTRUM**

quack-medicine vendor, charlatan: **MOUNTEBANK**

quadrangular: **TETRAGONAL**

quail, tremble or crouch, as in fear: **COWER**

quaint (British): **TWEE**

quaintness or fancifulness, as in a literary work: **WHIMSY**

quality, goodness, moral excellence: **VIRTUE**

qualm, doubt, apprehension: **MISGIVING**

quantity that a container lacks of being full: **ULLAGE**

quantity that is specified: **QUANTUM**

quarrel: **ALTERCATION**

quarrel, difference of opinion, discord: **DISSENSION**

quarrel, disagreement, estrangement: **FALLING-OUT**

quarreling, not able to agree: **AT LOGGERHEADS**

quarrel or argue noisily: **WRANGLE**

quarrelsome: **BELLICOSE**

quarrelsome: **CANTANKEROUS**

quarrelsome: **CONTENTIOUS**

quarrelsome: **LITIGIOUS**

quarrelsome: **PUGNACIOUS**

quarrelsome, vixenish: **TERMAGANT**

quarrel, wrangling: **JANGLE**

queenly: **REGINAL**

queer, eccentric: **CRANKY**

quench or satisfy, as a thirst: **SLAKE**

questionable, difficult to solve: **PROBLEMATIC**

questionable, suspicious: **EQUIVOCAL**

questionable, uncertain: **DUBIOUS**

question-and-answer method of instruction: **SOCRATIC METHOD**

question-and-answer method of teaching: **CATECHISM**

question a person insistently: **PLY**

question asked for effect and not calling for an answer: **RHETORICAL QUESTION**

question, consultational point of information: **QUERY**

question, examine: **INTERROGATE**

questioning or prying characterized by harshness: **INQUISITION**

questioning the existence of God: **AGNOSTICISM**

question mark: **EROTEME**

question searchingly and at length: **CATECHIZE**

question that suggests the answer sought by the questioner: **LEADING QUESTION**

question to be disputed: **QUODLIBET**

quibble: **CAVIL**

quibble, lie: **PALTER**

quibbler over small matters: **PETTIFOGGER**

quibbling: **CAPTIOUS**

quick disposal of a matter, as of a piece of business: **DISPATCH**

quick efficiency: **DISPATCH**

quickly: **LICKETY-SPLIT**

quickly, briskly, lively, in music: **VIVACE**

quickly or suddenly, in music: **SUBITO**

quickness of mind: **ACUMEN**

quick or ready in performance, easily achieved: **FACILE**

quick-tempered, irritable: **IRASCIBLE**

quick tempo, rapidly, swiftly, in music: **VELOCE**

quiet, abate, calm: **SUBSIDE**

quiet consent: **ACQUIESCENCE**

quiet down, soothe, mitigate, pacify:
    MOLLIFY
quiet, make peaceful: PACIFY
quiet, reserved, reluctant to speak:
    RETICENT
quiet, serene, calm: TRANQUIL
quilt: DUVET
quilt made of irregularly shaped pieces
    of variously colored and patterned
    fabric: CRAZY QUILT
quip: SALLY
quip, fun, playfulness: JEST
quirk, habit, mannerism peculiar to an
    individual: IDIOSYNCRASY

quiver, flutter, beat rapidly: PALPITATE
quizmaster (British): QUESTIONMASTER
quota for a race or class in admission
    to an academic institution:
    NUMERUS CLAUSUS
quotation mark (British): INVERTED
    COMMA
quotation marks in French (« »):
    GUILLEMETS
quotation or motto prefixed to a book:
    EPIGRAPH
quoting a person without using the
    exact words: INDIRECT DISCOURSE

"r" pronounced like "l" or "l" pronounced like "r" or "w": **LALLATION**

rabbit dwelling: **WARREN**

rabbit fur: **LAPIN**

rabbit stew as prepared in Germany: **HASENPFEFFER**

rabies: **HYDROPHOBIA**

race course's section farthest from spectators: **BACK STRETCH**

race course's straight portion forming the final approach to the finish: **HOME STRETCH**

racehorse that is male and four years of age or under, male foal: **COLT**

race improvement as a study or science: **EUGENICS**

race longer than the marathon (26.2 miles, 42.2 kilometers) in distance: **ULTRAMARATHON**

race on horseback along a course containing obstacles: **STEEPLECHASE**

races and ethnic groups as subjects of study: **ETHNOLOGY**

racetrack board showing the betting odds: **TOTE BOARD**

racial and ethnic groups brought together in legal and social equality: **INTEGRATION**

racial equalizing: **DESEGREGATION**

racially prompted property selling from exploited fears that a minority influx will adversely affect property values: **BLOCKBUSTING**

racial memory inherited by the individual: **COLLECTIVE UNCONSCIOUS**

racial or ethnic slur: **ETHNOPHAULISM**

racial segregation in South Africa: **APARTHEID**

racing finish so close that a camera is needed to decide the winner: **PHOTO FINISH**

racing gambling system in which the winnings of a previous race are placed on a later one: **PARLAY**

racing gambling system in which those backing the winners share in the total wagered: **PARIMUTUEL**

racketeers' money collector: **BAGMAN**

rack or frame on which to dry fish, cheese, bricks, etc.: **HACK**

rack or platform for drying food: **FLAKE**

racy, stimulating: **PIQUANT**

radar-presence detector in an automobile: **FUZZBUSTER**

radar warning system in North America: **DEW (DISTANT EARLY WARNING) LINE**

radiance, brilliance: **REFULGENCE**

radiance enveloping a sanctified being: **AUREOLE**

radiance, splendor: **EFFULGENCE**

radiant, transparent: **LUCENT**

radiate, diffuse: **EXUDE**

radiating, star-shaped: **STELLATE**

radical or liberal political figure: **LEFTIST**

radical or liberal political position: **LEFT**

radioactivity duration measure: **HALF-LIFE**

radio announcer who conducts a program of recorded music: **DISC JOCKEY**

radio-broadcasting or -listening commuter period: **DRIVE TIME**

radio-operating licensed amateur: **HAM**

radio or television station code letters:
CALL LETTERS
radio-reflecting layer of the ionosphere:
HEAVISIDE LAYER, E LAYER
radio word code for letters of the
alphabet, such as *Alpha* for A and
Zulu for Z: ALPHABET CODE
ragamuffin: TATTERDEMALION
ragged edge of handmade paper:
DECKLE EDGE
raggedly dressed person, usually a child:
RAGAMUFFIN
raging, fanatical: RABID
raging, frenzied: MADDING
raiding force or member of one:
COMMANDO
raid, invasion: INCURSION
raid, lay waste, pillage: HARRY
raid, plunder, invade for booty:
MARAUD
raid, plunder, pillage: FORAY
rail around the stern of a boat or ship:
TAFFRAIL
rail at, berate, find fault abusively:
VITUPERATE
railing, contentious, carping:
RABULISTIC
railroad building for repairing and
switching locomotives:
ROUNDHOUSE
railroad crossing X-shaped warning
sign: CROSSBUCK
railroad signal to go ahead: HIGHBALL
railway with a single track: MONORAIL
rainbow-like colors that shift:
IRIDESCENCE
rainbow trout along the Pacific coast:
STEELHEAD
rainfall study: HYETOGRAPHY
rainy: PLUVIOUS
rainy season that comes with the
summer wind along the Asian
coast of the Pacific: MONSOON
raised figures worked on a surface as
decoration: EMBOSSED
raised platform on which guests of
honor or speakers are seated: DAIS
raised sculpture in which figures project
slightly: BAS-RELIEF
raise trivial objections, carp: CAVIL
raise with a rope: TRICE
rake, profligate: LIBERTINE
rake, sensualist: ROUÉ
raking gunfire: ENFILADE

rakish in angle, as the way a hat is
worn: ARAKE
rakish, vulgar: RAFFISH
ramble, wander from main subject:
DIGRESS
rambling, aimless wandering:
MEANDERING
rambling and wordy talk: GARRULITY
rambling, confused: INCOHERENT
rambling, discursive, digressive:
EXCURSIVE
ramp, incline: GRADIENT
ramp that curves and ascends:
HELICLINE
ram's horn of ancient times still used in
synagogues: SHOFAR
ram that has been castrated: WETHER
rancorous, bitter: VIRULENT
random, accidental: HAPHAZARD
random, casual, aimless, disconnected:
DESULTORY
random, confused: INDISCRIMINATE
random, involving guesswork or
probability: STOCHASTIC
random shot or criticism: POTSHOT
range, extent, scope: PURVIEW
range in its entirety: GAMUT
range or limit, as of power or action:
TETHER
range, scope: LATITUDE
ranked as a tournament favorite:
SEEDED
rank formation or arrangement, as with
troops, fleets or airplanes:
ECHELON
rank in society, organization, business,
etc.: PECKING ORDER
rankle, irritate, cause bitterness: FESTER
rank or seniority order in the military:
CHAIN OF COMMAND
rank, spoiled-smelling: RANCID
ransack and rob: RIFLE
rapidly: LICKETY-SPLIT
rapidly, swiftly, galloping: TANTIVY
rapidly, swiftly, in a quick tempo, in
music: VELOCE
rapture or emotion that is
overpowering: ECSTASY
rare-book dealer: BIBLIOPOLE
rare person or thing: RARA AVIS
rascal, rogue: RAPSCALLION
rash: BRASH
rash and reckless person: HOTSPUR
rash, hasty, impulsive: IMPETUOUS

rash, incautious, thriftless: **IMPROVIDENT**
rashly, recklessly: **HEADLONG**
rash, reckless: **TEMERARIOUS**
Rastafarian braided hairstyle: **DREADLOCKS**
ratify, approve, permit: **SANCTION**
rational, calm, ordered, harmonious, balanced: **APOLLONIAN**
rational, clear, easily understood, bright, shining: **LUCID**
rationalization of matters of morals and ethics: **CASUISTRY**
rationalizing that what one doesn't or can't have, one doesn't really want: **SOUR GRAPES**
rattle, crackle: **CREPITATE**
rattle that is gourd-shaped and used to sound a rhythm: **MARACA**
rattling or clattering noise: **BRATTLE**
rave, speak violently: **RANT**
ravine or gulley in a desert region: **WADI**
raw cane sugar: **MUSCOVADO**
raw material: **STAPLE**
reachable, approachable, available, understandable: **ACCESSIBLE**
reaching out in services, charity, branches, etc.: **OUTREACH**
reach or arrive at a port: **FETCH UP AT**
react: **REDOUND**
reaction developed by training: **CONDITIONED REFLEX**
reaction in exaggerated form to a psychological defect: **OVERCOMPENSATION**
reaction of a violent nature: **BACKLASH**
readily, willingly: **LIEF**
readiness to comply, pliancy: **FACILITY**
reading ability impairment: **DYSLEXIA**
reading ability loss: **ALEXIA**
reading comprehension test in which words are deleted at intervals: **CLOZE**
reading disorder in which letters or words appear reversed: **STREPHOSYMBOLIA**
reading of a word or sentence is the same backward as forward: **PALINDROME**
reading, spelling, composition, etc., taught to develop fundamental language skills: **LANGUAGE ARTS**

read intently, study with care: **PORE OVER**
read or examine thoroughly, scrutinize: **PERUSE**
read or glance over hastily: **SKIM**
read quickly, glance at: **SCAN**
ready, easygoing, agreeable: **FACILE**
ready to be put into use: **OPERATIONAL**
ready-to-wear: **PRÊT-À-PORTER**
real, actual: **SUBSTANTIVE**
real existence of something in the mind, actual being: **ENTITY**
realism in art through use of everyday rather than heroic characters and situations: **VERISMO**
realistically tough and terse in writing style: **HARD-BOILED**
realistic to the point of looking real, as in art or decoration: **TROMPE L'OEIL**
realization, accomplishment of things worked for: **FRUITION**
realized or actual existence as opposed to mere potentiality: **ENTELECHY**
real, material, having definite shape: **TANGIBLE**
reappearance, fresh outbreak: **RECRUDESCENCE**
rear car of freight train: **CABOOSE**
rear end of a boat: **STERN**
rear, feed, support, raise: **NURTURE**
rear, toward the stern, on a boat: **AFT, ABAFT**
reasonable, apparently true but open to doubt: **PLAUSIBLE**
reasonable, practicable, suitable: **FEASIBLE**
reason by logical methods: **RATIOCINATE**
reason earnestly with someone, remonstrate: **EXPOSTULATE**
reasoned, sensible: **RATIONAL**
reasoning from the general to the particular: **DEDUCTION**
reasoning from the particular to the general: **INDUCTION**
reasoning rather than using intuition in reaching conclusions: **DISCURSIVE**
reasoning that is clever but unsound: **SOPHISTRY**
reasoning that is faulty or illogical: **PARALOGISM**
reason or justification for being: **RAISON D'ÊTRE**

reasons underlying something:
RATIONALE
reason, think: **INTELLECTUALIZE**
rebellious: **INSUBORDINATE**
rebellious: **INSURGENT**
rebellious action or speech: **SEDITION**
rebellious, insolent: **CONTUMACIOUS**
rebellious, irritable, unruly, cranky:
FRACTIOUS
rebel or ambitious advocate of change
within a group, establishment, etc.:
YOUNG TURK
rebirth politically or culturally, infusion
of new determination:
RISORGIMENTO
rebirth, restoration, reconstitution:
REGENERATION
rebound or skip of a bullet or stone
after it hits a surface at an angle:
RICOCHET
rebuff, reject, repel: **REPULSE**
rebuke, castigate, rake over the coals:
KEELHAUL
rebuke, censure, blame for a fault:
REPROACH
rebuke, criticize, find fault with, blame:
REPREHEND
rebuke, disapproval, censure: **REPROOF**
rebuke or censure severely: **REPRIMAND**
rebuke or chastise severely: **CASTIGATE**
rebuke sharply, upbraid, berate:
OBJURGATE
recall, cancel, rescind, annul: **REVOKE**
recalling or telling of past events:
REMINISCENCE
recalling past occurrences,
remembering: **RETROSPECTION**
recalling to mind: **ANAMNESIS**
recall to mind, remember: **RETRIEVE**
recant: **ABJURE**
recapitulation of an oration:
PERORATION
receptive: **HOSPITABLE**
recess period in work: **COFFEE BREAK**
recess, time between parts of a
performance or between events or
activities: **INTERMISSION**
recipient of benefits or favors:
BENEFICIARY
reckless, careless: **DEVIL-MAY-CARE**
reckless, careless, weak: **FECKLESS**
recklessly, rashly: **HEADLONG**
recklessly use or handle, squander:
PLAY DUCKS AND DRAKES WITH
reckless, rash: **TEMERARIOUS**

reckless ride in a stolen vehicle, ride for
pleasure: **JOY RIDE**
reclining, leaning, lying down:
RECUMBENT
recluse: **ANCHORITE**
recluse: **EREMITE**
recluse: **TROGLODYTE**
recognize as different, perceive:
DISCERN
recoil: **BACKLASH**
recoil, resume original shape after being
stretched: **RESILE**
recollection: **ANAMNESIS**
reconcile and blend, as various
philosophies: **SYNCRETIZE**
recorder (the musical instrument):
BLOCKFLÖTE
recording industry job of selecting
artists and approving and
promoting their recordings: **A&R**
(**ARTISTS AND REPERTORY**)
recording or program optical disk
usually less than five inches in
diameter: **CD** (**COMPACT DISC**)
record or souvenirs of happenings
worth remembering: **MEMORABILIA**
recover: **RECUPERATE**
recover, pay off: **REDEEM**
recover, remedy the consequences of,
regain, make up for: **RETRIEVE**
recovery of property pending a court
test: **REPLEVIN**
rectify, compensate: **REDRESS**
rectum and its diseases as a branch of
medicine: **PROCTOLOGY**
recurrence in the mind of the same
thought, tune, etc.:
PERSEVERATION
recurrent: **CHRONIC**
recurring at regular intervals,
intermittent: **PERIODIC**
recycled or unoriginal substance or
presentation: **REHASH**
red color that is dull: **STAMMEL**
reddening: **RUBESCENT**
reddish nose from drunkenness:
COPPERNOSE
redemption price of a bond if it is
higher than the face value:
PREMIUM
red, especially in heraldry: **GULES**
red-handed: **IN FLAGRANTE DELICTO**
redistrict a voting area so as to advance
the interests of a political party:
GERRYMANDER

red tape in government: BUREAUCRACY
reduce expenses: RETRENCH
reduce in quantity or force: ABATE
reduce in rank or position: ABASE
reduce in size, lessen, belittle: MINIFY
reduce to the smallest possible amount
    or degree: MINIMIZE
reduction of debt or liability, done
    gradually, as by installment
    payments: AMORTIZATION
reduction of personnel through
    retirement, death, etc.: ATTRITION
redundancy: TAUTOLOGY
redundancy, use of excess words:
    PLEONASM
refined but affected term, prudish
    euphemism: GENTEELISM
refined or delicate to an extreme:
    FASTIDIOUS
refined, polite, suave: URBANE
refined to excess, overly exotic or
    pretentious: RECHERCHÉ
refinement, well-bred in one's ways:
    GENTILITY
refine, purify: RAREFY
reflecting light, shining back, bright:
    RELUCENT
reflecting raised tiles instead of painted
    lines on a highway: BOTTS DOTS
reflective, serious, often melancholy:
    PENSIVE
reflect, think about, consider carefully:
    PONDER
refrain: ABSTAIN
refreshments: COLLATION
refuge for an animal: CREEPHOLE
refusal given bluntly: REBUFF
refusal to serve: NON SERVIAM
refuse scornfully, treat with contempt:
    DISDAIN
refuse, scorn, reject: SPURN
refuse to accept, disown, reject:
    REPUDIATE
refuse to deal with or patronize so as to
    punish: BOYCOTT
refuse to go forward, balk: JIB
refuse, waste matter: DROSS
refutation in syllogistic form: ELENCHUS
regain, as for a loss: RECOUP
regain, recover, make up for, remedy
    the consequences of: RETRIEVE
register of title deeds, charters, etc.:
    CARTULARY
register or enroll in a college or

university as a candidate for a
    degree: MATRICULATE
regret an action, feel contrite: REPENT
regret extremely: RUE
regret, plead against: DEPRECATE
regular fixed-dollar-amount method of
    purchasing securities: MONTHLY
    INVESTMENT PLAN
regular in repetition: CONTINUAL
regularly recurring, intermittent:
    PERIODIC
regulate, adjust, temper or soften:
    MODULATE
rehash, reworked literary material:
    RECHAUFFÉ
rehearsal: DRY RUN
reimburse: RECOUP
reincarnation: METEMPSYCHOSIS
rein thirty or more feet long at the end
    of which a horse moves for
    training and exercise: LONGE
reinvigorating: ANALEPTIC
reject, drive back: REPEL
rejection of customary belief,
    immortality and institutions:
    NIHILISM
reject, rebuff, repel: REPULSE
reject, refuse, scorn: SPURN
reject, refuse to accept, disown:
    REPUDIATE
reject with contempt, refuse scornfully:
    DISDAIN
rejoice greatly: EXULT
relapse: BACKSLIDE
related on the female or mother's side:
    ENATE
related on the male or father's side:
    AGNATE
related or alike in meaning, significance
    or effect: SYNONYMOUS
related or similar in structure, position,
    value: HOMOLOGOUS
related superficially: TANGENTIAL
related to a subject, relevant:
    PERTINENT
related to what is being discussed,
    relevant, pertinent: GERMANE
relationships within a group as a study:
    SOCIOMETRY
relationship that is close: AFFINITY
relaxant, sleep-producing medicine:
    OPIATE
release from care and pain, bliss:
    NIRVANA
release of repressed emotion by reliving

or talking about the original
situation, trauma, etc.:
ABREACTION
relentless: **INEXORABLE**
relevant only in part: **TANGENTIAL**
relevant, pertinent, related to what is
being discussed: **GERMANE**
relevant, related to a subject:
PERTINENT
relics' or holy objects' repository, as a
box or a shrine: **RELIQUARY**
relief design, as in metal: **REPOUSSÉ**
relieve of a burden: **DISBURDEN**
relieving irritation, soothing:
DEMULCENT
religious art that is cheap or vulgar:
BONDIEUSERIE
religious belief rejected: **ATHEISM**
religious belief that God has
foreknowledge of all and has
ordained the fate of human souls:
PREDESTINATION
religious devotion: **PIETY**
religious ecstasy: **THEOPATHY**
religious literature, traditions, etc.:
HIEROLOGY
religious movement based on literal
acceptance of everything in the
Bible: **FUNDAMENTALISM**
religious music or sacred poetry muse:
POLYHYMNIA
religious offering: **OBLATION**
religious order's candidate: **POSTULANT**
religious or meditative commune:
ASHRAM
religious or spiritual hermit: **EREMITE**
religious ritual: **LITURGY**
religious washing of hands: **ABLUTION**
relinquish, give up, forgo: **WAIVE**
reliquary: **FERETORY**
reliving a traumatic situation for release
from it: **ABREACTION**
reluctant, unwilling: **LOATH**
remainder after deducting all expenses,
outlays, etc.: **NET**
remainder, leftover part: **RESIDUE**
remarkable, strange, extraordinary:
UNACCOUNTABLE
remark, gesture, etc., that dispels initial
awkwardness, formality or tension:
ICEBREAKER
remark made in passing, comment that
is not binding: **OBITER DICTUM**
remark or observation that is brief,
clever and pointed: **EPIGRAM**

remark that is pointed, witty or
mordant: **ZINGER**
remarriage: **DEUTEROGAMY**
remarriage: **DIGAMY**
remedy: **TREACLE**
remedy, cure-all, panacea: **ELIXIR**
remedy for all ailments, cure-all:
PANACEA
remedy or cure for all ills: **CATHOLICON**
remedy that one swears by, medicine of
one's own invention, quack
medicine, cure-all: **NOSTRUM**
remedy the consequences of, get back,
regain: **RETRIEVE**
remembered or imagined with
photographic vividness: **EIDETIC**
remembering: **RETROSPECTION**
remembering in complete detail: **TOTAL
RECALL**
remember, recall to mind: **RETRIEVE**
reminder: **AIDE-MÉMOIRE**
reminder of mortality, as a symbol of
death: **MEMENTO MORI**
remind one of a mistake or fault in
order to taunt or annoy: **TWIT**
remission of sin: **ABSOLUTION**
remorse: **COMPUNCTION**
remove attention from: **PRESCIND**
remove obscene or otherwise
objectionable material: **EXPURGATE**
remove or dissociate from former
habits: **WEAN**
remove or drive away, as by scattering:
DISPEL
remove or take off, as clothing: **DOFF**
remove property to a distance or
beyond a jurisdiction: **ELOIGN**
removing by surgery: **ABSCISSION**
renaissance or revival politically or
culturally, infusion of new
determination: **RISORGIMENTO**
renaming a parent after his or her
child: **TEKNONYMY**
render null and void: **INVALIDATE**
renegade individual: **ROGUE ELEPHANT**
renew, repair: **RENOVATE**
renew, restore to perfection:
REDINTEGRATE
renounce: **ABJURE**
renounce: **ABNEGATE**
renounce claim to right or power:
ABDICATE
renounce, give up: **RELINQUISH**
renounce or abandon emphatically:
FORSWEAR

renovate, make over: REVAMP

renovation of buildings, a neighborhood, etc., to improve property values and occupancy or clientele socioeconomically: GENTRIFICATION

renowned, distinguished: ILLUSTRIOUS

renowned, important: PRESTIGIOUS

renown or splendor of reputation: ÉCLAT

rent that is unreasonable or exorbitant: RACK-RENT

repartee in classical and Elizabethan dramatic dialogue: STICHOMYTHIA

repay evil in kind, take revenge: RETALIATE

repay in kind, compensate: REQUITE

repay or pay, make up for, as a loss: RECOMPENSE

repeal: ABROGATE

repeal, revoke, abrogate: RESCIND

repeat: ITERATE

repeated: CONTINUAL

repeatedly appearing: RECURRENT

repeated song or phrase in music: REPRISE

repeating another's or others' words: ECHOLALIA

repeat meaningless words over and over, babble: VERBIGERATE

repeat, say or do over and over: REITERATE

repel: REBUFF

repel, reject, rebuff: REPULSE

repent: RUE

repentant, sorrowful, mourning, humbled: IN SACKCLOTH AND ASHES

repetition needlessly in different words, a circular and meaningless statement: TAUTOLOGY

repetition of an initial sound in a series of words: ALLITERATION

repetition avoided of a word and a strained synonym used instead: ELEGANT VARIATION

repetition of a word or phrase: ANAPHORA

repetition of someone's words in senseless fashion: ECHOLALIA

repetition of the last word of one sentence at the beginning of the next sentence or clause: ANADIPLOSIS

repetition of written letters or words done unintentionally: DITTOGRAPHY

repetitiousness: BATTOLOGY

repetitive or monotonous, narrow, belabored: ONE-NOTE

replacement of injured or diseased body tissue by a synthetic implant: ALLOPLASTY

replacement, temporary, or fill-in in a job: LOCUM TENENS

replace, supplant: SUPERSEDE

replies that are quick and witty: REPARTEE

reply, please: RÉPONDEZ S'IL VOUS PLAÎT (R.S.V.P.)

reply sharply: RETORT

reply so as to prove someone or something wrong, retort: CONFUTE

report-drafting official for a conference or committee: RAPPORTEUR

report of proceedings: CAHIER

representative of a government, civil magistrate or officer: SYNDIC

representative of a special-interest group who tries to influence legislation: LOBBYIST

representative, official or not, who deals with opponents, difficult situations, etc.: POINT MAN

representative or symbol of something, as of a doctrine or a cause: EXPONENT

repression generally forced on a society: GLEICHSCHALTUNG

reprimand, scolding: RATING

reproach sarcastically: TAUNT

reproach, scold, censure: UPBRAID

reproduce, duplicate, repeat: REPLICATE

reproduction or imitation of the original: ECTYPE

reprove mildly: ADMONISH

reptiles and amphibians as a study: HERPETOLOGY

repudiate: ABJURE

repudiate a former belief: RECANT

repudiate, contradict, deny: DISAFFIRM

repugnant, disgusting, offensive, hateful: ODIOUS

repulsive: LOATHSOME

repulsive, evil, flagrantly bad: VILE

repulsive-in-appearance thing or person: EYESORE

repurchase agreement: REPO

reputation-damaging campaign, personal-attack propaganda,

political slander: CHARACTER ASSASSINATION

reputed, usually so considered, supposed: PUTATIVE

request or entreaty that succeeds, procuring: IMPETRATION

require as a matter of justice, demand rigorously: EXACT

require, claim: POSTULATE

required by long use or custom: PRESCRIPTIVE

required earlier than something that follows: PREREQUISITE

required, indispensable: REQUISITE

required, obligatory: MANDATORY

research and development: R AND D

resemblance in certain aspects of otherwise dissimilar things: ANALOGY

resembling or correlative thing, equivalent in a manner of speaking: COUNTERPART

resent another's possessions or enjoyment: BEGRUDGE

resentfully morose, glum: SULLEN

resentful or angry to a great degree: IN HIGH DUDGEON

resentment, anger: DUDGEON

resentment, injured feeling: UMBRAGE

resentment, offended pride: PIQUE

reservation, excuse: SALVO

reserve accumulation of goods: STOCKPILE

reserved, close-mouthed: TACITURN

reserved, coy, shy, modest: DEMURE

reserved, reluctant to speak, quiet: RETICENT

reserve of unfilled orders: BACKLOG

residence: ABODE

resignation or giving up an office: DEMISSION

resigned or adjusted to a situation: RECONCILED

resiliency of the market in a particular security in the face of changing prices: LIQUIDITY

resistance shown to established government, revolt: INSURRECTION

resistance to harmful influence or disease: IMMUNITY

resistant declaration ("I will not serve"): NON SERVIAM

resistant, immune: INSUSCEPTIBLE

resistant, not yielding to measures taken or treatment: REFRACTORY

resistant to change, cautious, moderate: CONSERVATIVE

resistant, unyielding: IMPREGNABLE

resisting, doubting or ignoring attitude: NEGATIVISM

resolved, unflinching, determined: RESOLUTE

resonant: SONOROUS

resounding, echoing: RESONANT

resounding loudly: REBOANT

respectable: SAVORY

respectable, legitimate, legal: ON-THE-UP-AND-UP

respect deeply: VENERATE

respect is demanded and criticism is forbidden for such a person or idea: SACRED COW

respect, reverence, homage: OBEISANCE

respects paid: DEVOIRS

respiration at an excessive rate depleting carbon dioxide: HYPERVENTILATION

responding involuntarily to a stimulus as an organism does: TROPISM

response developed by training: CONDITIONED REFLEX

response, echo: REPLICATION

responsibility, burden: ONUS

responsibility for all one's acts (Buddhism and Hinduism): KARMA

responsively sung or chanted hymn, psalm, verse, etc.: ANTIPHON

responsive reaction or evaluation: FEEDBACK

responsive to persuasion or change: AMENABLE

rest and recuperation, leave: R AND R (REST AND RECUPERATION)

restaurant: TRATTORIA

restaurant or bar that is small: BISTRO

restaurant or café that provides entertainment: CABARET

restaurant that is bar-like and informal: BRASSERIE

resting, leaning or weighing upon something: INCUMBENT

resting, nonactive: STATIC

resting place for travelers or pilgrims: HOSPICE

rest in peace: REQUIESCAT IN PACE

rest interval, postponement, delay: RESPITE

restlessly or nervously move: FIDGET

restlessness, anxiety: DISQUIET

restlessness, uneasiness: INQUIETUDE

restless, superficial, frivolous: YEASTY
restless, unruly, fidgety: RESTIVE
restoration, compensation, amends:
   REPARATION
restore friendship: RECONCILE
restore to perfection, renew:
   REDINTEGRATE
restore to rank, position or state of
   health: REHABILITATE
restore youthful feeling or vigor:
   REJUVENATE
restrained, moderate: TEMPERATE
restrain or check, as an impulse:
   INHIBIT
restraint in sexual activity, moderation:
   CONTINENCE
restraint, modesty and self-control,
   prudence, temperance:
   SOPHROSYNE
restriction, boundary: PALE
restriction on freight transportation:
   EMBARGO
restrict to a scanty amount: STINT
result: AFTERMATH
result, effect: RAMIFICATION
result or consequence that is normal:
   COROLLARY
résumé, career or biographical
   description or chronology:
   CURRICULUM VITAE
resuscitation: ANABIOSIS
retaining wall: REVETMENT
retaliation: REPRISAL
retaliation, repayment in kind: TIT FOR
   TAT
retarded person brilliant in one skill or
   field: IDIOT SAVANT
retch, heave as if to vomit: KECK
retentive, as memory: TENACIOUS
retinue, train of attendants: CORTEGE
retired from active service but retaining
   an honorary position: EMERITUS
retired on account of age:
   SUPERANNUATED
retired person, pension recipient:
   PENSIONER
retire-early incentive offered to an older
   employee: GOLDEN HANDSHAKE
retire, make oneself inconspicuous:
   EFFACE
retort that is sharp and swift: RIPOSTE
retouching or delicate-work paint
   atomizer: AIRBRUSH
retract: ABJURE
retraction: PALINODE

retreat to an earlier or worse condition:
   RETROGRESS
retroactive: EX POST FACTO
retrospect: HINDSIGHT
return by an offender to criminal acts
   or antisocial behavior: RECIDIVISM
return in kind or amount:
   RECIPROCATE
return like for like, repay evil with evil,
   take revenge: RETALIATE
return of part of the output of a system
   into the input: FEEDBACK
return to a former place, position or
   condition: REVERT
return to normal condition or better:
   RALLY
reveal, bring to light, disclose: EXHUME
reveal, give vent to: UNBOSOM
reveal or tell, as a secret: DIVULGE
revelation or insight dramatically
   symbolic in a literary work:
   EPIPHANY
revelry, usually lasting for a special
   season or period: SATURNALIA
revengeful, spiteful: VINDICTIVE
revenge sought by a country at the cost
   of war or violence: REVANCHISM
reverberation, aftereffect:
   REPERCUSSION
revere: VENERATE
reverence, homage, respect: OBEISANCE
reverie, reflection: BROWN STUDY
reversal of fortune in drama, literature,
   etc.: PERIPETEIA, PERIPETIA,
   PERIPETY
reversal of letters or words as a form of
   reading disorder:
   STREPHOSYMBOLIA
reversal of opinion: ABOUT-FACE
reversal of opinion: FLIP-FLOP,
   VOLTE-FACE
reversal or disruption, overthrow,
   disorder, confusion, upset:
   BOULEVERSEMENT
reverse counting of time: COUNTDOWN
reversed order of things or events, used
   as a figure of speech: HYSTERON
   PROTERON
reversed or opposite in order or effect:
   INVERSE
reverse of phraseology in the second of
   two parallel expressions: CHIASMUS
reverse reading of a word or sentence is
   the same as forward reading:
   PALINDROME

reverse side of a phonograph record:
FLIP SIDE, **B** SIDE

reversion, backward movement:
REGRESSION

reversion to a more primitive type:
ATAVISM

reversion to an earlier form or
condition: THROWBACK

reviewing past occurrences,
remembering: RETROSPECTION

revise, renovate: REVAMP

revise, vary, restrict, limit: MODIFY

revival, new birth: RENASCENCE

revival or return to former excellence:
COMEBACK

revive, bring or come back to life:
RESUSCITATE

revive, refresh, renew: RENOVATE

revoke, abrogate, repeal: RESCIND

revoke a legacy: ADEEM

revoke or reverse a command:
COUNTERMAND

revolting, detestable, abominable:
EXECRABLE

revolting monster, grave robber: GHOUL

revolve or rotate, usually around a fixed
point: GYRATE

revolving serving tray: LAZY SUSAN

revolving, whirling or circular in
motion: GYRAL

reward: GUERDON

rewarding partisan service with public
office: SPOILS SYSTEM

reward or compensation in a job:
EMOLUMENT

rewording of a statement with the
original meaning retained:
PARAPHRASE

reworked literary material, rehash:
RÉCHAUFFÉ

rhyme composed of words similar in
spelling but not in sound: EYE
RHYME

rhyme in which the stress falls on the
next-to-last syllable: FEMININE
RHYME

rhyme scheme in which a word within
the line of verse rhymes with the
final word of the line: LEONINE
RHYME

rhyming game in which a rhyme must
be given for a word or line given
by another: CRAMBO

rhythmic or measured flow: CADENCE

rhythmic pendulum device for keeping
the beat: METRONOME

rhythmic placement of a tone so that its
accent does not coincide with the
metric accent: SYNCOPATION

ribbon cluster or rosette worn as a
badge: COCKADE

ribbons and pins in a store: NOTIONS

ribbon worn as an insignia of honor or
rank: CORDON

rib or ridge, as on fabric: WALE

rice cooked in broth: RISOTTO

rich and fashionable young people,
gilded youth: JEUNESSE DORÉE

rich and resonant, as a tone: VIBRANT

rich customers or patrons: CARRIAGE
TRADE

riches, wealth: OPULENCE

rich man: CROESUS

rich or ambitious newcomer, upstart,
parvenu: ARRIVISTE

rich or influential man: NABOB

rich person who has become so only
recently: NOUVEAU RICHE

rickety: RAMSHACKLE

riddle involving a pun: CONUNDRUM

riddle, puzzle, obscure or ambiguous
saying: ENIGMA

ride for pleasure, reckless ride in a
stolen vehicle: JOY RIDE

ridge around a hatchway or skylight to
keep out water: COAMING

ridge or rib, as on fabric: WALE

ridges fixed across the fingerboard of a
guitar or other stringed instrument:
FRETS

ridicule or scorn publicly: PILLORY

ridicule or treat with scornful mirth:
DERIDE

ridicule or wit used to attack vices or
follies: SATIRE

ridiculous, absurd: LUDICROUS

ridiculous or ludicrous situation: FARCE

riding the crest of a wave toward shore
on a surfboard: SURFING

riding the waves on a sailboard:
WINDSURFING

rid oneself of: SLOUGH

rid oneself of a burden: DISBURDEN

rifle marksmanship and skiing
competition: BIATHLON

rifle with a short barrel: CARBINE

right- and left-handed: AMBIDEXTROUS

right-angled position of a line or place
to another: PERPENDICULAR

right-angled triangle's side that is opposite the right angle: HYPOTENUSE

right a wrong, make compensation: REDRESS

righteous or pious as a pretense: SANCTIMONIOUS

right-hand page of a book: RECTO

right of feudal lords to the first night with a bride: DROIT DU SEIGNEUR

right of the state to take over private property for public use: EMINENT DOMAIN

right or claim that is legal: DROIT

right or left part of something, side: FLANK

right side as opposed to the left side, especially in heraldry: DEXTER

right side of a vessel or plane as one faces forward: STARBOARD

right that is exclusive or a privilege: PREROGATIVE

right to left, a word or sentence reads the same as left to right: PALINDROME

right to vote: SUFFRAGE

right word or expression: MOT JUSTE

rigid, enlarged condition of the penis: ERECTION

rigid, inflexible: HARD-SHELL

rigidity of the muscles after death: RIGOR MORTIS

rigid, severe: STRINGENT

rigmarole: AMPHIGORY

ring, as for the finger, made up of two interlocked circlets: GIMMAL

ring for attaching a leash, as to a dog's collar: TERRET

ringing in the ears: TINNITUS

ringing of bells: TINTINNABULATION

ringing or tinkling sound: JINGLE

ring or disk used to make a connection watertight or gastight: GASKET

ring-shaped hard roll of bread: BAGEL

ring to strengthen a loose-leaf paper hole: REINFORCEMENT

riot, civil or political disturbance: DISTEMPER

riotous, wild: TURBULENT

rip apart forcibly: REND

ripen: MATURATE

ripple, bubble, heave: POPPLE

rise above: TRANSCEND

rise and float in the air: LEVITATE

rise or overflow of a stream occurring suddenly: FRESHET

rise somewhat from the water when moving at high speed: PLANE

rising again: RESURGENT

rising and falling gently, wavy in appearance: UNDULATING

rising and setting of a star, involving the: ACRONICAL

rising market: BULL MARKET

rising up in insurrection: INSURGENCE

risks taken to achieve some end: BRINKMANSHIP

risky: SPECULATIVE

risky and delicate, uncertain, precarious: TOUCH-AND-GO

risky or uncertain venture: CRAPSHOOT

risqué, indecent: SCABROUS

risqué, suggestive: RACY

rite considered ordained by Jesus as a means of grace: SACRAMENT

ritual of public religious worship: LITURGY

rival or vie with successfully: EMULATE

rivalry, competition: CONTENTION

river embankment built to prevent flooding: LEVEE

riverine, pertaining to a riverbank area: RIPARIAN

river mouth area of plain and streams: DELTA

river mouth where the stream's current meets the sea, an inlet of the sea: ESTUARY

river of oblivion, forgetfulness: LETHE

river of woe: ACHERON

river or rivers, pertaining to: FLUVIAL

river's head or supply of water: WATERSHED

road ascending a steep incline in a zigzag pattern: SWITCHBACK

road raised over marshy land or water: CAUSEWAY

road repairing utilizing forced labor: CORVÉE

roam about in search of diversion, gad about: GALLIVANT

roaming, homeless: NOMADIC

rob a truck or seize a plane in transit: HIJACK

robber or bandit, usually one of a group: BRIGAND

robber who assaults or threatens the victim and tries to flee quickly: MUGGER robber who smuggles goods out of an open store: SHOPLIFTER

robe or undercoat, long-sleeved and sashed: CAFTAN

robotic, computerized or mechanical autonomy, as in performing tasks, solving problems or playing games: ARTIFICIAL INTELLIGENCE

robot like a human being: ANDROID

robot like a human being in Jewish folklore: GOLEM

rob, strip, deprive of: DESPOIL

robust, sound and vigorous of health: HALE

robust, tough: HARDY

rocket's forward separable section designed to stand intense heat: NOSE CONE

rocket's head containing explosive: WARHEAD

rock projecting and isolated: SCAR

rock salt (sodium chloride): HALITE

rocks and their characteristics as a study: PETROLOGY

rocks' structure and composition as a scientific study: LITHOLOGY

rocky cliff that extends a distance: PALISADES

rocky hill or its craggy peak: TOR

rod that holds meat together for cooking: SKEWER

rod that is a symbol of royalty: SCEPTER

rod that is pointed and is used for cooking meat over a fire: SPIT

rogue, rascal: RAPSCALLION

rolled up, spirally curling: VOLUTE

rollicking type of square dance: HOEDOWN

roll made of dough in the shape of a crescent: CROISSANT

roll of film or magnetic tape in a case: CASSETTE

roll of hard bread that is ring-shaped: BAGEL

roll of minced meat or fish in a thin pastry: RISSOLE

roll of sliced meat filled with minced meat: ROULADE

roll or move tumultuously: WELTER

romance or Gothic historical novel: BODICE RIPPER

Romanian and Israeli folk dance in which dancers lock arms in a circle: HORA

Roman gladiator who fought with a short sword and a long shield: SAMNITE

Roman gladiator who fought with a small and often curved sword: THRACE

Roman gladiator who fought with a standard sword and shield: MIRMILLON

Roman gladiator who fought with a trident and a net: RETIARIUS

romantic, chivalric or daring in intentions but impractical: QUIXOTIC

roofed atop columns or pillars: HYPOSTYLE

roofed mall, court or promenade, often glass-enclosed: GALLERIA

roof support just above a column: ARCHITRAVE

roof that is rounded, dome: CUPOLA

roof tile with an unbalanced S shape: PANTILE

roof with a single slope whose upper edge abuts a wall: LEAN-TO

roof with two slopes on all sides, the lower having a steeper pitch: MANSARD

roof with two slopes on each of two sides, the lower having a steeper pitch: GAMBREL

room or territory for expansion: LEBENSRAUM

room with therapeutic dry heat: SAUNA

roomy: CAPACIOUS

rooster that is castrated to make the meat better for eating: CAPON

root-like: RHIZOID

root out, destroy wholly: EXTIRPATE

rope, cable or wire used to steady or secure something: GUY

rope for mooring at the front of a boat: PAINTER

rope-like cord that is elastic, often with hooked ends, and used to secure large packages, luggage, etc.: BUNGEE CORD, SHOCK CORD

rope or cable for mooring or towing: HAWSER

rope- or cable-winding shaft: CAPSTAN, WINDLASS

rope with a running noose used with horses and livestock: LARIAT

rosette, ribbon badge: COCKADE

rosy: RUBICUND

rotary combustion engine for automobiles: **WANKEL ENGINE**

rotate or revolve, usually around a fixed point: **GYRATE**

rotation force: **TORQUE**

rote repetition in speech, parroting: **PSITTACISM**

rotten: **CARIOUS**

rotten, corrupt: **PUTRID**

rotten-egg-smelling gas: **HYDROGEN SULFIDE**

rotten or dead flesh: **CARRION**

rough-and-tumble clash, fracas: **SCRIMMAGE**

rough, crude, unrefined: **UNCOUTH**

roughly handle, manhandle, abuse: **MAUL**

roughness: **ASPERITY**

rough, plain, simple: **RUSTIC**

rough sketch: **ESQUISSE**

roundabout: **AMBIGUOUS**

roundabout, hesitant or insincere in speech, not straightforward: **MEALYMOUTHED**

roundabout, indirect: **CIRCUITOUS**

roundabout talk: **CIRCUMLOCUTION**

round building or hall: **ROTUNDA**

round but somewhat flattened at the top and bottom: **OBROTUND**

round but somewhat flattened or concave at the poles: **OBLATE**

rounded, full, clear, as a voice: **OROTUND**

rounded mass: **GLOMERATION**

rounded out, plump: **ROTUND**

rounded, spherical: **ORBICULAR**

roundness: **SPHERICITY**

round up: **CORRAL**

rouse to action, stimulate, arouse: **GALVANIZE**

rousing speech: **STEMWINDER**

route followed in traveling: **ITINERARY**

routine, commonplace, ordinary: **MUNDANE**

routinely performed without interest: **PERFUNCTORY**

roving, wandering, straying, itinerant: **ERRANT**

rowboat with high sides and a flat bottom: **DORY**

rower's seat in a boat: **THWART**

royalty symbol in the form of a rod: **SCEPTER**

rub away: **ABRADE**

rubbery plastic used in dentistry and golf balls: **GUTTA-PERCHA**

rubbing against another for sexual stimulation: **FROTTAGE**

rubbing off or wearing off of particles: **DETRITION**

rubbish, junk, trash: **DRECK**

rubbish, nonsense: **TRUMPERY**

rubbish, refuse, leavings: **OFFAL**

rubble below a cliff: **SCREE**

rub out, erase, cancel, obliterate: **EFFACE**

rub the body with oil: **EMBROCATE**

ruddy: **SANGUINE**

ruddy, flushed: **FLORID**

rude, disorderly, boisterous: **RAMBUNCTIOUS**

rudeness, insolence: **IMPERTINENCE**

rudeness in speech that is insulting and scornful: **CONTUMELY**

rude or discourteous manner: **INCIVILITY**

rude or ill-natured person: **CHURL**

rude, sullen: **SURLY**

rudimentary: **ABECEDARIAN**

ruffle at the neckline or front of a bodice or shirt: **JABOT**

ruffled or pleated strip of fabric worn about the neck or wrists of a woman's costume: **RUCHE**

ruffle on a blouse or coat at the waist: **PEPLUM**

ruffle, upset the balance: **DISTEMPER**

rugged and weather-beaten: **GNARLED**

ruin, destruction: **HAVOC**

ruiner of a plan, project, etc.: **MARPLOT**

ruinous or fatal act: **KISS OF DEATH**

ruin, rout, sudden and ruinous breakdown or collapse: **DEBACLE**

ruin, wreck, pillage: **RAVAGE**

rule by the best or the most privileged: **ARISTOCRACY**

rule, moral guide, maxim: **PRECEPT**

rule or principle that is established: **CANON**

rule or standard by which a judgment can be made: **CRITERION**

rule or treat with cruel power: **TYRANNIZE**

ruler or similar instrument used to punish children: **FERULE**

rulers or sovereigns reigning in succession in one line of descent: **DYNASTY**

ruler who governs in place of a
    sovereign: **REGENT**
ruler who is supreme: **SOVEREIGN**
rules or directions printed for use in
    religious services: **RUBRIC**
rumble, move with rumbling noise:
    LUMBER
rum drink that includes lemon or lime
    juice and sugar: **PLANTER'S PUNCH**
rummage about for something: **FOSSICK**
rumor, gossip, the lowdown:
    SCUTTLEBUTT
rumor that is false: **CANARD**
rumpled, untidy, unkempt, tousled:
    DISHEVELED
run away to escape the law: **ABSCOND**
run-down, neglected, fallen into ruin or
    decay: **DILAPIDATED**
run, go in a hurry: **SCAMPER**
runic alphabet: **FUTHARK**
runners fastened to shoes for gliding
    over snow: **SKIS**
running at a slow pace: **JOGGING**
running together of final and initial
    sounds of two adjacent words:
    SANDHI
run with a steady swinging stride: **LOPE**
rural: **AGRESTIC**
rural and peaceful, idyllic: **PASTORAL**
rural or farming affairs, pertaining to:
    GEORGIC
rural or remote area, hinterland, sticks:
    BOONDOCKS
rush forward: **SALLY**
rush headlong: **HURTLE**
rush wildly: **CAREEN**

Russian citizen denied permission to
    emigrate: **REFUSENIK**
Russian country home: **DACHA**
Russian dance in which a squatting
    man kicks each leg out alternately:
    KAZATSKY
Russian for "comrade": **TOVARICH**
Russian for "goodbye": **DO SVIDANIYA**
Russian painted hollow wooden doll,
    somewhat bowling-pin-shaped and
    with a separable top half, that is
    one of several that "nest" one
    within the other: **MATRUSHKA**
Russian policy of openness regarding
    solving internal social problems:
    GLASNOST
Russian title equivalent to "Mr.":
    GOSPODIN
Russian triangular-shaped stringed
    instrument: **BALALAIKA**
Russian unit of length (about 3,500 feet,
    .66 miles, 1.07 kilometers): **VERST**
Russian vehicle drawn by three horses
    abreast: **TROIKA**
rustic, pastoral: **BUCOLIC**
rustic, pastoral and simple, peaceful:
    ARCADIAN
rustling as of silk, swish, fanciness:
    FROUFROU
rustling, whispering, softly murmuring:
    SUSURRANT
ruthless in compelling conformity:
    PROCRUSTEAN
rye or bourbon cocktail made with
    vermouth: **MANHATTAN**

sable fur: **ZIBELINE**
sack of canvas or duck used for
    carrying personal possessions:
    DUFFLE BAG, DUFFEL BAG
sacred books of any sect or religion:
    CANON
sacredness maintained, unbroken:
    INVIOLATE
sacred poetry or religious music muse:
    POLYHYMNIA
sacrificial offering, wholly consumed by
    fire: **HOLOCAUST**
saddened, dejected, gloomy:
    DISCONSOLATE
saddened or desolate through loss:
    BEREAVED
saddle hind part that projects upward:
    CANTLE
saddle lighter but better padded than a
    Western saddle and having no
    pommel horn: **ENGLISH SADDLE**
sadism and masochism, sadomasochism:
    S AND M, S & M
sadism or masochism: **ALGOLAGNIA**
sad, mournful, painful: **DOLOROUS**
sad or mournful, especially in a
    ludicrous manner: **LUGUBRIOUS**
sad, pitiful, causing sorrow: **PATHETIC**
safe or proof against attack:
    UNASSAILABLE
safety or hiding place for an animal:
    CREEPHOLE
said or done thing for effect or as a
    formality: **GESTURE**
sailboat pole, or spar, projecting from
    the bow: **BOWSPRIT**
sailboat's mast or boom: **SPAR**
sailboat that is small and usually with a
    cockpit: **SAILBOARD**

sailboat with a single mast and
    fore-and-aft rigging: **SLOOP**
sailboat with three parallel hulls:
    TRIMARAN
sailboat with two parallel hulls:
    CATAMARAN
sailing close to the wind: **LUFF**
sail of triangular shape ahead of the
    foremast: **JIB**
sailor ranking below an able-bodied
    seaman: **ORDINARY SEAMAN**
sailor's bag for belongings: **DITTY BAG**
sailor's close-fitting knitted navy-blue
    cap: **WATCH CAP**
sailor's dance: **HORNPIPE**
sailors' rhythmical working song:
    CHANTEY, CHANTY
sailor uniform neck flap:
    TALLYWHACKER
sailor who is a veteran, old salt:
    SHELLBACK
sail that is large and usually triangular
    and used when running before the
    wind: **SPINNAKER**
sainted: **CANONIZED**
saints and their lives as a study:
    HAGIOGRAPHY
Saint Vitus's dance: **CHOREA**
salary, pension, allowance: **STIPEND**
sale item priced near or below cost to
    promote sale of others: **LOSS
    LEADER**
sales-force manager in a store:
    FLOORWALKER
saliva, spittle: **SPUTUM**
salmon before it enters the ocean: **PARR**
salmon of a salty, smoked variety: **LOX**
salmon that has returned for the first
    time from the sea to fresh water:
    GRILSE

salty: **SALINE**
salty, briny: **BRACKISH**
salvage something usable from refuse:
    SCAVENGE
same: **DITTO**
same as the previous reference: **IBID.**
same kind of person or thing:
    CONGENER
sameness in style, tone, expression,
    color: **MONOTONE**
sample strip of fabric: **SWATCH**
sanctimonious: **PHARISAIC**
sanctuary especially sacred: **SANCTUM**
    SANCTORUM
sandals with uppers made of straps:
    HUARACHES
sandstone used to scour the wooden
    decks of a ship: **HOLYSTONE**
sandwich of Swiss cheese, corned beef
    and sauerkraut on grilled rye
    bread: **REUBEN SANDWICH**
sandwich with three slices of bread and
    two layers of filling:
    DOUBLE-DECKER
sandy area with vegetation blown away
    by the sand: **SANDBLOW**
sandy, gritty: **SABULOUS**
sandy whirlwind that is small: **DUST**
    DEVIL
sane, sound of mind: **COMPOS MENTIS**
sarcastic: **ACRIMONIOUS**
sarcastic, biting: **CAUSTIC**
sarcastic, caustic, cutting: **MORDANT**
sarcastic or humorous speech in which
    the opposite of what is said is
    meant: **IRONY**
sardine-like fish: **SPRAT**
sarong-style loincloth worn by Samoan
    natives: **LAVALAVA, PAREU**
sash, usually wide, worn as a
    waistband: **CUMMERBUND**
sassy: **CHEEKY**
sassy young woman: **BAGGAGE**
satanic: **CLOVEN-HOOFED**
sated, full, amply supplied: **REPLETE**
satire that is sarcastic or coarse and is
    posted publicly: **PASQUINADE**
satirize or abuse in humorous prose or
    verse: **LAMPOON**
satirizing a literary work by using a
    grand or epical style describing
    something trivial: **MOCK-HEROIC**
satisfaction felt from another's troubles:
    SCHADENFREUDE
satisfy or quench, as a thirst: **SLAKE**

saturate, permeate, fertilize:
    IMPREGNATE
sauce, as for fish, made of mayonnaise
    and chopped pickles, capers, etc.:
    TARTAR SAUCE
sauce made with mayonnaise and
    spices: **RÉMOULADE**
sauce of onions, butter and white sauce:
    SOUBISE
saucer-like concave large antenna used
    for extensive television signal
    reception: **DISH ANTENNA**
saucer of plastic streamlined for a
    throwing game: **FRISBEE**
sauce thickener made of fat and flour:
    ROUX
sauciness, impertinence: **FLIPPANCY**
saucy, brazen, shameless, bold:
    IMPUDENT
saucy, lively: **PERT**
sausage of smoked beef and pork:
    CERVELAT
sausage-shaped: **ALLANTOID**
savage, fierce, bloodthirsty, cruel:
    FEROCIOUS
savage, wild: **FERAL**
save by not spending, economize:
    SCRIMP
saved fund of money for future use:
    NEST EGG
saved material after a wreck, fire, etc.:
    SALVAGE
save from destruction: **SALVAGE**
saving occurrence or thing that is
    unexpected but timely: **GODSEND**
savory, pleasant-tasting: **SAPID**
saying long in use: **ADAGE**
saying or precept, formal statement:
    DICTUM
sayings ascribed to Jesus but not found
    in the Bible: **AGRAPHA**
saying something that one at the same
    time suggests is too obvious to say:
    PARALEIPSIS
sayings that are humorous, witty or
    ribald: **FACETIAE**
say or do over and over, repeat:
    REITERATE
scale ramparts by means of ladders:
    ESCALADE
scaly: **SQUAMOUS**
scanty: **SKIMPY**
scanty, inadequate, thin: **MEAGER**
scanty, small, diminutive: **EXIGUOUS**
scanty, stingy: **NIGGARDLY**

scapegoat: FALL GUY
scapegoat: WHIPPING BOY
scarcity, lack, famine: DEARTH
scarf, long and made of fur or fabric, worn over a woman's shoulders: STOLE
scarf, necktie: CRAVAT
scarf, often of lace, worn over a high comb on the head by Spanish women: MANTILLA
scarf worn about the head and shoulders by Spanish and Latin American women: REBOZO
scarf worn on the head by women: BABUSHKA
scar, scar-like marking: CICATRIX
scatter among other things, set here and there: INTERSPERSE
scatter, drive away, dispel: DISPERSE
scattered in focus, haphazard, dispersed, indiscriminate: SCATTERSHOT
scattered, not concentrated: SPARSE
scattered, wasted: DISSIPATED
scatter or diffuse, as if by sowing: DISSEMINATE
schedule, select: SLATE
scheme, plot: MACHINATE
scheming person (derogatory): JESUIT
scheming politically in a ruthless way: MACHIAVELLIAN
schizophrenia: DEMENTIA PRAECOX
schizophrenia, usually associated with puberty, characterized by unsystematic behavior and exaggerated mannerisms: HEBEPHRENIA
scholarly celebratory or anniversary publication: FESTSCHRIFT
scholarly interpreter, annotator or commentator: SCHOLIAST
scholarly, learned: ERUDITE
scholarly life: ACADEME
scholarly person: SAVANT
scholar of prodigious encyclopedic learning, polyhistor: POLYMATH
scholar of prodigious encyclopedic learning, polymath: POLYHISTOR
scholars' conference or seminar: COLLOQUIUM
scholarship displayed in an undiscriminating way: PEDANTRY
science of bullets, missiles, rockets, etc.: BALLISTICS
science of soil: AGROLOGY
science of the earth's surface and its

physical, political and social characteristics: GEOGRAPHY
scientific husbandry: AGRONOMY
scoff: JEER
scold, censure, reproach: UPBRAID
scolding: ABUSIVE
scolding and abusive woman, shrew: TERMAGANT
scolding, harsh reprimand: RATING
scold, rake over the coals, reprove severely: KEELHAUL
scold severely, upbraid, berate: OBJURGATE
scold, sharp-tongued woman: VIRAGO
scold, tell off: BERATE
scope: AMBIT
scope, range, extent: PURVIEW
scorched, colored as if by scorching: USTULATE
scorched, hot: TORRID
scorn, despise: CONTEMN
scornful rudeness in speech: CONTUMELY
scornful, sneering, cynical: SARDONIC
scorn or ridicule publicly: PILLORY
scorn, reject, refuse: SPURN
Scotch whisky and vermouth cocktail: ROB ROY
Scottish cap with a tight headband and a wide, flat top: TAM-O'SHANTER
Scottish dish containing animal's insides boiled in its stomach: HAGGIS
Scottish furred pouch worn in front with a kilt: SPORRAN
Scottish woolen long and creased cap with ribbons hanging at the back: GLENGARRY
scoundrel: BLACKGUARD
scoundrel: CAITIFF
scowl, look angry or sullen: LOWER
scowl sullenly: GLOWER
scrap, do away with: SCUTTLE
scrape away: ABRADE
scrape or grind harshly, cut, pierce: GRIDE
scrape, paw, scratch: SCRABBLE
scrap, fragment: SNIPPET
scratch, cut: SCOTCH
scratch, scrape, paw: SCRABBLE
scream, bawl, cry loudly: SQUALL
screen behind an altar: REREDOS
screen or shutter of overlapping adjustable horizontal slats: JALOUSIE
screw or nail something so that it lies

flush with or below the surface:
COUNTERSINK
screwy, giddy, disorganized, frivolous:
SCATTERBRAINED
scribble: **SCRABBLE**
scribble, draw aimlessly: **DOODLE**
scribble, illegible handwriting:
GRIFFONAGE
scribblings or drawings on wall:
GRAFFITI
scroll-like architectural ornament or
tablet: **CARTOUCHE**
scruffy, uneven: **SCRAGGLY**
scrutinize, examine or read thoroughly:
PERUSE
scrutinize, look at closely: **SCAN**
scuba-diving metal valve for the diver's
breathing: **REGULATOR**
sculptor's framework for modeling
material: **ARMATURE**
sculptured basket of fruit: **CORBEIL**
sculpture in which figures project
slightly: **BAS-RELIEF**
sculpture-like decoration or grayish
painting: **GRISAILLE**
scum, froth, foam: **SPUME**
scythe- or sickle-shaped: **FALCATE**
sea area with numerous islands:
ARCHIPELAGO
sea arm with a long and narrow path
and between high banks: **FJORD**
sea-green or yellowish-green in color:
GLAUCOUS
seal or plug edges or crevices: **CAULK**
seal or signet rings as a subject of
study: **SPHRAGISTICS**
seaman's short coat of heavy woolen
fabric: **PEA JACKET**
sear: **CAUTERIZE**
search for food or supplies: **FORAGE**
search for gold in abandoned mines:
FOSSICK
search for information, investigate:
DELVE
search out by careful investigation:
FERRET
search, pursuit, adventure: **QUEST**
search, scour, move rapidly: **SKIRR**
search thoroughly: **RANSACK**
search through: **ROOT**
search through refuse, as for food:
SCAVENGE
seas, lakes, rivers, etc., studied to
determine their use for navigation:
HYDROGRAPHY

season of warm, hazy weather in late
autumn: **INDIAN SUMMER**
sea spray: **SPINDRIFT**
seat behind the saddle on a horse or
motorcycle: **PILLION**
seated a great part of the time, settled,
inactive: **SEDENTARY**
seat for riders on an elephant or a
camel: **HOWDAH**
seat or small stool, usually without
arms or a back: **TABORET**
seat or sofa for two people: **LOVE SEAT**
seat or step in a series that rises:
GRADINE
seaward current of water beneath the
surface: **UNDERCURRENT**
seaweed or other marine vegetation cast
ashore: **WRACK**
secluded: **CLOISTRAL**
secluded: **SEQUESTERED**
secluded garden for quiet pleasure:
PLEASANCE
secluded or inactive for a period,
especially winter: **HIBERNATING**
secluded or solitary person: **RECLUSE**
secondary, casual, minor: **INCIDENTAL**
secondary phenomenon occurring with
another but having no power to
produce effects: **EPIPHENOMENON**
second marriage: **DEUTEROGAMY**
second marriage: **DIGAMY**
second seat on a motorcycle: **PILLION**
second self: **ALTER EGO**
second sight: **CLAIRVOYANCE**
second-time experience imagined when
it is actually only the first time:
DÉJÀ VU
secret, abstruse, unknown except by an
inner few: **ESOTERIC**
secret agreement, usually to defraud
someone: **COLLUSION**
secretary: **AMANUENSIS**
secret fund to be used for corrupt
purposes: **SLUSH FUND**
secret group joined in intrigue: **CABAL**
secret, hidden: **ARCANE**
secret, hidden, puzzling, occult,
mystifying: **CRYPTIC**
secret jargon, especially of thieves,
beggars, etc.: **CANT**
secret laboratory, facility, etc., for
innovative development, as to build
experimental aircraft: **SKUNK
WORKS**
secretly: **SUB ROSA**

secretly depart, escape the law:
ABSCOND
secretly informed: PRIVY
secretly, in private: IN PETTO
secretly meeting or planned, kept
hidden for an illicit purpose:
CLANDESTINE
secret meeting: CONCLAVE
secret meeting, as of a legislature:
EXECUTIVE SESSION
secret meeting, as of lovers:
ASSIGNATION
secret name: CRYPTONYM
secret or closed session is: IN CAMERA
secret or harbored purpose or concern:
HIDDEN AGENDA
secret or involving intrigue, plotting,
spying, etc.: CLOAK-AND-DAGGER
secret or mystical system: CABALA
secret or private things: PENETRALIA
secret or unofficial means of relaying
information, usually by talking:
GRAPEVINE
secret rendezvous, especially by lovers:
ASSIGNATION
secret reservation or concern, ulterior
motive: ARRIÈRE-PENSÉE
secret, sheltered: COVERT
secret underhanded group: CAMORRA
secret winning resource, advantage or
weapon held in reserve: ACE IN
THE HOLE
section of a city in which a minority
lives: GHETTO
secularize: LAICIZE
securities bought over a period, by
dollar worth rather than by
number of shares: DOLLAR COST
AVERAGING
securities list: PORTFOLIO
securities pledged as collateral for a
loan: HYPOTHECATION
security for discharge of an obligation:
COLLATERAL
security, pledge, challenge: GAGE
security selling that is not done on the
floor of a stock exchange:
OVER-THE-COUNTER
security that is transferable by delivery:
NEGOTIABLE
sedate, steady, sober: STAID
sedative, sleep-producing medicine:
OPIATE
seduce, corrupt, deprave: DEBAUCH

seducer of women, ladies' man:
LOTHARIO
seductive woman: SIREN
seed-bearing: SEMINIFEROUS
seed-bearing part of flowering plants:
PISTIL
seedy, cheap-looking, shabby: TACKY
seeing into the future: PRESCIENT
seeing, knowing: COGNITION
seeing things that are not visible:
CLAIRVOYANCE
seeming, apparent: OSTENSIBLE
seemly, proper: DECOROUS
see (reference in a book): VIDE
see-through, as a fabric: DIAPHANOUS
segment: CANTLE
seize and place in legal custody:
IMPOUND
seize, appropriate: CONFISCATE
seize by legal means: SEQUESTER
seize by violence: WREST
seize, capture, secure: CORRAL
seize, grip tightly, struggle, contend
with: GRAPPLE
seize or appropriate beforehand:
PREEMPT
seize or stop on the way, prevent from
reaching the destination:
INTERCEPT
seize the day, live now: CARPE DIEM
seizure of property in legal proceeding:
ATTACHMENT
selecting from diverse sources:
ECLECTIC
selections or fragments from literary
works: ANALECTS
select, pick out, sort: CULL
select, schedule: SLATE
select the best from, separate out: TOP
OUT
self-assertive, bold, indecent: IMMODEST
self-assurance: COCKINESS
self-assurance, composure, serenity:
POISE
self-centered: EGOCENTRIC
self-centered, as an ethnic or racial
group: ETHNOCENTRIC
self-confidence: APLOMB
self-confident, lively, brisk, dashing:
JAUNTY
self-confident to an extreme: COCKSURE
self-contradictory, false or ridiculous
statement: PARADOX
self-control and modesty, prudence,
restraint, temperance: SOPHROSYNE

self-denial: ABNEGATION
self-determination: AUTONOMY
self-discipline in religion or meditation:
 ASKESIS
self-esteem, self-respect, personal
 dignity: AMOUR PROPRE
self-evident statement: AXIOM
self-examination: INTROSPECTION
self-governing: AUTONOMOUS
self-important, overdignified,
 pretentious: POMPOUS
self-important, petulant: HOITY-TOITY
self-interested person: INTROVERT
selfish person: EGOIST
selflessness: ALTRUISM
self-love: NARCISSISM
self-mortification: ASCETICISM
self-oriented philosophy that the self is
 essentially all that exists and can
 know only itself: SOLIPSISM
self-protective reaction of an organism:
 DEFENSE MECHANISM
self-reproach, guilt feeling: REMORSE
self-satisfaction: COMPLACENCY
self-satisfied, complacent: SMUG
self-service meal: BUFFET
self-styled: SOI-DISANT
self-supporting, as a country:
 SUBSTANTIVE
self, the part of the psyche that
 organizes thought and governs
 action: EGO
self-training, by using monitoring
 instruments, to control
 physiological and emotional states:
 BIOFEEDBACK
sell goods in the street, peddle: HAWK
selling by quiet persuasion rather than
 high-pressure tactics: SOFT SELL
selling off by a company or corporation
 of holdings: DIVESTITURE
sell property for profit: REALIZE
semicircle: HEMICYCLE
semiconscious: HYPNOPOMPIC
semifluid, sticky, honey-like in
 consistency: VISCOUS
seminar or group of people who study
 together some subject or topic:
 WORKSHOP
semiskilled worker: BLUE-COLLAR
 WORKER
semitransparent: TRANSLUCENT
send back to one's own country:
 REPATRIATE

send forth or give off, as light or heat:
 EMIT
send from one place to another:
 TRANSMIT
send or order back: REMAND
senility: CADUCITY
senility: DOTAGE
senior or eldest member of a group:
 DOYEN, DOYENNE
sensation of one sort, as of color,
 stimulated by a different kind of
 stimulus, as sound or smell:
 SYNESTHESIA
senseless, absurd: IRRATIONAL
senseless or foolish talk: DRIVEL
senses being the source of pleasure:
 SENSUOUS
sensibility, perception: ESTHESIA
sensible, reasoned: RATIONAL
sensitive: SUSCEPTIBLE
sensitivity in the extreme to touch, heat,
 pain, etc.: HYPERESTHESIA
sensitivity to heat and cold:
 THERMESTHESIA
sensual, carnal, worldly: FLESHLY
sensualist: VOLUPTUARY
sensualist, rake: ROUÉ
sensuous, especially concerning food:
 EPICUREAN
sentence-analyze by giving the form,
 function and syntactical
 relationship of its words: PARSE
sentence in which each word has a
 letter or syllable more than that
 preceding: RHOPALIC
sentence in which sense and structure
 are not completed until the end:
 PERIODIC SENTENCE
sentence in which the main clause
 appears at the beginning and less
 important matter follows: LOOSE
 SENTENCE
sentence or phrase challenging to utter
 quickly because of similar sounds
 easily confused: TONGUE TWISTER
sentence or word that reads the same
 backward as forward:
 PALINDROME
sentence's conclusive clause that follows
 from the protasis, or conditional
 clause: APODOSIS
sentence's conditional clause that leads
 to the apodosis, or conclusive
 clause: PROTASIS

sentences' or clauses' separation by a comma, wrongly, rather than by a period or semicolon: COMMA FAULT, COMMA SPLICE

sentence whose two main clauses are, usually improperly, separated by a comma rather than by a conjunction, period, semicolon or colon: RUN-ON SENTENCE

sentence within which one grammatical construction changes to another: ANACOLUTHON

sentimental features incorporated in a play or story to evoke emotional response: HOKUM

sentimentality: BATHOS

sentimentality that is false: MAWKISHNESS

sentimentality to excess: SCHMALTZ

sentimentally pensive: LANGUISHING

sentimental or emotional, tearfully so: MAUDLIN

separate a group into small dissenting factions: BALKANIZE

separate, as the good from the bad: WINNOW

separate, disconnected: DISCRETE

separated, set apart: ISOLATED

separate from, break away: DISSOCIATE

separate into opposing groups or views: POLARIZE

separate into parts: DIFFRACT

separate into two parts: DICHOTOMIZE

separate, mark out boundaries or limits: DEMARCATE

separate or break up into parts, analyze: RESOLVE

separate out, select the best from: TOP OUT

separate, part, divide: DISSEVER

separate, set apart: SEQUESTER

sequence in logic or grammar: CONSECUTION

sequence in which the difference between numerical terms remains constant: ARITHMETIC PROGRESSION

sequence in which the ratio between each two numbers is the same: GEOMETRIC PROGRESSION

serene, calm, quiet: TRANQUIL

serene, calm, unmoved: IMPASSIVE

series of reactions or events in which results become causes: CHAIN REACTION

series, succession: CONSECUTION

serious and solemn person: SOBERSIDES

serious, reflective, somewhat melancholy: PENSIVE

sermon, especially one based on a biblical text: HOMILY

sermonize, lecture: PRELECT

sermon or story having a moral: EXEMPLUM

sermon writing and delivery as a study: HOMILETICS

serpent represented in the headdress of Egyptian kings: URAEUS

serpent reputed to be hatched from a cock's egg: COCKATRICE

servant: RETAINER

servant-like subordinate, menial person, drudge (British): DOGSBODY

servant, low person: MENIAL

servant or assistant, as of a magician or scholar: FAMULUS

services, charity, branches, etc., extended beyond the usual: OUTREACH

servile, compliant, slavish: SEQUACIOUS

servile, fawning follower: MINION

servile, fawning person: TOADY

servile follower, toady: LACKEY

servilely flatter: ADULATE

servile, obsequious: SUBSERVIENT

servile or lickspittle attitude: KOWTOW

servile, overly obedient, fawning: OBSEQUIOUS

serving, portion: DOLLOP

servitude, slavery: THRALLDOM

set apart, separate: SEQUESTER

set aside, as money for a special purpose: EARMARK

set here and there, scatter among or between other things: INTERSPERSE

set in from the margin, as the first line of a paragraph: INDENT

set of concurrent symptoms indicating a specific disease or condition: SYNDROME

set speech, recitation: DECLAMATION

set straight, undeceive: DISABUSE

setter of a pace for others, lead taker: PACESETTER

setting, surroundings or environment, as of a motion picture: MISE EN SCÈNE

settled matter in law: CHOSE JUGÉE
settlement of a dispute by the decision of a person or body chosen with the consent of both sides: ARBITRATION
settlement of a dispute that is advanced by friendly intervention of a conciliator: MEDIATION
settle one's debts: LIQUIDATE
settler on public or unoccupied land without permission: SQUATTER
set up, establish: INSTITUTE
setup to swindle somebody: STING
seven days, week: HEBDOMAD
sevenfold: SEPTUPLE
sevenfold or based on the number 7: SEPTENARY
seven, seven things: HEPTAD
seventh year in the ancient Jewish system: SABBATICAL YEAR
seven years, recurring every: SEPTENNIAL
several names used for one thing: POECILONYMY
several, various: DIVERS
severance of relations: RUPTURE
severe, allowing no letup: EXACTING
severe, rigid: STRINGENT
severe, stormy: INCLEMENT
severe, strict, grim: STARK
sewage: SULLAGE
sewer: KENNEL
sewer, cesspool: CLOACA
sewing together of the edges of a wound in a surgical operation: SUTURE
sew loosely: BASTE
sex bias, especially against females: SEXISM
sex differentiation being absent, as in clothes, hairstyles, etc.: UNISEX
sex glands in the male: TESTICLES
sexless, asexual: NEUTER
sexless, effeminate: EPICENE
sexual abstinence: CELIBACY
sexual activity involving licking or sucking of the female genitals: CUNNILINGUS
sexual activity involving licking or sucking of the male genitals: FELLATIO
sexual act of simultaneous oral stimulation: SOIXANTE-NEUF, SIXTY-NINE

sexual arousal and satisfaction by oneself, masturbation: AUTOEROTICISM
sexual attraction to or involvement with another person: ALLOEROTICISM
sexual, cheap: RAUNCHY
sexual climax in intercourse: ORGASM
sexual coupling: INTERCOURSE
sexual desire for a member of the same sex: HOMOEROTICISM
sexual desire in man that is uncontrollable: SATYRIASIS
sexual desire in women that is uncontrollable: NYMPHOMANIA
sexual desire lacking: ANAPHRODISIS
sexual desire or impulse: LIBIDO
sexual desire or lust: CONCUPISCENCE
sexual desire reducer: ANAPHRODISIAC
sexual desire's absence: ANAPHRODISIA
sexual desire that is abnormally strong: EROTOMANIA
sexual doings: HANKY-PANKY
sexual external organs of female animals: VULVA, CLITORIS
sexual go-between: PANDER
sexual gratification or obsession with an article of clothing, part of the body, etc.: FETISHISM
sexual intercourse: COITUS
sexual intercourse: CONGRESS
sexual intercourse: COPULATION
sexual intercourse between persons so closely related that marriage is forbidden them: INCEST
sexual intercourse forced on a woman: RAPE
sexually abandoned, lewd: LICENTIOUS
sexually appealing, attractive physically: FOXY
sexually arousing: EROGENOUS
sexually arousing in a physical way: SENSUAL
sexually attracted to persons of the opposite sex: HETEROSEXUAL
sexually attractive: BEDDABLE
sexually desirous regarding those of the same sex: HOMOSEXUAL
sexually having characteristics of both sexes: ANDROGYNOUS
sexually incapable of orgasm: NONORGASMIC
sexually preoccupied: CARNAL
sexually stimulating: EROTIC

sexually stimulating object that in itself is not erotic, such as a shoe: **FETISH**

sexually unrestrained: **INCONTINENT**

sexually wanton man: **SATYR**

sexually wanton woman: **NYMPHOMANIAC**

sexual maturing period: **PUBERTY**

sexual molesting by rubbing against: **FROTTAGE**

sexual organ of male animals: **PENIS**

sexual organs: **GENITALIA, GENITALS**

sexual or scatological language: **COPROLALIA**

sexual pervert: **DEVIATE**

sexual pleasure from being tied up or restrained and chastened or humiliated: **B & D (BONDAGE AND DISCIPLINE)**

sexual pleasure resulting from pain: **ALGOLAGNIA**

sexual potency of a man: **VIRILITY**

sexual practices between males, especially between men and boys: **PEDERASTY**

sexual restraint, moderation: **CONTINENCE**

sexual stage in early life in which one becomes interested in peers of the same sex: **SUIGENDERISM**

sexual stage in early life when one becomes interested in opposite-sex peers: **ALTRIGENDERISM**

sexual stimulant: **APHRODISIAC**

shabby, cheap-looking, seedy: **TACKY**

shabby, decayed, neglected: **DILAPIDATED**

shabby, decrepit: **FLEA-BITTEN**

shabby, dirty: **DISREPUTABLE**

shabby, drab: **DOWDY**

shackle, handcuff, fetter: **MANACLE**

shading, as in a picture, done with crossed lines: **CROSSHATCH, CROSS-HATCHING**

shading with close parallel or crossed lines: **HATCH**

shading, with parallel lines, to show elevation or steepness: **HACHURE**

shadow pantomime in miniature: **GALANTY SHOW**

shadow that does not completely cut off light: **PENUMBRA**

shady: **ADUMBRAL**

shady, providing shade: **UMBRAGEOUS**

shake slightly: **JOGGLE**

Shakespeare idolatry: **BARDOLATRY**

shake suddenly or forcibly: **SUCCUSS**

shake up and down, bounce, jolt: **JOUNCE**

shake up, elbow, push or crowd roughly, shove: **JOSTLE**

shaking or shivering motion: **TREMOR**

shaky, loose: **RAMSHACKLE**

shallow, cursory, limited to the surface: **SUPERFICIAL**

sham: **SIMULACRUM**

sham, deceptive, pretended: **FEIGNED**

shameful: **IGNOMINIOUS**

shameful: **OPPROBRIOUS**

shameless: **BRAZEN**

shamelessness: **IMPUDICITY**

shank, part of leg between the knee and the ankle: **CRUS**

shantytown at the edge of a city: **BIDONVILLE**

shape distortion: **ANAMORPHISM**

shaped or designed so as not to adhere to any rigid pattern: **FREE-FORM**

shapeless: **AMORPHOUS**

shapely of buttocks: **CALLIPYGIAN**

shape or artistic design in the form of five joined leaves, petals or lobes: **CINQUEFOIL**

shape or artistic design in the form of four joined leaves, petals or lobes: **QUATREFOIL**

shape or artistic design in the form of three joined leaves, petals or lobes: **TREFOIL**

shape, outline, form: **FIGURATION**

shared feeling or feelings: **COMPATHY**

share, portion, half: **MOIETY**

sharer of secrets: **CONFIDANT**

sharing the sensations of another as if one were participating in the action: **VICARIOUS**

sharp: **ACERB**

sharp: **ACUATE**

sharp and abrupt emphasis: **STACCATO**

sharp answer or reply: **RETORT**

sharp but pleasant-tasting, tart: **PIQUANT**

sharp-edged and pointed: **CULTRATE**

sharpen, as a razor: **HONE**

sharpen, excite, stimulate: **WHET**

sharp-eyed, sharp-sighted: **GIMLET-EYED**

sharp in taste: **ACRID**

sharp, keen, cutting, biting: INCISIVE

sharply affecting the mind: PUNGENT

sharp-tasting or -smelling: PUNGENT

sharp-tongued woman, scold: VIRAGO

shattering effect of an explosion:
BRISANCE

shatter, splinter into fragments: SHIVER

shave or pare the surface, as of leather:
SKIVE

shaving of the crown of the head:
TONSURE

shedding or falling off, as of petals,
leaves or fruit: DECIDUOUS

shedding or molting of skin:
EXUVIATION

shed, get rid of: SLOUGH

sheep-like: OVINE

sheep or goat newly born: YEANLING

sheepskin coat worn by Spanish
shepherds: ZAMARRA

sheer, transparent: DIAPHANOUS

sheet carrying advertising or
propaganda: BROADSIDE

sheet folded once and forming four
pages: FOLIO

shelf above a fireplace: MANTEL

shelf above the back of an altar to hold
ornaments, candles, lights:
RETABLE

shelf for holding small ornamental
items: WHATNOT

shell containing baked minced food:
COQUILLE

shelled sea gastropod, a mollusk, that
clings to surfaces: LIMPET

shell game that is fraudulent:
THIMBLERIG

shell lined with mother-of-pearl:
ABALONE

shell- or pod-covered insect stage:
CHRYSALIS, PUPA

shell, pod, husk: SHUCK

shell, protective or hard covering:
CARAPACE

shell study: CONCHOLOGY

shelter, disguise: COVERTURE

sheltered, secret, concealed: COVERT

sheriff's office, term or jurisdiction:
SHRIEVALTY

Sherlock Holmes–style gooseneck pipe:
MEERSCHAUM

Sherlock Holmes type of hat with flaps:
DEERSTALKER

sherry from Spain that is pale and dry:
AMONTILLADO

shield division in heraldry: CANTON

shield-like architectural ornament or
tablet: CARTOUCHE

shield-shaped: SCUTIFORM

shield-shaped surface with armorial
bearings: ESCUTCHEON

shifting of a disease from one part of
the body to another: METASTASIS

shift or movement to the eye of an
object due to a different point of
observation: PARALLAX

shift position or direction: VEER

shifty, elusive: LUBRICIOUS

shinbone: TIBIA

shingle knife: FROE, FROW

shining: IRRADIANT

shining back, reflecting light, bright:
RELUCENT

shining, illustrious: SPLENDENT

shining with brilliance, dazzling, vividly
bright: RESPLENDENT

ship being so far away that the hull is
hidden below the horizon: HULL
DOWN

shipboard drinking fountain:
SCUTTLEBUTT

ship for armed antisubmarine combat,
which is disguised as a merchant
ship: Q-SHIP, Q-BOAT

ship opening in the floor or deck giving
access to area beneath: HATCH

ship portion above the main deck:
TOPSIDE

ship's central or projecting part of the
hull's bottom, ship's backbone:
KEEL

ship's high-up lookout platform:
CROW'S NEST

ship's kitchen: GALLEY

ship's length: FORE AND AFT

ship's officer ranking next below the
captain: FIRST MATE

ship's or plane's left side as one faces
forward: PORT

ship's or plane's position checking by
radio signals from known stations:
LORAN

ship's or plane's right side as one faces
forward: STARBOARD

ship space where cargo is stored: HOLD

ship's permission to enter port:
PRATIQUE

ship's sailing close to the wind: LUFF

ship's small boat: JOLLY BOAT

ship's stand or mounting holding the compass: BINNACLE

ship's upper front part: FORECASTLE

ship that is large: ARGOSY

ship with two or more masts, rigged fore and aft: SCHOONER

shirt or jersey without sleeves, for athletes: SINGLET

shivering or shaking motion: TREMOR

shiver or a shudder, as from excitement or fear: FRISSON

shocked or nauseated easily, prudish: SQUEAMISH

shocking, vivid, sensational: LURID

shock the middle class: ÉPATER LES BOURGEOIS

shock to the body or system caused by an injury: TRAUMA

shoddy, poorly made, cheap, tacky: SLEAZY

shoe, for a woman, that grips the toe and heel and has no straps PUMP

shoe, for a woman, with an open back and a heel strap: SLINGBACK

shoe for women that has a wedge-shaped piece joining the heel and sole: WEDGIE

shoelace end covering: AGLET

shoe or slipper, for a woman, that is backless: MULE

shoe's upper front part: VAMP

shoe that is heavy and coarse: BROGAN

shoot (a liquid) in by mechanical or physical means: INJECT

shoot from a hiding place: SNIPE

shoot out copiously, as a liquid: SPOUT

shop that has long hours, insufficient pay and poor conditions: SWEAT SHOP

shop that is small and fashionable: BOUTIQUE

shore, beach: STRAND

shore, coastal region: LITTORAL

shoreline barrier to break the force of waves: BREAKWATER

shore uncovered by low tide: FORESHORE

shortage, scarcity: PAUCITY

short and fat, squat: FUBSY

short distance: STONE'S THROW

shorten: ABBREVIATE

shorten: ABRIDGE

shortened: TRUNCATED

shortened word form: CLIPPED FORM

shortening of a syllable that is naturally or by position long: SYSTOLE

short-fingered or -toed: BRACHYDACTYLIC

shorthand, especially in ancient times: TACHYGRAPHY

short-headed: BRACHYCEPHALIC

short-lived: FUGACIOUS

short-lived, of short duration: TRANSIENT

short-lived, transitory, fleeting: EPHEMERAL

shortly, soon, later: ANON

short of breath: PURSY

shorts of leather, worn with suspenders, in Bavaria: LEDERHOSEN

short-takeoff and -landing plane: STOL

shoulder bag, especially as used by soldiers: MUSETTE BAG

shoulder cord or braid on a uniform: AIGUILLETTE, FOURRAGÈRE

shoulder joint that is a common source of injury among baseball pitchers: ROTATOR CUFF

shoulder ornament, especially on the uniforms of military and naval officers: EPAULET

shout, bawl, exclaim loudly: VOCIFERATE

shout, violently denounce: FULMINATE

shove, shake up, elbow, push or crowd roughly: JOSTLE

showcase of glass for displaying art objects: VITRINE

show clearly, manifest, demonstrate convincingly: EVINCE

show consisting of skits, songs and dances: REVUE

shower, scatter, sprinkle: SPARGE

show, exhibit or present to advantage: SHOWCASE

showiness: OSTENTATION

showoff tendency: EXHIBITIONISM

show sympathy toward: COMMISERATE

showy and cheap: TAWDRY

showy and cheap, gaudy, tawdry, phony: BRUMMAGEM

showy and worthless, junky: GIMCRACK

showy, bombastic, florid: FLAMBOYANT

showy but valueless things or matter, junk: TRUMPERY

showy but without substance: SPECIOUS

showy, excessively ornamented: ORNATE

showy, useless ornaments: FURBELOWS

shrew: VIXEN

shrewd and unscrupulous person:
    SNOLLYGOSTER
shrewd businessperson, deal-maker,
    operator: WHEELER-DEALER
shrewd, practical, obstinate:
    HARDHEADED
shrewd, wise: SAGACIOUS
shrewish old woman: GRIMALKIN
shrewish wife: XANTHIPPE
shrew, scolding and abusive woman:
    TERMAGANT
shrill, grating: STRIDENT
shrink or crouch in servility: CRINGE
shriveled, shrunken, withered: WIZENED
shrubs or trees trimmed and arranged
    in fantastic shapes: TOPIARY
shrunken, withered, shriveled: WIZENED
shuffle cards by bending up the corners
    of two parts of the pack and letting
    the cards flutter together: RIFFLE
shun as unworthy: ESCHEW
shut, block or close off: OCCLUDE
shut one's eyes to wrongdoing:
    CONNIVE
shut out, exclude: OSTRACIZE
shut out, exclude, render impossible:
    PRECLUDE
shutter or screen of overlapping
    horizontal slats: JALOUSIE
shy, inept person: NEBBISH
shy, jumpy: SKITTISH
shyly embarrassed: SHEEPISH
shy, meek, apologetic person:
    MILQUETOAST
shyness: DIFFIDENCE
shyness, timidity, lack of confidence in
    self: DIFFIDENCE
sick: NAUSEATED
sickening, insipid: MAWKISH
sickening to an extreme: AD NAUSEAM
sickle moon: CRESCENT MOON
sickle or half-moon shape: LUNETTE
sickle- or scythe-shaped: FALCATE
sick-making: NAUSEOUS
sickness caused by eating or drinking
    too much: CRAPULENCE
sickness pretended to avoid work:
    MALINGERING
sideboard or buffet, usually without
    legs: CREDENZA
sideburns: BURNSIDES
sideburns low and wider at the jaw:
    MUTTONCHOPS
side by side: ABREAST
side by side state: JUXTAPOSITION

side by side, at the same or an equal
    rate, progressing together: PARI
    PASSU
side by side, close together: CHEEK BY
    JOWL
side or private entrance: POSTERN
side or sides of a main thing: LATERAL
sidepiece in a door or window sash:
    STILE
side, right or left part of something:
    FLANK
side sheltered from the wind: LEEWARD
    SIDE
sides touching: ABUTTING
side to side: ATHWART
side-to-side lurch or twist: CAREEN
side-to-side measurement: BREADTH
side track connecting with the main
    track of a railroad: SPUR TRACK
sideways-moving: LATERIGRADE
sidewise glance: ASKANCE
sieve-like: CRIBRIFORM
sift, examine or analyze minutely:
    WINNOW
sift through a coarse sieve: RIDDLE
sighing sound, as of the wind: SOUGH
sighting land: LANDFALL
sight loss without organic defect:
    AMAUROSIS
sight marred by specks or threads
    seeming to float before the eyes:
    MUSCAE VOLITANTES
sight- or eye-related: OCULAR
signal for a parley made by a drum or
    trumpet: CHAMADE
signal for pillage and destruction: CRY
    HAVOC
signature ending made with a flourish:
    PARAPH
signature, especially of a sovereign:
    SIGN MANUAL
signature that authenticates another
    signature: COUNTERSIGNATURE
signet or seal rings as a subject of
    study: SPHRAGISTICS
signify, hint at: IMPLY
signify, point out, indicate: DENOTE
sign language, deaf-mute alphabet:
    DACTYLOLOGY
sign of a solemn pledge: SACRAMENT
sign or abbreviation representing a
    word, as the dollar sign:
    LOGOGRAM
sign or dedicate a book for
    presentation: INSCRIBE

sign or mark supposed to exercise occult power: SIGIL

sign or trace of something absent: VESTIGE

sign, public or road, using symbols, stick figures, etc.: GLYPH SIGN

signs and symbols theory: SEMIOTICS

silence at a point in a broadcast: DEAD AIR

silence, in music: TACET

silence or feigned ignorance, as of wrongdoing: CONNIVANCE

silence, subdue utterly, crush: SQUELCH

silencing or putting down, as of a rumor: QUIETUS

silent, unspoken: TACIT

silk-screen process used by artists: SERIGRAPHY

silky: SERICEOUS

silky, light and fluffy: FLOSSY

silly, fickle: FRIVOLOUS

silly or empty talk: TWADDLE

silly, pointless, empty-headed: INANE

silly, vain or foppish behavior: COXCOMBRY

silver or bronze gilt: VERMEIL

silver or white in armorial bearings (heraldry): ARGENT

similar: AGNATE

similarity in form: HOMOMORPHISM

similarity in sound: ASSONANCE

similarity without identity: ANALOGY

similar, like, the same in composition throughout, uniform: HOMOGENEOUS

similar or related in structure, position, value: HOMOLOGOUS

similar or virtually identical person or thing, copy, imitation: CLONE

similar thing: ANALOGUE

simmer: CODDLE

simple, candid, artless, unaffected: NAIVE

simple, frank, innocent, naive, straightforward: INGENUOUS

simple or artless in style in a deliberate and often somewhat false way: FAUX NAÏF

simple, rough, plain: RUSTIC

simple, sincere: UNAFFECTED

simple, unaffected, in music: SEMPLICE

simplicity, innocence and peace being portrayed as associated with rural life: PASTORAL

simultaneous: CONCURRENT

simultaneous belief in two contradictory ideas: DOUBLETHINK

simultaneousness: SYNCHRONISM

sin as a study or science: HAMARTIOLOGY

sincere, candid, artless: GUILELESS

sincere, real: UNAFFECTED

sinful, at fault: PECCANT

sinful, obstinate: UNREGENERATE

sinful, wildly wasteful or extravagant, dissipated: PROFLIGATE

sing a tune heartily: TROLL

singing, as by a quartet, in an old-fashioned a capella style with close and mellow harmony: BARBERSHOP

singing by monks unaccompanied and without harmonizing: GREGORIAN CHANT

singing, in opera or oratorio, that is akin to ordinary speech: RECITATIVE

singing leader in church: PRECENTOR

singing that is partly recitational or speech-like: SPRECHSTIMME, SPRECHGESANG

singing without accompaniment: A CAPPELLA

sing in such a way as to alternate falsetto and normal chest tones: YODEL

single-colored: MONOCHROME

singled out for special honor because of excellence in one's achievements: LAUREATE

single file: INDIAN FILE

single file, one behind the other: TANDEM

single piece of stone used in architecture or sculpture: MONOLITH

single woman: FEME SOLE

single word applied to two thoughts, each of which gives it a different meaning: SYLLEPSIS

single word applied to two thoughts, with the linkage to one of them grammatically incorrect: ZEUGMA

sing with trills, as a bird does: WARBLE

sink a ship by cutting holes in the bottom of it: SCUTTLE

sink, collapse, fail: FOUNDER

sink in mud, bog down: MIRE

sink table of wood with a metal-lined

top well for a basin and usually cupboards below: DRY SINK

sinuous and gliding motion: UNDULATION

sinuous, winding: ANFRACTUOUS

sin, wrongful act, unjust thing or deed: INIQUITY

sir: SAHIB

sisterhood, female student organization: SORORITY

sister killer: SORORICIDE

sister sharing only one of one's parents: HALF SISTER

sisters or brothers: SIBLINGS

sit and hatch eggs, develop: INCUBATE

situation that is difficult, risky, tricky or awkward (British): STICKY WICKET

sixfold: SEXTUPLE

sixfold or based on the number 6: SENARY

six, group of: HEXAD

six-ounce bottle of a beverage: SPLIT

size, extent: MAGNITUDE

skeptic: DOUBTING THOMAS

skeptic: ZETETIC

skeptical, disbelieving: INCREDULOUS

sketchily outline: ADUMBRATE

sketch that is only rough or preliminary: ESQUISSE

skewer for broiling meat: BROCHETTE

ski down a straight, steep slope: SCHUSS

skiing and rifle marksmanship competition: BIATHLON

skiing cross-country run: LANGLAUF

skiing jump made from a crouching position: GELÄNDESPRUNG

skiing over ice or snow in tow of a horse or motor vehicle: SKIJORING

skiing race over a winding downhill course laid out between posts: SLALOM

skiing surface bump, lump of snow: MOGUL

skiing term for a pit in the snow left by a skier who has fallen backward: SITZMARK

skiing with many fast turns and the skis kept parallel: WEDELN

skill, ability: PROWESS

skill at a particular thing: KNACK

skilled craftsman: ARTIFICER

skillful, adroit: DEXTEROUS

skillful in use of bodily or mental powers: ADROIT

skillful, inventive, clever: INGENIOUS

skillfully or properly done: WORKMANLIKE

skill in avoiding giving offense: TACT

skill, knowledge: EXPERTISE

skill or dexterity in manipulation: SLEIGHT

skills or equipment needed, as in medicine: ARMAMENTARIUM

skill, style or technical mastery, as of an art: VIRTUOSITY

skim over water, glide: SKITTER

skin and its diseases as a study: DERMATOLOGY

skin disease: ECZEMA

skin hanging loosely, as from a cow's neck: DEWLAP

skin hanging loosely from the neck or throat, as on turkeys: WATTLE

skin markings made by pricking with a needle and inserting indelible colors: TATTOO

skin peeling off because of sunburn: BLYPE

skin, remove impurities from: DESPUMATE

skin's outer layer: EPIDERMIS

skip about playfully: CAPER

skip a flat stone across a water surface: SCOON

skip or bounce over water: DAP

skip or leap about, frolic: GAMBOL

skip or rebound of a projectile after it hits a surface: RICOCHET

skirt-like garment worn by both sexes in the Malay Archipelago: SARONG

skirt that is full and has a gathered waist: DIRNDL

ski-run bump or hump: MOGUL

skull: CRANIUM

skull-and-crossbones flag of pirates: JOLLY ROGER

skullcap worn by Orthodox and Conservative Jewish men: YARMULKE

skullcap worn by Roman Catholic clergymen: ZUCCHETTO

skull conformations as indicating degree of development of mental facilities: PHRENOLOGY

skull of a human being as a symbol of death: DEATH'S HEAD

skull study: CRANIOLOGY

skull symbol (death's head) or other reminder of death: MEMENTO MORI

sky, heavens: FIRMAMENT
skylight: ABAT-JOUR
skylighted or open central area in a building: ATRIUM
skylit or glass-roofed mall, court or promenade: GALLERIA
sky with streaks or rows of small clouds: MACKEREL SKY
slake thirst: QUENCH
slander: ASPERSE
slander: CALUMNIATE
slander, calumny, curse against someone: MALEDICTION
slander, defame: VILIFY
slander, mock: TRADUCE
slander, speak evil of: MALIGN
slanted, indirect: OBLIQUE
slanting kind of type, usually used for emphasis or differentiation: ITALIC
slanting line, diagonal: BIAS
slanting line in printing or writing: VIRGULE
slash mark in printing or writing: VIRGULE
slaughterhouse: ABATTOIR
slaughterhouse: SHAMBLES
slaughter, massacre: CARNAGE
slaughter of diseased animals: ABATTAGE
slavery: SERVITUDE
slavery's end in the United States: ABOLITION
Slavic alphabet: CYRILLIC
Slavic folk dance performed by a male and marked by the prisiadka step, in which from a squatting position each leg is kicked out alternately: KAZATSKY
slavish, servile, compliant: SEQUACIOUS
slavish, submissive: SERVILE
sleep, desire for, that is uncontrollable: NARCOLEPSY
sleep-deterring: AGRYPNOTIC
sleep drug-induced in psychiatric treatment: DAUERSCHLAF
sleeper staying in bed late: SLUGABED
sleep-inducing medicine, relaxant: OPIATE
sleep-inducing or soothing sounds or motions: LULL
sleepiness, yawning: OSCITANCY
sleeping bag that fits tightly, with a small face opening: MUMMY BAG
sleeping cap, nightcap: BIGGIN

sleeping car on a European railroad: WAGON-LIT
sleeping sickness: ENCEPHALITIS LETHARGICA
sleeping that is chronically excessive: HYPERSOMNIA
sleeplessness, the chronic inability to sleep: INSOMNIA
sleepless period, as in keeping vigil: WATCH
sleep-producing: HYPNAGOGIC
sleep-producing medicine: SOPORIFIC
sleep-producing, narcotic: SOMNIFEROUS
sleep that is unusually deep: SOPOR
sleepwalking, somnambulism: NOCTAMBULATION
sleepy: SOMNOLENT
sleepy, drowsy: SOPORIFIC
sleeveless Arabian garment: ABA
sleight of hand: PRESTIDIGITATION
sleight of hand, trickery, hocus-pocus: LEGERDEMAIN
slender, graceful young woman: SYLPH
slender, slim, willowy: SVELTE
slender, wand-like, straight: VIRGATE
slew, jumble, accumulation that is confusing: WELTER
slice thinly, as leather: SKIVE
slide or glide, as a snake: SLITHER
sliding skillfully down a slope of ice or snow, as in mountain climbing: GLISSADE
slight, gracefully slender: GRACILE
slighting: DISPARAGING
slightly, in music: POCO
slight suggestion, vague idea, notion, hint: INKLING
slim and tall of figure: ASTHENIC
slim, willowy, slender: SVELTE
sling for lifting or lowering a heavy object: PARBUCKLE
slink: SKULK
slip by, pass away (said of time): ELAPSE
slip, error, fault: LAPSE
slip-like undergarment: CHEMISE
slip of the tongue: LAPSUS LINGUAE
slip or falter into a former condition, relapse: BACKSLIDE
slippery-feeling, greasy: UNCTUOUS
slogan, rallying cry, password: WATCHWORD
slope along a plateau's rim: SCARP

slope, especially a defensive slope in front of a fortification: GLACIS

slope, incline, ramp: GRADIENT

slope linking different levels: RAMP

slope or inclination of countryside: VERSANT

slope that is steep: ESCARPMENT

slope, tilt: CANT

sloping edge: BEVEL

sloping steeply: DECLIVITOUS

slovenly in appearance: BLOWZY

slow, delay, hinder: RETARD

slow, dignified dance, or music for such a dance: PAVANE

slow down: DECELERATE

slowly but surely, gradually: INCHMEAL

slow movement, as in music: ADAGIO

slow person, straggler falling behind: LAGGARD

slow tempo: LARGO

sluggish: INERT

sluggish, dull, inactive: TORPID

sluggish, lacking in energy: LYMPHATIC

sluggishness, dullness, apathy: LETHARGY

sluggish, uninterested: STAGNANT

sluice gate: PENSTOCK

slur over in pronunciation: ELIDE

sly look: LEER

sly or indirect intimation, hint: INSINUATION

sly, sneaky, furtive: WEASELLY

sly, stealthy: FURTIVE

small: PETITE

small and fashionable shop: BOUTIQUE

small country that depends on a great power: SATELLITE

small, cramped: INCOMMODIOUS

small decorative object: BIBELOT

small, extremely: LILLIPUTIAN

small flower: FLORET

small, insignificant, trifling: MINUTE

small letters of the alphabet used in printing: LOWER CASE

smallness of the head that is abnormal: MICROCEPHALY

small or insignificant amount: IOTA

small portable stove: CHAUFFER

small portion or piece: COLLOP

smallpox: VARIOLA

small quantity: MODICUM

small quantity, insufficiency: PAUCITY

small, scanty, diminutive: EXIGUOUS

small space, crack: INTERSTICE

small space or cubicle between library stacks for private study: CARREL

small, stunted thing, as an imperfectly developed fruit or ear of corn: NUBBIN

small sum of money: PITTANCE

small-time, half-baked: TINHORN

small to such an extreme that it cannot be easily seen: IMPERCEPTIBLE

small to the point of being incalculable, microscopic: INFINITESIMAL

small, trifling: NOMINAL

small, trifling work: OPUSCULE

small vehicle of any sort: DOODLEBUG

smartness and orderliness, neatness: SPIT AND POLISH

smartness, style, dash: PIZZAZZ

smelling disagreeably: MALODOROUS

smelling good: ODORIFEROUS

smelling like cooked game, pungent: GAMY

smelling-related, involving the sense of smell: OLFACTORY

smile in a silly, self-satisfied way: SMIRK

smile or smirk self-consciously: SIMPER

smiling or grinning behavior caused by embarrassment: DRY GRINS

smoke from tobacco users to which others are exposed: AMBIENT SMOKE

smoke hole in volcanic terrain: FUMAROLE

smoker's pipe exclusive of the stem, including the bowl and the shank: STUMMEL

smoky, sooty: FULIGINOUS

smooth, flowing, graceful, expressive: FLUENT

smooth, glossy, well-groomed: SLEEK

smooth-haired, straight-haired: LISSOTRICHOUS, LEIOTRICHOUS

smoothness, tact, highly refined skill: FINESSE

smooth or toughen metal: PLANISH

smooth the way, as for a project or piece of work: EXPEDITE

smooth to an excessive degree, oily-tongued: UNCTUOUS

smooth-tongued, sweet of voice, honeyed: MELLIFLUOUS

smug: SELF-RIGHTEOUS

smug and overexacting person: PRIG

smuggling or smuggled goods: CONTRABAND

smug philistinism: **PODSNAPPERY**

snack, eat, nibble: **NOSH**

snack of nutritious or high-energy food: **GORP**

snag, annoyance, hindrance, complication: **FLY IN THE OINTMENT**

snag, catch, complication: **HITCH**

snag, malfunction, foul-up: **GLITCH**

snake-haired ugly woman, or Gorgon, of classical mythology, killed by Perseus: **MEDUSA**

snake-like, cunning: **SERPENTINE**

snake-shaped: **ANGUIFORM**

snake worship: **OPHIOLATRY**

snap back, resume the original shape after being stretched: **RESILE**

snappish, peevish, bad-tempered: **WASPISH**

sneak, coward: **DASTARD**

sneaking, stealthy: **SLINKY**

sneaky, degraded, skulking: **HANGDOG**

sneaky, furtive, sly: **WEASELLY**

sneering, ironical, taunting language: **SARCASM**

sneering, scornful, cynical: **SARDONIC**

sneer, laugh coarsely, jeer, deride: **FLEER**

sneeze or noise produced by it: **STERNUTATION**

sneeze-producing substance, snuff: **ERRHINE**

sniff, smell: **SNUFF**

snobbish person: **BRAHMIN**

snoring, making a snoring sound: **STERTOROUS**

snow on high mountains that becomes ice, glacial snow: **NÉVÉ**

snow that is coarse and granular: **CORN SNOW**

snowy: **NIVEOUS**

snub: **REBUFF**

snub, deliberate slight: **COLD SHOULDER**

snuggle for comfort, cuddle: **NESTLE**

soak in a liquid: **STEEP**

soapy: **SAPONACEOUS**

sober, sedate, steady: **STAID**

soccer: to kick the ball through an opponent's legs and run past him to recover it: **NUTMEG**

soccer: to move the ball by successive kicks: **DRIBBLE**

soccer dislodging of the ball by sliding feet first to kick it away from the ball handler: **SLIDE TACKLE**

soccer kick made upside down with a scissors-like motion of the legs: **BICYCLE KICK, SCISSORS KICK**

sociable: **CONVIVIAL**

sociable, associating habitually with others: **GREGARIOUS**

socially low, alienated or hopeless: **LUMPEN**

socially lowered in status: **DÉCLASSÉ**

social meal based on early Christian love feast: **AGAPE, LOVE FEAST**

social only or meaningless, as applied to talk: **PHATIC**

society contains a mixture of ethnic, racial, religious or cultural groups: **PLURALISM**

society or community dominated by women: **MATRIARCHY**

sock-like or tube-like cloth hung to show wind direction: **WINDSOCK**

Socratic in method: **MAIEUTIC**

sodomy, sexual relations between males: **PEDERASTY**

sofa or bench with a high back: **SETTEE**

sofa or couch with a low cushioned seat and with arm rests and back: **DIVAN**

soft and rich, as certain soils: **UNCTUOUS**

soften by soaking in liquid: **MACERATE**

soften colors or lines in a painting or drawing: **SCUMBLE**

softened or euphemistic terminology: **PARADIASTOLE**

softening: **MOLLESCENT**

softening, soothing or relaxing, especially to the skin: **EMOLLIENT**

soften in temper, yield: **RELENT**

soften, regulate, adjust or temper: **MODULATE**

softly or privately spoken, in an undertone, whispered: **SOTTO VOCE**

softly performed in music: **PIANO**

soft spot, vulnerable point: **ACHILLES' HEEL**

soil, besmirch, defile: **SULLY**

soil deposited by water: **ALLUVIUM**

soil, discolor: **SMIRCH**

soiled, untidy: **BEDRAGGLED**

soil-protective mix: **MULCH**

soil rather than climate being an affective factor: **EDAPHIC**

soils being soft and rich are: UNCTUOUS
soil science: AGROLOGY
soil study: PEDOLOGY
solar: HELIACAL
solar system model that moves by
    wheels: ORRERY
soldier doing extra-duty work for an
    officer: STRIKER
soldier's or bandleader's tall and stiff
    cylindrical headdress with a visor
    and plume: SHAKO
soldiers vulnerable to artillery, infantry:
    CANNON FODDER
soldier who is boastful: MILES
    GLORIOSUS
solemn and serious person: SOBERSIDES
solemn declaration: ASSEVERATION
sole of the foot or the palm of the
    hand, pertaining to: VOLAR
solicit for sexual purposes: ACCOST
solicit votes by going about a region:
    CANVASS
solid earth: TERRA FIRMA
solid, forthright, firm: FOURSQUARE
solid foundation: BEDROCK
solid ground, firm earth: TERRA FIRMA
solidifying: CONCRETION
solid, packed with meaning, terse:
    PITHY
solitary or secluded person: RECLUSE
solo melody in opera: ARIA
solution-impossible absurdly circular
    situation: CATCH-22
solution or final unraveling in a plot:
    DENOUEMENT
solution or remedy resorted to in an
    emergency: QUICK FIX
solution, usually in alcohol, of a
    substance, used in medicine:
    TINCTURE
solve a complicated problem: CUT THE
    GORDIAN KNOT
something in return for something else:
    QUID PRO QUO
so much the better: TANT MIEUX
so much the worse: TANT PIS
song for several male voices with no
    accompaniment: GLEE
song-like, melodic: ARIOSE
song, often contrapuntal: MADRIGAL
song of triumph or joy: PAEAN
song of unhappy love: TORCH SONG
song performed by a lover under a
    sweetheart's window: SERENADE
song sheet containing only the melody

line and sometimes chord notations
    and lyrics: LEAD SHEET
song's middle part: BRIDGE
song that is short and simple: DITTY
sonorous: ROTUND
soon, shortly, later: ANON
soothe, pacify: SALVE
soothe, put to sleep or calm through
    soothing sounds or motions: LULL
soothe, quiet down, mitigate, pacify:
    MOLLIFY
soothing: LENITIVE
soothing agent: ABIRRITANT
soothing, melodious, sweetly pleasant:
    DULCET
soothing pain reliever: ANODYNE
soothing, relieving irritation:
    DEMULCENT
soothing, softening or relaxing,
    especially to the skin: EMOLLIENT
sophisticated woman: FEMME DU
    MONDE
sophisticate, worldly person:
    COSMOPOLITE
soporific, sleep-producing:
    SOMNIFEROUS
sorceress, fortuneteller: SIBYL
sorcery: DIABLERIE
sorcery, casting of lots, witchery:
    SORTILEGE
sorcery, fortune-telling, black magic:
    NECROMANCY
sorcery or witchcraft practiced in the
    South, Africa and the West Indies:
    OBEAH, OBI
sordid, low: GROVELING
sordid or worst aspect of something:
    SEAMY SIDE
sore, inflamed: IRRITATED
sore or swelling from exposure to cold:
    CHILBLAIN
sorrowful, mournful: PLAINTIVE
sorrowful, mournful: WOEBEGONE
sorrowful, mourning, repentant,
    humbled: IN SACKCLOTH AND
    ASHES
sorrow or grief, to cause: AGGRIEVE
sorrow, sympathy-evoking atmosphere,
    situation, etc.: PATHOS
sort, class, kind: ILK
sorting of casualties to fix priorities for
    treatment: TRIAGE
sort out, pick, select: CULL
so-so, middling: COMME ÇI, COMME ÇA
soul: ANIMA

soul, spirit: PNEUMA
sound and scene reproduction,
    pertaining to: AUDIOVISUAL
sound, as that made by a sleep-aiding
    machine, to drown out undesired
    ambient noises: WHITE NOISE
sound-imitating by a word: ECHOIC
sound in speech involving chiefly the
    lips, teeth or tongue: CONSONANT
sound like cat's cries at rutting time:
    CATERWAUL
sound of sighing or murmuring, as
    made by the wind: SOUGH
sound or letter inserted into a word:
    EPENTHESIS
sound or vibration caused by the hitting
    of one body against another:
    PERCUSSION
sound, pertaining to: ACOUSTIC
sound-producing or -conducting:
    SONIFEROUS
soundproof: ANACOUSTIC
sound-reflecting structure: SOUNDING
    BOARD
sound-related: SONIC
sound reproduction: AUDIO
sound reproduction using two or more
    loudspeakers is: STEREOPHONIC
sounds in opposition in music:
    ANTIPHONY
sounds of speech as a study:
    PHONETICS
sounds or tones in multiplicity:
    POLYPHONIC
sounds rather than words used in jazz
    improvised singing: SCAT
sounds repeated at the beginnings of
    words or in accented syllables:
    ALLITERATION
sound track change from the original
    language to another: DUBBING
sound-transmitting apparatus used
    under water: SONAR
sound wave or light wave change that
    seems to accompany change in
    distance between source and
    observer: DOPPLER EFFECT
sound with a lead weight, on the end of
    a line, to test the depth of water:
    PLUMB
soup ingredients of dough casings filled
    with ground meat: KREPLACH
soup made with strained vegetables or a
    dish containing such vegetables or
    fruit: PURÉE

soup of cream and potatoes, usually
    served cold: VICHYSSOISE
soup that is clear: CONSOMMÉ
soup, thick and creamy: BISQUE
sour: ACERB
source: SPRINGHEAD
source, forefather: PROGENITOR
source of something: PROVENANCE
source or potential for development is:
    SEMINAL
sour fermented cabbage in shredded
    form: SAUERKRAUT
souring: ACESCENT
sour juice of green fruit: VERJUICE
sourness or sharpness of disposition:
    VERJUICE
sour, spoiled-smelling: RANCID
South African grassland: VELDT
South African racial segregation:
    APARTHEID
South African language, based on
    Dutch: AFRIKAANS
South American treeless grassy plain,
    prairie: PAMPA
souvenir: MEMENTO
sovereign control over a locally
    autonomous region: SUZERAINTY
sovereigns or rulers in one line of
    descent reigning in succession:
    DYNASTY
Soviet citizen denied permission to
    emigrate: REFUSENIK
Soviet policy of openness regarding
    solving internal social problems:
    GLASNOST
Soviet Union collective farm: KOLKHOZ
Soviet Union–forbidden but
    clandestinely printed literature:
    SAMIZDAT
Soviet Union's equivalent of a Cabinet:
    PRESIDIUM
space around the altar of a church:
    CHANCEL
spacecraft's landing on water:
    SPLASHDOWN
space for freedom of action, latitude:
    LEEWAY
space from which something is missing
    or has been omitted: LACUNA
spade-like tool for removing the roots
    of weeds: SPUD
spangle, small metal disk: PAILLETTE
Spanish American, West Indian or Gulf
    State inhabitant of European
    descent: CREOLE

Spanish diacritical mark, as over the "n" in "señor": TILDE

Spanish dialect with Hebrew elements: LADINO

Spanish estate, plantation or ranch: HACIENDA

Spanish fly: CANTHARIDES

Spanish for "farewell": ADIOS

Spanish for "good day": BUENOS DIAS

Spanish for "thank you": GRACIAS

Spanish pale dry sherry: AMONTILLADO

Spanish-speaking quarter or ghetto: BARRIO

sparing in eating and drinking: ABSTEMIOUS

sparkle, gaiety, vivacity, lively spirits: EFFERVESCENCE

sparkle, glitter, flash: SCINTILLATE

sparkle, glitter, shine: CORUSCATE

sparkle in intellect or action: SCINTILLATE

sparkling object: SPANGLE

sparks seen before the eyes: SPINTHERISM

spark, trace: SCINTILLA

spasm in a muscle: CLONUS

spasm of the muscle: HYPERKINESIA

spasms of pain: THROES

spasm, twitching: MYOCLONUS

spatter, shower, pelt: PEPPER

spat, trivial quarrel: TIFF

speak at great length: PERORATE

speak dogmatically: PONTIFICATE

speaker's stand on which books or notes may be placed: LECTERN

speaker who fascinates or enthralls the audience by his eloquence: SPELLBINDER

speak ill of another: BACKBITE

speaking fluently, glib, talkative: VOLUBLE

speaking impairment, difficulty in understanding speech: DYSPHASIA

speaking in a bombastic or pompous style: GRANDILOQUENT

speaking or using two languages: BILINGUAL

speaking or writing with ease: FLUENT

speaking style, language, idiom: PARLANCE

speaking trick that makes the voice seem to come from a source other than the speaker: VENTRILOQUISM

speak loudly or rhetorically: DECLAIM

speak or write more fully, elaborate: EXPATIATE

speak violently, rave: RANT

speak with clarity and exactness: ENUNCIATE

spear-like weapon of old with a battle-ax head: HALBERD

spear with prongs used in fishing: LEISTER

special-application, not general: AD HOC

special, select or respected, as a panel or committee: BLUE-RIBBON

specialty or strong point of a person: FORTE

specific-purpose and specific-situation committee: AD HOC COMMITTEE

specify: STIPULATE

specify exactly: CONCRETIZE

speckled or spotted as if by drops: GUTTATE

speck, particle: MOTE

specks or threads appearing to float before the eyes: MUSCAE VOLITANTES

spectacular exhibition or parade: PAGEANT

spectacular, fascinating, astonishing: EYE-POPPING

spectacular theater production: EXTRAVAGANZA

spectator who gives unwanted advice to card players: KIBITZER

specter, imaginary appearance: PHANTASM

speculative: ACADEMIC

speech constituting a bitter verbal oath: PHILIPPIC

speech delivered simply to obstruct action: FILIBUSTER

speech given at a formal event: ORATION

speechify: BLOVIATE

speech-like singing style: SPRECHSTIMME, SPRECHGESANG

speech-like sounds that are unintelligible: GLOSSOLALIA

speech manner: LOCUTION

speech manner or dialect of an individual: IDIOLECT

speech mechanism positions represented by phonetic symbols: VISIBLE SPEECH

speech of fiery denunciation: TIRADE

speech or discourse that is breezy: TOLUTILOQUENCE

speech or essay that is highly emotional: DITHYRAMB

speech pattern: INTONATION

speech peculiar to a locality or group: DIALECT

speech, sales talk: SPIEL

speech sound involving chiefly the lips, teeth or tongue: CONSONANT

speech sounds as a study: PHONETICS

speech sound that is the smallest unit of its kind and distinctive from others: PHONEME

speech that is bombastic or flowery: RHETORIC

speech that is glib and swift: PATTER

speech that is lengthy, loud and vehement: HARANGUE

speech that is long and tiresome: SCREED

speech that is short and witty or satirical: SQUIB

speech that is stirring: STEMWINDER

speech that is unintelligible, gibberish, jargon: BARAGOUIN

speed: VELOCITY

speedily: LICKETY-SPLIT

speed in music: TEMPO

speed, move at full speed: CAREEN

speed, promptness: DISPATCH

speed that is dangerous is: BREAKNECK

speed up, quicken, facilitate: EXPEDITE

spelled the same: SYNORTHOGRAPHIC

spelling in which a letter represents different sounds in different words: HETEROGRAPHY

spelling of words differently to represent dialect: EYE DIALECT

spelling or handwriting that is bad: CACOGRAPHY

spelling that conforms to accepted usage: ORTHOGRAPHY

spelling that varies from the accepted standard usage: HETEROGRAPHY

spending or giving generously: LAVISH

spending to impress: CONSPICUOUS CONSUMPTION

spendthrift, loafer: WASTREL

spend wastefully, squander: DISSIPATE

sperm duct removal: VASECTOMY

sperm whale's waxy substance, used in perfumes: AMBERGRIS

sphere of action: AMBIT

sphere of authority: BAILIWICK

spherical but somewhat flattened or concave at the poles: OBLATE

spherical, rounded: ORBICULAR

sphinx-like in having a human head and an animal body: ANDROCEPHALOUS

spies' secret place for message or document exchange: DEAD DROP

spiked wheel at the end of a spur: ROWEL

spinach-including style of food preparation: FLORENTINE

spinal-columned creatures: VERTEBRATES

spinal curvature: LORDOSIS

spindle-shaped: FUSIFORM

spineless: INVERTEBRATE

spinning like a top, top-shaped: TURBINATE

spinning, whirling, dizzy: VERTIGINOUS

spiny, bristly: HISPID

spiral: HELIX

spirally coiled: HELICOID

spirally curling, rolled up: VOLUTE

spire: FLÈCHE

spirit agency, medium: CHANNEL

spirit ancestors among Pueblo Indians: KACHINA

spirited, vital, joyful, vigorous: EXUBERANT

spiritlessness, weakness, fatigue, dreaminess, dullness, stagnation: LANGUOR

spiritless, not alive: INANIMATE

spirit or demon that has sexual intercourse with women as they sleep: INCUBUS

spirit regarded as existing independently matter: ANIMISM

spirits, health: FETTLE

spirit, soul: PNEUMA

spiritual, insubstantial, nonmaterial: INCORPOREAL

spiritualist's meeting to communicate with the dead: SÉANCE

spiritual, light, airy: ETHEREAL

spiritual sloth: ACEDIA

spiritual teacher or guide: GURU

spirit, wit: ESPRIT

spit: EXPECTORATE

spiteful, deliberately mischievous: MALICIOUS

spitefulness, enmity: RANCOR

spitefulness, peevishness, ill temper: SPLEEN

spiteful, revengeful: VINDICTIVE

spit or skewer used in broiling, usually small: BROCHETTE

spitting receptacle: CUSPIDOR

splash, flounder: SLOSH

splashing or sucking noise, as when one walks in deep mud: SQUELCH

splendor, brilliance, radiance: REFULGENCE

splendor, radiance: EFFULGENCE

splinter: SLIVER

splinter into fragments, shatter: SHIVER

splinters: FLINDERS

split into two parts, divide, separate: BIFURCATE

split or cut into long thin pieces: SLIVER

split separating factions in a church or other organization: SCHISM

splitting, cutting: SCISSION

splitting or breaking apart: FISSION

spoil by indulgence: COCKER

spoiled-smelling: RANCID

spoil, impair: VITIATE

spoiling for a fight: PUGNACIOUS

spoils, booty: PILLAGE

spoil someone, pamper or pet: COSSET

spoken error thought to disclose a person's true feelings or thinking: FREUDIAN SLIP

spoken in an undertone, privately: SOTTO VOCE

spoken, oral: VIVA VOCE

spoken statement of a false or defamatory nature: SLANDER

spokesperson: PROLOCUTOR

spokesperson: MOUTHPIECE

sponger, shirker, avoider of paying: DEADBEAT

sponsorship: AEGIS

sponsorship, approval, official affiliation or support: AUSPICES

sponsorship, support: PATRONAGE

spontaneous, casual, impromptu: OFF-THE-CUFF

spontaneous talk by a patient in psychoanalysis: FREE ASSOCIATION

spontaneous, unprepared: IMPROMPTU

sports car competition on a twisting course: AUTOCROSS

sports car long-distance race: RALLY, RALLYE

sports player in the front line of attack or defense: FORWARD

sports term for an extra period in a tied game during which the first side to score wins: SUDDEN DEATH

spot or blemish, blurred impression in printing: MACKLE

spot or indicative mark on a domino, die or playing card: PIP

spotted, especially in white and black: PIEBALD

spotted horse or pony: PINTO

spotted or speckled as if by drops: GUTTATE

spotted, streaked, blotched: MOTTLED

spotted, variegated: DAPPLED

spotting on animals or plants: MACULATION

spouse: CONSORT

spouse murder: MARITICIDE

spray device on a bottle: ATOMIZER

spread about loosely for drying, as mown hay: TED

spread apart or branch out at a wide angle, diverge: DIVARICATE

spread, as information: DISSEMINATE

spread false charges: ASPERSE

spread in all directions, circulate: DIFFUSE

spreading of a disease from one part of the body to another: METASTASIS

spreading or expanding wide, as tree branches: PATULOUS

spread or branch out, diverge: DIVARICATE

spread out, extend: SPLAY

spread out into divisions, divide: RAMIFY

spread, pour or send out in all directions: DIFFUSE

spread, publicize, disseminate: PROPAGATE

spread the word far and wide: DISSEMINATE

spread thinly: SPARSE

spread through completely, penetrate: PERMEATE

spread throughout: PERVADE

spree, fling, prank, reckless behavior: ESCAPADE

spring back, snap back, recoil, resume original shape after being stretched: RESILE

spring in its early stage, pertaining to: PRIMAVERAL

spring-like, youthful, fresh: VERNAL

sprinkle: ASPERSE

sprinkle, shower, scatter: SPARGE

sprinkle, suffuse or cover with a liquid or color: PERFUSE

sprout, breed rapidly, swarm: PULLULATE

sprout, proliferate: BURGEON

spruced up: SPIT AND POLISH

spur into action, urge on, stir up: INCITE

spurious: APOCRYPHAL

spur of the moment, offhand: IMPROMPTU

spur on, goad, incite, foment, provoke to some drastic action: INSTIGATE

spurt or gush of liquid from a narrow orifice: JET

spy, or double agent, within an enemy network for a long period: MOLE

spy or intelligence agent field training: TRADECRAFT

spy residence used for safety and secret meetings: SAFE HOUSE

spy who infiltrates opposing espionage system to betray it: DOUBLE AGENT

squabble, heated argument: HASSLE

squall, brief windstorm: FLAW

squander, spend wastefully: DISSIPATE

squander, use or handle recklessly: PLAY DUCKS AND DRAKES WITH

square dance of a rollicking kind: HOEDOWN

square dancing term for a change of step or figure: CALL

square made up of words that read the same vertically and horizontally: WORD SQUARE

square surrounded by buildings: PIAZZA

squat, short and fat: FUBSY

squatting Slavic dance step in which a man kicks out each leg alternately: PRISIADKA

squeak by in obtaining or getting: EKE OUT

squeamish: QUEASY

squint: SKEW

squirm in agony: WRITHE

squirt, gush forth: SPURT

S-shaped: SIGMATE

stable adjunct, enclosure for exercising horses: PADDOCK

stab, pierce or tear painfully: LANCINATE

stagecoach: DILIGENCE

stage curtain that can be raised and lowered: DROP CURTAIN

stage fabric, light and sheer, used as a backdrop: SCRIM

stage front: DOWNSTAGE

stage movements, mustering, sounds, etc., of soldiers: ALARUMS AND EXCURSIONS

stage of a theater including its arch: PROSCENIUM

stage performer without a speaking part, as in a mob scene: SUPERNUMERARY

stage scenery that is flat, on the side of the stage: COULISSE

stage surrounded by seats: ARENA THEATER

stagnation, weakness, fatigue, dreaminess, dullness, spiritlessness: LANGUOR

stained-glass strip of lead dividing or bordering panes: BREAKER

stain or drench, especially with blood: IMBRUE

stairway between boat decks: COMPANIONWAY

stale joke: CHESTNUT

stale or musty atmosphere (British): FROWST

stale recapitulation: REHASH

stall for time: TEMPORIZE

stammering: TRAULISM

stamp collecting: PHILATELY

stamped or hammered, as the figure or design on a coin: INCUSE

stamp out, stifle: SCOTCH

standard of quality: BENCHMARK

standard or criterion for testing the qualities of something: TOUCHSTONE

standard, ordinary, usual, commonplace: GARDEN VARIETY

standard or rule by which a judgment can be made: CRITERION

standards of polite society: PROPRIETIES

standing out, striking, conspicuous: SALIENT

stand on the hind legs and stretch out the forelegs: RAMP

stand on which a speaker may place notes or books: LECTERN

standstill because of disagreement by two forces: DEADLOCK

stand with shelves, usually ornamental: ÉTAGÈRE

stare at, make eyes at suggestively: OGLE

stare stupidly, gape: GAWK
stare with an angry frown: GLOWER
starfish-like: ACTINOID
star grouping: GALAXY
staring, as the eyes of a fish: WALLEYED
staring or gawking with curiosity:
    RUBBERNECKING
staring or glancing in a deadly way:
    BASILISK
star-like symbol in printing (*):
    ASTERISK
star-like very distant object that emits
    strong radio waves: QUASAR
star mapping: URANOGRAPHY
stars' and planets' daily positions in the
    form of a table or almanac:
    EPHEMERIS
star-shaped: ASTEROID
star-shaped, radiating: STELLATE
stars, of and pertaining to: SIDEREAL
star's rising and setting, concerning:
    ACRONICAL
start a discussion: BROACH
start, beginning: INCEPTION
star that suddenly becomes brilliant and
    then fades: NOVA
starting existence, newly conceived:
    NASCENT
starting or launching point:
    JUMPING-OFF PLACE
starting point, beginning that is
    opportune, jumping-off place:
    SPRINGBOARD
startle, thrill, arouse: ELECTRIFY
start of something: CONCEPTION
star used as guide in navigation, guiding
    principle or example: LODESTAR
star with six points and composed of
    two equilateral triangles: STAR OF
    DAVID
state, declare, detail: EXPOUND
stately, impressive, grand: IMPOSING
stately in beauty: JUNOESQUE
stately passage or movement of music:
    MAESTOSO
statement or assertion that is obvious or
    self-evident: TRUISM
statement that decides the matter:
    CLINCHER
state or affirm something on the basis of
    known facts or conditions:
    PREDICATE
state or authority that is watchful and
    repressive: BIG BROTHER
state positively: ASSEVERATE

state's right to take over private
    property for public use: EMINENT
    DOMAIN
stationary, resting: STATIC
station baggage handler, porter: REDCAP
statistician dealing with vital statistics,
    as of births, deaths, disease:
    DEMOGRAPHER
status of holding one's position on an
    enduring basis: TENURE
statute, especially of a municipal body:
    ORDINANCE
staunch, brave: YEOMANLY
staunch, uncompromising:
    DYED-IN-THE-WOOL
staves ready for assembling into barrels
    or boxes: SHOOK
stay or dwell temporarily: SOJOURN
steadfast, brave: UNFLINCHING
steadfast, firmly directed, unwavering:
    INTENT
steadily at work, diligent: SEDULOUS
steady, sober, sedate: STAID
steady stream, as of people or things:
    INFLUX
steal: PURLOIN
stealer of another's date: BIRDDOG
steal funds and especially public funds,
    embezzle: PECULATE
steal in a petty way: PILFER
stealing money off the books or
    concealing of profits: SKIMMING
steal slyly in small amounts: FILCH
steal, take by fraud: EMBEZZLE
stealthily approach game: STALK
stealthily move about: SKULK
stealthy, sly: FURTIVE
stealthy, sneaking: SLINKY
steam-whistle organ: CALLIOPE
steep: PRECIPITOUS
steep downward slope: DECLIVITY
steep slope: ESCARPMENT
steep slope: SCARP
steering instrument: RUDDER
stench: MEPHITIS
stencil process that forces ink through
    the open meshes of a silk screen:
    SILK-SCREEN PROCESS
step recorder to measure walking
    distance: PEDOMETER
steps at the entrance to a house or
    apartment: STOOP
sterile, barren, fruitless: INFECUND
sterilized, germ-free: AXENIC

U.S. State Nicknames

Aloha State	Hawaii
Badger State	Wisconsin
Bay State	Massachusetts
Beaver State	Oregon
Beehive State	Utah
Blue Grass State	Kentucky
Buckeye State	Ohio
Centennial State	Colorado
Cornhusker State	Nebraska
Cotton State, Heart of Dixie	Alabama
Coyote State, Sunshine State	South Dakota
Empire State	New York
Equality State	Wyoming
Evergreen State	Washington
First State, Diamond State	Delaware
Flickertail State, Sioux State	North Dakota
Garden State	New Jersey
Gem State	Idaho
Golden State	California
Gopher State, North Star State	Minnesota
Grand Canyon State	Arizona
Granite State	New Hampshire
Green Mountain State	Vermont
Hawkeye State	Iowa
Hoosier State	Indiana
Keystone State	Pennsylvania
Land of Enchantment	New Mexico
Land of Opportunity	Arkansas
Last Frontier	Alaska
Little Rhody	Rhode Island
Lone Star State	Texas
Magnolia State	Mississippi
Mountain State	West Virginia
Nutmeg State, Constitution State	Connecticut
Old Dominion	Virginia
Old Line State	Maryland
Palmetto State	South Carolina
Peach State, Empire State of the South	Georgia
Pelican State, Creole State	Louisiana
Pine Tree State	Maine
Prairie State	Illinois
Sagebrush State, Silver State	Nevada
Show Me State	Missouri
Sooner State	Oklahoma
Sunflower State	Kansas
Sunshine State	Florida
Tar Heel State, Old North State	North Carolina
Treasure State	Montana
Volunteer State	Tennessee
Wolverine State	Michigan

sterilizing steam-heat device for medical instruments: AUTOCLAVE

stern, gloomy, morose, ill-tempered: DOUR

sternward or to the rear or aft of a boat: AFT, ABAFT

stew of meat and vegetables well seasoned: RAGOUT

stick for beating, club, cudgel: TRUNCHEON

stick or pestle for stirring drinks: MUDDLER

sticking pins into a doll as a form of black magic: INVULTUATION

sticking together: COHERENT

stick or baton carried by a military officer: SWAGGER STICK

stick or small rod for stirring mixed drinks: SWIZZLE STICK

sticks joined by a chain or rope and used in martial arts: NUNCHAKU, NUNCHAKUS, NUN-CHUCKS, KARATE STICKS

stick-together synthetic wool-like patching used on fabric for fastening: VELCRO

sticky, adhesive: VISCID

sticky, honey-like, semifluid: VISCOUS

sticky or gummy substance, glue, adhesive: MUCILAGE

stifle, stamp out, suppress: SCOTCH

stigmatize: BRAND

still, placid: QUIESCENT

still-water-dwelling; living in ponds, swamps, etc.: LENTIC

stiltedly correct speech: HYPERCORRECTION

stimulate, enliven, arouse: QUICKEN

stimulate, excite, raise the spirits of: ELATE

stimulate, excite, rouse to action: GALVANIZE

stimulate, push or touch with a slight jar, shake lightly: JOG

stimulate, sharpen, excite: WHET

stimulating, arousing: PROVOCATIVE

stimulating, racy: PIQUANT

stimulus, incentive: FILLIP

stimulus that hastens a result: CATALYST

stimulus to action: INCENTIVE

stinginess: PARSIMONY

stingy or mean practice: CHEESEPARING

stingy or petty in a mean way: MINGY

stingy, poor: PENURIOUS

stingy, scanty: NIGGARDLY

stinking: MALODOROUS

stinking: MEPHITIC

stinking, foul in odor: FETID

stinking, offensive, disgusting, noxious: NOISOME

stipulation, condition: PROVISO

stir-crazy enclosed feeling: CABIN FEVER

stir or cut up the surface, as of topsoil: SCARIFY

stirrer-uper, agitator, fiery upstart: FIREBRAND

stirring pestle or stick used for mixed drinks: MUDDLER

stir up, instigate, incite: FOMENT

stir up, spur into action, urge on: INCITE

stitching that is loose and temporary: BASTING

stitch used in surgery: SUTURE

stock bought in order to repay stock previously borrowed, a short sale operation: SHORT COVERING

stock bought in such quantity as to give the buyer control over the price: CORNER

Stock Exchange, New York: BIG BOARD

stock in a corporation that entitles the owner of the shares to dividends after other obligations have been met: COMMON STOCK

stock issued but reacquired by a company: TREASURY STOCK

stock market on the decline: BEAR MARKET

stock market on the rise: BULL MARKET

stock-market playing illegally with privileged information: INSIDER TRADING

stock of a company known for its quality and, therefore, for its ability to make money for investors: BLUE CHIP

stock of a company with good prospects for future earnings: GROWTH STOCK

stock of goods of a business listed: INVENTORY

stock on which dividends must be paid ahead of those on common stock: PREFERRED STOCK

stock on which omitted dividends must

be paid before dividends are paid on common stock: CUMULATIVE PREFERRED

stock options to sell a fixed number of shares at a specified price within a certain period of time or to buy a fixed number of shares at a specified price within a certain period of time: PUTS, CALLS

stock or bond sales that are not made on the floor of a stock exchange are: OVER-THE-COUNTER

stock phrases: CANT

stock purchase at one broker and equivalent sale at another to make trading seem active: WASH SALE

stock purchaser does not receive recent dividend: EX-DIVIDEND

stock-purchasing form of blackmail of a company by buying much of its stock and posing a threat of takeover: GREENMAIL

stock's market price divided by earnings per share for a 12-month period: PRICE-EARNINGS RATIO

stocks selling at less than $1 a share: PENNY STOCKS

stock that is high-priced and good: BLUE CHIP

stock that is traded on a securities exchange: LISTED STOCK

stock trading of blocks smaller than the established 100-share unit: ODD-LOT

stocky, fleshy: PYKNIC

stomach ache resulting from muscular spasms: COLIC

stomach inflammation: GASTRITIS

stomach pit: SOLAR PLEXUS

stomach upset or diarrhea: COLLYWOBBLES

stone (capstone) atop two others (megaliths) as a prehistoric monument: DOLMEN

stone for sharpening knives: WHETSTONE

stone or block on which a column or statue stands: PLINTH

stone shaft that tapers to a pyramidal top: OBELISK

stone slab carrying an inscription or design: STELE

stones piled as a marker or memorial: CAIRN

stone to death: LAPIDATE

stone used for polishing: PUMICE

stone used to scour the wooden deck of a ship: HOLYSTONE

stony, hard: PETROUS

stony, stone-like: LITHOID

stool or small seat, usually without arms or a back: TABORET

stoop to an action or person, condescend: DEIGN

stop, impede, block, hinder: OBSTRUCT

stop, keep back, suppress: STIFLE

stop or check the flow of: STANCH

stop or pause at intervals or temporarily: INTERMIT

stop or seize on the way, prevent from reaching the destination: INTERCEPT

stoppage in the flow of any bodily fluid: STASIS

stoppage of growth: ATROPHY

stop someone or something from all activity: IMMOBILIZE

storage place for goods: REPOSITORY

store carrying general merchandise: EMPORIUM

store, gather, accumulate: GARNER

storehouse underground: MATTAMORE, MATAMORO

storm and stress, turmoil, great unrest: STURM UND DRANG

storm characterized by sudden burst of wind, usually with rain or snow: SQUALL

storm consisting of a whirling column of air: TORNADO

stormy, severe: INCLEMENT

stormy, violent: TEMPESTUOUS

story, always long, sometimes poetic, chronicling adventure or heroic acts: SAGA

story between two main floors, a partial balcony: MEZZANINE

story or anecdote that is humorously long and pointless, ludicrously anti-climactic tale: SHAGGY DOG STORY

story or sermon having a moral: EXEMPLUM

story or statement issued to news media: HANDOUT

storyteller of great skill: RACONTEUR

story that is highly improbable: COCK-AND-BULL STORY

story whose effect is to warn or remind: **CAUTIONARY TALE**

story with a moral: **PARABLE, FABLE**

story with hidden or symbolic meanings: **ALLEGORY**

stout: **PORTLY**

stove of cast iron that is open-faced and resembles a fireplace: **FRANKLIN STOVE**

stove that is small and portable: **CHAUFFER**

straggler, slow or falling-behind person: **LAGGARD**

straight and iceless, not added to, as an alcoholic drink: **NEAT**

straightforward, frank, innocent, simple, naive: **INGENUOUS**

straight line over a vowel indicating a long sound: **MACRON**

straight, slender, wand-like: **VIRGATE**

strained, as in aiming at effect: **AGONISTIC**

strained, done with great effort: **LABORED**

strained, forced: **FARFETCHED**

strain, stretch, irritate: **RACK**

strange, extraordinary, remarkable: **UNACCOUNTABLE**

strange, freakish: **OUTLANDISH**

strange, weird, unnatural, eerie: **UNCANNY**

strangle: **GARROTE**

strap encircling the body of a horse: **SURCINGLE**

strap passing across the forehead that helps to support a load carried on the back: **TUMPLINE**

stratagem or tactic to outwit someone: **PLOY**

stratagem that is a sudden, telling blow: **COUP**

stratagem to avoid or conceal, dodge: **SUBTERFUGE**

strategies in games, economics, warfare: **GAME THEORY**

straw bed that lies on the floor: **PALLET**

straw hat with a flat crown and ribbon for a band: **BOATER**

straw mattress: **PALLIASSE**

stray: **WAIF**

stray-animal enclosure: **PINFOLD**

stray from script: **AD LIB**

straying from the right course: **ERRANT**

stray or wander aimlessly: **DIVAGATE**

streaked, blotched, spotted: **MOTTLED**

stream, creek, channel: **KILL**

stream or bay leading into the land from a larger body of water: **INLET**

stream or brook that is small, rivulet: **RUNNEL**

stream that is small, brook: **RIVULET**

street for pedestrians, with stores on each side: **MALL**

street organ with a rotating cylinder, bellows and crank: **HURDY-GURDY, BARREL ORGAN**

street performer or entertainer: **BUSKER**

street savvy and toughness, urban wisdom: **STREET SMARTS**

street show, peep show: **RAREE SHOW**

street, usually narrow, lined with dwellings that were formerly stables: **MEWS**

strength or degree of some quality, feeling, action: **INTENSITY**

strength, vigor: **STAMINA**

stretchable, capable of being drawn out: **TENSILE**

stretcher with wheels: **GURNEY**

stretch out, swell, expand: **DISTEND**

strict: **EXACTING**

strict disciplinarian: **MARTINET**

strict, grim, severe: **STARK**

strict in religious or moral matters: **PURITANICAL**

strictness, exactness: **RIGOR**

strict, tightly enforced: **STRINGENT**

stride that is steady and swinging: **LOPE**

strike against, bump: **JAR**

strike against, fall upon: **IMPINGE**

strike hard: **SLOG**

strike in which workers stay at the plant but refuse to work: **SIT-DOWN**

striking, weighted weapon like a blackjack: **COSH**

striking worker's replacement: **SCAB**

stringed instrument used in Hindu music: **SITAR**

string looped over the fingers into intricate arrangements: **CAT'S CRADLE**

strip as of rights or possessions: **DIVEST**

strip blubber or skin from a whale or seal: **FLENSE**

strip, deprive, as of possessions: **DIVEST**

strip, deprive of, rob: **DESPOIL**

striped fabric of bright colors: **BAYADERE**

strip, edging or selvage, as of cloth:
   LIST
striped, grooved: STRIATED
strip of material sewn to a seam: WELT
strip of ornamentation, as along the top
   of a wall: FRIEZE
strip or denude of leaves: DEFOLIATE
strip or row of cut grass or grain:
   SWATH
strips of meat or vegetables cut very
   thin: JULIENNE
stripteaser: ECDYSIAST
striving: CONATION
stroll, walk leisurely: SAUNTER
strong: PUISSANT
strong and dark in color, said of cigars:
   MADURO
strong, determined, brave: STALWART
stronghold: REDOUBT
strong physically: POTENT
strong point of a person: FORTE
strong, sturdy, masculine: VIRILE
strong to a superhuman degree,
   powerful and earthy: ANTAEAN
structural unit used in planning or
   building: MODULE
structure, framework: FABRIC
structure or outline of something:
   CONFORMATION
structure that projects and is supported
   at only one end: CANTILEVER
struggle clumsily, move awkwardly,
   stumble: FLOUNDER
struggle of people that is confused and
   noisy: MELEE
struggle or contend with: GRAPPLE
strut, bluster: SWAGGER
strut or promenade: CAKEWALK
stubborn, cantankerous: CROTCHETY
stubborn, cranky: PERVERSE
stubborn, determined: HEADSTRONG
stubbornly wrong or incorrect person:
   MUMPSIMUS
stubborn, obstinate: PERTINACIOUS
stubborn, persevering: INDOMITABLE
stubborn, persistent, tough: TENACIOUS
stubborn, pitiless, hardhearted:
   OBDURATE
stubborn, rebellious, disobedient:
   RECALCITRANT
stubborn, unmanageable: REFRACTORY
stubborn, unruly, difficult:
   INTRACTABLE
stubborn, unyielding: INFLEXIBLE

stubborn, unyielding, pigheaded:
   OBSTINATE
studio: ATELIER
study intensively for an examination:
   CRAM
study of insects: ENTOMOLOGY
study or experiment dealing with its
   subjects over a period of time:
   LONGITUDINAL STUDY
study or read intently: PORE
study or write laboriously: LUCUBRATE
study space or cubicle between library
   stacks: CARREL
stumble or move clumsily: FLOUNDER
stumbling block, pivotal test or problem
   for a beginner: PONS ASINORUM
stun, amaze, bewilder: STUPEFY
stunted, small item, as an imperfectly
   developed fruit or ear of corn:
   NUBBIN
stupid: ADDLED, ADDLE-BRAINED,
   ADDLEPATED
stupid, crude and backward person:
   NEANDERTHAL
stupid, foolish person: SCHMO
stupid, foolish, unmoved, brutish:
   INSENSATE
stupid, graceless fellow: LOUT
stupid, idiotic, inane: FATUOUS
stupid in a gross way: CRASS
stupidity or a stupid act or utterance:
   BETISE
stupid person: IGNORAMUS
stupid person, blockhead, dunce: DOLT
stupid person, fool: BONEHEAD
stupid, senseless: VACUOUS
stupor, apathy: TORPOR
stupor, muscular rigidity and occasional
   mental agitation: CATATONIA
sturdy or athletic in physical structure:
   MESOMORPHIC
sturdy, strong, masculine: VIRILE
stuttering: TRAULISM
style of great brilliance: BRAVURA
style of speech or writing that is
   artificially elegant: EUPHUISM
style, skill, technical mastery, as of an
   art: VIRTUOSITY
style, smartness, dash: PIZZAZZ
style that is spirited, dash: PANACHE
stylishness, good manners: BON TON
suave, refined, polite: URBANE
subconscious mind exhibited in art and
   literature: SURREALISM
subdue or suppress by force: QUELL

subdue utterly, silence, crush: **SQUELCH**

subjective aspect of an emotion: **AFFECT**

subject to the law or rule of another or of an outside force: **HETERONOMOUS**

sublime, celestial, superior, fiery: **EMPYREAL**

sublimely contented or happy, blessed, blissful: **BEATIFIC**

submarine narrow superstructure, modern conning tower: **SAIL**

submission to or respectful regard for the wishes or opinions of another: **DEFERENCE**

submissive: **AMENABLE**

submissive, slavish: **SERVILE**

subsidiary business on certain premises: **CONCESSION**

subsidy to support a study or institution: **SUBVENTION**

substance produced chemically: **SYNTHETIC**

substitute: **SURROGATE**

substitute: **VICAR**

substituted but usually inferior: **ERSATZ**

substitute, deputy: **ALTER EGO**

substitute for an actor or actress: **UNDERSTUDY**

substitute for or authority to act for another: **PROXY**

substitute goals or abilities to make up for a personal lack: **COMPENSATION**

substitutes on an athletic team: **BENCH**

substitute, temporary, improvised: **MAKESHIFT**

substituting a roundabout word for another to avoid giving pain or offense: **EUPHEMISM**

substitution of a title or epithet for a proper name: **ANTONOMASIA**

subtle: **FINE-DRAWN**

subtle and gradual introduction: **INSINUATION**

subtle, as a distinction made: **NICE**

subtle or fine variation or gradation: **NUANCE**

subtle, vague: **INDEFINABLE**

subtraction term for the number from which the subtrahend is to be deducted: **MINUEND**

suburb, isolated and often affluent: **EXURB**

subverting person or group that

undermines from within: **TROJAN HORSE**

success from notoriety or shocking subject matter rather than from merit: **SUCCÈS DE SCANDALE**

successful or prosperous period: **FLORESCENCE**

successful venture, performance, etc., that is wildly or startlingly so: **SUCCÈS FOU**

success that is sudden and removes an obstacle to progress: **BREAKTHROUGH**

succor, aid: **SUBVENTION**

sucker, dupe, victimized person: **PATSY**

sucker, easily-taken-advantage-of person: **SOFT TOUCH**

sudden, abrupt: **PRECIPITATE**

sudden and overwhelming: **FOUDROYANT**

sudden and turbulent outburst: **PAROXYSM**

sudden burst of activity or energy: **SPURT**

sudden change of mind without adequate motive: **CAPRICE**

sudden impulse: **IMPETUOSITY**

sudden inspiration: **BRAINSTORM**

sudden sharp twist: **QUIRK**

sudden start: **SALLY**

sudden success that removes an obstacle to progress: **BREAKTHROUGH**

suffering, capable of feeling: **PASSIBLE**

suffering, distress, pain, anguish: **TRAVAIL**

suffering that affords pleasure: **MASOCHISM**

sufficient grounds, justification: **WARRANT**

suffocate someone to death: **BURKE**

suffocation: **ASPHYXIATION**

suffuse or cover with a liquid or color: **PERFUSE**

sugar-accompanying protein hormone lacking in diabetics: **INSULIN**

sugar-coated nut: **DRAGÉE**

sugar depletion in the blood: **HYPOGLYCEMIA**

sugared or candied, iced, frozen: **GLACÉ**

sugar raw in the cane: **MUSCOVADO**

suggest, imply: **CONNOTE**

suggestive in a delicate way: **SUBTLE**

suggestive, off-color: **RISQUÉ**

suggestive of something, fragrant: **REDOLENT**

suggestive, risqué: **RACY**
suggest or mention for the first time:
BROACH
suggest, propose: **PROPOUND**
suicidal Japanese air attack: **KAMIKAZE**
suicide: **FELO-DE-SE**
suicide by disembowelment as a
Japanese ritual: **HARA-KIRI,
SEPPUKU**
suitable: **APROPOS**
suitable, advisable, proper: **EXPEDIENT**
suitable, practicable: **FEASIBLE**
sulkily pugnacious: **TRUCULENT**
sullenly or angrily look, scowl: **LOWER**
sullen, stern, gloomy, morose: **DOUR**
summarize: **RECAPITULATE**
summary: **PROSPECTUS**
summary: **RÉSUMÉ**
summary, diagram, or synopsis, as of a
process: **SCHEMA**
summary, digest: **CONSPECTUS**
summary, general view of a subject:
SYNOPSIS
summary in concise form, abstract:
PRÉCIS
summary of a document: **ABSTRACT**
summary of the main points of a course
of study: **SYLLABUS**
summary or synopsis of the plot of a
dramatic work: **SCENARIO**
summary that is brief but
comprehensive: **COMPENDIUM**
summation of an oration: **PERORATION**
summer home in Russia: **DACHA**
summerhouse or similar structure:
GAZEBO
summerhouse, tent or canopy:
PAVILION
summer-related, occurring in the
summer: **ESTIVAL**
summer's beginning when the sun is
farthest north of the equator, about
June 22: **SUMMER SOLSTICE**
summer, to pass the: **ESTIVATE**
summon, draw or call forth: **EVOKE**
summons or formal demand:
REQUISITION
sum of the squares of the two legs of a
right triangle equals the square of
the hypotenuse: **PYTHAGOREAN
THEOREM**
sun at its greatest distance north or
south of the equator: **SOLSTICE**
sun being at the center: **HELIOCENTRIC**
sunburned skin that peels off: **BLYPE**

sundial's upright blade that casts a
shadow: **GNOMON**
sun-dried brick: **ADOBE**
sunken design, incised carving:
INTAGLIO
sunken or slanted window or door
recess: **EMBRASURE**
sun-protective helmet, often of pith:
TOPEE
sun-related, solar: **HELIACAL**
sun room: **SOLARIUM**
sunset, occurring at: **ACRONICAL**
sun worship: **HELIOLATRY**
superficial: **FACILE**
superficial follower of an art or science:
DILETTANTE
superficial knowledge or little
knowledge: **SMATTERING**
superfluous: **DE TROP**
superfluous: **EXCRESCENT**
superfluous, extraneous:
SUPEREROGATORY
superfluous or redundant word or
phrase: **PLEONASM**
superintendence, management:
INTENDANCE
superior in weight, influence:
PREPONDERANT
superiority worshiper who shows
contempt for supposed inferiors:
SNOB
superior to all others: **SUPERLATIVE**
supernatural: **PARANORMAL**
superstition or story passed on from
generation to generation: **OLD
WIVES' TALE**
superstitious regard for an object
thought to have magical powers:
FETISHISM
supplant, replace: **SUPERSEDE**
supple, agile, lithe, pliant: **LISSOME**
supplemental, supporting or derivative
group: **AUXILIARY**
supplementary: **ADSCITITIOUS**
supply or feed to excess: **SURFEIT**
support: **ABET**
support: **ADMINICLE**
support, approval, encouraging look:
COUNTENANCE
supported by columns or pillars:
HYPOSTYLE
supporter or originator of a cause:
PROPONENT
supporters, voters: **CONSTITUENCY**

support for a lever that lifts, moves or balances: **FULCRUM**

support for wood in a fireplace: **ANDIRON, FIREDOG**

supporting, aiding, auxiliary: **ANCILLARY**

supporting, supplemental or derivative group: **AUXILIARY**

support of wood or metal to keep a broken bone in place: **SPLINT**

support or advocacy, as of a cause: **ESPOUSAL**

support, sponsorship: **PATRONAGE**

support with short feet for a hot dish: **TRIVET**

suppose or conclude from incomplete evidence: **CONJECTURE**

suppressing or silencing, as a rumor: **QUIETUS**

suppression of truth to procure some favor or reward: **SUBREPTION**

suppress, keep back: **STIFLE**

suppress, keep secret: **HUGGER-MUGGER**

suppress, put down forcibly: **QUASH**

suppress, stamp out, stifle: **SCOTCH**

supreme and independent authority: **SOVEREIGN**

supreme command, absolute power: **IMPERIUM**

supreme or highest good: **SUMMUM BONUM**

sureness: **CERTITUDE**

surface elegance: **VENEER**

surfeit, glut: **SATIATE**

surgery on living animals for medical research purposes: **VIVISECTION**

surmountable, conquerable: **SUPERABLE**

surname: **COGNOMEN**

surname: **PATRONYMIC**

surname from the maternal side: **MATRONYMIC**

surpass, excel, beat: **TRUMP**

surpassing others: **PREEMINENT**

surplus merchandise, money or value: **OVERAGE**

surprise attack: **AMBUSH**

surrender a prerogative: **ABDICATE**

surround, beset: **BELEAGUER**

surrounded by land: **LANDLOCKED**

surroundings: **AMBIENCE**

surroundings: **ENVIRONS**

surroundings, environment or setting, as of a motion picture: **MISE EN SCÈNE**

surroundings, setting, environment: **MILIEU**

survey of a subject: **CONSPECTUS**

survey or map used for taxation basis: **CADASTER**

surveyor's instrument used on a tripod: **TRANSIT**

survey to gain information: **RECONNAISSANCE**

survival and perpetuation of forms of life that are the most fit or the most adaptable: **NATURAL SELECTION**

survival-conducive area for an animal or species: **ECONICHE**

survive, pass through, as a crisis: **WEATHER**

surviving, existing: **EXTANT**

susceptibility or tendency to something: **PREDISPOSITION**

suspend, supplant, annul: **SUPERSEDE**

suspenseful story: **CLIFF-HANGER**

suspense or state of anxiety: **ON TENTERHOOKS**

suspension of action: **ABEYANCE**

suspension or delay authorized in some specific activity: **MORATORIUM**

suspension, temporarily, of punishment or pain: **REPRIEVE**

suspicious, cautious, wary: **LEERY**

suspicious, questionable: **EQUIVOCAL**

sustained or held, in music: **TENUTO**

sustenance: **ALIMENT**

swagger, bluster: **FANFARONADE**

swaggering adventurer or swordsman, bravo, daredevil: **SWASHBUCKLER**

swaggering self-assurance: **COCKINESS**

swallow food: **INGEST**

swallowing difficulty: **DYSPHAGIA**

swallow up, overwhelm: **ENGULF**

swampy body of water: **BAYOU**

swarm, teem, breed rapidly: **PULLULATE**

swashbuckling: **DERRING-DO**

swastika: **FYLFOT, HAKENKREUZ**

swastika: **GAMMADION**

sway, totter, waver: **VACILLATE**

swear falsely, perjure oneself, renounce: **FORSWEAR**

sweat: **SUDOR**

sweater, knitted, collarless and long-sleeved, that opens down the front: **CARDIGAN**

sweating in an excessive or abnormal manner: **SUDATION**

sweating that is excessive: **HIDROSIS**

sweat that smells bad: **BROMIDROSIS**

sweat that smells bad: **KAKIDROSIS**

sweeping, general and undetailed: **BROAD-BRUSH**

sweeten ostensibly or superficially: **SUGARCOAT**

sweet life (the), the good life: **DOLCE VITA**

sweet of voice, smooth-tongued, honeyed: **MELLIFLUOUS**

sweet or dessert-like food: **CONFECTION**

sweet or rich to a great degree: **LUSCIOUS**

sweet-sounding: **EUPHONIOUS**

sweet-sounding, melodious, pleasant: **DULCET**

sweet to excess: **SACCHARINE, CLOYING**

swell, expand, widen: **DILATE**

swelling: **INTUMESCENCE**

swelling in the body: **EDEMA**

swelling, knot, knob: **NODE**

swelling of a mucous membrane: **POLYP**

swelling or sore from exposure to cold: **CHILBLAIN**

swelling or tumor formed by an effusion of blood: **HEMATOMA**

swelling, protuberance: **TUBEROSITY**

swelling, puffiness: **TUMEFACTION**

swell, stretch out, expand: **DISTEND**

swerve: **SKEW**

swift, dashing, large, vigorous: **SPANKING**

swift, dazzling, brilliant: **METEORIC**

swiftly, rapidly, at a gallop: **TANTIVY**

swimmer's breathing tube that projects above the water's surface: **SNORKEL**

swimming kick in which both legs are parted and bent at the knees, then thrust backward together: **SCISSORS KICK**

swimming overarm stroke using both arms together and a scissors kick: **TRUDGEN**

swimming pool indoors: **NATATORIUM**

swimming under water with equipment such as flippers and snorkel: **SKIN DIVING**

swindle: **BUNCO**

swindle: **SKIN GAME**

swindle after the victim's confidence has been won: **CONFIDENCE GAME**

swindle, cheat: **ROOK**

swindle, con trick or job: **FIDDLE**

swindler, cheat, corrupt official: **HIGHBINDER**

swine castrated after maturity: **STAG**

swing around: **SLUE**

swing to and fro, fluctuate: **OSCILLATE**

swirling motion of air, water, gas, etc.: **TURBULENCE**

swish, fanciness, rustling as of silk: **FROUFROU**

switch from the lofty to the commonplace: **BATHOS**

switching of letters or sounds that changes a word: **METATHESIS**

swiveling wheel or ball, as on a chair leg: **CASTER**

swollen: **BULBOUS**

swollen: **TUMESCENT**

swollen: **TUMID**

swollen, bulging: **VENTRICULAR**

swollen, distended: **TURGID**

sword bar separating the handle from the blade: **CROSS GUARD**

sword-like in shape: **XIPHOID**

sword-like knife: **SNICKERSNEE**

sword's cross-guard arm or half, two of which separate the blade from the handle: **QUILLON**

sword-shaped: **GLADIATE**

swordsman who swaggers: **SWASHBUCKLER**

sword that is blunted and worn ornamentally: **CURTEIN**

sword that is short and curved: **SCIMITAR**

sword without cutting edge used in dueling: **ÉPÉE**

sworn written statement: **AFFIDAVIT**

syllable or letter appended to a word: **PARAGOGE**

syllable or syllables placed at the beginning of a word: **PREFIX**

syllable or syllables placed at the end of a word: **SUFFIX**

syllable or syllables placed in the middle of a word: **INFIX**

syllable shortened although it is naturally or by position long: **SYSTOLE**

syllables do, re, mi, etc., used vocally in music: **SOLFEGGIO**

syllables used vocally in music: **SOLMIZATION**

syllable third from last in a word: **ANTEPENULT**

symbol for "and" (&): **AMPERSAND**

symbol (ə), like an upside-down "e," used in phonetics: SCHWA

symbol or emblem used by a publisher on the title page of a book: COLOPHON

symbol or picture representing a word, sound or object: HIEROGLYPHIC

symbol or representative of something, as of a doctrine or a cause: EXPONENT

symbols devised to represent phonetically the positions of the speech mechanism: VISIBLE SPEECH

symbols, stick figures, etc., as used on public or road signs: PASIGRAPHY

symbol to inspire courage, such as a battle flag: ORIFLAMME

symbol (~) used in printing to avoid writing out a word or word element previously noted: SWUNG DASH

symmetrical in a radial way, like a starfish: ACTINOID

sympathize: COMMISERATE

sympathize or grieve with someone: CONDOLE

sympathizer with the enemy: FIFTH COLUMNIST

sympathy evocation, sorrow: PATHOS

symptom of an approaching disease: PRODROME

symptoms indicating a disease or condition: SYNDROME

synonyms and antonyms arranged in categories in a book: THESAURUS

synonym use merely to avoid repeating a word: ELEGANT VARIATION

synopsis or summary of the plot of a dramatic work: SCENARIO

synopsis, summary or diagram, as of a process: SCHEMA

syntax: COLLOCATION

synthesis of separate elements of emotion or experience that constitutes more than the mechanical sum of the parts: GESTALT

syphilis: LUES

systematized course of living: REGIMEN

table for holding a tea service: **TEAPOY**

table plate with short feet on which to place a hot dish: **TRIVET**

table-sharing, eating together: **COMMENSAL**

table supported wholly or in part by brackets: **CONSOLE TABLE**

table that is rectangular with squared legs even with and of the same thickness as the top: **PARSONS TABLE**

tablet on a wall for decoration or to mark an event: **PLAQUE**

tableware: **FLATWARE**

table wine: **VIN ORDINAIRE**

table with hinged sides or ends that fold down: **DROP-LEAF TABLE**

table with swinging legs that support drop leaves: **GATELEG TABLE**

tactic or stratagem to outwit someone: **PLOY**

tact, knowledge of the right thing to say or do: **SAVOIR-FAIRE**

tactlessness: **GAUCHERIE**

tact, smoothness, highly refined skill: **FINESSE**

tadpole: **POLLIWOG**

tailless: **ACAUDAL**

tailor- or tailoring-related: **SARTORIAL**

tail part that is fleshy, in animals: **DOCK**

take apart: **DISMANTLE**

take apart a weapon for cleaning: **FIELD STRIP**

take attention away from: **PRESCIND**

take away a legacy: **ADEEM**

take away from, detract: **DEROGATE**

take back, recant: **RETRACT**

take exception to, hesitate, object: **DEMUR**

take off, remove: **DOFF**

take over property from the owner, usually for public use: **EXPROPRIATE**

take parts from one piece of equipment to use in another: **CANNIBALIZE**

take place, happen: **SUPERVENE**

take the place of: **SUPERSEDE**

take with careful consideration: **TAKE UNDER ADVISEMENT**

taking back a present: **INDIAN GIVING**

taking into consideration or allowing for attendant differences: **MUTATIS MUTANDIS**

taking note: **COGNIZANCE**

taking risks to achieve some end: **BRINKMANSHIP**

talisman, charm: **GRIGRI, AMULET**

talkative: **LOQUACIOUS**

talkative, foolish person: **BLATHERSKITE**

talkative, glib, speaking fluently: **VOLUBLE**

talkativeness: **GARRULITY**

talkativeness to an abnormal degree: **LOGORRHEA**

talk, conference of opposing sides: **PARLEY**

talk critically about or against something: **DEPRECATE**

talked-about object: **CONVERSATION PIECE**

talker who is boastful: **COCKALORUM**

talker who is learned in table conversation: **DEIPNOSOPHIST**

talk evasively, hedge, equivocate: **WAFFLE**

talk foolishly: **TWADDLE**

talk in a wandering, incoherent manner: **MAUNDER**

talk in a windy way, hold forth with cant, speechify: **BLOVIATE**

talking about a traumatic situation for release from it: ABREACTION
talking foolishly: BLITHERING
talking people as seen in close-up on television: TALKING HEADS
talk or chatter that is rapid, nonsensical or unintelligible: JABBER
talk quickly or incoherently: GABBLE
talk rapidly and incoherently: GIBBER
talk senselessly, chatter: PRATE
talk that is foolish or senseless: DRIVEL
talk that is idle: PALAVER
talk that sounds important but isn't: BOMBAST
talk to oneself: SOLILOQUIZE
talk unfavorably or meanly about another: BACKBITE
tall and slender of figure: ASTHENIC
tall building: HIGH RISE
tall, lean, often awkward: LANKY
tall story: COCK-AND-BULL STORY
Talmudic literature devoted to legal elements: HALAKHA
Talmudic stories and account of the Exodus read at Seder service: HAGGADAH
tangible, touchable: TACTILE
tangle, make intricate: INVOLVE
tank or well to hold water: CISTERN
tantrum: CONNIPTION
tantrum: HISSY
tap dance style with hopping and leg flings: BUCK AND WING
tap dancing without metal taps: SOFT SHOE
tapeworm or similar parasite: HELMINTH
tap firmly: PERCUSS
tapistry: ARRAS
tap or drum monotonously: THRUM
target or object conveniently criticized or rejected (British): AUNT SALLY
target with no chance: SITTING DUCK
tart or pleasantly sharp-tasting: PIQUANT
taste, flavor: SAPOR
tasteless, flat, bland, dull: INSIPID
taste loss or impairment: AGEUSIA
taste or flavor that is sickeningly sentimental is: MAWKISH
tastes cannot be profitably disputed: DE GUSTIBUS NON EST DISPUTANDUM
tasting saline and distasteful: BRACKISH
tasting, taste: GUSTATION
tasty, appetizing: SAVORY

tasty, savory: SAPID
taunt, gibe (British): GIRD
taunting, sneering, ironical language: SARCASM
taunt, jeer: GIBE
taunt or annoy by reminding of a fault: TWIT
tautological, wordy: REDUNDANT
tax: IMPOST
tax of one tenth: TITHE
teacher: PRECEPTOR
teacher, lecturer, tutor without faculty rank: DOCENT
teacher or guide, especially in spiritual matters: GURU
teacher who is narrow-minded or pedantic: PEDAGOGUE
teaching or learning through discovery and investigation: HEURISTICS
team member who is a fill-in or outsider: RINGER
teapot's padded covering to keep the tea warm: TEA COZY
tear apart, as in searching for plunder: RANSACK
tear apart forcibly: REND
tear, chafe or burn away strips of: EXCORIATE
teardrop-shaped: GUTTIFORM
tearful: LACHRYMOSE
tearfully emotional or sentimental: MAUDLIN
tearing away: AVULSION
tear raggedly, mangle: LACERATE
tear to pieces: DILACERATE
tease or disappoint by repeated frustration of expectations: TANTALIZE
tease, torment playfully: RAG
teasing talk, jesting: RAILLERY
teasing that is playful: BADINAGE
technical mastery, skill or style, as of an art: VIRTUOSITY
technicians as rulers: TECHNOCRACY
tedious, boring: WEARISOME
tedious passage: LONGUEUR
tedious, troublesome, tiresome: IRKSOME
teething, cutting teeth: DENTITION
telepathy, clairvoyance: CRYPTESTHESIA
telephone transactions in unlisted stocks: OVER-THE-COUNTER TRADING
television: VIDEO

television-captioned for the
hearing-impaired: CLOSED
CAPTIONED
television magnetic tape on which the
video and audio parts of a program
can be recorded: VIDEOTAPE
television or radio melodramatic series:
SOAP OPERA
television ratings period: SWEEPS
television's picture as distinguished
from its sound, or audio: VIDEO
television's sound as distinguished from
its picture, or video: AUDIO
tell, disclose, reveal: DIVULGE
tell off, scold: BERATE
temperate in eating and drinking:
ABSTEMIOUS
temperature sense lack, inability to
recognize heat or cold:
THERMANESTHESIA
temperature standard used to estimate
fuel requirements for heating of
buildings: DEGREE DAY
temper tantrum: HISSY
temple or tower of the Far East with
stacked roofs each curving upward:
PAGODA
temple slave: HIERODULE
tempo and expression of music at the
performer's pleasure: A CAPRICCIO
temporary: INTERIM
temporary, brief: TRANSIENT
temporary buildings for housing troops:
CANTONMENT
temporary camp, usually without
shelter: BIVOUAC
temporary, improvised, substitute:
MAKESHIFT
temporary inaction: ABEYANCE
temporary or makeshift, as applied to a
ship's rigging: JURY-RIGGED
temporary, provisional, for the time
being: PRO TEMPORE
temporary replacement or fill-in in a
job: LOCUM TENENS
temporary residence or stay: SOJOURN
temporary stitching: BASTING
Ten Commandments: DECALOGUE
tendency, bent: PROPENSITY
tendency, inclination: BENT
tendency or drift that is hidden:
UNDERCURRENT
tendency or inclination, usually toward
something objectionable:
PROCLIVITY

tendency, susceptibility:
PREDISPOSITION
tendency that is inborn: INSTINCT
tendency, trend, liking, leaning or bent:
INCLINATION
tendency, way of reacting: DISPOSITION
tender, emotional, sometimes mawkish:
SENTIMENTAL
tender part of a loin of meat:
TENDERLOIN
tending to a particular point of view:
TENDENTIOUS
tendon at the back of the human knee
and thigh: HAMSTRING
ten-fold or based on the number ten:
DENARY
tennis: SPHAIRISTIKE
tennis ball returned repeatedly before it
hits the ground: VOLLEY
tennis court's screened gallery for
spectators, especially in court
tennis: DEDANS
tennis doubles player's intercepting of a
ball that would normally be played
by his or her partner: POACHING
tennis extra game, with different
scoring, played after a tie at,
usually, twelve games: TIEBREAKER
tennis game juncture when the server
is one point away from losing:
BREAK POINT
tennis loss of a point because both serve
attempts fail: DOUBLE FAULT
tennis player's winning of a game
against the server: SERVICE BREAK
tennis return in which a softly stroked
ball barely clears the net: DROP
SHOT
tennis rule violation of failing to keep
both feet behind the base line when
serving: FOOT FAULT
tennis serve that is unreturnable: ACE
tennis serve that touches the net before
landing and is not counted: LET
tennis set in which the winner wins
every game: LOVE SET
tennis shot hit past the opponent when
he or she is near the net: PASSING
SHOT
tennis stroke at the ball after it has
bounced: GROUND STROKE
tennis stroke in which the ball is arched
high into the air: LOB
tennis stroke in which the hand holding
the racket hits the ball from the

opposite side of the body:
BACKHAND

tennis stroke made on the same side of the body as that of the hand wielding the racket: FOREHAND

tennis style in which the server rushes to the net after each serve: SERVE-AND-VOLLEY

tense, bewildered, agitated, worried: DISTRAUGHT

tenth part of anything: TITHE

ten-year anniversary: DECENNIAL

ten-year period, decade: DECENNARY

terminally ill, hospital or program for: HOSPICE

terminology, names: NOMENCLATURE

territory surrounded by that of another country or class: ENCLAVE

territory with a populace and tradition close to one state or country but ruled by another, as at a border: IRREDENTA

terse, concise, brief and meaningful: SUCCINCT

terse, pithy, axiomatic: SENTENTIOUS

terse, solid, packed with meaning: PITHY

test, by an action or statement, of public opinion or reaction: TRIAL BALLOON

test for diphtheria: SCHICK TEST

test for uterine cancer: PAP TEST

test or gauge the weight of by lifting: HEFT

test or initiation that is severe or an ordeal: BAPTISM OF FIRE

test that is a key or decisive one: LITMUS TEST

test that is crucial, pivotal or tough: ACID TEST

test the depth of water: SOUND

test-the-waters action or statement: TRIAL BALLOON

test word, password: SHIBBOLETH

that is: I.E. (ID EST)

that is to say, namely: TO WIT

that's life: C'EST LA VIE

theater bulletin board: CALLBOARD

theater fabric, light and sheer, used as a backdrop: SCRIM

theater forward section of mezzanine or balcony: LOGE

theater having the stage surrounded by seats: ARENA THEATER

theater space above the stage containing the drop curtain and lighting: FLY

theater's projecting entrance roof or oblong canopy: MARQUEE

theaters, tents, modified barns, etc., usually in resort areas, for plays and concerts: STRAW-HAT CIRCUIT

theater waiting room for performers when they are off-stage: GREEN ROOM

theater writer, playwright: DRAMATURGE

theatrical collection of works prepared for production: REPERTORY

theatrical direction for martial activity: ALARUMS AND EXCURSIONS

theatrical, overly emotional: HISTRIONIC

theatrical stage objects: PROPS

theft: LARCENY

theme used throughout a work of art to indicate, signal or remind of a certain person, event or idea: LEITMOTIF

theological branch dealing with facts and proofs concerning Christianity: APOLOGETICS

theoretical, as opposed to practical: ACADEMIC

theoretical, conjectural: SPECULATIVE

theoretical, not concrete: ABSTRACT

theory or supposition used as a basis for further investigation: HYPOTHESIS

therapy by suggesting positive life goals: PSYCHAGOGY

therapy using doses of medicines that produce symptoms of the disease treated: HOMEOPATHY

thermometer degree markings: GRADUATIONS

thesis established by showing its opposite to be absurd: APAGOGE

thick and dense, as heavy smoke: TURBID

thicken: INCRASSATE

thicken as by evaporation: INSPISSATE

thickening and degeneration of artery walls: ARTERIOSCLEROSIS

thickening and degeneration of artery walls with deposits of fatty substances: ATHEROSCLEROSIS

thicket: COPSE, COPPICE

thief: GANEF

thin and pale: PEAKED

thin biscuit or cooky: WAFER

thin down, emaciate: MACERATE
thin, flimsy, delicate: TENUOUS
thing that goes into a mixture:
INGREDIENT
think about, reflect, consider carefully:
PONDER
thinker, clever man: SOPHIST
thinking, using the intellect:
INTELLECTION
think of separately: PRESCIND
think out carefully, devise: EXCOGITATE
think, reason: INTELLECTUALIZE
thin, lean: SPARE
thinly diffused: SPARSE
thinned out, weakened, somewhat
strained: ATTENUATED
thinness induced pathologically by
extreme dieting: ANOREXIA
NERVOSA
thin, scanty, inadequate: MEAGER
thin sheets of fabric, wood, etc., being
bonded together are: LAMINATED
third anniversary: TRIENNIAL
third finger: MEDIUS
third-person pronoun use instead of
"I": ILLEISM
third syllable from the end in a word:
ANTEPENULT
thirst-causing, dry up: PARCH
thirteen: BAKER'S DOZEN
this side of the Atlantic: CISATLANTIC
thoroughfare, open space for crowds:
CONCOURSE
thoroughgoing: UNMITIGATED
thoroughly, to the fullest, completely:
À FOND
thorough, thoroughgoing: INGRAINED
thoughtful, serious, often melancholy:
PENSIVE
thought, idea: INTELLECTION
thought-involving, not concrete:
ABSTRACT
thoughtless, unthinking: INCOGITANT
thought or observation that is literary:
PENSÉE
thoughts and feelings of a character
evoked in a literary passage:
INTERIOR MONOLOGUE
thousand, thousand years: CHILIAD
thousand tons: KILOTON
thousand-year period: MILLENARY
thrash severely, punish or beat:
TROUNCE
threatening and dark, as the weather:
LOWERING

threatening, menacing: MINACIOUS,
MINATORY
threat or denunciation, especially from
a divine source: COMMINATION
three-dimensional image (when viewed
through tinted lenses) printed in
two overlapping colors: ANAGLYPH
three-dimensional life-like image
produced by a laser process:
HOLOGRAM
three-dimensional-view optical viewer
with two eyepieces: STEREOSCOPE
three-figure design with branches, arms
or legs coming from a common
center: TRISKELION
three-fold: TRIPLE
three-fold or based on the number
three: TERNARY
three-hulled boat with sails: TRIMARAN
three in a governing group: TROIKA
Three Kings' visit to Jesus observed:
EPIPHANY
three miles: LEAGUE
three persons or things: TRIAD
three rhyming lines: TERCET
three separate but related literary or
dramatic works: TRILOGY
three spots, as on a card or domino:
TREY
thriftless, rash, incautious:
IMPROVIDENT
thrift or economy in managing:
HUSBANDRY
thrifty: FRUGAL
thrifty, careful: CANNY
thrill, arouse, startle: ELECTRIFY
thriving period, height of power,
exuberance: HEYDAY
throat irritation often causing loss of
voice: LARYNGITIS
throbbing, pulsing: VIBRANT
throb regularly, vibrate: PULSATE
throw-away matter: RECREMENT
throw forth or forward: PROJECT
throw goods or cargo overboard:
JETTISON
throwing out of a window:
DEFENESTRATION
throw in, introduce abruptly: INJECT
throw things at: PELT
thrust away from, push down: DETRUDE
thumb: POLLEX
thumb one's nose: SNOOK
thumb rapidly through a book's pages:
RIFFLE

thumb the nose: COCK A SNOOT, COCK
    A SNOOK
thus passes away worldly glory: SIC
    TRANSIT GLORIA MUNDI
ticket selling above the regular rates:
    SCALPING
tickle or excite pleasurably: TITILLATE
tickle, pinch, nip, twitch: VELLICATE
tidal wave: TSUNAMI
tide occurring at or shortly after the
    new or full moon: SPRING TIDE
tide that is an often dangerous
    countertide that produces turbulent
    water: RIPTIDE
tide when the rise and fall show least
    change: NEAP TIDE
tidy: KEMPT
tie, a race in which two competitors
    finish together: DEAD HEAT
tie or draw, as in a game: STANDOFF
tie or fasten together: COLLIGATE
tie that connects, bond: LIGAMENT
tie together the four feet or the feet and
    hands: HOG-TIE
tighten up, make concise: CONDENSE
tightrope walker: FUNAMBULIST
tight spot, predicament: QUANDARY
tile-like, either in shape or arrangement:
    TEGULAR
tilt, slope: CANT
timber driven into the earth to support
    a building or pier: PILE
timber in a stand and not yet cut:
    STUMPAGE
time as indicated in the military (000,
    0100 . . . 2400 hours): MILITARY
    TIME
time between periods or events,
    meantime: INTERIM
time category of a verb form: TENSE
time-consuming tactics to obstruct
    action: FILIBUSTER
time counted in reverse, as in rocket
    launching: COUNTDOWN
time erroneously associated with an
    earlier or later event or thing:
    ANACHRONISM
time erroneously given as earlier than
    the fact: PROCHRONISM
time erroneously given as later than the
    fact: METACHRONISM
time flies: TEMPUS FUGIT
time-honored, venerable, classic:
    VINTAGE

time, in addition to length, width and
    thickness: FOURTH DIMENSION
time-measuring science: CHRONOLOGY
time or interval for accomplishing
    something: WINDOW
time or rate agreement arranged:
    SYNCHRONIZED
time out from work for a short period:
    COFFEE BREAK
time period memorable for important
    events or influence: EPOCH
timepiece: HOROLOGE
time to be off the streets: CURFEW
time-to-get-up signal on bugle or drum:
    REVEILLE
time when work is not being done,
    equipment is broken, etc.:
    DOWNTIME
timid: PIGEON-HEARTED
timid, cowardly: CHICKEN-HEARTED,
    CHICKEN-LIVERED
timid, fearful: TIMOROUS
timid, fearful, trembling: TREMULOUS
timidity, shyness, lack of confidence:
    DIFFIDENCE
tinder of decayed wood: PUNK
tingle annoyingly: PRINGLE
tin mine region: STANNARY
tinselly, glittering, showy: CLINQUANT
tint, light color: TINCTURE
tiny: LILLIPUTIAN
tiny amount: IOTA
tiny person: HOP-O'-MY-THUMB
tiny quantity: SOUPÇON
tiny, very small: MINUSCULE
tip: POURBOIRE
tip, gift of money: GRATUITY
tip, gratuity: DOUCEUR
tip-of-the-tongue phenomenon:
    LETHOLOGICA
tip or band of metal, as at the end of
    an umbrella, cane or table leg:
    FERRULE
tip or present, gratuity: CUMSHAW
tip or small bribe: BAKSHEESH
tirade: HARANGUE
tireless, unflagging: INDEFATIGABLE
tiresome, tedious, troublesome:
    IRKSOME
tiring, weakening: FLAGGING
tissue and tissue structure as a
    biological study: HISTOLOGY
tissue growing abnormally, as a tumor:
    NEOPLASM

tissue removed from a living organism for examination: BIOPSY

title of respect used with a name: HONORIFIC

title or epithet substituted for proper name: ANTONOMASIA

title or heading of a section in a law: RUBRIC

toady, cringe fondly: FAWN

toady, servile follower: LACKEY

toasted slice of bread that has been baked yellow: ZWIEBACK

toast or bread, in a small piece, dipped in gravy or sauce: SIPPET

tobacco ash left in a pipe after smoking: DOTTLE

tobacco grown in Louisiana, dark and strong: PERIQUE

tobacco moisture-retaining box or case: HUMIDOR

tobacco or tobacco smoke aversion: MISOCAPNIA

tobacco that stinks: MUNDUNGUS

toeless: ADACTYLOUS

toes linked by a membrane: WEB-FOOTED

toes or feet being characteristically turned in: PIGEON-TOED

toe with the joint bent downward: HAMMERTOE

together: IN CONCERT

together, as a group or as one: EN MASSE

together, cooperative: SYNERGETIC

toilet-bowl-like basin for bathing the genitals: BIDET

toilet for numbers of people, as in a camp: LATRINE

toilet in nautical language: HEAD

toil, work hard: MOIL

token, counter: JETON

token of a solemn pledge: SACRAMENT

tomato juice mixed with vodka as a cocktail: BLOODY MARY

tomato juice served as if it were a cocktail: VIRGIN MARY

tomboy: HOYDEN

tombstone inscription: EPITAPH

tomcat: GIB

tomorrow (Spanish): MAÑANA

tone color or quality, as of a voice or an instrument: TIMBRE

tongue kiss: CATAGLOTTISM

tongue-lashing: EXCORIATION

tongue-like: LINGUAL

tongue-like object, land formation, etc.: LANGUET

too glib, facile: PAT

too great or too numerous to be determined: INCALCULABLE

too much, in music: TANTO

too sweet: CLOYING, SACCHARINE

toothache: ODONTALGIA

toothbrush rubber tip for massaging gums: STIMULATOR TIP

tooth cleanser: DENTIFRICE

tooth extraction: EXODONTIA

tooth-gnashing: BRUXISM

toothless: EDENTATE

tooth that is broken or that projects: SNAGGLETOOTH

tooth with two points: BICUSPID

top, apex: VERTEX

top course of a wall or roof: COPING

top grade or quality: FIRST WATER

top having four lettered sides, used in a gambling game: TEETOTUM

topmost point, acme: PINNACLE

top or cap being difficult to remove: CHILDPROOF

top-ranked: PREEMINENT

top-shaped, spinning like a top: TURBINATE

torch, candlestick that is large and decorated: FLAMBEAU

tormented, oppressed: HAGRIDDEN

torment, tease, rant, browbeat, bluster: HECTOR

tornado: TWISTER

torpor: ACEDIA

Torrid Zone inhabitants whose shadows fall according to the season: AMPHISCIANS

tortoise-like: TESTUDINAL

tortuous, winding: ANFRACTUOUS

torture to force confession: QUESTION EXTRAORDINAIRE

tossing or twitching to an abnormal degree: JACTITATION

total, end-to-end: OVERALL

to the point: APROPOS

touchable: TANGIBLE

touchable, perceptible: PALPABLE

touchable, tangible: TACTILE

touch at the sides or ends: ABUT

touching: TANGENT

touching, emotionally moving: POIGNANT

touch or push with a slight jarring, shake lightly, stimulate: JOG

touchy, irritable: TETCHY
toughen or smooth metal: PLANISH
tough, robust: HARDY
tough, terse and realistic in writing style: HARD-BOILED
tough, unyielding: HARD-BITTEN
tough urban wisdom and savvy: STREET SMARTS
tourist's diarrhea suffered in a foreign country: TURISTA, TOURISTA
tournament: JOUSTS
tournament in which each player engages every other player: ROUND ROBIN
tour of the European continent: GRAND TOUR
tour rural districts: BARNSTORM
tousled, untidy, unkempt: DISHEVELED
toward the base: BASAD
toward the center: CENTRIPETAL
tower of a mosque that is slender and balconied: MINARET
tower or keep of a castle: DONJON
tower or temple of the Far East with stacked roofs each curving upward: PAGODA
tower that tapers to a point: SPIRE
town dweller, citizen, middle-class resident: BURGHER
town that is small, remote and unknown: PODUNK
trace out, portray verbally, describe: DELINEATE
trace, sign of something absent: VESTIGE
trace, slight hint: SOUPÇON
trace, spark: SCINTILLA
track-and-field event in which an athlete uses a long pole to leap over a high horizontal bar: POLE VAULT
track or trail behind any moving thing, such as a ship: WAKE
track, trail, footprint or other trace of a wild animal: SPOOR
tractable, yielding: PLIANT
trademark of a publishing house: COLOPHON
trader: CHANDLER
trader, dealer: MONGER
trading of votes and influence between politicians: LOGROLLING
trading unit on a stock exchange, usually 100 shares: ROUND LOT
traditionalists, conservative or entrenched element: OLD GUARD

tragic flaw, as dramatized in Greek tragedy: HAMARTIA
tragic muse: MELPOMENE
trail, track, footprint or other trace of a wild animal: SPOOR
training of employees to develop skills, etc.: IN-SERVICE COURSES
train of slaves, prisoners or animals fastened together, as for marching: COFFLE
train to a behavior pattern: CONDITION
traitor: RECREANT
traitor: BENEDICT ARNOLD
traitor, deserter: RENEGADE
traitorous leader, collaborator with the enemy: QUISLING
traitor, renegade: TURNCOAT
tramp, wanderer: VAGABOND
tranquil, calm, untroubled: SERENE
tranquillity: ATARAXIA
tranquil, serene, uniform: EQUABLE
transaction conditionally authorized when, as and if a security is issued: WHEN ISSUED
transference of an emotion to something other than the original object: DISPLACEMENT
transferring one's feelings or desires related to childhood repression toward the psychiatrist or another person: TRANSFERENCE
transform: TRANSMOGRIFY
transformable, changeable: MUTABLE
transformation: PERMUTATION
transformation: SEA CHANGE
transformation of form, character or appearance: METAMORPHOSIS
transform, convert: RESOLVE
transient, fickle, unstable, fleeting: VOLATILE
transitional form: INTERGRADE
transition or progression without pause, as in sequential musical numbers or topics of conversation: SEGUE
transitory, fleeting: FUGACIOUS
transitory, lasting a short time, fleeting, of short life or duration: EPHEMERAL
transitory quality: CADUCITY
translation literally of a word or construction from one language to another: LOAN TRANSLATION
translation word for word: METAPHRASE
translucent, limpid: PELLUCID

transmit to another: BEQUEATH
transmutation process: ALCHEMY
transparent, glass-like: HYALINE
transparent, lucid, pure, clear: LIMPID
transparent or translucent, as a cloth:
DIAPHANOUS
transparent or translucent plastic:
LUCITE
transparent, radiant: LUCENT
transparent when wet: HYDROPHANOUS
transporter of pedestrians, such as a
belt-like conveyor or an elevated
car: PEOPLE MOVER
transport service that goes back and
forth quickly or frequently:
SHUTTLE
transposing letters of a word to form
another: ANAGRAM
transposition of letters or sounds that
changes a word: METATHESIS
transposition of sounds or of parts of
words unintentionally:
SPOONERISM
trapeze acrobat: AERIALIST
trap or danger always possible or to be
feared: PITFALL
trapping or irresolvably circular
situation: CATCH-22
trap, situation with no escape:
CUL-DE-SAC
trash, junk, rubbish: DRECK
trash seller, junk dealer:
SCHLOCKMEISTER
trashy art or literature: KITSCH
travel a route: PEREGRINATE
travelers moving in a group: CARAVAN
traveler, wayfarer: VIATOR
traveling or going from place to place:
ITINERANT
traveling salesperson who sells or gives
away religious books: COLPORTEUR
travel service that goes back and forth
quickly or frequently: SHUTTLE
travel urge: WANDERLUST
tray: SALVER
treacherous: PERFIDIOUS
treacherous, wily, cunning: INSIDIOUS
treacherous woman: DELILAH
treachery, evildoing, murder: FOUL
PLAY
treachery, perfidy, falseness in word:
PUNIC FAITH
treason, offense against sovereign
authority: LESE MAJESTY, LÈSE
MAJESTÉ

treasure, collection, gathering: TROVE
treasurer: BURSAR
treatise: DISSERTATION
treatise, formal discourse: DISQUISITION
treatise or pamphlet, usually on a
political or religious subject: TRACT
treatment of disease by manipulation of
the joints: CHIROPRACTIC
treatment of disease by producing
incompatible conditions:
ALLOPATHY
treaty, contract, agreement: PACT
tree-bordered walk or promenade:
ALAMEDA
tree grown from seed: STAND
tree or shrub miniaturizing, a Japanese
art: BONSAI
tree rings used to estimate dates of past
events: DENDROCHRONOLOGY
trees as studied in botany and forestry:
DENDROLOGY
trees, like or living in: ARBOREAL
trees or shrubs trimmed and arranged
in fantastic shapes: TOPIARY
tree tract or garden displaying many
varieties: ARBORETUM
tree with its top cut to cause growth of
shoots: POLLARD
trembling paralysis: PALSY
trendy adoption of a radical or minority
cause by the rich: RADICAL CHIC
trespass for hunting or fishing: POACH
trespass, intrude, advance beyond the
proper limit: ENCROACH
trial action or statement to determine
likely public response: TRIAL
BALLOON
triangles and the relationship of their
sides and angles as a study:
TRIGONOMETRY
triangle with no sides of the same
length: SCALENE
triangle with two equal sides:
ISOSCELES
triangular jet aircraft: DELTA WING
triangular or wedge-shaped piece of
fabric set into a garment to provide
greater fullness: GORE
triangular roof feature: GABLE
triangular roof-like fronting in
architecture, classical gable:
PEDIMENT
triangular stringed instrument
(Russian): BALALAIKA
tribute, elaborate praise: PANEGYRIC

trick, cajole, entice by flattery or guile:
INVEIGLE
trick, cheat: HOODWINK
trick, cheat, deceive: FINAGLE
trickery: CHICANERY
trickery, deceitfulness, double-dealing:
DUPLICITY
trickery, deception: HOCUS-POCUS
trickery, hocus-pocus, sleight of hand:
LEGERDEMAIN
trickery, rascality, deceitfulness:
KNAVERY
trickery, underhandedness:
SKULDUGGERY
trick, maneuver, device for obtaining an
advantage: STRATAGEM
trick or deceive someone: BAMBOOZLE
tricky, fraudulent action: JOCKEYING
tricky, lewd: LUBRICIOUS
trifle: BAGATELLE
trifle, little something: QUELQUECHOSE
trifles, unimportant details: MINUTIAE
trifle with or flirt: COQUET
trifling or insignificant in size or
amount: NEGLIGIBLE
trifling or small work: OPUSCULE
trifling, small: NOMINAL
trifling, unimportant, frivolous thing:
FRIBBLE
trifling, unimportant, insignificant:
PETTY
trilling sound, as that of grasshoppers
or birds: CHIRR
trimming for women's gowns, as beaded
lace or braid: PASSEMENTERIE
trimming on edges or seams of material:
PIPING
trim or cut branches, as from a tree:
LOP
trinket: BIBELOT
trinket: GEWGAW
trinket, gewgaw: KICKSHAW
trinket, gewgaw: TCHOTCHKE
trinket or ornament either gaudy or
trifling: FALLAL
triple tablet, picture or carving, often
depicting a religious subject:
TRIPTYCH
triplicate: TERNATE
trite, commonplace, banal remark:
PLATITUDE
trite, commonplace or worn out by
overuse, as a phrase: HACKNEYED
trite expression: BROMIDE
trite, hackneyed: HACK

trite or stale story, song or saying:
CHESTNUT
trite, worn-out or overused expression:
CLICHÉ
triumphant, joyful: JUBILANT
trivial, of small importance:
FEATHERWEIGHT
trivial or worthless matter: CHAFF
trivial, petty: INSIGNIFICANT
trivial, petty: PICAYUNE
trivial, petty, contemptible: PALTRY
trivial, silly, unimportant: FRIVOLOUS
trivial, unimportant: INCONSEQUENTIAL
trolley in parallelogram shape that
draws current for an electric
locomotive: PANTOGRAPH
troop call for service, review, etc.:
MUSTER
troops highly trained for bold attack,
assault force: SHOCK TROOPS
trouble: TSOORIS
trouble, bother, inconvenience:
DISCOMMODE
trouble-free state: ATARAXIA
troublemaker: ENFANT TERRIBLE
trouble-making: PESTILENT
trouble or torment relentlessly: HARASS
troublesome, difficult or risky situation:
HORNET'S NEST
troublesome, tiresome, tedious:
IRKSOME
trouble with persistent demands:
IMPORTUNE
trousers of women resembling a skirt:
CULOTTE
trudge laboriously: PLOD
true apparently but open to doubt:
PLAUSIBLE
truism: PLATITUDE
truly so: VERITABLE
trumpet mute: SOURDINE
trumpet or drum signal for a parley:
CHAMADE
trusted adviser or counselor: MENTOR
trustee, guardian: FIDUCIARY
truthful, accurate: VERACIOUS
truthful representation, likeness to what
is real or true: VERISIMILITUDE
truth that is obvious or self-evident:
TRUISM
tube between the mouth and stomach:
GULLET
tube of small size, often graduated:
PIPETTE
tuberculosis, consumption: PHTHISIS

tube used to transfer liquid to a container at a lower level: SIPHON

tub for boiling and bleaching fabrics: KIER

tuck made in a garment to achieve a good fit: DART

tuft of ribbons, yarn, feathers: POMPON

tuft or clump, as of grass or hair: TUSSOCK

tumbler, vaulter: VOLTIGEUR

tumor-like swelling of a mucous membrane: POLYP

tumor that is malignant: SARCOMA

tumult, confusion: TURMOIL

tune an instrument: TEMPER

turbulent and dangerous condition or place: MAELSTROM

Turkish confection: HALVAH

Turkish cylindrical men's hat, usually with a tassel: FEZ

Turkish title of respect (formerly): EFFENDI

turmoil, confusion: HURLY-BURLY

turmoil, haste or excitement, prompted by: HECTIC

turmoil, storm and stress, great unrest: STURM UND DRANG

turn aside: SHUNT

turn aside, deflect, distract, amuse, entertain: DIVERT

turn aside, swerve: SKEW

turn aside, wander from the main subject: DIGRESS

turn aside, ward off, avoid: PARRY

turn, as the hand, so that the palm is downward or backward: PRONATE

turn, as the hand, so that the palm is upward or forward: SUPINATE

turn away from the straight course: DEVIATE

turncoat, traitor: RENEGADE

turned up at the tip: RETROUSSÉ

turning of one's concerns inward upon oneself: INTROVERSION

turning point in action, belief, etc.: WATERSHED

turnip with a large root: RUTABAGA

turn or go back to a former place, position or condition: REVERT

turn out finally, result ultimately: EVENTUATE

turn outward or inside out: EVERT

turn, rotate or swing, as around an axis: PIVOT

turreted like a castle: CASTELLATED

turtle's underside or ventral horny plate: PLASTRON

tutor, teacher or lecturer without faculty rank: DOCENT

tuxedo, semiformal attire: BLACK TIE

TV portable camera with a build-in VCR: CAMCORDER

twelve-fold or based on the number 12: DUODECIMAL

twentieth anniversary: VIGENTENNIAL

twenty-fold or based on the number 20: VIGESIMAL

twenty-four hours in occurrence or cycle, as certain biological processes: CIRCADIAN

twenty-one, a card game: VINGT-ET-UN

twenty-year period: VICENNIAL

twice a week: SEMIWEEKLY

twice a year, semiannual: BIANNUAL

twig-like handicraft work, furniture, etc.: WICKERWORK

twig or slender branch that is tough and flexible: WITHE

twilight, dusk: GLOAMING

twilight-like in dimness, obscure: CREPUSCULAR

twilight of the gods: GÖTTERDÄMMERUNG

twin-bearing: BIPAROUS

twinge of fear: QUALM

twist, bend, contort: WRITHE

twist, bend, misrepresent: DISTORT

twisted cord used for ornamentation: TORSADE

twisted or intricate, complicated, involved: CONVOLUTED

twisting or being twisted: TORSION

twist or bend out of shape: DISTORT

twist or lurch from side to side: CAREEN

twist or pull away: WREST

twitching or tossing to an abnormal degree: JACTITATION

twitching, spasm: MYOCLONUS

twitch, pinch, nip, tickle: VELLICATE

two bids made simultaneously are decided by a flip of a coin: MATCHED AND LOST

two dancers in a ballet figure: PAS DE DEUX

two dots over a Germanic vowel to indicate a sound change (ü): UMLAUT

two dots over the second of two

consecutive vowels to indicate different pronunciation: DIERESIS

two, double or paired: BINARY

two-edged battle ax: TWIBIL

two equally accented syllables making up a poetic metrical foot: SPONDEE

two-fold or double: DUPLE

two-footed animal: BIPED

two-god theology: DITHEISM

two-handed: BIMANOUS

two-hulled boat with sails: CATAMARAN

two meanings in a phrase, one of them often risqué: DOUBLE ENTENDRE

two months apart: BIMONTHLY

two months in duration: BIMESTRIAL

two names or two terms, involving: BINOMIAL

two negatives in a single sentence ("I don't have no pencil"): DOUBLE NEGATIVE

two or more academic or scientific disciplines being involved: CROSS-DISCIPLINARY

two or more distinct personalities as a psychiatric disorder: MULTIPLE PERSONALITY

two or more husbands at once: POLYANDRY

two or more wives at once: POLYGYNY

two-part division of groups or classes that are often opposed: DICHOTOMY

two people sharing the same delusion: FOLIE À DEUX

two persons sharing ruling power: DIARCHY

two prosecutions for the same offense: DOUBLE JEOPARDY

two sections or two opposed parts: DICHOTOMY

two-sided: BILATERAL

two tickets for the price of one: TWOFER

two tones rapidly alternated, in music: TRILL

two vowel sounds that blend into one syllable: DIPHTHONG

two years apart: BIENNIAL

tying up or binding together; also, two or more letters united in print: LIGATURE

type assortment of all the characters in one size and style: FONT

type in which the letters slant, usually to denote emphasis or to differentiate: ITALIC

type measure equal to square of the type body: EM

type measure half the width of an em: EN

type or kind, as in art or literature: GENRE

type plate containing a company's distinctive form of name, trademark, newspaper nameplate, etc.: LOGOTYPE

type set by printers that exceeds the space available: OVERSET

typesetter: COMPOSITOR

type style that is upright and conventionally used in most books and publications: ROMAN

type that is heavy and black: BOLDFACE

type that looks like handwriting: CURSIVE

typewriter operated by telephone: TELEX

typewriter's roller: PLATEN

typewriter standard keyboard: **QWERTY**

typewriter white liquid for mistakes: CORRECTION FLUID, WHITEOUT

type twelve points high used as a unit of measurement in printing: PICA

typical example, model, pattern: EXEMPLAR

typical or specific language, style, etc., as in art or literature: IDIOM

typify: PERSONIFY

typographical error: TYPO

typographical ornament or symbol: DINGBAT

typographical term for the part of a letter that extends below the line: DESCENDER

typographical term for the part of a letter that extends upward: ASCENDER

typographical unit of measurement equal to twelve points: PICA

tyrannical subordinate official: SATRAP

tyrant: DESPOT

ugly and malicious old woman:
BELDAM
ugly, unpleasant in appearance,
disagreeable: **ILL-FAVORED**
ugly woman: **GORGON**
ulterior motive, secret reservation or
concern: **ARRIÈRE-PENSÉE**
ultimate or crucial test: **ACID TEST**
umbrella that is a lightweight sunshade:
PARASOL
umpire: **ARBITER**
unable to produce the desired effect:
INEFFECTUAL
unable to survive: **INVIABLE**
unabridged: **IN EXTENSO**
unacceptable, unwelcome person:
PERSONA NON GRATA
unaccompanied singing is: **A CAPPELLA**
unadorned, as speech or writing:
LITERAL
unaffected by pain or pleasure: **STOICAL**
unaffected, simple, candid, artless:
NAIVE
unalike, varied: **DIVERSE**
unalive, spiritless: **INANIMATE**
unambiguous: **UNEQUIVOCAL**
unattractive, dingy: **SNUFFY**
unavoidable, authoritative, urgently
necessary: **IMPERATIVE**
unavoidable, certain: **INEVITABLE**
unavoidable, inevitable: **INELUCTABLE**
unaware, unmindful: **OBLIVIOUS**
unbearable: **INSUFFERABLE**
unbeliever: **INFIDEL**
unbelieving, irreligious: **HEATHEN**
unbending: **INTRANSIGENT**
unbiased: **INDIFFERENT, DISINTERESTED**
unbiased, detached: **OBJECTIVE**
unbiased, impartial: **DISPASSIONATE**

unbiased, objective, impartial:
DISPASSIONATE
unbreakable: **INFRANGIBLE**
unbreakable: **IRREFRANGIBLE**
uncalled-for: **GRATUITOUS**
unceasing: **INCESSANT**
uncertain: **AMBIVALENT**
uncertain: **VACILLATING**
uncertain, delicately risky, precarious:
TOUCH-AND-GO
uncertain or unforeseen but possible
event: **CONTINGENCY**
unchangeable: **IMMUTABLE**
unchangeable: **INVARIABLE**
unchangeable, fixed: **INFLEXIBLE**
unchanged, undamaged, whole: **INTACT**
unchaste, morally unrestrained:
LIBERTINE
unchecked, wild: **RAMPANT**
uncivilized person, boor: **YAHOO**
unclean: **UNSAVORY**
unclear: **AMBIGUOUS**
unclear, hazy, misty, vague: **NEBULOUS**
uncle-like: **AVUNCULAR**
uncomfortably small, cramped:
INCOMMODIOUS
uncommunicative: **TACITURN**
uncommunicative, quiet, reserved:
RETICENT
uncompromising, staunch:
DYED-IN-THE-WOOL
unconcealed: **ABOVEBOARD**
unconcealed, open, evident: **OVERT**
unconcerned, apathetic: **INDIFFERENT**
unconcerned, lighthearted, carefree:
INSOUCIANT
unconquerable, impregnable:
INEXPUGNABLE
unconquerable, not capable of being
injured: **INVULNERABLE**

unconscious, lethargic, torpid:
COMATOSE
unconsciously perceived or intended to
be: SUBLIMINAL
unconsciousness caused by injury or
disease: COMA
unconsciousness caused by too little
oxygen: ASPHYXIA
unconscious part of the psyche regarded
as the source of instinctual drives:
ID
unconscious spell: SYNCOPE
uncontestable, indisputable:
IRREFRAGABLE
unconventional, odd: OUTRÉ
unconvincing, inadequate, fragile:
FLIMSY
uncultivated, unseeded: FALLOW
uncultured, unpolished, crude: INCULT
undamaged, whole, unchanged: INTACT
undeceive, free from false or mistaken
ideas: DISABUSE
undecided, wavering: IRRESOLUTE
undefendable: UNTENABLE
undeniable: INCONTROVERTIBLE
undependable person in a group:
WEAK SISTER, WEAK LINK
underdeveloped countries, especially in
Asia and Africa: THIRD WORLD
underdeveloped, inferior in growth or
numbers, few in varieties:
DEPAUPERATE
underdone, poorly made: SLACK-BAKED
under-floor or under-roof low space:
CRAWL SPACE
underground chamber or passageway:
CATACOMB
underground-dwelling gnome, in
German folklore: KOBOLD
underground Soviet Union literature:
SAMIZDAT
underground storehouse: MATTAMORE,
MATAMORO
underground structure or vault:
HYPOGEUM
underground water layer: AQUIFER
underground water source:
GROUNDWATER
underhanded and secret activity, plot:
INTRIGUE
underhandedness, trickery:
SKULDUGGERY
underhanded or shady dealing:
CHICANERY

underlying meaning, message or theme:
SUBTEXT
undermine the morale of, corrupt:
SUBVERT
understandable, clear: PELLUCID
understandable with ease, rational,
clear, bright, shining: LUCID
understanding agreement: ENTENTE
understanding, compatible: SIMPATICO
understanding, knowledge, grasp of
ideas or things: PERCEPTION
understand, interpret, puzzle out:
FATHOM
understatement for effect, a form of
litotes: MEIOSIS
understood, implied: IMPLICIT
understood only by an inner group:
ESOTERIC
understood or implied matter in
addition to what is expressed:
SUBAUDITUR
undertone, in an: SOTTO VOCE
underwater breathing apparatus: SCUBA
underwater euphoria and poor
judgment from excessive
bloodstream nitrogen in diving;
rapture of the deep: NITROGEN
NARCOSIS
underwater mountain on the sea floor:
SEAMOUNT
underwater work chamber: CAISSON
underwater worker or dweller for an
extended period, professional or
scientific diver: AQUANAUT
underwear concealer or negligee jacket:
CAMISOLE
underworld gods, spirits, etc., relating
to: CHTHONIAN, CHTHONIC
underworld vocabulary: ARGOT
undeveloped: LATENT
undisclosed, beyond what is spoken of:
ULTERIOR
undiscovered, unused, untrod hitherto:
VIRGIN
undo, void: NULLIFY
undying, unfading: AMARANTHINE
uneasiness, anxieties, restlessness:
INQUIETUDE
uneasiness, misgiving: QUALM
uneasy: QUEASY
uneatable: INEDIBLE
uneducated, illiterate: UNLETTERED
unemployed people or vagrants:
FLOTSAM
unending: AD INFINITUM

unequal: DISPARATE
unequaled: PEERLESS
unequaled: SANS PAREIL
unequaled, matchless: NONPAREIL
unerring: IMPECCABLE
unerring: INFALLIBLE
unessential: UNIMPORTANT
unethical clash of public duty and
   self-interest: CONFLICT OF
   INTEREST
unexpected and lucky gain or
   acquisition: WINDFALL
unexpected but timely occurrence or
   thing that is most welcome:
   GODSEND
unexpectedly, without warning:
   UNAWARES
unexplainable, beyond science:
   PARANORMAL
unexplored land or area: TERRA
   INCOGNITA
unexpressed, unspoken: INARTICULATE
unfading, undying: AMARANTHINE
unfair: INEQUITABLE
unfair attacker or exploiter:
   CHEAP-SHOT ARTIST
unfair or undeserved accusation or
   judgment, false verdict: BUM RAP
unfaithful, cowardly: RECREANT
unfavorable, inauspicious: UNTOWARD
unfeeling, emotionless, dispassionate:
   AFFECTLESS
unfeeling, hardened: INDURATE
unfeeling, impassive: STOLID
unfeeling, invulnerable: IMPASSIBLE
unfeeling, stupid, foolish: INSENSATE
unfilled orders: BACKLOG
unflagging, tireless: INDEFATIGABLE
unflinching, resolved, determined:
   RESOLUTE
unfocused, general, undirected,
   uncommitted: FREE-FLOATING
unfortunate: STAR-CROSSED
unfortunate, unlucky: HAPLESS
unfriendly: DISAFFECTED
unfriendly: ILL-DISPOSED
unfriendly: INIMICAL
unfruitful, barren: STERILE
ungentlemanly man, offensive intruder,
   cad: BOUNDER
ungodliness, lack of reverence: IMPIETY
ungrateful person: INGRATE
unified: INDISCRETE
uniformity, subordination, repression,

etc., forced on a society by a
   government: GLEICHSCHALTUNG
uniform, similar, like, of the same
   composition throughout:
   HOMOGENEOUS
uniform worn by male household
   servants or employees: LIVERY
unify, bring together into a whole, fit
   together: INTEGRATE
unifying or shaping through art or
   imagination: ESEMPLASTIC
unimaginative: LITERAL
unimportant, frivolous or trifling thing:
   FRIBBLE
unimportant or small details, trifles:
   MINUTIAE
unimportant person or thing: CIPHER
unimportant person or thing:
   NONENTITY
unimportant, trivial: INCONSEQUENTIAL
unimportant, trivial, petty: FRIVOLOUS
uninjured, unpunished, untaxed:
   SCOT-FREE
unintelligible: INCOMPREHENSIBLE
unintelligible speech or sounds:
   GLOSSOLALIA, SPEAKING IN
   TONGUES
unintentional: INADVERTENT
uninterested: APATHETIC
uninterrupted or extended:
   CONTINUOUS
uninvolved, carefree, easygoing: DÉGAGÉ
union members alone allowed to be
   employed: CLOSED SHOP
union membership not required for
   employment: OPEN SHOP
union membership required after
   employment: UNION SHOP
union member who represents fellow
   workers: SHOP STEWARD
union-strike enemy in the form of a
   substituting worker: SCAB
unique, one-of-a-kind: SUI GENERIS
united: IN CONCERT
united in opinion, all assenting:
   UNANIMOUS
United States and Soviet Union:
   SUPERPOWERS
uniting of atomic nuclei into one of
   heavier mass: NUCLEAR FUSION
unit of trading on a stock exchange,
   usually 100 shares: ROUND LOT
unit that is indivisible: MONAD
unity of purpose in relations or
   interests: SOLIDARITY

universal and all-embracing knowledge:
  PANSOPHY
universal, everywhere in presence,
  omnipresent: UBIQUITOUS
universal, widespread, generally
  epidemic: PANDEMIC
universal, worldwide, general, especially
  concerning churches: ECUMENICAL
universe, especially when viewed as a
  unity: MACROCOSM
universe in miniature: MICROCOSM
universe-origin theory that the cosmos
  began with a cataclysm: BIG BANG
  THEORY
universe or the theories of its creation,
  structure, etc.: COSMOLOGY,
  COSMOGONY
unjust: INIQUITOUS
unjustifiable: INSUPPORTABLE
unjustifiable, unprincipled:
  UNCONSCIONABLE
unjustly: UNDULY
unkempt, tousled, rumpled, untidy:
  DISHEVELED
unknowable through perception:
  NOUMENAL
unknown except by a few specially
  instructed individuals, secret,
  abstruse: ESOTERIC
unknown or hidden difficulty: JOKER
unlawful dispossession: DISSEISIN,
  DISSEIZIN
unlawful manner of performing a lawful
  act: MISFEASANCE
unlawful, unauthorized: ILLICIT
unlike, dissimilar, unequal: DISPARATE
unlike, dissimilar, unrelated:
  HETEROGENEOUS
unlikeness: DISSIMILITUDE
unlikeness, inequality: DISPARITY
unlimited as to subject, duration, etc.,
  or, in an investment company, as
  to number of shares: OPEN-ENDED
unlimited authority in a government:
  ABSOLUTISM
unlimited money or authority made
  available: BLANK CHECK
unlucky: ILL-STARRED
unlucky, frustrated, tormented, blighted:
  SNAKEBITTEN
unlucky, unfortunate: HAPLESS
unmanly, woman-like, weak, soft:
  EFFEMINATE
unmarried, abstaining from sexual
  congress: CELIBATE

unmindful, unaware: OBLIVIOUS
unmolested, uninjured, unpunished:
  SCOT-FREE
unmoved, calm, serene: IMPASSIVE
unnatural or disfiguring outgrowth,
  such as a wart: EXCRESCENCE
unoccupied, idle: VACUOUS
unorganized: AMORPHOUS
unorthodox: HETERODOX
unorthodox or liberal in attitudes or
  beliefs: LATITUDINARIAN
unpardonable: IRREMISSIBLE
unperceivable by the sense of touch:
  IMPALPABLE
unperceptive: PURBLIND
unpleasant in appearance, ugly,
  disagreeable: ILL-FAVORED
unpleasant-to-look-at thing: EYESORE
unplowed land near a fence or at the
  end of furrows: HEADLAND
unpolished, crude, uncultured: INCULT
unpolished, uncouth: AGRESTIC
unpractical, though romantic or
  chivalric in intentions: QUIXOTIC
unpredictable, uncertain:
  INCALCULABLE
unpremeditated: EXTEMPORANEOUS
unpremeditated: SPONTANEOUS
unpremeditated homicide in a sudden
  fight: CHANCE-MEDLEY
unprepared, spontaneous: IMPROMPTU
unprincipled, unjustifiable:
  UNCONSCIONABLE
unprovoked, unjust, malicious: WANTON
unpunished, uninjured, unmolested:
  SCOT-FREE
unquestionable: VERITABLE
unquestionable, certain: INDUBITABLE
unquestionable, unassailable:
  INCONTESTABLE
unreadable: INDECIPHERABLE
unreal, false, invented: FICTITIOUS
unreal, fanciful, high-flown: AIRY-FAIRY
unreal or removed refuge: IVORY
  TOWER
unreasonable: ABSONANT
unreasoning: IRRATIONAL
unreasoning devotion to one's race,
  country, etc.: CHAUVINISM
unreasoning passion, foolish love:
  INFATUATION
unreceptive, not open: IMPERVIOUS
unrefined, coarse, natural: EARTHY
unrefined, rough, crude: UNCOUTH

unrelated to the matter at hand, coming from without: EXTRANEOUS

unrelated, unlike, dissimilar: HETEROGENEOUS

unrelenting, merciless: IMPLACABLE

unreliable: IRRESPONSIBLE

unreliable: SKITTISH

unremediable, incurable: IRREMEDIABLE

unreserved, absolute: IMPLICIT

unrestrained: IMMODERATE

unrestrained, excessive: WANTON

unrestrained in speech or action: INTEMPERATE

unrestrained, unchecked: INCONTINENT

unrestricted authority: CARTE BLANCHE

unrivaled: INAPPROACHABLE

unruffled, calm: IMPERTURBABLE

unruly, boisterous: OBSTREPEROUS

unruly, difficult, stubborn: INTRACTABLE

unruly, fidgety, restless: RESTIVE

unruly, loud: RAUCOUS

unruly, malicious, fierce: VICIOUS

unruly, rebellious, irritable, cranky: FRACTIOUS

unscrupulous: UNCONSCIONABLE

unscrupulous and shrewd person: SNOLLYGOSTER

unseeable because of smallness: IMPERCEPTIBLE

unseeded, uncultivated: FALLOW

unseemly: INDECOROUS

unseen or unexamined purchase: PIG IN A POKE

unselfish devotion to others: ALTRUISM

unsettled, difficult to solve: PROBLEMATIC

unsettled, vague: INDETERMINATE

unskilled worker: BLUE-COLLAR WORKER

unsociable, fierce, wild: FAROUCHE

unsophisticated, artless, unaffected, uninstructed, simple: NAIVE

unsophisticated, narrow: PROVINCIAL

unspoken, silent: TACIT

unspoken, unexpressed: INARTICULATE

unstable, changeable: LABILE

unstable, fleeting, transient, fickle: VOLATILE

unsteady or irregular movement at sea: YAW

unsteady, wavering: FLUCTUATING

unsteady, wavering, wobbling: TITUBANT

unsubstantial, flimsy, weak: TENUOUS

unsuccessful, fruitless: INEFFECTUAL

unsuccessful, futile: UNAVAILING

unsuccessfully conclude a project: ABORT

unsuccessful, short of one's goal: MANQUÉ

unsuitability: INAPTITUDE

unsuitable, inappropriate, at odds with: INCONGRUOUS

unsuitable, untimely: INOPPORTUNE

unsure, risky: PRECARIOUS

unsurmountable: INSUPERABLE

untanned skin of a calf or lamb: KIP

unthinking, thoughtless: INCOGITANT

untidy in appearance: BLOWZY

untidy or careless person: SLOVEN

untidy or slovenly woman: SLATTERN

untidy, slovenly: UNKEMPT

untidy, soiled: BEDRAGGLED

untidy, unkempt, tousled, rumpled: DISHEVELED

untimely, unsuitable: INOPPORTUNE

untrustworthy person: SNAKE IN THE GRASS

untruthful: MENDACIOUS

unusable: IMPRACTICABLE

unused, brand-new or original condition: MINT CONDITION

unused condition, neglect: DESUETUDE

unusual happening: PHENOMENON

unutterable: INEFFABLE

unwavering, firmly faithful: STEADFAST

unwavering, steadfast, firmly directed: INTENT

unwelcome or unacceptable person: PERSONA NON GRATA

unwholesome and noxious atmosphere, influence, effect, etc.: MIASMA

unwieldly, ponderous, enormous: ELEPHANTINE

unwilling, reluctant: LOATH

unwise: INADVISABLE

unwise, imprudent: INDISCREET

unworkable, not usable or achievable: IMPRACTICABLE

unyielding: ADAMANT

unyielding: INDUCTILE

unyielding, aggressive: TRUCULENT

unyielding, refusing to compromise or come to terms: INTRANSIGENT

unyielding, resistant: IMPREGNABLE

unyielding, stubborn: INFLEXIBLE

upbraid, denounce scathingly: EXCORIATE

up for consideration: ON THE TAPIS
upheaval that is violent: CATACLYSM
upholstery or drapery fabric with
    varicolored stripes of satin or
    moiré: TABARET
uplift, enlighten, benefit: EDIFY
upper-class, aristocratic: PATRICIAN
upper-class customers or patrons:
    CARRIAGE TRADE
upper-class rule: ARISTOCRACY
upright kind of type, used in most
    printing: ROMAN
uprightness, correctness of judgment:
    RECTITUDE
uproar: BALLYHOO
uproar: BROUHAHA
uproar, brawl, conflict, fight: FRAY
uproar, confused sound: HUBBUB
uproar of a crowd: TUMULT
uproar, ruckus, confusion:
    HULLABALOO
uprooted, displaced, away from one's
    native place: DERACINATED
uproot, eradicate, dislocate, extirpate:
    DERACINATE
uprooting, forcible extraction:
    EVULSION
uproot, pull up by the roots, destroy
    utterly, erase: ERADICATE
upset, confuse, distract, throw off:
    DISCOMBOBULATE
upset, confuse, frustrate: DISCONCERT
upset, disturb, alarm: PERTURB
upset, irritate: RUFFLE
upside down: TOPSY-TURVY
upstart: JACKANAPES
upstart, newly rich or influential person:
    PARVENU
up-to-date: AU COURANT
upward leap made by a trained horse:
    CAPRIOLE
upward stroke of a small letter
    (typography): ASCENDER
upward trend in stock market prices:
    UPSIDE
urban complex: CONURBATION
urbane, cheerful, lively: DEBONAIR
urbane, gracious: SUAVE

urge by earnest appeal, recommend
    strongly, advise: EXHORT
urgent: IMPERIOUS
urgent, demanding immediate action:
    EXIGENT
urgently necessary, unavoidable,
    authoritative: IMPERATIVE
urge on, drive or force to action: IMPEL
urge on, stir up, spur into action:
    INCITE
urinary system as a branch of medicine:
    UROLOGY
urinate: MICTURATE
urinating backward, as a female:
    RETROMINGENT
urination-increasing substance:
    DIURETIC
urination that is excessive: DIURESIS
urination that is involuntary: ENURESIS
urine of cattle or horses: STALE
urn of metal for heating water for tea:
    SAMOVAR
usage-based law, rather than legislation:
    UNWRITTEN LAW
used to, accustomed to, habituated:
    WONT
useful or valuable in a functional way,
    practical: UTILITARIAN
useless: INUTILE
useless, ineffectual: OTIOSE
useless person or thing: DEADWOOD
useless work: BOONDOGGLE
U-shaped or horseshoe-shaped:
    HIPPOCREPIFORM
U-shaped piece of metal with pointed
    ends, used as a fastener: STAPLE
usurp: ARROGATE
utensils and serving dishes that are
    concave or bowl-like:
    HOLLOWWARE
uterine cancer test: PAP TEST
uterus's partial or complete removal:
    HYSTERECTOMY
uterus tissue removal through medical
    scraping: DILATION AND
    CURETTAGE (D & C)
utilitarian, prosaically practical or
    functional: BANAUSIC

vacation or paid leave of absence for one year, as for a professor to do research, originally granted every seven years: **SABBATICAL**

vacillate, veer, shift about: **WHIFFLE**

vagrant on the beach living off what he can find: **BEACHCOMBER**

vagrants, unattached persons: **FLOTSAM**

vague: **AMBIGUOUS**

vague concept, general idea: **NOTION**

vague, confused: **HAZY**

vague idea, notion, slight suggestion, hint: **INKLING**

vague, indefinite: **INTANGIBLE**

vague state between two others: **LIMBO**

vague, subtle: **INDEFINABLE**

vague, unclear, hazy, misty: **NEBULOUS**

vague, unsettled: **INDETERMINATE**

vain, silly or foppish behavior: **COXCOMBRY**

valiant, courageous: **METTLESOME**

valley or mountain pass that is narrow: **DEFILE**

value, in proportion to: **AD VALOREM**

valueless or worthless thing: **TINKER'S DAMN**

valueless though showy things or matter, junk: **TRUMPERY**

value of a bond, as it appears on the security: **FACE VALUE**

value of a business in excess of liabilities: **EQUITY**

value of a nation's annual output of goods and services before any deductions: **GROSS NATIONAL PRODUCT (GNP)**

value per share, calculated by totaling market price and deducting all liabilities: **NET ASSET VALUE**

valve or faucet used to drain off water or air: **PETCOCK**

vanish gradually, disappear by degrees: **EVANESCE**

vanquish, as in battle, or defeat the purposes of: **DISCOMFIT**

variation or inflection of words: **ACCIDENCE**

variations or changes occurring irregularly, as of fortune: **VICISSITUDES**

varied, diverse to a great degree: **MULTIFARIOUS**

varied, unalike: **DIVERSE**

varied, with many forms: **MANIFOLD**

varied without limit: **OMNIFARIOUS**

variegated in color or other elements: **MOTLEY**

variegated, spotted: **DAPPLED**

variety of things, miscellaneous collection: **OMNIUM-GATHERUM**

various, several, many: **DIVERS**

vary or change often and in irregular manner: **FLUCTUATE**

vary or diversify by interjecting something different: **INTERLARD**

vary, revise, restrict, limit: **MODIFY**

vary the products of a business so as to expand it: **DIVERSIFY**

vary the tone or pitch of the voice, modulate: **INFLECT**

vast and indefinite in number, innumerable: **MYRIAD**

vast, limitless: **INFINITE**

vat used by brewers for fermenting: **TUN**

veal cutlet breaded and garnished: **WIENER SCHNITZEL**

veal or chicken stuffed or layered with

ham and cheese before sautéing:
CORDON BLEU

veal thin-sliced and sautéed:
SCALOPPINE

veer, vacillate, shift about: WHIFFLE

vegetables and often a dip as appetizer:
CRUDITÉS

vegetable slicer in the form of a slanted
board with an adjustable blade:
MANDOLINE

vegetarian who also eats dairy products:
LACTARIAN, LACTOVEGETARIAN

vegetarian who also eats eggs and dairy
products: OVOLACTARIAN,
LACTO-OVO-VEGETARIAN

vegetate, become dull or inert:
STAGNATE

vegetation: VERDURE

vehemently censure: INVEIGH

vehicles traveling together: CARAVAN

vehicle that carries passengers for a
small fee: JITNEY

vehicle with three wheels moved by
pedaling: PEDICAB

veiling or seclusion of women: PURDAH

velvety, covered with soft hairs:
VELUTINOUS

venerable, classic, time-honored:
VINTAGE

vengeance or just retribution as
identified with an antagonist or
thing: NEMESIS

veranda furnished and used as a living
room: LANAI

verbal contention, argument about
words: LOGOMACHY

verbal fencing in classical and
Elizabethan dramatic dialogue:
STICHOMYTHIA

verbally compressed: HOLOPHRASTIC

verbal noun: GERUND

verb form that relates to the time of
action: TENSE

verb mood used to express hypothesis,
possibility, or a nonfactual
condition: SUBJUNCTIVE

verb of weak form that links subject
and predicate: COPULA

verbose: PROLIX

verbose: REDUNDANT

verbose, wordy: DIFFUSE

verb that forms its past tense by an
internal vowel change: STRONG
VERB

verb that forms its past tense with

suffixes but not by internal vowel
change, as "rain": WEAK VERB

verb that is a copula, serving mainly as
a connection between the subject
and predicate: LINKING VERB

verse containing eight lines and two
rhymes (a-b-a-a-a-b-a-b) with the
first line repeated as the fourth and
seventh, and the second as the
eighth: TRIOLET

verse form of three-line groups, or
tercets, in which the first and third
lines rhyme with the second line of
the preceding tercet (aba, bcb, cbc,
etc.): TERZA RIMA

verse free of conventional meter and
rhyme: FREE VERSE

verse, humorous and about a person,
containing four lines and the
rhyme scheme a-a-b-b: CLERIHEW

verse, humorous and often bawdy,
containing five lines with the
rhyme scheme a-a-b-b-a: LIMERICK

verse in praise of wine and sensual
pleasures: ANACREONTIC

verse of three stanzas and an envoy,
with the last line of each the same:
BALLADE

verse rhythm analysis: SCANSION

verse's feet analyzed: SCANNED

verse that ends with a lack of a syllable
in its final foot: CATALECTIC

verse that is humorous, metrical and
usually rhymed: LIGHT VERSE

verse that is trivial and awkwardly
written: DOGGEREL

verse using different meters:
POLYMETRY

verse with two feet to the line:
DIMETER

vertical: PERPENDICULAR

vertical sidepiece in a door or a window
sash: STILE

vertical-takeoff and -landing plane:
VTOL

very much: BEAUCOUP

vessel that services another at sea:
TENDER

veto effected by the U.S. president by
not signing a bill by the time
Congress adjourns: POCKET VETO

vex, annoy, weary: IRK

vibrate, throb regularly: PULSATE

vibrating effect produced on a stringed

instrument or with the voice:
TREMOLO
vibration or sound caused by the hitting
of one body against another:
PERCUSSION
vibration sensitivity or awareness:
PALLESTHESIA
vicarious sharing of another's emotions
or feelings: EMPATHY
vice-ridden and corruption-ridden area
of a city: TENDERLOIN
vicious, inhuman, cruel: FELL
victimized or injured by one's plans to
injure another: HOIST BY ONE'S
OWN PETARD
victimized person, dupe, sucker: PATSY
victims of poverty or discrimination:
UNDERPRIVILEGED
victory at great cost, Pyrrhic victory:
CADMEAN VICTORY
viewer with two eyepieces for
combining slightly divergent images
for a three-dimensional effect:
STEREOSCOPE
view in all directions: PANORAMA
vie with or rival successfully: EMULATE
view of the proportional relation of
parts to the whole, as in art or
architecture: PERSPECTIVE
vigilant, watchful: JEALOUS
vigor, dash: VERVE
vigor or youthful feeling restored:
REJUVENATION
vigorous, interesting: SUCCULENT
vigorous, large, swift, dashing:
SPANKING
vigorous, lively: VIBRANT
vigor, strength, endurance: STAMINA
vile, base, degraded: SORDID
vile, contemptible: DESPICABLE
vile, evil: NEFARIOUS
vileness, depravity, baseness:
TURPITUDE
vilify, abuse: REVILE
village: HAMLET
villain: BLACKGUARD
vinegary: ACETOUS
vineyard on a hillside: COTE
violation of a law or a pledge:
INFRACTION
violation of conventional language
usage: SOLECISM
violation or profaning of anything
sacred: SACRILEGE

violent and loud denunciation:
FULMINATION
violent disturbance: CATACLYSM
violent, impetuous, ardent: VEHEMENT
violent, intermittent: SPASMODIC
violently destructive: BERSERK
violent outbreak: RAMPAGE
violent reaction: BACKLASH
violent, stormy: TEMPESTUOUS
violent, sudden outburst: PAROXYSM
violinist who leads his section of an
orchestra and is considered
assistant conductor:
CONCERTMASTER
violin-like instrument that is slightly
larger and tuned lower: VIOLA
Virgin Mary holding the body of Jesus
represented in art: PIETÀ
virgin, woman of pure character:
VESTAL
visible or observable occurrence or
experience: PHENOMENON
visible to the naked eye: MACROSCOPIC
visionary, dreamer: FANTAST
visionary or imaginary semblance:
SIMULACRUM
vision being dimmed: PURBLIND
vision blurring or temporary loss caused
by oxygen deficiency, experienced
especially by pilots: GRAYOUT
vision defect in which specks or threads
appear to float before the eyes:
MUSCAE VOLITANTES
vision less distinct by day than by
night, day blindness:
HEMERALOPIA
vision of something not actually
present: HALLUCINATION
vision or discernment faultiness:
MYOPIA
vision that is distorted: ASTIGMATISM
vision that is normal at twenty feet:
20-20 VISION
visitor who frequents a place: HABITUÉ
visual arts involving the use of lines or
strokes on a flat surface, as
painting or drawing: GRAPHIC
ARTS
visual defects treated by exercises:
ORTHOPTICS
visualizing objects previously seen:
EIDETIC IMAGERY
vital principle: ANIMA
vital statistics, as of births, deaths,
disease: DEMOGRAPHY

vivacity, enthusiasm, dash: ÉLAN

vivacity, lively spirits, gaiety, sparkle: EFFERVESCENCE

vivid: GRAPHIC

vividly bright, shining with brilliance, dazzling: RESPLENDENT

vivid, sensational, shocking, violent: LURID

vocabulary of a class or group: ARGOT

vocabulary or jargon of a profession or class: LINGO

vocabulary that is specialized or technical and used by members of a particular group: JARGON

vocabulary, words in a language: LEXICON, LEXIS

vocalist's runs and trills: COLORATURA

vocal quality that is dry and rough or coarse is: HUSKY

vodka-and-orange-juice cocktail: SCREWDRIVER

vodka-and-tomato-juice cocktail: BLOODY MARY

vogue word, especially in government, business or science: BUZZWORD

voice-affecting throat irritation: LARYNGITIS

vocal improvisation in jazz: SCAT

voice in a motion picture or on television commenting on the picture or narrating: VOICE-OVER

voice of a male higher than a tenor: COUNTERTENOR

voice of the people: VOX POPULI

voice tone or pitch variations or modulations: INFLECTION

voiding, nullifying: DEFEASANCE

voiding, nullifying: DIRIMENT

void, undo: NULLIFY

volatile, lively, changeable: MERCURIAL

volcanic cone-like mound: CINDER CONE

volcanic hole emitting gases: FUMAROLE

volume of bids and offers on stocks is relatively low: THIN MARKET

vomit: REGURGITATE

vomiting: EMESIS

vomiting action causing strain: RETCH

vomiting-causing medicine: EMETIC

vomitously heave, retch: KECK

voodoo or witchcraft sticking of pins into a doll: INVULTUATION

vote against: BLACKBALL

vote by the people on a special issue or proposed measure or law: REFERENDUM

voters, supporters: CONSTITUENCY

votes and influence being traded between politicians: LOGROLLING

votes for a candidate in excess of the number cast for his nearest opponent: PLURALITY

vote that is unofficial and used to determine group opinion: STRAW POLL, STRAW VOTE

vote to obtain the people's will on an issue: PLEBISCITE

voting right: SUFFRAGE

vowel change for changed tense: ABLAUT

vowel insertion into a word: ANAPTYXIS

vowel lost at the beginning of a word: APHESIS

vowel marking (straight line) over a vowel to indicate a long sound: MACRON

vowel that is neutral, occurring in unstressed syllables in English: SCHWA

V-shaped: VULVIFORM

V-shape-headed can opener: CHURCH KEY

V-shaped insignia: CHEVRON

vulgar, common: PLEBEIAN

vulgar, disreputable, tawdry: RAFFISH

vulgar language or behavior: BAWDRY

vulgar, obscene: FESCENNINE

vulgar or coarse joking: RIBALD

vulgar, sexual, cheap: RAUNCHY

vulgar talk: BILLINGSGATE

vulnerable: PREGNABLE

vulnerable point: ACHILLES' HEEL

wad of compressed cotton or lint used for a wound: **PLEDGET**

wages remaining after payroll deductions: **TAKE-HOME PAY**

Wagnerian tenor: **HELDENTENOR**

wagon maker: **WAINWRIGHT**

wagon without sides: **LORRY**

wail, howl, hoot: **ULULATE**

wail in lament for the deceased: **KEEN**

wail, whimper, cry: **PULE**

waistband that is broad and worn with men's formal clothes: **CUMMERBUND**

waist flap attached to a garment, short shirt-like section: **PEPLUM**

waist measure: **GIRTH**

waiter or waitress at a drive-in restaurant: **CARHOP**

wait for and accost: **WAYLAY**

waiting or not acting as a strategy: **WAITING GAME**

waiting room in a theater used by performers when they are off-stage: **GREEN ROOM**

wakefulness-preceding, just before waking: **HYPNOPOMPIC**

walk, able to: **AMBULATORY**

walk about idly or aimlessly, gad about: **TRAIPSE**

walk around something: **CIRCUMAMBULATE**

walk by a performer that makes the feet seem to glide: **MOONWALK**

walk clumsily with short steps while swaying from side to side: **WADDLE**

walker: **PEDESTRIAN**

walk heavily: **CLUMP**

walk in a leisurely way: **AMBLE**

walk in a leisurely way, stroll: **SAUNTER**

walking as a health regimen: **CONSTITUTIONAL**

walking or moving about, itinerant: **PERIPATETIC**

walking space that is narrow and elevated: **CATWALK**

walking with short, dainty steps: **MINCING**

walking with the toes or feet characteristically turned in: **PIGEON-TOED**

walk laboriously, trudge: **PLOD**

walk or promenade bordered by trees: **ALAMEDA**

walk with a latticework roof, arbor: **PERGOLA**

wall bracket that holds candles or lights: **SCONCE**

wall crack filler: **SPACKLE**

wall hanging attached to a roller, devised by Japanese: **KAKEMONO**

wall molding close to the floor: **BASEBOARD**

wall-mounted, ornamental and often mirrored bracket for candles: **GIRANDOLE**

wall offshore to break the force of waves: **BREAKWATER**

wall of stone, cement, etc., for protective purposes: **REVETMENT**

wall or partition within a boat: **BULKHEAD**

wall painting by an artist: **MURAL**

wall paneling of wood or marble: **WAINSCOT**

wall plaster, whitewash coating: **PARGET**

wall scribblings or drawings: **GRAFFITI**

wall support that is a rectangular column: **PILASTER**

wan, colorless: PALLID
wanderer, tramp: VAGABOND
wanderer without a permanent home:
   NOMAD
wander from the main subject: DIGRESS
wander idly or without plan: MEANDER
wandering from the point, passing
   quickly from one subject to
   another: DISCURSIVE
wandering, roving, straying, itinerant:
   ERRANT
wander or stray aimlessly, digress:
   DIVAGATE
wand or staff of Mercury, symbol of the
   medical profession: CADUCEUS
wanted, desired or aimed-for thing:
   DESIDERATUM
wanting one's own way: WAYWARD
wanton, lewd: CYPRIAN
warding off, preventing: PREVENTIVE
ward off: STAVE OFF
ward off, avoid, turn aside: PARRY
ward off, drive back: REPEL
wardrobe or large cupboard that is
   usually ornate: ARMOIRE
wardrobe with drawers on one side:
   CHIFFOROBE
warhead of a missile: PAYLOAD
war-like, brave, disciplined: SPARTAN
warm, glowing, earnest: FERVENT
warmth, increasing warmth:
   CALESCENCE
warmth toward others, cordiality,
   friendliness that is effusive:
   EMPRESSEMENT
warning: CAVEAT
warning notice: MONITION
warning off, as an animal emitting a
   spray or sound or changing its
   coloration: APOSEMATIC
warning, omen, portent: PRESAGE
warning or danger sign, especially in
   zoology: SEMATIC
warning or reminding story:
   CAUTIONARY TALE
warning system by radar in North
   America: DEW (DISTANT EARLY
   WARNING) LINE
warn, presage, foreshadow: PORTEND
war-provoking event: CASUS BELLI
war-strategy game played in miniature:
   KRIEGSPIEL
wart-like skin protrusion near the
   genitals or anus: CONDYLOMA
wart or other skin growth: KERATOSIS

war, treaties and international relations,
   concerning: FETIAL
washing the body: ABLUTION
wasps, wasp colony: VESPIARY
waste: RECREMENT
wasted, scattered: DISSIPATED
wasteful, extravagant, lavish: PRODIGAL
waste matter from the body: EGESTA
waste matter from the bowels, feces:
   EXCREMENT
waste matter, refuse: DROSS
waste-matter-removing, as by the
   kidneys or intestines: EMUNCTORY
waste or entrails of a butchered animal:
   OFFAL
waste time, be idle, fool around: FUTZ
waste time, dawdle: PIDDLE
waste time, dawdle, fool around:
   LALLYGAG, LOLLYGAG
waste time, dawdle, loiter:
   DILLY-DALLY
waste time, loiter: DAWDLE
wasting away: TABESCENT
wasting or withering away: ATROPHY
watchful, alert: VIGILANT
watchful and repressive authorities,
   government, etc.: BIG BROTHER
watchful, eagle-eyed, alert: ARGUS-EYED
watchful supervision or care,
   monitoring from above: OVERSIGHT
watchful, suspicious: JEALOUS
watching and guarding carefully: WARY
watch kept over one: SURVEILLANCE
watch kept, usually at night: VIGIL
watchman, keeper, guard: WARDER
watch pocket: FOB
water-and-land vehicle or creature:
   AMPHIBIAN
water bag for military troops: LISTER
   BAG
water channel made with a gate to
   regulate the flow: SLUICE
water channel or apron to divert excess
   flow: SPILLWAY
water clock (flow of water to measure
   time): CLEPSYDRA
water-collecting hole or pit at the
   bottom of a shaft or hole: SUMP
watercolor: AQUARELLE
watercourse used for energy or
   industry: RACE
water craft with wing-like structures
   that lift the hull above the water at
   certain speeds: HYDROFOIL
water cure: HYDROPATHY

waterfront or river vessels laborer: ROUSTABOUT

water layer separating the warmer surface layer from a colder one below: THERMOCLINE

water layer underground: AQUIFER

water nymph: NAIAD

water nymph of folklore, who could obtain a soul by marrying a human and bearing his child: UNDINE

water of the soil not available to plants: ECHARD

waterproof broad-brimmed hat: SOUTHWESTER

water rushing onto the beach with the tide: SWASH

water search with a divining rod: DOWSE

water self-lifesaving technique: DROWNPROOFING

water signs as a means of divination: HYDROMANCY

waters of the earth as a study: HYDROLOGY

water source geologically, as for springs and wells: AQUIFER

water source underground: GROUNDWATER

water sprite in Germanic folklore: NIXIE

water storage receptacle: CISTERN

waters under the jurisdiction of a state: TERRITORIAL WATERS

water surface of a lake's waving movement: SEICHE

watertight chamber for construction in a body of water: COFFERDAM

water vertical pipe or tower: STANDPIPE

watery: AQUEOUS

wave, flood: SPRING TIDE

wave-like or watered appearance, as in fabrics: MOIRÉ

wavering, undecided: IRRESOLUTE

wavering, unsteady: FLUCTUATING

wavering, wobbling, unsteady: TITUBANT

waver, sway, totter: VACILLATE

waves that are long and don't crest: SWELLS

wave's upward convex hump, ascending to the crest: SCEND

wave that breaks on a reef, rock or shore: BREAKER

waving motion: WAFTURE

wavy-edged, bordered with notches or undulations: SCALLOPED

wavy in appearance or motion: UNDULATING

wavy- or curly-haired: CYMOTRICHOUS

wavy, winding: SINUOUS

wayfarer, traveler: VIATOR

waylay: AMBUSH

way of entry: ACCESS

weak: ANILE

weak and emaciated condition: CACHEXIA

weak, barren: EFFETE

weak, careless, reckless: FECKLESS

weak, cowardly: PUSILLANIMOUS

weaken by degrees, impair secretly: UNDERMINE

weaken, destroy the affection of: DISAFFECT

weakened, thinned out, somewhat strained: ATTENUATED

weaken, hang down: FLAG

weakening, tiring: FLAGGING

weaken, make feeble or languid: DEBILITATE

weaken, pine, droop gradually: LANGUISH

weaken, sap the strength of, devitalize: ENERVATE

weak, flimsy, unsubstantial: TENUOUS

weak, ineffective: IMPOTENT

weak, listless, lacking animation: LANGUID

weak, loose: SLACK

weakness, fatigue, spiritlessness, dreaminess, dullness, stagnation: LANGUOR

weakness or a failing in one's character: FOIBLE

weak person: WIMP

weak, self-indulgent: EFFEMINATE

weak, unconvincing, fragile: FLIMSY

wealth as a science: CHREMATISTICS

wealth pursuer: CHREMATIST

wealth, riches: OPULENCE

wealthy and powerful industrialist: TYCOON

wealthy, fashionable people: JET SET

wealthy man: CROESUS

wealthy person who has become so only recently: NOUVEAU RICHE

wealthy, privileged or status-conscious as consumers: UPSCALE

wealthy young woman or debutante typically belonging to the Association of Junior Leagues of

America, a civic and charitable organization: JUNIOR LEAGUER

wean: ABLACTATE

weaponry-rich status, power or might in arms: ARMIPOTENCE

wear away by friction: ABRADE

wearied, exhausted, sated, worn-out, dulled from overindulgence: JADED

wearing away or eating away of a substance: CORROSION

wearing off or rubbing off of particles: DETRITION

wearisome, boring: TEDIOUS

weary, vex, annoy: IRK

weather and atmospheric conditions as a science: METEOROLOGY

weather-beaten and rugged: GNARLED

weather that is dark and threatening is: LOWERING

weave together, combine, blend: INTERLACE

web-footed or web-fingered: SYNDACTYL

wedding-night noisy serenade by friends: CHARIVARI, SHIVAREE

wedding song or poem: HYMENEAL

wedged or packed firmly: IMPACTED

wedge-shaped, especially as used in ancient writing: CUNEAL, CUNEIFORM

weed killer: HERBICIDE

weeping or grief that is false: CROCODILE TEARS

weigh down, burden, hamper: CUMBER, ENCUMBER

weighing, resting, leaning upon something: INCUMBENT

weight: HEFT

weight a missile can lift and carry to a target: THROW-WEIGHT

weight being visibly lost, abnormally lean: EMACIATED

weightlessness in space is caused by: ZERO GRAVITY

weight of a container deducted to find the weight of its contents: TARE

weight unit for gems: CARAT

weird, eerie: ELDRITCH

weird, ghostly: EERIE

weird, unnatural, eerie, strange: UNCANNY

welcome in the form of an outburst of applause: OVATION

welcome or acceptable person: PERSONA GRATA

welfare assistance (Canadian): POGEY

welfare of all, general good: COMMONWEAL

well-being or happiness as found in a life of moderation: EUDEMONIA

well-being, relaxation, happiness: EUPHORIA

well-bred, distinguished, dignified: DISTINGUÉ

well-bred ways, refinement: GENTILITY

well-chosen, apt, agreeable in manner or style: FELICITOUS

well-groomed: SOIGNÉ

well-groomed, smooth, glossy: SLEEK

well-off, privileged or status-conscious as consumers: UPSCALE

well-to-do customers or patrons: CARRIAGE TRADE

Welsh eloquence or emotional oratory: HWYL

Welsh singing-and-poetry festival: EISTEDDFOD

werewolf: LYCANTHROPE

werewolf: LOUP-GAROU

Western cord-like necktie: BOLO TIE

Western Hemisphere: OCCIDENT

Western hill or mountain with a usually flat top: BUTTE

West Indian, Spanish American or Gulf State inhabitant of European descent: CREOLE

wetland grass, sedge: BULRUSH

whale oil: TRAIN OIL

whales as a study: CETOLOGY

whale (sperm whale) waxy substance used in perfumes: AMBERGRIS

wharf for loading and unloading vessels: QUAY

wharf or pier to protect a harbor or beach: JETTY

what is appropriate: COMME IL FAUT

what will be, will be (Spanish): QUÉ SERÁ, SERÁ

wheedle: CAJOLE

wheedle, flatter: BLANDISH

wheel about: CARACOLE

wheel heavy enough to resist sudden changes of speed: FLYWHEEL

wheel on a fixed axis and containing seats hanging from frame: FERRIS WHEEL

wheel or ball mounted to swivel, as on a chair leg: CASTER

wheel-shaped: ROTIFORM

wheel, spiked or toothed, at the end of a spur: ROWEL

wheels with the rims slanted in or out from the hub are: DISHED

wheel with teeth or notches into which something can lock and stop motion: RATCHET WHEEL

Where are the snows of yesteryear?: OÙ SONT LES NEIGES D'ANTAN?

which was to be proved or demonstrated: Q.E.D. (QUOD ERAT DEMONSTRANDUM)

while away the time: BEGUILE

whim: CAPRICE

whim, fancy, peculiarity: CROTCHET

whimper, wail, cry: PULE

whimsical or lighthearted sense: PICKWICKIAN SENSE

whine, complain: KVETCH

whiner, nag, pest: NUDGE, NOODGE

whining, complaining, fretful: QUERULOUS

whiplash-like, long, slender and flexible: FLAGELLIFORM

whip, scourge: FLAGELLATE

whirling on the toes in ballet dancing: PIROUETTE

whirling, revolving or circular in motion: GYRAL

whirling, rotating rapidly: VORTICOSE

whirling, spinning, dizzy: VERTIGINOUS

whirlpool: MAELSTROM

whirlwind of sand that is small: DUST DEVIL

whirlwind, whirlpool: VORTEX

whisky-and-vermouth cocktail: MANHATTAN

whispered, softly or privately spoken, in an undertone: SOTTO VOCE

whispering, rustling, softly murmuring: SUSURRANT

whisper intended to be overheard: STAGE WHISPER

whistle or call that is derisive: CATCALL

whistle, slender and silver, used on ships: BOATSWAIN'S WHISTLE

white linen oblong garment worn around the neck by a priest: AMICE

whitening: ALBESCENT

whiten or turn yellowish, as a plant does when kept from sunlight: ETIOLATE

white or European gentleman or official in imperial India: SAHIB

white or European woman in imperial India, lady: MEMSAHIB

white- or gray-haired, ancient, venerable: HOARY

white-skinned and pink-eyed person: ALBINO

whitewash coating, wall plaster: PARGET

who goes there?: QUI VIVE?

whole composed of originally separate parts: SYNTHESIS

whole number: INTEGER

whole-oriented with regard to bodily health, mind and spirit: HOLISTIC

wholesaler: JOBBER

wholesome: SALUTARY

whole that is uninterrupted: CONTINUUM

whole, unchanged, undamaged: INTACT

whooping cough: PERTUSSIS

whore: HARLOT

whorehouse: BORDELLO

wicked: INIQUITOUS

wicked, atrocious: FLAGITIOUS

wicked, atrocious, odious: HEINOUS

wicked, erring: PERVERSE

wickedness, monstrous act: ENORMITY

wicked, ominous: SINISTER

wicked, vicious woman: JEZEBEL

wicked, vile: NEFARIOUS

wicker receptacle for documents or valuables: HANAPER

wickerwork material from a tough-stemmed palm: RATTAN

wide and random in focus, haphazard, dispersed, indiscriminate: SCATTERSHOT

wide-awake, on the alert: ON THE QUI VIVE

widely practiced, common: PREVALENT

widen, swell, expand: DILATE

wider at the top, flared upward: EVASÉ

widespread: RAMPANT

widespread, prevalent: RIFE

widespread, universal, generally epidemic: PANDEMIC

wife: HELPMEET

wifely: UXORIAL

wifely to an excessive degree, fond of or submissive to one's husband: MARITORIOUS

wife or husband: CONSORT

wife's scolding in bed or in private: CURTAIN LECTURE

wife who murders her husband: MARITICIDE

wig for a man: TOUPEE

wild: BERSERK

wild, frenzied, orgiastic, pagan, passionate: DIONYSIAN

wild, irresponsible, reckless: HARUM-SCARUM

wildly excited: DELIRIOUS

wildly wasteful or extravagant, sinful, dissipated: PROFLIGATE

wild or wanton revelry, drunken carousal, debauchment: ORGY

wild party: BACCHANAL

wild passion: AMOUR FOU

wild prank, escapade: CAPER

wild, riotous: TURBULENT

wild, savage: FERAL

wild, unchecked: RAMPANT

wild, unexpected action: VAGARY

wild uproar: PANDEMONIUM

will exercised: VOLITION

willful, capricious: WAYWARD

willing, desirous: SOLICITOUS

willingly, gladly: FAIN

willingly or unwillingly: WILLY-NILLY

willingly, readily: LIEF

willingness that is cheerful: ALACRITY

will maker, one who has left a will: TESTATOR

will-o'-the-wisp, delusion: IGNIS FATUUS

willowy, slender, slim: SVELTE

willpower loss, inability to decide or act: ABULIA

will rather than reason stressed as the active factor in man's role in a hostile world: EXISTENTIALISM

willy-nilly: NOLENS VOLENS

wily, treacherous, cunning: INSIDIOUS

win by cleverness: OUTWIT

wind, cold and dry, that blows from the north through southern France: MISTRAL

wind direction indicator consisting of a cone-shaped cloth bag, as at an airfield: WIND SOCK

wind-driven rain or snow: SCUD

wind from ahead blowing directly opposite to the course of a ship: HEAD WIND

wind from the east in Mediterranean regions: LEVANTER

wind from the Sahara that blows in the Middle East before the vernal equinox: KHAMSIN

wind, hot and dry, of Southern California: SANTA ANA

wind, hot and dusty, that blows from

the African coast to Europe: SIROCCO

wind, hot, dry and full of sand, especially in deserts: SIMOOM

wind in and out: SINUATE

wind in a sudden, violent burst, usually accompanied by rain or snow: SQUALL

winding: ANFRACTUOUS

winding: TORTUOUS

winding, bending, wavering, unsteady: FLEXUOUS

wind is blowing toward this direction: LEEWARD

wind moving in a cold, sudden, violent blast down a mountain to the sea: WILLIWAW

wind of the Argentine pampas: PAMPERO

window, balcony or porch with an excellent view, in Spanish architecture: MIRADOR

window dealer or fitter: GLAZIER

window division, a vertical dividing piece in the opening: MULLION

window frame: SASH

window in a spire: LUCARNE

window, often semicircular, over a door: FANLIGHT

window opening vertically in the middle as a double door does: FRENCH WINDOW

window or any small opening suggestive of a window: FENESTELLA

window or doorway covering that covers only the top half of an opening: LAMBREQUIN

windowpane's wooden dividing strips: MUTTIN

window side post: JAMB

windowsill or inside ledge: STOOL

window slats that are horizontal and overlapping: LOUVER BOARD

window that is narrow and acutely pointed: LANCET WINDOW

window that is round or oval: OEIL-DE-BOEUF

window that opens on hinges at the side: CASEMENT

window that projects from a sloping roof: DORMER

window, throw out of: DEFENESTRATE

wind science: ANEMOLOGY

windstorm that is brief, gust of wind: FLAW

wind that is dusty from Africa:
   HARMATTAN
wind that is soft and gentle: **ZEPHYR**
wind, warm and dry, that blows down
   a mountain into a valley: **FOEHN**
windy pomposity, pretentiousness:
   FLATULENCE
wine aroma: **BOUQUET**
wine bottle holding almost four quarts:
   JEROBOAM
wine bottle or large vessel, usually with
   a handle and spout, used for
   serving liquids: **FLAGON**
wine bottle twice the ordinary size:
   MAGNUM
wine-cask storage shed: **CHAI**
wine cup in church: **CHALICE**
wine drink with fruit juice and soda
   water: **WINE COOLER**
wine measure of about eighteen wine
   gallons: **RUNDLET**
wine merchant: **VINTNER**
wine named for the principal or the one
   grape from which it is made:
   VARIETAL
wine made from two or more types of
   grape: **GENERIC WINE**
wine of no distinction, cheap red wine:
   VIN ORDINAIRE
wines and winemaking as a study:
   OENOLOGY
wine steward: **SOMMELIER**
wing: **PINION**
winged horse: **PEGASUS**
wingless: **APTEROUS**
wings, pertaining to, having or
   resembling: **ALAR**
wink: **NICTITATE**
winning of every event, as in a series:
   SWEEP
win or gain for one entailing loss for
   another in a system, game, etc.:
   ZERO-SUM
win over, appease: **PROPITIATE**
winter's beginning, when the sun is
   farthest south of the equator, about
   Dec. 21: **WINTER SOLSTICE**
win the favor or confidence of others by
   deliberate effort: **INGRATIATE**
wintry: **HIBERNAL**
wintry: **HIEMAL**
wipe off, cleanse: **DETERGE**
wipe out: **EXPUNGE**
wipe out, destroy completely:
   OBLITERATE

wire, rope or cable used to steady or
   secure something: **GUY**
wisdom, discernment: **SAGACITY**
wise: **SAPIENT**
Wise Men's visit to Jesus observed:
   EPIPHANY
wise person, infallible authority:
   ORACLE
wise, prudent: **JUDICIOUS**
wise, prudent, diplomatic: **POLITIC**
wise saying, maxim: **GNOME**
wise, shrewd: **SAGACIOUS**
wise statement: **APHORISM**
wish or desire that is weak or
   unfulfilled, tendency, inclination:
   VELLEITY
witchcraft or voodoo sticking of pins
   into a doll: **INVULTUATION**
witches' sabbath on April 30, the eve of
   May Day: **WALPURGIS NIGHT**
withdraw a contestant from a race, etc.:
   SCRATCH
withdraw formally from an
   organization: **SECEDE**
withdraw in fear, lose heart: **QUAIL**
withdraw, move backward: **RECEDE**
withdraw or end by plan: **PHASE OUT**
withdraw or remove from former
   habits: **WEAN**
withered, shriveled, shrunken: **WIZENED**
withering, mercilessly severe, harsh:
   SCATHING
withering or wasting away: **ATROPHY**
with ice cubes: **ON THE ROCKS**
within the same school, college, etc.:
   INTRAMURAL
without a center: **ACENTRIC**
without a date being set (for the next
   meeting): **SINE DIE**
without dividend: **EX-DIVIDEND**
without ice cubes: **STRAIGHT UP**
without payment pending approval or
   acceptance: **ON SPEC**
without warning: **UNAWARES**
with reference to: **APROPOS**
witness's sworn statements in court:
   TESTIMONY
wit that is dry or delicate: **ATTIC SALT**
witticism: **SALLY**
witty and short saying: **MOT**
witty, characterized by higher and finer
   qualities of the mind: **SPIRITUEL,**
   SPIRITUELLE
witty or clever piece of writing, light
   vignette: **JEU D'ESPRIT**

witty, quick replies: REPARTEE
witty remark: BON MOT
witty remark, gibe: QUIP
witty, terse statement: EPIGRAM
wizard, sorcerer: WARLOCK
wobbling, wavering, unsteady:
     TITUBANT
woeful tale, complaint, lament:
     JEREMIAD
woman adviser: EGERIA
woman beside herself with frenzy or
     excitement: MAENAD
woman companion (elderly), governess,
     chaperon: DUENNA
woman exploiter, male parasite:
     LOUNGE LIZARD
woman-hater: MISOGYNIST
woman hired to be friendly to a bar's
     patrons: B-GIRL
woman hired to suckle the child of
     another: WET NURSE
womanhood, femininity: MULIEBRITY
woman interested chiefly in money or
     gifts from men: GOLD DIGGER
woman keeping less than respectable
     company: DEMIREP,
     DEMIMONDAINE
woman-like, unmanly, weak, soft:
     EFFEMINATE
woman living on the street with her
     possessions: BAG LADY
woman living under canon law in a
     community but not under vows:
     CANONESS
woman-man relationship without sexual
     activity is: PLATONIC
woman of beauty who is a courtesan or
     social opportunist: HETAERA
woman of the world: FEMME DU
     MONDE
woman or girl who is not Jewish:
     SHIKSA
woman or women forming the
     government: GYNARCHY
woman's dressing room: BOUDOIR
woman servant in the Orient: AMAH
woman's legal status in marriage,
     formerly: COVERTURE
woman's one-piece bathing suit or
     tights: MAILLOT
woman's paid escort: GIGOLO
woman's short trousers that resemble a
     skirt: CULOTTE
woman's simple and shapeless long
     dress: MOTHER HUBBARD

woman's sunshade: PARASOL
woman's work and domain
     traditionally: DISTAFF
woman to whom a man is engaged:
     FIANCÉE
woman who has borne no children:
     NULLIPARA
woman who is abusive and scolding,
     shrew: TERMAGANT
woman who is adulterous or
     promiscuous, sinful temptress:
     SCARLET WOMAN
woman who is aggressive and
     domineering: BATTLE-AX
woman who is a nosy gossip or
     meddler: YENTA
woman who is cheap and loose, doxy:
     BIMBO
woman who is disreputable,
     ill-tempered and perverse: JADE
woman who is divorced or separated or
     lives apart from her husband:
     GRASS WIDOW
woman who is dowdy and sometimes
     also ill-tempered: FRUMP
woman who is elderly, dignified,
     wealthy: DOWAGER
woman who is hideously ugly: GORGON
woman who is homosexual: LESBIAN
woman who is imposing in age,
     sophistication or bearing: GRANDE
     DAME
woman who is old and ugly: CRONE
woman who is sexually provocative but
     a virgin: DEMI-VIERGE
woman who is sharp-tongued, scold:
     VIRAGO
woman who is untidy or slovenly:
     SLATTERN
woman who is vicious or hateful:
     HARRIDAN
woman who is voluptuous but
     treacherous: DELILAH
woman who is wicked and vicious:
     JEZEBEL
woman who lives with a man but is not
     married to him: CONCUBINE
woman whose allure leads to the
     downfall of men: FEMME FATALE
womb, or a woman considered legally
     as a child bearer: VENTER
women in general: DISTAFF
wonderful or marvelous to tell:
     MIRABILE DICTU
wondrous year: ANNUS MIRABILIS

wood as a thin and flexible strip, as used for basketmaking: SPLINT

wooded: ARBORACEOUS

wooded area of short trees: COPSE, COPPICE

wooden double-A-shaped support used for sawing wood: SAWHORSE

wooden slats for flooring over a wet surface, as behind a counter or bar: DUCKBOARDS

wooden vessel for butter or lard: FIRKIN

wood from broad-leaved deciduous trees, as oak or maple: HARDWOOD

wood in a thin, broad piece, as that forming the back of a chair: SPLAT

wood layers glued together: PLYWOOD

wood-like or made of wood: LIGNEOUS

woods or forest, of or pertaining to: SYLVAN

woodsy, thickly treed or shrubbed: BOSKY

woodworking knife with a handle at each end: DRAWKNIFE

woodworking training system: SLOYD

woolly in loose bits, fluffy-particle-like, like soft flakes: FLOCCULENT

woolly- or crispy-haired: ULOTRICHOUS

word adopted from another language and partly or completely naturalized: LOANWORD

word alteration or distorted adoption when borrowed by one language from another: HOBSON-JOBSON

word authority, language expert: LOGOGOGUE

word blindness: ALEXIA

word categories, of which there are eight in English (noun, pronoun, adjective, adverb, verb, preposition, conjunction and interjection): PARTS OF SPEECH

word changing or creation by inserting into a compound: TMESIS

word choice in speaking or writing: DICTION

word coined for a single or special occasion: NONCE WORD

word derived from the same root as another: PARONYM

worded pretentiously or bombastically: LEXIPHANIC

word formed by combining parts of two words: PORTMANTEAU WORD, CENTAUR WORD, BLEND WORD

word formed by transposing the letters of another: ANAGRAM

word formed from the initial letters of lines: ACROSTIC

word formed from the initial letters or syllables of a series of words: ACRONYM

word-for-word: TEXTUAL

word game in which a rhyme must be given for a word or line given by another: CRAMBO

word group between punctuation stops: SENTENCE

word hard to pronounce: JAWBREAKER

word having a veiled meaning, political or sociological euphemism: CODE WORD

word having the same or similar meaning as another word: SYNONYM

word identical with another in spelling but having a different origin and meaning: HOMOGRAPH

wordiness: VERBIAGE

wordiness, circumlocution: PERIPHRASIS

wordiness that is repetitive: BATTOLOGY

word inflection: ACCIDENCE

wording that is deliberately mild or gentle: PARADIASTOLE

word inspired by one that would seem to be an inflection of it, as "typewrite" from "typewriter": BACK-FORMATION

word interpretation that is largely spiritual and mystical: ANAGOGE

wordless drama played with gestures: PANTOMIME

word list, with definitions, of technical, obscure or foreign words of a work or field: GLOSSARY

word misuse: CATACHRESIS

word modeled on another word: PATTERNED FORM

word never existing or a misspelling appearing in a dictionary: GHOST WORD

word of more than three syllables: POLYSYLLABLE

word opposite in meaning to another word: ANTONYM

word-order inversion: ANASTROPHE

word-order inversion: HYPERBATON

word or expression having only one recorded use: HAPAX LEGOMENON

word or expression that is not standard:
BARBARISM

word origin popularly conceived but
erroneous: **FOLK ETYMOLOGY**

word origins and development as a
study: **ETYMOLOGY**

word or phrase often repeated, as a
slogan: **CATCHWORD,
CATCHPHRASE**

word or phrase serving only to
complete a rhythm or a pattern:
EXPLETIVE

word or phrase that is an exclamation
or obscene oath: **EXPLETIVE**

word or phrase that is substituted for
another to avoid giving offense or
pain: **EUPHEMISM**

word or saying that is familiar to most
people: **HOUSEHOLD WORD**

word or sentence that reads the same
backward as forward:
PALINDROME

word or term to be defined:
DEFINIENDUM

word, phrase or clause inserted into a
sentence to add explanation or
comment: **PARENTHESIS**

word popular in current use or jargon:
BUZZWORD

word pronounced like another but
different in meaning, derivation or
spelling: **HOMOPHONE**

word puzzle, as an anagram:
LOGOGRIPH

word related to one in another
language: **COGNATE**

word's alteration by shifting to its
beginning the final consonant of a
preceding word: **PROVECTION**

words altered by transposing sounds or
parts unintentionally: **SPOONERISM**

words and word groups, their
development and their changes of
meaning as a subject of study:
SEMANTICS

word selection and arrangement:
PHRASEOLOGY

words in a language, vocabulary: **LEXIS**

words in a series each having the same
initial sound: **ALLITERATION**

words in phrases, clauses and sentences
in terms of their arrangement and
interrelationship: **SYNTAX**

word's last syllable: **ULTIMA**

word's meaning improving to a positive
or more favorable sense:
MELIORATION

words of hesitation or habit in speech,
such as "you know," "like" and
"um": **EMBOLALIA**

words of one language altered to
resemble words in another, usually
for humorous effect: **MACARONIC**

words of wisdom: **APOTHEGM, GNOME,
MAXIM, SAW**

words or book of an opera: **LIBRETTO**

words or expressions placed next to
each other, the second explaining
the first: **APPOSITION**

word spelled like another but having a
different sound and meaning:
HETERONYM

word spoken, considered only as sound:
VOCABLE

words spelled differently to represent
dialect: **EYE DIALECT**

words that reflect natural sounds, or the
use of such words:
ONOMATOPOEIA

word structure as a study:
MORPHOLOGY

words used without sincerity: **LIP
SERVICE**

word, syllable or letter omitted
inadvertently when it should
appear twice in a row:
HAPLOGRAPHY

word that has been coined or an
existing word that has been given a
new meaning: **NEOLOGISM**

word that is a rare and pedantic, often
Latin borrowing: **INKHORN WORD**

word that is a shortened form of
another word: **CLIPPED FORM**

word that is similar but wrong and
usually inadvertently humorous:
MALAPROPISM

word that makes a statement that is
misleading or ambiguous: **WEASEL
WORD**

word used as a different part of speech:
FUNCTIONAL SHIFT

word used humorously with two
meanings: **PUN**

word used in a sense opposite to its
meaning, ironically: **ANTIPHRASIS**

word used in cabalistic charms:
ABRACADABRA

word use that is effective: RHETORIC

word widely used without regard to its exact meaning: COUNTER WORD

word with no stress but pronounced as part of a following word: PROCLITIC

word with no stress but pronounced as part of preceding word: ENCLITIC

word with several different meanings: POLYSEME

word with the same spelling and pronunciation as another but a different meaning: HOMONYM

wordy, long-winded: DIFFUSE

wordy, superfluous: REDUNDANT

wordy, tedious: PROLIX

wordy, wearisome in conversation: VERBOSE

workable, practicable: VIABLE

work at: PLY

work-avoid by pretending sickness: MALINGER

work clumsily: BUNGLE

work crew selection, especially among longshoremen: SHAPEUP

work done and paid for by the piece: PIECEWORK

worked up, overexcited or easily excitable, high-strung: HYPER

worker, clerical or professional: WHITE-COLLAR WORKER

worker in a routine and unglamorous job: WORKING STIFF

worker or itinerant who takes odd jobs: ROUSTABOUT

worker, performer, player, etc., who is diligent and experienced but unremarkable: JOURNEYMAN

workers employed in excess of actual needs: FEATHERBEDDING

workers' organization in a single company and unaffiliated with other unions: COMPANY UNION

worker, unskilled or semiskilled: BLUE-COLLAR WORKER

worker who crosses a picket line: SCAB

worker who is ultraconservative: HARD-HAT

work expands to fill the time allotted to it: PARKINSON'S LAW

work for which one is particularly suited, forte: MÉTIER

work hard, toil: MOIL

working class: PROLETARIAT

working conditions as a science: ERGONOMICS, HUMAN ENGINEERING

working independently, as a writer or artist, rather than for one employer: FREE LANCE

working on a job in addition to one's regular occupation: MOONLIGHTING

working or moving, effective: OPERATIVE

working with the hands, work done by hand: HANDICRAFT

work of no importance assigned to keep a person busy: MAKE-WORK

work shift beginning at midnight: GRAVEYARD SHIFT

work shift usually from 4 P.M. until midnight: SWING SHIFT

workshop: ATELIER

work slowdown caused by employees' ostensibly following the rules closely: JOB ACTION

work tediously: PLOD

work that is dull and wearisome: DRUDGERY

world and life as viewed comprehensively: WELTANSCHAUUNG

world betterment: MELIORISM

worldly as distinguished from spiritual or religious: SECULAR

worldly, as opposed to narrow or parochial: COSMOPOLITAN

worldly person, sophisticate: COSMOPOLITE

worldly, sensual, carnal: FLESHLY

worldly-wise: SOPHISTICATED

worldly woman: FEMME DU MONDE

world-weariness: WELTSCHMERZ

worldwide, general or universal, especially concerning churches: ECUMENICAL

worn, gaunt or wild-looking, as from fatigue, hunger or anxiety: HAGGARD

worn-out, exhausted, depleted of purpose or energy: BURNED OUT

worn-out, exhausted, overstrained: RAGGED

worn-out, exhausted, sated, dulled from overindulgence: JADED

worn-out or enfeebled by age or use: DECREPIT

worried, tense, bewildered, agitated, crazed: DISTRAUGHT

worry-free, carefree: SANS SOUCI

worry-free state or situation, prosperity: EASY STREET

worry, harass: CHEVY, CHIVVY

worry, harass: HARRY

worry-obsessed person: WORRYWART

worry, torment relentlessly: HARASS

worse, inferior, morally degraded: DEGENERATE

worsen, as in quality or power: IMPAIR

worsening, declining, going backward: RETROGRADE

worsen, make worse or more severe, aggravate: EXACERBATE

worship given properly only to God, in the Roman Catholic Church: LATRIA

worshiping or venerating ancestors or tradition: FILIOPIETISTIC

worship of idols: IDOLATRY

worst-possible-outcome hypothesis or possibility: WORST-CASE SCENARIO

worthless: CHEESEPARING

worthless leftover matter: RECREMENT

worthless, meaningless: NUGATORY

worthlessness or futility imposed on something or someone makes it or him: STULTIFIED

worthless or valueless thing: TINKER'S DAMN

worthless things or matter, rubbish, nonsense: TRUMPERY

worth the investment or expense, economical: COST-EFFECTIVE

worthy, allowable, permissible: ADMISSIBLE

wounds resembling those that Christ received during the Passion and Crucifixion: STIGMATA

wrangle, bandy words: SPAR

wrangling, quarrel: JANGLE

wraparound brightly colored long cloth garment of the tropics: LAVALAVA, PAREU

wrapped in tight-fitting rubbery clear plastic: SHRINK-WRAPPED

wreckage that is afloat or washed up on shore: FLOTSAM

wreck, pillage, ruin: RAVAGE

wrestler or boxer weighing over 175 pounds: HEAVYWEIGHT

wrestler or boxer weighing between 127 and 135 pounds: LIGHTWEIGHT

wrestler or boxer weighing between 136 and 147 pounds: WELTERWEIGHT

wrestler or boxer weighing between 148 and 160 pounds: MIDDLEWEIGHT

wrestler or boxer weighing between 161 and 175 pounds: LIGHT HEAVYWEIGHT

wrestler weighing up to 134 pounds or a boxer weighing up to 126 pounds: FEATHERWEIGHT

wrestling hold in which an arm is passed under the opponent's armpit and the hand is pressed against the back of his head: HALF NELSON

wrestling hold in which opponent's arm is twisted behind his back and upward: HAMMERLOCK

wrestling hold in which the arms are under the opponent's armpits from the back and the hands are against the back of his neck: FULL NELSON

wrestling hold in which the wrestler's head is gripped between his opponent's arm and body: HEADLOCK

wrestling term for when the head is caught and held under the opponent's arm: CHANCERY

wrestling throw: FLYING MARE

wretched, cheerless, abandoned, deserted: FORLORN

wrinkle, pucker: COCKLE

wrist: CARPUS

writ authorizing seizure of property: ATTACHMENT

write: INDITE

write, mark or engrave, especially for some solemn or public purpose: INSCRIBE

write or speak more fully, elaborate: EXPATIATE

write or study laboriously: LUCUBRATE

write out, compose or edit: REDACT

writer of articles, books or speeches for someone else to whom the authorship will be attributed: GHOSTWRITER

writer of polemical pamphlets: PAMPHLETEER

writer's assumed name: PEN NAME, NOM DE PLUME

writer's cramp: GRAPHOSPASM

writers' manuscripts sent unsolicited to a publisher: SLUSH PILE

writer's name at the head of an article:
  BYLINE
writers, scholars, people of letters:
  LITERATI
writing describing a pleasant, peaceful
  scene: **IDYLL**
writing desk: **ESCRITOIRE**
writing difficult to decipher:
  HIEROGLYPHICS
writing dispassionately as if one were a
  camera: **CHOSISME**
writing in which lines alternately read
  left to right and right to left:
  BOUSTROPHEDON
writing of an ancient mode:
  PALEOGRAPHY
writing of words or phrases erroneously
  because of cerebral injury:
  PARAGRAPHIA
writing or printing with flowing lines:
  CURSIVE
writing paper measuring about 13 by 16
  inches: **FOOLSCAP**
writing prose in line lengths
  corresponding to the sense:
  STICHOMETRY
writings or artistic work of a person's
  youth: **JUVENILIA**
writing technique that records inner
  thoughts and feelings of characters:
  STREAM-OF-CONSCIOUSNESS
writing that is backward and readable
  in a mirror: **MIRROR-WRITING**
writing that is continuous and random
  as an attempt to express the
  unconscious: **AUTOMATIC WRITING**

writing that is good but on a trivial
  subject: **ADOXOGRAPHY**
writing that is long and tiresome:
  SCREED
writing that is obvious or worthless,
  drivel: **PABULUM**
writ ordering that a person be brought
  before a court: **HABEAS CORPUS**
written in rounded, largely capital-letter
  forms, as in ancient Greek and
  Latin manuscripts: **UNCIAL**
written in the form of a letter or letters:
  EPISTOLARY
written statement or graphic
  representation that is false or
  malicious and damaging to a
  person's reputation: **LIBEL**
wrongdoing, especially by a public
  official: **MALFEASANCE**
wrongdoing imputed, implied or
  charged: **INCRIMINATION**
wrongdoing or illicit activity:
  HANKY-PANKY
wrong early dating of something in
  time: **PROCHRONISM**
wrongful act not involving breach of
  contract but constituting a possible
  basis for a suit: **TORT**
wrongful act, unjust thing or deed, sin:
  INIQUITY
wrongful use: **ABUSE**
wrong: if anything can go wrong, it
  will: **MURPHY'S LAW**
wrong late-dating of something in time:
  METACHRONISM
wrong name: **MISNOMER**

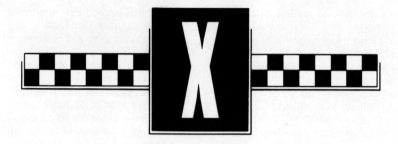

x-rays and nuclear radiation as a
medical field: **RADIOLOGY**

X-shaped: **DECUSSATE**

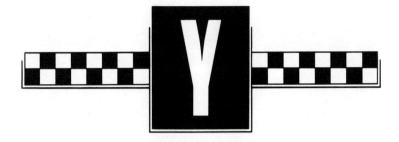

yard enclosure, close: **GARTH**

yarn length: **SPINDLE**

yarn length equaling 80 yards for wool, 120 for cotton, 300 for linen: **LEA**

yarn or thread wound in a coil: **SKEIN**

yawning, sleepiness: **OSCITANCY**

yearn, desire, crave: **HANKER**

year of wandering or traveling: **WANDERYEAR, WANDERJAHR**

year-old animal: **YEARLING**

year or period that is critical: **CLIMACTERIC**

year that is wonderful: **ANNUS MIRABILIS**

yellowed or yellowish brown, like pages of an old book: **FOXED**

yellowish-green in color, sea-green: **GLAUCOUS**

yellowish in complexion: **SALLOW**

yelp, bark: **YAWP**

yes, just so (used in parentheses after a quoted spelling, word or phrase to indicate that it is accurately reproduced): **SIC**

yesterday, pertaining to or occurring: **PRIDIAN**

Yiddish: **MAMALOSHEN, MAMA LOSHEN**

yielding courteously or respectfully to the wishes or opinions of another: **DEFERENCE**

yielding, persuadable: **PLIANT**

yielding readily in an emotional way: **SUSCEPTIBLE**

yield to or gratify, as one's desires: **INDULGE**

yield weakly or with bad grace, cringe: **TRUCKLE**

yokel, boor, hick: **MUCKER**

young advocate of change within a group, establishment, etc.: **YOUNG TURK**

young and innocent woman: **INGENUE**

young man who is remarkably talented or accomplished: **BOY WONDER**

young person, youth: **SPRIG**

young or becoming young: **JUVENESCENT**

young people who are rich and fashionable, gilded youth: **JEUNESSE DORÉE**

youthful days of freshness and inexperience: **SALAD DAYS**

youthful feeling or vigor restored: **REJUVENATION**

youthful, fresh, spring-like: **VERNAL**

you've scored a point, you've got me: **TOUCHÉ**

zeal that is extravagant or frenzied:
FANATICISM
Zen Buddhist spiritual or meditational
refuge: **ZENDO**
zenith, highest point of anything:
MERIDIAN

zest, enthusiasm: **GUSTO**
zestless, dull: **PERFUNCTORY**
zigzag course in sailing: **TACK**

Index of Target Words

bewitch 40
bewitching 128
B-girl 276
biannual 257
bias 66, 168, 227
biathlon 14, 208, 226
bibelot 228, 256
biblia abiblia 28
biblioclast 28
bibliography 28
bibliomania 146
bibliophile 28
bibliopole 200
bibulous 7, 73
bicameral 139
bicuspid 253
bicycle kick 229
bid 191
bidet 253
bidonville 221
biennial 258
bier 37, 45, 184
bifocals 86, 104
bifurcate 71, 234
bigamy 148
big bang theory 262
Big Board 164, 238
Big Brother 15, 105, 236, 270
bigfoot 10, 109
biggin 45, 164, 227
bight 21, 23
bijouterie 131
bikini 21
bilateral 258
bildungsroman 166
bilingual 232
bilious 120, 179
billet 142
billet-doux 143
billingsgate 268
bimanous 258
bimbo 193, 276
bimestrial 258
bimonthly 258
binary 72, 176, 258
binnacle 47, 223
binomial 258
biodegradable 62, 67
bioengineering 24, 150
biofeedback 218
biogenesis 140
biographical fallacy 88
biological clock 27

bioluminescence 104, 140
biopsy 83, 252
biostatics 9, 184
biparous 257
biped 258
birddog 236
birdie 105
biretta 35, 43
bisque 231
bissextile day 85, 138
bistro 206
bit, binary digit 48
bivouac 35, 249
biweekly 82, 98
blackball 173, 268
blackguard 17, 215, 267
blacklist 68, 133
blackmail 178
Black Maria 178, 186
Blackshirt 89
black tie 257
blandish 34, 93, 272
blank check 262
blasphemy 58, 128
blatherskite 95, 247
blazon 125, 195
bleachers 23
bleb 26
blepharoplasty 86
blindside 54, 114
blister pack 175
blithe 40
blithering 130, 248
blitz 96
blitzkrieg 15
blockbusting 154, 199
blockflöte 202
blood money 156
Bloody Mary 253, 268
bloomer 155
blooper 19
blouson 26, 101
bloviate 115, 232, 247
blowzy 89, 228, 263
blue chip 238, 239
blue collar worker 123, 147, 218, 263, 279
blue laws 47, 137
blue-pencil 52, 77
blue-ribbon 232
blue sky laws 137
bluestocking 28, 141
blurb 28
blype 226, 243

boater 240
boatswain's whistle 163, 273
boccie 129
bodega 114
bodice ripper 105, 210
body stocking 27
bogey 105
bogus 87, 88, 182
boilerplate 164
boiler room 114
boîte 34, 164
boldface 258
bollard 71
Boloism 63, 175
bolo tie 163, 272
bombast 248
bombinate 33, 118
BOMFOG (Brotherhood of Man, Fatherhood of God) 52, 106, 187
bona fides 40, 105
bondieuserie 204
bonehead 95, 241
bonhomie 105
boniface 125
bon jour 99
bon mot 43, 276
bonne bouche 11, 64
bonsai 130, 255
bon soir 99
bon ton 241
bonus baby 14
bon vivant 181
boondocks 212
boondoggle 264
boosterism 42, 47, 142
Boot Hill 106, 108
bordello 32, 273
Borsalino 111
borscht circuit, borscht belt 37
bosky 277
Boswell 24
botch 17
botched 44
bottom line 81, 121
Botts dots 203
botulism 95
boudoir 73, 276
bouillabaisse 93
boulevardier 146
bouleversement 174, 207
bounder 261
bounteous 102, 185

iamb, iambus 186
iatrogenic 71, 123
ibid. 214
icebreaker 143, 204
ichnography 107
ichor 94, 161
ichthyology 92
ichthyomania 146
icon 120, 182
iconoclast 65
iconography 120
icterus 131
id 260
ID card 119
ideation 119
idée fixe 93, 168
ideograph 106
ideologue 171, 181, 187
ideomania 146
ideophobia 181
idiolect 123, 232
idiom 182, 258
idiosyncrasy 147, 198
idioticon 66
idiot savant 152, 207
idolatrous 26, 66
idolatry 280
idyll 281
idyllic 183
i.e. (id est) 250
igneous 92
ignescent 93
ignis fatuus 274
ignoble 21, 63, 69
ignominious 69, 221
ignoramus 241
ignoratio elenchi 12, 88
ilk 43, 133, 230
illation 62, 124
ill-disposed 146, 261
illegal alien 119, 120
illeism 113, 170, 251
ill-favored 67, 259, 262
illicit 193, 262
illiquid 37
ill-starred 262
illuminate 62
illusion 88
illustrious 70, 88, 205
imago 124
imam 128, 155, 161
imbecile 152
imbibe 73
imbricate 174
imbrication 174

imbroglio 48, 50
imbrue 73, 235
imbue 126, 181
immaculate 43
immanent 123
immediacy 67, 127
immerse 80
immersion 63
immigrant 46
imminent 3, 120
immiscible 166
immobile 157, 166
immobilize 93, 239
immoderate 263
immodest 27, 122, 217
immunity 84, 206
immunology 120
immure 49, 79, 121
immutable 259
impacted 57, 175, 188, 272
impair 139, 280
impale 74, 93, 113, 183
impalpable 126, 262
impart 24, 68, 145
impartial 69, 87
impassible 128, 261
impassive 34, 219, 262
impasto 175
impeach 39
impeachment 4
impeccable 81, 89, 93, 261
impecunious 179, 187
impede 63, 114
impediment 168
impedimenta 18, 32, 73
impel 74, 97, 264
impending 3
impenetrable 64, 122
imperative 15, 259, 264
imperceptible 228, 263
imperial 176
imperious 12, 72, 264
imperium 3, 15, 244
impersonate 154
impertinence 126, 211
imperturbable 34, 263
impervious 44, 122, 262
impetrate 169
impetration 206
impetuosity 242
impetuous 111, 121, 200
impetus 74, 97, 122, 158
impiety 261

impignorate 178, 185
impinge 79, 88, 240
impious 25, 128
implacable 152, 263
implant 125
implement 36
implementation 196
implicate 50, 80, 128
implicit 3, 260, 263
implode 45
implore 22
implosion 128
imply 114, 128, 224
impolitic 121
importunate 64
importune 110, 180, 256
impose 124, 169
imposing 106, 121, 236
imposition 168, 179
impost 116, 248
impostor 62
imposture 188, 190
impotent 113, 189, 271
impound 217
impoverish 145
impracticable 263
imprecate 58, 189
impregnable 92, 206, 263
impregnate 91, 180, 214
impresario 146, 172
impress 39, 148
impressionism 13
imprest 142
imprimatur 169
imprinting 15, 138
improbity 69, 126
impromptu 169, 234, 235, 262
impropriated 77
improvident 122, 200, 251
improvise 128, 179, 192
impudent 27, 30, 214
impudicity 221
impugn 15, 39, 70
impuissance 135
impuissant 189
impunity 84, 98
imputation 4, 40
impute 13, 15
in absentia 3
inadvertence 174
inadvertent 261
inadvisable 263